THE
FOREIGN POLICY OF
SOVIET RUSSIA
1929–1941

THE
FOREIGN POLICY OF
SOVIET RUSSIA

1929–1941

MAX BELOFF

VOLUME II
1936–1941

Issued under the auspices of the
Royal Institute of International Affairs

OXFORD UNIVERSITY PRESS
LONDON   NEW YORK   TORONTO

Oxford University Press, Amen House, London E.C.4
GLASGOW NEW YORK TORONTO MELBOURNE WELLINGTON
BOMBAY CALCUTTA MADRAS KARACHI LAHORE DACCA
CAPE TOWN SALISBURY NAIROBI IBADAN ACCRA
KUALA LUMPUR HONG KONG

First published 1949
Fourth impression 1963

PRINTED IN GREAT BRITAIN

FOREWORD

I MUST renew my thanks to those inside and outside Chatham House who were named in the Foreword to Volume I. To an even greater extent than in the case of Volume I, I have been indebted to Mrs Jane Degras for her willing collaboration. I have also been in the fortunate position of having been able to make use in manuscript of her calendar of the documents of the subject. Mr. R. G. D. Laffan and Professor C. A. W. Manning have kindly given me access to manuscript studies written by them for the Institute.

I wish to thank Mr. Gerald Brenan and M. Luis Araquistain for assistance on the chapter dealing with Spain.

I must thank particularly Mrs. N. Good of the Institute's editorial section for invaluable technical assistance, and Mrs. R. Mitchison again and my wife for the index.

The preparation of this volume has suffered from the fact that important new material was appearing throughout the time it was in the press. As far as possible such material has been included at the proof stage if only in footnote form. It was felt that this was desirable even at the expense of literary elegance.

The publication has been considerably delayed by a fire at the printers which destroyed the proofs and part of the type. I am indebted to the publishers and to members of the Institute's staff for their help in overcoming these difficulties.

Oxford
October 1948

MAX BELOFF

CONTENTS

APPENDICES

MAPS

IV. THE BREAKDOWN OF COLLECTIVE SECURITY

Chapter One

INTRODUCTION

THE period between the German reoccupation of the Rhineland in March 1936 and the Munich crisis in September 1938 has a well-marked character of its own. In the preceding three years Soviet foreign policy had moved rapidly towards closer co-operation with non-Communist States, with the ostensible object of promoting European and world peace through a policy of 'collective security'. This object had been pursued along three separate but convergent paths. In the first place, the Soviet Union had succeeded in entering for the first time into normal diplomatic relations with States which had previously refused to recognize the Soviet régime, the most important of these being the United States of America. In the second place, the Soviet Union had entered the League of Nations and so undertaken the obligations placed upon it by the Covenant—obligations which it had formally carried out during the Italo-Ethiopian conflict. In the third place, it had attempted to make up for the Covenant's apparent weakness by supplementing that instrument with additional localized agreements for mutual assistance. This attempt achieved partial success with the passage and ratification of pacts of mutual assistance with France and Czechoslovakia.[1] At the same time, the Communist International, in which the Russian Communist Party remained the dominant element, had, for the time being at any rate, abandoned the direct promotion of revolutionary activity in favour of a policy of 'popular fronts', that is to say, of combining in every country all those forces which were likely to be opposed to the growth of Fascism at home and the aggressive designs of the Fascist and National-Socialist States abroad.

The years 1936 to 1938 witnessed the collapse of this security system and of the hopes which had been placed in it.[2] The

---

[1] The French Senate only ratified the Franco-Soviet Pact on 12 March 1936, that is to say, after the entry of German troops into the Rhineland.

[2] For a review of the Soviet Union's foreign policy towards the beginning of this period (August 1936) see the chapter by the well-known Tass correspondent, Andrew Rothstein: 'The Soviet Union in International Affairs' in *Problems of Peace*, Eleventh Series (Allen and Unwin, 1937). This was the

menace to the Soviet Union from outside developed with the progressive rearmament of Germany, and was made explicit by the 'Anti-Comintern Pact' between Germany and Japan in November 1936 and the adhesion thereto of Italy in November 1937. This was countered to some extent by the further development of the Soviet Union's own industrial and military potential under the second Five Year Plan. It was not, however, accompanied by any further *rapprochement* with France and Great Britain, the other two Great Powers who appeared to be menaced most by Germany's growing strength and increasing demands; nor did the outbreak of open war between Japan and China in July 1937 lead to any definite co-operation between the Soviet Union and the other Powers whose interests were thereby affected.

There were several reasons for holding that the change in Soviet policy had not as yet removed the suspicion with which it had been regarded among the Western Powers. Thus, the revision of the régime of the Straits by the Montreux Conference in the summer of 1936 was not effected without a fairly sharp clash between the Soviet and British viewpoints. On an even more important issue, that of the Spanish Civil War, which began in July 1936 and was still raging in September 1938, the formal adherence of the Soviet Union to the formula of non-intervention could not conceal very substantial differences in the attitudes of the Soviet Union and the Western Powers, both as to the origin and nature of the conflict and as to the measures required to deal with its European repercussions. Finally, at Geneva itself, the Soviet Union consistently advocated maintaining the security provisions of the Covenant as they stood, while the Western Powers were apparently prepared to envisage a watering-down of the Covenant, if by this 'reform' the Great Powers which had left the League or were about to leave it—the anti-Comintern Powers—could be brought back. The Soviet Union thus stood at this time for the policy which its leading spokesman in this period—the Foreign Commissar, Maxim Litvinov—summed up in the catchword: 'Peace is indivisible'. This policy involved drawing a distinction between the peace-loving and the aggressive States, and directing all political effort towards uniting the former group in order to frustrate the designs of the latter. British and French policy seemed to prefer to treat every international question on its merits, as it arose, with the primary

---

first contribution from the Soviet point of view to this annual series of lectures at the Geneva Institute of International Relations.

object of avoiding a head-on conflict with any other Great Power.

Certain features of the Soviet scene in these years were difficult to interpret in a reassuring sense from the point of view of the Western Powers. The stability and growing homogeneity of the Soviet State seemed to be demonstrated by the adoption, in December 1936, of a new Constitution incorporating certain features similar to those found in the democratic constitutions of the western European model. On the other hand the series of State trials which began in August 1936, and the accompanying 'purge' of the political, administrative, and military hierarchy which was still in progress in September 1938, tended to make people abroad discount the value of Soviet military support. Nor did the new 'line' of the Comintern make up for its renewed activity. The growth of Communism, particularly in France and Spain, was more frightening to right-wing and moderate elements, than the moderation of Communist policies was reassuring; and the actions of the local Communist Parties were often equivocal enough to give the suspicious some grounds for questioning the sincerity of their democratic and patriotic pretensions. At the same time, the Soviet Union's overt abandonment of the cause of international socialist revolution produced a new and embittered, but on the whole uninfluential, band of critics, this time on the left.

Direct contacts between Soviet citizens and foreigners became more limited than ever after the accusations at the State trials that such contacts had been used for treasonable purposes; and the Soviet Union seemed to be retreating into an ever-greater seclusion. The second Five Year Plan made no such calls upon foreign technical assistance and foreign trade as had its predecessor, and an important source of reliable estimates of conditions in the Soviet Union was thus lacking.[1]

Whatever the motives behind the policies of Great Britain and France may have been, the events of the summer and autumn of 1938 seemed to confirm Soviet suspicions. The increasing intransigence of the German attitude made it inevitable that the Western Powers, if they wished to treat with Germany at all, should do so without the Soviet Union; and the exclusion of the Soviet Union from the Munich Conference, and from all participation in settling the fate of Czechoslovakia, was taken as proof that the Soviet diagnosis of the attitudes of the Western

[1] For an interesting account of the effect of the internal events of these years upon Soviet productivity, as seen from the vantage-point occupied by a foreign engineer at the great steel centre of Magnitogorsk, see John Scott, *Behind the Urals* (Secker and Warburg, 1943).

Powers was correct. Their Governments were credited with a willingness to allow German expansion eastwards to proceed unchecked by action on their part, and this in turn was later on used to explain the reversal of the Soviet attitude in 1939. Because of the influence which they exercised on opinion abroad, it may be useful to preface the account of Soviet diplomacy of these years, with a consideration of certain domestic events. The principles of Soviet foreign policy at this juncture will then be considered in the academic but revealing light provided by the question of the proposed reform of the League of Nations Covenant. If the Soviet attitude on this question is contrasted with the British attitude, as it was officially and unofficially expressed, the immediate reasons for the inability of Soviet and British statesmen to find common ground for dealing with the political issues of the time should not be hard to grasp.[1] It is also desirable to say something more about the policy of the Comintern in this period.

The adoption by the Soviet Union of the new 'Stalin' Constitution of 1936 was the culmination of a series of measures designed to strengthen the régime by eliminating political and other forms of discrimination against those of non-proletarian origin, by revising the statutes of the collective farms to meet some of the grievances of the peasantry, and by remedying the defects in the educational system consequent upon the experimentalism and disorganization of the revolutionary period. The decision to 'democratize the Constitution' was announced during the seventh All-Union Congress of Soviets which met from 28 January to 6 February 1935. The draft of the new Constitution was published on 12 June 1936. It was presented in a slightly revised form to the eighth Congress on 25 November and unanimously accepted on 5 December.[2] The first elections under the Constitution were held on 12 December 1937.[3]

[1] A representative selection of British opinions on the subject can be found in *The Future of the League of Nations* (Oxford University Press, 1936), the record of a series of discussions at Chatham House held in May–July 1936.

[2] The Constitution provided for direct elections, universal suffrage with the equalization of rural and urban representation, and secret ballot. The single-party system was, however, maintained, and in the subsequent elections there was only a single candidate for each constituency, although a proportion of the candidates were not actually Party members.

[3] Liberal opinion in the outside world was impressed by the new democratic provisions of the Constitution, and the emphasis on these features of the Soviet State made easier the development of 'popular fronts' by Communist Parties outside the Soviet Union. The democratic character of the Constitution was emphasized by Molotov in his speech to the Congress of Soviets on 29 November 1936. V. M. Molotov, *The Constitution of Socialism*

Of international significance was the fact that the new document was shorn of the preamble of the 1923 Constitution with
its challenging statement that the world was henceforth divided
into the two camps of Capitalism and Socialism. The Soviet
Union retained, however, its international or supra-national
character, and the right to admit new constituent republics
(Article 14). The official emblem of the Soviet Union retained
the Communist slogan: 'Proletarians of all countries, unite!'
(Article 143). Soviet spokesmen also attached importance to
Article 17, which preserved to each constituent republic 'the
right of withdrawal from the U.S.S.R.', and claimed that this
was indicative of the Soviet Union's devotion to the principle of
self-determination in the internal and external aspects of its
policy.[1]

The new treaty obligations of the Soviet Union were recognized specifically in the powers granted to the Presidium of the
Supreme Soviet (between sessions of the latter) to proclaim a
state of war 'in case of armed attack upon the U.S.S.R. or in
case of the necessity for carrying out international treaty obligations for mutual defence against aggression' (Article 49,
Section J).

The new Constitution also contributed to the evolution of
the Red Army into a quasi-national force of a more conventional kind. By Article 132, all Soviet citizens were made liable
to military service with no distinction of class origin, and the
principle was exemplified in the new military statute promulgated during 1936 and by the new Field Service Regulations of
that year.[2] The new military oath introduced on 3 January
1939 marked a further step in this process.[3]

(Moscow, Co-operative Publishing Society of Foreign Workers in the
U.S.S.R., 1937). Litvinov, in a speech delivered on the previous day, had
emphasized the distinction between Soviet and 'bourgeois' democracy;
M. M. Litvinov, *The U.S.S.R.: A Powerful Bulwark of Universal Peace* (Moscow, Co-operative Publishing Society of Foreign Workers in the U.S.S.R.,
1937). Cf. S. Dobrin, 'The New Soviet Constitution', *Transactions of the
Grotius Society*, XXII, 1937, and N. S. Timasheff, 'Vertical Social Mobility
in Communist Society', *American Journal of Sociology*, July 1944, and references there.

[1] See I. Maisky, *Soviet Foreign Policy* (Address delivered at Oxford,
1 August 1936, to the Liberal Summer School), (Anglo-Russian Parliamentary Committee, 1936).

[2] D. Fedotoff White, *The Growth of the Red Army* (Princeton University
Press, 1944); M. Berchin and E. Ben-Horin, *The Red Army* (Allen and
Unwin, 1943); N. Basseches, *The Unknown Army* (Heinemann, 1943).

[3] The original oath of 1918 had included a paragraph which ran as follows: 'I pledge myself on the first call of the Workers' and Peasants' Government, to stand up for the Soviet Republic against all dangers and the

From the point of view of the non-Soviet world these signs of consolidation were eclipsed by the dramatic spectacle provided by the State trials and purges of these years. The number and status of the accused and the disgraced implied the existence of widespread discontent with the path which the Soviet Government had taken. The revelation that individuals formerly occupying the highest places in the Soviet State and Army were ready to use force in order to overthrow the existing Government, and were even prepared to seek the help of the sworn enemies of the Soviet State, was ill-calculated to promote confidence in the Soviet Union's potential value as a bulwark against aggression.

The violent upheaval within the régime may be dated from the severe repression which followed the murder of S. M. Kirov on 1 December 1934.[1] Apart from a large number of executions, two leading Bolsheviks, Zinoviev and Kamenev, received sentences of banishment. In August 1936 these two, along with others, were put on trial and found guilty of having organized an underground counter-revolutionary conspiracy under the auspices of the exiled Trotsky.[2] Further arrests were made and were followed in January 1937 by the trial of seventeen more prisoners, including such eminent Bolsheviks as Radek and Sokolnikov, on charges which included treasonable co-operation with agents of the German and Japanese Governments. The help of Japan and Germany was to have been rewarded by the cession to the former of the Maritime Province and other Siberian territory, and by the cession to the latter of the Ukraine, as well as by the grant of other political and commercial advantages.[3] This trial was followed by yet more executions, arrests, and expulsions from the Communist Party. During the remainder of the year, the 'purge' affected an increasingly large number of departments of Soviet life and extended to every part

---

endeavours on the part of all her enemies, and not to spare my strength and even my life in the struggle for the Russian Soviet Republic, *for Socialism and the brotherhood of nations.*' The corresponding paragraph of the new oath ran: 'I am always ready upon the orders of the Workers' and Peasants' Government to defend my country—the U.S.S.R.—and as a warrior of the Workers' and Peasants' Red Army I pledge myself to defend her courageously, efficiently, with decency and honour, not sparing my blood and even my life, *in order to achieve victory over the enemies.*' M. M. Laserson, *Russia and the Western World* (New York, Macmillan, 1945), pp. 47–8.

[1] *Survey for 1934*, pp. 366–8.

[2] *Survey for 1936*, pp. 376–8. The trial in August 1936 was referred to as the 'Trial of the Trotskyite-Zinovievite Terrorist Centre'.

[3] *Court Proceedings in the Case of the Anti-Soviet Trotskyite Centre*, 23–30 January 1937 (Moscow, Peoples' Commissariat of Justice of the U.S.S.R., 1937).

of the Soviet Union. In June, it was announced that Marshal
Gamarnik, one of the key figures in the Red Army, had committed suicide while in prison where he was awaiting trial on
charges of treason. This was followed by the trial (*in camera*) and
sentence of other prominent military personalities, including
Marshal Tukhachevsky, the most conspicuous figure in the
recent development of the Red Army, on charges of espionage
and treason.[1]

In March 1938, Bukharin, Rykov, Yagoda (former head of
the G.P.U. and N.K.V.D.[2]) and other prominent Bolsheviks
were charged with:

'having on the instructions of the Intelligence services of foreign
States hostile to the Soviet Union formed a conspiratorial group
named "the *bloc* of Rights and Trotskyites" with the object of
espionage on behalf of foreign States, wrecking, diversionist and
terrorist activities, undermining the military power of the U.S.S.R.,
dismembering the U.S.S.R., and severing from it the Ukraine,
Byelorussia, the Central Asiatic Republics, Georgia, Armenia,
Azerbaijan and the Maritime Region of the Far East for the benefit
of the aforementioned foreign States, and lastly, with the object of
overthrowing the Socialist social and State system existing in the
U.S.S.R. and of restoring capitalism, of restoring the power of the
bourgeoisie.'[3]

Nearly all the accused, like those at the previous trials, were
sentenced to death. The process came to an end only with the
fall of Yezhov, the head of the N.K.V.D., in December 1938
and with the subsequent 'purge' of that department as well.
In the present context two features of these proceedings call for
comment. In the first place, the 'purge' removed a very large

[1] *Survey for 1937*, pp. 11–22. On the place of Tukhachevsky in the development of Soviet military thought see E. M. Earle in chapter 14 of his
Makers of Modern Strategy (Princeton University Press, 1943).

[2] The G.P.U. (State Political Administration) was absorbed into the
newly created Commissariat of the Interior (N.K.V.D.) on 10 July 1934.

[3] *Report of Court Proceedings in the case of the Anti-Soviet 'Bloc of Rights and
Trotskyites'*, 2–13 March 1938 (Moscow, 1938), p. 5. Although Germany and
Japan were the foreign Powers chiefly in mind, it is worth noting that several
of the accused, like Trotsky, were declared guilty of working for the British
Intelligence service; some of them were also accused of working for the Polish
Intelligence service. A vast amount of controversy has gone on over the
'authenticity' of these trials. See P. Grierson, *Books on Soviet Russia*
(Methuen, 1943), pp. 128–31. It does not seem necessary to review these
discussions here. The expansionist aims of Germany and Japan require no
corroboration now, and from the Soviet point of view the importance of the
trials lies not so much in the specific charges made against the accused, as
in the evidence which they afforded of the internal stresses brought about
by the political vicissitudes of the régime, and in the effect of this evidence
abroad.

proportion of the officials and foreign representatives of the Commissariat for Foreign Affairs, so that Litvinov had to carry on with a diplomatic staff consisting almost entirely of new-comers. In the second place the 'purge' had important effects on the Red Army, and, as already noted, on that army's reputation abroad.

The suicide of Gamarnik underlined the failure and eclipse of the Political Administration of the Army (P.U.R.), the body responsible for its ideological conformity since Frunze's aboli-tion of the military commissars in 1924. On 10 May 1937, military commissars were reintroduced into the higher units of the army in disregard of the principle of 'unity of command'. The discarded 'collegiate' principle reappeared in the command of the military districts into which the Soviet Union was divided, and the complete duality between commanding officer and com-missar of the civil war period was brought back by the promul-gation on 15 August 1937 of a new statute of military commis-sars.[1] Military efficiency appeared to be in danger of being sacrificed once more to the requirements of political orthodoxy, and these events tended to make people forget that the Red Army was at the same time expanding its numbers and improv-ing its technical equipment. A decree of 11 August 1936 lowered the age of military service from 21 to 19.[2] The contingent called up that autumn numbered, apparently, 900,000 men (in-stead of the usual 600,000.)[3] Important additions to the Soviet Navy and Air Force were also announced.[4] Expansion in subse-quent years, difficult to follow in detail and variously assessed as to quality, was partially revealed by the striking increases in the annual military budget of the Soviet Union, which rose from 8 milliard roubles in 1936 to 22·4 milliard roubles in 1937, and 34 milliard roubles in 1938.[5] Addressing the Eighteenth Party Congress on 15 March 1939, the Commissar for Defence declared that the size of the Army had been more than doubled since 1934 and the Air Force increased by 130 per cent. The professionalization of the Red Army officers was not interrupted by the 'purge'.[6] On the other hand, prominence in the public

---

[1] White, op. cit., *passim.* [2] *Documents for 1936*, pp. 289–90.
[3] *Survey for 1936*, pp. 146–7. [4] ibid., p. 157. *Infra,* chap. 6.
[5] M. Werner, *The Military Strength of the Powers* (Gollancz, 1939), pp. 41–2. This student puts the strength of the standing army as 940,000 in 1935 and 1,300,000 by 1938. He makes clear the difficulty of interpreting Soviet military statistics. One question not dealt with by him is that of the troops directly under the control of the N.K.V.D. Their numbers in the period 1937–1938 have been put as high as a quarter of a million. D. Dallin, *The Real Soviet Russia* (Yale University Press, 1944), p. 242.
[6] Basseches, op. cit., p. 144; Earle, op. cit., p. 349.

eye was monopolized after the fall of Tukhachevsky by Stalin's close associate Marshal Voroshilov, an administrator and politician, rather than a soldier in the professional sense.

If Soviet leaders put their primary emphasis on the strength of the Red Army, their secondary instrument in the struggle for security was intended to be, at this time, the League of Nations.

A succinct definition of the Soviet attitude to the League and to proposed changes in its Covenant was contained in a lecture delivered by Andrew Rothstein to the Geneva Institute of International Relations in August 1937:

'The Soviet conception of how the affairs of this world can be settled goes very far beyond such an instrument as the League of Nations. It does not believe, has never believed, that the League of Nations can guarantee final peace, that the League is the only way to preserve peace, or even that it is the chief way to preserve peace. But even with a limited sphere it may act as something of a hindrance in the way of the war-makers. It may act as an obstacle, an impediment, something that hinders their action. The Soviet Union supports the League, as the Soviet Union has repeatedly supported other things, while not by any means believing that they were what their devoted and sometimes deluded supporters thought them to be —because the League still can play a positive part (be it ever so little) in hindering war.

'Because of that the Soviet Union is utterly and completely and uncompromisingly against any suggestion of "reform" of the League of Nations! The Soviet Union says that something which may, if its principles are applied 100 per cent, constitute an obstacle or impediment to war, does not require reforming. It does not require tinkering with, interfering with. It requires utilizing to the full.'[1]

The proposals for a reform of the League Covenant referred to by Rothstein arose directly out of the failure of the League in the Abyssinian crisis.[2] They took their urgency from the successive withdrawals of Japan, Germany, and Italy. An important impetus to the idea of reform was given by Neville Chamberlain on 10 June 1936, when he declared the policy of pursuing and intensifying sanctions against Italy to be 'the very midsummer of madness'. 'Surely', he said, 'it is time that the Nations who compose the League should review the situation and should decide to set limits to the functions of the League in future that they may accord with its real powers.' He went on to suggest that the existing coercive provisions of the League

[1] *Geneva and the Drift to War: Problems of Peace*, Twelfth Series (Allen and Unwin, 1938), pp. 179–80.
[2] For the proceedings of the League over the Abyssinian crisis, May–July, see *Survey for 1935*, II, pp. 482–514.

should be abandoned and that in future, under regional agreements approved by the League, sanctions and the accompanying risk of war should only be borne by nations directly interested in the various 'danger spots' of the world.[1]

A reform of the League on these lines would of course amount to releasing members from obligations which they found irksome; it had the additional advantage, from the point of view especially of some of the minor Powers, that it might permit the return of the absentee Great Powers and so remove from themselves the risk of being thought by these Great Powers to be members of a hostile organization. Discussions of League reform thus revolved round the two interlocked questions of removing its coercive character and of rendering it universal.[2] The initiative was taken by the Government of Chile, which on 26 June 1936 requested the League Council to take up the question of the 'reform of the Covenant'. The knowledge that the intention was to water down Articles X, XI, and XVI was no doubt the reason for the objections voiced by Litvinov to any general proposition for League reform.[3] The matter was postponed for discussion at the League Assembly, where Litvinov dealt with it in his speech on 1 July.[4]

After an analysis of the League's failure in the Abyssinian conflict, Litvinov challenged two of the principal contentions of the would-be reformers of the League. It was not universality which had been lacking, since some States-Members had disregarded their obligations under Article XVI, while the action of the United States had shown that the League could count on the co-operation of non-members if it chose to act energetically. It was likewise idle to attempt amending the Covenant to suit those members to whom it appeared unsatisfactory. For one thing, there was no agreement among the critics of the Covenant; for another, to recover by this means the adhesion of the Powers who had left the League was in fact to 'make the League safe for aggressors. Therefore the thing was to talk not of reforming the Covenant, but of making it explicit and stronger.' There must be a definition of aggression; economic sanctions must remain obligatory, and if it was too much to hope as yet for obligatory military sanctions, the latter should at least be embodied in regional pacts which should 'not super-

[1] *Survey for 1935*, II, pp. 463–4.
[2] The following paragraphs are based on S. Engel, *League Reform: an analysis of official proposals and discussions, 1936–9* (Geneva Research Centre, 1940). Much of the League material used for this analysis has not been published.
[3] *L.N.O.J.*, 1936, p. 752.   [4] *L.N.O.J. Spec. Suppl.*, 151, pp. 35–58.

sede the League Covenant but supplement it'. Pending the
realization of the ultimate ideal of universal disarmament all
one could do was

'to strengthen the League of Nations as an instrument of peace. To
strengthen the League of Nations is to abide by the principle of
collective security, which is by no means a product of idealism, but
is a practical measure towards the security of all peoples, to abide
by the principle that peace is indivisible.'

The Assembly resolved that the Governments of the States-
Members of the League should be invited to submit written
proposals for 'improving the application of the principles of the
Covenant'.[1]

The proposals from the Soviet Government were contained
in a communication to the League, signed by Litvinov and dated
22 August 1936.[2] Litvinov objected to the idea of proceeding
by way of formal amendment of the Covenant because the
requirements under Article XXVI would cause difficulty. Instead, the communication went on to suggest bases 'which if
accepted would . . . contribute to the more precise and effective
application of the principles of the Covenant in the sphere of
collective security, and which might with that object be adopted
either in the form of an Assembly resolution or by way of a
protocol open for signature by all members of the League'.

Under these proposals, it would in future be obligatory for
the Council to meet within three days of the notification to the
Secretary-General of the existence of a state of war. The Council
should reach within a maximum of three days a decision as to
whether the circumstances were such as to call into operation
the provisions of Article XVI. Such a decision should be attain-
able by the votes of three quarters of the members present,
excluding the States involved. The Council's decision should
have the automatic result of putting the offender into a state of
war with all the members of the League and so making it subject to sanctions. These sanctions should include military sanctions on the part of States bound to the State attacked by pacts
of mutual assistance, and on the part of other States, according
to Article XVI, 2, of the Covenant. The failure of the Council
to reach agreement should not affect the obligations of parties
to pacts of mutual assistance; action under them should not be
deemed aggression, and preparations for putting them into
effect should be permissible from the date upon which the notification of a state of war was first made to the Secretary-General.

[1] 'Documents relating to the Application of the Principles of the
Covenant', *L.N.O.J. Spec. Suppl.*, 154.
[2] ibid., pp. 10–11.

The Council should (again by a three-quarters vote) decide what non-military sanctions were obligatory under Article XVI, 1 and 3, and should permit these obligations to be wholly or partially suspended in the case of particular States in order to ensure concerted action and to minimize inequality of sacrifice. Economic measures should be taken against States not fulfilling their obligations with regard to economic sanctions. Where it was necessary for constitutional reasons, League members should pass the enabling legislation permitting the future imposition of economic sanctions without delay.

The concluding passages of this document are worth quoting as a further example of the consistency of the security pro-gramme of the Soviet Union at this time:

'XI. Mutual assistance agreements between States concerned in the maintenance of security in specific areas shall be recognized as constituting a supplementary guarantee of security within the frame-work of the Covenant. The following agreements which have been or which may in future be concluded between two or more States shall be recognised as constituting such a supplementary guarantee:

'1. Agreements which embody an undertaking to assist any signa-tory only when the latter is the victim of aggression;
'2. Agreements which make assistance obligatory in the same cases in which the Covenant itself acknowledges the right to furnish assistance;
'3. Agreements which are registered and published in conformity with Article XVIII of the Covenant.

'I think I should add that, in the opinion of the Government of the U.S.S.R., the putting into operation of these principles would be facilitated if it were also stipulated that for the purpose of the application of Article XVI of the Covenant, any State which has committed any act coming within the categories specified in the report on the definition of aggression submitted on 24 May 1933, by the Committee on Security of the "Conference for the Reduction and Limitation of Armaments"[1] shall be regarded as having resorted to war.'

The various suggestions for League reform were analysed in a report by the Secretary-General which was submitted to the Seventeenth Assembly when it met in September 1936. Further proposals were also made verbally. In his speech on 28 Sep-tember,[2] Litvinov dealt with a suggestion which had been made that the unanimity rule in Article XI should be revised. Much could be said in favour of revising this rule in regard to certain cases, but caution was needed since the rule had provided a

[1] This document will be found in *Documents for 1933*, pp. 217–30.
[2] *L.N.O.J. Spec. Suppl.*, 155, pp. 51–4.

dam by which the League was saved from being inundated 'with all kinds of petty claims having no connexion with the preservation of peace'. Furthermore, Article XI was only valuable in cases where some 'unexpected and accidental dispute' threatened grave consequences; it was ineffective in cases of intentional aggression. Article XI could only be effective when backed by Article XVI, and it was this article in which the unanimity rule should be rescinded. He also dealt with the suggestion that Article XIX of the Covenant should be 'activized' by pointing out that revision of international treaties would only be a fruitful undertaking if embarked upon with the preliminary consent of all the parties concerned, as in the case of the recent revision of the Straits Convention. Otherwise the discussion of such treaties by the League might merely have provided an encouragement to armed aggression. The Soviet delegation did not object to the (French) proposal for recalling the Bureau of the Disarmament Conference, while pointing out that disarmament to be effective required to be universal. Litvinov's main emphasis, however, was once more on the Soviet objections to any reform of the League Covenant designed to make its membership wider. There was no objection to negotiating with even 'the most aggressive countries' but they should not pay them 'premiums for being so kind as to negotiate'.

On 10 October 1936, the League Assembly set up a special committee—the Committee of 28—'to study all proposals . . . made by Governments regarding the application of the principles of the Covenant and the principles connected therewith'. The first session of this body was held from 14 to 17 December. The Chilean Government now carried its initiative a step further by proposing that countries outside the League should be consulted as to what reforms they would require before joining, or rejoining, it. This proposal was successfully resisted by the Soviet delegate Boris Stein, the Soviet Ambassador to Italy. It was decided to appoint rapporteurs on the various general issues involved and M. Stein was made *rapporteur* on the question of a possible regional or continental organization of the League.

The Chilean proposal was again discussed at the Committee's meeting on 10–11 September 1937.

'On the other hand, M. Stein resolutely opposed the idea of consulting non-members until the present members of the League reached agreement at any rate as to the main line of the proposed reconstruction of the Covenant. "All are [*sic*] aware", he said, "of the motive which had induced certain States to leave the League, and of the Articles of the Covenant which ran counter to the activities of those States." All know [sic] "the sort of League of Nations which those States would like to see at Geneva and to which they would be prepared to return".'[1]

The Chilean proposal was nevertheless revived at the Eighteenth Assembly (13 September–6 October 1937). Litvinov was once again the spokesman for the Soviet Union.[2] Once again his main theme was the uselessness of trying to reconcile the aggressors with the League by weakening the obligations of the Covenant, and he insisted that the suggested approaches to non-members were preparatory to a move in this direction. The matter was again referred to the Committee of 28, where Litvinov himself took part in a discussion on 25 September. Finally, the Assembly reached a compromise, it being decided by a resolution on 4 October that the Council should decide under what conditions the opinions of non-member States, or of States which had given notice, should be ascertained. Litvinov abstained from voting on the resolution.[3]

Litvinov reiterated the Soviet viewpoint in a speech at the meeting of the League Council on 27 January 1938.[4] The Committee of 28, meeting from 31 January to 2 February 1938, discussed a report drawn up by Lord Cranborne on the 'Participation of all States in the League of Nations', but failed to reach any agreement. Litvinov again attended in person and his speech was mainly devoted to a defence of Article XVI, which with its 'intrinsic possibilities' remained, despite all disappointments, 'the League's most valuable asset' and a ,potential of peace'.[5]

The Committee's report was considered at the meeting of the League Council on 11–14 May 1938. The Chilean delegate now declared that his country proposed to withdraw from the League of Nations, in view of its failure to persuade the League to remodel itself into 'an international organization of a non-coercive character'.

[1] Engel, op. cit., p. 44.
[2] Speech of 21 September 1937, L.N.O.J. Spec. Suppl., 169, pp. 79–83.
[3] L.N.O.J. Spec. Suppl., 169, pp. 112–13. The Assembly also resolved that the League of Nations should, in the event of war, or threat of war, seek to associate with its efforts non-members of the League bound by the (Briand-Kellogg) Pact of Paris or by the (Argentine) Treaty of Non-Aggression and Conciliation. M. Stein had the proviso inserted that the League should not on their account delay 'its own action in virtue of the Covenant'. The United States and Italy, as well as most of the Latin American States, were signatories of the Argentine Treaty. Documents for 1933, pp. 474–80.
[4] L.N.O.J., 1938, pp. 82–4.
[5] M. Litvinov, Against Aggression (Lawrence and Wishart, 1939), pp. 109–13.

The Nineteenth Assembly of the League (12–30 September 1938) again embarked on a discussion of Article XVI. Litvinov, in a speech on 21 September, restated the Soviet thesis and particularly the objections of the Soviet Government to any suggestion that Article XVI should lose its obligatory character:[1]

'The bitter taste of the remedy we are offered seems to be realized by the doctors themselves, since they propose to dilute it with syrup, in the shape of the suggestion that the unanimity rule be abolished in respect of the first paragraph of Article XI, dealing with what the League must do in the event of war or threat of war. Such a suggestion might have been welcomed if Article XVI were maintained, with its list of practical measures which the League can take. But when we are asked to nullify Article XVI, the aggressor will not be frightened of Article XI, which makes it possible only morally to condemn him.'

It was logical, as one delegate had had the courage to propose, to couple the abolition of Article X with that of Article XVI, went on Litvinov, since if 'collective measures for combating aggressors were abandoned', the undertaking to preserve the independence and integrity of States-Members would remain 'an empty declaration deprived of all practical significance'. In spite of the apparent defeat of all the hopes which had been placed in the League, the Soviet Union was far from regretting its decision to accept membership in it, 'if only because there would undoubtedly have otherwise been attempts to attribute the alleged impotence and collapse of the League to its absence'.

On 30 September, the Assembly accepted a report from the Committee of 28 of which the operative passage ran as follows:

'There is general agreement that the military measures contemplated in Article XVI are not compulsory. As regards the economic and financial measures, many Members of the League have stated that they could not in present conditions consider themselves bound automatically to apply such measures in any conflict. Some Members expressed the contrary view.'[2]

A protocol was adopted, under Article XXVI of the Covenant, incorporating amendments to the Covenant having the effect of

---

[1] *L.N.O.J. Spec. Suppl.*, 183, pp. 74–8.

[2] *L.N.O.J. Spec. Suppl.*, 183, pp. 142–4. The opposition of Poland and Hungary prevented the passage of a resolution to modify the unanimity rule in Article XI. A resolution was passed favouring 'technical and non-political' collaboration between the League and non-members. The Soviet Union showed little interest in this aspect of the League's work during the period of its membership.

separating the Covenant from the Peace Treaties. This protocol was not signed by the U.S.S.R.

Throughout these discussions, Litvinov was thus the representative of that school of thought which held that at a time when some of the world's major Powers were almost self-confessed aggressors, those nations which wished to preserve the peace could best do so by preserving and operating the existing machinery of the League. The policy was thus the opposite of what came to be known as appeasement—the policy of winning over the discontented and potentially aggressive nations by concessions to 'reasonable' demands, and of reviving the attraction of League membership for them by eliminating the coercive elements in the Covenant. It is perhaps worth pointing out that certain foreign observers (outside Germany, Italy, and Japan) were not prepared to accept this Soviet policy at its face-value. Soviet enthusiasm for Article XVI was, they asserted, motivated by the desire to see the remaining Great Powers involved in war with each other. This internecine conflict of the 'capitalist' States would then, it was insinuated, be used by the Communist International as an opportunity for renewing its efforts for revolution on a world scale.

Such for instance was one interpretation placed upon the speech made by Litvinov at the meeting of the League Council in London on 17 March 1936, in which he declared that the League of Nations had the duty of preventing the violations of treaties and of its own Covenant and that a League which confined itself to verbal protests would be worse than useless, since it might 'lull the nations into a sense of false security' and 'prevent them taking timely measures themselves for their self-defence'. The speech concluded by promising Soviet participation in any measures adopted by the Council in connexion with Germany's recent reoccupation of the Rhineland.[1] As has already been seen, this speech was described by Lord Lothian as 'the most sinister speech ever made at the Council of the League', and Soviet policy was declared by him to be based on the desire to maintain discord in Europe, with Communism as the beneficiary should the discord 'precipitate itself in war'.[2]

The activities of the Communist International in this period were guided by the decisions of the Seventh Congress which had met in the late summer of 1935.[3] The tasks of its various constituent parties, as defined by the General-Secretary, Dimitrov, could be summed up under the related headings of the 'struggle

---

[1] *Documents for 1936*, pp. 91–7.
[2] Speech at Chatham House, 2 April 1936, quoted in vol. I, p. 109 fn.
[3] See vol. I, chap. 15.

against Fascism' and the 'struggle against war'.[1] It was recognized that the actual course to be pursued would have to be varied in the different countries. But the basic tactics, to be applied especially in those countries where the Communist Party had a legal existence within the framework of democratic institutions, was the winning of mass support for the immediate objectives of the Comintern from the ranks of those who did not share its ultimate aims. This was to be achieved in two stages: first, by the formation of 'united fronts', that is by securing 'joint action by the supporters of the parties and organizations of the two Internationals, the Communist and the Second International'; and second, by using this as a basis for 'the formation of a wide, popular anti-Fascist front' in each country. The 'united front' was thus a purely proletarian formation, while the 'people's front' or 'popular front' knew of no such class limitation.

Since the struggle against war was conceived of as meaning collective resistance to Germany and Japan, since the struggle against Fascism demanded the defence of 'bourgeois-democratic' institutions, and since Communists were ordered not to allow the Fascists to monopolize the national appeal or to make themselves out to be 'supporters of national nihilism', it might have seemed that the Congress had prepared the way for a period of real collaboration between the Communists of the democratic countries and their labour and radical parties and organizations. But as Dimitrov himself made clear, there could in fact be no question of the Communists surrendering their right to independent action and independent propaganda, even if their tactical collaboration involved participation in a 'united front' or 'popular front' government. They were still to be free to carry on independent agitation and the propaganda of Marxism; trade union unity, an objective much stressed, was to mean the capture of trade union leadership by the Communists, and the joint struggle with social-democratic workers was not to prevent Communists from branding the leaders of the social-democratic parties as traitors. In other words, the common struggle for agreed objectives was to culminate in the winning of support for the Communist parties and the corresponding weakening of other left organizations. This basic dualism must be regarded as the main cause of the comparative ill-success of the Comintern's new course.

There were indeed some gains to record, and in both France

[1] See his report to the Congress of 2 August and his speeches of 12 and 20 August in G. Dimitrov, *The United Front* (Lawrence and Wishart, 1938), pp. 9–141.

and Spain the 'popular front' was of sufficient importance to warrant separate treatment. Elsewhere the big Socialist parties and trade unions showed considerable powers of resistance. Furthermore, the left wings of these movements were increasingly hostile to a policy which seemed to be ready to sacrifice all proletarian interests to the exigencies of the Soviet Union's foreign policy. There was, therefore, a final breach between the Communists on the one hand, and on the other hand, the French left-wing Socialists, the British Independent Labour Party, and the Austrian Socialists. Only the Young Communist League made real headway; for most left-wing youth organizations and some organizations, nominally unpolitical, were 'captured' by the Communists during the 'popular front' period.[1]

Attempts were renewed in this period to develop direct relations between the Communist International and the Labour and Socialist (Second) International. And there were fruitless exchanges in 1937 between leaders of the latter and certain Comintern representatives in western Europe. Another effort at 'working-class unity' was made along trade union lines. The Congress of the International Federation of Trade Unions at its meeting in London in 1936 passed a unanimous resolution to take up negotiations with all non-affiliated trade union movements and a copy of this was sent to the Russian Trade Unions. No reply was received by the next meeting of the General Council of the I.F.T.U., but after a further communication, the Russians agreed to negotiate and delegates from the I.F.T.U. visited Moscow in November 1937. The Russians put forward conditions for their adhesion. These were discussed at a meeting of the General Council at Oslo in October 1938, when it was decided by 14 votes to 7 not to conduct any further negotiations. The question was raised again by the British delegation to the Zürich Congress of the I.F.T.U. in July 1938, when they moved that the Russians be invited 'to affiliate on the basis of the statutes and rules of the I.F.T.U.' But the Congress ultimately voted by 60 votes to 5 with 18 abstentions, to confirm the Oslo decision.[2]

---

[1] One example of this comes from Great Britain. The Socialist societies in the British Universities accepted fusion with the Communist societies with the result that the federal body, the University Labour Federation, was inevitably dominated by the latter. On the outbreak of war in 1939, the University Labour Federation followed the new Communist line and opposed it. A similar attitude was taken by the National Union of Students which, although allegedly non-political, was also dominated by Communists at that time.

[2] John Price, *The International Labour Movement* (Oxford University Press, 1945), pp. 86–8, 139–41, 157–9, 214; *The Economist*, 24 February 1945.

In as far as a line of development can be drawn for these years, the most important thing to note is the increasing role given to questions of foreign policy in Comintern statements. In an article on 1 May 1936, Dimitrov insisted that the struggle against war must be interpreted as meaning the struggle against specific instigators of war. This naturally raised the question as to what position should be taken up by Communist parties in those countries whose foreign policy was opposed to that of Germany and Japan and whose governments were even, as in the case of France, linked by treaty with the U.S.S.R. Since power in these countries was in the hands of bourgeois governments, declared Dimitrov, the 'party of the working-class' could not take any 'political responsibility for the defensive measures of these governments and the military budget as a whole'. But Communists could abstain from voting on purely defensive measures, such as frontier fortifications, and might even speak and vote in favour of humanitarian measures, such as the provision of gas-masks for civilians. This answer was justified by the statement that the international situation was not comparable with that of 1914, when two 'military imperialist coalitions' were equally 'striving to establish their world hegemony'. It was now wrong to depict all countries as aggressors; the proletariat must support the League and sanctions.[1] In other words, in external as in internal affairs, the Communists were faced with an insoluble dilemma. To continue their previous opposition to all warlike measures was to weaken and perhaps destroy the military power of countries upon whose assistance the Soviet Union would have to depend in the event of war with Germany; to abandon their opposition altogether was to abandon left-wing leadership to parties unembarrassed by a connexion with the defence needs of the Soviet Union. The compromise satisfied no one and did little but increase suspicions of the Comintern and hence of the genuineness of the Soviet Union's policy of collective security.

It should of course be remembered in dealing with Communist policy and its repercussions that Communist propaganda was under legal restraints in most countries and the Communist Party outlawed in an increasing number of States. Only in the British Commonwealth, France, the United States, Czechoslovakia, Spain, Mexico, and in some of the lesser South American Republics were Communists given full political rights.[2]

[1] Dimitrov, op. cit., pp. 172–85.
[2] F. Eccard, 'La Legislation anti-Communiste dans le monde', *Revue Politique et Parlementaire*, July 1938.

The outbreak of the Spanish Civil War seemed to bring the danger of a general war in which the Soviet Union would be involved a great deal nearer. Writing in December 1936, Dimitrov claimed that events in France and Spain had justified the Comintern's policy.[1] But disappointments over the results of the 'non-intervention' policy and particularly over the actions of the French Popular Front Government increased the tension. This manifested itself in two contradictory ways. On the one hand, the local arrangements with non-Communist parties were weakened by the Communists' abuse of Socialist leaders.[2] On the other, there was an attempt to extend the field of anti-Fascist co-operation to embrace the totality of the working-class movement. Thus, after the bombardment by the German Navy of Almeria in Spain on 31 May 1937, the Comintern approached the Second International with abortive proposals for joint action.[3] An article by Dimitrov in July 1937 declared that the Fascist Powers were preparing for a world war and that working-class unity alone could save the situation.[4] Another article, in the following month, repeated this demand and coupled it with a denunciation of the ruling classes of Great Britain, France, and the United States, and of Trotskyists, and traitors of the Second International, for tolerating the blackmail of the Fascist Powers.

By now a further shift could be detected in Communist tactics—one particularly visible in France. Policy was still further subordinated to the supreme question of the defence of the U.S.S.R. In an article in November 1937 on 'The Soviet Union and the Working Classes of Capitalist Countries', Dimitrov claimed that the influence of Communism in the working-class movement was everywhere on the increase. The split in its ranks brought about by 'social-democratism' had been healed. Now two world-forces were clearly aligned against each other; but the criterion as to whether a particular individual or group stood with the forces of light or the forces of darkness was no longer one of proletarian origin or of Marxist ideology. The most certain criterion, declared Dimitrov, was the attitude towards the U.S.S.R.:

'The *historical dividing line* between the forces of Fascism, war and Capitalism on the one hand and the forces of peace, democracy and Socialism on the other hand is in fact becoming the *attitude* towards the Soviet Union, and not the formal attitude towards the Soviet Power and Socialism in general, but the attitude to the Soviet Union, which has been carrying on a real existence for twenty years already,

[1] Dimitrov, op. cit., pp. 197–216.
[2] ibid., pp. 225–38.   [3] ibid., pp. 245–52.   [4] ibid., pp. 262–9.

with its untiring struggle against enemies, with its dictatorship of the working class and the Stalin Constitution, with the leading role of the Party of Lenin and Stalin.'[1]

This unequivocal statement by its Secretary-General clearly represented the role of the Comintern at this time. Its *raison d'être* had for the moment nothing to do directly with promoting of Communism; its business was to supplement the efforts of the Soviet Foreign Office and the Red Army; its friends were those, and only those, who put the defence of the Soviet Union in the forefront of their policy.

On the other hand, the weapon was to be that of direct pressure by the working class of the capitalist States. On 21 June 1938, Dimitrov issued a four-point anti-Fascist programme calling on the workers of the world especially in France, Great Britain, and the United States, to bring effective pressure on their governments to join the U.S.S.R. in destroying the existing régimes in Germany, Italy, and Japan. Stalin, they were reminded, had promised them 'every possible form of organized assistance from the Soviet Union'. The four points were: (1) the international isolation of the Fascist aggressors and mass pressure in each country against all those who opposed this; (2) economic sanctions against Germany, Italy, and Japan; (3) united action by the international proletariat, not only against aggressive States but against bourgeois governments, to compel them to adopt a firmer policy against aggression and to break the influence of such leaders as Sir Walter Citrine; (4) a firm unbreakable pact between the working classes of capitalist countries and the Soviet people for all-round mutual support on the lines recently laid down by Stalin.[2]

During the following months, the course of internal events in France strongly favoured the Comintern's policy. The recrudescence of the activities of the Fascist leagues in the autumn of 1935 did more than the Communists' propaganda to persuade the other two major parties of the left to agree to joint action with them. Trade union unity, unattainable in the international field, was assured locally when the Socialist C.G.T. agreed upon fusion at its congress on 24–27 September 1935. The final details took some time to arrange, but the first congress of the united body was held on 2–4 March 1936.[3]

[1] ibid., pp. 270–80. The same note was dominant in the manifesto of the Comintern executive on the occasion of the Twentieth Anniversary of the Revolution in November 1937. This, however, summoned the workers in the democratic as well as the Fascist countries to follow Ruscia's example.

[2] *B.I.N.*, XV, pp. 591–2.

[3] E. Dolléans, *Histoire du Mouvement Ouvrier* (Paris, Armand Colin, 1936–9), vol. 2, p. 385.

The readiness of the Radical and Socialist Parties to co-operate with the Communists was stimulated by the approaching election campaign.[1] The 'rassemblement populaire', composed of the three parties and the smaller Socialist-Republican group, as well as of the two trade union bodies, and of four anti-war and anti-Fascist organizations, announced its formation on 11 January 1936, and published an agreed programme. This included the extension, particularly in eastern Europe, of a system of pacts modelled on the Franco-Soviet Pact.

The Government of Sarraut and Flandin, intended mainly to get the country over the election period, took office on 24 January 1936, at a time when vital decisions could not well be postponed. The first of these was to submit for ratification the Franco-Soviet Pact. The debates which followed have already been commented upon. It is only necessary to re-emphasize that the major danger detected by its opponents 'was of an internal order; the Pact legitimized, as it were, the French Communist Party, and gave it an air of national respectability; with the result that the Third International could in future ravage France with impunity'.[2] Philippe Henriot produced 'evidence' of cheques paid to French Communists by the Comintern, and Jacques Doriot, who had only left the Communist Party at the end of 1933, declared amid the cheers of the Right that, if war were to come, the Soviet Union would abandon France in the middle of it, and bring about a revolution there. Not all the Socialists were happy about an instrument which seemed likely to block any surviving hopes of reconciliation with Germany or of disarmament, and some may have voted for it only in order not to endanger the unity of the Left.

Meanwhile the lessons of the moment were being hammered home by Moscow's leading spokesmen. After the brutal assault on Léon Blum in February 1936, by the followers of Charles Maurras, Dimitrov produced an article which described the assault as 'a blow against the entire working class of France, a blow against the People's Front', and went on to assert that it was clear that certain leaders of the Second International were wrong in thinking that Fascism was on the decline.[3]

The evolution of the French Communist Party continued on the same lines right up to the elections at the end of April. The

[1] The French system of the 'second ballot' placed a premium on such combinations. The low representation which the Communists previously had in the Chamber was due to their aloofness from such electoral bargains. For this and the following paragraphs, see A. Werth, *The Destiny of France* (Hamilton, 1937), and *France and Munich* (Hamilton, 1939).

[2] Werth, *The Destiny of France*, p. 214.   [3] Dimitrov, op. cit., pp. 163-8.

national appeal figured ever more prominently in its propaganda. Tricolour posters identified the cause of the industrial magnates with that of the national enemy, Hitler. New 'patriotic' slogans were highly successful, as were references to 1789, 1792, and 1848. (The Commune of 1871 with its distasteful associations for the bourgeoisie and for all Catholics was allowed to drop out of view.) An effort was even made to exploit the appeal of the 'proletarian' Joan of Arc.[1]

The results of the election and the large majority which the combined parties of the left obtained in the Chamber seemed to justify these tactics. Even more striking was the individual success of the Communist Party, which increased its number of seats from 10 to 72. Moreover, in Paris and its industrial belt, the Communists were proved to be by far the strongest single party. The most significant testimony to the success of the new approach was, however, the heavy vote cast for the Party in some rural areas where, as in the Corrèze, it secured more than 20 per cent of the votes cast.

The next question was whether the Party would participate in a popular front government and so assume responsibility for a share in carrying out the common programme. On 11 May 1936, the Socialist Premier-designate, Blum, asked the Communist Party and the now partly Communist C.G.T. to enter the Government. Both refused, and the Communist press declared that the Party's role would be that of a 'sort of ministry of the masses' organizing, outside the Government, the most ardent and disciplined elements of the popular front. Blum no doubt realized from the start that the Communists had decided that they now had an opportunity to consolidate and even extend their gains, since the responsibilities of office would inevitably handicap the Government in the task of satisfying all the hopes placed in it. Blum made his appreciation of the position clear when, speaking on 30 May, he said:

'I am being spoken of as a Kerensky who is preparing the way for a Lenin. I can assure you that this is not going to be a Kerensky Government; and it is equally certain that if we fail we shall not be succeeded by a Lenin.'

The Communists were provided with an early opportunity of staking their claim to be the only genuine representatives of the wave of left-wing enthusiasm apparently sweeping France, in the outburst of 'stay-in' strikes which paralysed French industry at the end of May and the beginning of June 1936, and did not die down finally until the end of the year. It seems fairly

[1] For the ideology of the French Communist Party at this time see M. Thorez, *France Today and the People's Front* (Gollancz, 1936).

clear that the strikes were spontaneous manifestations by the rank-and-file of the workers, and that the Communists in their ranks were not acting under the direction of the party leaders. By about 7 June, when the Matignon agreements were signed between the employers and the C.G.T., agreements which heralded the subsidence of the movement, the Communist leaders were showing some uneasiness lest they should be left behind by the development of this new leftward movement. As its first impetus declined, however, they apparently managed to assert their authority. At a victory demonstration at Montrouge on 14 June, the victorious strikers were acclaimed as Communist heroes to the sound of the somewhat ill-adjusted slogans of 'Une France Libre, Forte et Heureuse' and 'Les Soviets Partout'. Thus began the Communist myth of the stay-in-strikes and the popular front.[1]

The result of this was to enhance the general belief among right-wing and moderate elements, both inside and outside France, that the Front Populaire Government was itself an instrument of the Comintern—a factor of considerable importance for the full understanding of France's role in the Spanish crisis.[2] The Communist clamour for intervention made caution on the part of the Government doubly necessary.

It was Spain indeed which provided the main plank upon which the Communists could safely denounce the Blum Government, in spite of the fact that, as Blum pointed out on 6 September 1936, the Soviet Government had itself signed the non-intervention agreement. And it was on the Spanish issue that, on 5 December, the Communists first withheld their vote from the Government on a confidence motion. A declaration was published on this occasion by the Communist party, stating that the party would loyally support the Government on other matters and that the popular front continued; but the divergences between the party and its partners in the arrangement became increasingly plain. As an historian of the Third Republic has put it:

'In every crisis the Communists were able to make the best of both worlds, to get credit for whatever gains were made by the

[1] For a version of French history, 1936–40, lauding the role of the Communists and vilifying that of the Socialists, see the novel by the Soviet journalist, Ilya Ehrenburg, *The Fall of Paris* (Hutchinson, 1943).

[2] An illustration of this belief can be found in an incident recounted by Blum at the 'Riom Trial' in March 1942. M. de Saint-Creusot, of the famous armaments firm of Schneider-Creusot, offered the Soviet Ambassador Potemkin a speeding up in the firm's deliveries of armaments to the Soviet Union, if he would influence Blum to exempt the firm from the projected measures of nationalization. *France*, 16 September 1942.

workers and to put on the shoulders of the Socialists and Radicals the blame for any disappointments . . . the "Front Populaire" was formed to save the Republic. . . . Well, the Republic was now safe, safe at any rate from its Fascist enemies. Was it safe from its new-found friends? Many Republicans and some Socialists had begun to wonder.'[1]

The continuous political effervescence which Communist tactics helped to maintain, reacted unfavourably upon the French attitude towards the Franco-Soviet Pact, quite apart from those who objected to that instrument for other reasons. The arguments of the Pact's supporters were also weakened by the repercussions of the Moscow trials:

'The execution of Marshal Tukhachevsky especially startled a country with a conscript army which, it was realised, might have found itself taking the field in alliance with a power whose high command was conspiring with the common enemy.'[2]

After Blum's announcement of a 'pause' in the application of the Government's programme, in his speech of 24 February 1937, the Communists took a turn to the left and Thorez publicly denounced 'Governments of the left who pursue a policy of the right'. The C.G.T., now strongly under internal Communist pressure, also showed some intransigence; but the tension abated in the early summer and on 16 June, after some apparent hesitation, the Communists voted in favour of the Government's Emergency Powers Bill. Once again, the explanation given was that it was necessary to preserve the popular front. After Blum's fall, the Communists duly supported the new popular front Government formed by the Radical-Socialist leader, Chautemps. The importance of maintaining the popular front was stressed by Dimitrov, who wrote that reactionary leaders were trying to sow mistrust between the Socialist and Communist Parties and 'preparing the conditions for the establishment of a coalition government of the bourgeois and Socialist parties directed against the Communists and the People's Front movement'.

The Communists' devotion to the popular front was strengthened by the evidence of Fascist conspiracies in France which came to light in the autumn of 1937. There was an obvious danger that a right-wing government might come into power which would be prepared to attempt an accommodation with Hitler and to jettison the Franco-Soviet Pact. The new strike-wave in December 1937 was thus not to the liking of Com-

[1] D. W. Brogan, *The Development of Modern France* (Hamilton, 1940), pp. 712, 717.
[2] ibid., p. 720.

munist leaders. But the Radicals seem to have decided that
even the tacit support of the Communist Party was prejudicial
to them, and it was a speech by the Prime Minister denouncing
the Communists, which made the position of the Socialist
ministers in the Government intolerable and brought about the
Government's fall.

During the ministerial crisis of 14 January 1938, Blum with
Communist support, launched the idea of a national government to include all parties from the centre to the extreme left—
'de Reynaud à Thorez'. This was, however, vetoed by radical
and centre opposition. After the interim government formed by
Chautemps had ended its existence on 8 March, at the height
of the Austrian crisis, Blum attempted to meet the dangerous
international situation by forming a national government extending still further to the right—'de Marin à Thorez'—excluding only avowed Fascist groups. Once again it was opposition
on the right of the proposed coalition which made the scheme
unworkable. The new Blum Government was based on the
original popular front coalition, but the popular front period
ended for good with Blum's resignation on 8 April. The ministry
formed by Daladier on 10 April was clearly of a different vin-
tage, although the Communist Party voted in favour of the
ministerial declaration of policy.

It is possible to trace in French developments the shift in the
Comintern line to a position in which ideological considerations
were almost wholly submerged by those deriving from the international position of the Soviet Union. But it is also clear that the
local needs of the Communists demanded at the same time an
ostensible devotion to left-wing action. The two were in the long
run incompatible and by the summer of 1938 the period of Franco-
Soviet collaboration, begun in 1933-4, had come to a close.

To sum up, it is as a period of renewed Soviet isolation that
the years 1936-8 should be regarded. There was something of
a paradox in the fact that they were also the years in which the
theory of collective security was most passionately expounded
by Soviet spokesmen and in which the Soviet Union was most
active at Geneva. The failure to make a reality of the new policy
must be ascribed to a combination of causes, not all of them
within the Soviet power to control. Not too much importance
should be attached to the fact that economic ties were less
significant than in the preceding period. Russia's foreign trade
remained at a comparatively low level.[1] In 1937 it was just

[1] For statistical analyses, see A. Baykov, *Soviet Foreign Trade* (Princeton
University Press, 1946), and M. V. Condoide, *Russian-American Trade* (Ohio
State University, 1946).

under, and in 1938 only just over, 1·1 per cent of the world's total trade (compared with 2·44 per cent in 1932, and 3·8 per cent in 1913). Credits had ceased to play an important part since the trade balance was favourable in every year between 1933 and 1937. In 1938 there was a slight negative balance owing principally to a sharp fall in Soviet exports, but the increasing production of gold could help to cover such imports as the rearmament programme required. More important than the economic causes of Soviet isolationism was an increasing mental isolationism. In some respects the Soviet leaders revealed themselves more percipient than many foreign statesmen but in others (and this is the importance of the Comintern aspect of affairs) they revealed that they still worked for objects which were not those of the liberal civilization of the West, and still spoke a language and lived in a world of mental concepts of their own. Finally, the apparent weakness of the Soviet State as such, discouraged all except professed Communists or fellow-travellers from attempting to understand this language or to examine these concepts. The collapse of the European system of security between the reoccupation of the Rhineland and 'Munich' cannot be dealt with merely as a series of diplomatic blunders.

Chapter Two

RUSSIA AND THE SPANISH CIVIL WAR

EVEN more clearly than events in France, the Spanish Civil War served to illumine the contradictions inherent in the Soviet attempt to combine diplomatic action at the side of the Western democracies with an active 'popular front' policy on the part of the Comintern. But both the motives and the nature of intervention in Spain by the Comintern and the Soviet Union were so largely misunderstood at the time that it is essential to consider briefly not only its diplomatic repercussions but also its actual influence on the Spanish situation itself.[1]

It is necessary to begin by trying to rectify some errors about the war and foreign intervention which still persis from the disputes of the time. The right considered it necessary to obscure the fact that Franco was incapable of winning without foreign backing, even at a time when Hitler and Mussolini themselves had long thrown off the pretence of non-intervention.[2] Similarly, the left in Britain and France was forced to ignore Russia's role in order to represent the Spanish Republic as a freely-functioning liberal democracy of the Western type. One side called the Spanish Republic 'Bolshevist', 'Moscow-controlled' and 'Red' in order to blacken its reputation among upholders of the existing social order everywhere; the other was not in a position to point out that in so far as the Communists were in control, their power was a guarantee against any large-scale internal changes. Russia was not in Spain to endow it with an immediate Communist revolution.[3]

[1] On this subject see *Survey for 1937*, II, and *Survey for 1938*, I, pp. 260 ff. Unfortunately the companion volume of documents has not appeared. The collection of documents edited by 'Hispanicus' entitled *Foreign Intervention in Spain* (United Editorial, n.d.) limits itself to intervention on the side of the rebels and ends with January 1937. Further documents are contained in N. J. Padelford, *International Law and Diplomacy in the Spanish Civil Strife* (New York, Macmillan, 1939).

[2] The extent of the German economic penetration of Spain even before the Civil War is emphasized in the Fabian Society pamphlet, *Spain in the Post-War World* (1945), by I. and A. Barea.

[3] The complete failure to understand the real role of the Communists or the real anxieties of the Soviet Union helped to make General Franco's friends in Great Britain quite useless as interpreters of what went on in Spain, and their evidence can be largely discounted. Unfortunately first-hand information from the Republican side is still scanty. Of the leading Spanish figures, the only one to have given his own version of events in English, in any detail, is J. Alvarez del Vayo, in his book, *Freedom's Battle*

28

The fact that the popular front triumphs in Spain and France occurred within so short a time of one another, should not have blinded anyone, and probably did not blind Moscow, to the essential differences between the situation in the two countries in the summer of 1936; it is certainly far from easy to trace any exact parallelism in the conduct of the Communist Parties of the two countries—although there can be no doubt that both were thoroughly responsive to Moscow's direction. The comparative weakness of Marxist as compared with Anarcho-Syndicalist ideas in most of Spain, and the fact that it was agrarian and not industrial relations which furnished the greater scope for agitation, largely explain the failure of the Spanish Communist Party to acquire a mass following in the pre-Civil War period.

Nevertheless, Spanish politics were not unaffected by the ideological conflicts which developed during the course of the Russian Revolution. The first impulse of the anarchist trade unions, the C.N.T., towards associating themselves with the Comintern in 1920 was weakened by the repercussions of the suppression of the Kronstadt rising in March 1921. In 1922, the C.N.T. declined all further contact with Moscow, a decision

---

(Heinemann, 1940). It is necessary to remember that he was the chief advocate of the Moscow connexion, outside the Communist party itself. Largo Caballero's point of view can be judged in part from the strongly anti-Communist and anti-Russian articles published in the American press in 1939 by Luis Araquistain, Caballero's Ambassador to France. (See, e.g. *San Francisco Chronicle*, 21 May; *Philadelphia Evening Bulletin*, 23 May; *Cincinnati Times-Star*, 6 June.) A personal narrative of great interest is that of A. Barea, *The Clash* (Faber, 1946). Some of the leading Russian personalities involved are thinly disguised in Ernest Hemingway's novel, *For Whom the Bell Tolls*. The attitude of aloofness towards both sides and the distinct antipathy betrayed towards all Spanish politicians have proved insufficient qualifications in the case of Salvador de Madariaga, for giving an objective account of the war; and the chapters devoted to it in the 1942 edition of his *Spain*, must be read with considerable caution; so must Louis Fischer's *Men and Politics* (Cape, 1941) and W. G. Krivitsky's *I was Stalin's Agent* (Hamilton, 1939). An interesting interpretation (by a left-wing non-Communist Dutch volunteer) is that of Jef Last in his *The Spanish Tragedy* (Routledge, 1939). The book by Henry Buckley, *The Life and Death of the Spanish Republic* (Hamilton, 1940), a useful account by an English journalist, tends to minimise Russian activities, largely no doubt because of the extreme caution which the Russians, like the Germans to some extent, but unlike the Italians, took to keep their activities unobserved. There is an excellent but all too brief epilogue on the politics of the Spanish War in Gerald Brenan's *The Spanish Labyrinth* (Cambridge University Press, 1943). F. Borkenau gives the result of his own observations and of his sociological studies in the *The Spanish Cockpit* (Faber, 1937), in chap. xxiv of *The Communist International* (Faber, 1938), and in his introduction to José Martin Blazquez' *I Helped to Build an Army* (Secker and Warburg, 1939); all these three books were published before the end of the war in Spain.

in which they were preceded by the Spanish Socialist Party. A
small Communist Party was founded from exile by Nin and
Maurin, ex-members of the C.N.T., in company with some
Socialists. But the Party remained insignificant and was indeed
too weak for Primo de Rivera to trouble to suppress it during
the dictatorship. At the end of 1931, Nin and Maurin, with
most of the Catalan membership of the Party, left it to form a
left Marxist (Trotskyist) group and as such took part in the
Catalan rising of 1932. This group itself split after the 1933
elections on the question of whether to co-operate with the
Socialists. In February 1934, Largo Caballero's *Alianza Obrera*,
an attempt at a united front under left-wing Socialist leadership,
was joined by the Trotskyists but not by the Anarcho-Syndi-
calists or the Communists. The Communists eventually acceded
to it in accordance with the new Comintern line a few days
before the Asturias rising in October 1934. The dissident left
Marxists also joined. The conduct of the Communists during
the Asturias rising added to their following—they had returned
only one member to the 1933 Cortes—but they were still
numerically insignificant. They remained until 1936, when the
popular front was formed, a sternly revolutionary party, rather
reluctantly following the new path taken by the Comintern.[1]
Their working-class following outside the Asturias was confined
to Seville and their membership in March 1936 has not been
reckoned at more than 3,000. The rise in their representation
in the Cortes to 14, must be attributed in large measure to their
electoral coalition with the Socialists and Republicans. On the
other hand, in Spain, as elsewhere, Communist influence extended well outside the ranks of the Party itself. The amalgamation of the Socialist and Communist youth organizations which
Alvarez del Vayo carried through after his return from Russia in
April 1936 gave the Communists control of the united organization. In Catalonia, where local separatism further complicated
political issues, the Socialists and Communists were united in
July 1936 into a single party, the P.S.U.C., which accepted the
authority of the Comintern. The two minor Marxist factions
in Catalonia had come together in February to form the
P.O.U.M. The Party was criticized by Trotsky, who retained
a small Catalonian following outside it, but it was denounced
as 'Trotskyist' by the Communists and their associates.[2]

For, in addition to the Marxist-Bakuninist feud, which lived
on in Spain, the rivalry of the Stalinist and anti-Stalinist com-
petitors for the Marxist heritage was also projected on to the

[1] Blazquez, op. cit., pp. 124–5.
[2] For the history of the Spanish left up to July 1936, see Brenan, op. cit.

Spanish scene. It is indeed just possible that this alone would have caused some Russian intervention in Spanish affairs, even had there not been the compelling political and strategic motives provided by Spain's geographical position. The Soviet public proved receptive to the enthusiasm for revolutionary Spain enjoined by the Soviet press from August 1936. But from the Soviet viewpoint it was essential that the ideology of the Spanish Republic should have no room for trends hostile to those dominant at Moscow. 'So far as Catalonia is concerned,' wrote *Pravda* on 17 December 1936, 'the cleaning up of the Trotskyist and Anarcho-Syndicalist elements has already begun and it will be carried out with the same energy as in the U.S.S.R.' The price of Communist support for the Spanish Government was hostility to the Anarcho-Syndicalist programme, even though the C.N.T. was represented in the Caballero Government between its reconstruction on 4 November 1936 and its fall on 15 May 1937, and again in Dr. Negrin's Government after 5 April 1938. If a *modus vivendi* with the Spanish disciples of Bakunin had to be found after the revelation of the C.N.T.'s strength in the Catalan crisis of December 1936, Soviet hostility towards those tarred with the Trotskyist brush was implacable. The severe action taken against the P.O.U.M. after the Barcelona rising of May 1937 was wholly in accordance with Soviet wishes. This does not, however, exhaust the connexion between the internal politics of the Soviet Union and those of loyalist Spain. If the great Russian 'purge' provided a sombre background to events abroad, it was the more important in its Spanish context, in that many of the victims were prominent figures in the world of international Socialism. The charges brought against them did nothing to cement and much to disrupt the forces of the left in Spain as elsewhere. It should also be noted that the 'purge' sooner or later engulfed almost all those who had played a leading role in the Soviet Union's assistance to Spain, in its earliest and most intense phase from October 1936 to February 1937. The public figures of this period, the Ambassador Rosenberg, his second-in-command and successor Gaikis, Michael Koltsov, nominally correspondent of *Pravda*, Generals Kléber and Goriev disappeared, and the political direction of affairs in Spain was left to secondary Comintern figures like André Marty whose influence was wholly unhealthy.

The information at present available permits nothing like a detailed account of Soviet intervention; and even its main phases can be distinguished only with difficulty. The first decision, influenced no doubt by the wish to maintain collabora-

tion with France, was not to intervene.[1] There seems no doubt
that the Soviet Government would have preferred to keep to
non-intervention had it been possible to secure the withdrawal
of foreign aid from the other side, and with it the collapse of
the rebellion.[2] Indeed the first Russian ships which arrived in
Spain at the end of October were laden with food,[3] the same
sort of humanitarian assistance for which the Communists were
later to scoff at the parties of the Second International. When
it became clear that while the French Government was not
going to assist the Spanish Government, the London committee
would not prevent foreign help going to the rebels, the Soviet
Government decided to take action. The revised attitude of the
Soviet Government, of which there had been hints earlier in
the month, was first made public on 23 October, when M.
Maisky informed the Non-Intervention Committee that the
Soviet Government could not consider themselves 'bound by
the agreement for non-intervention to a greater extent than
any of the remaining participants'.[4] But the decision at Mos-
cow was obviously taken at an earlier date. On 16 October
Stalin sent the first public message of Soviet sympathy for the
Spanish cause in a telegram to José Diaz, the secretary of the
Spanish Communist Party. On 28 October, Russian tanks were
in action in Spain for the first time, and on 8 November the
International Brigade arrived on the Madrid front. Recruited
through the machinery of the Comintern, but including no
Russians—there was a nucleus of foreign Communists long
resident in Russia—the Brigade deserves to be regarded as a
very important part of the Soviet contribution to the Republican military strength. Whatever may have been true at later
stages of the war, there can be little doubt that it was Soviet
intervention which, in the autumn of 1936, prevented the fall of
Madrid. The importance of Soviet help at this stage meant that
the Russians had for a time the main responsibility for military

[1] There is a brief account of Soviet diplomacy in regard to the Spanish
conflict in *Istoria Diplomatii* (A History of Diplomacy), ed. V. P. Potemkin,
vol. 3 (Moscow, 1945), pp. 575–86.

[2] See on Russia's reasons for accepting the idea of non-intervention,
Litvinov's speech to the League Assembly on 28 September 1936, which
stressed the fear of war felt by a friendly country (i.e. France). *L.N.O.J.
Spec. Supp.*, 155, pp. 62–4. The Soviet Union's declaration of its adhesion to
the principle of non-intervention, dated 23 August 1936, and the order of the
People's Commissar for Foreign Trade prohibiting the export of war supplies to Spain, dated 28 August, are printed in Padelford, op. cit., pp. 228,
300. Cf. Potemkin's speech at the League Council on 11 December.

[3] Blazquez, op. cit., pp. 246–51.

[4] *Survey for 1937*, II, p. 251; J. R. Bloch, *Espagne, Espagne!* (Paris, Editions
Sociales Internationales, 1936), Pt. II, chap. iv.

operations on the central front. The field commander from November was General Kléber.[1] Russian military personnel was always limited in numbers. Krivitsky's maximum estimate is 2,000; Fischer declares that there were never more than 700 Russians in Spain at any one time.[2] After the first months of the war, the most important aspect of Soviet aid was the fact that Comintern agents were available to assist in the purchase of arms—with Spanish funds. These arms were mostly not of Russian manufacture, but were purchased in different parts of Europe and America as occasion afforded. The chief difficulty throughout was one of transport rather than of supply or finance. The Russians were guaranteed against financial loss by the deposit in Moscow at the beginning of November 1936, of a large part of the gold reserve of the Bank of Spain.

There is no reason to doubt that political developments on the Republican side were conditioned by the importance of Soviet help. This was the easier to achieve in that the local and party nature of the early military formations enabled arms shipments to be directed to specific ports where they would come into the hands of elements which the Soviet authorities regarded as reliable. The Communists had two main political aims. The first was to increase the importance of the Party and its weight in the administration and in the armed forces. From the beginning they opposed the setting up of Revolutionary Committees and the creation of a workmen's militia. They stood for the creation of a centralized, disciplined, professionalized army. In the autumn of 1936, when Alvarez del Vayo was General Commissar for the Army, they secured the institution of a body of political commissars (with functions similar to those of their prototypes in the Red Army) who were the main agents of Communist influence in the Spanish forces. It has been suggested that the cancellation of some of these appointments by Largo Caballero was one of the reasons for his overthrow by the Communists in favour of the Negrin-Prieto combination.[3] The discipline and feeling for organization of the Spanish Communists made them an invaluable toughening element on the Republican side from the beginning of the war.[4] Afterwards, however, the revelation of their complete lack of any principle

---

[1] Krivitsky, op. cit., pp. 114–34; Fischer, op. cit., p. 374.

[2] Krivitsky, op. cit., p. 96; Fischer, op. cit., p. 470. The Soviet Government's decree of 20 February 1937, prohibiting the recruitment of volunteers for Spain, is printed in Padelford, op. cit., p. 364.

[3] See, however, Alvarez del Vayo, op. cit., pp. 124–5. Cf. Brenan, op. cit., p. 328.

[4] This is made abundantly clear in the already cited work by the strongly anti-Communist professional army officer, José Martin Blazquez.

other than their devotion to the policy of the Soviet Union and
of their apparently limitless opportunism lost them the respect
which they had gained.[1] But numerically their advance in the
early part of the war was striking.

The second political task assigned to the Spanish Communists was to prevent any large-scale social upheaval on the
Republican side, which might detract from military efficiency
and further prejudice the Western democracies against the
Republic. This was true from the beginning of the rising. The
Communists' first slogan was: 'This is not a proletarian revolution; it is only a democratic movement.' After a few days this
was altered to 'This is not a revolution at all; it is only the
defence of the legal government.' The visit of Rosenberg to
Moscow in December 1936 resulted in a letter to Largo Caballero, dated the 21st, and signed by Stalin, Voroshilov and,
Molotov.[2] In it they suggested that special consideration should
be given to peasant interests, that the middle and lesser bourgeoisie should be attracted to the side of the Government or
at least kept neutral by guaranteeing their economic interests,
that nothing should be done to alienate the Republican (non-
Socialist) leaders, so as to prevent Spain from being branded as
a Communist State, and that assurances should be given regarding foreign property and interests in Spain. At the same time
the Soviet leaders promised to send further military specialists
to help the Spaniards. It is a little difficult to accept the rather
disingenuous argument of Alvarez del Vayo that the moderation
of Stalin's advice proves that the Soviet Union did not intervene in Spanish internal affairs.[3] On the other hand it is
arguable that it was not Russian pressure which prevented the
Republican régime from developing on more radical lines. The
Russians merely assisted Caballero in his task of imposing
internal discipline on the Republican side.[4] The measures
taken included the dissolution of the Revolutionary Police which
had organized the execution of right-wing elements in the first
few weeks of the rising, and the re-instatement of the old police
who were used against the Communists' political rivals on the
left.

The most active period of Russian intervention came to an
end in February 1937 with the replacement of Rosenberg by
Gaikis and the removal of General Kléber. On 4 February

[1] Brenan, op. cit., pp. 325-7.
[2] The letter is reproduced in facsimile in Luis Araquistain's article in
the *Cincinatti Times-Star* of 5 June, and is printed in the original French in
Madariaga, op. cit., pp. 472-4.
[3] Alvarez del Vayo, op. cit., pp. 76-7.
[4] Borkenau, *The Spanish Cockpit*, pp. 286 ff.; Brenan, op. cit., pp. 316-17

Stalin sent Largo Caballero a further letter promising 'help in the future within the measure of our possibilities'.[1]

The results of the Communists' acting as the right wing of the Republican coalition, protecting the peasants against collectivization and even the Church against anarchist excesses, could be seen in the character of their newly increased membership.

'Unable to draw to themselves the manual workers who remained firmly fixed in their unions, the Communists found themselves the refuge for all those who had suffered from the excesses of the Revolution or who feared where it might lead them. Well-to-do Catholic orange growers in Valencia, peasants in Catalonia, small shopkeepers and business men, Army officers and Government officials enrolled in their ranks.'[2]

The Comintern view of events in Spain and of the position in the early spring of 1937 may be gathered from the report of the general secretary of the Spanish Communist Party made to the enlarged Plenum of the Executive on 5 March.[3]

'We are fighting for a democratic republic, for a *democratic republic of a new type*. The object of the struggle in Spain is not the setting up of a democratic republic on the model of the French or similar republics in the other capitalist countries. No, the democratic republic for which we fight is another republic. We fight in order to destroy that material foundation on which was based reaction and Fascism, for without the destruction of this foundation a real political democracy is impossible.

'We are fighting for the *destruction* of the material basis of semi-feudal Spain, in order finally to tear out the roots of Fascism.

'We must liquidate the class of great landowners, who have all without exception taken part in the military-Fascist coup; we must nationalize their lands and hand them over to the agricultural labourers and peasants, so that they can utilize them as they wish—individually or collectively.

'It is essential to destroy the economic and political power of the Church, which was the centre of the Fascist plot and the main stronghold of semi-feudal Spain, and to do that the property of the Church must be confiscated and nationalized. The struggle against the semi-feudal economic and political role of the Church does not signify a war against religion—on the contrary, only a republican and democratic Spain can guarantee the freedom of religion.

'We must also strive to liquidate the caste spirit of the old army,

---

[1] Facsimile in *Cincinatti Times-Star*, 5 June 1939.
[2] Brenan, op. cit., p. 325.
[3] José Diaz, in *Kommunisticheski Internatsional* (Communist International), 1937, No. 3, reprinted in *O Mezhdunarodnom Polozhenie* (On the International Situation) (Moscow, 1937), pp. 135–6.

which was at the service of semi-feudal Spain and was the weapon used to destroy progressive movements.

'We must put an end to the financial oligarchy of bankers and manufacturers, which is closely connected with the landowners and the hierarchy, and which has hampered the growth of the national economy. We must proceed to the nationalization of the Bank of Spain and the main branches of the country's industry. That is the only way of meeting the needs of the front and the country.

'Apart from these fundamental points, which when accomplished will have wiped out the semi-feudal castes which rule in Spain, and lead to the rebuilding of the material and social bases of our new democratic parliamentary republic, we must also have a truly universal franchise, so that the whole people may participate in the political and economic life of the country.

'This is the new kind of democratic and parliamentary republic for which our Party is fighting, and with our Party the whole of the Spanish people.

'In all the provinces under the authority of the Government there are no more big landowners, no more big churches as ruling powers, no more big bankers and big manufacturers. The best guarantee that we shall retain what we have won is the fact that there are arms in the hands of the people, in the hands of the anti-Fascists, in the hands of workers, peasants, intellectuals and petty bourgeoisie. And in that lies the best pledge that there will be no return to the past. And just because our gains are guaranteed, we must not lose our heads and leap beyond the bounds of reality, attempting to instal "libertarian Communism" (anarchism), or busy ourselves with "socialisation" in the factories and villages. The stage of the establishment of a democratic republic through which we are now passing makes it necessary for all anti-Fascist forces to take part in the struggle, and such experiments could only turn them aside from it.'

It has been suggested that Russian supplies were deliberately held back in order to secure the fall of Largo Caballero and his replacement by Negrin and Prieto.[1] Prieto himself is said to have advocated fusion between the Socialist and Communist Parties in the summer of 1937, a move which other Socialist leaders had contemplated earlier.[2] The Comintern's 'line' had swung so far in a popular-front direction that the Comintern was apparently prepared, so Dimitrov indicated to Fischer, to allow such a new combination to join the Second International, in order to overcome the objections of Negrin, who feared that Communist domination of the united party would be inevitable.[3] (At the same time, Dimitrov himself was using the Spanish situation to argue in the Russian press that united fronts were

[1] Luis Araquistain in *San Francisco Chronicle*, 21 May 1939.
[2] Alvarez del Vayo, op. cit., p. 69.   [3] Fischer, op. cit., p. 417.

necessary everywhere and that the Second International was the chief obstacle to their conclusion.)[1] Eventually Prieto would seem to have shown too much independence[2] for the Communists' liking, and it has been suggested that Russian supplies were once more held up in order to secure his departure from the Government in April 1938.[3] It was after his fall that Communist influence reached its height, but it declined with the falling off of Russian supplies later in the year.[4]

The fluctuation in the Soviet attitude towards the war in Spain must be considered in the light of the general political situation. There seems no reason to doubt that at the beginning of the war, the Russians hoped that the Western Powers would intervene and thus further strengthen the combination against Germany. As Dr. Negrin put it later:

'Moscow tried to do for France and Britain what they should have done for themselves. The promise of Soviet aid to the Spanish Republic was that ultimately Paris and London would awake to the risks involved to themselves in Italian and German intervention in Spain and join the U.S.S.R. in supporting us.'[5]

Instead of this, the progress of the war witnessed two simultaneous processes, both equally unwelcome to the Russians: the drawing together of Germany and Italy as aggressor States and the step-by-step retreat of the Western democracies before this threat.

At the same time as the hostility of the European Axis became more and more open, Russia's fears of developments on her eastern frontier became still more acute. Help for Spain had to be balanced against other calls on Russian resources and suffered from the continual disadvantage of obstacles placed by the French on the transit of arms by land, while the Russians could not themselves keep open the Mediterranean route to Spain.[6]

The Russians were no doubt influenced in their policy after the early months of the war by the knowledge of the growth of a spirit of compromise among some circles on the Republican side.

[1] See Dimitrov's three articles of June 1937, reprinted in *O Mezhdunarodnom Polozhenie* (On the International Situation): 'God geroicheskoy borby ispanskovo naroda'; 'Uroki Almerii'; 'Ispania zovet k edinstvu' (A year of the heroic struggle of the Spanish people; The lessons of Almeria; Spain calls to unity).

[2] Last, op. cit., p. 39. Borkenau puts the recovery of independence by the Spanish parties before the fall of Almeria and regards the departure of Rosenberg as its consequence. *The Spanish Cockpit*, p. 275.

[3] Araquistain, loc. cit.   [4] Brenan, op. cit., p. 329.

[5] Quoted in Alvarez del Vayo, op. cit., p. 76, from an address given in New York in May 1939.

[6] *Survey for 1938*, I, pp. 314–21; Fischer, op. cit., pp. 384–5, 470.

'Having become convinced', writes Luis Araquistain, 'that the inhibitions of the democracies in the face of the Spanish war and the drop-by-drop help that Russia gave us—little war material and a good deal of it useless—made almost impossible a Republican victory, I started negotiations at the beginning of 1937, from Paris, to obtain through possible concessions, the withdrawal of Italy and Germany. . . . On one occasion in Paris I informed Alvarez del Vayo, Foreign Minister, about the negotiations I had undertaken on my own initiative. He said they were "very interesting". He went to Geneva . . . and on his return to Paris he had changed his mind. "Litvinov", he said, "says that an arrangement of this nature would be a bonus paid to the aggressor." '[1]

In May 1937, President Azana himself is said to have tried to get the Western Powers to take up the question of mediation, approaching them through Julian Besteiro, Spain's representative at the coronation of King George VI.[2]

By 1938 the tide of aggression had swept much closer to the Soviet Union's own frontiers, and Spain became a mere diversionary side-show. The ultimate importance of the Spanish War is its role in sowing distrust between the Soviet Union and the Western democracies. The word 'non-intervention' itself came to be used by the Russians as symbolic of the attitude which had made the Litvinov policy of 'collective security' impossible of fulfilment.

'Far be it from me', said Stalin in his speech of 10 March 1939, 'to moralize on the policy of non-intervention, to talk of treason, treachery and so on. It would be naïve to preach morals to people who recognize no human morality. Politics is politics, as the old case-hardened bourgeois diplomats say. It must be remarked, however, that the big and dangerous political game started by the supporters of the policy of non-intervention may end in a serious fiasco for them.'[3]

[1] *The Philadelphia Evening Bulletin*, 23 May 1939; cf. Fischer, op. cit., pp. 549–50.
[2] ibid., p. 398.
[3] J. Stalin, *Leninism* (Allen and Unwin, 1940), pp. 627–8.

Chapter Three

RUSSIA, TURKEY, AND THE STRAITS

THE revision of Soviet foreign policy in the years 1934–1935 and the growing international tension in the Mediterranean area put a new complexion upon the historic problem of Russia's position with regard to Turkey and the Straits.[1] The régime of the Straits which the Soviet Union and Turkey accepted at the hands of the Western Powers in the Lausanne Treaty of 1923, and which was still in force, was unpalatable to both Powers and had never been ratified by the Soviet Union.[2] The Turkish claim to full sovereignty in the Straits was nullified by the demilitarization of the littoral and by the existence of an international commission of control. The complete closure of the Straits to the warships of Powers foreign to the Black Sea, which had been the foundation of Russia's policy, was set aside. The only limitations on the rights of foreign Powers in time of peace were that no one Power might send into the Black Sea a larger force than the most powerful fleet maintained there by any Black Sea Power; and that each of the Powers could send into the Black Sea at most three ships, none of them exceeding 10,000 tons. This would not prevent a hostile coalition from building up in the Black Sea a fleet more powerful than that of the Soviet Union. In time of war, Turkey being neutral, the limitations did not apply to belligerent warships to the detriment of their belligerent rights in the Black Sea.

The willingness to fall in with the demands of the Western Powers which Turkey showed at the Lausanne Conference had caused a cooling-off in Soviet-Turkish relations, which had been very intimate since the Soviet assistance to Kemal in 1922. But this cooling-off proved only temporary, and the isolation of the two Powers drew them together. The Russo-Turkish Treaty of 17 December 1925—a treaty of neutrality and non-aggression —gained added significance when the provisions of the Lausanne Treaty were taken into account, since it guaranteed to Russia freedom of passage in the Straits, although the Lausanne provi-

[1] For a summary of the history of the Straits Question see J. T. Shotwell and F. Déak, *Turkey at the Straits* (New York, Macmillan, 1940); cf. A. N. Mandelstam, 'La Politique Russe d'Accès à la Méditerranée au XXème Siècle', *Académie de Droit International, Receuil des Cours*, 1934; H. N. Howard, *The Partition of Turkey, 1913–23* (University of Oklahoma Press, 1931).

[2] For the Lausanne Conference, see *Lausanne Conference on Near Eastern Affairs*, Cmd. 1814, 1923.

sion with regard to belligerent rights made it impossible for the Straits to be closed to Russia's enemies.[1] This Treaty did not end all friction between Soviet Russia and Kemalist Turkey. The suppression by Kemal of the Turkish Communists showed on what very different lines the two revolutions were developing. An article in *Pravda* in November 1928 pointed out that it was absurd to talk of the Kemalist bourgeoisie as a revolutionary force when it stood by a semi-feudal agrarian system. It was the enemy of the agrarian revolution, the enemy of the workers and peasants.[2] The Russian press denied that the Kemalist repudiation of Pan-Turkism and Pan-Turanianism meant the end of such ambitions in Turkey. The final demarcation of the frontier in 1926 allowed Turkey to retain the districts of Kars and Ardahan ceded to her by the peace treaty of 16 March 1921.[3] The existence of an Armenian republic within the U.S.S.R. provided a lever for raising the question again should the situation change. And in spite of a trade treaty on 11 March 1927, there was a certain amount of economic friction between the two countries.[4]

On the whole, however, the differences between Turkey and the Western Powers remained of more account than those dividing her from the Soviet Union, and she remained outside the League of Nations while adhering more and more closely to the Soviet security system. Thus, on 1 April 1929, Turkey adhered to the Litvinov Protocol, and on 17 December a protocol to the treaty of 1925 prolonged the validity of that instrument until 1945. This protocol forbade its signatories to make treaties with each other's neighbours without prior consultation between themselves, and was clearly designed to prevent too close relations between Turkey on the one hand and Roumania and Poland on the other.[5]

In January 1930 some alarm was caused to the other Black Sea Powers by the unobserved entry into the Black Sea of the Soviet battleship, *Parizhskaya Kommuna* and the cruiser *Profintern*. Although there was no legal obstacle to this particular passage, the event did demonstrate how dependent the Lausanne Con-

---

[1] M. W. Graham, 'The Soviet Security System', *Int. Conc.*, 1929, pp. 362–4.
[2] *Pravda*, 11 November 1928, quoted by B. A. Borian, *Armenia, mezhdunarodnaya diplomatia i SSSR* (Armenia, International Diplomacy and the U.S.S.R.), (Moscow, Gosizdat, 1929), II, p. 408.
[3] Text of Treaty, *British and Foreign State Papers*, vol. 118.
[4] V. Conolly, *Soviet Economic Policy in the East* (Oxford University Press, 1933).
[5] 'UdSSR und die Neue Türkei', *Osteuropa*, August 1932, vol. vii, pp. 632–44.

vention was for its enforcement on the goodwill of the Turks, and the affair came in for some anxious comment in England.[1]

In September 1930 the Turkish Foreign Minister Tewfik Rüstü Bey visited Moscow, and the symbolic value of the gesture was enhanced by its coincidence with the first meeting of the commission of inquiry into the Briand plan for European Union, to which neither Russia nor Turkey had been invited. The presence of the two warships in the Black Sea had altered the naval position in Russia's favour and to this may be traced the acceptance by Turkey of the protocol on naval armaments concluded between the two countries at Ankara on 7 March 1931. On 16 March, a commercial treaty was signed which put an end to the specially privileged status which Turkey, along with Russia's other Asiatic neighbours, had previously enjoyed, although it in fact only confirmed what had been the position in practice since Karakhan's visit to Turkey in December 1929. In the same month, Molotov in his speech to the Sixth Congress of Soviets emphasized the new strengthening of Russia's ties of friendship with Turkey.[2]

In October 1931 Litvinov visited Ankara and on the 30th a new protocol prolonged the treaties of 1925 and 1929 as well as the naval arrangement. No doubt the visit had other ends in view besides the routine prolongation of treaties, and his presence may be explained perhaps by a desire to counter any too great influence which the pro-French Venizelos might have acquired after the Greco-Turkish treaty of the previous year.[3] In May 1932, the Turkish Prime Minister and Foreign Minister visited Moscow and negotiated a non-interest bearing credit for the purchase of Russian industrial equipment.

The revised attitude of the Soviet Union may have helped to bring about Turkey's entry into the League of Nations in September 1932.[4] Turkey was a signatory of the London Convention for the Definition of Aggression in July 1933, and the Soviet Union was represented by Voroshilov at the celebrations that autumn of the tenth anniversary of the setting up of the Turkish Republic. It has been suggested that Turkish mediation helped to bring about recognition of the U.S.S.R. by Roumania in 1934.[5]

The most important event in relation to the question of the Straits was the signature of the Franco-Soviet Pact in May 1935.

[1] P. P. Graves, *The Question of the Straits* (Benn, 1931), pp. 196–7.
[2] *Osteuropa*, vol. vi, p. 416.
[3] On Turkish-Greek relations, see *Survey for 1930*, pp. 157 ff.
[4] *Survey for 1934*, pp. 216 ff.
[5] A. J. Fischer, in the *New Statesman and Nation*, 15 January 1944.

The new entente would depend for its effectiveness in part at least on the possibility of maintaining the links between the two countries in time of war, or threat of war. France, one of the sponsors of the Lausanne arrangements, could not favour the prolongation of a régime of the Straits which the Soviet Union regarded as a menace to her security. Great Britain, however, was anxious to conciliate Germany and still hankered after a wider security scheme; there was therefore no enthusiasm on the British side for any change in the Lausanne Convention. 'It is profoundly to be hoped,' wrote a British military expert in 1935, 'that the solution of the thorny Straits question effected at Lausanne will achieve permanency. . . . We may be sure that if Turkey ever does demand the abrogation of the Straits Convention of 1923, it will be at the instigation of or under pressure from Russia.'[1] The same writer was, however, constrained to admit that unfortunately the idea seemed to have gained ground since then in the minds of Turkish nationalists that the régime of the Straits 'imposes unfair restrictions on their sovereignty over the international waterway'.[2] The Turks had, in fact, on several occasions, beginning with the meeting of the General Commission of the Disarmament Conference in May 1933, called attention to their grievances in the matter of the demilitarization of the Straits region, and their complaints on this score had received Soviet support at the meeting of the League Council in May 1935.[3] The opinion of the British expert that it was not improbable that the 'whole agitation' had been 'instigated throughout by Moscow',[4] might, however, be regarded as an exaggeration, since the Turks had ample cause for alarm in the imperialistic gestures of Mussolini's Italy. It was indeed the tense situation in the Mediterranean brought about by the Abyssinian campaign and the imposition of sanctions which forced the question of the Straits to the foreground in the autumn and winter of 1935.

Italy's violation of the League Covenant, and Germany's all too successful flouting both of the Versailles and the Locarno Treaties in the matter of the reoccupation of the Rhineland,

[1] J. H. Marshall-Cornwall, *Geographic Disarmament* (Oxford University Press, for R.I.I.A., 1935), p. 119.

[2] ibid., p. 168.

[3] For the Montreux Conference and its preliminaries, see the detailed account by D. A. Routh, in *Survey for 1936*, pp. 584–651. The accessibility and thoroughness of this study makes it unnecessary to go here into the detailed process by which the Montreux Convention was ultimately arrived at. The proceedings are printed in *Actes de la Conférence de Montreux* (Paris, Pedone, 1936).

[4] Marshall-Cornwall, op. cit., p. 169.

made France's previous objections to all treaty revision now somewhat academic. As far as the demilitarization clauses of the Lausanne Convention were concerned, the question was only whether the coming change should be a unilateral act on the part of Turkey or revision by general consent. The Turkish suggestion for a conference made on 10 April was accepted by the Soviet Government in a note on the 16th.[1]

The Conference of Montreux (22 June–20 July 1936) and its diplomatic preliminaries revealed clearly the true attitudes of the Powers towards each other, and showed some interesting similarities with, as well as contrasts to, the positions they had occupied at the time of Lausanne. Whereas all the Powers concerned (except the absentee, Italy)[2] were ready to accede to Turkish demands for a restoration of her sovereign rights on the littoral—Great Britain hoping thereby to attract Turkey out of the Russian orbit into her own—they diverged sharply in the discussion of the Turkish draft convention, which 'it is more than probable . . . was the result of Turco-Soviet collaboration',[3] and which for the first time revealed that the Turks intended to press for a general revision of the régime of the Straits.

These divergences arose over the question of the passage of warships and of oil-tankers, which in an age of mechanized warfare were coming to have almost equal strategic importance, and they 'resolved themselves into a duel between the British and the Soviet delegations with France and the Balkan Entente Powers playing seconds to Russia'.[4] The positions of Soviet Russia and Great Britain remained the same as in 1923; it was France and her Balkan associates whose positions had altered. Great Britain's only supporter was Japan, to whom the closing of the Straits to the egress of Russian warships had been of great advantage in the war of 1904–1905.

The terms of the Turkish draft were indeed 'highly favourable to the U.S.S.R. For whereas the total tonnage which non-riverain Powers might send into the Black Sea was drastically curtailed . . . the only new limit imposed on the egress of the Soviet fleet from the Black Sea . . . was one of the size and form of the units actually passing the Straits at any one time and

[1] A Soviet account of the Montreux negotiations is to be found in *Istoria Diplomatii*, vol. 3, pp. 567–71.

[2] For Italy's dislike of the Montreux Convention, see M. H. H. Macartney and P. Cremona, *Italy's Foreign and Colonial Policy* (Oxford University Press, 1938), pp. 188–9. Italy notified its adherence to the Convention on 2 May 1938.

[3] Routh, loc. cit., p. 618. The draft Convention is printed as Annex 1 to *Actes de la Conférence de Montreux*.

[4] Routh, loc. cit., p. 619.

not of the total tonnage. . . . The Soviet fleet, in other words, would now obtain a preponderant position within the Black Sea without sacrificing its potential influence in the Mediterranean, and in case of war would be able to attack a hostile fleet in the Mediterranean and then retire to the Black Sea without risk of effective pursuit. This, together with the fact that Turkey might give permission to any fleet of any size to pass the Straits during a war in which she herself was a belligerent, meant that so long as Turco-Soviet relations continued to be as good as they had been in the past, the position of Soviet Russia would be greatly strengthened.'[1]

Great Britain tried to counter this by claiming, in default of unlimited access to the Black Sea, a corresponding limitation upon the Black Sea Powers' right of egress. It was feared in London that the addition of this new factor to the rapidly altering Mediterranean balance of power, and the increase of Russian naval building in the Black Sea yards, which the proposed convention would undoubtedly encourage, would cause Germany to invoke the escape clause of the Anglo-German naval convention of June 1935 and provoke a general race in naval armaments.[2] The suggestion that the entire British attitude at Montreux was instigated by Germany[3] is no doubt extreme, but the point about naval construction was certainly a material one in Russian eyes.[4]

British policy was embodied in a new draft convention which was adopted as a basis for discussion in the second phase of the Conference's work. This draft included a compromise worked out by Litvinov, Eden, and Paul-Boncour in the form of a new 'escalator' clause allowing the fleets of non-riverain Powers permitted in the Black Sea to be increased *pari passu* with new Soviet construction. But other features of the proposals were sufficiently objectionable to the Russians to bring the Conference to the verge of a breakdown. These differences, while in part going over familiar ground, also touched upon one point which arose directly out of the new international situation.

The Russians had sought to amend the Turkish proposals for the régime of the Straits in the event of Turkey being neutral during a war. Their amendment was to the effect that none of

[1] ibid., p. 617.

[2] G. M. Gathorne-Hardy, *A Short History of International Affairs* 3rd ed., (Oxford University Press, 1942, R.I.I.A.), pp. 423–4.

[3] H. N. Howard, 'The Straits after the Montreux Conference', *Foreign Affairs*, October 1936.

[4] See Litvinov's speech on 23 June 1936, *Actes de la Conférence de Montreux*, pp. 33–4.

the limitations on the passage of warships imposed by the article in question should 'be taken to interfere with the rights of warships of whatever Power to pass the Straits for the execution of engagements under the Covenant of the League or under regional pacts concluded within the framework of the Covenant, nor of the warships of the Power to whom that assistance' was due. A similar amendment was put forward to the equivalent proposals of the British draft. The British had already modified their suggestion that limitations on non-riverain warships should be waived in favour of Powers exercising their belligerent rights in a war in which Turkey was neutral, a suggestion directly opposed to Soviet claims for special treatment. In other words, 'the Soviet delegation wanted to make perfectly sure that in addition to recognizing the special position of Russia in the Black Sea, the new Convention would make full allowance for the working not only of Article 16 of the League Covenant, but also—and this was where the Russian view conflicted with the British—of regional agreements such as the Franco-Soviet Pact'.

The British dislike of the system of regional pacts caused anxiety in other than Soviet circles, and rather than render itself responsible for a complete débâcle, Britain put forward and secured assent to a compromise by which exception was only to be made in virtue of 'a treaty of mutual assistance *binding Turkey* and concluded within the framework of the Covenant'.

The Montreux Convention satisfied Turkey in the matter of restoring her unfettered sovereignty in the Straits region and permitting her in the interests of her own security to close the Straits to the warships of all nations when herself belligerent or when threatened with imminent danger of war (subject to a two-thirds veto of the League Council). It also seemed to give important advantages to Russia.[1] When Turkey was at peace Russia had the right of unlimited egress for surface vessels, including tankers, subject only to the limitation that warships of over 15,000 tons had to proceed singly. Russian submarines could only pass through the Straits for the purpose of rejoining their bases in the Black Sea or to be repaired in dockyards outside it. They had to pass through the Straits, singly, on the surface, and by day only. There was no right of passage either way for military aircraft. Instead of limiting the tonnage which individual non-riparian Powers might send into the Black Sea, aggregate tonnage was limited, and the only category permitted, 'light warships', included neither pocket-battleships nor air-

[1] The Montreux Convention with the parallel articles of the Lausanne Convention is printed in *Documents for 1936*, pp. 648 ff.

craft-carriers. The stay of non-riparian warships in the Black Sea was also limited in point of time. No warships passing through the Straits were allowed to make use of their aircraft. In time of war, Turkey being neutral, belligerent warships were, as already noted, only to be allowed passage in fulfilment of obligations to assist a victim of aggression where such assistance was part of action taken under the League Covenant, or under a treaty of mutual assistance binding Turkey and concluded within the framework of the Covenant.

From the Soviet point of view the Montreux Convention, in spite of certain shortcomings, presented considerable advantages, and its conclusion was regarded as a big success for Soviet diplomacy.[1] Foreign comments which stressed these advantages were based on the presumption that Turkey would itself adhere to the Franco-Russian pact. Turkey was, however, somewhat worried by the Soviet attitude at Montreux and veered towards Great Britain. 'Close collaboration between Great Britain and Turkey . . . was not the least of the gains which Turkey, thanks to her increased desirability as a friend under the new Convention, took away from Montreux. Its corollary was a cooling off of the friendship hitherto existing between Turkey and the U.S.S.R., which had already been so evident on several occasions during the Conference as to evoke from the Soviet press the complaint that Turkey was yielding to the pressure of imperialist Powers.' This coolness was marked enough for the Germans to be able to point to it as a reason for expecting that Russia's apparent gains under the Convention would thereby be neutralized. Germany indeed officially informed Turkey on 26 February 1937, of its dislike of the Convention, and in particular of the clauses relating to the Soviet right of egress through the Straits, only to receive a reminder that she herself was neither a signatory of the Convention nor a Mediterranean Power.[2]

This incident, while productive of no immediate result, may be taken as marking the point at which the already involved inter-relationships between Russia and Great Britain over the problem of the Straits became further complicated by the arrival on the scene of a third major Power—Germany. This reproduced for Turkey the pre-1914 situation. Henceforth Axis pressure signified not merely Italy's Mediterranean ambitions but also the new German *Drang nach Osten*, and Ankara became

[1] *Istoria Diplomatii*, vol. 3, p. 571.
[2] ibid., pp. 571–2; *Survey for 1936*, pp. 646–8. For Italian moves to secure a curtailment of the Soviet Union's privileges in return for Italy's adhesion to the Convention, see ibid., pp. 648–51.

(like Constantinople before 1914) a focus of political and economic diplomacy of the first importance.[1]

On the other hand, the new Turkey, if weak in the industrial equipment required for serious military strength, was less vulnerable than the old Ottoman Empire, and clearly felt that the existing constellation of the Powers permitted her to exploit to the full the bargaining values of her position.

So long as the prospect of Russian co-operation with the Western democracies remained alive, Turkey's position was a strong one, and the cooling off in relations with Russia after Montreux did not appear of lasting significance. When a Pact of Friendship between France and Turkey was initialled on 4 July 1938 as a preliminary to the settlement of their dispute over Alexandretta, 'it was rumoured that Turkey would permit British, French, and Soviet battleships to pass freely through the Straits in time of war in return for partial or complete Turkish control of Alexandretta'.[2] Russo-Turkish relations appear to have been unaffected by the conclusion of the Middle Eastern (Saadabad) Pact of 8 July 1937, although of its four participants, three, Turkey, Iran, and Afghanistan—the other was Iraq— might seem by it to have signified their final emancipation from that dependence on Moscow which had been so marked in the previous decade.[3] This pact, together with the Balkan Pact of 9 February 1934,[4] made Turkey 'the pivot of an embryonic security system spreading from the Danube to the frontiers of India',[5] and should not have been unwelcome to a Power so markedly on the defensive as Soviet Russia in these years, but Soviet comment upon Turkey's policy was and remained very guarded.[6]

Some observers indeed professed to regard this apparent cordiality as only superficial. The suspicions which all non-Communist neighbours of Soviet Russia cherished in some degree were bound to be especially acute where, as in this case, the political frontier did not coincide with a clear ethnic boundary and accounted for most of the rumours of friction. The troubled

---

[1] For the economic aspects of the German drive in Turkey see *Survey for 1937*, I, p. 460; *Survey for 1938*, I, pp. 43–69.

[2] F. L. Schuman, *Europe on the Eve* (Hale, 1939), pp. 372–3; cf. *Survey for 1938*, I, pp. 479–92; *Documents for 1937*, pp. 515–17.

[3] For the Middle Eastern Pact, see *Survey for 1936*, pp. 793–803; *Documents for 1937*, pp. 531–3.

[4] For the Balkan Pact, see *Survey for 1934*, pp. 508–36.

[5] B. Ward, *Turkey* (Oxford University Press, 1942), p. 103.

[6] See the speeches by M. Litvinov and the Turkish Foreign Minister, Rüstü Aras, on the occasion of the latter's visit to Moscow on 12–17 July 1937, and the joint communiqué then issued. *Documents for 1937*, pp. 432–6.

history of post-1917 Transcaucasia and the occasional echoes of
pan-Turanianism were bound to have their effect.[1] But compared with the growing threat from the Axis, that from Russia
must have seemed remote.[2] The Soviet Vice-Commissar for
Foreign Affairs, Potemkin, was given a cordial reception when
he visited Ankara in April-May 1939, and to all outward
appearances relations were again excellent.[3]

[1] Pan-Turanianism, the idea of detaching the Turkish-speaking areas of
Soviet Central Asia and forming them into a federation with Turkey itself
continued to exercise an attraction on Turkish émigré circles. The idea was
linked with the plan for emancipating the peoples of the Caucasus from
Russian rule, the so-called Promethean movement. In the early nineteen-
thirties Paris was the centre of this activity, but from about 1937 it came
under the patronage of Germany. In spite of the official hostility of the
Turkish Government to Pan-Turanian ideas, they had a certain following in
Turkey itself, where they were disseminated by exiles from Soviet Turkestan.
Links with Pan-Turanian agents were among the charges brought against
the accused in the Soviet State Trial in March 1938. *Report of Court Proceedings in the case of the Anti-Soviet 'Bloc of Rights and Trotskyists'*, pp. 212–13,
229, 339, 671; cf. R. Schlesinger, *Federalism in Central and Eastern Europe*
(Kegan Paul, 1945), p. 382; A. Henderson, 'The Pan-Turanian Myth in
Turkey To-day', *Asiatic Review*, January 1945.

[2] The Russians do not appear to have intervened in any way during the
serious disturbances among the Kurds in 1937–8. W. G. Elphinston, 'The
Kurdish Question', *International Affairs*, January 1946; W. L. Westermann,
'Kurdish Independence and Russian Expansion', *Foreign Affairs*, July 1946.

[3] *Hitler's Route to Bagdad* (Fabian Society: Allen and Unwin, 1939),
p. 344. See the quotation from the joint communiqué of 7 May, *B.I.N.*,
XIV, p. 530.

Chapter Four

SOVIET DIPLOMACY IN EUROPE: FROM THE RHINELAND COUP TO THE ANTI-COMINTERN PACT

THE German reoccupation of the demilitarized zone of the Rhineland which began on 7 March 1936 was a direct challenge to any system of European security based upon France's ability to assist countries in Eastern Europe to resist German aggression.[1] Were the remilitarization of the area to be carried through without hindrance, the military value of the Franco-Soviet Pact, from the Soviet point of view, would be greatly diminished. It was the object of German propaganda, directed primarily to Great Britain and to right-wing elements in France, to obfuscate the military issues and to justify Germany's action by considerations of equality of rights and of self-protection against Bolshevik aggression.[2] In the memorandum addressed by Germany to the other Locarno Powers on 7 March it was stated that the Locarno Pact had 'lost its inner meaning and ceased in practice to exist' owing to France's 'military alliance with the Soviet Union exclusively directed against Germany'. The German proposal for a new series of non-aggression treaties as a foundation for European peace was significantly silent as to the role of Soviet Russia.[3]

The memorandum was quoted by Hitler in his speech to the Reichstag on the same day: 'If my international opponents reproach me to-day,' he said, 'that I have refused this co-operation with Russia, I make them the following declaration: I do not and did not reject this co-operation with Russia but with Bolshevism which lays claim to a world rulership.' Close diplomatic relations with the Soviet Union would provide a path for the entry into Germany of the Communist infection, and if France also became Communist, Moscow alone would be able to unleash the forces provided by the Franco-Soviet Pact. 'This gigantic mobilization of the East against Central Europe is opposed not only to the letter but above all to the spirit of the Locarno Pact.' Nevertheless, Hitler did not proceed to the logical conclusion of such a train of thought—a complete rupture

[1] There is a full account of the Rhineland crisis in *Survey for 1936*, pp. 252–370.
[2] The susceptibility of the French right to propaganda of this kind is discussed in C. A. Micaud, *The French Right Wing and Nazi Germany, 1933–9* (Durham, N.C., Duke University Press, 1944).
[3] Cmd. 5118.

with the U.S.S.R.: 'with this Bolshevik section of Europe we desire no closer contact than the ordinary political and economic relations.'[1]

From the Soviet point of view, the immediate significance of the Rhineland crisis was not therefore that it made the threat from Germany more imminent, but rather that it provided a test of the resolution of the Western Powers and in particular of France. It is not necessary to examine here the steps by which France, after an initial declaration of great firmness, came to accept the *fait accompli* and to waive before the year was out even the minimum demand that no permanent fortifications should be built in the Rhineland zone.

The Soviet Government, not being directly affected, was able to declare itself for a policy of firmness without making any move which might aggravate substantially its relations with Germany. On 7 March the Soviet Ambassador in Paris saw the French Foreign Minister, Flandin, and offered him Soviet support in any steps he might take, emphasizing the dangers of condoning Germany's action. Similar views were expressed in London by Maisky to Lord Cranborne, the British Under-Secretary for Foreign Affairs. But British reactions, as first expressed by Eden on 9 March, were so much less hostile to Germany's action than those of the French, that it must have been evident to the Soviet Union that the possibility of military action was remote. While French official opinion was still outwardly adamant against any idea of separating the security of Eastern Europe from that of Europe as a whole, British opinion was on the whole averse to further commitments, and was not disposed to allow Eastern European anxieties to preclude the chances of a new settlement in the West. Thus while France's immediate fears were to some degree allayed by the guarantee of British support given her on 9 March and included in the Locarno Powers' proposals of 19 March,[2] it was clear that Britain's ultimate objective was to include Germany in a new Locarno. It was felt in some French quarters that this would mean that any future intervention by France in Eastern European affairs would in fact depend on British and Italian consent.[3] There can be little doubt but that this reflection was also very present in the minds of the Soviet statesmen.

Conversations between the Locarno Powers other than Ger-

[1] *Hitler's Speeches*, ed. N. H. Baynes (2 vols., Oxford University Press: R.I.I.A., 1942), pp. 1271–1302.

[2] Cmd. 5134.

[3] 'Pertinax' (André Géraud), 'L'Assistance Mutuelle Franco-Britannique', *Politique Etrangère*, April 1937.

many were held in Paris and London from 10 to 19 March. While these talks were in progress, the League Council began (on the 14th) a series of meetings in London. On the 16th, the Council proceeded to discuss a Franco-Belgian resolution establishing the fact of Germany's violation of the Versailles Treaty. It was during the discussion of this resolution that Litvinov made his speech of 17 March, in which the Soviet attitude was set out in detail.

Litvinov pointed out that, as in the case of the German reintroduction of conscription and of Italy's attack on Abyssinia, the matter was not one in which the Soviet Union was directly concerned:

'These circumstances have not in the past prevented, and will not in the present case prevent, the representative of the Soviet Union from taking his place among those members of the Council who register in the most decisive manner their indignation at a breach of international obligations, condemn it, and support the most effective means to avert similar infringements in the future.'

Litvinov pointed out that the German claim that the Franco-Soviet Pact was incompatible with the Locarno Treaty had not been accepted by the Treaty's other two signatories, Great Britain and Italy; furthermore, Germany's assertion would not hold water in view of the entirely defensive nature of the Pact. The Pact would not begin to operate unless Germany attacked the U.S.S.R. or France.

'But if the Soviet Union becomes the victim of an attack by Germany, the Locarno Treaty gives France, as any other member of the League, the unquestionable right to come to the assistance of the Soviet Union. In this event, an unmistakable definition of the aggressor is facilitated by the absence of a common frontier between Germany and the Soviet Union. If the German armed forces cross the boundaries of their own country, and pass through the States and the seas dividing the two countries in order to invade the territory of the Soviet Union, the German aggression will be quite apparent and vice versa.

'This is perfectly obvious to the German Government too, and therefore it hastens to call to its assistance a far-reaching hypothesis of the possibility of a change of the social system in France.'

Litvinov went on to discuss the more general justification of Germany's action, and made effective use of *Mein Kampf*, to show that Germany's policy was based upon the determination to ensure by force of arms that there were never two military powers on Germany's frontiers. 'It is a question of setting up the hegemony of Germany over the whole European continent, and I ask you, must and shall the League of Nations condone the promotion of this objective?'

Finally he dealt with the new proposals which Germany had submitted. The new arrangements for the West amounted to a revival of Locarno—a treaty which Germany had just repudiated—but for twenty-five years instead of in perpetuity, and shorn of the guarantee of the demilitarized zone.

The pacts which Germany was prepared to sign with her other neighbours would not even have the safeguard which the British and Italian guarantees were meant to provide in the West.

'The Soviet Union', continued Litvinov, 'has itself signed pacts of non-aggression with all its neighbours (excepting Japan which rejects such a pact up to this day). But the Soviet Union has always attached great importance to the point that these pacts should not facilitate aggression against third parties. We therefore always included in these pacts a special clause, freeing either of the contracting parties from any obligations under the pact if the other party commits an act of aggression against a third State. Such a clause, however, will be absent from the pacts proposed by Mr. Hitler, according to the model which he has indicated. And, without such a clause, the proposed system of pacts reduces itself to the principle of localization of war which is preached by Mr. Hitler. Every State which has signed such a pact with Germany is immobilised by her in the event of Germany attacking a third State.

'This proposal of Mr. Hitler's gives me the impression that we are faced with an attempt to divide Europe into two or more parts, with the object of guaranteeing non-aggression for one part of Europe in order to acquire a free hand for dealing with other parts. . . .

'The whole sense of Mr. Hitler's statements, and of his proposals in the sphere of international political relations, amounts to the organization of a campaign against the peoples of the State I represent, and to a formation of a coalition against them of the whole of Europe—if possible the whole of the world.'

In spite of the admitted candour of these remarks, Litvinov was as usual careful to anticipate any charge of war-mongering:

'Let me express the hope that I shall not be misunderstood, and that the conclusion will not be drawn from what I have said that the Soviet Union is proposing only registration, condemnation, severe measures and nothing else; that it declares itself against negotiations and a peaceful settlement of the severe dispute which has arisen. Such a conclusion would represent a completely false picture of our conception. We are not less but on the contrary more interested than others in the maintenance of epace, both to-day and for decades to come, and not only in one area of Europe, but throughout the whole of Europe and all over the world. We are resolutely against anything that might bring war nearer by even a single month. . . .'

The Soviet Union would, however, be willing to support the Council in any action which it might prove willing to take on the present unilateral infringement by Germany of her obligations.[1] The Franco-Belgian resolution was adopted on 18 March. On the following day, the Council was apprised of the proposals of the Locarno Powers. These included a recommendation that Germany should be invited to submit to the Permanent Court of International Justice the juridical question as to the compatibility of the Treaty of Locarno with the Franco-Soviet Pact.

Finally, on 24 March, the Council, while nominally adjourning the discussion, actually brought to an end its part in the matter, leaving it to the Locarno Powers to try to find a way out of their differences. In the discussion on the Council's resolution, Litvinov showed his concern for the maintenance at least of the outward dignity and independence of that body, by protesting against the inclusion of the statement that the Council had 'taken cognisance' of the Locarno Powers' proposals and by securing the substitution of a less offensive phrase.[2]

On 26 March, the Central Executive Committee of the Soviet Union duly ratified the Franco-Soviet Pact. The negotiations between Germany and the Western Powers which followed did not directly concern the Soviet Union. The German memorandum of 31 March 1936 rejected the suggestion that the Permanent Court of International Justice should pronounce on the juridical aspect of the German claim; and Germany's own proposals were once again limited to suggested pacts of non-aggression with 'the States on Germany's south-eastern and north-eastern frontiers'.[3] This point was taken up in the British questionnaire of 7 May which commented on the ambiguity of this definition of the countries concerned. 'His Majesty's Government', continued the British document, 'cannot but feel that the general settlement would be very greatly facilitated if the German Government could see their way to interpret these words so as to cover at least also the Soviet Union, Latvia, and Estonia, as well as the States actually contiguous to Germany.'[4] To this questionnaire no reply was ever given.

The direct effect of the *coup* of 7 March on Soviet-German relations was less than Litvinov's speeches might have suggested. It is true that the trade talks between the Soviet Union and

[1] *L.N.O.J.*, April 1936, I, p. 319.
[2] *L.N.O.J.*, April 1936, I, pp. 346–7.   [3] Cmd. 5175.   [4] ibid.

Germany then in progress in Berlin were broken off. The American Ambassador noted that very few Germans were present at a reception at the Soviet Embassy on 16 March and none in official positions.[1] But there were voices raised on both sides in favour of maintaining peaceful relations. On the German side these came mainly from military circles and were sharply different in tone from those of the increasingly strident official propagandists of the Nazi Party. On the Soviet side the most important indication of conciliatory tendencies was an interview given by Molotov in Moscow to the Editor of *Le Temps*.[2] 'The main trend among our people,' he said, 'the trend which determines the policy of the Soviet Government, considers an improvement in relations between Germany and the Soviet Union possible. . . . The participation of Germany in the League of Nations would be in the interest of peace and would be favourably regarded by us.' 'Even of Hitler Germany?' asked the French journalist. 'Yes,' replied Molotov, 'even of Hitler Germany.'[3]

Soviet press comment was withheld for a fortnight after the publication of this pronouncement. On 6 April, however, an article by Radek appeared in *Izvestia*. The Soviet Union, he stated, was still willing to see Germany return to the League on a basis of equality provided that the League's guarantees of security to its members were strengthened. Germany should have a place of equality in drawing up a collective plan for peace, but 'if Germany, having strengthened herself by arming and by occupying the Rhineland, should not wish to take that place', and had 'no desire to receive security in exchange for giving security, then that system should be created in spite of Germany'.

'In any case,' continued Radek, 'the main object of Hitler's diplomatic strategy is clear. It is to *confront France with the alternative, either of renouncing her allies*, or of having no peace from Germany. The meaning of Hitler's proposals is to offer France *territorial security, at the price of her abdication as a Great Power, capable both of seeking and of giving help against an aggressor.*'

The bilateral pact, which Hitler proposed to make with Czechoslovakia, was denounced by Radek as a device which would enable Germany to attack Austria without Czechoslovakia intervening.

[1] W. E. Dodd, *Ambassador Dodd's Diary* (Gollancz, 1941), p. 329.
[2] The interview, given on 12 March, was published in *Pravda* on the 24th.
[3] German willingness to re-enter the League of Nations in certain rather ill-defined eventualities had been indicated in the memorandum of 7 March.

This exposé of Soviet policy may be taken as marking the end of the period of tension due to the Rhineland Pact, and on 29 April a new trade agreement for one year between Russia and Germany was duly signed.

Any German hopes that Soviet purchases in Germany might again reach the high levels of the later years of the first Five Year Plan were not justified in the event. But Soviet-German trade did revive considerably in 1936 despite the political tension. Soviet purchases from Germany rose from 39 million Rm. in 1935 to 126 million Rm. in 1936. This made Germany first among Russia's sources of supply. On the other hand, Soviet exports to Germany fell from 215 to 93 million Rm. In 1937 German exports to the Soviet Union fell to 117 Rm. and Germany was replaced by the United States as Russia's chief supplier. In 1938 her exports to Russia fell to only 32 million Rm. Russia's exports to Germany continued to decline: to 65 million Rm. in 1937 and to 47 million Rm. in 1938.

Official declarations of German policy during the summer months of 1936 were mainly concerned with emphasizing Germany's pacific intentions and did not directly aggravate Soviet-German relations.[1] On the other hand, German propaganda was unmistakably playing up to British mistrust of Soviet intentions. As far as the British Government was concerned, this propaganda appeared to make no headway, and relations between the Soviet and British Governments continued to be outwardly friendly.[2] On 30 July it was announced that the Soviet Union was to receive British credits of up to ten million pounds under the export-credits scheme, and on the same day it became known that the Anglo-Soviet naval conversations which had been in progress since the middle of May had resulted in an agreement, but the conclusion of a formal naval treaty was held up pending the conclusion of a similar treaty between Great Britain and Germany.[3]

In September General Wavell headed a British party to the

---

[1] On 18 May 1936, the German Foreign Minister Neurath told W. C. Bullitt, later American Ambassador to France, that it was the policy of the German Government to do nothing active in foreign affairs until the Rhineland had been digested; *The Trial of the German Major War Criminals: Proceedings of the International Military Tribunal sitting at Nuremberg, Germany* (London, H.M. Stationery Office, 1947–8; subsequently referred to as *Nuremberg Trial*), Part 5, p. 133.

[2] Maisky, in his speeches, repeatedly returned to the point that the Franco-Soviet Pact of 1935 was in no way exclusive. See his speeches of 19 March 1936 and 15 May 1936, quoted by W. P. and Z. K. Coates, *A History of Anglo-Soviet Relations* (Lawrence and Wishart and Pilot Press, 1943), pp. 551–2.

[3] See chap. 5, *infra*.

Red Army manœuvres near Minsk, and in October a naval attaché was appointed to the British Embassy for the first time since the Revolution.[1] The pacific nature of Soviet foreign policy was the theme of a speech made by the Soviet Ambassador Maisky on 1 August.[2] After emphasizing the common interest which the Soviet Union and Great Britain possessed in the maintenance of peace, Maisky turned to the question of European security. On the substance of the talks still going on among the Locarno Powers, he preferred to reserve judgment until their outcome could be seen:

'But', he went on, 'I would like to say just this: The Soviet Union would sincerely welcome every equitable settlement of the recent European difficulties, but she cannot help thinking that such a settlement is possible only on a basis which includes the whole of Europe, and not some particular corner or corners of that continent. . . . If it should degenerate into a piecemeal arrangement destined to divide Europe into water-tight compartments, some with a semblance of temporary security and others without security at all, then it will bring not peace but war.'

Maisky then went on to state the familiar Soviet point of view on League of Nations 'reform':

'Regional pacts must be the first line of defence and the League of Nations the second line. The existence of regional pacts in no way relieves the other members of the League from their obligations under the Covenant; it simply gives them a little time to mobilize their forces, economic, financial and other, against the aggressor.'

Less than a fortnight before this speech, the outbreak of the Spanish Civil War (to which Maisky did not refer) had added a new element of discord to the relations between the Soviet Union and the Western Powers. In these circumstances much depended on the policy of the new French Government under Blum which took office at the beginning of June. Its attitude towards Germany, it has been said, 'was marked from the outset by a greater spirit of conciliation and less inclination to drive hard bargains and to insist upon the letter of the law than had generally been shown by governments further to the right'.[3] A Conference in London on 23 July decided tacitly to accept the *fait accompli* in the Rhineland and announced that a meeting of the five Locarno Powers to negotiate a new Rhineland Pact was

[1] Coates, op. cit., p. 557.

[2] Maisky, *Soviet Foreign Policy*. Until the reversal of Soviet foreign policy in September 1939, Maisky continued to be the most indefatigable exponent of the doctrine of collective security.

[3] *Survey for 1936*, p. 345.

the first item on the international agenda. If progress were made at such a meeting, it would be natural, it was declared, to look forward to the widening of the area of the discussion with the collaboration of the other interested Powers.[1] It was no doubt this declaration that Maisky had in mind on 1 August when he made the remarks which have already been quoted.

The French readiness to follow the British lead was equally marked in the case of the Spanish Civil War; and the reaction to this of the French Communist Party did not help in creating harmony between the French and Soviet Governments. The latter accepted the French proposal for an agreement among the Powers not to intervene in the Spanish War by sending munitions to either party, and was represented when the Non-Intervention Committee met in London on 9 September. But it was made clear from early on that the Soviet Union would not permit the Committee to be used as a shield for intervention by other Powers. On 6 October the U.S.S.R. accused Portugal of allowing its territory to be used as a base of operations by the rebels, and in a note of 7 October it declared that it could in no case consent to 'turn the agreement into a screen shielding the military aid given to the rebels by some of the participants', and that it would consider itself released from its obligations if violations of the agreement were not immediately stopped. Maisky, the Soviet representative on the Committee, announced on the 23rd that the Soviet Union would not consider itself bound to adhere to the principle of non-intervention to a greater extent than any other country, and a further statement to this effect was made on 28 October.[2] On the 24th, factory meetings were held at many places in the Soviet Union at which resolutions were passed applauding Maisky's stand—this being the normal way of emphasizing a Soviet move in foreign affairs. And these heralded, as has already been seen, active Soviet intervention on the Republican side.

Meanwhile the Spanish War had provided an occasion for the renewal of the German attack on Communism—a propaganda campaign no doubt designed to prepare the way for the Anti-Comintern Pact. The actual signal for a renewal of German outbursts was given by the Soviet decree of 11 August lowering the age for military service. This was violently denounced in the German press and attention was called to other manifestations of the increasing military strength of the

[1] *Documents for 1936*, pp. 218–19.
[2] The proceedings of the Non-Intervention Committee at London are dealt with in *Survey for 1937*, II, pp. 222 ff., and in *Survey for 1938*, I, pp. 307 ff.

E—11

U.S.S.R. At the same time the Soviet system of non-aggression pacts was attacked as forming a network of alliances directed against Germany.[1] The lengthening of the period of military service in Germany itself, announced on 24 August, was accompanied by an official commentary stressing the danger from Communism as the reason for the change: 'History has taught us that it is better, if necessary, to make great sacrifices for external peace rather than to be overwhelmed in the Bolshevist chaos.'[2]

The principal theme of the speeches at the Nazi Party rally held at Nuremberg from 8 to 14 September was the danger from Communism and from the Soviet Union. In a speech on 12 September, Hitler told his hearers that the Bolsheviks had made nothing of the vast resources at their disposal, whereas the Nazis would work wonders with them if they were under their control:

'If we had at our disposal the incalculable wealth and stores of raw material of the Ural mountains and the unending fertile plains of the Ukraine to be exploited under National-Socialist leadership, then we would produce, and our German people would swim in plenty.'[3]

On the 12th and 13th, even more inflammatory speeches were delivered by Hitler, but again the logical conclusion was missing, and his speech on the 14th was something of an anti-climax, it being once again suggested that the more cautious advice of the military experts had won the day.[4]

[1] *Hitler's Speeches*, p. 1327.

[2] On 14 August 1936, Ribbentrop spoke to the Polish Under-Secretary for Foreign Affairs of the necessity for Polish-German collaboration: 'Both Poland and Germany were faced with a serious danger arising from the fact that the Soviets had not renounced the conception of world revolution. Moscow could not renounce this conception, and Stalin was bound to carry on a corresponding policy, otherwise there would be a breakdown of the whole Bolshevik system, which aimed at levelling down and destroying all the achievements of Western civilization and culture. Chancellor Hitler could not make any compromise in relation to Russia, because the slightest deviation from his own present policy must open the way for the reign of Bolshevism in Germany. M. von Ribbentrop considered that Poland was menaced by the danger of Bolshevism equally with Germany, and that the only way of counteracting this danger was the prevention of the catastrophe by crushing at their roots even the smallest signs of communism.' *Polish White Book*; Official Documents concerning Polish-German and Polish-Soviet Relations, 1933–1939 (London, Hutchinson, published by Authority of the Polish Government, n.d.), pp. 33–4.

[3] *Survey for 1936*, p. 381.

[4] It was considered symptomatic of the German wish not to make relations with the Soviet Union altogether impossible, that the passage quoted from Hitler's speech was published in the German press in a revised and less

The Soviet reply was delivered by Voroshilov in a speech at Kiev on 17 September:

'I can assure you that the Soviet Ukraine will remain an impregnable outpost of our Great Socialist Fatherland. . . . I can assure the workers of the Ukraine that our Red Army will be fully able to meet the enemy wherever he prefers or whenever he turns his crazy attacks on Soviet territory.'[1]

The bellicose tone of German propaganda was maintained throughout October 1936. A further menace seemed implicit in the rapid *rapprochement* at this time between Germany and Italy. This had followed upon Ciano's appointment in June 1936 as Italian Foreign Minister and had been facilitated by the agreement between Germany and Austria on 11 July.[2] The latter was a source of disquiet in itself, since it appeared to place Czechoslovakia, the Soviet Union's ally, in the forefront of Germany's potential victims, and make Czechoslovakia in fact 'the most dangerous of the several danger-zones of Europe'.[3] Actual co-operation between Germany and Italy followed in the wake of the Spanish war but took some time to develop. The Nuremberg speeches in September aroused little echo in Italy, where the press uttered warnings against Italian embroilment in the conflict of ideologies, and declared Italy's indifference to the form of government in the Soviet Union itself. On the other hand, Italy was hostile to the Montreux Agreement and to the greater scope which it gave to the Soviet Union in Mediterranean affairs.[4]

At the end of October, Ciano visited Germany and in a statement on the 25th, referred significantly to 'the supreme obligation assumed by Germany and Italy to defend the great

provocative version: 'If the Urals with their incalculable wealth of raw materials, the rich forests of Siberia and the unending corn-fields of the Ukraine *lay in Germany* under National-Socialist leadership the country would swim in plenty. We would produce and every single German would have enough to live on.' It has been pointed out that this version was more in accordance with the conclusion of Hitler's argument, which was a declaration of the need for autarky; ibid., p. 382 *n*.

[1] *Documents for 1936*, pp. 296–7. In a further speech on the 25th the Soviet Defence Commissar declared that the Red Army was intended solely for defence, that an assault on the Soviet Union might come at any moment but would find the country ready to meet it.

[2] *Documents for 1936*, pp. 320–6; *Survey for 1936*, pp. 402–69.

[3] *Survey for 1936*, p. 481. German-Czechoslovak tension in 1936 is analysed, ibid., pp. 469–501.

[4] Macartney and Cremona, *Italy's Foreign and Colonial Policy, 1914–1937*, pp. 11, 118–9.

institutions of Europe'.[1] It is probable that the actual results of these talks were more far-reaching than was indicated by the official pronouncements upon them. The result was in fact a 'further Italian identification with the German anti-Bolshevik policy'.[2]

The new phase in Italian foreign policy was given unmistakable emphasis in a speech by Mussolini on 1 November 1936.[3] With the agreement of 11 July between Germany and Austria 'an element of dissension between Berlin and Rome' had disappeared; Germany had 'practically recognized the Empire of Rome' even before Ciano's visit.

'It is not a matter for surprise that to-day we hoist the flag of anti-Bolshevism. . . . What is known as Bolshevism or Communism does not date from to-day . . . but is a State super-capitalism raised to its fiercest extreme. . . . And it is high time to end placing in contrast Fascism and Democracy. . . . If any of these Ministers, members of Parliament and people of the same kind who speak on hearsay, would decide at last to cross the Italian frontier, they would be convinced that if a country does exist where true Democracy has been realized, that country is Fascist Italy.'

The Russians countered these statements by pointing out that the real implications of Italy's new policy lay in the adhesion of that country to the German revisionist camp, at least for the time being. An article in the *Journal de Moscou* of 3 November pointed out that the new developments marked the final failure of Laval's policy of trying to detach Italy from Germany. Even if one doubted the solidarity of the new accord and expected Hitler and Mussolini to betray each other, Italy would in fact support Germany in matters of vital interest to France. France had therefore been as unsuccessful in paying court to Mussolini as Great Britain had been in paying court to Hitler. But Soviet attempts to make use of these events in order to strengthen the Franco-Soviet pact seemed unlikely to succeed.[4]

---

[1] *Documents for 1936*, pp. 340–3.

[2] Macartney and Cremona, op. cit., p. 165.

[3] *Documents for 1936*, pp. 343–7.

[4] 'Pertinax' writes that Soviet Russia suggested to France in October 1936 that the two countries should jointly study the problem of the defence of Czechoslovakia. According to him, British hostility to such a move prevented the French from accepting the proposal; 'Pertinax' (André Géraud), *Les Fossoyeurs* (New York, Maison Française, 1943), vol. ii, p. 101. According to Pierre Cot, Air-Minister in the popular front governments, the Russians informed the French several times in 1936 and 1937 that they were disposed to extend the Franco-Soviet Pact into the military field. He gives as the French reasons for rejecting the idea: first, doubts as to Soviet military power—doubts fostered by W. C. Bullitt, who became American

Litvinov had occasion to discuss the general international situation when he received the Order of Lenin on 11 November 1936, three days after a speech by Hitler, devoted to the theme of Germany's impregnability against a Bolshevik attack. Litvinov outlined the difficulties in the way of persuading other countries to accept the policy of collective security. In fact, only two paths were open to them; collective security or a *rapprochement* with the aggressors. The U.S.S.R. was strong and could afford to wait for the other Powers to come round to her point of view. They could not achieve peace without her. He indicated that the German menace could not be canalized so as to threaten Russia alone. 'I stress that it is not a question of isolating her but of isolating other countries so as to render them defenceless and to subjugate them.'[1]

Meanwhile developments on the Non-Intervention Committee had done little to ease the prevailing tension. Since 24 October the Committee had been occupied with a scheme for controlling the different channels through which war materials might reach Spain. The policy of the governments supporting the Spanish 'nationalists' appears to have been directed towards delaying the application of such a scheme, in the belief that they would in the meantime be able decisively to outstrip the Soviet Union in the sending of supplies. The representatives of Germany, Italy, and Portugal managed to delay until 2 December the submission of the proposed scheme to the contending parties in Spain.

Ambassador in Paris in September 1936—and, second, the Government's conviction that any such move would alienate Great Britain; P. Cot, *Triumph of Treason* (New York, Ziff Davis, 1944), pp. 357–8. Evidence of Bullitt's hostility towards the Franco-Soviet Pact and of his sympathies for the idea of a French *rapprochement* with Germany is given in the diary of W. E. Dodd, the American Ambassador in Berlin, under the date 13 December 1936. *Dodd's Diary*, pp. 376–7. Bullitt's hostility to the Soviet Union is described in *Istoria Diplomatii*, vol. 3, pp. 609–10. General Schweisguth, who was France's representative at the Russian autumn manœuvres in 1936, is said to have reported that the object of Soviet policy was to thrust back to the West a storm she felt to be mounting towards the East. Russia did not wish to be involved in the next European conflict but to play, like the United States in 1918, the role of an arbiter in an exhausted Europe; G. Bonnet, *Défense de la Paix: De Washington au Quai d'Orsay* (Geneva, Editions du Cheval Ailé, 1946), p. 124.

Franco-Soviet relations in the years 1934–8 are dealt with by Paul Reynaud in *La France a Sauvé l'Europe* (Paris, Flammarion, 1947), vol. i, pp. 108–35.

[1] *The Times*, 12 November 1936. A further cause of Soviet-German friction was the news of the arrest of some German nationals in Russia. Recriminations on this subject went on throughout the month; *Survey for 1936*, p. 383.

On 18 November, with the fall of Madrid apparently in prospect, Germany and Italy had actually recognized the government of General Franco. A threat by General Franco on 17 November, to prevent war supplies from reaching the Spanish Government through Barcelona by blockading and bombarding that port, led to a British decision, announced on 23 November, to introduce a bill prohibiting the carriage of arms to Spain by British ships; and this became law on 3 December. The prospects for the Spanish Republic, now more than ever dependent on Soviet aid, were thus extremely gloomy.[1]

It was at this juncture that the Soviet Union received formal confirmation of rumours which had been accumulating throughout the year, regarding a *rapprochement* between its principal potential enemies in Europe and Asia. On 17 November, it was stated in Moscow that the Japanese Foreign Minister had informed the Soviet Ambassador Yurenev that the Japanese Government and 'a third party' had been discussing ways and means of combating Communism but that these discussions had no bearing upon relations between Japan and the Soviet Union.[2] Moscow comment was to the effect that the 'third party' in question was Germany, and that the agreement against Communism was intended to serve as an excuse for concerted military action should either of the partners be at war.[3] On 18 November, it was denied at Tokyo that a military alliance formed any part of the German-Japanese Agreement now admittedly under negotiation. On the 19th, Yurenev informed the Japanese Foreign Office that these explanations were unsatisfactory and that any such agreement would have a detrimental effect on Russo-Japanese relations.[4]

The 'Agreement against the Third International' or 'Anti-Comintern Pact', as it came to be called, was actually signed in Berlin on 25 November.[5] On the face of it the text of the agreement did little more than reiterate what was common form among the spokesmen of the two Powers:

'The Government of the German Reich and the Imperial Japanese Government, recognizing that the aim of the Communist International, known as the Comintern, is to disintegrate and subdue existing States by all the means at its command; convinced that the toleration of interference by the Communist International in the

[1] *Survey for 1937*, II, pp. 246–59.
[2] Soviet-Japanese relations and the effect upon them of the Anti-Comintern Pact are discussed *infra*, chap. 8.
[3] *The Times*, 17 November 1936; *New York Times*, 18 November 1936.
[4] Soviet communiqué of 20 November; *Daily Telegraph*, 21 November 1936.
[5] *Documents for 1936*, pp. 297–9.

internal affairs of the nations not only endangers their internal peace and social well-being, but is also a menace to the peace of the world; desirous of co-operating in the defence against Communist subversive activities; have agreed as follows:

Article I

'The High Contracting States agree to inform one another of the activities of the Communist International, to consult with one another on the necessary preventive measures, and to carry these through in close collaboration.

Article II

'The High Contracting Parties will jointly invite third States whose internal peace is threatened by the subversive activities of the Communist International to adopt defensive measures in the spirit of this agreement or to take part in the present agreement.'

By Article III, the agreement was to remain in force for a period of five years, before which an understanding was to be reached as to methods of further co-operation.

By a supplementary protocol, signed on the same day, Germany and Japan pledged severe action against direct or indirect agents of the Comintern and announced their intention of setting up a permanent committee to consider measures necessary for the struggle.

In a statement published on the same day, Ribbentrop, the German signatory of the Pact, referred to Spain as 'the latest victim of the desire for destruction shown by the Bolshevist virus' and pointed out that 'several states, as for instance America', had made ineffective protests against the decisions of the Seventh Comintern Congress.

'To-day', he declared, 'a strong line of defence has been formed by two nations who are equally determined to bring to destruction every attempt at intervention in their two countries by the Communist International. Japan will never permit any dissemination of Bolshevism in the Far East. Germany is creating a bulwark against this pestilence in central Europe. Finally, Italy, as the Duce informs the world, will hoist the anti-Bolshevist banner in the south. I am convinced that those nations which are to-day still unaware of the danger of Bolshevism, will one day thank our Führer for his clear and seasonable recognition of this unique world-menace.'[1]

The extent of Germany's ultimate ambitions with regard to the recruitment of other nations under the anti-Communist banner was revealed by Goebbels in a speech on 26 November.

'We should be more than short-sighted if we were to wish that France should be ruled by a Bolshevist régime. Fundamentally the disputes between European peoples, as compared with the advancing

[1] *Documents for 1936*, pp. 299–300.

Bolshevist danger, are only a kind of family quarrel. If France were prepared to act honourably it would be easy to establish peaceful relations with Germany. The crisis arose when France entered into a military alliance with the Soviet Union; in the face of that we could not remain passive.'[1]

The Congress of Soviets which met in Moscow on 25 November 1936, in order to pass the new Constitution, provided an opportunity for the Soviet Union to reply to this challenge. In a speech on 26 November, Lubchenko, Prime Minister of the Ukrainian Republic, declared that Germany and Japan were preparing 'a holy crusade against the Soviet Union'.

'Our answer', he said, 'to the Nazi dream of invading the Ukraine is an old Ukrainian saying: Just as a pig can never look at the sky, so Hitler will never be able to see our cabbage patch. . . .
'The Ukrainian people are ready to defend the Socialist Republic by force of arms. If a Fascist army dares to approach the Soviet Union our army under Voroshilov will deliver such a blow as has never been seen before.'[2]

The heads of the fighting services made confident reports on the Soviet Union's ability to resist aggression.

On 28 November, Admiral Orlov, the Commander-in-Chief of the Navy, told the Congress that since 1933 the Soviet Union's strength in submarines had increased seven-fold and its strength in seaplanes five-fold, while it had trebled the number of small coastal defence craft and doubled the number of batteries of long-range and anti-aircraft artillery.[3] On the following day, General Khripin, the assistant commander-in-chief of the Soviet Air Force, made the startling claim that the Soviet Air Force was now the most powerful in the world. The number of fighting planes, 60 per cent of which were bombers, had been quadrupled since 1932 and by the end of the year there would be 100,000 pilots available.[4]

---

[1] ibid., p. 301. See also the speech by Hess, ibid., p. 303.
[2] ibid., p. 301.
[3] Orlov was dismissed on 5 October 1937, and his execution was announced on 20 August 1938. See *infra*, chap. 6.
[4] *Survey for 1936*, p. 157.

Chapter Five

SOVIET DIPLOMACY IN EUROPE: FROM THE ANTI-
COMINTERN PACT TO THE NYON CONFERENCE

THE most important comment upon the Anti-Comintern
Pact from the point of view of the U.S.S.R., was that
made by Litvinov when he addressed the Congress of
Soviets on 28 November 1936.[1] The speech, while largely
devoted to the Spanish issue, included a long disquisition on the
role of Fascism as a method of dealing with the inherent contradictions of bourgeois society, and on the distinction between the
decrepit bourgeois conception of liberty and the new rich content which the Soviet Union had given to the idea, as exemplified in the draft Constitution.

'In becoming the bulwark of democracy and freedom, the Soviet
Union does not, however, call for the creation of an international
bloc to struggle against Fascism, which rejects democracy and freedom. We, as a State, are not concerned with the internal Fascist
régime of this or that country. Our collaboration with other
countries and our participation in the League of Nations are based
on the principle of the peaceful co-existence of two systems—the
Socialist and the capitalist—and we consider that the latter includes
the Fascist system. But Fascism is now ceasing to be an internal
affair of the countries which preach it.'

Mussolini had recently come over to the view, always held
by German National-Socialism, that Fascism was an article for
export; Germany already had agencies all over the world, carrying on political agitation. But this activity presented no danger
with which the Soviet Union could not easily cope.

The foreign activity of Fascism was more serious, declared
Litvinov, when it took forms such as the intervention in Spain.

'In the case of Spain, we have the first sally of Fascism beyond
its borders. . . . If this attempt were to succeed, there would be no
guarantees against its repetition on a wider scale in relation to other
States.
'It is necessary to bear in mind that Fascism is not only a specific
internal State régime, but that it represents at the same time preparation for aggression, preparation for war against other States.'

Fascism prepares by implanting a chauvinist mentality in the
population, by extensive rearmament, and

[1] Litvinov, *Against Aggression*, pp. 58–80.

65

'by releasing itself unilaterally from all international obligations binding it or by simply violating them when it suits it; by avoiding all international co-operation for the strengthening of the peace; by attempting to undermine the international organizations which are called upon to protect peace, by waging a campaign for disuniting other countries and by preventing the collective organization of security'.

Fascist hostility towards the Soviet Union had grown parallel with the Soviet Union's efforts to strengthen the collective system. Fascist propaganda against the Soviet Union had the objects

'firstly of destroying the ties that exist between (other) countries and the Soviet Union as members of the League of Nations, and, secondly . . . of receiving financial assistance for strengthening its armaments, which can be directed against other countries, not necessarily against the Soviet Union'.

Finally, Fascism, in order to conceal its isolation, had appealed to the few other equally isolated countries which shared its hostility to the League of Nations and to the organization of peace and had concluded a bloc with them, ostensibly for the struggle against the 'international Communist menace'.

'To be exact, I must point out that it is not a general bloc which has been concluded between the three States, but one between Germany and Japan.

'Incidentally, we have exact information that Italy, anxious to follow at all costs in the footsteps of her new mentor, Germany, has proposed to Japan that she conclude an agreement with her similar to the published part of the Japanese Agreement.'

Italy's decision, after more than a decade of 'highly proper relations with the Soviet Union' was, he said, clearly due to the Soviet Union's loyal participation in sanctions and to the Soviet stand against Fascist military intervention in Spain.

Litvinov pointed out that the Anti-Comintern Agreement meant, on the face of it, an admission that the two signatories, in spite of their efforts, were faced with an internal Communist danger too great for each to be able to meet without foreign assistance. The two meagre articles which had been published had scarcely required fifteen months of negotiations in the greatest secrecy between a Japanese general and a German 'super-diplomat'.

'I would recommend you', he said, 'not to seek for any meaning in it, since it really has no meaning, for the simple reason that it is only the cover for another agreement which was simultaneously discussed and initialled, probably also signed, and which was not published and is not intended for publication.'

In fact what now existed was an agreement of an aggressive character, in which Communism was not even mentioned, and in which Italian Fascism was (so Litvinov's denunciations assumed) a full participant.

On the other hand, the Soviet Union remained faithful to her policy of peace and ready to co-operate with other States for that end.

'The Soviet Union, however, does not beg to be invited into any unions, any blocs, any combinations. She will calmly let other States weigh and evaluate the advantages which can be derived for peace from close co-operation with the Soviet Union, and understand that the Soviet Union can give more than receive. . . . Other States, other territories are menaced most. Our security does not depend upon paper documents or upon foreign policy combinations. The Soviet Union is sufficiently strong in herself.'

The speech thus ended upon the same note as that which had been predominant throughout the Congress, one of confidence in the internal strength of the Soviet Union, as if in direct contradiction to the rumours which the 'purge' was multiplying throughout the world. But the fact that Litvinov also took care to begin and end his address with considerations of an internal order, was perhaps equally significant. It may be argued that this speech marks what was in fact a turning-point in Soviet foreign policy—the beginning of a movement away from collective action, and towards a new isolation.[1]

Litvinov's suspicions about Italy were not at once justified, since the Italian Government maintained a reserved attitude, in spite of the applause which the Pact received from the Italian press. The immediate British reaction was frankly hostile.[2] The anxieties of the Soviet Union must therefore have been confined to the question of the possible reactions of the countries of eastern Europe.

Of Czechoslovakia's fidelity to her engagements to Russia there could be little question. German pressure against Czecho-

[1] It is perhaps worth noting that a number of rumours were in circulation early in 1937 about a direct approach to Germany by the U.S.S.R. The German press denied that anything but economic matters was discussed. Suritz, the Soviet Ambassador to Berlin, denied the truth of these reports in a conversation with the American Ambassador on 10 April; *Dodd's Diary*, p. 402. Cf. D. J. Dallin, *Russia and Post-War Europe* (Yale University Press, 1943), p. 108.

[2] A speech by Eden on 14 December in which he asserted that Britain's task, as proved by the Spanish War, was to work for a comprehensive European settlement and that Britons could not live secure in a Western European glass-house, was warmly welcomed by *Izvestia* on the 16th. Coates, *A History of Anglo-Soviet Relations*, pp. 558–9.

slovakia during 1936 had taken the form of inciting the German minority to make demands designed to weaken the structure of the Czechoslovak State, as well as of a direct campaign of intimidation.[1] The object of the latter was to discredit Czechoslovakia in the eyes of the West, by picturing the country as a hotbed of Bolshevism, and to intimidate Czechoslovakia into adopting a position of diplomatic isolation, on the model outlined for Belgium in King Leopold II's speech of 16 October 1936.[2] In its pursuit of the former object, German propaganda made some progress, the full fruits of which were not gathered until 1938.

On 25 March 1936, the British Foreign Secretary assured the House of Commons that the Czechoslovak Government had given the British Minister in Prague a categorical assurance that no arrangement was in existence between the Czechoslovak and Russian Governments for the use of aerodromes on Czech territory by the Russian Air Force. Speaking on 28 May, the Czech Foreign Minister Krofta referred to the denial of this rumour and also of the story that Soviet troops were stationed in Slovakia. It was, he declared, only natural that Czechoslovak relations with the Soviet Union, since the conclusion of the Treaty of 1934, should have become steadily more friendly.[3] These stories were revived again by the news of the arrival in Prague on 15 July 1936 of an important Soviet Air Force mission. And President Benes found it necessary to revert to the subject in a speech on 19 August:

'In coming together with the Soviet Union we accomplished a good work for the maintenance of peace in Western and Eastern Europe—we had no other aims in that connexion. All the fantastic rumours of what is going on between us and Moscow are tendentious inventions. The deductions that we have become the instrument of Communist politics in Europe are simply ridiculous. . . . Communism has no foothold and can have no success among us.'[4]

The allegations were, however, repeated by Goebbels and Rosenberg in their speeches at Nuremberg on 10 September and

---

[1] For the local background of Czechoslovakian affairs which was to figure so prominently in international debate for the next three years, see E. Wiskemann, *Czechs and Germans* (Oxford University Press, 1938); R. J. Kerner (ed.), *Czechoslovakia: Twenty Years of Independence* (University of California Press, 1940); R. W. Seton-Watson, *A History of the Czechs and Slovaks* (Hutchinson, 1943). It should not be overlooked that as late as 1933 Communists abroad had professed no sympathy for Czechoslovakia, and that the Comintern had formerly advocated autonomy and even secession for its minorities.

[2] *Documents for 1936*, pp. 223–7.

[3] ibid., p. 365.   [4] ibid., pp. 373–4.

the Czechoslovak Government made an official protest about them on 23 September.[1]

Whatever the extent to which Soviet-Czech preparations for mutual assistance were in fact carried, there can be no doubt that Czechoslovakia was the principal barrier to Germany's eastward expansion. In the event of war 'the Russian alliance was the keystone to Czechoslovakia's hopes of emerging on the winning side'. Air support was the only immediate aid which Czechoslovakia could expect as far as resisting Germany itself was concerned, although the Soviet alliance was calculated to have a deterrent effect upon Polish and Hungarian ambitions at Czechoslovakia's expense.[2]

It was later revealed by Dr. Benes that Germany proposed at this juncture a non-aggression pact with Czechoslovakia on the model of that with Poland. The proposal was made by two special emissaries of Hitler on 11 October.[3]

Any hope that Czechoslovakia would voluntarily abandon the Soviet alliance was dispelled by Krofta's speech on 22 October 1936.[4] Her only hope, he declared, was to remain faithful to her existing alliances and to strive to strengthen and extend them. He once more denied the reports about the establishment of Soviet bases on Czechoslovak soil and reiterated Czechoslovakia's refusal to join in any ideological bloc. The treaty with Soviet Russia had been concluded 'practically as a partial substitute for the proposed Eastern Pact' and in no way implied that Czechoslovakia had become the tool of Moscow.

The signing of the Anti-Comintern Pact did nothing to alter Czechoslovakia's policy. The German proposals for a non-aggression pact were apparently repeated in December. These did not demand that Czechoslovakia should denounce her existing engagements but merely that she should undertake not to implement them if occasion arose. Dr. Benes said that counter-proposals based on the Locarno Treaty were sent to Berlin in January but remained without reply.[5] German

[1] *Survey for 1936*, pp. 485-6.

[2] G. E. R. Gedye, *Fallen Bastions* (Gollancz, 1939), pp. 386-8. According to Pierre Cot negotiations took place in 1937 for a tripartite air pact (between the U.S.S.R., France, and Czechoslovakia), of which the operation was to be subordinated to the League Covenant. The pact, he asserts, was ready for signature when he left office in January 1938; Cot, *Triumph of Treason*, pp. 359-63.

[3] This was revealed by Dr. Benes in a press conference at Chicago on 27 May 1943. B. Bilek, *Fifth Column at Work* (Lindsay Drummond, 1946), pp. 13-15.

[4] *Documents for 1936*, pp. 375-92.

[5] Bilek, loc. cit. Dr. Ripka states that these negotiations made such progress that it was considered certain that an agreement with Germany

attacks upon Czechoslovakia continued, if intermittently, in the new year.[1] There was another scare about Soviet aerodromes in January and February. Further German press campaigns followed in the summer and autumn.

Less reassuring from the Soviet point of view was the attitude of Czechoslovakia's partners in the Little Entente. Yugoslavia, now actively courted by Germany, had no wish to abandon its standing hostility towards the Soviet régime. More important was the unwillingness of Roumania, in the face of the increasing German backing for 'revision', to follow Czechoslovakia's course and to improve its relations with the Soviet Union. In the first place, in Roumania, as in other countries of south-eastern Europe, the unbalanced nature of the social structure, and the consequent narrow basis of the existing political régime, made the anti-Communist aspect of German policy by no means unwelcome to the ruling class.[2] In the second place, German propaganda in these countries went hand in hand with a process of economic penetration which, in spite of some set-backs, was pursued with increasing intensity from 1936 onwards.[3] This penetration helped these countries to solve some of their most pressing problems, at the price of permitting Germany to acquire an ever-growing hold over their national policies.[4] In the third place, German anti-semitism helped to reconcile to German penetration groups which in other respects claimed to represent the purest nationalism.

Communist Parties were illegal in all these countries[5] and

would be reached. 'The agreement', he writes, 'did not materialize for several reasons. The decisive reason was perhaps the hope held in Berlin that Stalin's opponents, of whom the most important was Marshal Tuchachevsky, would succeed in overthrowing his régime and in constituting a new government which would come to terms with Germany. The German government considered it advisable to wait for this radical change in the balance of power in Eastern Europe.' H. Ripka, *Munich: Before and After* (Gollancz, 1939), p. 98.

[1] See the speeches by Goebbels on 4 and 12 February 1937; *Documents for 1937*, pp. 175–8. On 12 January 1937, the Czechoslovak General Staff sent a note to the military attachés of foreign powers in Prague, repudiating German propaganda about the presence of Soviet officers among the Czechoslovak forces. Bilek, op. cit., pp. 86–7. Cf. Krofta's speech of 2 March 1937, *Documents for 1937*, pp. 354–5.

[2] Hugh Seton-Watson, *Eastern Europe between the Wars, 1918–1941* (Cambridge University Press, 1945), *passim*.

[3] *Survey for 1936*, pp. 526 ff.; *Survey for 1937*, I, pp. 459 ff.; *Survey for 1938*, I, pp. 43 ff.

[4] H. Seton-Watson, op. cit., pp. 382–96.

[5] The dates upon which Communist Parties in these countries were declared illegal are as follows: Hungary 1919, Roumania 1920, Yugoslavia 1921, Bulgaria 1934. Communists began to be active in Greece in about

Soviet propaganda, having to work underground, was limited in scope. Nor could it derive much assistance from Soviet economic policy.[1] In the case of Roumania, the Bessarabian questioned remained a source of anxiety, since the increasing military importance of the Soviet Union made it unlikely that it would consent much longer to leave the question in abeyance.[2]

As late as May 1936, the Little Entente appeared firm in its devotion to collective security and ready to continue the path of improved relations with the U.S.S.R., which had been entered upon in 1934.[3] But it soon became evident that this solidarity, as far as relations with the Soviet Union were concerned, was dependent in Roumania on the personal ascendancy of the Foreign Minister Titulescu.[4] His replacement on 30

1932. Their centre was the Macedonian tobacco-manufacturing town of Kavalla. In January 1936, fifteen Communists were returned to the Greek Parliament, and the Party held the balance between monarchists and republicans. The Party was suppressed after General Metaxas established his dictatorship in August. A. W. Gomme, *Greece* (Oxford University Press, 1945), pp. 70–3.

[1] A Russo-Roumanian economic agreement was signed on 17 February 1936; *Excelsior* (Bucarest), 22 February 1936. Commercial agreements between the U.S.S.R. and Greece were signed on 14 January 1936 and 27 February 1937.

[2] On 5 April 1937, the Soviet Foreign Office denied a Roumanian report that the U.S.S.R. was about to renounce its claim to Bessarabia. Cf. Seton-Watson, op. cit., pp. 336–8. Russia had secured part of Bessarabia by the Treaty of Bucarest in 1812 and the remainder by the Treaty of Berlin in 1877–8, in spite of the fact that the Roumanians had fought with them against the Turks. In the first world war, the Central Powers had promised the whole of Bessarabia to Roumania if she would enter the war on their side. On 2 December 1917, the local Council of Bessarabia had declared it to be a Moldavian Democratic Republic and part of the Russian Federal Republic. When the Bolsheviks entered Kishinev in January 1918, the Bessarabians appealed to Roumania for assistance and on 24 January the Council declared Bessarabia's independence. On 5 March the Roumanians signed an agreement with the Russians that they would evacuate the province. On 9 April the Council voted the province's adhesion to Roumania (which was confirmed by plebiscite later in the year). Chicherin protested against this on behalf of Russia on 18 April. J. Bunyan and H. H. Fisher, *The Bolshevik Revolution, 1917–18* (Stanford University Press, 1934), pp. 462–4; cf. A. Popovici, *The Political Status of Bessarabia* (Washington, Georgetown University Press, 1931).

[3] Communiqué of the Permanent Council of the Little Entente, Belgrade, 7 May 1936. *Documents for 1936*, pp. 349–51.

[4] According to M. Paul-Boncour, Litvinov discussed with Titulescu during the Montreux Conference, the possibility of Soviet troops passing through Roumania in the event of an act of aggression against Czechoslovakia, and agreed with him provisionally on a formula binding the Soviet Union to withdraw any troops remaining west of the Dniester after the end of hostilities. M. Paul-Boncour also relates that he received from King Carol during a conversation in Paris in February 1936 when he was

August 1936 by Antonescu meant above all that the King had accepted the view that Titulescu's policy of overt friendship with France and Czechoslovakia, and tacit acceptance of collaboration with the Soviet Union, was too dangerous.[1]

The first statement of the new Roumanian Foreign Minister suggested an effort to maintain at least the façade of continuity. 'Our alliance with the Little Entente constitutes an essential element of our foreign policy . . . we shall continue to maintain and develop our relations of good neighbours with Soviet Russia.'[2]

The Czechoslovak Foreign Minister Krofta, for his part, speaking on 22 October, was at pains to deny that Titulescu's departure meant any change in Roumanian foreign policy. King Carol's visit to Prague at the end of the same month, and the meeting of delegates from the parliaments of the three Little Entente States on 1 December, provided further occasions for stressing the solidarity of the Little Entente. And the Anti-Comintern Pact received no immediate welcome in these countries.

On the other hand, given the existing state of Polish-Soviet and of Polish-Czechoslovak relations, there was something disquieting in the marked cordiality between Roumania and Poland which followed the fall of Titulescu.[3] For if Roumania

---

Minister of State, assurances that he would bring Roumania round to accept an entente with the Soviet Union. A year later he found the King's sentiments had altered. J. Paul-Boncour, *Entre Deux Guerres* (Paris, Plon, 1946), vol. 3, pp. 58–61.

[1] *Survey for 1936*, pp. 522–3. It may be noted that on 26 August the Hungarian press had published a report from Bucarest that there was to be an air force conference at Prague between Russia, France, Czechoslovakia, and Roumania. There had been a rumour in July that the Roumanian Government had agreed to the building of a strategic railway for the transport, if necessary, of Russian ground forces to Czechoslovakia. This was officially denied by the Roumanian Government on 12 August, i.e. after the fall of Titulescu, which the rumour may have helped to precipitate.

[2] *Documents for 1936*, pp. 394–5. The Communiqué issued by the Permanent Council of the Little Entente after its meeting on 13–14 September stressed again its members' devotion to collective security and to the principle of non-intervention in the affairs of other nations (ibid., pp. 351–4). While the signatories no doubt had Spain in mind, it should be remembered that the extreme right-wing parties in Roumania, outside the Government, were receiving increasing support from Germany on a basis of hostility towards the French as well as the Soviet orientation of Roumanian policy.

[3] A Polish publicist has since claimed that the 'credit' for the overthrow of Titulescu should largely go to Arcizewski, Polish Ambassador in Bucarest from 1933 onwards, who, he asserts, had continually stimulated opposition to the former's 'pro-Soviet' policy; S. Mackiewicz, *Colonel Beck and his Policy* (Eyre and Spottiswoode, 1944), pp. 97–100.

were to align her policy definitively with that of Poland, it would mean that Russia would be cut off from her Czechoslovak ally by a continuous belt of neutral if not unfriendly territory. The close relations between Roumania and Poland continued into 1937, culminating in King Carol's visit to Warsaw at the end of June.

Czechoslovakia naturally did its best to counteract the tendency in Roumanian policy represented by the Polish connexion. The Roumanian Prime Minister Tatarescu visited Prague on 23–24 March 1937 and 'a comprehensive detailed agreement was concluded concerning the financing of Czechoslovak supplies for the Roumanian Army'.[1] A meeting of the Permanent Council of the Little Entente on 1–2 April 1937 once more declared the unity of the three States in regard to the European problems of the moment.[2]

Commenting upon this solidarity, Krofta, in his speech of 21 May, emphasized its significance with regard to the Soviet Union:

'In discussing the Little Entente I should like to refer to a matter which is often designated as a stumbling-block, and so to say, an indisputable proof of dissensions within the Little Entente. This is the question of our relations with the Soviet Union. As is well known, the Soviet Union was recognized by Roumania and Czechoslovakia in June 1934. This recognition was accorded on the basis of the express concurrence of Yugoslavia with the step taken by Roumania and Czechoslovakia, a concurrence which was given several months in advance, and accompanied likewise by the express consent of Roumania and Czechoslovakia that Yugoslavia should in this matter adopt the course which she deemed best for herself. When Czechoslovakia had in mind the negotiations for a treaty of mutual aid, subsequently signed in May 1935, our two allies Roumania and Yugoslavia were constantly informed from beginning to end about our negotiations, and were asked for written concurrence which they have given both to the negotiations and to the treaty. I am not revealing any secret when I say that this concurrence on the part of our two allies has been confirmed again and again on various occasions without reserve. Our two allies cannot really desire that Czechoslovakia should throw over her purely defensive pact with Russia, any more than Czechoslovakia has ever wished, or would wish, for example, that Roumania should renounce her treaty of alliance with Poland. The questions of the recognition of the Soviet Union and of the Czechoslovak-Soviet Pact have thus

---

[1] *Documents for 1937*, pp. 383–4.
[2] ibid., pp. 340–2. It has been stated that it was on this occasion that the Yugoslav Premier Stoyadinovic first intimated to Czechoslovakia that in his view she should come to terms with Germany; H. F. Armstrong, *Where There is no Peace* (Macmillan, 1939), p. 34 *n.*

from the very outset been absolutely clear within the ranks of the Little Entente. There is complete unanimity there concerning it, despite the various individual attitudes of the three States to the Soviet Union, determined in each case by special individual reasons which are fully recognized by the other two members of the Little Entente.'[1]

Speaking on the same day, however, Antonescu, although careful to deny that the recent visit of Beck had marked a change in Roumanian foreign policy, was not over-enthusiastic about relations with Russia: 'Our relations with the Soviet Union are friendly. They are developing to the satisfaction of the two countries. They could be intensified.'[2]

It was thus not only in virtue of her own strength, but as an influence on other countries, that Poland's role continued to be of the first importance.[3] By the time of the Rhineland *coup*, the Poles were somewhat disenchanted with the results of their *rapprochement* with Germany in 1934. Economic relations were not as satisfactory as it had been hoped they would become, and the growth of Nazi influence in Danzig was a major source of anxiety. The Poles began therefore to try to strengthen their much-weakened links with France. On the other hand, they showed no more enthusiasm than before for a security system of the type envisaged in the eastern pact negotiations of 1934–5. Poland's ultimate objectives were to retain her temporary Great-Power status, threatened by the military recovery of Russia and Germany, and to avoid becoming the battle-ground of eastern Europe. Above all she wished to avoid the entry of the Red Army into those non-Polish territories acquired from Russia by the Treaty of Riga in 1921.

Poland's policy was thus to build up some kind of bloc in eastern Europe which might insulate the potential belligerents on either side of it. This policy, as has been seen, awakened sympathetic echoes in Roumania, in spite of Poland's friendship for Hungary. It also possessed an appeal for the Baltic States and for some circles in western Europe.[4]

---

[1] *Documents for 1937*, pp. 366–7.   [2] ibid., p. 382.
[3] For a general survey of Polish policy at this time see *Survey for 1936*, pp. 393–40. Cf. Léon Noël, *L'Agression Allemande Contre la Pologne* (Paris, Flammarion, 1946).
[4] The Latvian Foreign Minister Munters had a conversation with Mr Joseph E. Davies at Riga in the middle of August 1937 on the steps which should be taken for an eastern European settlement in the event of a settlement being reached in the west. 'In that connection he stated that several months ago he had had a long political discussion with Neville Chamberlain, which developed the idea that the solution for the peace of eastern Europe might be found under an arrangement between Germany and the

There was thus no change in Poland's relations with the Soviet Union. Poland's attitude towards the Rhineland *coup* had been too reserved for Russia's liking, although the two Powers were at one in resenting the way in which the Locarno Powers, during the crisis, appeared to disregard the rights of other members of the League Council to full participation in the London discussions. In Poland's case, however, it was its own dignity as a Great Power, not the position of the League, which was the issue. Poland was indeed foremost among those States which were seeking to minimize the obligations of the Covenant, and to limit League action, so as not to be involved in matters outside the sphere of their 'direct interests'. It had seemed possible nevertheless that Russian and Polish suspicions of the possible revival of the Four-Power pact idea would lead to a *rapprochement* between them. Molotov, in the interview which he gave to the editor of *Le Temps* in March 1936 had expressed his belief in a possible amelioration of Russo-Polish relations; but Litvinov's passage through Warsaw on 31 March was disregarded by the Polish authorities. There were rumours that Litvinov would pay the Polish capital an official visit to mark the fifteenth anniversary of the Treaty of Riga (signed on 18 March 1921). In mid-April, however, the Soviet press dismissed as premature current speculation about a possible re-orientation of Polish policy. Communist disturbances in Poland in April were among the handicaps to any growth of cordiality on the Polish side.[1] On 13 May, Litvinov saw Beck in Geneva but no great importance was attached to this meeting.[2] At most one could say that during the remainder of the year there was something in the nature of a *détente*.[3]

Poland's efforts in the autumn of 1936 to improve her relations

---

Baltic States, Poland and Roumania, whereby Germany would enter into the same kind of treaties with these states, respectively, which the U.S.S.R. had with these states. With such pacts of non-aggression, together with a clear definition of what constituted the aggressor, peace would be assured as far as treaties could effect that end and thereby there would be created a roof between Germany and Russia which would relieve the situation of the necessity for Russia and Germany to enter into a contract or treaty as it was thought that Hitler would under no circumstances "sign any contract with the Soviet Union at this time".' J. E. Davies, *Mission to Moscow* (Gollancz, 1942), pp. 350–1; cf. ibid., p. 146.

[1] J. Donnadieu, *La Lutte des Aigles aux Marches Orientales* (Paris, Alcan, 1939), p. 155. It would seem that the Polish Communist Party, which had been forced to work underground since Pilsudski's *coup* in 1926, was increasing in strength as a result of the economic depression; H. Seton-Watson, op. cit., p. 166.

[2] *Manchester Guardian*, 14 May 1936.

[3] Donnadieu, op. cit., p. 219.

with France were watched with interest in Moscow.[1] On 24 September, the Soviet press commented on the recent visit to Paris of General Smigly-Rydz, which had taken place three weeks previously. It was stated that Poland had given France more than verbal assurances in return for a promise of French financial assistance for Polish rearmament.[2] A split was apparent between Smigly-Rydz himself and Beck, and a definite change in Polish foreign policy had begun. Any genuine friend of France, it was argued, must of necessity be a friend of the Soviet Union and of Czechoslovakia.[3] But if this comment indicated a new Soviet bid for a mutual-assistance pact with Poland, it was destined to be ineffective. Litvinov again passed through Warsaw on 14 October without meeting the Polish leaders.[4] Nevertheless, the Polish Government maintained an aloof attitude towards the Anti-Comintern Pact.[5] On 26 November its London embassy denied a report that Poland had been approached with a view to its becoming a signatory.[6]

In his statement on 18 December Beck said:

'The work done by us in co-operation with our Eastern neighbour, the Union of Soviet Socialist Republics, continues to yield useful results. We transact our common neighbourly business without any shocks or serious misunderstandings.'[7]

This remark came in for severe criticism in the Soviet press. *Izvestia* expressed surprise that Beck could talk of co-operation with the Soviet Union or of Poland as a defender of the Baltic States. The Smigly-Rydz visit to Paris had brought about no alteration in Polish policy, and Beck would give his approval to the League of Nations only when its members were as free to commit acts of aggression as non-members. *Pravda* drew a parallel between the policy of Poland and that of Hungary. Beck's silence on the question of Czechoslovakia showed that

[1] In the second week in August, General Gamelin visited Warsaw and had an interview with General Smigly-Rydz who told him of his objections to the eventual passage of Soviet troops through Poland or Lithuania. M. Gamelin, *Servir* (Paris, Plon, 1946), vol. 2, pp. 230–1.

[2] In fact no undertakings of any kind had been secured from Poland in return for the 'Rambouillet' Agreement. Nöel, op. cit., pp. 138–50, cf. Reynaud, op. cit., vol. 1, pp. 126–7.

[3] *Manchester Guardian*, 25 September 1936.

[4] *The Times*, 15 October 1936.

[5] Germany made further attempts to enlist Poland directly in her anti-Soviet schemes. See Szembek's minute of his conversation with Ribbentrop on 14 August 1936. *Polish White Book*, pp. 33–4.

[6] 'It is said that Japan did her best to get Poland to participate in the arrangement with Germany but without success.' Grew, on 1 January 1937, *Ten Years in Japan* (New York, Simon and Schuster, 1944), p. 175.

[7] *Documents for 1936*, pp. 406–15.

Poland was prepared to fall in with the plans of the German aggressors, for it was no secret that Germany contemplated an attack on Czechoslovakia. The solidarity between Poland and Italy over sanctions showed that Poland also contemplated aggression.[1]

Polish-Czechoslovak hostility continued to be an important obstacle to any further improvement in Poland's relations with the Soviet Union.[2] So also were Poland's efforts to weaken the ties between Roumania and Czechoslovakia.[3] Espionage in favour of Poland was one of the charges made against some of the victims of the Soviet 'purge', while the press of each country kept up its usual barrage of criticism concerning the social structure and political régime of the other.

The Baltic States also felt the repercussions of the increased tension in Russo-German relations. Without sharing Poland's ambitions, they shared her fears of becoming one of the battle-grounds of the rival Powers and of the rival ideologies. To an outside observer, the three States seemed 'to be wavering be-tween the assumption of a posture of detachment which might prove untenable in a crisis and the incompatible alternative policy of throwing themselves upon the protection of the U.S.S.R., as a more practical means of obtaining security against Germany'. At the end of April 1936, the chiefs of staff of the three Republics visited Voroshilov at Moscow, and this was followed by a meeting of the Baltic Entente at Tallinn on 7–9 May. The terms of the communiqué issued at the conclusion of this meeting suggested that the Baltic States 'were still hesitat-ing to follow Czechoslovakia's example of seeking security by joining the Franco-Russian military alliance. The motive that weighed with the Baltic Governments appears to have been not a fear of Soviet penetration but rather an anxiety to avoid giving offence to Germany and Poland'. Meanwhile, Germany was doing her best to keep the Baltic States out of the Soviet

[1] Quoted in Le Temps, 23 December 1936.
[2] There was a détente in Polish-Czechoslovak relations in 1936 but it did not last long. Noël, op. cit., pp. 167–8.
[3] Poland's task was made easier by an unfortunate incident. In January 1937 M. Seba, who had been Czechoslovak Minister in Bucarest since 1932, published a book (which received a prize from the City of Prague) entitled Russia and the Little Entente in World Politics. This work gave great offence in Poland and Roumania alike by the regrets which it appeared to express over the fact that Czechoslovakia and the U.S.S.R. did not possess a common land frontier; also by certain strictures, in which the author indulged, on the Roumanian social system, and on the conduct of the Roumanian Army during the War of 1914–18; Survey for 1937, I, p. 406. Cf. Davies, op. cit., p. 63, where it appears that the book had a preface by the Czechoslovak Foreign Minister.

orbit 'by the triple means of threats, blandishments, and propaganda'.[1] Germany's assets for all three purposes included the German minorities in these countries. Her principal and most unexpected success in this sphere was to bring about a *rapprochement* with Lithuania, which was marked by the temporary shelving of the Memel question and by the conclusion on 5 August 1936 of a commercial treaty.[2]

The primary reaction of the Baltic States to the news of the Anti-Comintern Pact was fear lest new pressure on the Soviet Union in Asia should weaken its power to defend them against Germany. Nevertheless the Soviet authorities do not seem to have been altogether reassured. On 29 November 1936 Zhdanov, the secretary of the Communist Party for the Leningrad Province, in the course of his speech to the Congress of Soviets, uttered what could only be described as a threat:

'Round us are small countries which dream of great adventures or allow great adventurers to manipulate their territory. We are not afraid of these little countries but if they do not mind their own business, we shall be compelled to open our borders and it will be too bad if we are compelled to use the Red Army on them.'

There seem to have been second thoughts as to the wisdom of this outburst, for on 2 December the Soviet Minister in Riga assured the Latvian Foreign Minister Munters that the speech reflected no aggressive intentions on the part of the U.S.S.R. towards the Baltic States.[3]

The Latvian Foreign Minister delivered a pessimistic speech on the general European situation when the Baltic Entente held a meeting at Riga a week later. While the Baltic States had always preferred collective action they admitted that other methods might yield good results, although it would be a mistake to adopt them in a spirit of intransigence. In spite of this hint of its readiness to consider neutrality of the Scandinavian type, the conference reaffirmed its confidence in the League.[4] The

[1] *Survey for 1936*, pp. 536–7.

[2] 'In the first weeks of September it was reported that Germany had offered Lithuania a non-aggression pact as a first step towards the conclusion of pacts of this kind with all three Baltic States.' ibid., p. 539. On 21 May 1935 Hitler had said that the Memel question made a non-aggression pact with Lithuania impossible; *Hitler's Speeches*, p. 1236. The report of September 1936 seems to have had no sequel.

[3] Zhdanov's speech caused something of a stir abroad and was referred to by Beck in his statement on 18 December: 'It gives me great satisfaction to confirm that the explanation received does not give any ground for disquietude. I had the opportunity of hearing that the Soviet Government attaches equal importance to good and normal relations with all the States situated on its western borders.' *Documents for 1936*, p. 408.

[4] *The Baltic States* (R.I.I.A., 1938), p. 86.

Soviet reply took the form of a speech at Kaunas by the Soviet Minister Karsky, who was about to leave to take up important duties at Moscow. Russo-Lithuanian friendship was an important factor of peace. The Baltic States could not remain outside a conflict in Europe and declarations of neutrality only excited the greed of the aggressor. Only the Soviet Union was in a position to protect the Baltic States.[1] This last remark was no doubt prompted by Beck's friendly remarks about Latvia, 'our neighbours by land and water' in his speech of 18 December.

Relations between the Soviet Union and the Baltic States remained reasonably good in 1937. In February, Marshal Egorov, the Soviet Chief of Staff, visited the three Balkan capitals.[2] There was also a visit to Riga by the Soviet battleship *Marat*.

In June, Munters visited Moscow, and Litvinov made a speech at a reception held in his honour on the 15th. In this speech, he referred to the seventeen years of good neighbourly relations between the Soviet Union and Latvia and declared that Latvia's geographical position made it impossible for the Soviet Union to disinterest itself in the maintenance of Latvian integrity and independence in conformity with the League Covenant.[3]

Relations with Finland, where Communism had been proscribed since 1929–30, continued to be less satisfactory than those with the Baltic States proper.[4]

In 1934–5 there was evidence of considerable trouble in the

[1] *Le Temps*, 26 December 1936.
[2] Egorov was later on a victim of the 'purge'.
[3] *Journal de Moscou*, 22 June 1937. Interesting notes on the position in the Baltic States in July–August 1937 are to be found among the dispatches of Joseph E. Davies, who paid visits at this time to the three Baltic capitals. Davies, op. cit., pp. 139–40, 320–2. Estonia: 'Their attitude to Russia is friendly and formal. They want to get along with their big neighbour, but they still remember the unsuccessful Communist *putsch* of 1924. . . . In the last analysis, however, England now dominates Estonia. . . . From the military point of view, in the event of a German attack on Russia, they seem to think that they are outside the danger zone.' Latvia: 'A balance and a strict neutrality between Germany, Poland and the U.S.S.R. are . . . imperative. . . . As near as I could sense, the officials are more favourably disposed towards Poland than to either the U.S.S.R. or Germany. England is their largest customer and has dominant influence.' Lithuania: 'It is in the heart of the danger zone as between the Soviet Union and Germany and while desirous of maintaining strictly formal relationships with Germany it is the most friendly to Russia of all the European states adjacent to the U.S.S.R. . . . the government and the entire population are bitterly hostile to Poland.'
[4] On Finland, see J. Hampden Jackson, *Finland* (Allen and Unwin, 1938).

Soviet republic of Eastern Karelia, to which the building of the White Sea–Baltic canal had given new importance, and which Finnish nationalism regarded as an irredenta.[1] Much of the indigenous Finnish population was deported from Eastern Karelia and also from Ingria in connexion with the building there of frontier fortifications by the Soviet Union. In July 1935, the Finnish Government requested an explanation of these deportations, which was refused on the ground that the matter was a purely internal one.[2] In November, the Finnish-born Premier of the Eastern Karelian Republic was dismissed from his post and expelled from the U.S.S.R. and other Finnish-born dignitaries of the Republic were also replaced by Russians.[3]

Meanwhile the Finnish Government, although suspected by the Russians of too great friendliness to Germany, had been at pains to maintain a neutral attitude. This was the more natural in that Finland, unlike the Baltic States proper, might hope to keep out of a future Russo-German conflict. In April 1935, the Finnish Prime Minister denied in a speech to the Diet that Finland had any hostile designs with regard to the Soviet Union, but made it clear that Finland would not follow the example of the Baltic States should they conclude pacts of mutual assistance with the U.S.S.R. He also complained of Finland's unfavourable trade balance with the Soviet Union and expressed the hope that Finnish exports to the Soviet Union would increase.[4] In July, he again found it necessary to deny allegations of hostility to the Soviet Union.[5]

Relations were aggravated by the long-drawn-out trial at Helsinki of a Finn, Antikainen, on the charge of atrocities committed by him while fighting on the Soviet side in Eastern Karelia in 1921–2. Antikainen, whom the Finns believed to be one of the Comintern's most important agents abroad, was finally condemned in May 1936 to penal servitude for life. There were also a number of other espionage and frontier incidents. In August 1936, the Moscow press alleged that

[1] The White Sea–Baltic canal was completed in June 1933.

[2] *New York Times*, 16 May, 18 August, 13 October 1935; *The Times*, 10 July, 14 October 1935.

[3] *New York Times*, 7 November, 10 November 1935; *The Times*, 7 November 1935.

[4] *Le Temps*, 18 April 1935; *Berliner Tageblatt*, 25 April 1935. The U.S.S.R. sold to Finland goods worth 3,500,000 roubles in 1935, 7,600,000 roubles in 1936, and 9,400,000 roubles in 1937, and bought from Finland goods worth 1,400,000 roubles in 1935, 3,600,000 roubles in 1936, and 3,800,000 in 1937. (The figures for 1936 and 1937 should be divided by 4·38 to get the equivalent in the old roubles used for reckoning in 1935.) Trade in both directions fell off in 1938.

[5] *The Times* 20 July 1935.

Finnish plans for 'commercial' airfields in eastern Finland were really for military airfields to be put at the disposal of Germany. The Finnish Chargé d'Affaires at Moscow protested against this accusation, which, he said, was designed to separate Finland from the other Scandinavian countries. The Soviet Government, however, as usual, declined responsibility for the Soviet press.[1]

On the Soviet side of the frontier there seem to have been extensive military preparations and fortifications.[2]

The danger to Finland of the growing friction with the U.S.S.R. was appreciated at Helsinki. In October 1936 the Prime Minister Kallio made a speech advocating an alliance with the Baltic States. Finland showed no interest in the Anti-Comintern Pact. At the beginning of January 1937, it was announced that the Finnish Foreign Minister, Holsti, had accepted an invitation to Moscow. In an interview on the 21st, he declared that Finland had always been faithful to the League Covenant, that she was not involved in any anti-Soviet combination, and that Germany exercised no undue influence upon her foreign policy.

Holsti's visit to Moscow took place on 8–10 February. Molotov gave a dinner for him—an honour previously only enjoyed by Eden and Laval—and this was attended by Voroshilov, Egorov, and Budyenny. Litvinov's speech of welcome was couched in friendly tones and the visit was generally regarded as a sign of improved relations.[3]

It is likely that this move on the part of Finland was the outcome of her obvious desire for closer relations with the Scandinavian states, particularly Sweden, with whom her *rapprochement* reached a climax in the spring of 1936. Finland had for some months been discussing informally the possibility of her being accepted as a member of the neutral Scandinavian bloc and had been informed that a prerequisite of this, was for her to convince the Soviet Union of the genuineness of her neutrality.[4]

A further improvement in Soviet-Finnish relations was brought about by the result of the presidential election in Finland on 15 February 1937. *Izvestia* described the defeat of Svinhufvud by Kallio as having deprived Berlin of an important trump in the diplomatic-military game.[5] The election was followed by a statement from Holsti:[6]

[1] *New York Times*, 14 August 1936.   [2] Davies, op. cit., pp. 348–9.
[3] *Le Temps*, 10 February 1937; *The Times*, 11 February 1937.
[4] Davies, op. cit., pp. 56–7, 63, 140–1, 145–6.
[5] *New York Times*, 17 February 1937.   [6] *Survey for 1936*, p. 536.

'I have no desire or intention that Finland shall join either a so-called Communist or (a so-called) anti-Communist front in Europe. The front which I wish to strengthen is the front of the democratic Powers, and especially of Great Britain, France, the Scandinavian countries and the League countries in general.'

His visit to Moscow had had an economic as well as a political purpose, in view of the fall in Russian imports from Finland in the last four years.

'I wanted to dispel the anxieties felt in Moscow that Finland might have made secret arrangements with a Great Power whereby Finland should be the jumping-off ground for an attack on the Soviet Union. No such secret arrangements exist, and the Finnish Government has no plans for warlike adventures of any kind.'

Nevertheless, towards the end of July 1937, new Soviet press attacks on Finland were evoked by a German naval visit to Helsinki, and Finland remained the most sensitive spot as far as the northern flank of the Soviet Union's European territory was concerned.

An attempt was also made to improve Soviet relations with the Scandinavian countries themselves. At the beginning of July 1937, the Swedish Foreign Minister, Sandler, visited Moscow. Sandler held that Article 16 of the Covenant should be modified in order to relieve the smaller nations of the burden of sanctions and to enable them to maintain their neutrality within the framework of the League. The Scandinavian bloc, to which Finland was regarded as adhering, would thus 'contract out' of any future European conflict, and Sandler was opposed to any further pacts of mutual assistance. Litvinov expressed himself very bitterly on this subject to the American Ambassador. Sweden was playing Germany's game. He objected in particular to Sandler's use of the obviously fallacious argument that the United States would be willing to join the League if the Covenant were revised.[1] Litvinov's speech on the occasion of a reception to Sandler on 9 July, was largely devoted to emphasizing that the task of the moment was to 'consolidate the potential of peace', and that to 'weaken the League Covenant even theoretically' would have the contrary effect.[2] The Tass communiqué of 11 July dealing with these talks, declared that both countries were faithful to collective security based on the Covenant and the Kellogg Pact—the mention of the latter being no doubt a concession to the Swedish viewpoint.

In so far as the Baltic was the point of intersection of the

[1] Davies, op. cit., pp. 117–18, 140–1, 346–7.
[2] Litvinov, *Against Aggression*, pp. 86–7.

interests of three Great Powers, the U.S.S.R., Germany, and the commercially preponderant Great Britain, the most important aspect of Soviet policy in this zone appeared in 1936–7 to be the negotiations for the limitation of naval armaments— negotiations in which the Scandinavian States, Finland, and Poland were also involved.[1]

The London Treaty of 25 March 1936 had been signed by Great Britain, the United States, and France. It had provided for the exchange of information on naval armaments, for the advance notification of new construction, for agreed maximum limits of tonnage and gun-calibre for capital ships, aircraft carriers, cruisers, and submarines and for 'a holiday' in the construction of heavy cruisers until the expiry of the treaty in December 1942. The utility of the agreement to its signatories was diminished by the absence from their number of so many naval Powers. The Italian Government had proved unwilling to sign a treaty with the Powers who were imposing sanctions against it, and Japan had withdrawn from the conference as a protest against the refusal to grant her 'parity'. France had refused to allow Germany to be invited, and it was anyhow considered unlikely that Germany would have attended, had the U.S.S.R. also been invited, as would then have been inevitable. But, even from the European point of view, Japan's absence was the decisive factor, since a large new building programme by Japan would have forced Great Britain to revise her programme and that would in turn have entitled Germany to a proportionate increase under the Anglo-German naval treaty of 1935. The solution adopted was for Great Britain to set about negotiating treaties separately with Germany and the U.S.S.R. and for Great Britain and France to delay their ratification of the original instrument pending the conclusion of these negotiations.[2]

The talks between Great Britain and Germany were the first to begin, but Germany refused to accept quantitative limitations until the U.S.S.R. had given a similar undertaking. Anglo-Soviet talks were initiated in the middle of May, and, as has already been noted, it was announced at the end of July 1936 that agreement in principle had been reached. This agreement involved the acceptance by Great Britain of the Soviet Union's two major conditions for adhering to the London Treaty—that any form of limitation accepted by the U.S.S.R. must also be binding on Germany and that in the event of Japan actually exceeding the treaty limits, the U.S.S.R. should be permitted

[1] *Survey for 1936*, pp. 49 ff.; *Documents for 1936*, pp. 598–664.
[2] The treaty itself also contained an 'escape clause' with regard to the proposed 'holiday' in the building of heavy cruisers.

to increase its own construction in the Far East. There was also a provisional agreement that the U.S.S.R. might build two 16-inch-gun battleships.[1]

Objections raised by Germany to certain provisions in the Anglo-Soviet draft led to lengthy negotiations, and it was only on 17 July 1937 that the final agreements were signed.[2]

The Anglo-Soviet agreement provided that the limitations and restrictions of the London Treaty, which were accepted, in so far as the Russian Black Sea and Baltic fleets were concerned, should not apply to the Russian Far Eastern Fleet, unless an agreement on the subject were reached between the Soviet Union and Japan, but the Soviet Union undertook not to exceed these limitations and restrictions unless Japan took the initiative. Should Japanese action force the Soviet Union to undertake such construction, Great Britain would be informed and would be empowered to communicate the information in confidence to Germany, and to the original signatories of the London Treaty. The Soviet Union was freed from any obligation to furnish information about naval construction in the Far East not in excess of treaty limits, pending the acceptance of a similar obligation by Japan. The reservation about the Far East did not entitle the Soviet Union to transfer to other waters vessels constructed there which might exceed the treaty limits.

In view of the fact that the Soviet Union had already embarked upon the construction of seven 8,000-ton cruisers mounting 7.1-in.-guns (instead of the 6.1-in.-guns allowed by the London Treaty), all three Powers were allowed to exceed the treaty limit in this respect. It was also agreed that Germany might build five 'A' type cruisers (10,000 tons with 8 in.-guns) instead of the three agreed to in 1935. Germany, however, undertook not to avail herself of this permission unless 'special circumstances' arose, and then only after informing Great Britain who would pass on the information to the U.S.S.R. and to the London Treaty Powers.[3]

The prominence which Litvinov gave to the Spanish question in his speech of 28 November 1936 was symptomatic of its great importance in the foreign outlook of the Soviet Union.

[1] 16-in. became the general upper limit after the Japanese notified their refusal to accept the 14-in. limit in March 1937.

[2] No agreements could be reached with the minor naval Powers with whom talks were also held.

[3] It does not appear that the U.S.S.R. insisted on its earlier claim to build up to ten cruisers if the German limit was raised to five. Report by Davies on 26 March 1937 of his conversation with Litvinov; Davies, op. cit., p. 81. The agreements were ratified on 4 November 1937, Cmd. 5518. 9.551 The London Treaty had come into force on 29 July.

'In the case of Spain, we have the first sally of Fascism beyond its borders. Here is an attempt at a forcible implantation in Spain from without of a Fascist system. . . . If this attempt were to succeed, there would be no guarantee against its repetition on a wider scale in relation to other states.'

By interpreting 'the word "non-intervention" in the sense that it itself was not to intervene in the intervention in Spanish events', the London Committee had 'sanctioned in advance all future infringements of obligations on the part of the Fascist States'. This explained the Soviet Union's declaration that it did not consider itself morally bound by the non-intervention agreement to a greater extent than the other participants.[1]

On the day before Litvinov's speech, 27 November, the Spanish Government had appealed to the League under Article 11 of the Covenant, and an extraordinary session of the Council was fixed for 10 December. The majority of the Powers concerned exerted themselves to prevent the proceedings from assuming too great an importance, and the U.S.S.R. fell in with these plans to the extent of not sending Litvinov as its representative.

The Soviet representative, Potemkin, speaking on 11 December, once more defined the Soviet attitude to non-intervention and contrasted the Soviet Union's faithful fulfilment of its undertakings with the open intervention by other Governments on the side of the rebels, emphasizing the need for effective supervision over the execution of the non-intervention agreement, and promising to co-operate in efforts to bring hostilities to a close.[2] The Council's resolution expressed in general terms the duty of States to respect each other's integrity and independence, and commended the efforts of the London Committee.

Meanwhile the London Committee itself, having on 2 December 1936 submitted its control scheme to the contending parties decided on the 4th to examine the question of preventing the dispatch of foreign 'volunteers' to Spain.[3] Since it was clear that the Fascist Powers were in a better position to send assistance of this kind, the Soviet Union supported the attitude of France and Great Britain on this matter.

On 4 December, Great Britain and France asked the Soviet,

[1] Litvinov, *Against Aggression*, pp. 64–70.

[2] *L.N.O.J.*, January 1937, pp. 16–17. A Tass communiqué of the same date denied that there were any Soviet troops in Spain.

[3] The 'International Brigade' had played an important part in stemming the 'nationalist' advance on Madrid in November. At the end of November and during December, thousands of Germans arrived to join Franco and between December and February still larger numbers of Italians arrived.

German, Italian, and Portuguese Governments to join with them in pressing on with the organization of a fully effective control and to attempt to bring the conflict to an end by means of mediation. The Soviet Government was the only one to welcome the latter proposal, which the attitude of both sides showed to be hopeless. The former proposal met on the part of Germany, Italy, and Portugal, with a series of objections, clearly designed to delay matters until the side which they supported had secured the upper hand. Not until 21 February did a ban on the enlistment and dispatch of 'volunteers' become part of the obligations of the adherents of the non-intervention agreement.

The operation of a scheme for the control of supplies was still further delayed. Here, one obstacle was the attitude of the Soviet Government to the question of the control of maritime traffic. It at first demanded that control should be by a single international fleet. When this was turned down in favour of separate control-zones, it demanded that one such zone should be assigned to the Red Fleet, and further delay was caused before this claim was withdrawn. The final scheme was adopted on 8 March 1937 and came into effect on 30 April. Meanwhile, as has been seen, direct Soviet assistance to Spain had become less intensive.

The Soviet Government had further anxieties over the general tendencies of British policy at this time, since the British Government's main concern was not so much Spain itself, as the removal of obstacles to a general agreement among the Western Powers. An outcome of this concern was the Anglo-Italian declaration signed at Rome on 2 January 1937. The two Powers proclaimed their intention of respecting each other's Mediterranean interests and disclaimed any desire to modify the *status quo* regarding the national sovereignty of territory in the Mediterranean area. As interpreted by Mussolini in an interview published in the *Voelkischer Beobachter* on 17 January, this agreement and the preceding exchange of notes entitled Italy to see that Franco's Government was enabled to exert its authority over the whole of Spain and prevent a rival Spanish or Catalan Government from setting itself up in Valencia or Barcelona.[1] In fact, from the beginning of 1937, it was Italy which took upon itself more and more of the burden of supporting Franco, while Germany remained, comparatively speaking, in the background.

Italian denunciations of Communism were now coupled with an increased emphasis on the identity of Italian and German policies. For these reasons a *rapprochement* between Great Britain

[1] *Survey for 1936*, pp. 652 ff.; *Documents for 1937*, pp. 87–9, 265.

and Italy, however innocent the motives of the former, could not but appear of sinister import in Soviet eyes.[1]

The gloomy international outlook was referred to by Kalinin in a speech on 15 January 1937, when he described the Soviet Union as surrounded by foes, and declared that the class war had now taken on an international character, as was proved by events in Spain and by the revelations of the Russian State trials.[2]

As far as Anglo-Italian relations were concerned, Soviet anxieties were in fact premature; for the improvement was a very temporary one, and the situation remained tense until the summer. On the other hand the negotiations for a new Western pact were still not regarded by the British Government as wholly at an end. They received a new impetus when Hitler, speaking on 30 January 1937, denied that Germany's policy was one of isolation and, while indulging in new denunciations of Bolshevism, made friendly references to Great Britain and France.[3] He also offered to meet Belgium's wish to become only a guaranteed and not a guarantor Power by offering to conclude with Belgium (and with Holland) a pact of non-aggression. On 2 March, Mr. Eden declared in the House of Commons that since the Spanish conflict, which had been one of the chief obstacles to progress in the Western pact negotiations, was now 'less likely to spread beyond the borders of Spain', the British Government felt the time was ripe for another effort. On 12 March, replies were at last received in London from Germany and Italy to the British memorandum of 19 November 1936.

The German and Italian notes had been drawn up in consultation, and were identical in substance. Although they were not published, their contents were made known through summaries in the German and Italian press:

'In brief the Italo-German suggestions seem to have been that the independence and integrity of Belgium should be guaranteed by the four European Great Powers, on condition that she should undertake to remain neutral in the event of any conflict; that France and Germany should conclude an agreement of non-aggression under the guarantee of Great Britain and Italy; that the two guarantor Powers should receive reciprocal guarantees; that in the event of a breach of the Franco-German non-aggression agreement the responsibility for deciding which party was the aggressor should rest upon the guarantor Powers and not upon the Council of the League; and that these provisions should be applicable also to the

[1] On 25 and 27 December the Soviet press carried articles on attempts to squeeze the Soviet Union out of a European settlement.
[2] *Journal des Nations*, 17–18 January 1937.
[3] *Hitler's Speeches*, pp. 1334–7.

contingency of a Franco-German dispute arising out of events in Eastern Europe.'[1]

It was clear that Germany would thus secure her objective —a free hand in eastern Europe—and that France was being asked to submit the operation of her eastern European alliances to the veto of two Powers, one of which was a partner in the Rome-Berlin 'Axis'. Even so, some members at least of the British Government seem to have been prepared to continue discussions on this basis, rather than admit total defeat— possibly with the hope that some kind of settlement for eastern Europe might be arrived at later.[2]

An Anglo-French declaration of 24 April, assenting to the new status requested by Belgium, was followed by discussions between Great Britain and France, in which the former strove to persuade the latter of the advantages of keeping the Western pact negotiations in being. On 9 June, a French note on the subject was sent to London.

'Though it was rumoured that it marked a certain advance in the direction of meeting German and Italian wishes (for instance, by hinting at the possibility that somebody other than the League Council—perhaps the Permanent Court of International Justice— might be entrusted with the task of deciding whether and by whom an act of aggression had been committed), the British Government apparently did not feel that it offered a suitable basis for further discussion with Germany and Italy.'[3]

In the course of July the negotiations lapsed by tacit consent.[4] The Soviet point of view on all these proceedings was ex-

---

[1] *Survey for 1937*, I, p. 355.

[2] The conversation between Munters and Chamberlain on this subject has already been referred to. On the other hand, when writing to Sumner Welles on 28 June 1937, Davies said: 'Last winter Eden rejected the German overtures with reference to economic aid through colonies or otherwise unless political security were assured in Eastern as well as Western Europe.' Davies, op. cit., p. 111. On 3 March 1937 Halifax quoted in the Lords a parliamentary answer given on 8 February by Viscount Cranborne in which the latter had denied that there was any commitment 'whereby under the Franco-Russian Pact Great Britain could be involved in a European war', and made it clear that while Great Britain could not subscribe to the thesis: 'I will only fight when I am myself a victim of attack', it was not prepared to say 'I will fight in every case on behalf of peace which is one and indivisible'.

[3] *Survey for 1937*, I, pp. 362–3.

[4] Some British circles were sympathetic to the German view that the Franco-Soviet pact was a justification for Germany refusing to undertake new engagements. See the address by Lord Lothian given at Chatham House on 29 June 1937, in which he praised many aspects of the Nazi régime, and also the subsequent discussion; *International Affairs*, 1937, pp. 870 ff.

pounded by Litvinov to Davies on 4 February 1937.[1] He declared his failure

'to understand why England and France were "continually bothering" with Hitler in Germany; that he could not understand why they should project notes and questionnaires and constantly stir up the German situation and thereby accentuate Hitler's importance and "feed his vanity" into his self-conception that he (Hitler) is the dominating figure in Europe, that he thought they ought to let him "stew in his own juice"; that Hitler's policy had not changed from that which he had announced in his book *Mein Kampf*; that he was dominated by a lust for conquest and for the domination of Europe; that he could not understand why Great Britain could not see that once Hitler dominated Europe he would swallow the British Isles also. He seemed to be very much stirred about this and apprehensive lest there should be some composition of differences between France, England and Germany.'

Litvinov returned to the subject in a conversation on the 15th, concerned with reports that Great Britain and America were contemplating economic assistance to Germany. He appeared 'very much disturbed about it and again voiced his almost bitter attitude that France and England should be engaging in discussions at all with Germany'. Davies asked Litvinov

'whether he did not see an indication in Hitler's speech of a differentiation between the Russian people and the Russian government and an opening that would permit some statement from an official spokesman of the Russian government to the effect that it would engage itself not to project propaganda in Germany provided Germany would not project its propaganda into Russia'.[2]

Davies suggested that such a statement would deprive Hitler of his chief argument against Russia. Litvinov's reply, he reported,

'was negative; that Germany was concerned solely with conquest and it was a mistake to magnify its importance by engaging in discussions of the character which France and England were projecting'.

[1] Davies, op. cit., pp. 48–50.

[2] ibid., pp. 61–2. The passage in Hitler's speech which Davies presumably had in mind ran: 'I demand from every German workman that he shall not have any relations with these international mischief makers and he shall never see me clinking glasses or rubbing shoulders with them. Moreover any further treaty connexions with the present Bolshevik Russia would be completely worthless for us. It is out of the question to think that National-Socialist Germany should ever be bound to protect Bolshevism or that we on our side, should ever agree to accept the assistance of a Bolshevik State. For I fear that the moment any nation should agree to accept such assistance it would thereby seal its own doom.'

On the following day Goering, on a visit to Warsaw, expounded Hitler's meaning for the benefit of Smigly-Rydz:

'It was quite obvious that a strong Poland with access to the sea, a Poland with whom Germany could agree her policy, was incomparably more necessary and useful to the Reich than a weak and mutilated Poland. For Germany realized that an isolated Poland would be much easier to subdue, and then the whole Russian avalanche would strike directly against the German frontier.

'Before Chancellor Hitler came to power, German policy had made many dangerous mistakes. The dangerous policy of Rapallo had been followed in relation to Russia. As the result of this policy Germany helped Russia in military matters, armed her, sent her instructors, assisted her to build up her war industry. The old Reichswehr had had many advocates of *rapprochement* with Soviet Russia, but an end was put to this by the elimination of all such elements from the German Army. It is true that General Schleicher had said that he wanted to fight Communism internally, but externally he had sought contacts with the Soviets. These were serious mistakes which must never be repeated. M. Hitler had reversed the policy, and laid down the principle against which there was no appeal, that all contacts with Communism were prohibited. He had explicitly stressed his attitude when Marshal Tukhachevski had passed through Berlin. Not only did he not receive him personally, but he had not allowed anyone from military circles to have any contact with him.

'It should not be forgotten that the new Germany had come into existence in the same way as the new Poland. Germany would never return to a pro-Russian policy. For it should always be remembered that there was one great danger coming through Russia from the East, and menacing both Germany and Poland alike. This danger existed not only in the form of a Bolshevik and Communized Russia, but of Russia generally, in any form, be it Monarchist or Liberal. In this respect the interests of Poland and Germany were entirely one. . . .

'In Berlin, he went on, they had no illusions that Stalin was not preparing to let loose world revolution. They possessed information that although the Soviets had withdrawn from revolutionary activity in South America, and, after the conclusion of the German-Japanese Pact, in the Far East, they had increased their propaganda in Poland, Roumania, the Baltic States and Austria. . . .'[1]

Public expression to Soviet anxieties was given by Maisky in a speech in London on 13 March.[2] The danger to the U.S.S.R. had increased during the past fifteen months; the anti-Communist pact was virtually a military alliance. It was no part of Soviet policy to strive for autarky. They were out for

---

[1] *Polish White Book*, pp. 36–8.
[2] G. Bilainkin, *Maisky* (Allen and Unwin, 1944), pp. 174–6.

economic independence, not for economic exclusiveness; but in the case of an emergency like war, they were already in a position to carry on for an indefinite period on the basis of a self-supporting economy. Echoing Litvinov's speech of the previous 28 November, the Ambassador declared that the Soviet Union was strong enough from the military as well as from the economic point of view, to repel any attack single-handed, but it could not single-handed prevent war from breaking out. Therefore it clung to the ideal of collective security through the League of Nations. Europe had the choice between collective security and the localization of war. The latter meant in fact retreat before the aggressors.[1]

It is possible that the Soviet Government received some re-assurances at about this time from the Western Powers, for Davies found Litvinov more optimistic at their next meeting which he reported in his dispatch of 28 March.[2]

Litvinov then expressed the view that the democratic nations ought to tell Mussolini that they would not tolerate the sending of more Italians to Spain and declared that neither Germany nor Italy were adequately prepared for war. Davies stated that he had 'heard rumours that the Soviet Union was apprehensive lest France and England might possibly make a peace in Western Europe with Germany and Italy, leaving Russia to face Germany alone.' Litvinov 'stated very positively that in his opinion that was not a fact'. Davies then suggested that the five Powers might relieve the situation by agreeing 'to preserve the territorial integrity of Europe and through trade agreements [to] provide Germany with raw materials and thereby the assurance that she could live.' Litvinov said that any body of opinion there might be in Germany which could be attracted by such a scheme could not prevail against Hitler and the domi-nant military and political forces. He then said that

'the only hope for the preservation of European peace was a prompt, firm declaration of the democracies of Europe that they were stand-ing together for peace; he named France, Russia and Czecho-slovakia. He then said that if the United States were to join in such a declaration it would mean not only European but world peace as well.'[3]

On 26 March 1937 the note of alarm was sounded again when the Soviet press published a speech made by Stalin on

---

[1] This speech created rather a stir and it was believed in some circles that it heralded more active asssitance by the Soviet Union to Spain. Davies, op. cit., pp. 90–1.

[2] ibid., pp. 79–81.

[3] The omission of Great Britain here is curious, if it was intentional.

3 March, dealing with the struggle with Trotskyism, in which Germany and Japan were several times mentioned as working with Trotsky.

Another attempt was made at this time to give a military content to the Franco-Soviet pact. The Soviet Ambassador at Paris, Potemkin, saw M. Blum on 17 February and discussed means by which Russia could help France and Czechoslovakia in the event of war. He declared that there were two possibilities. If Poland, France's ally, and Roumania, allied to both France and Czechoslovakia, agreed to the passage of Soviet troops, then full support with all arms would be forthcoming provided there was preliminary agreement. If Poland and Roumania refused passage, Russia would send troops to France by sea and give France and Czechoslovakia direct air support. Economic help would also be given. But what would France do? Asked why he did not mention a possible passage through Lithuania, the Ambassador said that only passage through states friendly to France was envisaged. If there were other possibilities it was for France and the Soviet Union to prepare them. Gamelin was asked to prepare a reply to the Soviet inquiry and this was handed by him to Daladier, the War Minister, on 10 April. Gamelin declared that France could not supply Russia with armaments since she would require all she had for herself. There was no hope to be derived from the conversations with Poland and Roumania of a rapid solution to the question of permitting the passage of troops through their territories. Only motorized troops could be used in any case, since both countries would need all their railway facilities for their own troops. According to Gamelin, no further discussions of a military kind took place.[1]

From March onwards, discussions in the Non-Intervention Committee largely turned on the withdrawal of 'volunteers' from Spain. After the rout of the Italians at Guadalajara, the Italian attitude on the question stiffened. This led Maisky on the 24th to make, against the Italian Government, detailed charges of 'ever-increasing military intervention in the affairs of Spain'. It was only after insistence by France and Britain that the Russians were persuaded to withdraw their demand that a commission of investigation be sent to Spain. In May, the British Government suggested that an attempt should be made to arrange an armistice under cover of which it would be possible to withdraw the foreign elements. The Soviet Union, while accepting the idea in principle, stipulated that the 'nationalists' should take the initiative and that Franco's

[1] Gamelin, *Servir*, vol. 2, pp. 285-7.

Moorish levies should be among the troops withdrawn. The plan made no progress.

On 18 May Litvinov made an effort to re-animate the embers of Franco-Soviet cordiality by holding conversations in Paris with Blum and Delbos.[1] The communiqué on these conversations declared that the participants

'were glad to be able to take note of the friendly relations existing between the two countries, as also of their common aim to maintain the organization of indivisible peace by means of collective security. They reaffirmed their fidelity to the pact uniting the two nations, and their determination to pursue within the framework of the League, and in accordance with its principles, a loyal policy of international collaboration.'[2]

A test of the realities behind this declaration was afforded at the meeting of the League Council on 24 May, since Spain had again made an appeal to Geneva. The U.S.S.R. was on this occasion represented by Litvinov himself, who again stressed the Soviet view that but for foreign assistance to the rebels the war in Spain would long ago have been over.

'Thus one of the members of the League has been subjected to foreign invasion and the danger of violation of its territorial integrity and political independence.

'But it is not only a question of Spain. The events in Spain have created one of the greatest dangers to European and world peace. This menace arises in consequence of an attempt at armed intervention in the internal affairs of a European state, an attempt to thrust upon the people of the state an internal régime and, mainly, a foreign policy orientation alien to it. . . . If this attempt succeeded and went unpunished there would be no guarantee that it would not be repeated in other countries.'

Litvinov declared that the Soviet Union had little concern with the Spanish State as such. At the beginning of the outbreak the Soviet Union had had no active diplomatic or consular relations with Spain, and there had not been a single Soviet subject on its territory. All they wanted was that Spain should have a freely elected government, and they were therefore prepared to support any action designed to remove foreign combatants from Spain. The Spanish Government were fully justified in appealing to the League, in spite of the attitude of some people who regarded 'any appeal to the League in any serious international affair' as an 'attempt upon the existence of the League'.[3]

---

[1] Delbos, Foreign Minister in the Blum Government, retained his post in the Chautemps Government formed on 23 June 1937.
[2] *Le Temps*, 19 May 1937.   [3] *L.N.O.J.*, May-June 1937, pp. 321-3.

Eden and Delbos, however, did their best to maintain that the situation had actually improved since the Council had considered it in December; and the Council was once again content to note and approve the actions of the London Committee.

The next crisis arose over the maritime aspect of intervention. As early as mid-December 1936, the Soviet press had expressed great indignation over the sinking of the Soviet ship *Komsomol*. It had then appeared to be the intention of the Soviet Government to take reprisals if similar incidents occurred in future. They were said to have abandoned this intention at the instance of the French Government, who pointed out the dangers inherent in a policy of individual reprisals. Throughout the first five months of 1937, Soviet shipping had suffered along with that of other nations from Franco's maritime activities. According to a Soviet statement to the London Committee on 5 May, eighty-four Soviet ships were interfered with in the period 30 October 1936–10 April 1937, only one of which was actually bound for a Spanish port. 'The Soviet authorities do not appear to have taken steps to prevent vessels flying the Soviet flag from suffering molestation and little or no publicity was given to incidents involving Russian ships.'[1] This is a rather curious fact, considering the vehemence with which British sympathizers with the Spanish Government (and with the Soviet Union) attacked the British Government for its failure to ensure respect for the British flag. It must be taken as one more proof of the Soviet Union's determination not to attract attention to its own assistance to the Spanish Government, and to avoid any direct clash with the 'Axis' Powers.

It was the Spanish Government which itself precipitated matters. On 29 May the German battleship *Deutschland* was bombed from the air (in disputed circumstances) and, two days later, the Germans retaliated by shelling the town of Almeria from the sea. The London Committee were simultaneously notified that both Germany and Italy were withdrawing from the naval patrol.

Every effort was made by Britain and France to bring the two Powers back into the naval control scheme, for fear the whole non-intervention system might break down. But an agreement which had been reached was abandoned after allegations that the German cruiser *Leipzig* had been attacked by a submarine. The German and Italian withdrawal from the naval patrol became definite on 23 June.

Thus by the midsummer of 1937, the international situation had undergone a further deterioration. The Soviet Union's

1 *Survey for 1937*, II, p. 306.

prestige declined further as a result of the most sensational of all the events of the great 'purge', the condemnation and execution, early in June, of Tukhachevsky and seven other high military personalities on charges of conspiring with a foreign Power and the suicide of Gamarnik, the head of the Army Political Administration.

Davies, returning to Moscow from leave at the end of the month, found much less disturbance than might have been expected, and by 4 July was writing that 'it looks as though the loyalty of the army to the Stalin government has not been weakened'. The pity of it all though, he added, is that Stalin

'has destroyed the confidence of western Europe in the strength of his army and the strength of his government; that has also weakened the confidence of both England and France in the strength of the Russian army and has weakened the democratic bloc in western Europe, and that is serious, for the only real hope for peace is a London-Paris-Moscow axis'.[1]

This was the moment for yet another of those incidents which seemed now and then to crop up in defiance of those who believed in the inevitability of a Russo-German clash. In April it was made known that Suritz, the Soviet Ambassador in Berlin, was to be transferred to Paris.[2] Suritz was replaced in Berlin by Yurenev, Ambassador at Tokyo since 1933. The latter was received by Hitler himself on 21 July. The speeches exchanged were in the circumstances remarkably friendly. Hitler said:

'Your declaration that you desire to direct your efforts towards the creation and maintenance of normal relations between Germany and the U.S.S.R., I have heard with satisfaction. I share your view that such relations between the German Reich and the Soviet Union will correspond with the necessity, greater to-day than ever it was, for non-intervention in the affairs of other States, and will thus correspond also with the interests of both countries and contribute to the cause of general peace.'[3]

Otherwise the tension over Spain showed no signs of slackening. On 2 July the German and Italian Governments, acting jointly as was now normal, proposed that both parties in Spain be granted belligerent rights, a measure which would clearly be of advantage to the 'nationalists'. The Soviet representative on

[1] Davies, op. cit., pp. 116, 129–38.
[2] Suritz is said to have worked hard in Paris to strengthen the ties between the U.S.S.R. and France and to have warned French statesmen repeatedly not to force the U.S.S.R. to choose between France's security and its own; Cot, op. cit., p. 52.
[3] *Hitler's Speeches*, p. 1335.

the Non-Intervention Committee immediately voiced strong disapproval and there was evidence that the French attitude would also stiffen. The British Government was responsible for a compromise plan, adopted by the Committee on the 16th, as a basis for discussion. This linked together three questions: the recognition of belligerency, the withdrawal of volunteers, and a plan for control at the ports to replace the naval control scheme. On 29 July Chamberlain, who had become Prime Minister on 28 May, is said to have tried to overcome Soviet opposition to this plan, in a personal interview with Maisky, but Maisky's speech at the Committee on the following day showed no change in the Soviet attitude.[1] It was evident that the Soviet Government would not consider the granting of belligerent rights until all 'volunteers' including the Moors had left Spain.

The deadlock was rendered more dangerous by events at sea in August. These amounted to a series of indiscriminate attacks upon merchant shipping in the Mediterranean, made by surface warships, aircraft, and submarines without regard to the nationality of the vessel attacked, the nature of its cargo or its destination. The aircraft were almost certainly those of the Spanish 'nationalists', but the question of the identity of the submarines was never officially cleared up. The Spanish Government, however, declared in an appeal to the League on 21 August and in a note to the European Powers on the 22nd, that the attacks on their ships were the work of Italian destroyers and submarines. The Russian Government gave open support to the Spanish claims, while the 'nationalists' retorted that Russian submarines were to blame, without indicating why Russian submarines should attack Russian and Republican Spanish merchantmen. Matters were rendered more difficult for the other Powers, by reason of the fact that the Italian press was now boasting openly of Italy's intervention in the war.

A speech by Mussolini on 20 August included the following passage:

'Another reality of which account must be taken is that which is commonly known as the Rome-Berlin axis. One does not reach Rome by ignoring or going against Berlin, and one does not reach Berlin by ignoring or going against Rome. You understand me when I say that there is an active solidarity between the two régimes. Let it be said in the most categorical manner that we will not tolerate in the Mediterranean Bolshevism or anything of a similar nature. As soon as these disturbances created by a people absolutely foreign to the Mediterranean have been crushed, I shall be pleased to issue an appeal for peace to all those countries which

[1] Bilainkin, op. cit., p. 182.

are bathed by that sea where three continents have brought together three civilizations.'[1]

In view of past experience the British and French Governments decided that the only hope of dealing with this question of 'piracy' in the Mediterranean was to take it out of the hands of the Non-Intervention Committee. They therefore issued invitations for a conference to be held at Nyon on 10 September, to all the Mediterranean and Black Sea States except Spain, and to Germany. A note from the Soviet Government to the Italian Government on 6 September, alleging the latter's responsibility for the recent sinking of two Russian ships, and demanding compensation and the punishment of those responsible, was probably intended to ensure that Italy did not attend the conference.[2] On 9 September the Governments of Germany, Italy, and Albania notified their refusal to take part in the conference.[3]

[1] *Documents for 1937*, pp. 288–9. On 27 August, the Italian press published congratulatory telegrams exchanged between Mussolini and Franco, a list of Italian casualties in recent fighting, and the names of 12 Italian generals then serving with Franco.

[2] The Soviet Government appears to have feared that such a conference would increase the isolation into which she had been put by her recent stand on the question of belligerent rights, and that Italy and Germany would use the occasion for another plea in favour of this step, from which Franco stood to gain.

[3] All the other Governments accepted the invitation, although the Soviet Union's note of acceptance criticized the invitation to Germany which was not a Mediterranean or Black Sea Power, and the omission of the Spanish Government from the list.

Chapter Six

SOVIET DIPLOMACY IN EUROPE: FROM THE NYON CONFERENCE TO THE ANSCHLUSS

THE atmosphere in which the Nyon Conference assembled on 10 September 1937 was not propitious from the point of view of the Soviet Union's relations with the Western Powers. As recently as 1 August, *Izvestia* had blamed Great Britain for the non-intervention deadlock, and asserted that Great Britain was prepared to let Franco be victorious in the belief that his subsequent need for financial assistance would force him into the British camp. Soviet suspicions of British motives were not connected solely with Spain; for the British attempts to arrive at a direct understanding with Italy were now paralleled by equally determined efforts to reach a general agreement with Germany. These may be said to have begun with the arrival in Berlin of a new British Ambassador, Sir Nevile Henderson, who presented his credentials to Hitler on 11 May 1937.[1]

It was in July 1937 that Anglo-Italian relations began to show signs of rapid improvement. A personal exchange of letters between Chamberlain and Mussolini was followed, on 6 August, by an intimation that discussions for a settlement of outstanding differences would begin through diplomatic channels in September. From the Soviet point of view this was the more disconcerting in that the Italian Government showed no sign of abating its hostile attitude towards the Soviet Union or of departing from its now well-marked German orientation.

On 7 September an Italian delegation attended the annual Nazi rally at Nuremberg and took part in an anti-Communist demonstration.[2] In his speech at Nuremberg on the 13th,

---

[1] For these efforts see the account in Sir Nevile Henderson, *Failure of a Mission* (Hodder and Stoughton, 1940).

[2] The rally was for the first time attended by the British Ambassador (as well as by his French and American colleagues). Henderson had another chance to talk to Goering when he went to stay at the latter's shooting-lodge in the first week in October. In spite of the increasing accent upon the question of colonies which had been notable throughout the year in German propaganda, Goering's idea of the basis for an Anglo-German agreement included the recognition of the 'supreme position of Great Britain overseas'. Great Britain, on the other hand, 'would recognize the predominant continental position of Germany in Europe, and undertake to do nothing to hinder her legitimate expansion. It was the theory of the free hand for Germany in Central and Eastern Europe'. Nevile Henderson,

98

Hitler explained German and Italian policy in Spain as motivated by their anxiety

'that the balance of power [should] not be altered by an increase in the power of Bolshevism. . . . Just as, on the one hand, people in England and France tend to be anxious for fear lest Spain should be occupied by Italy or Germany, so, on the other, we are disturbed by the possibility that Spain might be conquered by Soviet Russia. This conquest need not be carried out in the form of an occupation by Soviet troops, but it will nevertheless be an accomplished fact the moment a Bolshevized Spain becomes a section, that is to say, an integral part of the Bolshevist Moscow Centre.'

With an eye no doubt to the capitalists of the Western Powers, Hitler also pointed out that a Communist triumph in Spain would close that country to foreign trade; there were thus sound economic as well as political reasons for Germany's policy.[1]

Meanwhile the opening meeting of the Nyon Conference had provided Litvinov with an opportunity to repeat the Soviet charges against Italy, although without mentioning that Power by name.[2] In the absence of Germany and Italy, the proceedings were very rapid. By the evening of 11 September, a draft agreement for countermeasures against Mediterranean 'piracy' was reached. The major share of responsibility under its provisions fell upon the British and French fleets, with the riparian

---

op. cit., pp. 69–79 and 91–2. In the circumstances, there is nothing surprising about Soviet suspicions of all negotiations with Germany.

[1] Litvinov took occasion to deal with this argument when he addressed the League Assembly on 21 September (*L.N.O.J. Spec. Suppl.*, 169, p. 79). 'Sometimes the founders of this (anti-Communist) ideology themselves begin to doubt its cogency and acceptability as a leading international idea. . . . Then we learn . . . that anti-Communism has also a geological meaning and denotes a craving for tin, zinc, mercury, copper, and other minerals. When even this explanation proves inadequate, anti-Communism is interpreted as a longing for profitable trade. We are told this trade might be lost if Spain is tarred with the Communist brush. . . . But we know the example of at least one Communist State, rich in minerals and other raw material, which has not refused to export these minerals and raw material to other countries, to trade with them on a very wide scale whatever the régime ruling in these countries, including even the Fascist and National Socialist régimes.' Anyhow there had been and was no Communist order in Spain, he concluded. The German Government cannot in fact have intended this particular point of Hitler's to be taken very seriously. On the contrary, in his speech in Berlin on 28 September, Mussolini referred to their endeavours to attain economic autarky, as an additional resemblance and bond between his country and Nazi Germany. *Survey for 1937*, I, p. 335.

[2] The diplomacy of the Spanish conflict from September to December 1937 can be followed, ibid., pp. 305–76. On 12 September, Stalin and Molotov took the salute at a mass demonstration in Moscow directed primarily against Italian 'piracy'.

Powers of the Eastern Mediterranean taking their share within their own territorial waters. Litvinov was one of the delegates who felt it necessary to refer the agreement to their Governments before signing and this held up its signature until the 14th. In his closing speech, Litvinov regretted that, in spite of Soviet opposition, Spanish Government vessels had been excluded from the protection provided by the scheme, on the ground that their inclusion might be held to signify intervention in the conflict. His conclusion was, however, optimistic:

'At a time when aggression, international lawlessness, adventurist impudence have been accustomed to success, any action combating these phenomena which takes the form not merely of discussion, protests and declarations but of practical steps must be particularly welcomed, while to-day we have before us an international agreement with very material backing.'[1]

In point of fact the Nyon agreement does seem to have put an immediate end to the activities of the submarines, although attacks on shipping by aircraft continued on a reduced scale.[2]

The meeting of the League Council on 10 September, followed by that of the Assembly, brought the Spanish question as a whole once more onto the international agenda. Litvinov's speech to the Assembly on the 21st, coupled the war in Spain with that which had opened two-and-a-half months previously in China. The international repercussions of the latter were already tending to overshadow the Spanish issue, and Soviet diplomacy was more than ever obliged to keep both fronts in mind.[3] Nor could Litvinov overlook the fact that the excuse for intervening in Spain might serve Germany equally well elsewhere.

'We often hear it said that all democratic parliamentary régimes are on the eve of Bolshevization . . . countries which by general opinion are earmarked for the next aggression are beforehand declared to be Bolshevized or fallen under Bolshevist influence for the purpose of subsequent justification of the intended aggression.'

On Spain itself, Litvinov did little more than restate the familiar Soviet case; but Hitler's speech of 13 September had left the way open for a retort:

[1] Coates, *A History of Anglo-Soviet Relations*, pp. 565–6.
[2] Negotiations for bringing Italy into the scheme, to which the Russians seem to have raised no objection, were initiated by the French, and Italian participation became effective on 30 November.
[3] This may explain the falling off in Soviet supplies to Spain which was noticeable in the autumn of 1937; *Survey for 1937*, II, p. 367.

'A few days ago the campaign to justify the aggression in Spain was capped with a new absurdity to the effect that the Soviet Union is intent on the conquest of Spain or, at least, is out to secure political influence over Spain and thereby disturb the equilibrium in the Mediterranean. The truth was spoken here a few days ago by the Spanish Premier, Señor Negrin, who said that, throughout the Spanish conflict, the Soviet Union has requested nothing from Spain, has not tried to get anything and is making no attempt. The Soviet government has neither mineralogical, economic, nor strategic interests in Spain, nor even interests in the so-called equilibrium.'[1]

The resolution presented to the Assembly by its political committee came much nearer to the Soviet viewpoint than any previous League pronouncement on this question had done. It included the recognition that there were on Spanish soil 'veritable foreign army corps' which represented 'foreign intervention in Spanish affairs'. Having appealed to the Powers to make 'a new and earnest effort' to secure their withdrawal, it declared that in the event of failure, the League Members concerned would 'consider ending the policy of non-intervention'. The resolution did not obtain the requisite unanimity because Portugal and Albania voted against; the thirty-two States voting for it included, in addition to the Soviet Union, Great Britain, and France, all but four of the other members of the Non-Intervention Committee represented at the Assembly.

During the Franco-Italian conversations on 22 September, Delbos had been assured that Italy would not take control of the Balearic Islands, would not leave her troops in Spain for an indefinite period, and would not send further reinforcements. But hopes that the deadlock in the Non-Intervention Committee might be solved by this new approach were not enhanced by the belligerent demonstrations of Italo-German solidarity which marked Mussolini's visit to Berlin on 25–29 September, since both the Italian and the German press referred to the Anglo-French initiative as designed to separate Italy from Germany in relation to Mediterranean affairs.

'Not only', said Mussolini on 28 September, 'have Nazism and Fascism everywhere the same enemies, who serve the same master —the Third International—but we have many conceptions of living and historical order in common. . . . This community of ideas in Germany and Italy is found at present in the fight against Bolshevism. Fascism has fought against it with words and with arms, because, if words have no effect and circumstances require it, arms must speak. This is what we have done in Spain, where thousands of Italian and Fascist volunteers have fallen for the salvation of

[1] *L.N.O.J. Spec. Suppl.*, 169, p. 79.

European civilization, which can even now have a rebirth if it turns away from the false and lying gods of Geneva and Moscow.'[1]

On 10 October the Italian Government formally declined the Franco-British invitation to direct talks on Spain, and took the opportunity to declare categorically that it would not participate in any negotiations to which Germany was not also invited and in which she did not take part. Nevertheless, in spite of alarming rumours in the first half of October, it appeared that Italian assistance to Franco was if anything diminishing, and the French Government was persuaded not to proceed with its intention of opening the Spanish frontier to the passage of arms.

The question of foreign volunteers came before the London Non-Intervention Committee when it renewed its suspended activities on 16 October 1937. Maisky had first held fast to the old Soviet refusal to consider the granting of belligerent rights to the parties in Spain until all foreign combatants had left the country, and continued to denounce the violations of the non-intervention agreement:

'Non-intervention was from the beginning violated by certain Powers, but lately, especially during the last six or seven months, it has become a complete farce. Violations of non-intervention have finally reached such dimensions and have acquired such a flagrant nature that they have become an international scandal of the first magnitude.'[2]

Early in October Maisky intimated that the Soviet Union would refuse to make further contributions to the expenses of the Non-Intervention Committee as a proof of its conviction that the system should now be abandoned and the Spanish Government's liberty of action restored.[3] Germany and Italy, however, proved more conciliatory and prepared to work on the basis of the British plan of 14 July. On 20 October they accepted the proposal that international commissions should be sent to the two sides in Spain so as to enable the Committee to decide 'in what manner and in what proportions' the withdrawal of foreign volunteers should take place. Soviet support was not forthcoming at the time, but on 26 October Maisky made the first concession by suggesting that the Soviet Union might be ready to consider the granting of belligerent rights when the bulk of the foreigners had been withdrawn. Instead of voting in the negative on the suggested procedure, the Soviet Union

---

[1] *Survey for 1937*, I, pp. 334-5. Mussolini's visit to Berlin was followed on 22-24 October by a visit of Ribbentrop's to Rome, during which the Japanese Ambassador to Berlin also put in an appearance.

[2] Coates, op. cit., p. 566.

[3] This intimation was formally confirmed on 28 October.

abstained, and Italy and Germany ultimately agreed to proceed without Soviet participation, subject to the reservation that some compensatory provision should be made in the event of the Soviet Union persisting in its refusal to grant belligerent rights.

In an interview with Davies on 30 October Litvinov gave his version of Soviet policy in this matter:[1]

'He outlined at considerable length the attitude of the Soviet Union in the Non-Intervention Committee and stated that Ambassador Maisky in London had taken the position that the Soviet Union could not assume any responsibility in connection with the British-French plan, but that nevertheless because it did not wish to embarrass the possibility of results in the projection of peace, therefore, it would not vote against the plan but would simply abstain from voting. Italy, he stated, had refused to accept that attitude. . . . Both France and England had urgently pressed upon his government that it should co-operate in this situation, as to do otherwise would place the Soviet Union before the world as a nation that was blocking the possibilities of peace, and that such action would necessarily "isolate the Soviet Union". His reply to them, he said, was that it would be better to be isolated and to be right than to be wrong in good company and to be foolish as well. He then went on to add that the Soviet Union was definitely prepared to be "isolated" and was quite prepared for this contingency. This confirms a statement which was made to me last July, and which I reported to the Department at the time, which was made by a high official of the government, indicating the indifference of the Soviet Union to the attitude of outside governments and even to the attitude of Great Britain and France, and that the governing powers here had definitely decided to proceed along the lines of policy which they had determined upon and quite independently, if necessary, confident of their ability to withstand enemies either on the west or the east. In reply to my inquiry as to whether the instructions to Maisky would hold and that the policy as heretofore outlined would persist, he stated positively that the policy would stand.'

Nevertheless, when, on 4 November, the full Committee met, Maisky indicated the Soviet Union's withdrawal from its original standpoint:

'If and when the Soviet Government is satisfied that the bulk of non-Spanish nationals has actually been withdrawn, that new reinforcements for the rebels have ceased to arrive and that there can therefore be detected on the part of the respective governments a sincere desire to stop interference in Spanish affairs, then it might perhaps consent to consider the question of granting belligerent

[1] Davies, *Mission to Moscow* (dispatch of 9 November 1937), pp. 161–4.

rights even before a 100 per cent evacuation has taken place. But of course the Soviet Government must reserve the right to decide whether the necessary prerequisites do exist for such a step.'[1]

On 16 November Maisky announced that the Soviet Government had now accepted in principle the plan to grant belligerent rights to the two sides, when a substantial withdrawal of foreign volunteers had taken place, 'leaving along with other Governments its interpretation of the term "substantial withdrawal"' until the question came up for consideration by the Committee. This diplomatic retreat must have been due to the Soviet Government's unwillingness to find itself isolated from Great Britain and France in a matter upon which they had reached agreement with Germany and Italy.[2] It was also significant of the diminishing importance now attached to the Spanish question by the Soviet Government.

Davies's account of this conversation with Litvinov on 30 October included the latter's statement (with reference to Ribbentrop's visit to Rome) that Italy had been brought into the Anti-Comintern Pact:

'In reply to my inquiry as to whether in his opinion this amounted to a definite offensive and defensive military alliance between the Powers, he stated that there was no necessity for a formal declaration of commitments of a military character as between these parties because of modern conditions under which wars occurred, without formalities of declarations thereof.'

In the same dispatch, the Ambassador noted that a large section of the Commissariat of Heavy Industry had recently been put under direct administration by the Army, and that there were signs of 'somewhat feverish activity' in negotiations for the procurement of war materials, lorries, &c. Official propaganda was constantly stressing the menace of war and the possibility of attack, while there were many indications that the masses of the people were extremely 'war conscious' and 'apprehensive'. In another interview (apparently on the 29th

[1] Maisky also suggested that the matter of the Soviet Union's financial contribution to the system might be reconsidered. Litvinov denied to Davies on 30 October that the Soviet Union had discontinued its contribution; Davies, op. cit., p. 163.

[2] On 11 November, Great Britain agreed to exchange 'agents' with Franco. In a meeting at the Reich Chancellery on 5 November Hitler explained that from the German point of view 'a one hundred per cent victory by Franco' was not desirable; they were more interested 'in a continuation of the war and preservation of tensions in the Mediterranean'; *Nuremberg Trial*, Part I, p. 162.

or 31st), Davies again found Litvinov extremely pessimistic about the general European situation.[1]

Italy's formal accession to the Anti-Comintern Pact took place on 6 November 1937. The text of the protocol was accompanied by a short statement from Ciano:

'As a result of the signature of the Tripartite Pact, three Great Powers—Italy, Germany and Japan—are arrayed together against the insidious attacks of Bolshevism. With them the sound and constructive forces of all civilized countries will be solid. The pact has no secret aims. It is not directed against any other country, and any other States which wish to associate themselves with this common action are free to join it. It is an instrument placed at the service of peace and civilization, which Fascism intends to defend and preserve against all dangers.'[2]

Once again there was no response to the implied invitation to other Powers, among whom Poland, Hungary, Austria, and Portugal had been mentioned as possible adherents.[3]

On 5 November a German-Polish joint declaration was published on the subject of their respective minorities in each other's territories. In a discussion on the previous day between Goering and the Polish Under-Secretary Szembek, the former had 'repeated the statement he had made to Marshal Smigly-Rydz on former occasions, that the Third Reich would not collaborate either with the Soviets or with Russia in general irrespective of her internal régime. He reiterated what he had said so many times before, that Germany needed a strong Poland.' The Polish Government took good care, however, to let it be known that it would be impervious to German blandishments as far as the Pact was concerned.[4]

Italy's own adhesion to the Anti-Comintern Pact provoked a sharp reaction from the Soviet side. On 8 November the Soviet

---

[1] Davies, op. cit., pp. 164–5. [2] *Documents for 1937*, pp. 307–8.

[3] *Survey for 1937*, I, pp. 43–5. On 1 October, Poland and Japan had raised their respective legations to the rank of embassies.

[4] Note from Beck to Polish missions abroad, 9 November 1937: 'So far no proposals to join the Italo-German-Japanese Protocol (Anti-Comintern Pact) have been received by Poland. In any case, Poland could not be a party to that Protocol in view of her special position as a neighbour of the U.S.S.R. as well as her objection in principle to the formation of any bloc. If inquiries are made on this subject please reply in the above sense.' *Polish White Book*, pp. 38–43. There were some further indications of Polish sympathies with Japan at the meeting of the League Assembly in October 1937, and Council in January-February 1938. On 2 February Poland refused to vote for the resolution on the Chinese Government's appeal, on the ground that it had been drawn up in advance by selected Powers working outside the machinery of the League. *L.N.O.J. Spec. Suppl.*, 177, pp. 25–6; *L.N.O.J.*, 1938, p. 124.

Ambassador in Rome conveyed to Ciano the Soviet view that the signing of the Pact was not only an unfriendly gesture towards the Soviet Union, but an actual breach of the Italo-Soviet non-aggression pact of 2 September 1933. This was of course a departure from the customary Soviet attitude that the Communist International was a separate institution with which the Soviet Government was not directly concerned, and deserves notice on that account. But the main effect of the further deterioration in Italo-Soviet relations was economic.[1]

Trade between the U.S.S.R. and Italy had not been of great importance to either State since the conclusion of the first five year plan, and, as has already been seen, it was further affected by the imposition of 'sanctions'.[2] In 1936 Italy supplied the U.S.S.R. with 0·4 per cent of her imports (as compared with 5·1 per cent in 1934), and took 3·1 per cent of her exports (as compared with 4·6 per cent in 1934). Italy's purchases from the Soviet Union in 1936 still totalled 164 million lire against sales to the Soviet Union worth only 9 million lire. After the lifting of sanctions in July 1936, Italy proceeded to negotiate a new series of trade treaties based on the principle that the trading account with each country should balance and should not call on Italy's part for any expenditure of foreign currency. Ciano reported on the progress of these negotiations in his speech on 13 May 1937:

'Only with Russia, of all the countries with which we were in contact, was it impossible to conclude negotiations successfully, because that country demanded a balance in her favour of many tens of millions and we were unable to see why such exceptionally favourable treatment should be accorded to the Soviet Union.'[3]

In 1937 Italy's adverse balance was 96 million lire. On 15 January 1938 it was stated in Moscow that the Government had suspended all payments due to Italian firms for goods supplied, on the ground that Soviet organizations had not been paid for goods purchased by Italy, particularly oil, for about a year.

---

[1] It has been stated that Communist propaganda in Italy was intensified in the autumn of 1937; R. G. Massock, *Italy from Within* (Macmillan, 1943), p. 73.

[2] See vol. I, Appendix A.

[3] It was probably Italy that Litvinov had in mind when, in his speech at the League Assembly on 21 September, he said: 'Communism is not a hindrance to international trade with any State, on condition, of course, that the latter observes at least elementary international proprieties, does not indulge in Billingsgate, does not play the hooligan or announce openly that the proceeds will be spent in increasing armaments to attack the country it is trading with.' *L.N.O.J. Spec. Suppl*, 169, p. 79.

What in fact took place was an almost complete commercial rupture between the two countries. Italy's exports to the Soviet Union dropped from 9 million lire in 1937, to 1 million lire in 1938, and her imports from 105 million lire to 7 million.[1]

It was in this highly charged atmosphere that the twentieth anniversary of the Revolution was celebrated in Moscow. The usual military and civil parades took place. Davies, who gave a long account of the ceremonies in a dispatch on 15 November, mentioned one significant feature:[2]

'It was noted that there was a marked difference in this celebration as contrasted to that of last year in the absence of slogans, transparencies, and picturizations assailing capitalistic countries and fascist enemies. Personally I noticed only three caricatures aimed at Germany.'[3]

In his speech on 7 November, Voroshilov acclaimed twenty years of Soviet progress, which would, he asserted, have been even greater but for enemies inside and outside the country. This connexion between external and internal enemies continued to furnish a main theme of Soviet propaganda.[4]

Attention now became focused on Anglo-German relations. On 12 November it was announced that Halifax, Lord President of the Council, would shortly visit the Berlin Hunting Exhibition and while in Germany would visit Hitler. This decision was generally regarded as a defeat for those members of the Government, notably the Foreign Secretary, Eden, who supported the

[1] By an arrangement made in 1933, the Italian Government was to build two cruisers, one at Leningrad and one at Leghorn, for the Soviet Government. After the rupture, it has been said 'the Italians immediately seized the funds which the Soviet Government had in a Milan bank to pay for the cruiser the Orlando shipyard at Leghorn was building for the Russian Navy. Work on the cruiser was suspended. Eventually the ship was completed and the Soviet Embassy at Rome, by paying the full price in cash, was able to send the new cruiser to join her sister-ship at Leningrad only six months before World War II broke out in September 1939.' Massock, op. cit., p. 71.

[2] Davies, op. cit., pp. 153–60.

[3] As noted earlier, the Executive Committee of the Comintern gave one of its infrequent signs of life at this period, by issuing a manifesto urging the masses in Fascist and democratic countries alike to follow Russia's example in carrying through a revolution. They could always count on the full assistance of the Soviet Union as a pioneer and a bulwark in the struggle against Fascism and capitalism. It praised the popular front movement as a weapon against German, Italian, and Japanese aggression and pointed to its success in Spain and China and against reactionary elements in France. It was their attitude to the Soviet Union which distinguished the friends from the enemies of the working class. The struggle against Fascism in Spain and China should be turned into the ending of Fascism in the world.

[4] In September, for instance, German and Finnish agents were said to be implicated in a plot to seize a section of the Murmansk Railway.

principle of collective security and were opposed to what was coming to be called 'appeasement'.[1] Halifax arrived in Berlin on 17 November, saw Hitler at Berchtesgaden on the 19th and arrived back in London on the 22nd.[2] The substance of these Anglo-German conversations remained a closely guarded secret.[3] But the Russians may well have been worried by current press comment in Great Britain and other countries.[4]

In a speech in London on 24 November Maisky gave a strong, if decently camouflaged, hint, that it did not rest with the Western Powers alone to decide who should pay the expenses of appeasement. Suppose, he asked his audience, one were to imagine the world of to-day as it would have looked had there been no Russian revolution:

'I see indeed a terrible picture. Tsarist Russia would by now be either crushed by other aggressive Powers and made their vassal, or she would have joined the Fascist League of aggressors, which is making the present world so unsafe and dangerous.

'In both cases there would have been a tremendous bloc of aggressive States, stretching from the Far East to the North Sea, and Western Mediterranean, having at its disposal unlimited resources in men, materials and technique, ensuring its absolute invincibility in any struggle with the rest of the world. The Western democracies would be in mortal peril.

'Even the intervention of the U.S.A. would not change essentially the correlation of forces in such circumstances. . . .

'Let them ponder on this, those who, while protesting their interest in the cause of progress and democracy, are apt to cast a stone against the real or imaginary shortcomings of the U.S.S.R. The mere existence of the Soviet Union greatly assists all forces of progress and peace and puts a check on all forces of reaction and war.'

[1] Part of the credit for bringing about Halifax's journey was later claimed by Lord Londonderry, a well-known exponent of closer relations with Germany and of distrust of the U.S.S.R. Londonderry, *Ourselves and Germany* (Hale, 1938).

[2] A German record of the conversation is given in *Documents and Materials Relating to the Eve of the Second World War.* vol. I (Moscow, 1948), pp. 14–45.

[3] On 29 or 30 November, the French were informed that Hitler had indicated that the Czechoslovaks would have to accept the federalization of their State so as to place Czechs, Slovaks and Germans on an equal footing. Bonnet, *Défense de la Paix: De Washington au Quai d'Orsay*, p. 49.

[4] See, e.g. the passages quoted from J. L. Garvin's article in the *Observer* on 14 November 1937, by Bilainkin, *Maisky*, pp. 185–6: 'the scheme of counter-alliance between Britain, France, Russia, and a few satellites, is not a calculation but a gamble. That way lies madness.' On 19 December, the same influential journalist wrote: 'It is no longer reconcilable with the life and safety of the Empire, that we should seek to block the Reich in mid-Europe; to oppose the closer union of the German race; or to meddle in any way with the future relations of Berlin with Austria and Czechoslovakia.' ibid., p. 190.

If all the peace-loving forces of the world were to speak and act as circumstances demanded, then perhaps at the eleventh hour, a halt might be called to the monster of war which threatened to overwhelm the world.[1]

On 27 November Litvinov gave another account of the Soviet attitude to the international situation in the form of a speech to his Leningrad constituents.[2] Litvinov, who had just returned from the Brussels conference on the Far Eastern crisis, spoke in his usual sarcastic vein about the procession of official and unofficial emissaries to the aggressor States, whose purpose was merely to request confirmation of their openly-declared intentions—intentions which, in Spain and China, were already being put into practice. For its own part, the Soviet Union accepted the statements of the aggressor States, although it was of course aware of the fact that they did not always indicate precisely where their next blow would fall. Sometimes when aggression was preparing against one sector, attention would be diverted to some totally different one. Certain States even used such naïve tricks as pretending that they had united their land, sea, and air forces for the peaceful purpose of shooting down the ideas of the Communist International. Some of the aggressive countries had so exhausted their economic resources in war preparations, and in adventures already embarked upon, that they could not venture on a long serious war, and in their future aggressions they would look for the line of least resistance. 'We know', he declared, 'and they know that they will not find this line of least resistance on our frontiers.' This was due to the Soviet Union's attention to its defences and to the extirpation of spies and wreckers.[3]

The implications of Litvinov's speech were underlined in an interview which he gave to an American journalist shortly afterwards, but which was not published at the time. The Anti-Comintern Pact, he said, was really a threat to the Western Powers, not to the Soviet Union. Spain was not itself vital to the Soviet Union, and Soviet help had been given because

[1] ibid., pp. 187–8. The speech was made before a Socialist and trade union audience. Other attempts were made at this time to appeal to non-Communist working-class organizations in support of the Soviet viewpoint.

[2] Litvinov, *Against Aggression*, pp. 102–8. The first Soviet elections under the new Constitution were held on 12 December.

[3] Between November 1937 and February 1938 the 'purge' was felt particularly severely by the Soviet Foreign Office and diplomatic corps. In December, the German Government were informed that Yurenev was not returning to his post and rumours of his arrest were current. Of Litvinov's collaborators only Maisky, Suritz, and for a short time yet, Stein in Italy, remained.

Spain was a neighbour to France with which the Soviet Union had a pact and which was under a popular front government. Before attacking the Soviet Union, the Germans would go west; and when ready to do so those 'bandits' would come to Moscow and ask for a pact. Meanwhile, Austria was first on the agenda, and Czechoslovakia next. German designs on Czechoslovakia would not involve the Soviet Union in war because the pact between the Soviet Union and Czechoslovakia only came into operation if France fulfilled her own obligations to that country; and, said Litvinov, France will not fight.[1]

In a speech to his Moscow constituents on 9 December Molotov also struck a pessimistic note. 'We have had the danger of war every spring,' he said, 'and we have been glad for the sixteen years' peace in which to build up our socialist society.' They had crushed the domestic enemy, but the Fascist States had called in 'wreckers and diversionists' to aid them. On 15 January 1938, Davies noted in his diary: 'Apparently the Kremlin was really scared last summer and still remains so.'[2]

In the same month, January 1938, the Soviet Union embarked upon a policy of still further curtailing its contacts with the outside world by insisting on a reduction of the number of foreign consulates in Russia. The principle was to be that no State should keep more consulates in Russia than there were Soviet consulates in its own territory; and the number of Soviet consulates abroad was drastically reduced.[3] On 19 January Molotov, speaking in the newly elected Supreme Soviet, declared that certain foreign consulates had in fact been 'engaged in hostile anti-Soviet spying activities on Soviet territory'.

It has been plausibly suggested that the main object of the Soviet Government was to reduce the number of foreigners in Leningrad, where large-scale naval preparations were going forward. On 15 January Molotov told the Supreme Soviet that the refusal of Italy and Japan to limit their fleets, together with Italy's claim to supremacy in the Mediterranean, made it necessary for the Soviet Union to build more large warships. Germany had signed an agreement for limitation but, he said, 'we know what Germany's signature means'. There seems to have been no official German reaction to this statement.[4]

[1] J. T. Whitaker, *We Cannot Escape History* (New York, Macmillan, 1943), pp. 266–70.

[2] Davies, op. cit., p. 172.

[3] This resulted in the ending of all British consular representation in the U.S.S.R. It had not been restored by June 1941. Coates, op. cit., p.p 583–4.

[4] For negotiations on naval armaments in 1938 see *Documents for 1938*, vol. i, pp. 510–18.

There appears to have been at about this time a definite decision to increase not only the scale of Soviet naval construction but also the scope of Soviet naval policy.[1] In place of the defensive role hitherto assigned to the Soviet navy, the new slogan became 'to transfer the war on sea to the waters of the enemy and to beat him'. The official programme became that of a navy second to none, and the theme was repeated with increasing insistence throughout 1938 and 1939.[2] A Naval Commissariat separate from the Defence Commissariat was created 31 December 1937, and in 1939 a Commissariat for Shipbuilding was added. Nevertheless, progress seems to have been slow, particularly as far as the construction of large vessels was concerned. It was submarine building which seems to have been pushed ahead most rapidly. On 23 July 1939, the Soviet Naval Commissar Kuznetsov declared that the Soviet Union possessed more submarines than any other Power and more than Germany and Japan combined.

The new naval policy was not introduced without opposition, and the purge of the higher ranks of the Soviet Navy in August 1938 was admittedly connected with criticism of the new programme as over-ambitious, and with alleged sabotage in its execution.

In December 1937 the French Foreign Minister, Delbos, undertook a tour of the eastern European capitals. The tour, which included Warsaw, Bucarest, Belgrade, and Prague, was no doubt designed to test the extent to which France could count on her eastern alliances in case of need, and the omission of Moscow from the itinerary was the more ominous.[3]

[1] On this, see D. J. Dallin, *The Big Three* (Yale University Press, 1945), pp. 186–99.

[2] On 17 May 1939 *Izvestia* wrote: 'Historical and geographical circumstances have bestowed upon our country the role of a great sea Power.' On 20 May *Pravda* wrote: 'We are a Great Power and we must have a powerful fleet which can not only defend our maritime borders but can deal the enemy a crushing blow in his own waters. We are building a big High Seas Fleet.' Quoted by E. Wollenberg, *The Red Army* (Secker and Warburg, 1940), 2nd ed. pp. 326–7. Cf. R. J. Kerner, 'Russian Naval Aims', *Foreign Affairs*, January 1946. Developments in the Soviet transport system were also of strategic significance. See Paul Wohl, 'Transport in the Development of Soviet Policy', ibid., April 1946. For an important aspect of this see T. A. Taracouzio, *Soviets in the Arctic* (New York, Macmillan, 1938).

[3] *Survey for 1937*, I, pp. 340–5; *Documents for 1937*, pp. 142–54; Werth, *France and Munich*, chap. 1; Noël, *L'Agression Allemande contre la Pologne*, pp. 174–6. In November, the French trade union leader Léon Jouhaux had visited Moscow. The Soviet statesmen whom he saw complained that nothing had been done to make the Franco-Soviet pact effective and that the French press was making attacks on the Soviet Union; Reynaud, *La France a Sauvé l'Europe*, vol. 1, pp. 129–30.

Whether or not the omission was in deference to Polish feeling, Delbos had little reason to believe that Poland was any more willing than before to co-operate in a wider security system. Polish hostility to all suggestion of strengthening the coercive powers of the League was one of the main points in a review of her policy made by Beck on 10 January 1938.[1] On Polish-Soviet relations all he found to say was:

'the past year has brought no essential changes. Our attitude and policy continue, as in the past, to be based on the Pact of Non-Aggression of 1932 with all its supplements, so that the current problems which have arisen have been settled in an atmosphere of objective negotiation.'

The attitude of the Yugoslav Government, whose head had just returned from Italy at the time of Delbos's visit, was not essentially different from that of the Polish Government.[2] Czechoslovakia's policy remained unchanged. The most equivocal position was that in Roumania, where King Carol was trying to keep on good terms with both Roumania's partners in the Little Entente. On the whole, Roumanian policy in the second half of 1937 was less disquieting from the Soviet point of view, if only because Roumanian-Polish relations seemed rather less intimate. The change seems to have come about during King Carol's visit to western Europe in July 1937 and may have been partly due to French influence. On the other hand, while Carol was actually in England, the Soviet press, in discussing the Roumanian-Polish *rapprochement*, had indicated that the Bessarabian question could easily be raised again should Roumania's policy develop unfavourably from the Soviet standpoint, and this may have decided Carol in favour of caution.[3] Roumania's attitude at the time of Delbos's visit to Bucarest could be regarded as satisfactory and the definition of his country's position made by Antonescu in a speech on 9 December had the true Litvinov stamp:

'We are partisans of collective security, but we consider that this doctrine has one meaning. The security of Western Europe cannot be disassociated from the security of Central and Eastern Europe.'

The position altered abruptly soon after Delbos's departure as a result of the Roumanian general election on 20 December

[1] *Documents for 1938*, vol. i, pp. 306–11.

[2] Yugoslavia and Italy had signed a pact of non-aggression on 25 March 1937.

[3] *L'Œuvre*, 23 July 1937. Late in September 1937, according to General Gamelin, King Carol said that he would allow Russian troops to pass through the north of his territory in order to reach Czechoslovakia, but wished the matter discussed in Roumania; Gamelin, *Servir*, vol. 2, p. 279.

and the accession to office on 28 December of a Government under the right-wing extremist leader Goga.[1] Moscow's attitude to the new Government was naturally very suspicious. Poland received the chief share of blame in the Soviet press for having brought about a change which menaced France and Czechoslovakia, and which, like Stoyadinovic's régime in Yugoslavia, was bound to result in a weakening of the Little Entente. It was Poland, it was asserted, which had persuaded Roumania that she could have good relations with Germany without sacrificing her ties with France. The cordiality in Roumanian-Soviet relations brought about by Titulescu had suffered under the Tatarescu Government; it was now in greater jeopardy than ever.[2] In fact, in spite of internal measures which won the approval of the Axis, and of some amicable gestures towards Germany and Italy, the new Government professed no intention of departing from the main lines of the country's foreign policy, and addressed assurances to that effect to Prague and to Moscow. British and French pressure brought about the fall of the Goga Government on 10 February 1938. Roumanian foreign policy became henceforth more than ever a monopoly of the Crown.

Delbos's tour, whatever reassurance it may have brought to France, did nothing to increase France's standing in Moscow.[3] Communist hostility to the French Government grew more vehement. On 14 January 1938 the Government resigned and the new Chautemps Government, formed on 18 January without Socialist participation, marked the end of the popular front.

On the previous day, the Soviet Foreign Commissariat, although not Litvinov himself, had been criticized in a speech in the Supreme Soviet by Zhdanov. His criticism was based on the alleged weakness of the country's foreign policy in regard to Japan and France; the latter, he declared, had been tolerant of anti-Soviet activities in a manner incompatible with the duties of a loyal ally. The point was duly taken up by Molotov in his speech on the 19th:

'Up to the present, notwithstanding the existence of friendly relations between the Soviet Union and the French Republic, the territory of France offers a refuge to all sorts of adventurers and criminal organizations which are nothing but nests of vipers, nests of

[1] *Survey for 1937*, I, pp. 429–30.
[2] *Journal de Moscou*, 4 January 1938. Beck's efforts to persuade Roumania not to allow Soviet help for Czechoslovakia to cross her territories, and his wider scheme for a 'Helsinki-Bucarest axis' are discussed in Noël, op. cit., pp. 208–9.
[3] There were rumours that Delbos urged the Czechs to make concessions to Germany; Schuman, *Europe on the Eve*, p. 314.

terrorists and diversionists, which openly pursue their hostile and anti-Soviet activities under the eyes and under the protection of the French authorities. These facts can clearly not be justified by the right of asylum for foreigners. It may well be asked who finds it necessary to encourage all sorts of criminals of Russian or non-Russian bourgeois origin, who engage in terrorist and anti-Soviet activity on French territory and openly perpetrate their crimes against Soviet representatives and organizations. Why are these persons protected in France, and how does this accord with the Franco-Soviet pact of friendship? Our People's Commissariat for Foreign Affairs will certainly have to concern itself with this question.'[1]

Molotov was referring to incidents connected with the disappearance from Paris in September of General Miller, a former general of the 'White' Russian armies and a leader of the Russian monarchist emigration in France.[2] The French police claimed to have discovered a vast Soviet counter-espionage organization in the course of their investigations, but the indignation of the Soviet spokesmen expressed a more far-reaching distrust of general French policy.

The Non-Intervention Committee was concerned throughout December 1937 with the British plan for withdrawing volunteers from Spain. Early in January 1938, it became clear that Italy would oppose one of the principles upon which a tentative scheme had been based: that the withdrawal of foreign combatants should be proportional to the total number of them serving on either side. The matter was therefore once more left to private negotiations between the principal parties interested, to be undertaken on British initiative.[3]

Anglo-Italian conversations looking towards a general settlement began in London on 10 February 1938.[4] While testimony conflicts as to the exact sequence of the diplomatic exchanges in the course of the next ten days, it is clear that the majority of the Cabinet were prepared to waive Eden's demand that comprehensive negotiations must be preceded by substantial withdrawals of Italian troops from Spain. According to Eden, the Italian approach carried with it something in the nature of a threat, since it proffered the establishment of good relations on a 'now or never' basis. Eden's resignation on the 20th was followed on the 21st by the announcement that Italy had

[1] *Documents for 1938*, vol. i, p. 313.
[2] *The Times*, 24, 25, 27 September; 2, 15, 22 October 1937.
[3] The development of the Spanish War from January 1938 to March 1939 and its diplomacy, is dealt with in *Survey for 1938*, I, pp. 260 ff.
[4] *Survey for 1937*, I, pp. 345-6; *Survey for 1938*, I, pp. 129-37; *Documents for 1938*, vol. i, pp. 1-27.

accepted a British formula regarding the withdrawal of volunteers from Spain and the granting to the Spanish parties of belligerent rights. During the last week of February it became known that it had been generally agreed that 10,000 troops should be withdrawn from the side employing the smaller number of foreign combatants (i.e. the Republicans), and a proportionately larger number from the other side, and that thereupon belligerent rights should be granted. The Soviet Union, however, insisted upon a figure of 20,000 instead of 10,000. This was almost certainly more than the total number of foreigners on the Republican side and the Soviet move was consequently interpreted as a device to prevent the negotiations from proceeding further.

Meanwhile Franco's recapture of Teruel in the third week in February, and the successful completion, on 15 April, of his armies' drive to the sea, which cut into two the diminishing territory of Government Spain, made it appear possible that the whole dispute might become academic through an outright collapse of the Spanish Government's resistance. These fears were, however, premature. A new stabilization of the front owed something to the relaxation in March of French control over the frontier. This permitted a considerable supply of munitions to reach Spain during the next three months. What proportion of these were Russian, it is not possible to say.

Eden's departure from the British Cabinet was generally regarded as significant for the British attitude towards Germany as well as towards Italy.[1] Eden said in his resignation speech that there was 'a real difference of outlook and method' between himself and the Prime Minister. There has been, he said, 'within the last few weeks', a 'fundamental' difference upon 'one most important decision of foreign policy which did not concern Italy at all'. This may have had to do with the Halifax mission to Berlin, which was actually decided upon while Eden was at the Far Eastern Conference at Brussels.[2]

The new storm centre was Austria,[3] whose Chancellor had been forced on 12 February 1938 to agree to include Nazi

[1] Another portent of a general change in British policy has since been seen in the transfer of Sir Robert Vansittart on 1 January from the position of Permanent Under-Secretary to the Foreign Office to that of Chief Diplomatic Adviser to the Government.

[2] *Survey for 1938*, I, p. 133 *n.* Cf. Schuman, *Europe on the Eve*, p. 320.

[3] For the Austrian crisis, see *Survey for 1938*, I, pp. 179 ff.; Schuman, *Europe on the Eve*, pp. 297–331, and the bibliography in *Hitler's Speeches*, pp. 1374–6. A summary of the steps taken by Germany to absorb Austria will be found in the relevant portion of the prosecution's case in *Nuremberg Trial*, Part I, pp. 211–64.

sympathizers in key positions in his Government. On the day of Eden's resignation, the 20th, Hitler made a long speech, largely devoted to denunciations of Bolshevism, in which the British Foreign Secretary was singled out for abuse.[1]

On his attitude to the Soviet Union, Hitler was more categoric than ever, although he made it plain that he did not blame 'the Russian people' for the misdeeds of their rulers and exploiters:

'There is only one State with which we have not sought to establish relations, nor do we wish to establish relations with it: Soviet Russia. More than ever do we see in Bolshevism the incarnation of the human destructive instinct. . . .

'Great Britain has repeatedly assured us through the mouth of her responsible statesmen of her desire to maintain the *status quo* in the world. This should apply here too. Whenever a European country falls a prey to Bolshevism, a shifting of position becomes apparent. For the territories thus Bolshevized are no longer sovereign States with independent, national lives of their own, but are now mere sections of the Moscow Revolutionary Centre. I am aware that Mr. Eden does not share this view. M. Stalin does, however, and is perfectly frank about it. In my opinion M. Stalin is still at the moment of speaking a much better judge and interpreter of Bolshevist views and aims than a British Cabinet Minister! Therefore we look upon every attempt to spread Bolshevism, no matter where it may be, with utter loathing, and where it menaces us, there we shall oppose it.'

Anti-Communism explained, he declared, Germany's attitude to Japan, which he signalized again by announcing the German recognition of 'Manchukuo'; Germany supported Japan in the Far East because China was not able to resist the virus of Communism.

[1] *Hitler's Speeches*, pp. 1376–1409. On 14 January, Hitler had had a conversation with Beck in the course of which he 'dwelt at length on his attitude to Communism, indicating very decidedly that his negative attitude was immovable. In this connexion he mentioned certain views which existed as to the possibility of an evolution in Russia in a national sense. Such opinions had been shared by the Reichswehr also. They had considered that Soviet military elements would be in a position to continue to impose their opinions. The contrary had occurred and present day Russia was in a complete state of Communism while the Generals were dead.' *Polish White Book*, pp. 43–4. This statement throws some light perhaps on the relations between the executed Russian generals and elements in the German General Staff. It may also have some connexion with the sweeping changes made in the German Army command on 4 February 1938. On the same day Neurath was replaced as Foreign Minister by Ribbentrop; *B.I.N.*, 19 February 1938, pp. 3–6; N. Henderson, op. cit., pp. 107–11. Henderson's appraisal of these events has been called naïve by a more thorough student of Germany. See J. H. Morgan, *Assize of Arms*, (Methuen, 1945), vol. 1, p. 249.

'The Italo-German friendship, springing as it does from definite causes, has become an element of stabilization in the appeasement of Europe. The connection of both States with Japan presents the most powerful of all obstructions to the further advance of the menacing power of Russian Bolshevism.'

Eden was again attacked in connexion with British press 'slanders' on the Nazi régime.

It was therefore possible to argue that the British Foreign Secretary had been sacrificed to the wrath of the dictators and the reflection was pertinent that he was the member of the British Government most prominently connected with the Anglo-Russian *rapprochement* of 1934-5.[1] It was noticeable that in his own speech on 21 February, Chamberlain defended his policy with the words: 'the peace of Europe must depend on the attitude of the four major Powers of Europe: Germany, Italy, France and ourselves'. The omission of Russia can scarcely have been accidental or regarded as such by Moscow; it was indeed the prelude to a year when every mention of the Soviet Union seemed to be systematically excluded from the pronouncements of British statesmen.[2]

How the Soviet Union would react to these further symptoms of its isolation was by no means clear. In an article in *Pravda* on 14 February, Stalin had declared that the Soviet Union had solved its internal problem by achieving 'the victory of Socialist construction in a single country'. But since they lived not on an island but in a system of States, several of them hostile, he went on, 'we say frankly and honestly that a victory of Socialism in our country is not yet final. But from this it follows that the second problem (that of external relations) has not yet been solved and it will still have to be solved.' This could be done only by joining the serious efforts of the international proletariat with the still more serious efforts of the whole Soviet people. International proletarian connexions of the working-

[1] For British press comments, see Coates, op. cit., p. 581-2; for French opinion, see Werth, *France and Munich*, pp. 38-41.
[2] See *Documents for 1938*, vol. i, pp. 1-132, 'Declarations of British Foreign Policy'. Eden was replaced as Foreign Secretary by Halifax. British foreign policy between this date and the outbreak of war in the West seems to have been very largely in the hands of the Prime Minister.
In a conversation with the American Ambassador on 3 March 'Litvinov expressed the opinion that Hitler and Mussolini had Chamberlain on the spot: that Chamberlain would be required to make good before his public by making some sort of arrangement; that the dictators would either drive a hard bargain with him so as to make it impossible, or Chamberlain would be required to make a paper peace that would really amount to nothing more than a sham for home consumption.' Davies, op. cit., p. 175.

classes in the Soviet Union with those in bourgeois countries should be strengthened. Political assistance from the working-class of the bourgeois countries to those of the Union, in the event of an armed attack, should be organized and vice versa. Finally, the Red Army and Air Force should be strengthened and the whole people kept in a state of mobilization and preparedness in the face of the danger of an attack. In a speech on the 22nd, Voroshilov called the Red Army 'the champions of the workers of the world to free them from the yoke of capitalism'. It appears to have been decided, however, that such statements were too likely to destroy whatever chance still existed of co-operation with the democracies, and on 1 March the Soviet press published a statement saying that the article in *Pravda* had been misunderstood. Soviet foreign policy was not directed against any peaceful foreign State but only against Fascism. The Union had two enemies, the imperialism of Japan and the Fascism of Germany and Italy, and both the Soviet Union and the Comintern were collaborating loyally against Fascism with all other countries. Stalin's words had been directed exclusively against aggressive countries and the Soviet Union only wanted peace with the others. But it was certain that an armed clash would come with Fascism, developing into a great war in which one of the sides would be destroyed.

The events in Great Britain seem to have been interpreted in Germany as meaning that action in regard to Austria would not be resisted. The Austrian question, and the right of the Germans in Czechoslovakia to autonomy in cultural and other matters, took up a good deal of Hitler's side of the conversation at the interview which Henderson secured on 3 March 1938, in order once again to suggest a general settlement of Anglo-German differences.[1] On the question of disarmament, which the Ambassador also raised, Hitler 'referred to the threat to Germany of the Franco-Soviet pact and of Czechoslovakia's accession thereto'. It was, he said, for that reason that Germany had to be so heavily armed, and any limitation of armaments depended therefore on the U.S.S.R. The problem was, he continued, rendered particularly difficult 'by the fact that one could place as much confidence in the faith in treaties of a barbarous creature like the Soviet Union as in the comprehension of mathematical formulae by a savage. Any agreement with the U.S.S.R. was quite worthless and Russia should never have been allowed into Europe'. It was for instance impossible, he added, to have any faith in any Soviet undertaking not to use poison gas.

[1] N. Henderson, op. cit., pp. 114–18.

The German move into Austria on 11–13 March was thus a climax which can have taken none of the Powers by surprise.[1]

[1] On 13 March, the day on which Hitler announced the incorporation of Austria in the Reich, the last of the great Moscow trials, that of Bukharin and other former leading figures in the Party, concluded with the condemnation of the accused on charges which included plotting with foreign States to dismember the Union by delivering up the Ukraine, White Russia, Soviet Central Asia, and the Far Eastern Maritime Province to foreign States.

Chapter Seven

SOVIET DIPLOMACY IN EUROPE:
FROM THE ANSCHLUSS TO 'MUNICH'

THE crisis over Czechoslovakia which began with the. Anschluss is generally regarded as a turning point in the history of the inter-war period, and of major importance in the development of Soviet foreign policy. But in spite of frequent assumptions to the contrary its history cannot yet be written with confidence.[1]

The incorporation of Austria by Nazi Germany was an obvious and immediate threat to the security of Czechoslovakia.[2] German hostility towards Czechoslovakia had become

---

[1] The absence of official documentation for the period January September 1938 is very marked, although considerable light on German policy has been thrown by the Nuremberg Trial. See *Nuremberg Trial* and the documents in *Nazi Conspiracy and Aggression* (Washington, U.S. Government Printing Office, 1946–7), vol. 3, pp. 295–379. The Polish and German White Books are reticent to the point of silence where major issues of policy are concerned. 'This reticence', it has been observed, 'finds its counterpart in the French Yellow Book and the British Blue Book which open properly only after the two, let us call them "major operations" of 1938 had been performed. During the nine pregnant months of 1938, all the "Coloured Books" suffer from vapours and faintness and from a most remarkable mental blackout.' L. B. Namier, *Diplomatic Prelude, 1938–9* (Macmillan, 1948), p. 33. The Czechs have published no 'coloured book': 'they were weak, were wronged, and a statement of their case would have produced irritation'; ibid., p. 4. But Dr. Hubert Ripka (later to become a minister in the Czechoslovak Government in exile) in his book, *Munich, Before and After*, adds a number of documents from the Czech side. For Russia itself we are as usual confined to public pronouncements or to evidence at secondhand. See *Documents for 1938*, vol. ii, with useful introductory notes giving a chronology of the crisis. For a bibliography, see *Hitler's Speeches*, pp. 1476–87; 1890–5. A brief Soviet account of the crisis is given in V. P. Potemkin, *Politika Umirotvoreniya Aggressorov i Borba Sovetskovo Soyuza za Mir* (The Policy of appeasing the Aggressors and the Soviet Union's Struggle for Peace), (Moscow, 1943). This emphasizes the Soviet Union's fidelity to her obligations. On the French side, there is the book by Georges Bonnet, *Défense de la Paix: De Washington au Quai d'Orsay*. Cf. P. Reynaud *La France a Sauvé l'Europe*, vol. i, pp. 553–72. Little new light is thrown by K. Feiling, *Neville Chamberlain* (Macmillan, 1947). Mr. J. W. Wheeler-Bennett's book *Munich, Prologue to Tragedy* (Macmillan, 1948), was still unpublished when this chapter was written. For a summary of the crisis, see S. Harrison Thomson, *Czechoslovakia in European History* (Princeton University Press, 1943), chap. 15.

[2] The actual strategic effects of the change were estimated rather variously. A. Henderson, *Eyewitness in Czechoslovakia* (Harrap, 1939), pp. 20–3.

less overt in the last weeks of 1937.[1] But in his speech on 20 February, Hitler said: 'Over ten million Germans live in two of the States adjoining our frontiers. . . . The interests of the German Reich' included 'the protection of those fellow Germans who live beyond our frontiers and are unable to ensure for themselves the right to a general freedom, personal, political, and ideological.'[2] The replies of the Czechoslovak Prime Minister and President in their statements of 4 and 5 March advisedly placed more emphasis on the friendship of the Western Powers than on the Soviet alliance.[3] By 13 March 1938 nearly seven million of the ten million Germans mentioned by Hitler were German citizens: would the fate of the remainder be the same?

From the formal point of view, the immediate situation was not unsatisfactory, since the Czechoslovak Minister in Berlin received categorical reassurances from Goering on 11 and 12 March.[4] Neurath also told the Minister on 12 March that Germany considered herself bound by the German-Czechoslovak arbitration convention of 16 October 1926.[5] Czechoslovakia assured Germany on the evening of 11 March that she would refrain from mobilizing. On 14 March the French Government categorically reaffirmed its intention of honouring its pledges to its ally.[6] The Soviet Government seems to have

---

[1] At the time of Delbos' visit to Prague there had been rumours of a German-Czechoslovak non-aggression pact. These rumours were officially denied; *Survey for 1937*, I, pp. 447–8. The Nazi leaders had decided on 5 November 1937 to absorb both Austria and Czechoslovakia even at the risk of a general war. Hitler believed as early as this that 'in all probability England and perhaps also France had already silently written off Czechoslovakia'; *Nuremberg Trial*, Part I, p. 161.

[2] *Hitler's Speeches*, pp. 1404–6.   [3] *Documents for 1938*, vol. ii, pp. 113–20.

[4] Halifax, *House of Lords Debates*, 14 and 16 March.

[5] Text in A. Berriedale Keith, *Speeches and Documents on International Affairs 1918–1937*, 2 vols. (Oxford University Press, 1938), vol. i, pp. 117–24.

[6] *French Yellow Book*. Diplomatic Documents 1938–1939 (London, Hutchinson, published by authority of the French Government), pp. 2–7. The Chautemps Cabinet had fallen on 10 March. Cabinet-making was held up by the refusal of the centre and right to serve in a 'national' government with the Communists. On 13 March, Blum formed a government of Socialists and Radicals with the League of Nations enthusiast Paul-Boncour as Foreign Minister. France's intention to support Czechoslovakia was reaffirmed by Blum on 17 March and by Paul-Boncour on 23 March. According to Bonnet, op. cit., pp. 223–4, General Gamelin and General Vuillemin, at a meeting of the French Permanent Committee of National Defence, expressed great scepticism as to both the political and technical prospects of Soviet aid for Czechoslovakia. According to 'Pertinax', French obligations had been extended in October 1937 to cover the case of a German-engineered internal rising in Czechoslovakia; 'Pertinax', *Les Fossoyeurs*, vol. i, p. 10.

waited to see what the reactions of the other Powers would be to the new situation created by Germany's action. On 15 March a Soviet spokesman told the press that the Soviet Union would go to the help of Czechoslovakia if the latter were attacked provided that France did likewise. On 17 March Litvinov handed a statement to the foreign press.[1]

After the customary references to the Soviet Union's efforts for collective security, Litvinov emphasized the new feature in the latest example of aggression. The other outbreaks had taken place outside Europe or on its outskirts, 'this time the violence has been perpetrated in the centre of Europe and has created an indubitable menace not only for the eleven countries now contiguous with the aggressor, but also for all European States and not only European ones'.

After referring specifically to Czechoslovakia and to the Polish-Lithuanian crisis, Litvinov pointed out the responsibility which these events placed on all peace-loving States and especially on the Great Powers:

'The Soviet Government being cognizant of its share in this responsibility and being also cognizant of its obligations ensuing from the League Covenant, from the Briand-Kellogg Pact and from the treaties of mutual assistance concluded with France and Czechoslovakia, I can state on its behalf that on its part it is ready as before to participate in collective actions, which would be decided upon jointly with it and which would aim at checking the further development of aggression and at eliminating the increased danger of a new world massacre. It is prepared immediately to take up in the League of Nations or outside of it the discussion with other Powers of the practical measures which the circumstances demand. It may be too late to-morrow, but to-day the time for it is not yet gone if all the States, and the Great Powers in particular, take a firm and unambiguous stand in regard to the problem of the collective salvation of peace.'

In the course of the discussion which followed, Litvinov reiterated the statement that the Soviet Union would stand by its treaty with Czechoslovakia if France did likewise, but that if France did not march it would feel free to act as it chose. Asked how the Soviet Union could reach its ally, Litvinov said:

[1] *Documents for 1938*, vol. i, pp. 314–15. On the same day, the United States Ambassador in Moscow noted in a letter: 'Along with the rest of Europe this country is extremely war-conscious. Enormous shipments are being sent to the Far East. The shipments include war materials and food stuffs. There are many indications of shortage here in food that did not obtain last winter, in spite of the huge crop last summer. There are indications that the government is going more isolationist than ever before. War is terribly close.' Davies, *Mission to Moscow*, pp. 188–9.

'if the non-aggressive nations take up that problem seriously it can be solved'.[1]

On the following day, the 18th, the Soviet Government presented notes to the British, French, and American Governments proposing that representatives of these four countries should meet to decide what steps could be taken to prevent further aggression.

Meanwhile the weakening of the precarious structure of European security was shown by Poland's taking advantage of the situation to settle accounts with Lithuania. The crisis came to a head on 17 March, when Lithuania was faced with an ultimatum demanding the immediate establishment of diplomatic relations. The Polish demands were accepted on 19 March.[2]

Litvinov mentioned the Polish-Lithuanian crisis alongside the danger to Czechoslovakia in his statement on 17 March. He also took the occasion to say to the correspondent of the Polish official news agency:

'Your Government says it did not address an ultimatum to Lithuania, but it smells like one to me. If you say the situation is not serious I hope you are right; but it looks serious to me. We informed your Government in the friendliest manner about our anxiety over this point.'[3]

Although Litvinov told Davies on 23 March that Germany was actually 'opposed to the seizure of Lithuania by Poland, because she, Germany, was greedy for that territory herself' and because 'Hitler had designs on all the Baltic States as well', the American Ambassador thought that Poland's move had made the Russians very anxious indeed.[4]

[1] *B.I.N.*, XV, p. 320. 'The implication generally accepted here,' wrote Davies to the Secretary of State on 26 March, 'was that the U.S.S.R. was serving notice on Poland in particular, and possibly on Roumania as well, that if necessary the Soviets would violate territorial boundaries to go to the aid of Czechoslovakia.' Davies, op. cit., p. 191.

[2] *Documents for 1938*, vol. i, pp. 301–6, 'The Polish-Lithuanian Crisis'; *B.I.N.*, 2 April 1938.

[3] *B.I.N.*, XV, p. 350.

[4] Davies, op. cit., pp. 189–90. Litvinov also 'expressed the view that within a very short time, Germany would take over the Polish Corridor and Danzig and informed me that he had been told here by the German Military Attaché that the German government would pay nothing in return.' It was presumably Litvinov's intention that this remark should be passed on to the Poles. Davies gave a more detailed account of the crisis in a report to the Secretary of State on 26 March; ibid., pp. 190–2. 'The anxiety here was very serious. The fear was that Poland had some secret agreement with Germany whereunder Germany would support a Polish purpose to

At a meeting with Davies on 23 March Litvinov spoke of the Czech crisis and the policy of the Western Powers:

'He said . . . that he felt very sure that Czechoslovakia would cause trouble this summer; that the German minorities in Czechoslovakia were exerting pressure on Hitler to move in that direction. He made the rather startling statement that there was danger that Czechoslovakia might voluntarily yield to Germany because she had no confidence in France and was completely surrounded. For that matter, Litvinov stated frankly, "France has no confidence in the Soviet Union and the Soviet Union has no confidence in France" . . . the only thing that would prevent complete Fascist domination of Europe was a change in government or policy in Great Britain. . . . He expressed the view that if Fascist Germany does become dominant over Europe, the long Russian frontier will have nothing to fear from Germany because she, Germany, will have her hands full in the states bordering it.'[1]

On the following day a speech was made by Chamberlain which seemed to justify Litvinov's gloomy forebodings on the likely direction of British policy. The British Government declined the Soviet proposal for a conference on the grounds that its object would be to negotiate 'mutual undertakings in advance to resist aggression' which Great Britain could accept only in regard to limited areas with which she was particularly concerned; furthermore, to promise military action in the event of aggression against Czechoslovakia or to give France an assurance that in the event of her being called upon to fulfil her undertaking under the Franco-Czechoslovak treaty 'we would

---

absorb Lithuania and find an outlet to the sea, in consideration for which Poland would relinquish the Polish Corridor to Germany. . . . If such were the actual facts of the situation, there was a general conviction here that the Soviet Union would be compelled to come to the aid of Lithuania and that war would result. While the governments of France and England were bringing pressure upon Poland to restrain its attitude, the Soviet Foreign Office here also took a strong position apparently with both parties.' According to Davies, Litvinov had told the Poles that the Soviet Union was vitally concerned with Lithuania's continued independence and was afraid that if she gave way further demands would be made which would effectively destroy it. On the other hand, Litvinov told him that he had advised the Lithuanians to give way on the immediate demands so as to avoid the possibility of invasion. The Soviet attitude seems to have been a disappointment to the Lithuanians; ibid., p. 189. In a letter to Sumner Welles also dated 26 March, Davies declared that the Lithuanian crisis had a favourable effect as far as the Soviet Union's relations with Finland, Esthonia, and Latvia were concerned. There seemed to be 'some indications' of their 'being impressed by the success of German aggression' and of 'a recognition of the desirability of the friendship of Russia as a bulwark and support to their independence as against possible German or Polish aggression'; ibid., p. 196.

[1] ibid., pp. 189–90.

immediately employ our full military force on her behalf' would be to take the choice between peace and war out of the hands of the British Government.[1]

Chamberlain's references to the League and to collective security were dismissed in *Pravda* on 26 March as indicating the need for his Government to find means of disarming the growing opposition in Great Britain. To every question directly related to resisting the aggressors, his answer, so it was said, had been an unqualified negative.

'On the whole there remains a thoroughly well-based impression that Chamberlain's rejection in his declaration of any "new obligation" whatever with regard to co-operation with the peace-loving nations was so definite for the simple reason that he has already entered upon some undertakings towards the aggressors. That is simply the conclusion which suggests itself.'[2]

Summing up the situation in a letter written from Moscow to Sumner Welles on 26 March Davies said:

'England and France have been playing into the hands of the Nazi and the Fascist aims. The Soviet Union is rapidly being driven into a complete isolation and even hostility to England and indifference to France. This may extend to the point where there might be developed a realistic union of these forces with Germany in the not distant future. . . . In any event Hitler is threatened in the East unless his Eastern door is closed. That is a classic accepted by German strategists as a basis for any war against the Western Powers.'[3]

The Nazi leaders met on 21 April and decided to launch an attack on Czechoslovakia not later than 1 October.[4]

In Czechoslovakia itself, the German annexation of Austria was almost immediately followed by increased intransigence on the part of the German minority, culminating in its leader Henlein's 'Eight Points' speech at Karlsbad on 24 April. The granting of these demands as far as the internal government of the country was concerned would in fact have involved the creation of a State within a State.[5] But the demands went still

[1] *House of Commons Debates*, 24 March 1938. Cf. Halifax in House of Lords, 24 March 1938, Viscount Halifax, *Speeches on Foreign Policy* (Oxford University Press, 1940), pp. 131–8; and his attack on 29 March on 'diplomacy by collective action', ibid., pp. 139–43.
[2] Cf. 'Les Faux Calculs de M. Neville Chamberlain', *Journal de Moscou*, 29 March 1938; 'Chamberlain's Foreign Policy spurs Fascist Aggression', *Moscow Daily News*, 30 March 1938.
[3] Davies, op. cit., p. 194. Cf. ibid., pp. 196, 205, and 208.
[4] *Nuremberg Trial*, Part I, pp. 8, 164–5.
[5] *Documents for 1938*, vol. ii, pp. 130–7. 'In actuality, there was never the slightest possibility that a complete acceptance of Sudeten demands at any period of the tension would have meant any permanent alleviation of the

further and involved a total revision of Czech foreign policy
and the abandonment, in Henlein's own words, of 'the dangerous view, which flies in the face of all historical development,
that it is the mission of the Czech people as Slavs, to form a
Slav bulwark against the Germans. . . . It would,' he added,
'be an error for Czech policy to rely solely upon its alliances
with France and Russia without itself making a decisive contribution to securing the peace of Europe.'[1]

While tension in Czechoslovakia was rising, the Western
Powers were showing signs of contemplating an attempt to
appease Germany at Czechoslovakia's expense. In France, the
Blum-Paul-Boncour Government came to an end on 8 April,
and on the 10th, Daladier formed a new cabinet without
Socialist participation and with Bonnet as the Foreign Minister.
On the 12th, *Le Temps* published an article by the well-known
jurist Joseph Barthélemy in which he argued that France was
not obliged to go to war in order to save Czechoslovakia. If the
Russian Army were to fight, the Soviet régime would collapse
and another Brest-Litovsk would ensue. How, he asked, could
Russia's forces come to the aid of Czechoslovakia, when the
airfields they required would all be overrun in three weeks.
According to a statement made to the French Cabinet by
Bonnet on 27 September, doubts of Russian aid had been
expressed by the Committee of National Defence on 15 March.[2]

It was also known that there was considerable scepticism in
British as well as French circles as to the military strength of
the Soviet Union itself after the 'purges'. In his able defence

---

crisis.' Thompson, op. cit., p. 334. The evidence at the Nuremberg trial
has confirmed this verdict.

[1] For conditions in Czechoslovakia and particularly the Sudetenland at
this time see Henderson, *Eyewitness in Czechoslovakia*, pp. 20–49; S. Morrell,
I Saw the Crucifixion (Peter Davies, 1939), pp. 9–24. The Slovak autonomists
were also showing an alarming tendency to borrow the Nazi ideology. On
24 March, their leader Hlinka had said: 'We are in the midst of a decisive
struggle against internationalism and Bolshevism.' Schuman, *Europe on the
Eve*, p. 368. Fears that Czechoslovakia might be only a stepping-stone to
wider German ambitions were enhanced by the popularity among Nazi
official circles at this time of a book by a writer of German origin, Sanders,
Um die Gestaltung Europas, which claimed for Germany a right to incorporate
the Ukraine and the Caucasus on pseudo-historical grounds; W. E. D.
Allen, *The Ukraine* (Cambridge, 1940), p. 385.

[2] *Carnets Secrets de Jean Zay* (Paris, Editions de France, 1942), p. 19. General
Faucher, head of the French military mission in Prague, 1926–39, said
after his return that the Russian 'support given during the early days would
certainly have been weak', but that 'the Czech aerodromes were so exceptionally well situated from a strategic point of view that it would have been
possible to obtain excellent results with very little material'; *L'Epoque*,
24 December 1938, quoted by Ripka, op. cit., pp. 296–7.

of British foreign policy in the Munich crisis, Mr. J. A. Spender made much of this point.[1] There were also reports of a serious setback to Russia's industrial production.[2]

Soon after assuming office, M. Bonnet asked Léon Noël, the French Ambassador to Warsaw, to pay a short visit to Prague where he had previously been posted, in order to investigate the situation there.[3] M. Noël's visit brought home to him the importance of the fact that neither the Franco-Soviet nor the Czechoslovak-Soviet treaty had been completed by military conventions. Benes told M. Noël that he had no intention of concluding a military agreement with the Soviet Union unless France and Great Britain had first taken this step. M. Noël's advice that, in the circumstances, Czechoslovakia should be warned that France would not be in a position to fulfil her engagements, was not accepted by the French Government.[4]

On 28–29 April, talks were held in London between Daladier and Bonnet and members of the British cabinet.[5] Extracts from the *procès-verbal* of these meetings have since been made public. It appears that the British representatives argued that Prague should be pressed to make concessions to Germany, and that Mr. Chamberlain took the view that Hitler did not in fact want to destroy Czechoslovakia itself, but did not see how he could be prevented from doing so, if such was his intention.

[1] J. A. Spender, *Between Two Wars* (Cassell, 1943). The only member of the British Government at the time who has given the public his subsequent reflections on British policy is Viscount Maugham in his *The Truth About the Munich Crisis* (Heinemann, 1944). But although he adduces the same general theory of unpreparedness as Spender, the force of his argument is weakened by his defence of the Munich settlement as such. See the review of this book under the title: 'Verdict on Munich' in the *Economist*, 18 March 1944. Russia's attitude during the crisis is summed up by Lord Maugham as follows: 'The attitude of Russia under the Pact seems to have been "correct"; but their aid would not apparently have been of a very speedy kind except as against Poland, and she had of course no right of access to Czechoslovakia while Roumania and Poland were neutral.' op. cit., p. 46 n.

[2] Soviet statistics by no means bear out such reports; Yugow, *Russia's Economic Front for War and Peace* (Watts, 1943), p. 16. Reports about Russian weaknesses 'were much less of a deterrent to Prague than to any other capital because the Czechs had unique sources of accurate information as to Russia and many direct military and industrial contacts'; R. W. Seton-Watson, *Munich and the Dictators* (Methuen, 1939), p. 90.

[3] Noël, *L'Agression Allemande contre la Pologne*, pp. 198–202.

[4] The historian G. Vernadsky, in an article published in 1942, argues that the Franco-Soviet Pact was, as the Russian leaders knew, doomed from the beginning because of the lack of sincerity on the part of France, for whom the alliance was 'an interim diplomatic move without solid significance' and that a straight Soviet-Czechoslovak alliance would have been stronger; 'A Review of Russian Policy', *Yale Review*, Spring 1942.

[5] *Survey for 1938*, I, pp. 143–4.

Both the British and the French took the view that Russia's armed forces had been seriously weakened, although M. Daladier called attention to the still formidable character of the Soviet air arm. The maximum to which the British Government would assent was to inform Berlin that, if Germany used force against Czechoslovakia, France would be bound to intervene, and that Great Britain could not guarantee she would not be drawn into the conflict.[1]

By their agreement with Italy of 16 April the British Government undertook *inter alia* to recognize the Italian annexation of Abyssinia, provided the League Council could be induced to release League members from their pledge not to do so.[2] This outcome had been forecast by Litvinov in a conversation with the American Ambassador on 23 March, and he had then declared that he would not attend the meeting of the League Council in May unless some new circumstances arose to make it necessary.[3] Nevertheless, Litvinov did attend and his opposition helped to prevent the British proposal going through.[4] In his speech on 12 May, Litvinov pointed out that it was wrong to assert that non-recognition had a purely academic significance:[5]

'It must be made even more clear that the League of Nations has not changed its opinion on the general principle of non-recognition of the accomplished fact produced by aggression and on the appropriate resolutions adopted by the League on other occasions. The latter particularly applies in cases where the States which have been the victims of attack have aroused the amazement and admiration of the world by the valiance of their citizens, who continue to fight the aggressor with unweakening energy, obstinacy and fortitude. It must be clear that the League of Nations has no intention of changing its attitude, whether to the direct seizure and annexation of other people's territory, or to those cases in which such annexations are camouflaged by the setting up of puppet "national" governments, allegedly independent, but in reality serving merely as a screen for and an agency of the foreign invader.'

The course of events in Spain, to which Litvinov was obviously referring, was giving renewed cause for anxiety, since it seemed probable that as a result of the French visit to London and of the Franco-Italian negotiations, the relaxation of frontier

---

[1] Speech by E. Daladier in the French National Constituent Assembly, 18 July 1946.

[2] Cmd. 5726; *Survey for 1938*, I, pp. 137–43. On 22 April, conversations with Italy were begun by France. On 1 April the French Communist paper *L'Humanité* had advocated a French agreement with Italy in order to save Italy from total dependence on Germany.

[3] Davies, op. cit., p. 190.   [4] *Survey for 1938*, I, pp. 144–52.

[5] *Documents for 1938*, vol. i, pp. 258–61.

control by France would come to an end. On 13 May a Spanish resolution calling upon the League to bring the non-intervention system to an end was rejected by the votes of Great Britain, France, Poland, and Roumania against those of the U.S.S.R. and Spain, with the remaining members abstaining.[1]

In supporting the Spanish proposal, Litvinov denied that there would be a danger of war in the event of the abandonment of the non-intervention policy.

'I believe the concept of non-intervention was faulty from the very beginning, in that both parties in the conflict were regarded as sides having a claim to equal rights and equal treatment . . . we were unable to persuade other governments to follow a different policy, and we had to agree to a policy of non-intervention into which we entered with very slight hope that perhaps it might at least bring about some real result.'[2]

More alarming to Russia than 'appeasement' in the Mediterranean was the evidence of increasing British sympathy for the German case in regard to Czechoslovakia. There were a number of indications that influential circles in Britain were coming round to the view that nothing short of the cession of the German-speaking areas of that country to the Reich would be sufficient.[3]

In the Soviet Union itself, the reaction was an increased emphasis on the likelihood of war, which the Far Eastern situation rendered all the more plausible, on the ability of the Soviet Union to defend itself singlehanded, and on the compliance of the bourgeois democracies with the demands of the aggressors.[4]

The Soviet Government was informed on 9 May of the joint Anglo-French *démarche* at Prague on the 7th. The two Ministers told the Czechoslovak Government that Britain and France

[1] *Survey for 1938*, I, pp. 317–19.   [2] *L.N.O.J.*, 1938, pp. 531–2.
[3] A leading article in *The Times* on 22 March said: 'If we were to involve ourselves in war to preserve Czech sovereignty over these Germans without first clearly ascertaining their wishes, we might well be fighting against the principle of self-determination. A dangerous situation thus exists, the remedy for which is to ascertain the wishes of the Sudeten Germans. The best means of doing this would be an international plebiscite, on the lines of that held in the Saar territory in January 1935.' Cf. correspondence in *The Times*, beginning 7 May. Speaking at Bristol on 8 April, Halifax declared that if the British tried to organize a new pattern of collective security against Germany by the existing League Powers, they would be doing the very thing which would be destructive of the hope of winning Germany and other Powers back to European co-operation and would be dividing Europe into rival blocs. Cf. his speech in the House of Lords on 18 May.
[4] See the quotations from Voroshilov's speech on 1 May and the *Izvestia* leading article of that date in Coates, *A History of Anglo-Soviet Relations*, pp. 586–7.

hoped the problem of the German minority would be solved within the framework of the Czechoslovak State, and offered their services to that end.[1] At the same time evidence that British and French official circles contemplated a more radical solution was accumulating.[2]

In contrast to this the Soviet Government seemed determined not to provide any excuse for such vacillation and to encourage the Czechs to resist any pressure that might be applied.

On 11 May Kalinin made a statement to the leader of a Czechoslovak labour delegation:

'The Soviet Union has invariably fulfilled all its treaties concluded with other States in all their consequences and will do so in this case also. It will if called upon fulfil to the last letter all its obligations to Czechoslovakia and France. The Soviet Union possesses ores, iron, petrol, foodstuffs, cotton, everything, in fact, that is necessary

[1] N. Henderson, *Failure of a Mission*, p. 132. Halifax is said to have told the Czechoslovak Minister in London on 2 May that more far-reaching concessions than those hitherto contemplated would have to be made to the German minority. Armstrong, *Where There is no Peace*, p, 168. Reports that the British and French ministers had urged concessions or particular measures on the Czechs were denied by the British Under-Secretary for Foreign Affairs in the House of Commons on 16 May.

[2] The view that Russia neither could nor would fight for Czechoslovakia and that France would not, was apparently expressed by Neville Chamberlain at a private luncheon with American and Canadian journalists on 10 May 1938. He is also said to have revealed plans for a Four-Power Pact between Britain, France, Germany, and Italy to the exclusion of the U.S.S.R. The claim that the British Prime Minister had indicated a cession of the Sudetenland as the best solution of the Czech crisis was made in a message to the *Montreal Daily Star* of 14 May, from Joseph Driscoll of the *New York Herald Tribune* and by an article by 'Augur' (V. Poliakoff) in the *New York Times* of the same date. Two days' discussions in the House of Commons failed to produce a denial of the authenticity of these reports and Sir Archibald Sinclair specifically called attention to the disastrous effect of trying 'to exclude Russia from Europe'; *House of Commons Debates*, 21, 22, and 27 June. On 16 May, *The Times* advocated the neutralization of Czechoslovakia. The veering of British opinion was encouraged by a visit to London of Henlein on 12–14 May. He must have been impressed by the widespread willingness to accept much of the German case. For his own part, he appears to have convinced a number of opponents of 'appeasement' of the moderation and justice of his claims. R. W. Seton-Watson, *Munich and the Dictators*, pp. 38 and 56 n.; *History of the Czechs and Slovaks*, pp. 393–4; A. Henderson, *Eyewitness in Czechoslovakia*, pp. 51–2; Winston Churchill, who on 9 May had declared that Great Britain would be 'improvidently foolish . . . to put needless obstacles in the way of the general association of the great Russian mass with the resistance to an act of Nazi aggression', appears subsequently to have gone back on this view for a time. Compare his articles of 23 June, 23 July, 18 August, and 15 September; *Step by Step* (Cassell, 1939), pp. 247–50; 255–8; 264–73; 273–6. Only in the last of these is joint action with Russia advocated.

for the conduct of any war whatsoever. France does not possess all these things in the same quantities. If the pact of friendship between the Soviet Union, France, and Czechoslovakia were as firmly established as we could wish, it would firmly influence England to follow a different course in her policy, and the pact would have great international significance and weight.'[1]

In a conversation with Litvinov on 12 May Bonnet asked him what the Soviet attitude would be in the event of a conflict between Germany and Czechoslovakia. Litvinov replied that if France fulfilled her obligation, the U.S.S.R. would act likewise. Pressed as to how the U.S.S.R. would get over the obstacle caused by Polish and Roumanian objection to the passage of Soviet forces, Litvinov said that the U.S.S.R. would not act without the consent of these countries; it was up to France which had treaty relations with both to secure their consent. That of Roumania would be the easier to get. But Bonnet found the Roumanian Foreign Minister, M. Comnène, obdurately opposed to any such suggestion.[2]

During the third week in May 1938, reports of German troop movements on the borders of Czechoslovakia (and of the assembly of Polish troops) became current, and these came to a head on 19 and 20 May. It is in fact almost certain that these reports were vastly exaggerated.[3] During the early hours of the 21st, the Czechs called up five classes and the frontiers were manned.[4] France also took some partial measures of mobilization. Henderson had two interviews with Ribbentrop on the 21st:

'After notifying him of the action which His Majesty's Government were taking in Prague with a view to inducing the Czech Government to come to a settlement direct with Henlein, I warned His Excellency that France had definite obligations to Czechoslovakia and that if these had to be fulfilled, His Majesty's Government could not guarantee that they would not be forced by events to become themselves involved.'[5]

---

[1] *Documents for 1938*, vol. ii, p. 139.

[2] Bonnet, op. cit., pp. 125–7. Cf. *Documents and Materials Relating to the Eve of the Second World War*, vol. I, pp. 139–40, 149.

[3] Noël, op. cit., pp. 203–4; Daladier speech of 18 July 1946; Professor Thomson accepts the contrary version and declares that Hitler was foiled by 'Benes's quick and courageous action'; op. cit., p. 335.

[4] Bilek, *Fifth Column at Work*, p. 38.

[5] N. Henderson, *Failure of a Mission*, pp. 134–40; cf. Chamberlain's statement in the House of Commons, 23 May 1938. Henderson asserts that by 23 May 'all but the most intractable had become convinced that the stories of German troop concentrations were in fact untrue'. This version (that the crisis was wholly imaginary) does not seem to have found general acceptance.

On the same day, Bonnet received the diplomatic representatives of Great Britain, the United States, the U.S.S.R., Poland, and Czechoslovakia, to explain the French attitude.

On 22 May the British Government sent a note to the French Government declaring that if British pressure in Berlin were to fail, Great Britain would not take immediate military measures in conjunction with the French to aid Czechoslovakia but would come to France's assistance in the event of an unprovoked attack upon her by Germany. The British Government was of the opinion that the military situation was such that France and Great Britain, even in the event of their receiving help on the part of Russia, would not be in a position to prevent Germany from overwhelming Czechoslovakia. The only effect of their intervention would be to bring about a European war of which the outcome must be considered doubtful. At the same time both Poland and Roumania showed themselves hostile to the passage of Soviet aid for Czechoslovakia, the latter's attitude differing only in being less rigidly formulated.[1]

No further steps were taken and the atmosphere of crisis subsided by the end of the month. The German press showed great indignation at the general assumption elsewhere that Germany had suffered a diplomatic set-back, and mingled attacks on British interference with renewed denunciations of Czechoslovakia and its Russian patrons.

It is now known that it was on 28 May that Hitler gave orders that preparations for military action against Czechoslovakia should be complete by 2 October and that there should meanwhile be a speeding-up of the work on the Western defences of the Reich.[2]

On 30 May Hitler issued a military directive: 'It is my unalterable decision to smash Czechoslovakia by military action in the near future.'[3] It is unlikely that Germany's purpose can have remained unobserved by foreign Powers during the summer, and certainly on the Soviet side a resort to force by Germany was confidently predicted. It was no doubt in this light that the Soviet Government judged the policies of the Western Powers. No direct approach was made publicly by them to the Soviet Government during the 'May crisis' itself, but it has since been stated that in the summer of 1938 there

[1] Daladier, speech of 18 July 1946.

[2] Speeches of 14 September 1938 and 30 January 1939, *Hitler's Speeches*, pp. 493–7 and 1570–3. *Nuremberg Trial*, part II, p. 6. Cf. N. Henderson, *Failure of a Mission*, pp. 140–2; A. Henderson, *Eyewitness in Czechoslovakia*, pp. 116–23.

[3] *Nuremberg Trial*, part II, p. 7. Hitler considered that Russia would probably assist Czechoslovakia with her air force.

were several exchanges of views between the French and Litvinov, notably in May.[1] The first indication of the official Soviet reaction to the 'May crisis' had been a speech made in New York by the Soviet Ambassador, Troyanovsky, on 25 May:

'Our people in a military sense and psychologically are prepared to repulse any foreign invasion and the aggressors probably would prepare to take many preliminary steps before attacking Soviet Russia. Among these preliminary steps would be to fight against Spain, Austria, Czechoslovakia, Roumania, Poland, France, and even Great Britain. But, though our country does not appear to be menaced by immediate danger, we cannot wash our hands of the present European situation. We have our principles and we are tied by our treaties. We will be faithful to those principles and those treaties. We are ready with France to defend Czechoslovakia in the event of aggression. We are ready to defend France itself. We shall perhaps be summoned to defend other Great Powers. We do not want to be isolated in international affairs. A firm stand against the aggressors is the fundamental solution of the present international tension.

'The attitude of the Czechs is an encouraging factor, which shows the way to deal with those aggressors. With the end of the lethargy and "jitters" of certain Powers, the end of the present international troubles should come very soon. We are ready to contribute to this aim. . . .'[2]

On the following day, 26 May, the Soviet press published articles declaring that the Soviet Union would fulfil all the obligations entered into with France and Czechoslovakia. The aggressive plans of Germany had only been postponed and the Soviet Government was vigilantly watching developments. Czechoslovakia was the citadel of peace and must be defended. It was not on negotiations nor on concessions to an unappeasable aggressor, but on Czechoslovakia's strength and the possibilities existing for its defence that everything depended. During an interview with the French Ambassador M. Coulondre in the first half of June, Litvinov again asked the French to secure Roumania's assent to the passage of Soviet troops. The request was passed on to the Roumanian Government by the French Minister in Bucarest, who informed his Government on 9 July, that the Roumanian Government's attitude was unaltered, and referred to the clause in the Roumanian Constitution of 27 February 1938 specifically forbidding the passage of foreign troops without special legislation. He also made it clear that

[1] Daladier, Speech of 18 July 1946.
[2] *Documents for 1938*, vol. i, p. 315.

even if the political objection could be overruled, the technical facilities for the passage of land troops were very limited.[1]

The Soviet outlook on the European situation as a whole was summarized by Stalin in an interview given to the American Ambassador on 5 June.[2] As reported by Davies to his Government, Stalin said that

'the outlook for European peace was very bad and the summer might induce serious trouble. He then went on to say that the reactionary elements in England represented by the Chamberlain government were determined upon a policy of making Germany strong as against Russia. He stated that in his opinion Chamberlain did not represent the English people and that he would probably fail because the Fascist dictators would drive too hard a bargain. He said that the Soviet Union had every confidence that it could defend itself.'[3]

The speech made by Litvinov in Moscow on 23 June was largely an elaboration of the same theme, if in a rather less blunt fashion.[4] After dealing with the revival of Germany's strength after her defeat in the Great War, Litvinov said:

'The entire diplomacy of the Western Powers in the last five years resolves itself into an avoidance of any opposition to Germany's aggressive actions, to compliance with her demands and even her caprices, fearing to arouse her dissatisfaction and disapproval even in the slightest degree. . . . Of that formidable force which the League should have represented only a pale shadow has remained. Thus still another achievement of the World War is being liquidated, one on which the victors particularly prided themselves.'

The Soviet Union, he declared, could not stand aside from these events:

'Germany is striving not only for the restoration of her rights violated by the Versailles Treaty, not only for the restoration of her pre-war imperial boundaries, but is building her foreign policy on unlimited aggression, even going so far as to talk of the subjection to the so-called German race of all other races and peoples. She is conducting an open, rabid, anti-Soviet policy . . . and publicly abandons herself to dreams of the Ukraine and even of the Urals.'[5]

---

[1] Bonnet, op. cit., pp. 163–5, 303–4.   [2] Davies, op. cit., pp. 220–6.

[3] *The Times* on 3 June 1938 suggested plebiscites to decide whether or not Czechoslovakia's German, Polish, and Hungarian minorities should secede.

[4] *Documents for 1938*, vol. i, pp. 315–22. On 21 June, the Secretary-General of the Comintern issued a manifesto calling on the workers of the world and especially those of France, Britain, and the United States to bring pressure to bear on their Governments to join the U.S.S.R. in a firm policy against the three 'Fascist' aggressors.

[5] There were no outward indications that German hostility to the Soviet Union was weakening during the summer of 1938. On 9 June, however,

He then extolled the Soviet Union's disinterested and active role in the League of Nations:

'When the proposed Eastern regional pact was frustrated by Germany and Poland, the Soviet Union concluded pacts of mutual assistance with France and Czechoslovakia. . . . In face of the menace which now hangs over Czechoslovakia, it should be clear to the whole world that the Czechoslovak pact . . . is the most, if not the sole, major factor in relieving the tension around Czechoslovakia. It must be said that in promising to assist the victim of aggression, the Soviet Government does not use this assistance as a means of bringing pressure to bear on this victim in order to urge it to capitulate to the aggressor and act in such a way that assistance would be superfluous.'

This direct attack on Anglo-French policy over Czechoslovakia was followed by a reminder of the Soviet Union's action after the Anschluss:

'Even quite recently it reminded the peaceful Powers of the need for urgent collective measures to save mankind from the new sanguinary war that is approaching. This appeal was not heard but the Soviet Government, at least, has relieved itself of responsibility for the further development of events.'[1]

After pointing out the precarious position in which the victors of the Great War had placed themselves by their so-called realism, Litvinov went on to discuss the position of the lesser European Powers:

'With the exception of Czechoslovakia, the Western European Powers have no longer any allies among the middle and small States of Europe. Some of these States have openly entered the orbit of the aggressor countries, others for fear of the latter are mumbling about neutrality. By their declaration of neutrality it is as though they say that they reject the assistance of the League of Nations, the assistance of friends and invite anyone who wishes to violate them. There can be no doubt whatsoever that the aggressor countries, who have to-day been able to inspire such fear in those countries as to extort such declarations from them, will on the very day after

---

Molotov told the American Ambassador 'that they had been offered very large credits by Germany in the very recent weeks which they were not going to accept under any conditions'; Davies, op. cit., p. 342. In his speech of 31 May 1939 Molotov referred to the rejection of this offer in rather different terms. *Infra*, p. 250. Hitler's reception of the newly accredited Soviet Ambassador, Alexei Merekalov, on 13 July, was markedly cold; *Hitler's Speeches*, p. 1464.

[1] Halifax did not mention the U.S.S.R. during a review of British foreign policy on 21 June 1938; *Speeches on Foreign Policy*, pp. 174–8.

mobilization, compel these countries to violate their neutrality and force them into their service.'[1]

Earlier in his speech, Litvinov had called attention to the weakening in the strategic position of England and France through the joint German and Italian 'occupation' of a considerable part of Spain, the Balearic islands and Spanish Morocco. He gave the customary justification of the acceptance of the original non-intervention scheme by the Soviet Government—the Soviet belief that the Spanish Government could cope with the rebels unaided, provided external help for the latter could be prevented. But here, too, the policy of Great Britain and France had been one of 'endless concessions' to the aggressors.

'Under such conditions the Committee not only did not in the slightest degree succeed in ensuring non-intervention, but it is listing more and more to Franco's side. Our role in the Committee now resolves itself to attempts to straightening out this list to the best of our ability and as far as possible, and at least to prevent the intervention of the Committee itself in Spanish affairs on Franco's behalf.'

After the meeting of the League Council in May, Soviet diplomacy had seemed to be fighting a rearguard action against the British plan for combining the granting of belligerent rights to both sides with the withdrawal of foreign volunteers and with the restoration or strengthening of land and sea controls.[2] On 26 May the Soviet delegate withdrew his previous objection to the figure of 10,000 as the basis for the first propor-

---

[1] One of the States which may have been in Litvinov's mind was Yugoslavia. The Yugoslav Prime Minister, Stoyadinovic, had been cordially received in Berlin in January 1938 and by Ciano in Venice in mid-June; *Documents for 1938*, vol. i, pp. 293–8; *B.I.N.*, XV, p. 579. It has been stated that during the summer, Stoyadinovic 'found means to let President Benes know that he thought the zero hour had come when Czechoslovakia must follow Yugoslavia's example and make the best terms possible with the new dominant forces in Europe'. Armstrong, op. cit., p. 34. There is considerable evidence of strong sympathy among the Yugoslavs for the Czech cause. This was demonstrated for example at the remarkable rally of the 'Sokols' in Prague early in July, when there were delegates from all the Slav peoples except from the Poles and those in the Soviet Union. Morrell, op. cit., pp. 71–6. But when a British journalist travelled through Yugoslavia between 'Godesberg' and 'Munich', he found little evidence that its Government intended to come to the help of Czechoslovakia. A. Henderson, *Eyewitness in Czechoslovakia*, pp. 226–8. The Yugoslav Government is said to have informed the French Government at about the beginning of June, that it did not consider that its engagements to Czechoslovakia went beyond help in case of an attack by Hungary. Bonnet, op. cit., pp. 162–3.

[2] 'The Non-Intervention Committee on Spain', *B.I.N.*, 18 June 1938.

tional withdrawal of volunteers. Other differences over procedure were not ironed out until 21 June.[1]

Since the Anglo-Italian agreement would not come into force until the Spanish issue had been settled, the British Government was pressing strongly for the acceptance of its scheme. This was achieved on 5 July, at the first plenary session of the Non-Intervention Committee since the previous November.[2]

The operation of the scheme depended upon the consent of both sides in Spain itself. The Republican Government sent word on 26 July that they would accept the plan subject to certain minor amendments, but there was a long delay before Franco replied. When he did so on 16 August, the reply contained so many qualifications as hardly to constitute an acceptance. Soviet comment was to the effect that the course of military events had gone contrary to Franco's expectations and to those of the British and French Governments, since his delay in answering had been due to hopes of a speedy advance upon Valencia, with the aid of the additional military resources recently received from abroad. Such a victory would have liquidated the Spanish problem and thus have been satisfactory to Great Britain and France. Even after the rebuff which they had now received from Franco, it was likely that the only result would be that they would proceed to further concessions.[3]

Ciano, when pressed by the British for information on reports of increasing Italian aid to Franco, did not deny that new contingents had been sent, but claimed that they only amounted to necessary replacements and that they were sent because of reports that France was again permitting the transit of war material to Spain from Czechoslovakia and the U.S.S.R.[4]

Early in September it was decided that the Secretary of the Non-Intervention Committee, Mr. Hemming, should go to Spain and endeavour to persuade Franco to abandon his opposi-

[1] The Soviet Government maintained their refusal to contribute to the cost of looking after the German and Italian volunteers while they were being withdrawn. In fact the Soviet Government had paid nothing towards the expenses of the control scheme since September 1937.

[2] On this occasion the Soviet representative, M. Kagan, gave his consent to the adoption of the scheme only in his personal capacity; formal Soviet acceptance of the scheme was notified on 8 July. The International Brigade made its last appearance in the Ebro offensive on 12 July.

[3] *Pravda*, 24 August 1938.

[4] Interview with British Ambassador, 20 August 1938. As has already been noted (*supra*, chap. 2), Soviet supplies had in fact been more plentiful since the fall of Prieto in April 1938 and the establishment of Communist ascendancy in the Spanish Government which followed. But Ciano's statement that considerable supplies were coming through France does not appear to be substantiated.

tion to the Committee's plan. By the middle of the month all the Powers except the U.S.S.R. had agreed to this procedure. But in October, after the Munich crisis had still further widened the breach between the U.S.S.R. and the Western Powers, it was decided to dispense with Soviet consent, and allow Mr. Hemming to go to Burgos.

The situation had meanwhile been altered by the announcement of the Spanish Government at the League Assembly meeting on 21 September 1938, that it was prepared to part with all the volunteers on its own side irrespective of what action Franco might take. It was also announced that the League Council had been requested to appoint a commission to supervise the withdrawal.[1]

On the Sixth (Political) Committee of the Assembly to which the matter was referred, the suggestion to send a commission was opposed by Hungary, Portugal, Poland, and Roumania—an ominous combination from the Soviet point of view. Speaking on 29 September, Litvinov referred to 'the noble and self-sacrificing declaration' of the Spanish Government. He pointed out the distinction in the nature of the 'volunteering' on the two sides. The opponents of the Spanish request had wished the matter referred to the 'so-called Non-Intervention Committee', but this organization had already proved itself a failure. If the Non-Intervention Committee had anything to boast of, it was that it had seriously interfered with the supplies for the legitimate Republican Army and for the provision of food for the civil population, in the territory occupied by the latter. How far, he asked, might the Committee not have gone in supporting the rebels but for the brake applied through Soviet participation in its proceedings.[2] The Committee referred the matter to the Council, which on 30 September approved the Spanish Government's request.

Franco-British conversations in Paris on 19–22 July coincided with the publication of a new set of far-reaching demands which had been made by the Sudeten Germans on 7 June.[3]

During the conversations, the French were informed of the British intention to send Lord Runciman to Czechoslovakia.[4] These conversations were preceded by a visit to London from Captain Wiedemann, a confidential emissary of Hitler's. The nature of his talks with Halifax was not disclosed, although it

---

[1] *L.N.O.J. Spec. Suppl.*, 183. The Spaniards may have been made aware that they could not expect further assistance from the Soviet Union in any considerable quantity.

[2] *L.N.O.J. Spec. Suppl.*, 189, pp. 70–2.

[3] *Documents for 1938*, vol. i, pp. 151–62.   [4] Bonnet, op. cit., pp. 173–4.

was generally assumed that he had gone away empty-handed.[1]
Such were the preliminaries to the announcement of Lord
Runciman's mission made to the House of Commons on 26
July, without preliminary notification to the Soviet Govern-
ment.[2]

On 10 August the Czechoslovak Communist paper *Rote
Fahne* claimed to have been informed by a prominent member
of the British Liberal Party that Lord Runciman's 'chief efforts
in Prague will be in the direction of weakening as much as
possible the Czechoslovak-Russian alliance'.[3] The Soviet press
took much the same line, declaring that Runciman's purpose
was to insist on the neutralization of Czechoslovakia and on its
consequent reduction to a state of helplessness. Polish circles
were said to be discussing the inevitable liquidation of Czechoslovakia and to be planning the seizure of Teschen and
Ruthenia.[4]

Meanwhile Soviet suspicions as to the intentions of some

[1] R. W. Seton-Watson, *Munich and the Dictators*, pp. 45–9.
[2] *Documents for 1938*, pp. 167–8. R. W. Seton-Watson, *Munich and the
Dictators*, p. 92. Nevile Henderson had telegraphed to Halifax that he did
not believe that an independent mediator could succeed. Instead he
suggested asking Italy to join in proposing to Germany and France a four-
Power Conference to settle the problem. At that moment, however, it was
feared that it would be difficult to exclude other Powers from such a
Conference. Hence the decision to send Runciman; N. Henderson, *Failure of
a Mission*, pp. 141–2. The inference is legitimate that what was lacking was
public consent in Great Britain and France to the exclusion of Czechoslovakia and Russia.
[3] A. Henderson, *Eyewitness in Czechoslovakia*, p. 157.
[4] *Manchester Guardian*, 17 August 1938. Cf. Noël, op. cit., pp. 205–9.
On 19 July, the Polish Foreign Minister had been attacked for a series of
visits he had been paying to the Baltic capitals. *Pravda* alleged that he was
trying to create a so-called 'bloc of neutral States extending from the Black
Sea to the Arctic Ocean' which was in reality a Fascist organization intended
as an instrument against Russia. Esthonia, it was alleged, had already fallen
victim to the schemes of 'Hitler's tool', Beck; *B.I.N.*, XV, pp. 672–3. In a
statement made on 16 July, before his departure from Latvia, Beck repeated
that Poland was unwilling to regard Article XVI of the Covenant as other
than optional; ibid., p. 664. On 23 August, *Pravda* returned to the theme of
Beck's diplomacy in the Baltic and Scandinavian countries and in Roumania,
and indicated that his efforts had been unavailing, particularly in Roumania.
An even more violent attack upon Beck appeared in *Pravda* on 31 August in
connexion with the forthcoming session of the League Council and Assembly.
He was accused of trying to wreck the League at the behest of Hitler and
Mussolini, of having blocked action against Japan, and showing hostility
to the Spanish Government. At the same time he was trying to extricate
Poland from the undertakings given by Smigly-Rydz to France in September
1936. Poland was, however, by no means secure itself against German
penetration and aggression, and a recent article to this effect by the Polish
General Sikorski (then in opposition to the Government) was quoted with
approval.

circles in Great Britain may have been stimulated by the fierce controversies between supporters and opponents of the British Prime Minister. 'If you or anyone else', wrote Lord Rothermere to Wickham Steed on 10 August in a letter published on 16 August, 'are so foolish as to believe Great Britain and her Dominions will fight for the Moscow-owned Prague government, you are labouring under some strange delusion.'[1] In France there were reports that the Soviet Union could not be relied on, since it would soon come to terms with Germany.[2]

The Russian press adopted an attitude of comparative detachment towards the continued political and diplomatic activity in Czechoslovakia, drawing attention, however, to foreign reports of German military preparations and of reactions to these reports in other countries concerned.[3]

A more acute phase of the crisis opened on 26 August with the sudden recrudescence of alarming reports about tension in the Sudetenland itself.[4] Speaking at Lanark on 27 August, Sir John Simon restated the objectives of the policy of appeasement and its relations to Czechoslovakia.[5] A warning to the German Government not to proceed to the use of force was intended, however, in one passage:

'There is no need to emphasize the importance of finding a peaceful solution. For in the modern world there is no limit to the reactions of war. This very case of Czechoslovakia may be so critical

[1] *Daily Herald*, 16 August 1938.

[2] One writer asserted that Stalin having had Tukhachevsky and his associates executed for planning a *rapprochement* with Germany, was now preparing to adopt his policy as his own. It was claimed in support of this thesis, that the German Army crisis of February 1938 had resulted in the elimination of the elements most strongly opposed to collaboration with Russia, and attention was drawn to the still important economic contacts between the two countries. J. de Saint-Chamant; 'Après le Procès de Moscou: Les Contacts Germano-Russes', *Revue des Deux Mondes*, 1 July 1938.

[3] After the Conference of the Little Entente on 21–22 August and the conclusion of an agreement to recognize Hungary's claim to equality of rights in the matter of armaments in return for the latter's agreeing to enter into non-aggression pacts with them, *Pravda*, which had discounted the possibility of such a conclusion to the talks, printed a report of a German-Hungarian agreement directed against Czechoslovakia; *Documents for 1938*, vol. i, pp. 282–4; *Pravda*, 22, 23, and 26 August 1938. On 25 August orders were issued to the German Air Force as to its operations against England and France, should these Powers intervene; *Nuremberg Trial*, part II, p. 76.

[4] It was understood that German diplomatic representatives in Belgrade and Bucarest had given warnings that Germany might have to intervene and that she would not consider this as justifying intervention by any other State. There was also a report that the German representative in Moscow had been warned that such intervention would be considered a *casus belli* under the Soviet-Czechoslovak treaty. Cf. Wheeler-Bennett, op. cit., p. 86.

[5] *Documents for 1938*, vol. i, pp. 89–91.

for the future of Europe that it would be impossible to assume a limit
to the disturbance that a conflict might involve, and everyone in
every country who considers the consequences has to bear that in
mind.'

On 29 August, *Pravda* quoted *L'Humanité* as saying that Simon
was wrong to put the Czechs and Henleinists on the same footing, although it admitted that the speech marked a step forward
on England's part. But in an article in *Pravda* on 30 August,
on 'England and the Czechoslovak question', Simon's speech
was declared to advance things no further. He had said that
England could not remain unaffected by an outbreak of war in
Central Europe, but he had made no concrete suggestions, and
had had nothing to add to Chamberlain's statement that he
could not undertake any responsibilities for guaranteeing the
independence of Czechoslovakia. 'The days of May showed
that an aggressor can only be restrained by collective action . . .
Simon's speech contains no word about collective resistance to
an aggressor.' The British Cabinet (due to meet on the 30th)
should realize that only collective action by peaceful countries
including Great Britain was of any use. In that respect the
Reuter communiqué on the meeting, which *Pravda* quoted next
day, could give little satisfaction.

On 1 and 2 September Henlein saw Hitler and at Runciman's request also conveyed a message from himself. It appears
that the final time-table of the crisis was established by the
German Government at about this time, since, according to the
Nuremberg trial indictment, 'by 3rd of September 1938, it
was decided that all troops were to be ready for action on
28 September 1938.'[1] Reports on German military preparations continued to appear in the Soviet press, coupled with
reports tending to show widespread dissatisfaction in Germany
with the bellicose policy of the German Government.

In face of the evidence that no plan so far produced by the
Czechoslovak Government would be acceptable, and that
German pressure was increasing, the attitude of the Western
Powers had to be redefined. The position in France was complicated by the increasing internal opposition to Daladier's
Government. In spite of their simultaneous demands for a
firm front against aggression, the French Communists took the
lead in this and on 31 August, *L'Humanité* denounced as an attack
by the '200 families' upon the working-class, a decree of
Daladier sanctioning unlimited overtime in the defence industries and further overtime in others. The internal political
strife in France received a good share of attention in the Soviet

[1] *Nuremberg Trial*, part I, p. 8.

press. Spender attaches considerable importance to an unfavourable report on Soviet military strength said to have been
made by the French Intelligence in August and passed on to
the British.[1] On 4 September, however, Bonnet declared in a
public speech, with specific reference to Czechoslovakia: 'In
all cases, France will remain faithful to the pacts and treaties
which she has concluded. She will remain faithful to the engagements which she has made.'[2]

At the end of August and the beginning of September the
British Government gave a series of warnings to Germany; this
was made public in a Reuter communiqué of 11 September. But
the British attitude was criticized for its indecisiveness by the
Geneva correspondent of *Pravda* on 13 September.[3]

While Great Britain was thus endeavouring to restrain
Germany, her diplomacy was no less active at Prague.[4]

A leading article in *The Times* on 7 September, suggesting
that Czechoslovakia cede outright the 'fringe of alien popula-

[1] This report was, he asserts, reproduced in substance in an article which
appeared in a French review after 'Munich' ('Le Traité Franco-Soviétique
du 2 mai 1935 et ses conséquences', *Revue de Paris*, 1 January 1939). The
article argues that Russia could not intervene against Germany if the latter
should attack France and therefore that France should denounce the Franco-
Soviet Pact as purely one-sided. The description which the author gives of
Russia's fighting forces can be summed up in his own words: 'the Russian
Army at the present time is strong in numbers, organized and equipped in
an up-to-date fashion but mediocre as to its cadres and high command.'
He further emphasizes the unsuitability of Russia's western frontier, apart
from the Galician plain, for the deployment of her large mechanized armies
and stresses the poor development of railways in the frontier zone. On the
political side, 'the Russian Army is not a national army; it is not merely a
class army, but the instrument of the world revolution of the proletariat'.
To this is ascribed in part the hesitation of both Poland and Roumania, a
reluctance fortified in the case of the latter by the Roumanian Constitution's specific prohibition of the transit of foreign troops without special
legislation. This point might have been regarded as academic. Other
authorities attach importance to the influence of the American airman
Lindbergh, then resident in England. Lindbergh returned to London on
10 September 1938, after visiting Moscow, and was reported to have
declared that the Soviet Air Force was demoralized and that the Nazi Air
Force could easily defeat that of Great Britain, France, Czechoslovakia, and
the U.S.S.R. together. On 10 October, while the Soviet press featured
reports of Lindbergh's pro-German activity, the airman went to Germany
'to be fêted by Nazi air officials'. Schuman, *Europe on the Eve*, pp. 468–9.

[2] *Documents for 1938*, vol. ii, pp. 177–8. On the following day, certain
military precautions were announced; ibid., vol. i, p. 217. Further military
measures in France and naval precautions in Great Britain were reported
during the following days.

[3] N. Henderson, *Failure of a Mission*, pp. 144–7.

[4] On this see Lord Runciman's report on his mission. This was made
orally to the Cabinet on his return on 16 September, and was published in
the form of a letter to the Prime Minister on the 21st; Cmd. 5847.

tions who are contiguous to the nation with which they are united by race', was not propitious for a negotiated settlement within the framework of the Czechoslovak State, which was still the ostensible object of British diplomacy.[1] The publication of this article was indeed reported in *Pravda* on 8 September under the headline, '*The Times* supports Hitler's plans'.

In contrast to the activity of the Western Powers, the diplomacy of the Soviet Union in the early days of September was marked by its now customary passivity. In the pamphlet already referred to, the Soviet historian, Potemkin, asks: 'Is it not a fact that the French Government received an absolutely definite declaration on this question from the Soviet Government in reply to its inquiry made at the beginning of September 1938?'[2] Following a conversation in Paris between Bonnet and Suritz on 26 August, the French Government telegraphed to M. Payart its Chargé d'Affaires in Moscow on the 31st instructing him to inquire what methods of helping the Czechs were envisaged in view of the obduracy of Poland and Roumania. M. Payart saw Potemkin on 1 September and Litvinov on 2 September. According to the Soviet version of these talks Litvinov gave a categorical assurance that the U.S.S.R. was prepared to fulfil its treaty obligations and suggested that immediate staff talks should be held between Moscow, Prague, and Paris and that the Czechs should formally invoke Article XI of the Covenant.[3] According to M. Daladier the French Government took the initiative and sent a telegram to Moscow to inquire what methods of helping Czechoslovakia were envisaged. In the subsequent interview Litvinov said that the Soviet Union was determined to fulfil her obligations if France did so. He wanted to know what actual measures the French proposed. M. Payart insisted on keeping to general questions and declared that France's position had been clearly defined and that he wanted to know the Soviet Union's position in the matter. M. Payart's report of the conversation continued as follows: 'Litvinov indicated to me that in view of the negative attitude adopted by Warsaw and Bucarest he could see only one practical step, that of a recourse to the League of Nations. He mentioned, but only to exclude it *a priori*, the eventuality of a passage by force of Soviet troops, apart from a decision at Geneva, through Poland and Roumania.' In the circumstances, asserts

---

[1] The British Government denied on the same day that the article represented an official viewpoint.
[2] p. 14.
[3] This was revealed in Litvinov's speech before the League Assembly on 21 September; *L.N.O.J. Spec. Suppl.*, 183, pp. 74–8.

M. Daladier, he was determined that France should not declare war on Germany alone and made this clear to Prague.[1] It is uncertain whether the Soviet Union did anything to clarify its attitude by a direct intimation to Germany.[2]

On 7 September, *Pravda's* London correspondent declared that no one doubted that the U.S.S.R. would fulfil its obligations to Czechoslovakia, but that there were very grave doubts as to whether France would honour her undertakings, both because of opposition from right-wing circles inside France, and because of pressure not to do so which would be forthcoming from the British Government, and on 8 September, Maisky discussed the position with Halifax. On the same day *Pravda* denounced the British pressure on Czechoslovakia which had brought about the offer of the '*Fourth Plan*', or, as the Russians regarded it, the acceptance of Henlein's Karlsbad Programme. Henceforth the Soviet press attacks on Great Britain grew ever more direct, although they were couched normally in the usual Soviet form of quotations from the foreign press (British, French, and American).

On 8 September, also, *Pravda* called attention to Polish moves to take advantage of Czechoslovakia's plight,[3] but the Soviet press of the time does not give the impression that the crisis was regarded as one which might at any moment plunge the Soviet Union itself into war. Suggestions that the Soviet Union itself might act were confined to an occasional report of some demand by a British opposition group that the British Government ought to seek to co-operate with the French and Soviet Governments in resisting further aggression.[4] No notice was

[1] Daladier, speech of 18 July 1946. Cf. Bonnet, op. cit., pp. 197–9. The extracts given by Bonnet from Payart's report of his conversation with Litvinov make no mention of the proposed staff talks. See *infra*, p. 166.

[2] There was a report on 5 September that Litvinov had told the German Ambassador in Moscow that the U.S.S.R. was prepared to fight for Czechoslovakia if necessary; *B.I.N.*, XV, p. 794. The evidence at the Nuremberg trial shows that the Germans seem to have reckoned with the possibility that the Russians might give some assistance to the Czechs. Military precautions are said to have been taken in White Russia and the Ukraine; André Pierre, 'L'URSS et la Tchécoslovaquie', *Europe Nouvelle*, 15 October 1938.

[3] On 8 September, the first meeting took place between representatives of the Sudeten Germans and the leaders of the Slovak, Magyar, and Polish minorities. The semi-official Polish press made furious attacks on the Czechs, and the Poles renewed former protests against the alleged anti-Polish intrigues of a Comintern agency in Prague; Noël, op. cit., p. 215. Hungary's willingness to assist Germany provided the attitude of the other members of the Little Entente was assured, was established during the visit of Horthy to Berlin on 21–26 August 1938; *Nuremberg Trial*, part II, pp. 14–16.

[4] On 9 September, *Pravda* reported a resolution to this effect by the British National Council of Labour.

taken of the German propaganda campaign designed to discredit Czechoslovakia as an outpost of Bolshevism.

Hitler himself took the lead in this with an adroit declaration to a French newspaper correspondent which appeared in *Le Journal* on 2 September:

'From the time of Ivan the Terrible and Peter the First, Russia, considered historically, has developed along inherently necessary lines, at least that is how it seems to me. . . . I am even tempted to say that, in the Soviet régime, Russia has found a form of organization fairly well suited to her. But for the rest of Europe this form of organization could only lead to major disaster.

'I believe moreover that the Russian Bolshevik mentality differs too greatly from the mentality of other European nations for co-operation in any common undertaking to be possible between them.

'As to the absorption of other territories by Bolshevism, it is impossible to be indifferent to this question. We are not living in a closed room, in a vacuum. Interchanges with other nations are going on all the time. . . .

'Now, I no longer believe in the victory of Bolshevization in countries like Holland, Belgium, or France. . . . In these countries Russo-Asiatic Communism has been defeated.

'Had Germany given way, there would be no hope left for Europe. . . . It was Germany which at the last moment halted the onrush of a tragic fate.'[1]

We know, said Goering at Nuremberg on 10 September, 'that it is not these absurd pygmies [the Czechs] who are responsible. It is Moscow and the eternal grimacing Jewish-Bolshevist rabble behind it.'[2] On the same day Goebbels amplified the charge:

'We know all about Bolshevist wireless and film propaganda. We know all about Moscow's influence with the Prague Press—particularly with the bourgeois democratic papers—and we know that the Czech Government looks on with approval at these activities of Moscow. What is not so well known is that Prague represents the organizing centre of Bolshevist plots against Europe.'[3]

With the opening of the meeting of the League Council at Geneva on 9 September, and of the Assembly on the 12th, the focus of diplomatic activity was shifted there. Litvinov included in his entourage the Soviet representatives in Paris, Rome, Berlin, London, and Stockholm. On 11 September Litvinov repeated to Bonnet the assurances as to the Soviet attitude

---

[1] *Hitler's Speeches*, pp. 1466–9. In the proclamation opening the Nuremberg Rally, Hitler talked of 'the Bolshevist danger of a destruction of the life of peoples' rising more threatening than ever over the world; ibid., pp. 1469–72.

[2] *Documents for 1938*, vol. ii, p. 189.   [3] *Hitler's Speeches*, p. 1471.

already given to M. Payart.[1] But at the same time he made it clear that any military action by the Soviet Union was out of the question until the League Council had persuaded Roumania to allow the passage of Soviet troops and aircraft, and until Roumania had agreed to this course.[2]

On 12 September it was reported that he had secured agreement from the Roumanian Foreign Minister for the passage of Soviet aid for the Czechoslovaks across Roumanian territory, subject presumably to a League designation of the aggressor.[3]

[1] Bonnet, op. cit., pp. 198–200. *Pravda*, reporting on the 12th that Litvinov had seen Bonnet and the Roumanian Foreign Minister, gave no indication of the subject of the talks. It has been alleged that Bonnet on this as on other occasions misled his colleagues as to the nature of his information on Soviet policy. See e.g. 'Pertinax', op. cit., vol. i, p. 106. For the extent to which Bonnet ran a personal as contrasted with a Cabinet policy in 1938–9, see Noël, op. cit., *passim*. It should be noted, however, that whatever Bonnet's guilt in the matter of misrepresenting Soviet purposes may have been, it lay well within the power of the Soviet Government to make their position clearer to the French and British Governments and to their peoples than in fact they did; their reticence about the possibility of their being involved in war made it all too easy for those who wished to demonstrate that no such possibility existed. The first unmistakable public pronouncement of Soviet policy was that by Litvinov on 21 September, when matters were already a long way advanced towards the ultimate settlement.   [2] Noël, op. cit., p. 225.

[3] M. Petrescu-Comnène became Foreign Minister in Carol's reconstructed Government of National Concentration and remained so until replaced by M. Gafencu on 21 December. In a statement of policy on 7 April, he had declared his Government's intention of working 'in all sincerity for the development of the good neighbourly relations which exist between Roumania and the U.S.S.R.' (*Documents for 1938*, vol. i, pp. 291–2.) On the whole these relations seem to have been uneventful during the summer. It is difficult to discover how far the Roumanian Foreign Minister declared his country ready to go during this interview with Litvinov. M. Ripka says that 'every arrangement was made for the passage of Soviet troops over Roumanian territory on their way to Czechoslovakia'; op. cit., pp. 338–9; cf. Thomson, op. cit., p. 338. *L'Europe Nouvelle* (24 September 1938) declares that Roumania, asked for a direct right of passage, had insisted instead on a previous action by the League, under pressure from Poland that the Polish-Roumanian alliance would otherwise be denounced (p. 1030). According to M. Gafencu, Roumania declared itself ready to assist Czechoslovakia and persisted in this loyal attitude until the eve of Munich, but she was unable to bring herself to undertake in advance to allow the passage of Soviet troops through her territory; G. Gafencu, *Derniers Jours de l'Europe*, (Paris, Egloff, 1946), p. 148. Schuman suggests that Petrescu-Comnène's attitude was equivocal on the 12th; on the 20th, he declares, it was made known that Roumania would only permit passage by Soviet troops if France were also fighting for Czechoslovakia (*Europe on the Eve*, pp. 401 and 420). One Czechoslovak view at the time was that Roumania would not have been able to resist Soviet demands if they were made for fear that the Russians would raise the Bessarabian question; E. Lennhoff, *In Defence of Dr. Benes and Czech Democracy* (Rich and Cowan, 1938), p. 152.

But it is now fairly clear that this agreement had not in fact been secured.[1]

Hitler wound up the Nuremberg Rally on 12 September with a speech in which he violently attacked Bolshevism and the Czechs, declaring Germany's determination to see that the Sudeten Germans got 'the free right of self-determination'. He also warned the Western Powers against intervention, underlining his warning by pointing to the massive defences which had been in construction along Germany's western frontier ever since 28 May.[2] *Pravda* reported that the speech had violently attacked Czechoslovakia but gave no other indication of its contents and proceeded to quote hostile comments upon it from the foreign press.

On the night of 13–14 September the French and British Governments agreed that Chamberlain should fly to see Hitler, and this decision was announced on the evening of the 15th.[3] The full international significance of the situation was seen when on 14 September, a Japanese official statement included the following remarks:

'For the present complication of the Sudeten question the responsibility lies largely on the machinations of the Comintern, which is pulling the strings behind the Czechoslovak Government. . . . Since the position of Czechoslovakia as a base for the Comintern's machinations for the bolshevization of Europe is exactly similar to that of China in East Asia, we can readily see the ways of the Comintern in Europe. And Japan is prepared as ever to join forces with Germany and Italy for fighting against the Red operations in accordance with the spirit of the Anti-Comintern agreement.'[4]

Italian press comment followed similar lines.[5]

The Soviet Government were not informed in advance of Chamberlain's project. Indeed, every step taken by the British and French Governments throughout the crisis was taken with-

---

[1] Bonnet, op. cit., pp. 200–3 and 304 *n.*, where he quotes an article by M. Comnène himself.

[2] *Hitler's Speeches*, pp. 1487–99.

[3] It is worth noting in this connexion that one member of Chamberlain's Cabinet has since stated that it was on 13 September that the French Government definitely decided they would not go to war in defence of Czechoslovakia; Maugham, op. cit., p. 36.

[4] *Documents for 1938*, vol. ii, pp. 204–5.

[5] *B.I.N.*, 24 September 1938, pp. 40–1. Signor Mussolini's unsigned open 'Letter to Lord Runciman', published on the 15th, was more cautious, attacking freemasonry instead of Bolshevism. *Documents for 1938*, vol. ii, pp. 206–8. But in a speech on the 18th, he talked of the 'campaign of Moscow' hindering a solution, ibid., pp. 239–40.

out prior notification to the Russians.[1] The reaction of the
Soviet press on the 15th to the news of Chamberlain's flight
was as hostile as the previous comments on British policy.[2] On
17 September *Pravda* devoted a long article to the subject:

'It is necessary to clarify the situation and for that it is necessary
to consider what can have persuaded the British Prime Minister to
ask Hitler for an interview. The British Prime Minister, one must
assume, was disturbed by the following circumstances: (1) The total
failure of the Runciman mission, which on the one hand did not
succeed in bringing about the capitulation of the Czechoslovak
Government, and which on the other hand revealed, perhaps against
its own will and desires, the utter hopelessness of the effort to
negotiate with the Henleinists. (2) The fact that the Henleinist
putsch and its accompanying circumstances have given extreme
actuality to the possibility of an armed conflict, to the possibility of
an open attack by Germany on the Czechoslovak Republic. In
that case France would be obliged to act and Great Britain would
seem faced with the prospect of being drawn into the conflict not on
the side of Germany but against her.

'Mr. Chamberlain's conception of foreign policy is well known—
he stubbornly advocates an accord and a deal with the aggressor.
Of that even the German Fascist press is a witness. For instance, the
Deutsche Allgemeine Zeitung wrote with reference to Chamberlain's
journey: "To Germany there travels a man, who has staked his
political career upon achieving an understanding with the authori-
tarian (i.e. the Fascist) States."

'There can be no doubt that if Mr. Chamberlain wished to
declare in the name of his Government, that Great Britain, together
with other peace-loving countries, would not permit the violation
of the independence and integrity of the Czechoslovak Republic,
there would be no need for the "dramatic gesture" to which the
British Prime Minister has had recourse. It is quite clear that the
journey to Germany had the purpose of a deal, for which it is wished

---

[1] 'Ni le 15 septembre lorsque Chamberlain partit pour Berchtesgaden, ni
le 22 quand il se rendit à Godesberg, ni le 28 quand Anglais et Francais
proposèrent la conférence, les Russes n'avaient été avertis à temps, eux, alliés
ou si l'on veut associés.' 'Pertinax', op. cit., vol. ii, p. 111. Later claims
that consultation had been adequate, such as that made in the House of
Commons by Sir Samuel Hoare on 3 October, were contradicted by Tass.
'In the course of the interviews of M. Bonnet with M. Suritz and of Lord
Halifax with M. Maisky, which took place during the final period, the two
Ambassadors of the Soviet Union were given no information other than what
had appeared in the daily press. There was no sort of a conference and
still less an agreement between the Governments of the U.S.S.R., France,
and England with regard to the fate of the Czechoslovak Republic or to the
question of concessions to the aggressor. Neither France nor England
consulted the U.S.S.R., but confined themselves merely to informing the
Soviet Government of what had already happened.' *Pravda*, 4 October 1938.

[2] *B.I.N.*, XV, pp. 850–1.

to make Czechoslovakia pay. It is by no means an accident that the French and British press openly wrote that the Berchtesgaden talks would turn on the holding in the Sudeten region of a "plebiscite" on the model of that which was held in the Saar.

'At the moment there are no detailed reports on the results of the discussions between Chamberlain and Hitler. At any rate it is now possible and indeed essential to make plain the following: the British Government has not followed the path of collective security, opposing to the aggressor a front of peace-loving States. Neville Chamberlain, as it is said, has the intention of trying to call a conference of three or four Powers, that is to say Great Britain, France, and Germany and perhaps Italy, for the consideration of the Czechoslovak problem, alongside other European problems. In other words, the famous "four-Power pact" project, which Chamberlain will in no way be able to carry out, is again being taken from the archives.

'The British Conservative papers, and Conservative circles which support Chamberlain, wish to make political capital out of the notion that an understanding with Fascist Germany, new concessions to Hitler, would eliminate the possibility of an armed conflict and save Europe from war. There is no more fallacious belief. The policy of coming to an understanding with the aggressor does not put war off but brings it nearer. The facts declare this eloquently enough.

'The days of May showed that only a lasting front of the peace-loving Powers can halt the aggressor. No other methods can influence the incendiaries of war. It is easy to see what the results of the new concessions to Hitler would be if Czechoslovakia, under pressure from Great Britain and France, accepted them. The German Fascists demand the annexation of the Sudeten region to Germany. One must be blind not to see that this would put an end to the independence of Czechoslovakia and would open the way for Fascist Germany to establish its hegemony over central and southeastern Europe. This would mean that Fascist Germany, secure in its rear and its sources of raw materials, would be able sharply to increase its intervention in Spain. This would mean the Fascist encirclement of France, depriving her of her last points of support in Europe.

'One of the most decisive factors in the present situation is the position of France. If France takes up the firm position that the Czechoslovak Government has just assumed, then no efforts of Chamberlain will avail to persuade Czechoslovakia to give way before the aggressor. If France turns out to be following Chamberlain's lead, then the meeting in Berchtesgaden may prove to involve consequences from which both the cause of peace will suffer, and, in the first place, the safety of France and Great Britain.

'Chamberlain's journey to Berlin is an effort to deceive world opinion, to deceive the peoples, and beneath the flag of peace-bringing gestures to bring off an agreement with the aggressors. It is an effort with unworthy means whose import will be revealed in the very near future.'[1]

This analysis of the situation, with its omission of any mention of the possibility that the U.S.S.R. might itself be involved in the conflict if France did stand firm, is certainly significant. The mention of the 'four-Power' pact—what amounts indeed to a forecast of Munich itself—links the Soviet attitude over the Czechoslovak crisis to its earlier and later attitudes to European affairs. It remains to be seen how far the Soviet attitude was consistent with this during the remainder of the crisis.

On 18 September there was a conference in London between the British and French Ministers. Their communiqué, besides declaring that they were agreed upon their policy towards Czechoslovakia, expressed the hope that thereafter it would be possible 'to consider a more general settlement in the interests of European peace'. What this involved was seen when the Anglo-French proposals were submitted to the Czechoslovak Government on 19 September.[2] The most immediate stipulation was that for the cession of all districts containing more than 50 per cent of Germans. But from the Soviet point of view, the most significant paragraphs were the following:

'5. We recognize that, if the Czechoslovak Government is prepared to concur in the measures proposed, involving material changes in the conditions of the State, they are entitled to ask for some assurance of their future security.

'6. Accordingly H. M. Government in the United Kingdom is prepared as a contribution to the pacification of Europe, to join in an international guarantee of the new boundaries of the Czechoslovak State against unprovoked aggression. One of the principal conditions of such a guarantee would be the safeguarding of the independence of Czechoslovakia by the substitution of a general guarantee against unprovoked aggression in the place of existing treaties which involve reciprocal obligations of a military character.'[3]

When Lord Runciman's report was published on the 21st,

---

[1] On the 17th Prague had made a semi-official proposal to cede certain portions of the disputed territory containing a population of 800,000 or 900,000 Sudeten Germans; Daladier, speech of 18 July 1946. Daladier reported to his Cabinet on the 19th that Chamberlain was still against any British commitment in central Europe; *Carnets Secrets de Jean Zay*, pp. 4-7; Anatole de Monzie, *Ci-devant* (Paris, Flammarion, 1942), pp. 31-2. Cf. Bonnet, op. cit., pp. 238-41.

[2] The proposals were first published on 28 September in the British White Paper, Cmd. 5847; but their contents were no secret from the start.

[3] M. Bonnet claims that he thus secured the promise of a British guarantee for the new Czechoslovakia *in addition* to the existing treaties between Czechoslovakia and France, and Czechoslovakia and the U.S.S.R., op. cit., pp. 238-41, 260.

the reasoning which underlay the proposals was made clearer. He wrote:

'I believe that the [political side of the] problem is one of removing a centre of intense political friction from the middle of Europe. For this purpose it is necessary permanently to provide that the Czechoslovak State should live at peace with her neighbours and that her policy, internal and external, should be directed to that end. Just as it is essential for the international position of Switzerland that her policy should be entirely neutral, so an analogous policy is necessary for Czechoslovakia—not only for her own future existence but for the peace of Europe.'[1]

The Czechoslovak note rejecting these proposals was based on the territorial cessions demanded and was intended to permit further negotiations.[2] Comment on the suggestion that the country's international status should be changed was confined to the following remarks:

'The Czechoslovak Government are sincerely grateful to the Great Powers for their intention of guaranteeing the integrity of Czechslovakia; they appreciate it and value it highly. Such a guarantee would certainly open the way to an agreement between all the interested Powers, if the present nationality conflicts were settled amicably and in such a manner as not to impose unacceptable sacrifices on Czechoslovakia.'

It was on 19 or 20 September that Benes is said to have put verbal inquiries to Alexandrovsky, the Soviet Minister in Prague. The first—whether the Soviet Union would honour her pact—was answered in the affirmative. The second was what Russia's advice would be in the event of France dishonouring her signature. The reply was that Czechoslovakia should appeal to the League and that upon Germany being branded as an aggressor for failing to make a case, the U.S.S.R. would come at once to the assistance of the Czechs whatever the other Powers might do.[3]

'It would', remarks Dr. Ripka, 'have been more than dangerous to ask Russia to act independently of France and the League of

[1] In addition to remodelling her foreign policy 'so as to give assurances to her neighbours that she will in no circumstances attack them or enter into any aggressive action against them arising from obligations to other States', Czechoslovakia was recommended to forbid, if necessary by legal measures, agitation by parties and persons 'who have been deliberately encouraging a policy antagonistic to Czechoslovakia's neighbours', i.e. the Communist party. Cmd. 5847.

[2] *Documents for 1938*, vol. ii, pp. 214–16; Czechoslovak Government communiqué of 20 September 1938; *Pravda*, 21 September.

[3] G. Vernadsky, loc. cit., p. 520. Cf. Gedye, *Fallen Bastions*, pp. 425–6; R. W. Seton-Watson, *History of the Czechs and Slovaks*, p. 364. The latter adds, however, that 'Moscow never attempted to define the exact manner in which assistance would be made effective'. See Note 2, p. 166 *infra*.

Nations, for Britain and France, who were supporting German claims in the dispute and who were therefore opposing us, would have considered such Russian intervention on our part as a dangerous expansion of "Bolshevism" in Europe. . . . To ask help from Soviet Russia alone would have been dangerous from internal Czechoslovak reasons also, for although all our political parties were united in favour of seeking help from France and Russia combined, the parties of the Right would certainly have protested against accepting help from Russia alone.'[1]

The version of these events made public by Litvinov in his speech to the League Assembly on 21 September was less dramatic.[2] He said that on the 19th, a formal inquiry had been addressed by the Czechoslovak Government to the Soviet Government as to whether it was prepared 'in accordance with the Soviet-Czech Pact to render Czechoslovakia immediate and effective aid, if France, loyal to her obligations' were to render 'similar assistance'. To this the Soviet Government, according to Litvinov, gave a clear answer in the affirmative.

From 18 to 20 September, the Soviet press continued to print foreign press comment on the development of the situation and to present it in a manner thoroughly hostile to the reported Anglo-French plans. Attention was also focused on the steps by which Poland and Hungary came to range themselves openly on Germany's side and to demand that their minorities in Czechoslovakia should benefit equally from any concessions granted to the Germans.[3]

---

[1] Ripka, op. cit., pp. 85–7. Cf. R. W. Seton-Watson, *Munich and the Dictators*, pp. 69–70; 90–1. B. Schmitt in *Czechoslovakia, Twenty Years of Independence* (edited R. J. Kerner), p. 424.

[2] *L.N.O.J. Spec. Suppl.*, 183, pp. 74–8. Dr. Ripka says: 'During the critical days before and after Berchtesgaden, the Czechoslovak Government put two questions to the Soviet Government: (1) Would the U.S.S.R. fulfil their obligations under the Pact of Mutual Assistance? (i.e. would they come to the assistance of Czechoslovakia if France did so?) The answer was in the affirmative. (2) Would the U.S.S.R. fulfil their obligations arising out of their membership of the League of Nations? The answer was again unconditionally in the affirmative.' op. cit., pp. 145–7.

[3] Hungarian and Polish representations were made in London on 19 and 20 September and in Prague on 21 and 22 September. Chamberlain, *House of Commons Debates*, 28 September 1938.

On 21 September Lord Halifax received the Polish Ambassador, who presented his Government's case for the cession to Poland of the area in Teschen containing the Polish minority in Czechoslovakia. The Hungarian Minister in London was also understood to have told the Foreign Office that his Government considered any concessions made to the Sudeten Germans should also be made to the Magyar minority, who would not be satisfied with autonomy if the Germans were allowed to secede; Hungary's views were further conveyed to the Czechoslovaks on 26 September. *Documents for 1938*, vol. ii, p. 344. On 19 September Beck demanded the cession of

On 20 September, it was reported from Geneva that the Soviet delegation there had definitely denied suggestions that the U.S.S.R. had declined to fulfil its obligations.[1] On 21 September *Pravda* (for the first time) devoted a front-page leading article to the crisis: 'Playing with Fire'. The emphasis was again on the danger to England and France of their connivance in Germany's aggressive plans. 'Self-determination' could hardly appeal for long to Powers with vast dependent empires. The path of concessions to the aggressor would lead to further demands and was destroying all confidence in international agreements and in promises of support from Great Britain and France. With regard to manifestations of Polish interest in the question of Czechoslovakia's minorities, *Pravda* commented as follows:

'If one were to reckon how many Poles live in the Ukrainian and White Russian territories of the Polish State, it is doubtful whether the result of this calculation would serve as an argument in favour of these provinces belonging to Poland. Further, if one is to interest oneself in ticklish questions, the answer to the question by what right of national self-determination, and generally speaking by what right, Poland rules the Ukrainian and White Russian population, would be no less eloquent.'

In conclusion, the Soviet Union's own position was stated:

'The Soviet Government is the only government which supports firmly and to the end the cause of general peace, of international law and security. Our country, which has ended every form of subjugation within its own boundaries, appears as the firm opponent of every form of national and colonial subjugation, wherever it may take place. The Soviet Union views with equanimity the question as to which imperialist robber gives orders in one or other colony, in one or other vassal State; for it sees no difference between German and English robbers. But these questions cannot be a matter of indifference to the "democratic countries" of Western Europe. In agreeing to robbery at Czechoslovakia's expense and in giving it their blessing, Great Britain and France are *playing with fire*; for

---

Teschen and on the 21st, Poland denounced the Polish-Czechoslovak Minorities Convention of 1925; Noël, op. cit., p. 215; cf. Bonnet, op. cit., pp. 255–60. Both sets of demands were strongly supported by Mussolini, in his speeches on 18 and 21 September; *Documents for 1938*, vol. ii, pp. 239–41. On 25 September, the Roumanian and Yugoslav Governments notified their intention of fulfilling their obligations under the Little Entente treaties, if Hungary attacked Czechoslovakia; Ripka, op. cit., p. 145. Cf. 'La Politique de Bucarest', *Europe Nouvelle*, 1 October 1938. The same article pointed out, however, the existence of strong pro-Axis currents in Roumania and said that some circles were prepared to make territorial cessions to Hungary if an anti-Soviet war were to permit Roumania to annex Soviet Moldavia.

[1] *B.I.N.*, XV, p.297.

tomorrow the same questions may be put before them with reference to some territories in Asia or Africa under the domination of the "democratic" Powers.'

Thus, from dividing the world into 'Fascist aggressors' and 'peace-loving' States, the Soviet interpreters had come full circle, back to their impartial condemnation of all 'imperialist' States. The logic of the later Soviet-German Pact of August 1939 is implicit in this argument. And once again, the possibility of the Soviet Union itself being involved in war, is overlooked.[1]

During the night of 20–21 September the Czechoslovak Government, under extreme pressure from Great Britain and France, accepted the Anglo-French proposals.[2]

The surrender of the Czechoslovak Government had not been made public when Litvinov spoke at the League Assembly on the 21st.[3]

'One of the oldest, most cultured, most hard-working of European peoples, which acquired its independence as a State after centuries of oppression, to-day or to-morrow may decide to take up arms in defence of that independence.'

Later on, he pointed out that the Soviet Government had not offered any advice to the Czechoslovak Government on the problem of the Sudeten Germans

'considering it inadmissible that it should be asked to make concessions to the Germans, to the detriment of its interests as a State, in

[1] E. Wollenberg refers to this article and to that of 17 September in the course of his endeavour to prove that the Soviet Government made no attempt to prepare its people for war over the Czechoslovak issue; *The Red Army*, pp. 283–5.

[2] It does not seem appropriate here to go into the course of events during the 20th and 21st. See R. W. Seton-Watson, *Munich and the Dictators*, pp. 65–72; Armstrong, op. cit., pp. 68–76; Morrell, op. cit., pp. 190–5; A. Henderson, *Eyewitness in Czechoslovakia*, pp. 201–7; H. Beuve-Méry, *Europe Nouvelle*, 29 October 1938; H. Hauser, ibid., 12 November 1938; Schuman, op. cit., pp. 419–22; Ripka, op. cit., pp. 78–119. The text of the telegram from Lacroix to Bonnet conveying Benes' request for a formal notification of France's repudiation of her obligations is in P. Lazareff, *De Munich à Vichy* (New York, Brentano, 1944), pp. 61–2. Cf. de Monzie, op. cit., p. 47; Noël, op. cit., pp. 226–7. There was also a report on the 20th that Benes had asked the French to demand that the dispute should be submitted to arbitration according to the German-Czechoslovak Treaty of 16 October 1925; *Carnets Secrets de Jean Zay*, pp. 16–17. It seems clear that, for reasons already discussed, the Czechoslovak Government would not consider asking for Soviet assistance alone. Speaking to Munters, the Latvian Foreign Minister, on 3 October 1939, Stalin is reported to have said: 'The Czechs wanted to fight and also the heads of the army but the leaders spoilt this.' *Latvian White Book* (Washington, 1942), p. 101.

[3] *L.N.O.J. Spec. Suppl.*, 183, loc. cit.

order that we should be set free from fulfilling our obligations under the treaty bearing our signature.'

Litvinov then disclosed, as already described, the assurances which had been given to France and Czechoslovakia:

'It is not our fault, if no effect was given to our proposals, which I am convinced could have produced the desired results, both in the interests of Czechoslovakia, and in those of all Europe and of general peace. Unfortunately other steps were taken which have led, and which could not but lead to such a capitulation as is bound sooner or later to have quite incalculable and disastrous consequences.'[1]

The note of 21 September from the Czechoslovak Government in reply to the Anglo-French proposals 'accepted these proposals as a whole, from which the principle of a guarantee ... cannot be detached', but did not specifically mention the proposed denunciation of Czechoslovakia's existing treaties. A Czechoslovak Government broadcast on the same evening, after referring to the fact that Great Britain and France would not have helped in the event of a German attack, continued as follows:

'since the Soviet Union could afford us military help only in company with France, or alternatively, if France would not act, (not) until Germany had been declared an aggressor by the League of Nations, we found ourselves faced with the threat of a war, which would endanger not merely the present boundaries of our State but even the very existence of the Czechs and Slovaks as one indivisible nation.'[2]

There was no hint of any offer from the Soviet Union of unconditional assistance. *Pravda* declared on 22 September that the official Czechoslovak news agency, in reporting the Government's surrender, had tried to compromise the U.S.S.R. by repeating the report, printed in the paper of the Czechoslovak Agrarian Party, that Russian help could not be relied upon, and in adding to the account of the Soviet Union's suggestion

---

[1] There would seem to be a contradiction between Litvinov's statement that Czechoslovakia might soon have to take up arms and his remarks about a 'capitulation', unless indeed he was guessing correctly at the course of events at Godesberg on the following days. Litvinov's speech, together with a leading article, which added nothing to it, filled most of the front page of *Pravda* on 22 September. Prominence was also given to an announcement that Poland had denounced the treaty of 1925 with Czechoslovakia which governed the position of the Polish minority in that country. Cf. Ripka, op. cit., pp. 113–16.

[2] *Documents for 1938*, vol. ii, pp. 217–18.

for approaching the League, that in existing circumstances this was a hopeless business.

On 22 September the Hodza Government was replaced by a new one under General Syrovy, which the *Berliner Tageblatt* promptly described as composed of 'deputies of Stalin'.[1] Benes broadcast the same evening, without however throwing any light on relations between Czechoslovakia and the Soviet Union.[2]

Chamberlain met Hitler at Godesberg on 22 September to discuss the method of carrying into effect the Anglo-French plan, and this meeting revealed very considerable differences between the British and German viewpoints.[3]

At 4 a.m. on the morning of 23 September the Soviet Acting Commissar for Foreign Affairs, M. Potemkin, gave the Polish Chargé d'Affaires a note stating that the Soviet Union would denounce the non-aggression treaty of 25 July 1932, if Polish troops invaded Czechoslovakia.[4] This fact did not appear in the Soviet press until the 26th.

There were no meetings at Godesberg on the 23rd, but Chamberlain and Hitler exchanged letters in which their differences were clarified.[5] Chamberlain declared himself unable to do more than pass on to Prague the German proposals, of which the kernel was a demand that the whole area in dispute as defined by Germany should be handed over by 1 October.

During the afternoon of 23 September, Litvinov spoke in the Sixth (Political) Committee of the League Assembly, and again referred to the Soviet attitude to the crisis:

'After his statement in the Assembly [on the 21st] on the Soviet attitude towards the Czechoslovak problem, M. Litvinov had heard it said that, seeing that the Soviet Government made its help to Czechoslovakia conditional upon similar help by France, it would appear to be equally culpable of breaking its Pact of mutual assistance with Czechoslovakia. People who said that were obviously unaware, or pretended to be unaware, that the Franco-Soviet and

[1] R. W. Seton-Watson, *Munich and the Dictators*, p. 74.

[2] *Documents for 1938*, vol. ii, pp. 226–7.

[3] It is now clear that during the Godesberg and Munich conferences, Germany was going forward with military plans for the occupation by force of the whole of Czechoslovakia. *Nuremberg Trial*, part II, pp. 34–9.

[4] Beck replied that this threat did not add a new element to the situation and that Poland's demands would be achieved in conformity with the pact. Noël, op. cit., p. 216. On 25 September, *Pravda* reported from Prague that Poland's demands upon Czechoslovakia had been restated in the form of an ultimatum. On 27 September it was announced from Prague that negotiations with the Poles for a peaceful settlement were under way.

[5] Cmd. 5847.

Soviet-Czechoslovak Pacts of mutual assistance were the result of action undertaken for the creation of a regional Pact of mutual assistance, with the participation of Germany and Poland, based on the principle of collective assistance. In consequence of the refusal of those two countries, France and Czechoslovakia had preferred instead of a single Soviet-Franco-Czechoslovak Pact, the conclusion of two bilateral Pacts. Moreover, it was the Czechoslovak Government that had at the time insisted that Soviet-Czechoslovak mutual assistance should be conditional upon assistance by France: that was reflected in the treaty in question.

'Thus, the Soviet Government had no obligations to Czechoslovakia in the event of French indifference to an attack on her. In that event, the Soviet Government might come to the aid of Czechoslovakia only in virtue of a voluntary decision on its part, or in virtue of a decision by the League of Nations. But no one could insist on that help as a duty, and in fact the Czechoslovak Government—not only out of formal, but also out of practical considerations—had not raised the question of Soviet assistance independently of assistance by France. Czechoslovakia, after she had already accepted the German-British-French ultimatum, had asked the Soviet Government what its attitude would be; in other words, would it still consider itself bound by the Soviet-Czechoslovak Pact if Germany presented new demands, if the Anglo-German negotiations were unsuccessful and Czechoslovakia decided to defend her frontiers with arms? That second inquiry was quite incomprehensible since, after Czechoslovakia had accepted an ultimatum which included the eventual denunciation of the Soviet-Czechoslovak Pact, the Soviet Government had undoubtedly had the moral right also to renounce that Pact. Nevertheless, the Soviet Government, which, for its part, did not seek pretexts for evading the fulfilment of its obligations, had replied to Prague that, in the event of France granting assistance under the conditions mentioned in the Czechoslovak inquiry, the Soviet-Czechoslovak Pact would again enter into force.'[1]

In the evening Litvinov had a conversation with Earl de la Warr, the Lord Privy Seal, who had specially been sent to Geneva, and Mr. R. A. Butler, who was representing Britain at the League Assembly. Maisky was also present. This appears to have been the only direct consultation over the crisis between the Soviet and British Governments. No official account of it was made public.[2]

On the same evening, the 23rd, the Czechoslovak Government was informed that the French and British Governments

---

[1] L.N.O.J. Spec. Suppl., 189, pp. 34-5.
[2] According to one unofficial version of the conversation, Litvinov repeated his Government's intention to assist Czechoslovakia if France did so and suggested a three-Power conference between Soviet Russia, Great Britain, and France, indicating his readiness to meet Halifax and Bonnet in London. Bilainkin, Maisky, p. 213.

could no longer 'take the responsibility of advising them not to mobilize'.[1] Czechoslovak mobilization followed.

On 24 September Mr. Chamberlain returned to England with the German terms, which were passed on to the Czechoslovak Government during the afternoon. The Prague radio announced that new assurances of assistance had been received from France, Soviet Russia, Roumania, and Yugoslavia.[2] According to one historian's narrative, Soviet Russia now advised the Czechoslovak Government to appeal to the League, and itself prepared for military action.[3] This, it is said, was done circumspectly in order not to give new openings for anti-Bolshevik propaganda in the West.[4]

On 25 September the Czechoslovak Government rejected the Godesberg terms. On that day and the following one, Franco-British conversations took place in London. The situation was once again apparently fluid and *Pravda* took occasion, on the 26th, to point out that Great Britain still had an opportunity to remedy its errors and to take a firm stand, but gave no hint that this would involve the U.S.S.R. in war. On the evening of the 26th, a British official statement was issued which included the following passage:

'If in spite of all efforts made by the British Prime Minister, a German attack is made upon Czechoslovakia, the immediate result must be that France will be bound to come to her assistance and Great Britain and Russia will certainly stand by France.'[5]

[1] Czechoslovak Government note to British Government, 25 September 1938, Cmd. 5847.

[2] Armstrong, op. cit., p. 213. There were reports of Russian troop concentrations on the Polish frontier. *B.I.N.*, XV, p. 928.

[3] It has been stated on the authority of Dr. Hodza that after the Godesberg terms had been made known, the Soviet Union offered to help Czechoslovakia even if France did not act. Vernadsky, loc. cit.

[4] R. W. Seton-Watson, *A History of the Czechs and Slovaks*, p. 366. At about this time Lord Londonderry received a letter from Goering in which the latter declared that the Germans had no claims beyond those on Czechoslovakia and sincerely desired the friendship of Great Britain. 'You must not, moreover,' he wrote, 'forget that behind Czechoslovakia there is Russia. If Russia herself has no desire to make war and is completely incapable of doing so, she wishes all the more intensively to entangle the other European Powers in war, because Bolshevism alone stands to gain thereby. I am greatly concerned at Russia's attitude, in supporting and inciting Czechoslovakia in her intention of provoking war in order to attain her aim of reducing Europe to chaos. It is to be hoped that there are statesmen in England who likewise understand the position correctly.' Lord Londonderry passed on this letter to Sir Horace Wilson just before the latter left for Munich with Mr. Chamberlain on 29 September; Marquess of Londonderry, *Wings of Destiny* (Macmillan, 1943), pp. 200–4.

[5] *Documents for 1938*, vol. ii, p. 261. In accounting for this sudden reference to the U.S.S.R., Lord Maugham refers only to Litvinov's speeches of 21

Meanwhile, on the same day, Hitler delivered in a speech at Berlin his final defiance to the Czechs and their supporters, making it clear that he would not wait beyond 1 October.[1] Apart, however, from remarking that Benes and his diplomats were hoping that Chamberlain and Daladier would be overthrown, that revolutions were on the way, and that the Czechs placed 'their hope on Soviet Russia', Hitler did not attack the U.S.S.R., and with his previous speeches in mind the omission was noticeable.[2]

Nevertheless Hitler's speech was described in the Russian press as a piece of 'political blackmail and bluff'. Doubts were also expressed as to the military preparedness of Germany and her capacity to face a protracted European war.[3]

Indeed foreign observers in Moscow began to see signs of definite intentions to act on the part of the Soviet Government. On 26 September one British correspondent telegraphed from Moscow:

'All Russia was told officially for the first time to-day of the Soviet warning to Poland—that if the latter attacked Czechoslovakia, Moscow would denounce the Soviet-Polish non-aggression Pact. . . . At the same time it made public here the text of the Soviet-Czechoslovak treaty and Russia's obligation to assist Czechoslovakia if attacked is emphasized.'[4]

A Havas report from Moscow on 27 September defined the Soviet Union's position as follows:[5]

'High authorities in Soviet Russia who had previously considered the situation as somewhat involved now consider that it has been

---

and 23 September, and ignores the de la Warr-Butler interview with the Soviet Foreign Commissar; *The Truth about the Munich Crisis*, pp. 45-6. Professor Thomson writes, however: 'There can be no question of French fear that Soviet Russia would not take immediate military action against Germany in fulfilment of the letter and spirit of her treaties with France and Czechoslovakia. M. Litvinov categorically reiterated Russia's certainty of action in this eventuality to French and British officials at Geneva on September 25 and 26.' op. cit., pp. 345-6. The Russians can scarcely have been unaware of the efforts made by circles close to the French Foreign Minister to discredit the British communiqué as unauthorized. Cf. Bonnet, op. cit., pp. 267-74. On contacts with Russia see also Gamelin, op. cit., vol. 2, pp. 348-60.

[1] *Hitler's Speeches*, pp. 1508-27.
[2] 'La Politique Russe et la Crise Européenne', *Europe Nouvelle*, 1 October 1938.
[3] *B.I.N.*, XV, p. 76. The Soviet press was very eager throughout the crisis to pick up suggestions that there was internal opposition to the war in Germany itself. Marxist analysis was still faithfully distinguishing 'German Fascism' from 'the German people'.
[4] *News Chronicle*, 27 September 1938.   [5] Ripka, op. cit., pp. 150-1.

cleared up. France and England have taken a stand on the side of Czechoslovakia, and there is no doubt whatsoever that President Roosevelt's declaration to Herr Hitler and Dr. Benes has had a powerful effect in favour of world peace.[1] It is considered that the world is only two inches removed from war and that only the close collaboration of the peace-loving Great Powers can prevent war. The diplomatic representatives of the Powers which are friendly towards Czechoslovakia, for their part, are quite convinced that the Soviet Government is perfectly sincere in its decision to fulfil all its obligations towards Czechoslovakia with all its powers. It is considered to-day that the requisite conditions exist for the realization of common agreement and for close military collaboration between England, France, and Soviet Russia. The Soviet Government is willing to commence forthwith discussions to that end.'[2]

The report went on to give an account in general terms of military preparations in the Soviet Union.[3]

After the failure of Sir Horace Wilson on 27 September to get any concessions from Hitler, and the latter's declaration to him that German action would take place on the following day, new British proposals for carrying out the substance of Germany's demands were presented at Prague. These were in line with the previous British attitude, since, after dealing with the territorial issue, they included (paragraph 5) the following significant provision:

'Later negotiations will follow between Germany, Great Britain, France, and Czechoslovakia . . . (b) for the revision of the present system of alliances of Czechoslovakia and the introduction of a system which would jointly guarantee the new Czechoslovakia.'[4]

[1] On 26 September President Roosevelt addressed to Benes, Hitler, Chamberlain, and Daladier an appeal that negotiations for a peaceful settlement of the dispute should not be broken off; *Peace and War*. United States Foreign Policy 1931–1941 (Washington, United States Government Printing Office, 1943), pp. 425–6.

[2] Professor Thomson writes that Russia's determination to live up to her treaty obligations was 'openly re-avowed' on 27 September; op. cit., p. 345.

[3] One obscure point is whether Czechoslovakia, whose smooth mobilization was favourably commented upon in the Soviet press, received any material help from Russia during the crisis. 'It is now known', writes Louis Fischer, 'that several mighty squadrons of Soviet planes were actually standing on Czechoslovak airfields at the time of Munich.' *Men and Politics*, p.537. Other estimates gave between 500 and 900 as the number of planes flown from Russia to Czechoslovakia during September; *Europe Nouvelle*, 24 September 1938, p. 1030; Armstrong, op. cit., p. 227. After Czechoslovakia's mobilization, runs another account, and 'in readiness for the arrival of Soviet troops, quantities of rolling-stock were hurried down to the Roumanian frontier.' A. Henderson, *Eyewitness in Czechoslovakia*, p. 221.

[4] Hitler's Godesberg plan had dropped the idea of an international guarantee.

These proposals were accepted by the Czechoslovak Government on 28 September.[1]

Meanwhile, on 27 September American diplomatic representatives accredited to all Governments from which the United States had not already heard, were instructed to bring Roosevelt's appeal of 26 September to the notice of such Governments and to ask them to take parallel action. A special message to this effect was sent to Mussolini, and another in reply to Hitler's answer to the first appeal.[2] The latter telegram suggested if necessary an 'immediate conference of all the nations directly interested in the present controversy', to be held in 'some neutral spot in Europe'.

A reply from the Soviet Government was delivered on 28 September to Mr. Kirk, the American Chargé d'Affaires at Moscow. This pointed out that the Soviet Government was 'investigating the obstacles' which were preventing 'Anglo-American mediation between Czechoslovakia and Germany' and referred to the Soviet proposal for an international conference, made after the German occupation of Austria: 'Faithful to its desire for peace, the Soviet Government is even now willing to support the proposal of the United States that an international conference should be called and is willing to participate actively in such a conference.'[3]

This would appear to be the last formal pronouncement by the Soviet Government on their attitude towards the Czechoslovak crisis; for they were not consulted during the moves which led up to the Munich Conference on 29–30 September. The Soviet Union was thus in no way associated with the Conference or its outcome.[4]

The principle of an international guarantee for the new truncated Czechoslovakia was reaffirmed in the annex to the Munich Agreement.[5] In expounding and justifying the Agreement in the House of Commons on 3 October 1938, Mr. Chamberlain made no mention of the Soviet Union. After Opposition criticism during the debate which followed, Sir John Simon expressed the hope that the U.S.S.R. would participate in the proposed collective guarantee.[6] This could not, however,

[1] Ripka, op. cit., pp. 193–203.
[2] *Peace and War*, pp. 426–9. The replies to the first appeal are in *Documents for 1938*, vol. ii, pp. 262–6.
[3] *Pravda*, 29 September 1938, translation in Ripka, op, cit., pp. 152–3.
[4] The inclusion of Mussolini was regarded in Moscow as 'monstrous'; *Izvestia*, 29 September 1938, quoted *B.I.N.*, XV, p. 76. The same paper complained of the Soviet Union's exclusion.
[5] Cmd. 5848.
[6] *House of Commons Debates*, 5 October 1938.

obscure the fact that Germany had achieved, with the agreement of the Western Powers, the truncation of the Soviet Union's ally and its virtual neutralization as a factor in European politics.

It remains important to know how far the question of the Soviet Union's attitude influenced Czechoslovakia's final surrender on 30 September. Broadcasting that evening, the Czechoslovak Minister of Propaganda, M. Vavrecka, spoke as follows:

'We had to consider that it would have taken the Russian Army weeks to come to our aid—perhaps too late, for by that time millions of our men, women, and children would have been slaughtered.

'It was even more important to consider that our war by the side of Soviet Russia would have been not only a fight against Germany but it would have been interpreted as a fight on the side of Bolshevism. And then perhaps all of Europe would have been drawn into the war against us and Russia.'[1]

This statement seems to imply that Czechoslovakia had the option of receiving Soviet help and resisting, even at the last moment.[2]

Russian sources give few clues as to the Soviet attitude in the concluding stages of the crisis.[3]

Apart from what could be gathered from the quotation of hostile foreign comment on the Munich Agreement and its associated settlements, and in particular on the successful Polish ultimatum of 30 September, the Soviet attitude was not specifically defined. The method taken to dissociate the U.S.S.R. from what had happened was, as so often, an indirect one. On 2 October *Pravda* printed the following Tass communiqué:

'The Paris correspondent of the United Press informs New York that the Soviet Government appear to have empowered Daladier

[1] Quoted Morrell, op. cit., p. 291.

[2] Benes stated on 27 May 1943 that the Czechoslovak Army had offered to fight after the Munich terms were made known; Bilek, op. cit., p. 75. According to one Czechoslovak source, Benes made a late inquiry as to what the Soviet attitude would be should Czechoslovakia decide to fight with, without or even against France. The Soviet reply which arrived after Czechoslovakia had accepted the Munich terms, was said to be a promise of support in all three eventualities; Arne Lansing, former editor of the *Prager Presse*, in *New York Post*, 29 April 1939, quoted by Vernadsky, loc. cit. The view that the Russians were prepared to fight for the Czechs alone if the Czechs resisted is accepted by Mr. Wheeler-Bennett in his *Munich : Prologue to Tragedy*.

[3] The statement in *B.I.N.*, XV, loc. cit. that the Soviet press published no information about the Munich conference on 30 September is incorrect. *Pravda* published a Reuter report on the proceedings of the night of 29–30 September. The full text of the Munich settlement was printed on 1 October.

to speak in its name at the four-Power conference at Munich. Tass is empowered to state that the Soviet Government clearly gave no powers to M. Daladier, just as it did not have and has not got any connexion with the Munich Conference and its decisions. The message of the United Press is a clumsy fabrication from beginning to end.'

A leading article in *Pravda* on 4 October, accompanying a further Tass communiqué which has already been quoted, referred to this Paris report and to one reproduced in a Prague paper which said that the U.S.S.R. had been kept fully informed by the Western Powers throughout the crisis. Both these reports were declared to be the outcome of strenuous efforts by Chamberlain and Daladier to shift on to the Soviet Union a part of the blame for the Munich decisions. For a true picture of the Soviet attitude, reference was again made to Litvinov's speech of 23 September. The straightforwardness of the Soviet attitude had, it was claimed, been widely appreciated in Czechoslovakia. *Pravda* found an unexpected witness to this in the person of the Agrarian Party leader Rudolf Beran, who was reported as saying to a Czechoslovak youth delegation:

'The Western and other allies (i.e. presumably the Little Entente), not only betrayed us, but threatened us with armed intervention. The only ally who remained faithful to Czechoslovakia was the U.S.S.R. It guaranteed us real assistance under all possible circumstances.'[1]

Historians of these events have constantly disagreed as to the amount of support received by the Czechs from their Soviet ally.[2] One British historian declares that 'it is not too much to affirm that the attitude of Russia was clear and consistent throughout the crisis'.[3] But, as has been seen, it was confidently asserted at the time by supporters of the policy of the French and British Governments that Russia would not, or as a result of the purges could not, fight Germany. It is interesting to note

[1] Beran is generally described as one of the chief obstacles to the acceptance of Soviet help. On 1 December, after the fall of the Syrovy Government, Beran became Prime Minister, a position which he still held when Czechoslovakia was occupied as a whole in March 1939.

[2] 'Of the states east of Germany only Czechoslovakia sought their (the Soviets') support, and thereby at once increased the hostility of her neighbours, Poland in particular, without getting any solid backing in return.' C. A. Macartney, *Problems of the Danube Basin* (Cambridge University Press, 1942), p. 119. 'By all evidence,' declares an authoritative reviewer, 'Russia was the only one of her friends who was ready to stand by Czechoslovakia at the time of Munich.' D. Mitrany, *International Affairs, Review Supplement*, June 1943, p. 643.

[3] R. W. Seton-Watson, *History of the Czechs and Slovaks*, p. 367.

how the Russian aspect of the matter is summed up by J. A. Spender in his book *Between Two Wars*.

Spender argues with some force that the real turning-point in Britain's foreign policy in the inter-war period came in November 1936 when Baldwin, explaining Britain's decision to rearm, pointed out the advantages in the matter of speed which dictatorships possessed over democracies who might 'lag two years behind'. This speech, writes Spender, 'marks the point at which the possibility of coming to terms with Hitler by conciliation and disarmament had passed out of the hands of the League and after which nothing remained but an effort to prolong the peace until the democratic Powers had made good the worst of their deficiencies'. He further asserts that it was known from quite early on that the earliest date by which this could be accomplished was March 1939.

If this is correct, and if Spender is also right in crediting Stalin with the belief that a German attack was 'ultimately the greatest danger threatening Russia' and in regarding him as 'fully entitled to reap such advantage as he could from his greatest enemy being worn down by a previous war against the Western Democracies', then he and his friends must be taken as assenting to the counter-proposition that the Western democracies were entitled to try to get Hitler to wear out his strength on Russia first.[1] Time has shown how great were the

[1] The Soviet interpretation of British policy in the 'Munich' period can be gauged from the 1938 edition of the *Short History of the All-Union Communist Party*: 'The "democratic" states are of course stronger than the fascist states. The one-sided character of the developing world war [sic] is the absence of a united front of the "democratic" states against the Fascist Powers. The so-called democratic states, of course, do not approve of the "excesses" of the Fascist States and fear any accession of strength to the latter. But they fear even more the working-class movement in Europe and the movement of national emancipation in Asia, and regard Fascism as an "excellent antidote" to these dangerous movements. For this reason the ruling circles of the "democratic" states, especially the ruling Conservative circles of Great Britain, confine themselves to a policy of pleading with the overweening Fascist rulers "not to go to extremes" and at the same time give them to understand that "they fully comprehend" and on the whole sympathize with their reactionary policy towards the working-class movement and the national emancipation movement.' (Russian ed. p. 319. English ed. (1939), p. 331.) Professor Schuman, writing in 1939, treated the whole 'appeasement' policy as dictated by the almost unanimous conviction on the part of the British ruling class that the Soviet Union and not Germany was the real enemy and regarded the Munich crisis as a deliberate artificial scare designed to overwhelm popular objections to a course which the British Government had long determined to pursue; op. cit., chaps. ix–xi. Another American writing in 1944, gave much the same analysis: 'There appear to have been two factors which influenced the Western Powers to ignore Russia: (1) the dread of Communism, which was strong in capitalistic

risks involved in either calculation. There is no reason to doubt but that this was clear at the time to some people in Russia as well as in Britain. What is in dispute is whether or not, even at this late hour, the Russians genuinely tried to carry out the alternative policy of combining together all the forces which might be rallied to resist German aggression. It has often been argued that because the Soviet Union chose the path of appeasement in August 1939, it was preparing to do likewise in the event of war coming a year earlier. The argument is a legitimate one but by no means conclusive.[1]

Spender does not ignore the fact that the question of Soviet policy at the time of 'Munich' is bound to be raised. He points out indeed that there had always been a 'curious reluctance to put a direct question' to Russia as to how far she was in fact prepared to go to resist 'aggression'. This had been so in the case of the Abyssinian war; and further confusion was caused by the vacillation of Soviet policy over Spain. 'In September, 1938, Russia was the only Power that could have brought Czechoslovakia the immediate assistance that could have saved her from a German attack, but once again the direct question was not asked, and what she might have done if she had been asked, was left to become a damaging reflection on the British and French Governments that failed to ask her.'[2]

To sum up, the Soviet record in the 'Munich' crisis will certainly stand up to examination, even though the only diplomatic *démarche* of which there is indisputable record dealt solely with the secondary menace from Poland. But had it

---

countries, especially during the years of economic depression; (2) the memory that it had been the quarrel between Slav and Teuton over the mastery of the Balkans that had precipitated the war in 1914. The underlying meaning of the appeasement policy was the granting to Germany of a free hand in the East. Munich was the climax, and its sequel showed the perils to which Britain and France had exposed themselves. The British sharply reversed themselves and tardily set to work to organize a "Stop Hitler" coalition.' R. W. Van Alstyne, *American Diplomacy in Action* (Stanford University Press, 1944), p. 381 n. Cf. A. Wolfers, *Britain and France between Two Wars* (New York, Harcourt Brace, 1940), pp. 132–41, 279–382, 304–10.

[1] In an after-dinner conversation at Yalta (January–February 1945), Stalin said that the Soviet Union would never have entered into the Non-Aggression Pact with Germany had it not been for the attempt at Munich to appease Hitler and the failure of Britain and France to consult Russia on the subject. J. F. Byrnes, *Speaking Frankly* (Heinemann, 1947), p. 283.

[2] Spender, op. cit., p. 109. After the crisis the British Government's attitude was that 'we were content to let the French Government take the lead in consulting with the Russian Government whose position was analogous to theirs'; Sir Samuel Hoare, *House of Commons Debates*, 30 October 1938.

intended action, the Soviet Government could have gone further in making its position known after Litvinov's speech on 23 September. There is also very little evidence that it was preparing its own people for the possibility that it would itself be involved in war as a result of what its press dealt with under the heading of 'the situation in central Europe'. Russia is not in central Europe. It is therefore arguable, that the Soviet Union was certain from very early on that France and Great Britain would not fight for Czechoslovakia and that Czechoslovakia would not resist without their support. In these circumstances, Soviet diplomats could go to the limit in pledging their country's readiness to resist aggression. At all events the attitude of the Western Powers was sufficient to dispel most of the remaining hold which the 'collective security' idea may have had in Soviet circles, and it is obvious that the retreat into isolation now gathered further momentum.

Note 1.   The opposition of Roumania to the passage of Soviet aircraft is further brought out in Appendix IV to M. Bonnet's second volume : *Fin d'une Europe* (Geneva, 1948).

Note 2.   According to Mr. Wheeler-Bennett, the Russians were prepared to come to the support of the Czechs as soon as the League was seized of the case, without waiting for a decision, op. cit., p. 127.

Chapter Seven : Additional Note. On the same day as Litvinov saw Payart, the contents of his remarks were conveyed to Mr. Winston Churchill by Maisky in an interview at Chartwell, described by Mr. Churchill in a letter to Lord Halifax on 3 September. This confirms that Litvinov's suggestion had been that the League be invoked in order to overcome Roumania's objections, and that the Soviet Union suggested immediate staff talks between Czechoslovakia, France, and the Soviet Union as to the way in which assistance might be given. He also recurred to the suggestion of a joint declaration by France, Great Britain, and the U.S.S.R., orginally put forward on 17 March. Lord Halifax replied on 5 September that he did not think an appeal to the League under article 11 would be helpful at that time. W. S. Churchill, *The Gathering Storm* (Cassell, 1948), pp. 229–32, 239. See *supra*, pp. 143–4.

Chapter Eight

RUSSIA AND THE FAR EAST, 1936–1939

THROUGHOUT the period of increasing tension in Europe, between the spring of 1936 and the spring of 1939, Soviet policy was largely influenced by anxieties in the Far East. The friction with Japan, which more than once led to actual fighting, was the outstanding feature of the Far Eastern scene. This in turn explains the growth of comparatively friendly relations between the Soviet and the Chinese Governments, despite their differences over Sinkiang and Outer Mongolia and the still more fundamental problem presented by the Chinese Communist movement.[1] It helps to explain the continued attempts by the Soviet Union to win at least the benevolence of the United States.

Soviet calculations must in turn have been affected by the knowledge that there were considerable differences between the various Japanese political and military groups as to the course their country should follow in the immediate future. But, throughout 1936, it was the Soviet Union rather than China which seemed generally marked out as the likely victim of the next stage of Japanese aggression.[2]

Japanese policy in this direction rested upon their estimate of the forces which the U.S.S.R. could spare for the Far Eastern front, and on the chances of assistance from Japan's other partners in the ideological crusade, but it is reasonable to assume that, in Japan's case, protestations about her fear of Communism were more genuine than in Germany's, and were not wholly a cover for her territorial ambitions.[3] In an article on the 'Tokyo War Guilt Trial' published on 10 March 1947, the Tokyo correspondent of *The Times* wrote: 'The evidence has made it clear that up to 1940 Japan's primary concern was to find a suitable opportunity for waging war against the Soviet

---

[1] See vol. 1, App. C. D. E. Cf. O. Lattimore, 'The Outer Mongolian Horizon', *Foreign Affairs*, July 1946; E. Lattimore, 'Report on Outer Mongolia', *Far Eastern Survey*, 6 November 1946.

[2] H. Byas, *Government by Assassination* (Allen and Unwin, 1943), pp. 156–60.

[3] See the address on Russo-Japanese relations given by O. Lattimore at Chatham House on 5 May 1936; *International Affairs*, XV. In an address delivered there on 25 February 1937, Major E. Ainger stressed the Japanese fear of Russia's growing military and air-power in the Far East; ibid., XVI, p. 388–402.

Union so as to remove the "Communist menace" from East Asia.' Moreover, Japan's hope of establishing economic domination in China by agreement with the Chinese Government encountered left-wing nationalist opposition.

Although the Soviet Government received assurances that the *coup* by the Japanese militarists in February 1936 was an internal matter, and that Mr. Hirota's new Government would seek to better Soviet-Japanese relations, no very definite moves were made in this direction.[1] The press on both sides became less overtly hostile and Japanese statesmen, including the Foreign Minister Mr. Arita, made some friendly gestures.[2] In spite of the fact that Japan, no less than China, showed indignation at the announcement on 8 April of the Soviet Union's pact with Outer Mongolia, by the end of the month an agreement had been reached that a joint commission should delimit the easternmost portion of the disputed Manchurian frontier (that between Lake Khanka and the Korean border). No progress was made towards implementing this decision.[3]

It has been suggested that it was now Japan that was most interested in improving relations between the two countries, and that the U.S.S.R., with its military preparations in better shape, showed itself less prone to follow a policy of appeasement than at the time of the sale of the Chinese Eastern Railway.[4] Some evidence of the Soviet Government's determination to take a firm line was provided by the bargaining for the renewal of the fisheries agreement due to expire on 31 May 1936.[5] Negotiations, which had been broken off in June 1935, were begun again on 13 March 1936, but the two sides had not drawn much closer together in the interval. The Japanese regarded the proposed Soviet terms as indicating a determination to exclude them from the fisheries altogether. This charge was repudiated in the Soviet press and on 25 May the old convention was extended until the end of the year.

Meanwhile new frontier incidents and other occasions of friction, including disputes over the payment of the C.E.R. instalments, indicated that the situation was still tense. The

---

[1] On 4 April the Soviet Ambassador in Berlin mentioned to the American Ambassador the lessening of tension between Soviet Russia and Japan; *Dodd's Diary*, p. 333.

[2] Hirota was his own Foreign Minister when the cabinet was formed on 19 March, but gave way to Arita on 2 April.

[3] For the details of Soviet diplomacy in the Far East and of Soviet press comment thereon, this chapter is much indebted to Harriet L. Moore. *Soviet Far Eastern Policy, 1931–1945* (I.P.R., Princeton University Press, 1945).

[4] *Survey for 1936*, pp. 929–38.   [5] See vol. 1, chaps. 6 and 13.

Soviet press continued to insist that the Soviet offer of a non-aggression pact still held good, but at the same time it drew attention to the increasing menace from the Japanese militarists, whose hold over their country appeared to be growing steadily. On 18 June *Izvestia* accused the Hirota Government of being no more than a screen for aggressive elements in the Japanese army and pointed out the one-sidedness, for obvious geographical reasons, of the Japanese proposals for a demilitarized zone along both sides of the disputed Manchuria frontier.[1]

German diplomacy, wishing to maintain good relations with both China and Japan, tried to embroil the latter with the U.S.S.R.[2] According to information obtained during interrogations of leading Germans in the autumn of 1945, and in particular to that given by Dirksen, the German-Japanese contacts began with the formation in 1935, of a German company for the economic exploitation of Manchuria, in which leading Nazis including Goering participated. A secret German military mission went to Japan in 1935, and towards the end of the year political contacts began. The negotiations leading up to the signature of the Anti-Comintern Pact were carried on not through the Foreign Office but through the Ribbentrop Büro (i.e. the Dienststelle Ribbentrop) in Berlin, the chief negotiator on the German side being a certain von Raumer.[3] Japan may have feared, however, that Germany's challenge to the Western Powers would force them into some form of co-operation with the U.S.S.R. in which case Germany would be unable to give any serious assistance should Japan decide upon war. Such fears would have been strengthened by the news on 30 July 1936, of the provisional naval agreement between Great Britain and the U.S.S.R., which provided an escape clause for the latter should Japan not accept limitation.[4]

This would help to explain the new Russo-Japanese *détente* in the autumn. In October, negotiations began again over the question of the Outer Mongolia-Manchuria border commission; on the 10th, Tass announced that the basis for an agreement on a new fisheries convention had been reached and, on the same day, the Soviet Commissariat of Heavy Industry signed a new agreement with the Japanese oil concessionaires on Sakhalin.

[1] See vol. 1, App. B.
[2] Note by the American Ambassador in Tokyo, 18 June 1936; Grew, *Ten Years in Japan*, p. 188.
[3] De Witt C. Poole, 'Light on Nazi Foreign Policy', *Foreign Affairs*, October, 1946.
[4] *Supra*, chap. 5. The Washington Naval Treaty of 1922 expired on 31 December 1936.

But when relations between the Soviet Union and the Western Powers had deteriorated, and joint action seemed unlikely, Japanese reluctance to commit the country still further to Germany was to some extent overcome. On 25 November 1936, the Anti-Comintern Pact was signed.[1] This could be of no assistance to Japan in her Chinese ambitions. And in spite of Japanese assurances, given over a week previously, that the Pact was in no way directed against the Soviet Union, Soviet diplomats abroad gave it to be understood that Soviet patience was exhausted.[2] As has already been noted, Litvinov took the occasion of his report to the Congress of Soviets on 28 November to announce his conviction that the agreement concealed a military alliance for purposes of aggression, and that Italy had proposed a similar agreement to Japan.[3]

'The reputation for sincerity of the Japanese Government will not be enhanced; this Government assured us of its desire for the estab-

[1] The translation of the secret addendum is given in De Witt Poole, loc. cit., as follows:

'1. Should either of the High Contracting States become the object of an unprovoked attack or an unprovoked threat of attack by the U.S.S.R., the other High Contracting State engages itself to enter upon no measures of a kind which would have the effect of relieving the position of the U.S.S.R.

'Should the case indicated in the foregoing paragraph arise, the High Contracting States will immediately consult on what measures to take for the safeguard of their common interests.

'2. During the continuation of this agreement the High Contracting States will not without reciprocal concurrence conclude any sort of political treaties with the U.S.S.R. which are not in keeping with the spirit of this agreement.'

At the Nuremberg trial, Ribbentrop admitted the responsibility of his office for the conclusion of the Anti-Comintern Pact. On being asked whether the Pact had practical aims or was purely ideological, Ribbentrop replied: 'It is certain that this pact—as a basic principle, I should say—had an ideological aim. It was meant to oppose the work of the Comintern in various countries at that time. But naturally it also contained a political element. This political element was anti-Russian at the time, since Moscow was the centre of the Comintern idea. Therefore it occurred to the Führer and me that through this pact a certain balance or counterbalance against Russian efforts or against Russia would be created in a political sense as well, because Russia was in opposition to Germany with regard to ideology and also, of course, to politics.' Ribbentrop was not questioned as to the existence of the secret articles. *Nuremberg Trial*, part X, pp. 163–4.

[2] *Survey for 1936*, pp. 924–9.

[3] *Supra*, chap. 5. On 30 November the Japanese Prime Minister told the American Ambassador that no agreement existed between Japan and Italy. 'The simple facts were that Italy was going to open a consular office in Manchukuo and Japan would eventually do the same in Abyssinia and that this was all there was to it.' Grew, op. cit., p. 190. Another provocative action by Japan was the announcement of a convention for intellectual co-operation with Poland; ibid., p. 203.

lishment of peaceful relations with the Soviet Union and urged us for the sake of this, to meet it in the settlement of several questions in dispute in which it was interested. Now, however, it has concluded a secret agreement with Germany. The Japanese Government also assured us that it was still considering the non-aggression pact we proposed to it and that such a pact might be concluded after the settlement of all questions in dispute; now, however, it has made the conclusion of such pacts dependent upon Germany's consent, lessening thereby the independence of its own foreign policy.'

In spite of official Japanese denials that anything more than joint 'police measures' were contemplated under the Pact—denials which lost some of their effect through the bellicose and exultant attitude of a section of the Japanese press—the opinion of foreign diplomats in Tokyo, as reported by the American Ambassador, was that a secret military understanding between Japan and Germany had in fact been established. The British Ambassador, Sir Robert Clive, was reported to believe that German arms would now be shipped to Manchuria in return for various commodities including soya beans.[1]

'The Soviet Ambassador is convinced that while the agreement as published is merely a façade to hide a secret agreement for joint action in the event of war with the Soviet Union, this alleged secret agreement is nevertheless aimed also at Great Britain and he insists that an agreement or understanding exists for the division between Germany and Japan in case of need of certain British possessions overseas as well as the Dutch East Indies. The Soviet Ambassador considers the alleged secret pact as part and parcel of Germany's need for colonies and of Japan's southern expansion programme. These ideas, although they may be far-fetched, are in accord with the perhaps not unreasonable suspicions of Japanese intentions and activities usually held by the Soviet Ambassador, who has informed the American Ambassador that the Soviet Government has indisputable evidence that a military agreement exists. He has informed the British Ambassador that at an opportune moment this evidence might be published.

'The Japanese Prime Minister (Hirota) made a significant remark to the American Ambassador to the effect that relations between Germany and Japan would become closer the more communistic activities and the influence of the Comintern spread abroad.'[2]

The Soviet Government now refused, in view of the changed situation, to sign the draft fisheries convention. In conversa-

---

[1] A trade pact between Germany and Japan (including Manchukuo) had been signed in April; K. Bloch, *German Interests and Policies in the Far East* (I.P.R., 1940), p. 35.

[2] Grew to Secretary of State, 4 December 1936; *Peace and War*, pp. 340–2. Cf. *U.S. Foreign Relations: Japan, 1931–41*, vol. 2, pp. 153–61.

tions with the Japanese Ambassador Shigemitsu on 8, 9, and 14 December, Litvinov made it clear that from the Soviet point of view, the conditions for Japan's exercise of her fishing-rights under the existing treaties should be determined by the Soviet Government alone. On 28 December a year's extension of the existing fisheries convention was agreed to. With regard to the other principal matter under dispute, Litvinov insisted that the frontiers of the Soviet-Chinese treaty of 1924 must be recognized by Manchukuo and that Japan could not be accepted as a third party to the frontier negotiations but must act jointly with Manchukuo.

Meanwhile a considerable change was taking place in the prospects for Russo-Chinese relations, which had been fairly cool since the Chinese protest in April 1936 against the Soviet pact with Outer Mongolia.[1] The Chinese Government had not responded to suggestions from the Chinese Communists for the formation of a 'united front' against Japan. Indeed, ever since February 1936, intermittent conversations had been taking place between the Chinese and Japanese Governments, on the latter's initiative. Japan's object was a general economic agreement and the adoption of a common policy against Communism.[2]

Various anti-Japanese incidents during the summer led to a redefinition of these demands and they now appear to have included an undefined extension of Japanese control in North China and the brigading together of Japanese and Chinese troops for joint action against the Communists. By October 1936, a considerable measure of agreement seems to have been reached. But in the following month a number of events helped to bring the *rapprochement* to an end. The most important of these was the unsuccessful revolt in the Suiyan province of Chinese Inner Mongolia, which was supported by the Japanese Kwantung Army in Manchuria. The object of the rebels was said to be the formation of an independent Mongol State under Japanese protection as a counter-weight to Soviet-dominated Outer Mongolia.

In December the events connected with the kidnapping of Chiang Kai-shek at Sian, by the troops of Marshal Chang Hsueh-liang, provided a further and, as it proved, final, obstacle to an agreement between Japan and the Chinese Government. As has already been seen, the extreme perplexity

---

[1] The Soviet press treated the Chinese protest as the outcome of Japanese pressure on Nanking. See the article from *Pravda*, 9 April 1936, translated in Moore, op. cit., pp. 230–3.

[2] *Survey for 1937*, pp. 908–24.

of the Soviet press at the news of the Sian *coup* and its expressions of suspicion as to its motives, strongly suggest that neither the Chinese Communists nor the Russians were privy to the plot.[1] But by the end of the month, Soviet commentators had changed their mind, and were applauding the prospect of the union of China's national forces, including the Communists, in a common front against Japan, under the indispensable leadership of Chiang Kai-shek.[2]

In a long analysis of the Japanese situation on 1 January 1937, Grew devoted considerable attention to Soviet-Japanese relations:[3]

'Good relations between Japan and Soviet Russia in the present political era are an anachronism. Apart from frontier incidents and other minor troubles it is perfectly obvious that Russia's well-justified fears of eventual Japanese expansion into Mongolia and Siberia on the one hand, coupled with Japan's fear of the spread of Communism in neighbouring territory on the other hand, are in themselves sufficient to prevent the development of any basis of mutual confidence. . . .

'[The] temporary amelioration of Soviet–Japanese relations . . . was rudely shattered by the conclusion by Japan of the anti-Comintern pact with Germany. . . . Political opponents of the cabinet in Japan maintain that if the news of this pact had not been permitted to leak out before 20 November, the Soviet-Japanese fisheries treaty would have been signed and all would have been well and they therefore charge the Foreign Minister with a grave blunder in allowing this leakage. But it is inconceivable that Moscow was not well aware, long before that date, of what was going on in Berlin, and the blunder, if such it was, would seem to lie not with the leakage before a certain date but in entering into any such pact at all,

'The explanation is simple. The pact and whatever secret agreement may be attached to it were concluded by the Japanese military, the negotiations with Germany having been largely carried on by Major-General Oshima, the Japanese Military Attaché in Berlin. We do not know whether these negotiations were conducted with the blessing of the Japanese Foreign Office, but since the Foreign Office has long been assiduously working to improve and stabilize Japan's relations with the U.S.S.R. as a matter of major policy, it is reasonable to question whether the shattering effect on those relations of a pact with Germany would not have been abundantly clear in advance and whether the civil Government in Tokyo could have been in sympathy with so sharp a divergence in the political orientation of

[1] See vol. 1, App. C. Owen Lattimore, *Solution in Asia* (Cressett Press, 1945), chap. iv. It should be pointed out that some authorities on Far Eastern affairs continue to believe that Moscow had a hand in the plot from the beginning.

[2] See the article from *Izvestia*, 27 December 1936, translated in Moore, op. cit., pp. 234–6.   [3] Grew, op. cit., pp. 192–204.

Japan's diplomacy. . . . We may be sure that the Soviet government will continue to act on the principle that the only language understood by the Japanese is force, and that when struck, whether by a minor frontier incursion or by some broader form of aggression, the wisest policy to follow is promptly to strike back with double force.

'That the treaty between Japan and Germany envisages anything in the nature of a pact of military mutual assistance in case of war seems highly unlikely. It is said that Japan did her best to get Poland to participate in the arrangement with Germany but without success, and with Poland independent of commitments, and with France at Germany's back, it is hardly likely that Germany would undertake to attack Russia in the case of a Soviet war with Japan. Nevertheless, the existence of an agreement for an exchange of military information and for the supply of arms and ammunition and technical aid to Japan in return for commercial commodities from Manchuria is a reasonable hypothesis . . . it is evident that a new orientation has arisen in Japan's policy.'

The Soviet attitude to events in the Far East in the first half of 1937 was to prove less simple than such forecasts suggested. Its outward manifestation continued to be the endemic friction with Japan, culminating at the end of June in the so-called 'Amur' incident. In spite of the outward intransigence of the Kuomintang, it seems clear that the negotiations between Chiang and the Communist leaders resulted during the spring in some kind of working military agreement; and it is not surprising that this should have led to the belief that a Soviet-Chinese pact was under consideration.[1] There are indications that talks between the two Governments were pushed ahead after the return to Nanking on 1 April 1937 of the Soviet Ambassador Bogomolov.[2]

[1] *Survey for 1937*, I, pp. 154–8; A Pierre, 'L'U.R.S.S. et le parti communiste de Chine', *Politique Etrangère*, June 1937. J. E. Davies noted in his journal on 26 March 1937, a conversation with Tsiang Ting-fu, the Chinese Ambassador in Moscow. 'My impression', he wrote, 'is that relations between China and the Soviet Union have improved immeasurably within the past few days; that a definite understanding has been arrived at; that there is an agreement that the Soviet Union will refrain from Communistic activity in China which was antagonistic to the present Chinese government; that this specifically involved that the U.S.S.R. would lend no support to any independent communistic Chinese military forces or local governments; that this means a very great deal to China and gives much promise for the strengthening of the situation in China; that on their part the Chinese government will make provision to take care of those people in China who will thereby be deprived of means of support.' *Mission to Moscow*, pp. 96–7.

[2] According to an article in *Izvestia* on 30 August 1937, accompanying the text of the Soviet-Chinese non-aggression pact of 21 August, the negotiations for the treaty had been 'carried on for more than a year' (translation in Moore, op. cit., pp. 244–5).

In his survey of the position on 1 January 1937, the American Ambassador had noted that one of the brakes on Japanese activity was that the Japanese Army had 'at last awakened to the fact that in the event of a Japanese war with Soviet Russia, Great Britain might not preserve even a benevolent neutrality'.[1] Such a conclusion on the part of the Japanese might well have followed a consideration of the increasing signs of hostility in Great Britain towards Japanese expansionism and of the growing practical assistance which Great Britain was giving China. The British attitude was indeed bound to be of decisive importance in determining the policy which Japan should pursue in China. The peaceful penetration of China, in agreement with Nanking—a policy favoured by powerful civilian elements in Japan—could only be achieved with the aid of foreign capital, that is to say only with the goodwill of London or New York.[2]

According to a speech made on 7 January 1939 by Sun Fo, President of the Chinese Legislative Yuan, the U.S.S.R. proposed to China on 1 April 1937 that the latter should call a Pacific peace conference, that a Soviet-Chinese non-aggression pact should be signed, and finally that a Soviet-Chinese mutual assistance pact should be concluded. It has been suggested that the Chinese declined the proffered alliance because it might prejudice British and American aid and because they believed that the Soviet Union would give them assistance anyhow in the event of an attack from Japan. H. P. Howard, 'The Diplomatic Prelude to the China War', *Pacific Affairs*, September 1941. In an address delivered in 1939, Dr. W. W. Yen, a former Chinese Ambassador to the Soviet Union, referred to such reports and suggested that the possibility of a Soviet-Chinese agreement may have precipitated the Japanese attack; 'Some Aspects of China's Relations with the Soviet Union', *Asiatic Review*, April 1940. The American journalist Hallett Abend recounts a conversation with Bogomolov in which the Soviet Ambassador told him that the Soviet Union had adopted a new policy towards China just before the Sian *coup*. The purpose of the policy was to make a war in Asia less likely by assisting in the unification of China. According to this account, the Russians hoped that the agreement discussed in April 1937 would include the following points: the Soviet Union to supply China with petrol and heavy machinery on long credits; Sinkiang to be restored to 'Chinese sovereignty' and a rail link to be built between Urumchi and Lanchow under joint ownership, the Chinese to build a railway from Lanchow to the existing railhead at Sian; an air-line under joint ownership to be organized between Ulan Bator, Ninghsia, Lanchow, and Sian; Soviet consulates to be reopened in Hankow and Canton; a treaty to open trade along the borders of the U.S.S.R., Outer Mongolia and China; Moscow to give no assistance to the Chinese Communists and China not to conclude any agreements with foreign Powers for their suppression; Chinese sovereignty over Outer Mongolia to be re-affirmed but the existing position to be maintained in view of the Japanese threat; China and the U.S.S.R. to propose, circumstances permitting, an all-embracing Pacific non-aggression pact; *My Life In China, 1926–1941* (New York, Harcourt Brace, 1943), pp. 237–9.

[1] Grew, op. cit., p. 197.   [2] *Survey for 1937*, I, pp. 146–7.

These civilian elements seemed to have secured a greater
share in the determination of Japan's policy after the change
of government in January 1937. In a speech on 8 March the
Foreign Minister, Mr. Sato, proclaimed the necessity for a 'new
deal' with China and for the re-establishment of friendly
relations with Great Britain.[1] With a view to carrying out this
part of the programme, economic talks with China were begun
almost at once. Progress was slow, and it soon became evident
that the Japanese Foreign Office was not strong enough to
counteract quite different tendencies on the part of the Japanese
military in North China and Manchuria.[2] The demand for
the return of Manchuria to China figured in the forefront of the
programme of the Chinese Communists, whose *rapprochement* with
Nanking was an admitted source of anxiety to the Japanese.[3]
The Japanese were also being influenced in favour of extending
rather than diminishing the area of Inner Mongolia under their
control by the restlessness of the Mongol inhabitants who
'looked with increasing envy on the one side at the large
measure of independence enjoyed by their kinsmen in Outer
Mongolia, and on the other side at the subsidies which the Mongolian Political Council in Suiyuan received from Nanking'.[4]

During the first week in May it became known that Yoshida,
the Japanese Ambassador in London, had made an approach
to the Foreign Office.[5] In a speech on 17 May, Sato referred
in general terms to these talks and remarked that from the
standpoint of Japan's 'foreign relations in general', it was
'highly desirable to secure firmly' the country's 'friendship with
Great Britain'.[6]   On 24 June it was announced that the

[1] ibid., pp. 161–80.

[2] E. C. Carter, 'Before the War in China', address given at Chatham House
on 5 October 1937; *International Affairs*, XVI, pp. 833–52; Howard, loc. cit.

[3] Cf. T. H. White and A. Jacoby, *Thunder out of China* (Gollancz, 1947),
pp. 52–3.

[4] *Survey for 1937*, I, p. 173.

[5] In spite of British assurances that there was no intention of reviving the
policy of spheres of influence or of revising treaties concerning China without
her consent, the news of the talks caused considerable alarm in China.
This is reflected in some American accounts of this episode. 'There is no
question that the basis for a mutually profitable and agreeable understanding between Japan and Great Britain existed in the spring of 1937. There
is no way of knowing yet just how far the diplomats had proceeded in
reconciling their conflicting claims. But history may very well show that
the British had actually acquiesced in the Japanese programme in China,
only to have that victory annulled by the impatience of the Japanese
militaristic leaders.' C. A. Buss, *War and Diplomacy in Eastern Asia* (New York,
Macmillan, 1941), p. 305.

[6] *Documents for 1937*, pp. 650–2. On 28 May Mr. Baldwin was replaced
as Prime Minister by Mr. Chamberlain. On 31 May the Hayashi Cabinet

Japanese Ambassador had received instructions enabling him to start discussions on concrete issues affecting China and Anglo-Japanese commercial relations; on the following day Mr. Eden spoke optimistically of the future relations between the two countries.[1]

In the existing state of Soviet relations with Japan, these moves were bound to be regarded with suspicion. In a review of the international situation on 10 May *Pravda* wrote:

'The Anglo-Japanese conversations do not affect the interests of Japan alone. By handing over North China to the Japanese, London in fact allows and encourages Tokyo to engage in large-scale military adventures on the borders of the Soviet Union and the Mongol People's Republic. In that is hidden the secret object of the manoeuvres of London and Tokyo.'

Comments of this kind revealed that the suspicion which the Soviet Union increasingly voiced in this period—namely, that the object of British and French diplomacy was to canalize Nazi aggression towards eastern Europe—was matched in the Far East by the suspicion that Great Britain cherished the hope that Japanese aggression could be diverted from South China and the South Seas towards Mongolia and Eastern Siberia.

Ten days after the appearance of the article already quoted, *Pravda* returned to the same theme at greater length.[2] It was pointed out that the press of the two countries concerned gave suspiciously different explanations of the import of the Anglo-Japanese talks. The Japanese spoke of them in connexion with the new non-aggressive stage of their policy in China. The British press looked forward hopefully to the delimitation of new 'spheres of influence', or, in less diplomatic language, to being allowed to exploit the centre and south of 'semi-colonial' China, in return for a free hand to Japan in the north. (In the Far East, it was easier than in Europe to equate the British policy of appeasement with 'imperialism' in the Leninist sense.) The author went on to point out the inroads made upon Britain's position in China by Japan, ever since the latter's conquest of Manchuria. In spite of Britain's recent attempts to strengthen her strategic position in the Far East, European complications made it difficult for her to do as much as she would have desired

---

which had been defeated in the elections a month earlier, resigned. On 4 June Prince Konoye became Prime Minister with Mr. Hirota as Foreign Minister.

[1] *House of Commons Debates*, 25 June 1937.

[2] G. Anbor, 'Britain's Policy of Concessions and its Results', *Pravda*, 20 May 1937.

in this direction. But it was not to be overlooked that Japan's aggressive policy, as hitherto pursued, had landed her too in considerable difficulties, both political and economic. Japan could not afford an all-out struggle in China; hence the new 'peaceful' policy there, and the anxiety to impress this change upon the minds of the British statesmen, who, full of misgivings and uncertain of their country's strength, were prepared to seek safety in concessions to their rival and competitor.[1]

Japan also hoped that Britain would use its influence with Nanking to forward Japanese hopes in China. By its approach to Britain, Japan hoped to weaken that wing of the Kuomintang which favoured Britain and the United States and to strengthen the pro-Japanese group of Wang Ching-wei. Japan needed the help of Britain for the furthering of her aggressive plans in the Far East, and hoped at the same time to worsen relations between Britain and the United States. 'In this deal,' the author concluded, 'the losing side is undoubtedly England, unless she gives up in time the policy of encouraging and giving in to the aggressor. The interests of general peace demand from her decisive action in regard to the incendiaries of war.'[2]

In Asia, as in Europe at this time, the trials and purges of 1937 were generally considered to have diminished the Soviet Union's military strength.[3] At the trial of Piatakov, Sokolnikov, Radek, and others in January 1937, several of the accused admitted sabotage in conspiracy with a Japanese agent. In May, over forty railway officials in Eastern Siberia were executed on charges of sabotage under Japanese orders, and of selling military secrets to Japan. Further executions followed in June and July; and the alleged activities of Japanese in the Far Eastern territories and Outer Mongolia were given wide publicity.[4]

This may explain why the new Japanese Cabinet, which was doubtless already preparing for the next stage of aggression in

---

[1] Japan's internal weakness was generally stressed in Soviet writings at this time. The novel *Na Vostoke* (In the East) by P. Pavlenko, published in 1937, dealt with the development and strengthening of the Soviet Far East since 1932 and went on to describe a future world war in which Japan's initial assault on Russia was followed by risings inside China and Japan and eventually by world revolution. The book was translated into English by S. Garry under the title *Red Planes Fly East* (Routledge, 1938).

[2] On 21 May 1937 *Izvestia* printed an article welcoming the suggestion of a Pacific non-aggression pact which had been proposed by Australia at the Imperial Conference in London. (Translation in Moore, op. cit.. pp. 231–9.)

[3] Cf. Sir John T. Pratt, *The Expansion of Europe in the Far East* (Sylvan Press, 1947), p. 191.

[4] See the two long articles on 'The subversive activities of Japanese agents' in *Pravda*, 9 and 10 July 1937.

China, thought the moment propitious for a preliminary test of Soviet strength.

In spite of the usual minor incidents, there was no serious deterioration in Soviet-Japanese relations before June. Goods in payment for the C.E.R. were shipped satisfactorily.[1]

In a speech on 17 May, Sato had referred to the vigour and speed with which military works and the creation of war industries were being pressed in the Soviet Far East, and to his own Government's efforts to 'eliminate all unnecessary friction between the two countries'. The Soviet Government can hardly have taken kindly to his remarks that 'the internal political condition' of the Soviet Union appeared to be 'quite complicated judging from the so-called anti-revolutionary conspiracy trials' of August 1936 and January 1937, nor to his vigorous defence of the Anti-Comintern Pact from which 'great benefits' were expected.[2]

It does not appear that at this juncture, Japan intended to do more than threaten the U.S.S.R. On 9 June, General Tojo, then Chief of Staff of the Kwantung Army in Manchuria telegraphed the Army General Staff at Tokyo that, with reference to the attack on the Soviet Union, he believed it advisable first to dispose of the 'Nanking régime' so as to remove the menace from the rear.[3]

On 16 May 1937 it was announced in Tokyo that the U.S.S.R. had declared its intention of abrogating the 1934 waterways agreement with 'Manchukuo', which dealt with navigational facilities along the rivers forming the frontier. On 27 June the headquarters of the Kwantung Army reported that on the 21st Soviet forces had occupied two islets in the Amur which were claimed by Manchukuo. On 28 and 29 June

---

[1] Moore, op. cit., p. 81. The course of Soviet trade with the Far Eastern countries in this period can be seen from the following table. S. P. Turin, *The U.S.S.R.: An Economic and Social Survey* (Methuen, 1944), p. 60. The values are in 1936 gold roubles. Cf. Moore, op. cit., App. III.

	China (excluding Sinkiang)	Sinkiang	Outer Mongolia	Japan
Soviet Exports: ('000 roubles):				
1936	573	36,145	50,433	27,679
1937	623	34,753	65,822	11,743
1938	767	43,381	69,838	6,086
Soviet imports ('000 roubles):				
1936	12,791	25,671	32,120	61,968
1937	14,958	25,774	33,694	54,375
1938	33,302	35,159	38,510	17,597

[2] *Documents for 1937*, pp. 650-2.   [3] *The Times*, 10 March 1947.

Shigemitsu protested in Moscow against this action and demanded the withdrawal of the troops. Litvinov insisted that the islets were Soviet territory, and suggested that both sides should move their forces from the vicinity pending a settlement of the question of sovereignty.[1]

While the Kwantung Headquarters and Tokyo were being consulted on the Soviet proposals, an armed clash took place (on 30 June). There were casualties on both sides and a Soviet gunboat was sunk. After receiving assurances, however, on 2 July, that the Japanese forces had been removed from the area, the Soviet Government issued instructions for the evacuation of the neighbourhood.[2] The evacuation was complete on 4 July, and, two days later, one of the disputed islets was occupied by Manchukuoan troops. In spite of a Soviet protest to Tokyo on 9 July, these retained their position and with the grave developments in China monopolizing attention, the Soviet Government allowed the matter to drop. On the face of it, then, the Soviet Union appears to have acted in an extremely conciliatory fashion and to have been most unwilling to take up the challenge.[3]

[1] *Pravda*, 30 June 1937. 'At the root of this dispute over a couple of unimportant islands lay possibly a desire on the part of the Soviet military authorities to keep Japanese and Manchukuoan craft well away from the Russian bank of the Amur, so as to prevent observation of the defences they were erecting.' *Survey for 1937*, I, p. 151.

[2] *Pravda*, 2 and 3 July 1937.

[3] 'The settlement was hailed in Tokyo as a diplomatic victory, seeing that the Russians had withdrawn from the islands without any agreement on the question of sovereignty having been reached or guarantees given against the subsequent occupation by "Japanese-Manchukuoan" forces, of the places in dispute. Undoubtedly the moral drawn by the Japanese military was that the Red Army was . . . in no state to take the field. The affair had begun as a minor affray between local forces—the one hundred and eighty-fifth incident of the kind on the Soviet-"Manchukuo" border— but it had furnished the Japanese Government with a valuable means of testing the strength of the Soviet Union in the Far East, and the latter's pacific demeanour could be, and almost certainly was taken as proof of Moscow's consciousness of unpreparedness for a serious conflict. So far from diverting Japanese pressure on China, the Amur incident, by convincing the Japanese military that there was no immediate likelihood of Russian intervention, acted as a spur to the extremists to risk a resort to arms in order to force the issue in North China.' *Survey for 1937*, I, p. 152.

Davies, who saw both Litvinov and Shigemitsu during the 'Amur incident', writes that 'later in 1938 in Europe, a high Japanese official told him that the Japanese Government had deliberately projected these tests of Soviet resistance and military strength; and that the Japanese were surprised and impressed with the mechanized strength and effectiveness of the Red Army in the Far East'; op. cit., pp. 113-15. This version of the incident and its results is accepted by Moore, op. cit., pp. 81-3. Cf. Lattimore, op. cit., p. 63.

The outbreak of Sino-Japanese hostilities in July 1937 was regarded in Moscow from the beginning as of much more than local significance, and Great Britain was blamed for having encouraged Japan to assume that there would be no outside interference with her plans of aggression.[1] In an analysis of the situation on 22 July, *Izvestia* affirmed that the Lukuochiao incident heralded 'the beginning of the long and basically-prepared second step in the conquest of China by the Japanese imperialists', and that, as in 1931, Great Britain seemed prepared to swallow the Japanese assurances that the conflict would be localized. But there were important differences between the existing situation and that of 1931; not to mention 'such a decisive factor as the extraordinary growth of the power of the Soviet Union' there was the growth of a national spirit of resistance among the Chinese and a weakening of Japan's domestic strength.[2]

The Soviet Union marked its approval of China's resistance to the new Japanese attack by offering it a pact of non-aggression, which was signed on 21 August.[3] The text was made public on 30 August.[4] No indication was given in Soviet comment that active assistance was contemplated, although *Pravda* described it as a practical application of the principle of the 'indivisibility of peace' and 'collective security'.[5] Japanese

---

Another suggestion is that the Japanese may have intended to deter the Chinese from seeking a Soviet alliance by proving that the Soviet Union itself was in danger. Howard, loc. cit.

[1] *Pravda*, 11 July 1937.   [2] Translation in Moore, op. cit., pp. 240–3.

[3] *Istoria Diplomatii*, vol. 3, p. 593. See Grew's memorandum of 1 September 1947, *Foreign Relations of the United States: Japan, 1931–41*, 2 vols. (Washington, United States Government Printing Office, 1943), vol. 1, p. 360.

[4] *L.N.T.S.*, vol. 181, p. 102.

[5] *Pravda*, 30 August 1937, quoted *Istoria Diplomatii*, loc. cit. Cf. the article in *Izvestia* of the same date, printed in Moore, op. cit., pp. 244–5. 'The Kremlin is definitely "playing down" any possibility of active Soviet participation against Japan. . . . There is no doubt in my mind but what Russia is innately desirous of helping China. What deters her is fear of possible German attack in the event of her participation and possibly also fear as to the solidarity of her eastern military forces until the internal situation has cooled off and solidified after the shootings and "purgings" that have been going on. In the event that Japan through China should seriously threaten the railroad line of communications and Lake Baikal, the Soviet Union would undoubtedly get into the fight.' Davies to Secretary of State, 1 September 1937, op. cit., pp. 146–7. Germany, which still had important links with the Chinese Government, did not relish Japan's forces being locked up in a struggle with China and made several efforts to mediate a peace between October 1937 and the beginning of the following year. D. H. Popper, 'The Western Powers and the Sino-Japanese Conflict',

reports of secret military clauses were officially denied in Nanking. The pact could indeed be interpreted as a Soviet diplomatic victory, since China was precluded by it from purchasing peace from Japan at the price of accepting Japan's offer of a place in the anti-Comintern group of Powers. On the other hand, relations between the Soviet Union and Japan were such as to render seemingly superfluous Soviet pledges of non-co-operation with the Japanese aggressor. For the same reason, it was unlikely in any circumstances that Japan would feel free to remove troops from Manchuria for use in the interior of China.[1] Japanese allegations that the Nanking Government had now become an agent in the bolshevization of China were met by a Chinese official statement that Article 6 of the Sino-Russian treaty of 1924 was unaffected by the new pact and that by this article both countries had undertaken not to support revolutionary groups or to spread propaganda in each other's territories.[2]

The Chinese appeal to the League of Nations gave Litvinov an opportunity of stating his Government's position with regard to the conflict during his speech before the Assembly on 21 September.[3] He drew a parallel between the Spanish and Chinese conflicts and declared his conviction that the League of Nations, even with its existing composition, could afford both countries more aid than they had asked for. In the Far Eastern Advisory Committee on 27 September, Litvinov drew attention to the fact that the concentration of the British and French delegates on the inhumanity of Japan's aerial warfare should not be taken as evidence that the committee condoned other forms of attack. The Assembly's resolution of 6 October indicating, though not naming, Japan as the aggressor, and asking League members to consider what aid they could individually afford China, was accepted by the Soviet delegation as a step forward.[4] But the proposed conference of the signatories of the Nine-

Foreign Policy Reports, XIV; L. K. Rosinger, 'The Far East and the New Order in Europe', Pacific Affairs, December 1939. By 26 January 1938 however, as a confidential report from the German Ambassador, Dirksen reveals, the German Government changed its policy towards Japan in anticipation of a Japanese victory over China. The Times, 10 March 1947.

[1] A memorandum by the U.S. Military Attaché sent by Grew from Tokyo on 29 September said that it was held in army circles in Japan that there was a serious possibility of war with the Soviet Union and that steps had been taken to reinforce the Kwantung Army: 'however plans to bring on another Russo-Japanese war soon have not been made.' Foreign Relations of the United States: Japan, 1931–41, vol. 1, p. 378.

[2] Survey for 1937, I, pp. 295–8   [3] L.N.O.J. Spec. Suppl., 169, p. 79.
[4] L.N.O.J. Spec. Suppl., 177, pp. 13–14, and 31.

Power Pact was regarded in Moscow as a method of shelving the issue as far as collective action was concerned, and the Soviet Union objected to the whole idea of direct contact with the aggressor which this proposal implied.[1]

In spite of Japan's refusal of the invitation to the Brussels conference, Soviet opinion remained pessimistic:

'The composition of the Brussels Conference, even in the case of Japan's absence, makes it impossible in advance for the Conference to reach any positive decisions. The basis for activity in these circumstances can result only in empty chatter under cover of which the Japanese militarists will continue their criminal war against Chinese peoples.'[2]

The Brussels Conference met on 3 November 1937, and Litvinov in his opening speech gave another warning against the dangers of seeking peace through direct contacts between international organizations and the aggressors:

'In the progress of negotiations connected with consistent concessions to the aggressors, it is possible to overstep the lines on which persons, undoubtedly inspired by the best intentions slip, without noticing it themselves, into the viewpoint of the aggressor, commence to speak in his language, actually justifying and encouraging his actions.'[3]

The Conference nevertheless issued another invitation to Japan and this was likewise rejected. By then any hope of a definite outcome had been abandoned and Litvinov had departed. At the meeting on 13 November, the Soviet representative Potemkin merely indicated that his Government would accept any solution likely to lead to a pacific settlement.[4]

[1] On 15 October, Hirota told Grew that Chiang's attitude had hardened since the Sino-Soviet pact and that he was no longer a free agent; in his view, the pact contained secret clauses; Memorandum by Grew, 15 October 1937, *Foreign Relations of the United States: Japan, 1931–41*, vol. I, pp. 402–3.

[2] *Pravda*, 28 October 1937. The Russians particularly resented the presence of Italy which on 6 November, while the Conference was actually in session, put its signature to the Anti-Comintern Pact. Speaking to Davies before leaving for Brussels, Litvinov declared that 'the vital interests of the Soviet Union were less affected by the situation in the Far East . . . than those of either Great Britain or France and that he had little confidence in the final outcome of the Conference, due mainly to what he considered the weakness of the British and French attitude . . . the Soviet Union was already prepared to take a strong stand if it were in co-operation with France, England, and the United States'. Davies to Secretary of State, 11 November 1937, op. cit., pp. 164–5.

[3] *Documents for 1937*, pp. 726–8.

[4] The final resolution of the Conference agreed to on 24 November was weaker than that of the League Assembly of 6 October; *Survey for 1937*, I, pp. 285–93. The account of the Conference in *Istoria Diplomatii* concludes

Speaking at Leningrad on 29 November 1937, Litvinov reviewed the course of international diplomacy with regard to
the Far Eastern crisis and sarcastically hinted that the bourgeois States were simply seeking to come to terms with the
aggressor.[1]

The question for Russia was how much assistance it could
afford to give, without weakening its own security and without
provoking the aggressor into a direct attack upon the Soviet
Union itself. The rumoured divergences of opinion on this
subject may well have corresponded to fact.[2] It does, however,
appear that some material help was given from a very early
date and it is possible that an informal agreement on Soviet
credits was also made.[3] In January 1938 a Chinese mission
under Sun Fo went to Moscow to press for further assistance,
but reports as to the success of the mission varied.[4]

During 1938 and 1939 considerable supplies were sent to
China by the Sinkiang route.[5] Japanese protests on the subject
were answered by Litvinov in a statement which declared that
'the sale of arms including air planes to China is entirely in
accord with international law . . . especially in view of the fact
that arms are provided to China, just as incidentally to Japan,
by many countries'.[6] Russian 'volunteers' also served with the
Chinese forces as pilots, technical advisers, and instructors, but
they were not of the same high rank or as influential as their
German predecessors.[7] The latter were withdrawn between

by suggesting that the object of Great Britain and the United States was to
force the Soviet Union into a war with Japan on China's behalf; vol. 3,
pp. 594–5.

[1] *Documents for 1937*, pp. 755–6.
[2] On 13 December 1937 the Russian Chargé d'Affaires in Berlin told
the American Ambassador that England, France, and the United States
wanted Russia to save China without their assistance. Russia would not do
that but would co-operate in any general measures which might be taken;
Dodd's Diary, p. 443.
[3] Davies, op. cit., pp. 165–7; letter to Secretâry of State, 16 November
1937, ibid., pp. 168–9.
[4] Popper, loc. cit., pp. 114–15.
[5] O. Lattimore, 'Chinese Turkistan-Siberian Supply Road', *Pacific
Affairs*, December 1940; G. Hogg, *I see a New China* (Boston, Little, Brown,
1944), pp. 146–9.
[6] *Izvestia*, 5 April 1938. The Japanese protested again in May and were
reported to have declared that China had received 500 planes, 200 pilots,
and large quantities of equipment. *China and Japan*, 3rd ed. (R.I.I.A., 1941),
p. 95.
[7] *Survey for 1938*, I, p. 568. The Soviet personnel was apparently withdrawn in haste during the European crisis in August 1938. E. F. Carlson,
The Chinese Army (New York, I.P.R., 1940), p. 73.

May and July 1938, Germany having decided apparently to throw its weight wholly on to the side of Japan.[1]

Soviet economic aid for China, although little publicized on the Soviet side, continued to grow. Chinese sources indicate that credits of 50,000,000 dollars were granted to China in October 1938 and in February 1939, in connexion with arrangements for the exchange of machinery and munitions for tea, minerals, and other raw materials. According to Chinese spokesmen, no political conditions were attached to these credits.[2]

A trade treaty between the Soviet Union and China was signed in Moscow on 16 June 1939.[3] This extended most-favoured-nation treatment to both sides and provided diplomatic status and immunities for the Soviet trade delegation. This was followed by a further credit of 150,000,000 dollars in August 1939.

The importance which Sinkiang acquired as the channel for Soviet supplies to China made the affairs of that turbulent province a matter of more than local interest.[4] Things had not run altogether smoothly since order had been restored there, with Soviet assistance, in 1934. Serious political trouble began again towards the end of 1936.[5]

One account of the rising blames 'ill-timed and inappropriate reforms' and the Government's over-great reliance on an 'elaborate secret police service operating in characteristic Russian fashion'. Another suggests Turki hostility to anti-religious propaganda. Once again the revolt was a Moslem affair with both Turkis and Tungans (under Ma Ho-san) taking part. Once again divergences between the two races ruined their chances of success and Ma Ho-san was finally defeated in the summer of 1937 by forces which are said to have included Soviet troops and aircraft.

[1] W. H. Chamberlin, 'The Anti-Communist Front', *Asia*, December 1938. K. Bloch, 'The New Berlin-Tokyo Axis', ibid. In his speech on 20 February 1938, Hitler had announced Germany's decision to recognize Manchukuo, and, while stating that Germany remained neutral in the Sino-Japanese conflict, had declared that a defeat for Japan would only benefit Russia, since China was not strong enough, spiritually or materially, to resist Bolshevism; *Hitler's Speeches*, pp. 1395–7.

[2] Moore, op. cit., p. 118.

[3] The treaty was ratified by the Presidium of the Supreme Soviet on 5 January 1940, and ratifications were exchanged in Chungking on 16 March 1940. A translation of the Russian text, published on 15 June 1940, is given in Moore, op. cit., pp. 189–99.

[4] See vol. I, App. D.

[5] *The Times*, 5 January 1938. S. Hedin, *The Silk Road* (Routledge, 1938). Appendix.

Although the Chinese Central Government had not given any active support to Governor Sheng, civil officials were sent to Sinkiang, perhaps with a view to counterbalancing Soviet influence.[1] The latter, however, increased with the development of the supply route and early in 1938, a report spoke of a number of students from Sinkiang at the Tashkent military college.[2] The Soviet trading agency Sovsintorg was very active and many Soviet technicians were employed as advisers. One experienced student of Sinkiang affairs described the province as afflicted with a strongly Russianized and highly bureaucratic administration and as deluged with 'anti-imperialist' propaganda.[3] The latter manifested itself in agitation for driving out of Sinkiang all foreign elements other than the Russians. Edicts published by the Sinkiang Government in March 1939 ordered all foreign traders in Khotan and Yarkand to surrender their goods and leave within a week. This was obviously directed against the Indians and various forms of unpleasant pressure were brought to bear upon the British consular authorities. A visit to Urumchi by the British Consul in July was unsuccessful and the expulsion of the traders continued while attempts were also made to get rid of the foreign missionaries.[4] Russia continued to exercise preponderant influence in Sinkiang until after her entry into World War II.[5]

The Brussels Conference marked the end of any serious prospect of China receiving help through international action. But the Soviet delegation gave full support to Chinese requests for further League assistance made at the Council meetings of January-February and May 1938, and January 1939.[6]

More important was the effect of Soviet policy on China's internal politics. Indeed, in a list of the reasons which had led the Japanese to precipitate their attack in July 1937, a Soviet commentator included 'the rumours of active co-operation

[1] In October 1937 Chen Li-fu, Chinese Minister of Mass Training and Propaganda said: 'It is natural that Sinkiang and Russia have close relations particularly in the economic sphere, since the geographical isolation of Sinkiang from China and its proximity to Russia makes for easier communications. But no attempt is being made to "communize" the province which is developing along the lines of the rest of China under General Sheng who is completely loyal to Nanking.' Moore, op. cit., p. 132.

[2] *The Times*, 11 February 1938.

[3] M. Cable, 'The New Dominion', *J.R.C.A.S.*, 1938.

[4] *The Times*, 13 November 1938, 25 March, 1 and 16 October 1939.

[5] There was a report of another plot against Governor Sheng in August 1939; Soviet circles seem to have put it down, like most untoward events in Sinkiang, to Japanese intrigue. A. L. Strong, 'Airplane from the U.S.S.R.', *Asia*, January 1942.

[6] *L.N.O.J.*, February 1938; May-June 1938; February 1939.

between Nanking and the Red Armies of China'.[1] The co-operation between the Kuomintang and the Communists continued to make steady progress after the outbreak of the Sino-Japanese war.[2] In July 1938 the Chinese Government acknowledged, at the first session of the People's Political Council, that the Communists had faithfully observed the conditions for unity laid down by the Kuomintang.[3] In October, after the loss of Canton and simultaneously with the all-out Japanese assault on Hankow, the Sixteenth Plenum of the Chinese Communist Party met at Yenan and passed resolutions further detailing the Party's programme and making recommendations for the next stage of the war. Mao Tse-tung explained the Communist theory of the nature of the war and the methods by which alone victory could be achieved, and suggested for the purpose an organic union of all parties engaged in the anti-Japanese struggle, promising that this would not be used in order to build up secret Communist organizations within the Kuomintang.[4] The Party's general attitude remained indeed throughout the year the same as that outlined by Mao to an American admirer in May: 'The Chinese Communist party', runs the summary of his statement, 'hopes to continue the present entente with the Kuomintang, looking to the establishment in China of a real democracy with a two-party government. We believe that the state should own the bank, mines, and communications. We believe that consumers' and producers' co-operatives should be developed. We favour the encouragement of private enterprise and we desire that cordial relations should be established and maintained with all foreign nations which are willing to meet China on a basis of equality.'[5]

The prevailing optimism as to the future was reflected in the Soviet press. This stressed the role of the Border Government in the North-West and ascribed to its example the praiseworthy activities of the Central Government in the economic and social sphere. While the interest in the U.S.S.R. prevailing in China, and its popularity there were stressed, events in China were not presented as a triumph for Communism nor was the war presented as in any way a competition between the U.S.S.R. and Japan.[6]

[1] *Bolshevik*, 1 August 1937. Quoted in H. Moore, 'The Soviet Press and Japan's War on China', *Pacific Affairs*, March 1938.

[2] See vol. 1, App. C.

[3] *China Year Book* (Tientsin, Tientsin Press), 1939.

[4] L. Epstein, *The People's War* (Gollancz, 1939), chap. 14.

[5] Carlson, op. cit., p. 72.

[6] M. R. Norins, 'The War in China and the Soviet Press', *Pacific Affairs*, June 1939. A picture of the Red Army in this period is given in Carlson,

The most important aspect of Communist participation in the war was the organization of partisan warfare inside areas nominally controlled by the Japanese. The first 'guerilla government', an all-party coalition, was set up in January 1938, at Fuping in Western Hupeh.[1]

The accord was not destined to be a lasting one. At the end of 1938, a military clash occurred in north Honan between the Eighth Route Army and troops of the Central Government. In 1939 there was friction both in the guerrilla areas and on the frontiers of the North-West Border Region, and what had appeared to be isolated incidents came to be seen as symptoms of a general political change at Chungking.[2] In January 1939, a proposal for an organic union (the old idea of dual membership) between the Kuomintang and the Communist Party was turned down by the former. In February a Supreme Defence Council was formed without the inclusion of a single Communist.[3] The legal ban on the Communists (as well as on all other minority parties) remained effective and the practical toleration granted to them continued to be of a very limited kind.[4] Soviet aid to China had thus not succeeded in altering the basic outlook of the country's ruling group; on the other hand, the Japanese were by the spring of 1939 so deeply involved in their Chinese campaign as to give the Russians less cause for anxiety than for a long time past.

Russo-Japanese relations had continued to be extremely tense throughout the period since the Lukouchiao incident.

---

op. cit., pp. 35–42. A first-hand description of conditions in the Shensi Special Area is given by Nym Wales in 'The Passing of the Chinese Soviets', *Asia*, February 1938. 'One of the major social experiments of our generation has ended,' she writes, '—a Leninist attempt to establish Soviets in a semi-colonial land'. Cf. V. Cressy Marcks, *Journey to China* (Hodder and Stoughton, 1940), Pt. IV, for an account of a visit to North Shensi in 1938. An interpretation of the situation from a Communist standpoint is given in A. L. Strong, 'How Red is China Now?', *Asia*, August 1938. This admits that the Chinese Communists, believing their struggle is bound up with events all over the world, co-operate through the Comintern with Communist Parties in other countries but denies any contact with or help from the Soviet Government. Cf. A. Smedley, *China Fights Back* (Gollancz, 1939); L. K. Rosinger, 'The Politics and Strategy of China's Mobile War', *Pacific Affairs*, September 1939.

[1] White and Jacoby, op. cit., pp. 51–6.

[2] L. K. Rosinger, *China's Wartime Politics* (I.P.R., Princeton University Press, 1944), pp. 38–9. Cf. White and Jacoby, op. cit., pp. 75–7.

[3] At this time, according to one estimate by a sympathizer, the Communists controlled about a tenth of the nation's armed forces and ruled over a million people in the Special Border Area; Epstein, op. cit., p. 373.

[4] Linebarger, *The China of Chiang Kai-shek* (Boston, World Peace Foundation, 1941), p. 160.

In August 1937 there were raids on the Soviet consulates in Tientsin and Shanghai. In August, Manchukuo again suspended pension payments to former employees of the C.E.R. There were new disputes over the Sakhalin concessions and no improvement in the situation on the Mongolia-Manchuria border. In September the Soviet Government withdrew recognition from the Japanese consulates at Odessa and Novosibirsk, a fore-runner of more drastic action with regard to foreign consulates at the beginning of the following year. The Soviet Government protested against the Japanese bombing of Nanking and against provocative anti-Soviet utterances by General Araki.[1] In December 1937 a Soviet mailplane came down in Manchuria and there were strong protests at the failure to release its crew and hand over its cargo. On 29 December the fisheries agreement was once again prolonged for a year but the Soviet press charged the Japanese with concealing the news from its public in order to stimulate anti-Soviet feeling.[2]

In his speech of 17 January before the Supreme Soviet, Zhdanov declared that the Soviet Foreign Commissariat 'should be more resolute in its attitude towards the arrogant, hooligan, and provocative conduct of the agents of Japan and that puppet State called Manchukuo'.

Speaking on 19 January Molotov said:

'I will speak first of all of our reciprocal relations with Japan, and of the effrontery of certain agents of the Government of Japan and of the Government of Manchukuo, which latter, notorious as it is, is nothing but a puppet Government. You are aware, Comrades, that the Soviet Government has repeatedly been obliged to protest against certain inadmissible acts of the Japanese and Manchukuo authorities. We expect to be in a position to safeguard the interests of the Soviet Union fully against all these insolent acts and others

[1] In November, the Japanese protested about the treatment of the Korean settlers in the Soviet Far East, who, it was believed, were being moved from there and resettled in Soviet Central Asia. Replying on 28 November, Litvinov was understood to have denied Japan's right to intervene since the Koreans were Soviet citizens. *B.I.N.*, XIV, p. 574. The Koreans were all deported to Kazakhstan. See 'Divided Korea', *The Economist*, 5 January 1946.

[2] Speaking on 22 January 1938, the Japanese Foreign Minister Hirota said a *modus vivendi* had been necessary owing to the attitude of the Soviet authorities. 'I should add however,' he continued, 'that since the Soviet government are proceeding with the necessary internal preparations for the conclusion of an agreement providing for a revision of the treaty now in force, we are taking steps for the continuance of the negotiations and the signing of the new agreement at the earliest possible date.' With regard to the Sakhalin concessions Hirota declared that Japan would 'never allow these rights and interests derived from the Soviet-Japanese Basic Treaty to be nullified through unreasonable pressure.' *Documents for 1938*, vol. i, p. 344.

of the same kind on the part of foreign States. We can assure you, Comrades, that we shall actually apply all the measures which may be necessary on our part.'[1]

In fact a series of measures and counter-measures followed on both sides.[2] On 4 April 1938 the Soviet Ambassador Slavutsky (who had succeeded Yurenev on 2 September 1937) suggested to Hirota that there should be a general settlement of the matters in dispute. The Japanese Government insisted that some of the questions involved should be taken up with the Manchukuo Government direct, that the Soviet Government should indicate what concessions it was prepared to make in the Sakhalin disputes, agree to sign a new long-term fisheries convention and consent to Japan's retaining consulates at Khabarovsk, Blagoveshchensk, and elsewhere.

The Japanese demands were rejected by Moscow at the end of the month, and the situation remained tense in spite of a simultaneous Soviet offer to settle the smaller issues which did not bear 'on the general policy of both Governments' and were 'the cause of inconvenience to one side without any advantage to the other'.[3]

---

[1] *Documents for 1938*, vol. i, p. 313.

[2] In January 'Moscow took retaliatory action against Japan by suspending parcel post connexions with Manchuria. In February and March the Japanese seized and held two Soviet ships which had called at Japanese ports, evidently with the object of forcing the Soviets to exchange the Japanese they had arrested as spies for the Russian passengers and crews. Thereupon the Soviets detained eight Japanese previously scheduled for deportation. Finally, Manchukuo refused to honour the obligations for the final payment on the Chinese Eastern Railway in March 1938 on the ground that the Soviet government still owed considerable debts in connexion with the line. In answer, the Soviets seized more Japanese fishing smacks, demanded the closing of the Japanese consulate at Okha on Sakhalin and refused to grant certain requests by the Sakhalin concessionaires.' Moore, op. cit., p. 97. Davies reported to the Secretary of State a conversation with Litvinov on 23 March 1938, in which the latter told him that aggression by Japan against the Soviet Union had been rendered out of the question by China's resistance. Davies also mentioned a recent confident statement on the Soviet Union's strength in the Far East made by Marshal Bluecher. In a further dispatch on 1 April he added: 'This (the Soviet) government does not conceal its deep sympathy for China but is meticulously careful to maintain peace with Japan, at least for the present.' Davies, op. cit., pp. 195-6.

[3] *Izvestia*, 28 April 1938, quoted by Moore, op. cit., p. 98. On 16 May 1938, Grew reported on a press conference held by Hirota on 9 May: 'The Soviet Union, he said, was insisting that only urgent pending questions be discussed between the two countries, while Japan wished that as many questions as possible be taken up including that of the fisheries; no break with the Soviet Government was anticipated, even if Soviet-Japanese negotiations for the settlement of outstanding questions should fail; and

In a speech in Moscow on 23 June 1938 Litvinov devoted considerable attention to Japan's record of aggression.[1] He pointed out that Japan was not limiting herself to the boundaries of China, but like Germany, sometimes permitted herself to dream about Soviet lands. This speech heralded a new acute phase in Soviet-Japanese relations.

On 15 July the Japanese Ambassador Shigemitsu demanded the withdrawal of Soviet troops from a hill called Changkufeng, west of Lake Hasan, near the junction between Manchuria, Korea, and the Soviet Union, which they had occupied on

---

Soviet assistance to China, although conspicuous, had been less in extent than expected by China; and in his (Mr. Hirota's) opinion, the Soviet Government would stop such assistance realizing it had been extended in vain.' *Foreign Relations of the United States: Japan, 1931–41*, vol. 1, p. 466. The American Ambassador in Moscow made the following entry in his journal under the date 4 June: 'The following is my best judgement as to the situation here with reference to Japan:

'Soviet-Japanese relations are very difficult; constant difficulties were being experienced in the Island of Saghalien (Sakhalin) in connection with the operation of Japanese concessions; where necessary reliance was placed in large part upon Soviet employees; these difficulties, it is claimed by some, arise primarily from the fact that such Soviet employees, fearing charges of being Trotskyites, Japanese spies, and wreckers, refused to have anything to do with the Japanese; that there were also other matters of serious difference.

'I have the impression that the attitude of Russian diplomacy is definitely hardening towards Japan and more aggressive than last summer.

'According to reliable information there are approximately 450,000 to 600,000 Soviet armed troops in the eastern area. It is stated, however, that the Japanese believe that for every Japanese soldier in Manchukuo, the Soviets maintained in Manchuria [*sic*] three Soviet soldiers. The Japanese armed forces in Manchuria are estimated to be from 150,000 to 200,000 in number. This checks with other information current here.

'Litvinov recently advised me that the Japanese were extensive buyers of Soviet rubles "outside"; that this accounted for the rise in price of the "black" ruble, and that in his opinion Japan was procuring rubles for the purposes of bribery in the East.' Davies, op. cit., pp. 216–17. In his final report to the Secretary of State, dated 6 June, Davies seems to have revised these estimates. He now gave the strength of the Soviet Far Eastern Army at from 350,000 to 450,000 men and said that it was reported to be the fixed intention of the Soviet Government to keep two soldiers in the Far East for every Japanese soldier in Manchuria. He also reported the existence of a Pacific fleet claimed to number 40 submarines and of an air force of 1,500 planes in the Far East; ibid., p. 266. A month or two later the Soviet paper *Red Fleet* estimated the Kwantung Army as 250,000 men with 600 tanks, 1,000 guns, and 450 planes (about 20 per cent of Japan's total air strength), and the Japanese Army in Korea as 60,000 men, with 200 guns, 50 tanks, and 100 planes. The Manchukuo Army was said to be 80,000 strong and to be officered by 10,000 Japanese instructors. See 'The Manchukuo Border: Soviet-Japanese Clash', *B.I.N.*, 13 and 27 August 1938.

[1] *Documents for 1938*, vol. i, pp. 315–22.

11 July. This demand was rejected on the ground that the area in question lay within the Soviet frontier. Further unsuccessful diplomatic exchanges were followed by actual fighting around the disputed zone which began about the 27th.

On 4 August the Japanese put forward proposals for a settlement. They suggested a return to the position as it had stood before 11 July and a commission to demarcate the frontier. Litvinov insisted as usual that the Japanese recognize existing Sino-Russian agreements as the only basis for settling the frontier disputes and that Japanese troops be withdrawn from Changkufeng itself, which they had taken on the 29th.[1] No agreement could be reached on this basis and no further progress was made when the Japanese Ambassador saw Litvinov again on 7 August. On this occasion Litvinov declared that the affair could hardly be treated as a frontier incident since heavy artillery was now in action. He went on to state that the Soviet Government would not tolerate further Japanese attacks on its frontier guards or Japanese incursions into its territory 'Let the Japanese Government force the Kwantung and Korean armies to respect the existing frontier. It is time to put an end to the endless incidents and clashes on the frontier.' In an editorial on 8 August, *Pravda* charged the Kwantung Army with trying to 'drag Japan into war with the U.S.S.R.' This outspoken attitude on the part of the Soviet Union was backed up by accounts in the Soviet press of mass meetings in farm and factory calling for the defence of the Soviet fatherland and for the defeat of the Japanese invader.

Soviet militancy did not, however, necessarily indicate that a show-down with Japan was desired, and after further fighting Litvinov on 10 August proposed a truce. His suggestion was that the respective forces should hold existing positions (the Soviet troops having apparently recovered some of their lost ground) and that the frontier should be 'redemarcated' by a mixed commission to consist of two representatives of the U.S.S.R., two of Japan and Manchukuo, with an outside arbitrator to be jointly agreed upon. This basis was substantially accepted for the truce which came into force the next day; but the idea of an arbitrator was dropped and no agreement was reached as to the documentary basis on which the commission should do its work. No progress in settling the frontier was in fact made. There seems reason to believe that in practice the Soviet authorities made good their claim to the disputed hill.

The Changkufeng incident was the most serious of the affrays

[1] The Soviet claim was made on the basis of a protocol signed in 1886 to the Sino-Russian treaty of Hunchun of 1869.

which had so far taken place on the borders of the Soviet Far East.[1] But once again it looked as though neither side had really wished for an all-out clash. On the other hand, the Soviet attitude gave evidence of much more confidence in Soviet strength than had been apparent a year earlier, and this in spite of the fact that the crisis in its military and naval leadership was not yet over.[2]

Some Soviet spokesmen treated the incident as having been provoked by the Japanese with a view to distracting Soviet attention from events in Europe.[3]

[1] Soviet estimates of the casualties were: Russians: killed, 236; wounded, 611. Japanese: killed, 600; wounded, 2,500. Japanese estimates were: Russians, killed and wounded over 1,700; Japanese, killed 158, wounded 723.

[2] Marshal Bluecher was reported to have arrived at Novokievsk on 9 August in order to take charge of operations in person.

'This particular incident', wrote the American Ambassador in Tokyo, 'seems to have been more serious than usual and reminded us of the trouble over the islands in the Amur River last year, when the Japanese appeared to be trying out the Soviet strength. In the present case it may be that the Russians were testing the Japanese strength and determination, or they may have staged the incident in order to draw Japanese troops away from the drive on Hankow with a view to co-operating with the Chinese. If this was their purpose, they seem to have been at least partially successful, for considerable troop movements to the north are reported, and Japan can now hardly afford to omit preparations for any eventuality in that area.

'Being convinced that the Soviets do not want war with Japan at present, and equally convinced that the Japanese cannot now afford any such venture, I was not greatly perturbed by the incident and felt from the beginning that it would be localized. General Ott, the German Ambassador, who has close relations with the highest Japanese military officers, told me that these high officers had said to him that they want no trouble with Russia at present because they are far too much occupied in China and that they would therefore not allow the incident to develop.' Grew, op. cit., pp. 250–1. The document from which this is taken is dated 1 August; this is obviously a mistake since Grew goes on to mention the armistice (of 11 August).

Walter Duranty writes that the Japanese object in wishing to seize Chang-kufeng was that the hill gave artillery control over Possiet Bay, where the Russians were planning a new submarine and air base. He estimates the forces engaged as from seventy to eighty thousand on either side; U.S.S.R. (Hamilton, 1944), pp. 244–5.

[3] During the crisis reports varied as to the attitudes of Japan's European associates. There was a report that on 6 August, the German and Italian Ambassadors at Tokyo represented to the Japanese Government that the time was not propitious for a clash between the anti-Comintern Powers and the U.S.S.R. Reports of some kind of promise of help by Germany were, however, provoked by a visit of the Japanese Ambassador in Berlin to Ribbentrop on the 9th; the German Government refused to comment on these reports. The evidence at the Tokyo War Guilt Trial seems to have shown that the affair was brought about by the Japanese in order to test Soviet strength. *The Times*, 10 March 1947.

In a speech on 9 November 1938 Molotov said: 'The whole question of events in the district of Lake Hasan was actually decided not in Tokyo, but in another place, somewhere in Europe, and most probably in Berlin. The Japanese military probably wanted to support their Fascist friends in Germany.'[1]

Meanwhile, the other differences dividing the Soviet Union from Japan had come no nearer a solution. The Soviet Ambassador, who had left Tokyo before the Changkufeng affair, was not replaced until November 1939. The most important Soviet grievance was Manchukuo's refusal to pay the last instalment of the C.E.R. purchase. The Soviet Government refused to consider the Japanese request for a long-term agreement on the fisheries until this sum was paid. Litvinov offered in December 1938 to prolong the existing agreement for yet another year but with certain changes involving the withdrawal of certain areas previously open to the Japanese, 'for reasons of the conservation of the fisheries or for strategic reasons'. As a result, negotiations were prolonged, and it was only on 2 April 1939 that a compromise was reached. The agreement signed then extended the existing convention until 31 December 1939 but with the alteration necessary to meet the new Soviet demand.[2] In February 1939 there was a new frontier incident, and there were further Japanese complaints about Sakhalin, while the anti-Comintern motif continued to bulk large in

[1] Voroshilov, however, speaking on 7 November, described the incident as an attempt by 'not very clever people to acquire cheaply a bit of Soviet territory and then to shout about the Red Army's weakness'. In November 1938, Matsuoka, who became Japanese Foreign Minister in 1940, is said to have devised a plan, with the knowledge of Konoye, the Japanese Prime Minister, for the joint purchase by the United States and Japan of all Siberia east of Lake Baikal. This he declared to be essential to avoid an otherwise inevitable war with Russia. He is also said to have revealed that he attached great importance to discontent alleged to exist among the Ukrainians and Cossacks of Eastern Siberia and that the Japanese were tolerating a secret organization working for their autonomy with headquarters in Harbin; Hallett Abend, *Pacific Charter* (Lane, 1943), pp. 146 ff. Japan had shifted its main support from Semenov to General Rodzaevsky and his Russian Fascist Union, and to an even greater extent to the associated Russian Emigrants' Bureau founded in 1934 and headed by General Kislitsin. In August 1946, Semenov, Rodzaevsky, Prince Uktomski and five others were found guilty by a Russian court of organizing Russian elements in the Far East in support of Japan. Five of the defendants, including Semenov were sentenced to death. *The Times*, 27 August, 31 August 1946.

[2] Article 8, Protocol A of the Convention of 1928 was omitted. This provided that lots once opened for exploitation could not thereafter be closed but had to continue to be offered for lease. The text of the 1928 Convention is printed in Conolly, *Soviet Trade from the Pacific to the Levant* (Oxford University Press, 1935), App. vi.

official Japanese pronouncements. Thus even before the outbreak in May of fresh fighting on the Manchuria-Mongolia
frontier, the Far Eastern situation must have played some considerable part in the Soviet attitude to international affairs
generally.

Relations between the Soviet Union and the United States
in the period under review continued to reflect the substantial
differences in their general international outlook. The Russians
went on hoping for some effort by the United States to assist in
checking aggression, particularly in the Far East. Whatever the
private opinions of the United States administration may have
been, public and Congressional sentiment, as reflected in the
Neutrality Act of 1 May 1937, made any such action no more
likely than before.[1] On the other hand, the United States policy
to Russia continued to centre round the old questions of trade,
debts, and propaganda.[2]

The trade agreement of 1935 was renewed for a year on
11 July 1936 and the Russian guarantee to purchase thirty
million dollars worth of American goods in the ensuing year
was also renewed.[3]

In August 1936 President Roosevelt offered the American
Embassy to J. E. Davies in succession to W. C. Bullitt, whose
mission had left a legacy of irritation on both sides. Davies
arrived in Moscow on 18 January 1937, and a meeting took
place on 5 February at which the question of the debt was raised
by the Russians. Those taking part in the discussion included
Rosengoltz, Voroshilov, Mikoyan, Vyshinsky, and Rosov, the
newly appointed head of Amtorg, the Soviet trading organization in America. It is fairly clear that the Russians would have
liked a settlement, but felt themselves precluded from formal
action through the Foreign Commissariat for fear of being
obliged thereby to take up again the much more considerable
claims of France and Great Britain. A further discussion took
place between Molotov and Davies on 19 February; Litvinov
was present on this occasion but took no part in the talks.[4]

During the summer, Davies took up the question of renewing
the trade agreement and pressed for the guarantee for Soviet
purchases to be raised to forty million dollars.[5] In this he was

---

[1] Litvinov expressed strong disapproval of the proposed neutrality legislation in an interview which Davies had with him on 15 February; Davies,
op. cit., pp. 61–2.
[2] See Davies' note of his talk with Sumner Welles on 15 December 1936,
soon after his nomination as Ambassador to the U.S.S.R.; Davies, op. cit.,
pp. 13–14. It was not apparently intended that the question of the debts
should be raised on the American side.   [3] *L.N.T.S.*, vol. 172, p. 434.
[4] Davies, op. cit., pp. 50–3, 65–6.   [5] ibid., pp. 121–2.

successful, and the agreement was renewed on 4 August.[1] It also provided for most-favoured nation treatment on the Russian side.

The outbreak of war in China focused attention on the political aspect of Soviet-American relations. On 21 July the text of Cordell Hull's statement on general American policy was officially communicated to the Soviet Government with a request for its comments.[2] On 23 July a reply from Litvinov was delivered to the American Embassy in Moscow. Litvinov declared that the principles enshrined in the American statement were not merely approved of by his Government but had in fact formed the basis of its own diplomatic activity and of its endeavours to strengthen the machinery of peace. He added that there were a number of ways open for carrying these principles into practical effect in ways parallel to the activities of the League of Nations, such as, for example, 'regional pacts of mutual assistance and other agreements'. He also attached great importance, he declared, to periodic manifestations of the solidarity of all peace-loving states and added that the Soviet Union was always prepared to take its full part in these, as in all efforts on behalf of international peace.[3]

The Roosevelt 'quarantine' speech at Chicago on 5 October 1937 may have raised hopes of some definite action by the United States.[4] But any such hopes were rapidly dissipated by the hostile reactions to the speech in America itself and by the American failure to give a strong lead at the Brussels Conference. Nevertheless, in a dispatch on 1 April 1938, Davies could assert that the United States mission had during the past year received more consideration than that of any other foreign Government, although, as he pointed out, this attitude did not deter the Russians in 'matters affecting their vital interests, as indicated by the debt and Comintern situation'.[5]

On 5 June Stalin gave Davies, on the eve of the latter's depar-

---

[1] United States Executive Agreement Series No. 105, *Documents on American Foreign Relations*, 1938–9 (Boston, World Peace Foundation), p. 383. The guaranteed figure was maintained at 40,000,000 dollars per annum from 1937 to 1940. Soviet trade with the United States was as follows (in millions of dollars):

	Exports to United States	Imports from United States
1936	21	33
1937	31	43
1938	24	70
1939	25	57

[2] Text of the American statement, *Peace and War*, pp. 370–1.
[3] *Pravda*, 8 August 1937.   [4] *Peace and War*, pp. 383–7.
[5] Davies, op. cit., pp. 200–1.

ture, the then unusual privilege of an interview. Stalin at first brought up the question of the difficulties which had arisen in connexion with the Soviet Government's attempt to contract for the building of a battleship in the United States. He then passed on to the question of the debts. The proposal was that the 'Kerensky' debt should be treated by itself as a debt to the United States Government, since this would avoid the question of claims by French and British nationals. But a payment made on this account would have to be accepted as a final settlement of all claims. Elaborating this suggestion on 8 and 9 June, Molotov again indicated that the matter should be handled through Rosov, and not through diplomatic channels. He declared that the Soviet Union, with its favourable balance of trade, did not require credits, and in fact had recently rejected the offer of a large credit from Germany. It was clear that it was for political reasons ('high regard for the United States, &c.') and not in order to escape from the provisions of the Johnson Act, that this proposal was being put forward. The proposal was further discussed after Davies's return to the United States but apparently came to nothing.[1]

In summing up his impressions of his mission in two dispatches to the Secretary of State on 6 June 1938, Davies said that the Comintern was the one issue over which serious friction might arise between the U.S.S.R. and the United States. For, although Comintern activity was not great, the Soviet desire to use the Comintern as an adjunct to its military forces in case of war, was too strong for it to be abandoned. He thought it quite clear that the Soviet Union was more friendly to the United States than to any other Power.[2]

Nevertheless, after Davies's departure from Moscow (which was almost simultaneous with the departure of Troyanovsky from Washington), no new American Ambassador to the Soviet Union was appointed and relations between the two Governments became very distant.[3] Speaking on 23 June 1938 Litvinov deplored the fact that 'in the great transatlantic republic' isolationism had made such great headway that little hope could be placed 'on her eventual co-operation', particularly if

[1] ibid., pp. 220-1, 228, 341-3, 239-42, 344-6. The trade agreement was renewed for another year on 5 August. *Documents on American Foreign Relations*, 1938-9, p. 384.

[2] Davies, op. cit., pp. 243-73.

[3] Oumansky, who became Chargé d'Affaires after Troyanovsky's departure from Washington, was appointed Ambassador at Washington later in the year. Davies' successor as Ambassador in Moscow, Lawrence Steinhardt, was not appointed until well into 1939 and only arrived in Moscow on 8 August.

no firm grouping opposed to aggression was formed in Europe.

As has been noted, the Soviet Government welcomed the American proposal for an international conference, made during the 'Munich' crisis, but there was no sequel to this solitary contact. The United States (like the other Western Powers), took up a less compliant attitude towards Japan after Konoye's pronouncement on the 'new order for East Asia' on 3 November 1938, and there were signs of a greater readiness to give assistance to China. But this had no apparent effect on Soviet-American relations, and in the spring of 1939 the two countries seemed politically as far apart as at any time since 1933.

Chapter Nine

RUSSIA AND THE MIDDLE EAST, 1929–1939

THE importance of the Middle East during the later stages of the expansion of Tsarist Russia, and during the early post-Revolutionary years, would seem to demand a separate treatment of that area for the period with which this study is concerned. In fact, the late nineteen-twenties saw the beginning of a period of relative and temporary stabilization. But considerations of internal as well as external policy made it impossible for Russia's rulers to be wholly uninterested in anything which went on among the broad belt of Moslem peoples which stretches all the way from the Aegean to north-western China. Turkey on the one hand, and Sinkiang on the other, having already been dealt with, there remains to be considered the policy of the Soviet Union with regard to Persia and Afghanistan.

Some account of Russian relations with Persia before 1929 is essential for an adequate survey of the period now under review. The lack of a clearly defined natural frontier north of the mountains, and the racial ties between certain of the peoples of northern Persia and those brought under Russian sway between 1860 and 1880, made this fruitful area—the Caspian provinces —a natural goal for further imperialist expansion. And from 1880 onwards Russian penetration into Persia was rapid. In addition to the economic advantages which might be achieved in the North and the possibility of territorial annexations, there was the remoter prospect of finding in the Persian Gulf that ice-free port which was the *ignis fatuus* of Russian imperialism. Finally, Persia had an obvious utility as a scene of diversionary pressure against Russia's British rival. The latter Power, primarily concerned with the defence of India, was ready to sub-ordinate Persian to Afghan policy in 1879–81,[1] and twenty years later to envisage with equanimity the predominance of Russia in the north and the prospect of a Russian commercial outlet on the gulf.[2]

The emergence of a nascent constitutionalist and nationalist

---

[1] J. G. Allen, 'British Policy towards Persia in 1879', *J.R.C.A.S.*, 1935.
[2] B. H. Sumner, *Tsardom and Imperialism in the Far East and the Middle East, 1880–1914* (Oxford University Press, for British Academy, 1942). For the Persian background, see Sir Percy Sykes, *A History of Persia*, 2 vols., 2nd ed. (Macmillan, 1931), vol. ii, chaps. lxxix to lxxxiv.

movement in Persia, with some support in British quarters, enabled the Russians to increase their hold on the country by intervening decisively on the side of political reaction. The necessities of world politics obliged Russia to enter into an agreement with Britain on 31 August 1907, by which her Government accepted that virtual partition of the country which the forward party in Asiatic affairs wished to avoid. Those elements in the country which favoured a German rather than a British alignment were particularly hostile to the agreement.[1] In Sazonov's negotiations with Germany in 1910–11 the latter Power did indeed show a not unnatural readiness to barter recognition of Russia's special position in Persia in return for assent to her own further penetration in the Ottoman territories.

In point of fact, as British critics of the agreement pointed out, the position of Russia was by no means a weak one. She tended to treat both the northern (Russian) zone and the middle (neutral) zone as her own preserve, with the ultimate annexation of the north as a scarcely concealed goal. Britain's own popularity and prestige among the Persians received a severe blow; but the importance of the southern oilfields, only revealed after 1907, made it unlikely that she would voluntarily permit an extension of the Russian hold to the whole country.

The war of 1914 led to the occupation of the north and north-west of the country by Russian troops and to a British landing in the south. By the secret agreement of 18 March 1915, Russia made considerable sacrifices in Persia—the inclusion of almost the whole of the neutral area within the British zone —as the price of the Allied concessions with regard to Constantinople and the Straits. On the other hand, Russia's intentions of annexing the north were made plainer than ever.[2] But the collapse of the Russian hold, after the Revolution, permitted Britain to occupy the whole country and by the treaty of 9 August 1919, to establish a virtual protectorate.[3]

Since the spring of that year, Persia had actually provided a base for British intervention in the Caucasus. But after the defeat of Denikin, and the Soviet reoccupation of Baku, the Red Fleet, in May 1920, took the Persian port of Anzali (Enzeli) where Denikin's defeated flotilla had taken refuge, and the Bolsheviks proceeded to entrench themselves in the province

[1] See the memorandum of February 1914 by P. N. Durnovo and the Duma speech of N. E. Markov of 23 May in F. A. Golder, *Documents of Russian History* (New York, Century, 1927), pp. 3–28.

[2] Temperley, *A History of the Peace Conference*, 6 vols. (Frowde, Hodder and Stoughton, 1924), vol. vi, pp. 4–9.

[3] ibid., chap. i, Part V; Sykes, *History of Persia*, vol. ii, chaps. lxxxv–xc.

of Gilan. This was followed by a gradual withdrawal of British forces from the country.

The Russians reappeared on the Persian scene in the unaccustomed role of liberators; for their policy as outlined in Karakhan's note of 26 June 1919, consisted in the abandonment of all the economic concessions which the Tsarist Government had acquired, as well as of the capitulations, as derogatory to Persian independence and sovereignty. Negotiations on this basis opened in the autumn of 1920 and Riza Khan's *coup d'état* in the following February enabled matters to be carried to a rapid conclusion. The Soviet-Persian treaty was signed in Moscow on 26 February 1921; the Anglo-Persian treaty was formally denounced by the Persians in June.[1] The Soviet-Persian treaty reaffirmed the Russians' renunciation of all the special advantages acquired by the previous régime and embodied certain territorial concessions to Persia. Russian assistance was to be forthcoming in case Persia was attacked from the direction of Turkey, while Russian troops were empowered to enter the country temporarily, if it again became a base for activities hostile to the Soviet régime.[2]

The position was complicated for a time by the existence in Gilan, which had been proclaimed an independent republic in June 1920, of a more or less Soviet régime. The meeting there, in the same month, of the first Congress of the Persian Communist Party, suggested that the sovietization of northern Persia and its consequent incorporation in the territories ruled by Moscow might not be far off. More cautious counsels prevailed, however, and the fear of provoking a British counter-action in the south led to the evacuation of the Soviet forces in May-June 1921, and to the occupation of the republic by Persian troops in the autumn.[3]

From the point of view of the struggle against Western 'imperialism', the policy of Riza Khan, as ruler of a 'semi-colonial' country, was not very congenial to the Russians. Like Kemal in Turkey, he persecuted the revolutionary movement

---

[1] The text of the treaty and an accompanying letter of interpretation will be found in M. W. Graham, 'The Soviet Security System', *Int. Conc.*, 1929. It was under the provisions of this treaty (clearly directed against Great Britain) that the Russians took action in conjunction with Britain and against Germany in August 1941. U.S.S.R. note to Iran of 24 August, summarized in *B.I.N.*, 6 September 1941.

[2] L. Fischer, *The Soviets in World Affairs*, 2 vols. (Cape, 1930), vol. 1, pp. 287–91.

[3] ibid., pp. 428–32. A. Wilson, *Persia* (Benn, 1932), pp. 146–8. The Soviet version is that the Gilan republic was fatally weakened by dissensions between Communist and non-Communist elements. See the article 'Persia' in vol. 45 (1940) of the *Bolshaya Sovietskaya Entsiklopedia*.

relentlessly, and although until 1925 he was considered by the Russians to be playing a useful part on the international scene as the instrument of the local nationalist bourgeoisie against the British, his assumption of the crown in that year was held to be a betrayal of the republican movement, carried out with the aid of reactionary elements and with British support. The dictatorial nature of his government was stressed in Soviet writings and the settlement of the nomad peoples of his realm described as being achieved at the price of their national independence. The programme of agrarian reform was criticized as insincere and doomed to failure owing to the opposition of the landlord classes, and the country was described as predominantly feudal in its agrarian structure. Two-thirds of the peasants lacked both land and implements and the entire rural population was subject to forced labour and heavy taxes. Significance was naturally attached to the peasant revolts in Gilan in 1926, in Persian Baluchistan in 1928, and in Khorasan in 1929. The industrialization programme was stigmatized as a burden upon the masses and the monopolistic trading companies created under the laws of 1931 described as fortifying the economic hold of the landowners and larger merchants. It was noted that industrialization was creating a new proletariat, and the condition of the masses was said to have become worse as a result of the world economic crisis of 1929–33, while the bourgeoisie were accused of having sought external support at the price of economic concessions to the imperialist Powers. The Anglo-Persian oil agreement of 1933 was analysed in Soviet writings from the point of view of its possible effect upon the Persian class-structure and revolutionary movement.[1]

To what extent the hopes of a serious Communist movement in Persia after 1921 were genuine or well-founded is questionable. 'In political life,' writes a British student of Persian affairs, 'Islam and the Islamic tradition have played an important part in deciding the reaction of the people to modern political doctrines, especially communism. Broadly speaking communism is regarded by the people with horror.'[2] If resis-

---

[1] See *Bolshaya Sovietskaya Entsiklopedia*, loc. cit.; Rendjar, 'Zemelnaya "reforma" Riza-Shah', (The land 'reforms' of Riza-Shah), *Revolutsiony Vostok*, 1933, no. 6. 'Anglo-Persidskoe neftianoe soglashenie' (The Anglo-Persian Oil Agreement), *Materiali po natsionalny-kolonialnym Problemam*, 1933, nos. 1 and 6. For British accounts of Iran under Riza Shah, see L. P. Elwell-Sutton, *Modern Iran* (Routledge, 1941); V. Conolly, 'The Industrialisation of Persia', *J.R.C.A.S.*, 1935.

[2] A. K. S. Lambton in *Islam Today*, ed. A. J. Arberry and Rom Landau (Faber, 1943), p. 173. Cf. the same author's article 'Persia', *J.R.C.A.S.*, 1944.

tance to Soviet propaganda has indeed been attributable to Islam, the Soviets might have been expected to profit at second-hand by the general weakening of Islamic influences as a result of the official westernization movement.[1]

If the Russians' plans still envisaged annexations in Persia it is probable that they attached more importance to the disintegrating effects of racial differences and to the effect of the leading minorities being represented on both sides of the frontier. The Soviet Encyclopaedia (in a volume published in 1940) credited the Persians with accounting for only 50 per cent of the population of their country, with 25 per cent of Turko-Mongols and 10 per cent of Kurds as their principal minorities.[2] There is, however, no evidence available to show that any minority in Persia (with the possible exception of the Armenian diaspora) has been particularly susceptible to Soviet propaganda. The Russians' continued special interest in the northern provinces was shown by the publication by the Narkomindel in 1933 of a series of recent consular reports (1927–30) from northern Persia—reports which went into some detail on the social and economic life of the areas concerned.[3]

Commerce was the main element in Russo-Persian relations in the decade after the treaty of 1921, and in this sphere the pattern for the next decade was dictated by the general evolution of Soviet economic policy with regard to its Asiatic neighbours.[4] Thus Persia profited by its exemption in the early years from the strict application of the foreign trade monopoly. The provisional agreement of 1927, forced upon Persia by a Russian boycott of her goods in the previous year, turned the balance of trade strongly in favour of Russia, and by 1928–9 she had regained her position as Persia's most important supplier. When this treaty expired in 1929, the Persian merchants finally lost their right to trade in Russia, although the Russian organizations were well established in Persia.[5]

This exploitation by Russia of northern Persia's economic

---

[1] On the westernization of Iran, see W. S. Haas, *Iran* (Columbia University Press, 1946), pp. 136–7.

[2] Cf. R. Forbes, 'British and Russian relations with modern Persia', *J.R.C.A.S.*, 1931. The chequered racial pattern and history of Central Asia works both ways of course. At the Peace Conference in 1919, Persia claimed boundaries which would have given her Transcaspia, Merv, and Khiva, and part of the Caucasus including Erivan, Derbent and Baku. Sykes, *History of Persia*, vol. ii, p. 519.

[3] *Sbornik Konsulskikh dokladov Severnaya Persia*, 1933. The districts covered were Khorasan, Astarabad, Gilan, Azerbaijan, and Kurdistan.

[4] V. Conolly, *Soviet Economic Policy in the East*, chap. i.

[5] ibid., chap. iii. *Survey for 1925*, I, pp. 534–46. *Survey for 1928*, pp. 347–74. Cf. Fischer, *Soviets in World Affairs*, vol. 2, pp. 726–34.

dependence upon Russian markets at the expense of Persian traders and consumers did not for a time prevent the continuance of fairly cordial political relations. These were dictated by Russia's general policy of attaching Turkey, Persia, and Afghanistan to herself by treaty arrangements, while encouraging these countries to settle the territorial and other disputes between themselves and to enter into bilateral pacts with each other. A Soviet-Persian treaty of guarantee and neutrality was signed on 1 October 1927, simultaneously with the economic agreements. This treaty, which substantially reproduced the provisions of the treaty of 1921, was ratified on 31 January 1928, a fortnight after the Russians had handed back to the Persians the port of Anzali (now renamed Pahlawi).[1] Persia became a signatory of the 'Litvinov Protocol' on 1 April 1929.

On the other hand some competent observers considered that this period in fact exhibited a general decline in Russia's influence in Persia, and it was certainly followed by a definite Persian effort to check the economic predominance which the Soviet Union had acquired and which, it was feared, might be exploited for political ends.

Some of the developments in industry and transport were anyhow bound to lessen dependence on Russia for vital supplies. The trans-Iranian railway, under construction in these years, would ultimately enable the northern provinces to find new outlets for their products, in particular for rice. By 1935 it could indeed be said that, although this latter objective had not yet been achieved, Persia was already less dependent on Russia for such principal imports as sugar and cotton piece-goods. These results had been obtained by deliberate control of foreign trade as well as by the stimulation of local industry. The 1930 'Bill for Commercial Reciprocity with foreigners' and the introduction of a foreign trade monopoly in February 1931 were both clearly directed against Russia. The new commercial treaty of 27 October 1931 limited Russian imports into the country by a system of fixed quotas. The Russian quotas were, however, still large, amounting in some cases to a monopoly, and it could be argued that Persia's gains were more nominal than real. The activities of Soviet trading organizations continued to cause a great deal of discontent. Imports from Russia

[1] The texts of these treaties are printed and their significance discussed in Graham, loc. cit.

Persia, however, remained throughout a member of the League of Nations as she had been since the end of 1919. (Turkey and Afghanistan were neither of them members: the former joined in 1932, the latter in 1934 along with the U.S.S.R. itself.) M. Mesbah Zadeh, *La Politique d'Iran dans la Société des Nations* (Paris, Pedone, 1936).

fell off considerably in 1932 and there was a temporary boycott of such goods in 1933. A settlement was reached, however, which covered both commercial questions and another old subject of dispute, the Caspian fisheries.[1]

The real turning point was, however, the new commercial treaty of 27 October 1935, after which trade between the two countries improved considerably.[2]

In 1936–1937 Russia took 12·5 per cent of the total exports of Iran (as Persia was now styled) and supplied 32·1 per cent of her imports; in 1937–1938 the corresponding figures were 32·5 per cent and 9·6 per cent.[3] 'Russian engineers and technicians began to pour into the country; contracts were obtained for flour mills and bakeries, granaries and workshops, Russian surveyors were employed on new road projects, and Russian pilots, aero, and tank experts began to appear in unusually large numbers.'[4] From about 1935 the Russians displayed much interest in Persian culture; and propaganda of a cultural type was soon in full swing.[5] On the surface there was no major change in the development of political relations between the two countries. Nevertheless, as an authority on Iran has pointed out, 'if there was a central idea in Riza Shah's foreign policy, it was his dread of Bolshevism and of the spreading of Bolshevik propaganda in his country'. In 1937 a number of people were sentenced to imprisonment for the spreading of Communistic ideas. It was this fear of Bolshevism which later made the Shah so susceptible to the blandishments of Nazi agents.[6]

Relations between Persia and her other neighbours continued to develop independently of Russia; this was particularly true

[1] Conolly, loc. cit. Elwell-Sutton, op. cit., p. 162. Department of Overseas Trade, *Economic Conditions in Iran, 1935*. Report by S. Simmonds (London, H.M.S.O., 1935). Cf. review by Conolly, *J.R.C.A.S.*, 1936.

[2] Department of Overseas Trade, *Economic conditions in Iran, 1937*.

[3] Soviet-Persian trade (in millions of roubles):

	Soviet Exports to Persia.	Soviet Imports from Persia.
1929–30	61·2	47·3
1930	60·2	44·4
1931	32·2	46·4
1932	25·3	49·9
1933	8·4	12
1934	11·8	14·3
1935	15·7	20·7
1936	63·3	91·1
1937	91·7	84·8
1938	58	63·8

For purposes of comparison, the figures from 1936 onwards should be divided by 4·38.

[4] Elwell-Sutton, op. cit., p. 162–3.

[5] *Survey for 1934*, p. 220–1.   [6] Haas, op. cit., pp. 222–3.

of relations with Turkey, with which a frontier agreement and a treaty of arbitration and conciliation were reached in 1932. The treaty of friendship in November 1933 was followed by Riza Shah's visit to Turkey in 1934.

Russia was to some extent the gainer from renewed friction between Persia and Great Britain—the dispute over Bahrein and the more important one over the Anglo-Persian Oil Company's concession which culminated in its cancellation in November 1932. Since a new agreement more favourable to Persia (and one which enabled the company to compete with Russian oil in the north) was arrived at in the following May, after mediatory action at Geneva, no more than tacit support was required from Russia during the controversy and this, it seems, was forthcoming.[1] On 3 July 1933 Persia was one of the signatories of the Russian-inspired Convention for the Definition of an Aggressor. The year also saw a visit to Persia by Karakhan, and Litvinov's references to Persia in his speech of 29 December were of the friendliest.[2]

During the years 1934–7, the States of the Middle East drew still closer together, and in the autumn of 1935 Iran took the initiative in proposing a Middle Eastern pact. Although negotiations were delayed pending the solution of a number of outstanding questions, the Saadabad Pact was duly signed at Teheran on 8 July 1937, by the representatives of Iran, Iraq, Turkey, and Afghanistan.[3]

A new turn was given to the affairs of the Middle East by the tour there of Dr. Schacht in November 1936. In consequence of the new agreement then concluded, there began a period of rapid growth in the trade between Germany and Iran, and in 1938–9 its volume surpassed that of Soviet-Iranian trade. Japan also became an important supplier of Iran's needs.[4]

German trade meant the infiltration of German personnel on the familiar model, and cultural and propagandist activities were carried on fairly intensively. The Soviet Union protested in March 1938 when planes of the Luft-Hansa service to Tokyo were allowed to land at Teheran, and Iran found it necessary to deny that the Germans had been given facilities at the mili-

---

[1] *Survey for 1933*, pp. 180–2.

[2] *Documents for 1933*, p. 432.

[3] The U.S.S.R. had in January 1935 signified its neutrality in the case of the most important of these disputes, that between Iran and Iraq over the Shattu'l 'Arab. For the text of the Saadabad Pact see *Documents for 1937*, pp. 531–3.

[4] As early as 1935, anxiety was expressed in the Soviet press at Japanese attempts to gain influence in Iran and Afghanistan; Moore, *Soviet Far Eastern Policy*, p. 38.

tary airport at Meshed.[1] In August 1938 the Russians again
protested against German activities in Persia.[2] Generally
speaking, the indications were that Riza Shah hoped to make
use of Germany to counterbalance Soviet influences, but that no
break with the Soviet Union was contemplated. Economic
relations with the U.S.S.R. continued to be of great importance to Persia.[3]

Soviet Russia's relations with Afghanistan in the period dealt
with showed a certain parallel to those with Persia.[4] The British
war with Afghanistan in 1919 (the Third Afghan War) left
that country a fully independent State, but the lingering suspicions of British designs made the country susceptible to the
influence of Soviet propaganda, which was vigorously pressed
forward in 1919–20. This was regarded in Moscow as all the
more important, since in Russian eyes Afghanistan could not
but retain its historic role as the gateway to India. The revolution in Bokhara in 1920, which brought to Afghanistan as
refugees the Emir and hundreds of his Uzbek supporters, caused
a revulsion of feeling against the Russians. Nevertheless, an
Afghan-Soviet treaty of friendship and alliance was signed on
28 February 1921 and ratified by the Emir in August.[5] This
treaty provided for the establishment of Soviet consulates and
for the grant to Afghanistan of financial and material aid. The
conclusion of a treaty between Afghanistan and Great Britain
on 15 November showed that Afghanistan did not intend to be
drawn altogether within the Soviet sphere of influence; but
Soviet propaganda within the country itself and, through
Afghanistan, among the Indian frontier tribes, continued unabated and led to a sharp diplomatic clash with Great Britain in
May 1923.[6] In line with the general development of the Soviet
Government's policy, Communist propagandist activities were
henceforward on a less important scale.

Soviet policy towards Afghanistan itself continued to be
affected by events in Soviet Central Asia. In 1921 Enver
Pasha, whose chances of returning to power in Turkey had

[1] Elwell-Sutton, op. cit., pp. 162–8. In April 1938, Davies reported that
the Soviet Union had serious border and other disputes with Iran as well
as with Afghanistan and Turkey; *Mission to Moscow*, p. 196.

[2] There was an article on German infiltration into Iran in *Pravda* on
22 September 1938.

[3] See the article 'Riza Shah Pahlevi, 1925–1941', in *J.R.C.A.S.*, October
1941.

[4] For Russian relations with Afghanistan, see Sir Percy Sykes, *A History
of Afghanistan*, 2 vols. (Macmillan, 1940).

[5] Text in Freund, *Russlands Friedens-und Handlesverträge, 1918–1923*
(Leipzig, 1924).

[6] For the 'Curzon ultimatum' on this issue see, Cmd. 1869; 1874; 1890.

ended with the Soviet agreement with Kemal in March, managed to find his way to Bokhara. He joined the 'Basmachi', the local insurgents against Bolshevik domination, and tried to enlist them for his Pan-Turanian ideology. King Amanullah of Afghanistan had hopes of profiting from this development in the event of Bokhara and Khiva (Khorezm) separating themselves permanently from Russia, and he gave some measure of support to Enver. The latter's defeat in June 1922, and his death six weeks later, put an end to any serious hopes of extending Afghan rule in this direction.[1]

The full Sovietization of Soviet Central Asia in 1924–5 and the creation of the Soviet Socialist Republics of Turkmenistan, Uzbekistan, and Tadjikistan was viewed with apprehension among the Afghans.[2] Conditions along the Soviet Afghan frontier became tense and there was an armed clash in December 1925. Following this an attempt seems to have been made to improve relations, and on 31 August 1926 a treaty of neutrality and non-aggression was signed.[3] This was followed by a period of considerable external cordiality culminating in Amanullah's reception in Moscow in the summer of 1928.[4]

Meanwhile, Soviet-Afghan economic relations had been steadily strengthened, particularly since 1925. A variety of Soviet goods found their way to Afghanistan in return for livestock, wool, and cotton—Soviet goods often quite unobtainable on the Russian home market.[5]

The Soviet railway touched the Afghan frontier at two points;

[1] Fischer, *Soviets in World Affairs*, vol. 1, pp. 383–91.
[2] For developments in Soviet Central Asia see W. M. Mandel, *The Soviet Far East and Central Asia* (New York, I.P.R., 1944); W. R. Batsell, *Soviet Rule in Russia* (New York, Macmillan, 1929), pp. 232–5; 346–9.
[3] *Int. Conc.*, 1929, pp. 408–11.
[4] Fischer, *Soviets in World Affairs*, vol. 2, pp. 785–94.
[5] The figures for trade between the Soviet Union and Afghanistan are as follows (in millions of roubles):

	Soviet Exports to Afghanistan.	Soviet Imports from Afghanistan.
1928–9	7	11·7
1929–30	7·3	10·3
1930	7·8	9·2
1931	11·5	11·6
1932	14·6	11·8
1933	7·1	5·6
1934	3·1	2·8
1935	3·5	3·9
1936	16·3	22·0
1937	17·0	17·0
1938	14·8	13·7

(From 1936, the figures should be divided by 4·38 for purposes of comparison.)

an air service between Tashkent and Kabul was inaugurated
and work was begun on linking together the two countries by
motor roads which it was planned to prolong into southern
Afghanistan, hitherto largely inaccessible to Russian trade.[1]
Nevertheless, it was symptomatic of the Afghan desire for
economic and political independence that no commercial
treaty was concluded with that country by the Soviet Union;
and in that respect, Amanullah's visit to Moscow was unproduc-
tive. The main issue in dispute was the Afghan demand for
transit rights across Russia for its imports from other countries.

The revolt against Amanullah after his return from Moscow
was attributed in the Soviet press to the machinations of Great
Britain. But Amanullah failed to secure Soviet aid in repressing
the revolt, although it does appear that one of his supporters was
permitted to levy a small force of Soviet Uzbeks and Turkomans.
Nadir Shah's restoration of the dynasty in 1929-30 was also
attributed to British influence by the Russians. But once his
rule appeared to be established, the Soviet Government accepted
his assurance of friendliness and on 31 June 1931 a non-aggression pact was concluded with him.[2] Afghanistan, like Turkey,
showed a marked sympathy for the Soviet viewpoint at the Disarmament Conference in 1932.[3] The usual provision was included in the non-aggression pact for the banning of activities
by organizations hostile to the other party. This seems to have
been rigorously observed on the Afghan side. Ibrahim Beg, one
of Enver's associates, was driven across the border into the arms
of Soviet forces. Moslem emigrés from Central Asia were
moved away from Russia's borders.[4] This prudent attitude was
no doubt dictated by the extreme vulnerability of Herat, Kan-
dahar, and the Oxus provinces, if not of the remainder of the
country, to an advance from the north. On 29 March 1936 the
non-aggression pact was renewed for ten years; ratifications of
the renewal were exchanged on 3 September.[5] On the other
hand, Afghan policy under Nadir Shah and his successor was
undoubtedly more favourably disposed towards Great Britain
than it had been previously.[6]

[1] The air convention of 28 November 1927 is given in Conolly, *Soviet
Economic Policy in the East*, App. III. British pressure had prevented the
Soviet Government being allowed to open consulates in this area.

[2] Text in M. M. Litvinov, *Against Aggression*, pp. 144-7. Cf. vol. 1, p. 24.

[3] See vol. i, pp. 51-2.

[4] J. Castagné, 'Soviet Imperialism in Afghanistan', *Foreign Affairs*, July
1935; R. Byron, 'From Herat to Kabul', *J.R.C.A.S.*, 1935, p. 207.

[5] *Documents for 1936*, p. 672.

[6] For a semi-official account of Afghan policy see Abdul Quadir Khan,
'Afghanistan in 1934', *J.R.C.A.S.*, 1935, pp. 211-20.

Afghanistan's attempt to achieve some degree of independence from both the formidable neighbours whose rivalries had for so long dominated its affairs was to some extent paralleled in the economic sphere. The Government tried to cut down its imports of sugar and textiles by encouraging the growing of beet and cotton.[1] But Soviet economic influence continued to be important. Trade went on increasing from 1928 to 1932, in which year the Soviet Union had for the first time a favourable balance. Goods made in Bokhara and Tashkent dominated the market at Herat, Afghanistan's second largest city.[2] Soviet-Afghan trade fell sharply in 1933–4; in 1935, there was a slight rally but the balance was again unfavourable to the Soviet Union. In 1936, a commercial agreement was signed, providing for a two-way exchange of goods to the value of £2,000,000 annually (about 38,500,000 million roubles). But the hoped for level had not been attained by 1938. So far from Russia importing Afghan cotton, it appears that Russian cotton was now used in Afghan mills and that refineries were constructed to deal with the seed.[3]

In retrospect it would appear that the Soviet Union hardly made as much use as might have been expected of its obvious advantages in dealing with the countries of the Middle East. Its Central Asian territories did not at that time seem to have the attraction for its comparatively backward neighbours which the protagonists of 'Socialism in one country' might well have looked forward to.

One possible explanation has been suggested by a British student of the problem:

'Soviet achievements, so manifold and so undoubted in many ways, and including the work for hygiene, education, and the emancipation of women might in fact have attracted millions of poverty stricken Iranians *inter alia* to the Soviet fold, if it were not for the constant stream of tell-tale refugees slipping across the frontier from the Soviet Union and all telling the same tale of ruthless oppression, semi-starvation, and Olympian disregard for the wishes and ways of the Central Asian native, and in particular for his deeply rooted Moslem faith.'[4]

[1] Sykes, 'The Role of the Middle East', *J.R.C.A.S.*, 1941.
[2] J. G. French, 'A Tour through Afghanistan', *J.R.C.A.S.*, 1933, pp. 27–45.
[3] J. C. le Clair, 'The West Eyes Afghanistan', *Asia*, January 1938.
[4] V. Conolly, 'The Development of Industry in Soviet Asia', *J.R.C.A.S.*, 1941.

V. THE SOVIET UNION AND 'THE SECOND IMPERIALIST WAR'

Chapter Ten

SOVIET DIPLOMACY IN EUROPE: FROM 'MUNICH' TO 'PRAGUE'

IN the interval between the Munich Conference and the German occupation of the remainder of Czechoslovakia, upon which Hitler was already determined, Soviet policy underwent no striking transformation.[1] While Soviet spokesmen continued to criticize the failure of the Western Powers to enforce a system of security, Soviet diplomacy seemed disinclined to take any large initiative, and prepared to accept the position of comparative isolation in which the country now found itself. It is nevertheless probable that it was in fact during this period that the Soviet Government came to accept the view that its purposes would best be served by some formal arrangement with Germany, if that Power could be induced to abandon the idea of an attack on Russia in favour of expansion elsewhere. Further trade talks which had no immediate result were carried on in Moscow with Schulenburg.[2] And it is not surprising that, before the end of the period, rumours to this effect began to circulate.[3] Such rumours were rendered the more credible by the emergence of a new note in Soviet propaganda—the analysis of the policy of the Western Powers as

---

[1] For German plans, see *Nuremberg Trial*, Part I, p. 145. For a short Soviet account of this period see V. P. Potemkin, *Politika Umirotvorenia Agressorov i Borba Sovetskovo Soyuza za Mir*, and *Istoria Diplomatii*, vol. 3, pp. 674-70. Cf. L. B. Namier, *Diplomatic Prelude, 1938-1939*, pp. 34-70; Schuman, *Europe on the Eve*, pp. 451-89; *Night over Europe* (Hale, 1941), pp. 31-122.

[2] Molotov, speech of 31 May 1939, *infra*, chap. 11.

[3] In the middle of December, the Bulgarian Prime Minister Kiosseivanov expressed to M. Ristelhueber, the French Minister to Sofia, his opinion that, particularly if the Comintern agreed to attenuate its propaganda, there might be a *rapprochement* between the U.S.S.R. and Germany. This, he said, had always been the dream of a part of the German General Staff and the day it was accomplished would see the fourth partition of Poland; *Documents Diplomatiques, 1938-9* (Paris, 1939), p. 41. On the other hand, German statesmen continued to stress the anti-Bolshevik foundations of German foreign policy. See the accounts of Ribbentrop's conversations with Bonnet on the occasion of the Franco-German declaration of 6 December 1938, and of Hitler's conversation with Beck on 5 January 1939; ibid., pp. 36-8; 45-7; *Polish White Book*, p. 53. Cf. Reynaud, *La France a sauvé L'Europe*, vol. 1, p. 575.

being designed above all to make a catspaw of the Soviet Union, and to urge Germany into a war with Russia from which they themselves could hold aloof.

The Soviet Union's dissatisfaction over its exclusion from the Munich Conference soon made itself felt. Bonnet asked for an interview with Litvinov on the occasion of the latter's passage through Paris on 1 October 1938, but found the Soviet Foreign Minister very cold as to the future prospects of Franco-Soviet co-operation.[1] On 2 October *Pravda*, as has been seen, denied a report that the U.S.S.R. had empowered Daladier to represent it at Munich. In Great Britain, criticism from the Opposition made it necessary for the Government to reply to charges that Russia had been wilfully and unnecessarily pushed aside. Speaking in the House of Lords on 3 October, Lord Halifax said that Hitler and Mussolini could not have been brought to confer with a Soviet representative, 'at least not without much preliminary discussion for which there was no time', and that time was vital if war were to be avoided. In the House of Commons, Sir Samuel Hoare tried to prove that consultation had in fact been adequate, with France, as was natural, taking the lead. Such assertions were, however, contradicted in a Tass communiqué which declared that the Soviet representatives in Paris and London had never been given any information other than that which they could have obtained from the daily press, and that talk of an agreement was even wider off the mark.[2] On 5 October another effort to mend matters was made—this time by Sir John Simon, speaking in the House of Commons: 'it is our hope that Russia will be willing to join in the guarantee of Czechoslovakia. It is most important that she should do so. The Government have no intention whatever of excluding Russia or trying to exclude Russia from any future settlement of Europe.'

Further Soviet comment gave little ground for hoping that the gulf between the Soviet Union and the Western Powers could now be bridged. A remark of Lord Winterton on 10 October, to the effect that Russia had not offered help in the Czech crisis but had 'only made very vague promises owing to her military weakness', was the subject of an official Soviet protest on the following day.[3] The Soviet Government seemed

[1] *Europe Nouvelle*, 24 September 1938.

[2] *Pravda*, 4 October 1938. The communiqué was discussed in a lengthy leading article which listed among the results of the Munich crisis an enhancement of the international prestige of the U.S.S.R., the only country whose policy was directed towards general peace and to the independence and freedom from Fascist aggression, of all nations.

[3] *B.I.N.*, 22 October 1938, p. 55.

extremely concerned to impress upon the public mind the belief that it was the only Power whose devotion to collective security was unwavering.

While the causes of the Czechoslovak *débâcle* were thus the subject of long-range debate, developments inside the country itself followed a more or less predictable course. The Communist Party was banned in Bohemia and Moravia on 20 October 1938 and this was followed by the suppression of the Communist press. On 21 October, after a visit to Berlin by the Czechoslovak Foreign Minister Chvalkovsky, the Soviet Minister in Prague was informed that the Czechoslovak Government was no longer interested in its pact with the Soviet Union.[1] Beran, now Prime Minister, did not mention relations with the Soviet Union in a speech on 13 December.[2]

In Slovakia, now autonomous, the anti-Soviet current set in even more rapidly. One of the first acts of its Government, which took office on 7 October, was to ban the Communist Party. In December, spokesmen of the Slovak Government began a violent campaign for the formal denunciation of the pact with the Soviet Union and for the final alignment of Czechoslovakia with the anti-Comintern Powers. During another visit by Chvalkovsky to Berlin (on 21 January 1939), similar demands were apparently urged upon him by Hitler and Ribbentrop. But the Czechoslovak Government still apparently held out against a formal repudiation of the Soviet alliance.[3]

More significant than the confirmation of the fact that the Czechs and Slovaks were now within the German sphere of influence was the revival, as an indirect result of the Munich crisis, of an international question, more or less dormant since 1921—the question of the Ukraine.[4] The revival of this question was to be of such great importance in the new period in the history of Soviet policy as to demand some consideration of its setting.[5]

---

[1] *B.I.N.*, 5 November 1938. As late as 10 December, a Czech minister denied that the pact had been denounced. Bonnet, *Fin d'une Europe*, p. 148.

[2] *Documents for 1938*, vol. ii, pp. 362–5. Cf. A. Henderson, *Eyewitness in Czechoslovakia*, pp. 261–7. But on the 14th, Chvalkovsky denied to the French Minister at Prague that a denunciation of the pact had ever been envisaged. Bonnet, *Défense de la Paix: De Washington au Quai d'Orsay*, p. 339.

[3] Ripka, *Munich, Before and After*, pp. 283–5.

[4] Noël, *L'Agression Allemande contre la Pologne*, pp. 260–5.

[5] For the following paragraphs, see Ripka, op. cit., pp. 260–6, 276–7, 325–30, 343–5; Schuman, *Night over Europe*, pp. 57–77; Henderson, *Eyewitness in Czechoslovakia*, pp. 246–94; Allen, *The Ukraine*, pp. 378–90; E. Wiskemann, *Undeclared War* (Constable, 1939), pp. 193–241; 'The Ukrainian Problem', *B.I.N.*, 14 January 1939. C. A. Manning, *The Story*

The inhabitants of Ruthenia formed the smallest of the four divisions into which the Ukrainian people fell as a result of the peace treaties of 1919–21.[1] It is indeed probable that but for the Bolshevik Revolution they would have come under Russian rule after the break-up of the Austro-Hungarian Empire. In the circumstances they accepted inclusion within the Czechoslovak State, with the promise of an autonomous status. And, although little progress was made towards the fulfilment of this promise, the position in Ruthenia does not seem to have led to any friction between the Soviet Union and Czechoslovakia. There was certainly no evidence of a nationalist movement comparable to the one which embittered the relations between Ukrainians and Poles in neighbouring Galicia. Nevertheless, the extreme poverty of the country and dissatisfaction at the way in which its affairs were handled by Prague, caused some growth of nationalist feeling, and in June 1937, a bill to give the Province greater autonomy was actually introduced into the Czechoslovak Parliament. Negotiations over it were very slow, partly because of the long-standing division of the nationalist movement into two main tendencies—Russian (Greek Orthodox) and Ukrainian (Greek Catholic, i.e. Uniate). Of the two tendencies, the Ukrainian would have appeared to command rather more support. It should, however, be noted that in the elections of 1935, the largest single party in Ruthenia proved to be the Communist Party with 26·5 per cent of the votes, which may be taken as evidence of a pro-Russian tendency.[2]

At the time of the Munich crisis, Hungary hoped to recover the whole territory and in this ambition she was strongly supported by Poland. Czech resistance to this was very forceful.[3] The Germans for their own reasons encouraged Czech resistance.[4]

---

of the Ukraine (New York, Philosophical Library, 1947), p. 268. For the general question of Ruthenia (Sub-Carpathian Russia), see O. Jaszi, 'The Problem of Sub-Carpathian Ruthenia' in *Czechoslovakia: Twenty Years of Independence*, edited by R. J. Kerner; C. A. Macartney, *Hungary and Her Successors* (Oxford University Press, 1937), pp. 200–50.

[1] According to the Czechoslovak census of 1930, the Ruthenes (Ukrainians) of Czechoslovakia accounted for 550,000 (5·7 per cent) of the population. The Roumanian census of the same year returned the total number of Ukrainians as about 575,000 (3·3 per cent) of the population. These were partly in Bukovina, where they retained contact with the Ukrainians of Polish Galicia, and partly in Bessarabia. H. Seton-Watson, *Eastern Europe Between the Wars*, pp. 179–82, 336–8, 430–4.

[2] The next largest party was also not a local one—the Czechoslovak Agrarians.   [3] A. Henderson, *Eyewitness in Czechoslovakia*, pp. 246–55.

[4] According to Bonnet, the Poles suggested to the Roumanians on 19 October that the latter annex Ruthenia. The Roumanians, with French approval, rejected the proposal; op. cit., p. 328.

On 11 October 1938 Ruthenia was granted autonomy on the same lines as Slovakia, and a coalition cabinet was set up representing the two autonomist tendencies with the 'Russophile' Andrej Brody as Prime Minister. One of the Government's early actions was to suppress the Communist Party. On 26 October Brody was dismissed, and three days later he was arrested on a charge of having plotted to hand over the country to the Hungarians. The new Cabinet, headed by Mgr. Augustin Volosin, with Julian Revay as its dominating figure, represented the extreme Ukrainian tendency, and proceeded to organize the country on accepted totalitarian lines complete with a nationalist militia, the Sitch.

The Vienna Award of 2 November 1938, by which Ribbentrop and Ciano fixed the new Hungarian-Czechoslovak frontier, deprived Ruthenia of considerable territory, including its capital Uzhorod.[1] The truncated State, forced to fix its capital at Chust, which was no more than a village, and with its main lines of communication cut by salients of Hungarian territory, was obviously incapable of independent existence and could expect little help from Prague.[2] Nevertheless, it had its own unmistakable place in the German scheme of things. It rapidly became the much publicized centre of the idea of a 'Great Ukraine'. Successfully relying on German support to stave off Hungarian and Polish intervention, Carpatho-Ruthenia or Carpatho-Ukraine, as it finally dared to call itself in January 1939, became the Mecca of Ukrainian nationalists from Poland and to a lesser extent from Roumania.[3]

Under German patronage, the Sitch developed on warlike lines and the spokesmen of the Chust Government talked more or less openly of the coming creation of a Great Ukraine and of the liberation of their kinsmen from the yoke of Poland and Russia. In January there were reports—later denied by Prague —of the departure from Berlin for Chust of the former Ukrainian Hetman Skoropadsky and of the Cossack General Popov. According to some accounts, the latter was acting in the interests of the Tsarist Pretender, the Grand Duke Vladimir, whose presence in Berlin had been reported in December 1938. The Soviet Government is said to have protested to Prague against the toleration of these anti-Soviet intrigues.

There seems little doubt that the Ukrainian accomplices (or

[1] *Documents for 1938*, vol. ii, p. 315.

[2] For a good first-hand account of these months in Ruthenia, see Michael Winch, *Republic for a Day* (Hale, 1939).

[3] Beck put forward a scheme for dividing Ruthenia between Poland, Hungary, and Roumania, but the Roumanians were opposed to it. Gafencu, *Derniers Jours de l'Europe*, p. 47.

dupes) of Germany visualized Poland rather than the Soviet Union as the first victim of the Ukrainian liberation movement. But their references to the latter could not pass unnoticed, and in a speech on 12 December 1938, M. Petrovsky, the Prime Minister of the Soviet Ukraine, declared that the Russians and Ukrainians would defend themselves together against aggression from any quarter.[1]

The effect of these developments in Poland was naturally more pronounced. For a time, indeed, the major effect of the revival of the Ukrainian question appeared to be a rebuilding of the bridges between Moscow and Warsaw, although the importance of what was done was exaggerated in quarters unacquainted with Beck's fundamental policy of 'independence' and 'balance'.[2] Early in October 1938, the Polish Ambassador in Moscow, M. Grzybowski, took the initiative in proposing to Potemkin concrete steps for the improvement of Polish-Soviet relations. Discussions, in which Litvinov took part, made slow progress, and it was only on 24 November that agreement was reached. The successful conclusion of the political talks was made public in a communiqué on 26 November 1938, which reaffirmed the two countries' fidelity to the existing pact of non-aggression. The trade talks forecast in the communiqué were opened in Moscow in mid-December, and were resumed after an interval in mid-January, a series of agreements being signed eventually on 19 February 1939.[3]

By this time, however, a certain coolness was manifest in Soviet-Polish relations and this may have been indirectly connected with further developments in the 'Great Ukraine' plan. For it had become clear that German official opinion was by no means unanimous in its favour. Possibly, the German High Command were discouraged by the absence of any visible repercussion of these activities in the Soviet Ukraine and by evidence that the Soviet régime and army had not after all been mortally weakened by the 'purge'.[4] It may be that the Germans were uncertain of their ability to direct Ukrainian nationalism precisely along the lines which suited them best, and that they had decided upon more direct methods of attaining their expansionist aims. By the beginning of 1939, there was evidence that the German interest in Ruthenia was evaporating. And, as an acute British observer had foreseen, the abandon-

[1] Ripka, op. cit., p. 347.
[2] Noël, op. cit., pp. 271–4.
[3] Polish White Book, pp. 181–3, 204–5.
[4] See the article by General W. Sikorski quoted from the Kurjer Warzawski of 31 December 1938 by Ripka, op. cit., pp. 345–7.

ment of the 'Great Ukraine' plan laid open the way to the German-Russian *rapprochement* which was already in the air.[1]

A dispatch from the French Ambassador to Berlin, dated 14 March 1939, indicated that Hitler had abandoned the 'Munich' policy as early as the end of December 1938, and that he was henceforth preparing to break up Czechoslovakia and to accept the (Italian) view that Ruthenia as a whole should go to Hungary.[2]

This reckoning would fit in with the impression given by Polish sources, that a tentative effort at a German-Soviet understanding began in the New Year. At Hitler's New Year reception, it was noticed that he spoke longer to the Soviet Ambassador than to anyone else, and this fact was widely commented on in Moscow. On 5 January, Hitler told Beck that he was interested in the Ukraine from an economic standpoint, but had no interest in it politically. On 8 January Litvinov advised Grzybowski to hasten the trade negotiations in order 'to forestall German intrigues'. Soon afterwards it became known that a German trade delegation under Dr. Schnurre was due to arrive in Moscow. This delegation actually reached Warsaw from Berlin on about 25 January but then turned back.[3] Germany appeared to be hesitating as to whether to conciliate Soviet Russia or Poland. Beck returned from a visit to Hitler on 5 January, confident of Germany's intentions regarding Poland and of Hitler's continued hostility to Russia and Communism.[4] Hitler's speech on 30 January 1939 did not

[1] 'A dangerous day for Britain and France will come should the Nazis decide that the dream of colonizing the Ukraine, of making it a German dominion, is a dream that can never become a reality.' A. Henderson, *Eyewitness in Czechoslovakia*, p. 287.

[2] Coulondre states that the Polish-Soviet *rapprochement* was believed to be partly responsible for Germany's change of front, that Hitler hoped to secure Polish neutrality in the event of a European conflict and also Hungarian co-operation against Roumania. Hungary was in fact brought still further within the German orbit at this time. On 24 February 1939, she signed the Anti-Comintern Pact (along with Manchukuo). On 2 March 1939, the U.S.S.R. severed diplomatic relations with Hungary on the ground that by its action the Hungarian Government had surrendered its independence in matters of foreign policy; *Manchester Guardian*, 3 March 1939. Evidence at the Nuremberg trial has since shown that Hitler's directive to the army to prepare for the absorption of the whole of Czechoslovakia was issued on 21 October 1938; a supplementary directive of 17 December explained that this was to be presented as an act of pacification and that no marked resistance need be expected; *Nuremberg Trial*, Part II, pp. 42–4. L. B. Namier, *Diplomatic Prelude*, pp. 405–416.

[3] *Polish White Book*, pp. 53 and 206–7.

[4] ibid., pp. 53–4; Noël, op. cit., pp. 285–9.

contain the customary anti-Communist diatribe, but his refer-ence to Poland was conspicuously friendly.[1]

At any rate, the Ukrainian agitation had served its purpose as far as the Germans were concerned. When German troops occupied Bohemia and Moravia on 15 March and permitted Slovakia to assume a fictitious independence as a German pro-tectorate, Ruthenia was abandoned.[2] After one day of independence, the Sitch was overwhelmed by the Hungarians, and on 16 March Budapest announced the reincorporation of Ruthenia in Hungary.[3]

The attention paid by the press of the Western countries to events in Ruthenia was interpreted in Moscow (as Stalin's speech was shortly to make clear), as evidence of the desire of these Powers to increase the likelihood of conflict between Germany and the Soviet Union. But it was only part of a general world-scene whose interpretation by Soviet spokesmen indicated their steadily increasing mistrust of Great Britain and France.

Events in Spain continued to contribute their quota to the occasions of disagreement, in spite of the fact that the Soviet Union had now abandoned any attempt to influence the course of the war by direct action. Early in October it was made known that about 10,000 Italian 'volunteers' would be with-drawn and that number actually sailed for home on the 15th.[4] The announcement was given in *Pravda* under the heading 'An Anglo-Italian deal at the expense of Spain'. Mussolini, it was asserted, had been prevailed upon by Chamberlain to call for the Munich Conference with the promise of the ratification of the Anglo-Italian agreement of 16 April; the Franco 'gesture' was intended to remove the obstacle to this; in the same way the revival of British proposals for international mediation between the belligerents was meant to provide a way to the recognition of the Franco Government.[5]

On 2 November the House of Commons fulfilled the Soviet prognostication by voting by 345 votes to 138 to bring into

---

[1] *Hitler's Speeches*, pp. 1567–8. During his visit to Warsaw at the end of January Ribbentrop again suggested that Germany and Poland should co-operate against Russia. Noël, op. cit., pp. 290–5; cf. R.Umiastowski, *Russia and the Polish Republic, 1918–1941* (Aquafondata, 1945), p. 122.

[2] For the final German moves to disrupt Czechoslovakia, see *Nuremberg Trial*, Part II, pp. 87–108.

[3] A letter from the Hungarian Regent Horthy, presumably to Hitler, two days before the German occupation of Bohemia and Moravia, shows that the fate of Ruthenia was pre-arranged. *Nuremberg Trial*, Part II, p. 94.

[4] *Survey for 1938*, I, pp. 332–5.

[5] *Pravda*, 10, 11 October 1938. Cf. the article 'The Anglo-Italian Plan to Strangle the Spanish Republic', ibid., 12 October.

immediate effect the Anglo-Italian agreement. Thereafter, the
Spanish War proceeded to its inevitable conclusion. On 18
January 1939 the British and French Governments gave their
final refusal to lift the arms embargo; on 27 February they
recognized the Government of General Franco; on 3 March
the Soviet Union announced the withdrawal of its representative from the Non-Intervention Committee on the grounds that
it had long ceased to function and had lost consciousness of its
own existence; on 29 March the Spanish War came to an end.

The conduct of Great Britain was still analysed in the light
of the theory of 'appeasement'; but after Munich increasing
attention was paid to the imperial aspects of British policy. It
was suggested that in her dealings with Germany, Britain was
above all determined to stave off a direct demand for the return
of Germany's former colonies and was worried particularly by
the threat to imperial communications involved in the attempted
German penetration of south-eastern Europe and Turkey.[1]
Class prejudice was the reason for the failure of the threatened
imperialisms to work in harmony with the Soviet Union.

Speaking in Moscow on 6 November 1938 Molotov said:

'The second imperialist war has already begun on an immense
field from Gibraltar to Shanghai. The democratic Powers allege as
a pretext their weakness in face of an aggressor, but in reality they
do not desire to intervene seriously against the aggressor, for they
are still more afraid of a workers' movement.'[2]

The events of the next four months did nothing to diminish
the force of Molotov's argument in Soviet eyes. The increasingly anti-Communist tone of the Daladier Government in
France, where the Communists were leading a campaign against
the more intensive productive effort demanded in the name of
national defence, became even more marked after the abortive
general strike of 30 November. Ribbentrop's visit to Paris and
the Franco-German declaration of 6 December were hardly
points in the French Government's favour.[3] Similarly, the visit
of Mr. Chamberlain and Lord Halifax to Rome on 11-14
January 1939, though barren of results, was bound to increase
Soviet suspicions. The optimistic tone of British official comment on the international situation in the new year, suggested
that the British Government had not given up the hopes placed

[1] G. Anbor, 'Great Britain and Germany', *Pravda*, 16 October 1938.
[2] *Documents for 1938*, vol. ii, pp. 322–3.
[3] ibid., pp. 220–3. Suritz was informed of the proposed declaration on
22 November, *French Yellow Book*, Doc. No. 27; cf. Noël, op. cit., pp. 274–81,
Reynaud, op. cit., pp. 574–5.

in appeasement in spite of increased German intransigence.[1]
And this impression was enhanced when it was made known
early in February, that Mr. Oliver Stanley and Mr. Robert
Hudson were due in Berlin for economic talks, in the middle of
March.[2]

The meeting of the Eighteenth Congress of the Communist
Party in March 1939 must be regarded as an event of considerable significance in the internal history of the Soviet Union,
since it marked the end of the period of uncertainty and upheaval which had begun not long after its predecessor in 1934.
The domination of the Party in the State, and of Stalin within
the Party, had never been more clearly apparent; and the
development of the Party from the spearhead of the proletariat
into an overwhelmingly non-proletarian organization of those
holding key positions in the administrative and economic fields
was well-nigh complete. Only the future relations between the
Party and the armed forces presented an element of doubt. And
the still recent army purges can have left little uncertainty as to
where ultimate victory would lie, although the methods by
which Party control was to be assured were still to be the subject
of experiment.[3]

Stalin's customary report was thus a speech of the utmost
importance; and the events of the next few months might have
given less cause for surprise if more attention had been paid,
outside the Soviet Union, to what he had to say on the subject
of foreign affairs.[4]

[1] In his speech on 30 January, Hitler had insisted on Germany's right to
colonies for 'economic reasons'. The assumption that good relations with
Germany could be nothing but a cover for a plot against Russia was of
course a natural one for the Soviet mind. The concept of general appeasement remained incomprehensible. In fact, at a confidential press conference,
'a few days before the Germans marched into Czechoslovakia' Mr. Chamberlain declared 'that the international position had so improved that he
had every confidence that a successful disarmament conference could be
held in the autumn'; F. Williams, *Press, Parliament, and People* (Heinemann,
1946), p. 143. This would obviously have involved co-operation with the
Soviet Union.

[2] Henderson, *Failure of a Mission*, pp. 198–9. On 21 February, a Havas
dispatch from Moscow declared that the U.S.S.R. considered itself released
from any obligation to France or Great Britain. R. C. K. Ensor, *A Miniature
History of the War* (Oxford University Press, 1944), p. 15. It would be
interesting to know whether French official circles were concerned to spread
a report which might assist the 'appeasers'.

[3] The proceedings of the Congress were published in Moscow (in English)
under the title, *The Land of Socialism, To-day and To-morrow*. Cf. F. L.
Schuman, *Soviet Politics at Home and Abroad* (New York, Knopf, 1946),
pp. 345–61.

[4] Speech of 10 March 1939; *Leninism*, pp. 619–70.

The first point of interest is the domination of his presentation of the world-scene by purely Marxist concepts. He began with the new recession in world production which had marked the latter half of 1937. This had started in Great Britain, France and the United States, but had by 1938 spread to Italy and Japan in spite of the war-footing of these countries' economies. There was therefore no reason to doubt that Germany would follow in the same path:

'The new economic crisis must lead, and is actually leading, to a further sharpening of the imperialist struggle. . . . It is now a question of a new redivision of the world, of spheres of influence and colonies by military action.'

Stalin went on to describe how the bloc of aggressor States had been formed out of the Powers aggrieved by the settlement which followed the 'first imperialist war', and how the post-war system based on the Versailles Treaty and Nine-Power Treaty had collapsed and led to what he had earlier called the new imperialist war, 'already in its second year'. The Anti-Comintern Pact was simply a cover for the aggressive designs of its signatories on British and French positions in Europe, and on British, French, and American positions in the Far East.

The question to be answered was why the non-aggressive Powers who were thus being attacked showed so feeble a resistance.

'Is it to be attributed to the weakness of the non-aggressive States? Of course not. Combined, the non-aggressive democratic States are unquestionably stronger than the Fascist States, both economically and in the military sense.'

This assessment of relative strength by Stalin must not be overlooked when we come to consider the Soviet Union's policy between August 1939 and June 1940. But it did not answer his immediate question; nor did he now accept Molotov's interpretation of the previous November.

'To what then are we to attribute the system of concessions made by these States to the aggressors?

'It might be attributed, for example, to the fear that a revolution might break out, if the non-aggressive States were to go to war and the war were to assume world-wide proportions. . . .

'But at present this is not the sole or even the chief reason. The chief reason is that the majority of the non-aggressive countries, particularly England and France, have rejected the policy of collective security, the policy of collective resistance to the aggressor and have taken up a position of non-intervention, a position of neutrality.

'. . . the policy of non-intervention reveals an eagerness, a desire, not to hinder the aggressors in their nefarious work: not to hinder

Japan, say, from embroiling herself in a war with China, or better still with the Soviet Union; not to hinder Germany, say, from enmeshing herself in European affairs, from embroiling herself in a war with the Soviet Union; to allow all the belligerents to sink deeply into the mire of war, to encourage them surreptitiously in this; to allow them to weaken and exhaust one another; and then when they have become weak enough, to appear on the scene with fresh strength, to appear, of course, in the interests of peace, and to dictate conditions to the enfeebled belligerents.'

After describing the way in which the Western Powers had, according to him, encouraged Japan to extend its penetration into China, Stalin continued:

'Or take Germany for instance. They let her have Austria despite the undertaking to defend her independence; they let her have the Sudeten region; they abandoned Czechoslovakia to her fate, thereby violating all their obligations; and then began to lie vociferously in the press about the "weakness of the Russian army", "the demoralization of the Russian air force", and "riots" in the Soviet Union, egging the Germans on to march further east, promising them easy pickings and prompting them: "Just start war on the Bolsheviks and everything will be all right." It must be admitted that this too looks very much like egging on and encouraging the aggressor.

'The hullabaloo raised by the British, French, and American press over the Soviet Ukraine is characteristic. The gentlemen of the press there shouted until they were hoarse that the Germans were marching on the Soviet Union, that they now had what is called Carpathian Ukraine, with a population of some seven hundred thousand, and that not later than this spring, the Germans would annex the Soviet Ukraine which has a population of over thirty millions, to this so-called Carpathian Ukraine. It looks as if the object of this suspicious hullabaloo was to incense the Soviet Union against Germany, to poison the atmosphere and to provoke a conflict with Germany without any visible grounds. . . .

'Even more characteristic is the fact that certain European and American politicians and pressmen, having lost patience waiting for "the march on the Soviet Ukraine" are themselves beginning to declare what is really behind the policy of non-intervention.'

They were, Stalin declared, as 'disappointed' that Germany was turning West and demanding colonies, instead of attacking the Soviet Union, as though the Sudetenland had been given to Germany as part of a bargain which the Germans were now refusing to carry out.

'Far be it from me to moralize on the policy of non-intervention, to talk of treason, treachery, and so on. It would be naïve to preach morals to people who recognize no human morality. . . . It must be remembered, however, that the big and dangerous political game started by the supporters of the policy of non-intervention may end in a serious blow for them.'

In fact, in spite of the unctuous speeches about further appeasement, Great Britain and France were pushing ahead with their armaments. The old slogans of pacifism and disarmament were dead.

This analysis can only be read as at once a warning to Great Britain and France that they would have to bid very high now for Soviet support, and give concrete pledges of their trustworthiness, and as an invitation to Nazi Germany with whom 'no visible grounds' of conflict existed.

It is thus not surprising that Stalin's defence of the Soviet Union's own recent policy was somewhat perfunctory, and that in defining its policy for the future, no mention was made of 'collective security', although a promise of support was made for countries actively resisting aggression.

In the light of the coming negotiations, the most significant passage was that in which Stalin defined the relations of the Soviet Union to its immediate neighbours.

'We stand for peaceful, close and friendly relations with all neighbouring countries which have common frontiers with the U.S.S.R. That is our position; and we shall adhere to this position as long as these countries maintain like relations with the Soviet Union, and as long as they make no attempt to trespass, directly or indirectly, on the integrity and inviolability of the frontiers of the Soviet State.'

The notion of indirect trespass was to have an eventful history in the months and years to come.

From the point of view of the Western Powers, the sting was in the concluding sentences of this section of the speech, where Stalin defined the tasks of the Party in foreign affairs:

'1. To continue the policy of peace and of strengthening business relations with all countries.

'2. To be cautious and not to allow our country to be drawn into conflicts by war-mongers who are accustomed to have others pull the chestnuts out of the fire for them.

'3. To strengthen the might of our Red Army and Red Navy to the uttermost.

'4. To strengthen the international bonds of friendship with the working people of all countries who are interested in peace and friendship among nations.'

The Soviet attitude to 'the second imperialist war' could hardly have been more precisely described.

Chapter Eleven

THE SOVIET UNION AND THE WESTERN ALLIES:
MARCH TO AUGUST 1939

STALIN'S speech of 10 March 1939, and the German occupation of Czechoslovakia five days later, may be taken together as heralding a new period in the relations between the Soviet Union and the outer world. The former stamped upon this period the designation of the Second Imperialist War, and the latter made the imminence of armed conflict on a global scale universally apparent. The period was brought to a close by the German attack on the Soviet Union on 22 June 1941, which turned the war into 'The Great Patriotic War of the Soviet Union', and marked the beginning of a new period outside the scope of this narrative.[1]

The Soviet-German agreement, concluded initially for ten years, must be taken as the formal expression of Soviet policy towards the war in Europe which broke out just over a week after its signature, since the German War Criminals were formally charged in 1945 with having 'deceitfully denounced' it at the time of the German attack.[2] But in a longer perspective this agreement, which was so generally regarded at the time as a complete reversal of the Soviet Union's foreign policy, falls into its place as part of a political strategy whose purposes arose naturally from the Soviet Union's international position and general outlook.

It is of course impossible to recount in any detail the diplomatic history of this period from the Soviet point of view.[3] All

---

[1] This is the title of the English translation of a collection of speeches, &c. made in wartime by Stalin. J. Stalin, *On the Great Patriotic War of the Soviet Union* (Hutchinson, 1943).

[2] *Nuremberg Trial Indictment*, Cmd. 6696, p. 11. Cf. Stalin's speech of 3 July 1941, op. cit., p. 6.

[3] The most ambitious attempt to do so is that of David J. Dallin, *Soviet Russia's Foreign Policy, 1939–1942* (New Haven, Yale University Press, 1942). From the point of view of international relations generally, the fullest treatment is Schuman, *Europe on the Eve*, which comes down only to November 1940. Soviet policy during and after this period is dealt with more specifically in the same author's *Soviet Politics at Home and Abroad*, which also contains on pp. 627–9 some critical notes on Dallin's work. The fullest Soviet account is that contained in chapters 25 and 26 of vol. 3 of *Istoria Diplomatii;* these chapters are by A. M. Pankratova and V. P. Potemkin. Cf. the latter's *Politika Umirotvorenia Aggressorov i Borba Sovetskovo Soyuza za Mir.* Both these accounts end with the outbreak of war in Europe in September 1939.

that can be done here is to give some indication of those developments of which sufficient is known to make them of value in a general appraisal of Soviet foreign policy.

For the sake of convenience the period can be divided into four. From March to August 1939, the Soviet Union still retained the choice between committing itself to the forces gathering to resist German aggression, and coming to an arrangement with the aggressor which would permit it to stand aside from the conflict. From September 1939 to March 1940, the Soviet Union was employed in gathering the fruits of its agreement with Germany, while Germany, fortified by the agreement, prepared for its assault on the west. Between April and November 1940, the situation was altered out of all recognition by the German victories in Western Europe—victories for which the Soviet Union's gains in the east were insufficient compensation. Molotov's visit to Berlin in November 1940 may be taken as marking the moment at which the possibilities of strengthening the Soviet position by further bargaining with Germany were found to be exhausted. From November 1940 to June 1941, Soviet diplomacy was clearly attempting the difficult task of trying to place obstacles in the way of further German expansion, while outwardly continuing the policy of appeasement in the hope of delaying the inevitable blow.[1]

The most important feature of the whole period, from the Soviet viewpoint, was the vast speeding-up in the disintegration of the political structure of the intermediate zone between Germany and the U.S.S.R. In 1938, when the process had begun with the Anschluss and the annexation by Germany of the Sudetenland, one of the governing factors in the situation had been Russia's lack of a common frontier with her ally, Czechoslovakia. On the other hand, it was equally true that at that time and even after March 1939, Germany could not attack the Soviet Union without securing the assistance, or violating the neutrality of, some other State or States. The Soviet Union was confirmed in this favourable position by the Anglo-French guarantees to Poland and Roumania, which indirectly brought to the Soviet Union many of the advantages it might have gained by a direct arrangement with the Western Powers. By June 1941, the situation had so changed that Hitler was able to throw the German Army and the

[1] Documents from the German archives dealing with Soviet-German relations in the period have been published by the American Government. *Nazi-Soviet Relations, 1939–1941*, ed. by R. J. Sontag and J. S. Beddie. (Washington, D.C. Department of State, 1948). For a German account see, Erich Kordt, *Wahn und Wirklichkeit*. (Stuttgart, 1947).

armies of a number of satellites against the whole length of the
Soviet frontier from the Arctic to the Black Sea.

The advance of the two frontiers—the Soviet and the Nazi
—towards each other had not been effected in an entirely one-
sided fashion. Russia had acquired certain strategic advantages
through the new frontier with Finland, and it was the *glacis* provided by the Baltic States that perhaps enabled the Red Army
to halt the Germans short of, if only just short of, Leningrad.
More doubtfully valuable, as it proved (even if ethnographically
more justifiable), were the territorial gains at the expense of
partitioned Poland and truncated Roumania. On the other
hand, Russia had to look on while Germany added to her lion's
share of Poland the control of a re-aggrandized Hungary, of the
Roumanian rump, of Yugoslavia, and Greece, and to a limited
degree, as far as Russia was concerned, of her ever-delinquent
protégé Bulgaria. Hitler, by June 1941, in fact, ruled more
Slavs than had ever lived beneath the sway of a Habsburg, a fact
which was to have some curious consequences.

It is perhaps the first period—between March and August
1939—which offers the greatest difficulties to the historian.[1]

It is possible that the German decision to seek agreement
with the Soviet Union at Poland's expense antedates March
1939.[2] Stalin's speech of the 10th was certainly taken as an

[1] No documents on the 1939 negotiations between the Western Powers
and the Soviet Union have been officially published by either side. A British
Blue Book was promised by the Prime Minister in December 1939; but on
21 February 1940, the Foreign Under-Secretary, Mr. R. A. Butler, announced that it had been held up pending consultations with France. On
6 March, Mr. Chamberlain announced that it had been after all decided
not to publish it. It was, however, possible to reconstruct the course of the
actual negotiations with only a slight margin for error, from official communiqués, from speeches made at the time, and from 'inspired' press
comment. This was done in the Russian works already referred to, in
the books by Schuman and Dallin, by W. P. and Z. K. Coates in *A History
of Anglo-Soviet Relations*, pp. 600–16, and by Bilainkin, *Maisky*, pp. 233–83.
Since these accounts were written, information of importance has been
divulged on the French side. See especially, Bonnet, *Fin d'une Europe*.

Istoria Diplomatii treats the negotiations under the heading: 'The rivalry
between the Anglo-French bloc and German-Fascist diplomacy for an agreement with the U.S.S.R.' p. 679, which suggests that the Soviet Union did
not take the initiative in either case.

[2] On 16 March 1940 Ciano told Sumner Welles that in the summer of
1939 Hitler had informed the Italians of German commercial negotiations
with the Soviet Union, saying that their object was to impede the negotiations between the Soviet Union and the Western Powers, and that they
were only a 'petit jeu'; S. Welles, *A Time for Decision* (New York, Harper,
1944), p. 67.

Istoria Diplomatii puts the German offer of a non-aggression pact in the
'summer' of 1939, vol. 3, p. 689. In a speech on 16 December 1939, Ciano

encouragement to the Germans to proceed with their court-ship.[1]

'In his report to the Eighteenth Congress, Comrade Stalin raised the question of the good neighbourly relations between the U.S.S.R. and Germany. This declaration of Comrade Stalin was properly understood in Germany. On the proposal of the latter, new negotia-tions were started for a convention on credit and commerce, which ended in the signing of the convention on 19 August 1939. Later Germany expressed its wish to improve political relations with the U.S.S.R. The previous conventions and that of 23 August 1939, mark a decisive turn in Soviet-German relations and are therefore an international event of the greatest historical significance.'[2]

The possibility of a Soviet-German accord if the negotiations between the Soviet Union and the Western Allies did not turn out to the former's satisfaction was not of course absent from the minds of the British and French statesmen concerned, and various warnings of this kind can be found in the French documents.[3] But it is impossible to distinguish between intelli-

---

stated that Berlin and Rome had arrived at an agreement during talks in April and May 1939 for 'a policy of *détente* with Russia . . . to keep her from entering the system of encirclement planned by the Great Democracies'. *B.I.N.*, XVI, p. 1441. Cf. R. G. Massock, *Italy from Within*, p. 153.

[1] Some light was thrown on this by the interrogation of leading Germans after the end of the war. 'The earliest definite sign of a reconciliation between Germany and Soviet Russia following the estrangement of 1932 and subsequently, occurred in the autumn of 1938, when the two Govern-ments formally agreed to reduce to tolerable proportions the attacks against each current in the public press of the other. The Germans saw a second and clearer sign when, in the spring of 1939, Stalin in a public address asserted that even violent contradictions in outlook and governmental forms need not constitute an obstacle to practical co-operation between two States having common interests in concrete matters, and Moscow let Berlin know informally (the Germans said) that this utterance was spoken with Germany particularly in mind.' De Witt C. Poole, 'Light on Nazi Foreign Policy', *Foreign Affairs*, October 1946. Cf. *Nazi-Soviet Relations*, p. 76.

[2] Quoted from the article 'Germany' in *Politicheski Slovar* (*Political Dictionary*) (Moscow, 1940), by Max M. Laserson, *Russia and the Western World*, p. 44.

[3] M. Henri Béranger, Chairman of the Foreign Affairs Commission of the French Senate, stated on 12 October 1939 that 'both Paris and London had been warned from reliable sources that an association was being prepared between Berlin and Moscow to divide among themselves the spheres of influence and even the territories from the Baltic to the Aegean Sea, between the Oder, the Danube, and the Dniester, from the Carpathians to the Balkans. The Western Powers had been informed that constant negotiations were being conducted between the Reich and the Kremlin in the diplomatic, military, and financial fields in order to link up the present with the past—that is to resuscitate the Chicherin-Rathenau agreement concluded in 1922 at Rapallo'. Quoted from *New York Herald Tribune*, 13 October 1939, by Schuman, *Europe on the Eve*, pp. 265–6; cf. Henderson, *Failure of a Mission*, pp. 226 and 228.

gent speculation and actual information that negotiations were in progress. Nor is it possible to give a conclusive answer to the question as to how much confidence the Soviet Union ever placed in the possibility of a favourable outcome to the negotiations with the Western Allies.[1] All that can be said is that the arguments which carried the day in favour of the German offer must have been apparent at least from the moment of the British guarantee to Poland.

The alternative lines of approach to the problems facing the Soviet Government can be indicated in the words of two highly qualified exponents of Soviet policy.

On 11 March, in Moscow, Manuilsky presented to the Congress of the Russian Communist Party, the report of the Party's delegation to the Communist International and described the international situation in words which echoed those of Stalin:

'The plan of the British reactionary bourgeoisie is to sacrifice the small States of south-eastern Europe to German Fascism so as to direct Germany eastward—against the U.S.S.R., to attempt by means of such a counter-revolutionary war, to retard the progress of socialism and the victory of communism in the U.S.S.R.; to buy off Germany with her imperialist claims on British colonies. At the same time, the British reactionaries would like to use the U.S.S.R. to draw the fangs of German imperialism, to weaken Germany for a long time to come, and to preserve the dominant position of British imperialism in Europe. . . .'

These plans were 'paving the way for the collapse not only of Fascism but of the entire capitalist system'. Manuilsky went on

[1] 'Early in May', according to German sources, 'the Germans took heart also from the replacement of Litvinov by Molotov as Foreign Minister. The lack of results from British negotiations with Russia was noted. Word came from Russian friends of Stalin's distrust of British intentions and dislike of the hesitant manner in which the negotiations with Russia were being carried on by the Western Powers'. Astakhov, Russia's representative in the trade negotiations with Germany, was doing his best to press for political talks. Hitler was adverse to this at first but became fearful lest the talks between Russia and the Western Powers might after all yield results. He decided to forestall such an eventuality by offering Russia rights in the whole zone from the Baltic to the Black Sea. Early in August he sounded Neurath (the latter said) about the wisdom of coming to terms with Russia, expressing doubt about the possible effect in the Nazi Party. 'New Light on Nazi Foreign Policy', *Foreign Affairs*, October 1946; Harold Deutsch 'Strange Interlude: The Nazi-Soviet Liaison of 1939–1941.' *The Historian*, Spring, 1947.

Professor Namier has examined the evidence contained in the affidavit of Friedrich Gaus, the legal adviser of the German Foreign Office, made at Nuremberg and dated 15 March 1946. This indicates that Ribbentrop began to consider a *rapprochement* with the Soviet Union from about the middle of June. L. B. Namier, *Diplomatic Prelude, 1938–9* (Macmillan, 1948), pp. 189–90, 281–3.

to forecast the salvation of the Soviet Union not only through its own armed resistance but by the stirring-up through the Soviet example of the 'whole world of labour'.[1]

Speaking in London on 15 March Maisky said:

'The foreign policy of the Soviet Government has always been a policy of universal peace. Not a peace at any price, but a peace based on law and order in international affairs. . . .

'Our two countries do not always see eye to eye as to the best methods for securing peace, but it is equally true—and the fact is of paramount importance—that at present there is no conflict of interest between the U.S.S.R. and the British Empire in any part of the world.

'You will find that in the last resort the fate of peace or war in our time depends on the kind of relations which exist between London and Moscow.'[2]

On the same day, the German seizure of the Czech lands provided another opportunity for seeing what those relations were and for testing the respective validity of the contradictory theses of the ex-Secretary of the Communist International and the Ambassador to the Court of St. James.[3]

[1] The membership of Communist Parties outside the Soviet Union had risen since 1934 from 860,000 to 1,200,000.

[2] Quoted by Coates, op. cit., pp. 602–3.

[3] The first British reaction to the news was very reserved, and it was not until 17 March that instructions to deliver a formal protest were sent to the British Ambassador in Berlin and that the Prime Minister in his Birmingham speech expounded the full gravity of the new situation. Professor Schuman bases upon this fact the assertion that what caused the abandonment of appeasement on 17 March was not the violation of the Munich agreement itself, but the revelation afforded by the Hungarian annexation of Carpatho-Ukraine that the Germans were not going to attack the Soviet Union. He supports this with arguments based on Coulondre's dispatches of 14, 15, 16, and 19 March and from his reading of documents from the Polish archives published by the German Government on 30 March 1940 (*The German White Book*, No. 3, with an introduction by C. Hartley Grattan, New York, Howell, Soskin and Co., 1940). Schuman, *Night over Europe*, pp. 114–22, *Soviet Politics*, p. 363; the only inference which can be drawn from this surprising suggestion is that henceforward, while accepting the prospect of a war with Germany, the British and French Governments preferred that the U.S.S.R. should be neutral or even hostile. But Sir Nevile Henderson reports himself as having declared to Hitler on 23 August 1939 that 'speaking quite personally and on purely moral grounds, if an agreement had to be made with Moscow he had rather Germany made it than Great Britain'; *Failure of a Mission*, pp. 247–8. Professor Schuman's assertion with regard to the events of 15 to 17 March is unconvincing if only because the German abandonment of any hopes based on the use of the Carpatho-Ukraine was common property considerably earlier. No authority is given for the statement in *Istoria Diplomatii* that Hitler considered Hungary's occupation of the Carpatho-Ukraine, which he had agreed to 'premature' and ordered her to withdraw her troops; vol. iii, p. 656.

On 17 March, with the German menace to Poland and Roumania becoming more clearly defined, diplomatic activity became intense, particularly in London.[1] On 19 March the Soviet note of protest against Germany's action in Czechoslovakia was delivered in Berlin.[2]

Meanwhile, an exchange of views between London and Moscow had begun. Its results were announced in a Soviet communiqué on 21 March.

'Poland and Roumania did not apply to the Soviet Government for help, nor did they inform that Government of any danger threatening them. What actually happened was that on 18 March [Saturday], the British Government informed the Soviet Government of the existence of weighty reasons to fear an act of violence over Roumania and inquired about the possible position of the Soviet Government in such an eventuality.

'In reply to this inquiry, the Soviet Government put forward a proposal for a calling of a conference of the States most interested— namely Great Britain, France, Poland, Roumania, Turkey, and the Soviet Union.

'In the opinion of the Soviet Government such a conference would give the maximum possibilities for the elucidation of the real situation and the position of all the participants at the conference. The British Government, however, found this proposal premature.'[3]

The British Government proposed instead a formal declaration to be signed by Great Britain, France, the U.S.S.R., and Poland, to the effect that the four Powers would immediately enter into consultations on any measures required to meet a threat to European peace and security.[4] This proposal was put

---

[1] See *German White Book* No. 2, nos. 263–72. For a reported German 'ultimatum' on trade relations delivered to Roumania on 17 March, see *B.I.N.*, XVI, pp. 292–3; for the German-Roumanian trade agreement of 23 March, see ibid., pp. 308–10. Schuman writes 'the Soviet Government gave promise of help for Roumania if the necessity arose'; *Night over Europe*, p. 226. Grigore Gafencu, who had become Roumanian Foreign Minister on 23 December 1938, had already indicated a wish to improve relations between Roumania and the Soviet Union which had been strained throughout 1938. No Soviet Minister to Bucarest had been appointed since the 'disappearance' of Mr. Butenko, the Chargé d'Affaires there, in February 1938. For Roumanian policy between January 1939 and June 1941 see the important book by Grigore Gafencu, *Prelude to the Russian Campaign* (Muller, 1945).

[2] Text in *B.I.N.*, XVI, pp. 243–4.

[3] Quoted from Coates, op. cit., p. 604. Professor Feiling points out that the Polish refusal to enter into contact with Russia was itself enough to prevent the proposed six-power conference; *Neville Chamberlain* (Macmillan, 1946), pp. 402–3.

[4] According to his biographer, Mr. Chamberlain himself worked out the formula for a four-Power declaration between 15 and 21 March.

to the Polish Government on 21 March. The reply conveyed to Lord Halifax on 24 March raised objections to the idea of a multilateral declaration. On 30 March the Poles were asked whether they would raise objections to a British assurance of support for Poland if that country's independence were threatened. This assurance was given in a declaration by the Prime Minister in the House of Commons on 31 March.[1]

In accordance with previous arrangements, Mr. Robert Hudson, Secretary of the British Department of Overseas Trade, had come to Moscow on the 23rd to initiate negotiations for a new trade agreement. The atmosphere had not been improved there by the publication, on the previous day, of the declaration of the Federation of British Industries and the Reichsgruppe Industrie announcing the establishment of a permanent machinery for consultation between the two bodies. On 23 March *Pravda* warned Great Britain and France that unless they showed more devotion to collective security, Soviet suspicions of the democracies would be further aggravated. The trade talks were inconclusive, but satisfactory enough for hopes to be held out that further discussions to be held in London would bring about the desired result. A Tass communiqué on 28 March declared that friendly discussions on international policy had brought out the points of contact in the position of the two countries and that the personal contacts made during them should be of use in strengthening Anglo-Soviet relations and international co-operation, in the interests of peace.[2] But on the same day, articles in *Izvestia* and *Pravda* complained that British and French policy was reverting to its old line of appeasement, now that the immediate panic over Roumania had subsided.[3]

[1] *Polish White Book*, pp. 69–72. Noël, *L'Agression Allemande contre la Pologne*, pp. 320–34. The situation had been rendered more acute by the German ultimatum to Lithuania on 21 March and the cession of Memel, and the German-Lithuanian non-aggression pact on 22 March. On 23 March a treaty between Germany and Slovakia was signed, subordinating the latter's foreign and military policy to German requirements; *Polish White Book*, pp. 59–60, cf. *Nuremberg Trial*, part 2, pp. 102–3. On the same day, the Germans and Roumanians signed a trade pact of far-reaching importance. Gafencu, *Derniers Jours de l'Europe*, pp. 38–63, 139–40.

[2] *Istoria Diplomatii*, vol. iii, p. 675.

[3] Schuman, *Night over Europe*, p. 226. On 26 March, Mr. Chamberlain wrote to his sister: 'I must confess to the most profound distrust of Russia. I have no belief whatever in her ability to maintain an effective offensive, even if she wanted to. And I distrust her motives, which seem to me to have little connection with our ideas of liberty, and to be concerned only with getting everyone else by the ears. Moreover, she is both hated and suspected by many of the smaller States, notably by Poland, Roumania and Finland'; Feiling, op. cit., p. 203.

The British guarantee to Poland was preceded by a rejection on Poland's part of German demands concerning Danzig and the 'Corridor', and of suggestions for Polish collaboration against the Soviet Union.[1] The news of the guarantee itself was greeted in Moscow with approval, but expressions of this approval were accompanied by extremely sceptical commentary. 'Independence' for Czechoslovakia had not precluded the giving up of the Sudetenland; did 'independence' for Poland preclude the surrender of Upper Silesia, Danzig, and the Polish sea-coast?[2] On the other hand the Soviet Government appeared in no hurry to supplement the guarantee by any positive step of its own. On the contrary, a Tass communiqué of 3 April repeated a previous denial (of 21 March) that the U.S.S.R. had given an undertaking should war break out to supply Poland with arms and to withhold raw materials from Germany. An article in *Pravda* on 4 April again revived the charge that Great Britain and France were trying to drag Germany and the Soviet Union into a war over the Carpatho-Ukraine.

On 6 April, while German pressure on Poland was being intensified, a reciprocal Anglo-Polish defensive agreement was announced from London.[3] This was followed by a slight détente in the German-Polish tension, a fact attributed by the French Chargé d'Affaires in Berlin to reluctance to launch a war in which she would have to fight a serious adversary on both fronts.[4] The conditions for a German approach to the Soviet Union were now plainly in existence.[5]

[1] Noël to Bonnet, 30 March, 30 April, Coulondre to Bonnet 8 May 1939; *Documents Diplomatiques*, pp. 99–100, 119, 131–5. In a conversation with Lipski on 21 March Ribbentrop emphasized that an understanding between Germany and Poland 'obviously . . . would have to include explicit anti-Soviet tendencies. He affirmed that Germany could never collaborate with the Soviet, and that a Soviet-Polish understanding would inevitably lead to Bolshevism in Poland'; *Polish White Book*, pp. 61–3. In a further conversation on 26 March, Ribbentrop said that 'Germany recognized Poland's priority of right in the Eastern sector'; ibid., pp. 66–9. Noël, op. cit., pp. 313–20. An order of Keitel's dated 3 April 1939 gave 1 September as the date by which the German armed forces were to be ready for the attack on Poland; *Nuremberg Trial*, part 2, p. 142.

[2] *Izvestia*, 2 April, quoted Schuman, *Night over Europe*, pp. 226–7.

[3] *British Blue Book*, Cmd. 6106, pp. 36–7. This agreement was concluded during a visit to London by Beck who showed his usual reluctance to have any dealings with the Soviet Union. 'I confess I very much agree with him', wrote Chamberlain to his sister, 'for I regard Russia as a very unstable friend . . . with an enormous irritative power on others'. Feiling, op. cit., p. 208.

[4] M. de Vaux St. Cyr to Bonnet, 11 April 1939, *Documents Diplomatiques*, pp. 107–9.

[5] According to the well-informed American journalists J. Alsop and R. Kintner, Germany suggested a trade pact to the U.S.S.R. after the Anglo-

Italy's seizure of Albania on 7–8 April, and the strong reaction produced by this in the Western capitals, led on 10 April to Soviet press and radio statements expressing gratification that the Soviet policy of collective security appeared to be gaining ground. But, it was argued, a mere British guarantee to Greece would be insufficient. Single guarantees, like the British guarantee to Poland, diverted the tide of aggression without checking it. What was needed was that Turkey, Roumania, and, above all, the Soviet Union should be enlisted to form a defensive bloc against the tide of aggression.[1] This was presumably the view urged upon Lord Halifax when he was visited by Maisky on 11 April.

By 11 April it was known that Great Britain was prepared to guarantee Greece. At a French Cabinet meeting on that day Daladier declared that the most important thing was to save Roumania. Bonnet pointed out that Poland had confirmed that it did not want Soviet assistance and that it had received no request for help from Roumania. The French had asked Roumania to request Poland for a promise of help. The British had been very wrong to give their guarantee to Poland without asking the latter to undertake the same obligations in favour of Roumania. Bonnet told the Cabinet that he had just had from Suritz the Soviet reply to his latest communication. This regretted the failure both of the Soviet proposal for a conference and of the suggested four-Power declaration, but affirmed the Soviet Government's readiness to examine any concrete proposal in favour of Roumania and Poland.[2]

Chamberlain's announcement in the House of Commons on 13 April of the British guarantees to Greece and Roumania

---

Polish agreement, and received a reply to the effect that the U.S.S.R. wanted closer political relations. Thereupon the Germans are said to have made yet another approach to the Poles for joint military action against the Soviet Union; *American White Paper* (Michael Joseph, 1940), p. 72.

[1] *B.I.N.*, XVI, p. 417. A French guarantee to Roumania and Greece was announced on the same day, as well as the confirmation of the Franco-Polish alliance; ibid., p. 381. The French statement was to be brought to the notice of Turkey, in particular, with which closer relations were impeded by the Hatay (Alexandretta) question; *Documents Diplomatiques*, p. 109.

[2] *Carnets Secrets de Jean Zay*, pp. 56–7. At a conference at the French War Ministry on 9 April, Bonnet had suggested that the French should ask the Russians through both diplomatic and military channels what they would do for Poland and Roumania. According to General Gamelin, British objections prevented the implementation of this suggestion until August; *Servir*, vol. ii, p. 406. This was not the case ; but the Soviet reply referred to Polish and Roumanian unwillingness to accept Soviet aid. Bonnet, op. cit., pp. 176–181.

did not meet the Soviet point, although in response to an interjection, the Prime Minister added that he hoped members would not assume, that if he had not mentioned the Soviet Union in his statement, that meant that his Government was not keeping in closest touch with that country's representatives.[1]

This announcement proved in fact to be the prelude to a resumption of direct discussions between the Soviet and British Governments.   Maisky saw Lord Halifax on the 14th and on the 15th Sir William Seeds handed new British proposals to Litvinov in Moscow.[2] On 17 April Litvinov gave the Ambassador the Soviet counter-proposals.

According to a Soviet account the Soviet offer was as follows:

'It put forward the suggestion that a three-Power pact should be concluded between the U.S.S.R., Great Britain, and France, for the protection of countries menaced by Fascist aggression. The Soviet

---

[1] On 14 April, the French submitted to Moscow a suggested text for a joint declaration. 'In case France and Great Britain should find themselves at war with Germany as the result of action taken by them to bring help to Roumania or Poland following upon unprovoked aggression against the latter, the U.S.S.R. would at once come to their aid. In case the U.S.S.R. should find itself in a state of war with Germany, as the result of action taken by it to bring help to Roumania or Poland, following upon unprovoked aggression against the latter, France and Great Britain would at once come to its aid. The three governments shall enter into discussions without delay on the forms of this assistance and take all measures to assure its full efficacy.' Bonnet, op. cit., p. 180.

[2] Sir William Seeds had replaced Lord Chilston at the Moscow Embassy in January 1939. The British note ran as follows: 'The British Government has noted the recent declaration of M. Stalin by the terms of which the Soviet Union declares itself in favour of assistance for nations which may become the victims of aggression. It seems therefore that the Soviet Government would act in complete accordance with this policy if it were to make now upon its own initiative a public declaration, in which, referring to the above mentioned declaration and to the declarations recently made by the British Government and the French Government, it were to repeat that in the event of any act of aggression against any neighbouring State to the Soviet Union which that State were to resist, the assistance of the Soviet Government would be given, if the desire for it were expressed, and would be made available according to the most appropriate method. . . . A positive declaration of the Soviet Government's at the present moment would have a calming effect upon the international situation and would constitute a concrete application of Soviet policy as it is defined above', Gafencu, *Derniers Jours*, p. 140. On the following day Kalinin sent to President Roosevelt a telegram of sympathy and congratulation on the 'noble message' which the President had sent Hitler on the 14th, and in which he had asked Hitler for a pledge that his troops would not invade any of thirty named States including Russia. The text of the Roosevelt message is in *Peace and War*, pp. 455–8.

Government added that the agreement which it proposed could be embodied in three acts: in the first place an agreement between the three Powers for mutual assistance; in the second place the conclusion between them of a military convention which would give to the mutual assistance pact real strength, and finally a guarantee by the three Powers to all States between the Baltic and the Black Sea.'[1]

On 18 April Maisky left London for a week of consultation with his Government. On 17 April, the Soviet Ambassador Merekalov called on the German State Secretary Weizsäcker for the first time since taking up his post in Berlin (in June 1938). The ostensible reason was the question of the fulfilling of certain contracts for supplying armaments to the Soviet Union entered into by the Skoda works in Czechoslovakia. From this the conversation passed to current political events and Merekalov significantly remarked that Soviet Russia had not exploited the friction between Germany and the Western democracies against Germany, nor did she desire to do so.

[1] *Istoria Diplomatii*, vol. iii, p. 674.
According to M. Bonnet, essential points in these proposals, which he dates 19 April, were that the Baltic States should be included in the agreement despite their opposition; that the three Powers (Great Britain, France, U.S.S.R.) should agree not to sign a separate peace; that British help to Poland should be restricted to the case of German aggression, and that the Polish-Roumanian alliance should be rewritten so as to apply against all comers and not merely the U.S.S.R.
In an interview with the Polish Ambassador, Grzybowski, at the end of the first week in May, Molotov is reported to have told him that the Soviet terms had included permission for Soviet troops to enter Poland by a northern and a southern route, the repudiation of the Polish-Roumanian alliance, and a declaration by Great Britain that her guarantee of Poland applied exclusively to Poland's *western* frontiers. This account, based on unpublished Polish sources, is given in Umiastowski, *Russia and the Polish Republic*, p. 130. He dates the interview 8 May. The *Polish White Book* gives Sunday, 7 May as the date, (p. 208).
Julian Lukasiewicz, at that time Polish Ambassador to France, states that the Soviet terms in the summer of 1939 included the above points (apart from the British declaration which is not mentioned) as well as a Soviet-Polish political treaty going beyond the existing pact of non-aggression, and a free hand in the Baltic States. Polish reserve, he declares, was due to its unwillingness either to accept the full Russian demands in connexion with Eastern Poland or to cause Britain and France to assent to another 'Munich'. The only acceptable form of assistance which the Poles could have had from the Soviet Union would have been in the form of materials of war, and this was never offered. J. Lukasiewicz, *Z Doswiadzen Przeszlosci* (From the *Experience of the Past.*) (Rome, 1944). In an article published in 1946, M. Lukasiewicz said that Bonnet informed him of the Russian reply on 25 April. It demanded an Anglo-French-Russian alliance, the extension of the guarantee to the Baltic States and the cancelling of the Polish-Roumanian alliance. Namier, op. cit., p. 155 *n*.

'There exists for Russia no reason why she should not live with us on a normal footing. And from normal, the relations might become better and better.'[1] Shortly afterwards the Soviet Ambassador in Berlin and the Military Attaché there also left for Moscow.[2] The moment was obviously a crucial one and it is abundantly clear that the stated attitudes of the Soviet Government and of the Western Democracies to the problem of security were very far apart.[3]

---

[1] Memorandum by Weizsäcker, *Nazi-Soviet Relations*, pp. 1–2.

[2] On 6 May a member of the French Embassy, Captain Stellin had a conversation with one of Hitler's entourage (General Bodenschatz). Referring to Hitler's speech of 28 April, in which he denounced the Munich agreement, the Anglo-German naval treaty, and the Polish-German non-aggression pact, the German said:

'Were you not struck by the fact that in his last speech [Hitler] made no allusion to Russia? Have you not noticed the understanding way in which this morning's papers—which, by the way, had received very precise instructions on this point—speak of M. Molotov and Russia? (Molotov had succeeded Litvinov as Foreign Commissar three days earlier.) You have had some wind,' he continued, 'of certain discussions in progress and of the journey of the Soviet Ambassador and military attaché to Moscow. The former was received on the eve of his departure by Ribbentrop, and the second at the Army High Command, and has been made thoroughly familiar with the views of the German Government. I can really tell you no more about it but you will learn some day that something is going on in the East [dass etwas im Osten im gange ist]. . . in brief . . . the situation can be summed up as follows: the Poles believe they can be insolent towards us, feeling themselves strong in the support of France and Great Britain and believing themselves able to count on the material aid of Russia. They are mistaken in their calculations. Just as Hitler did not feel able to settle the question of Austria and that of Czechoslovakia without Italy, so he does not now think of settling the German dispute with Poland without Russia. . . . There have been three partitions of Poland. Well, believe me, you will see a fourth.' He added that the uncertainties of Japanese policy had been one of the factors which had led Hitler to revive his Russian policy. The prospects for a German-Soviet *rapprochement* were fully discussed by Coulondre in the dispatch enclosing the report of this conversation. Coulondre to Bonnet, 7 May 1939, *Documents Diplomatiques*, pp. 127–31. It has also been said that von Papen, who presented his letters of credence as German Ambassador at Ankara on 29 April, entered almost at once into discussions with Terentiev, the Soviet Ambassador there; H. W. Blood-Ryan, *Fritz von Papen* (Rich and Cowan, 1940), pp. 15, 309–16.

[3] According to M. Gafencu, the British attitude to the negotiations was stated as follows in a document of 29 April: 'The policy pursued by H.M. Government in its contacts with the Soviet Government has for its object to reconcile the following considerations: (a) Not to neglect the chance of receiving help from the Soviet Government in case of war; (b) not to compromise the common front by neglecting the susceptibilities of Poland and Roumania; (c) not to alienate the sympathy of the entire world by giving a

A report from the Polish Ambassador in London on 26 April
has been published by the Germans:

'Without any doubt England wants Russian participation in the
relations of the Powers, but does not want to bind itself formally or
too closely. From the explanations made to me by the permanent
Sub-secretary (sic) Cadogan of the Foreign Office, it is inferred that
England and France wish to limit themselves to obtaining a declaration from Russia stating that in case of war it would maintain a
benevolent attitude so that, in this way, assurance may be had of
access to basic materials, &c. This could be accomplished through
a partial statement of the Soviet Government which would state
that in the case of a German attack on Poland or Roumania, Russia
would make known its attitude beforehand. But the counter-
proposal of the Soviet, which desires to arrange a pact of mutual
aid, in either an Anglo-Russian bilateral form corresponding to the
French-Soviet treaty, or as an accord among France, England, and
Russia, was unacceptable to England according to Cadogan, nor did
France want it. Cadogan referred to the necessary consideration of
the reactions that would be provoked in other countries, mentioning
among others Poland, Roumania, Yugoslavia, Spain. At the same
time Cadogan underlined the difficulties that the British Government
would have; he did not want to give a negative answer in such a
way as to cause anger. Also Minister Gafencu has been informed of
this point of view.[1] From his conversations he became convinced
that the British Government was avoiding a closer relationship with
the Soviet. The Roumanian Foreign Minister expressed his opinion
before me that actual Anglo-Soviet negotiations would be fruitless.
Because of this, English policy, which still does not want to make
any exclusively anti-German arrangements, tries to avoid any direct
tie-up with the Soviet. But the future development of the international situation may take such a turn as to make the maintenance
of this line impossible.'[2]

---

pretext to the anti-Comintern propoganda of Germany; (d) not to compromise the cause of peace by provoking violent act on the part of Germany.' This document again put forward the British suggestion for a unilateral declaration by the U.S.S.R. On the same date, the French Government are said to have proposed a new formula by which the U.S.S.R. on the
one hand, and France and Great Britain on the other, would give each other
help in the event of either side finding itself at war with Germany as the
result of intervening to prevent the modification by force of the status quo
in central or eastern Europe. Derniers Jours, pp. 165–7. Professor Namier
identifies this document as the aide-mémoire presented by the British to the
French Government.

[1] Gafencu visited London on 23–26 April, Derniers Jours, pp. 107–22.
[2] German White Book, No. 3, pp. 68–9. The account given here resembles
closely the analysis of the British attitude made by the London correspondent of a French weekly in a message dated 18 April: 'The Soviet Government would not merely guarantee Poland and Russia (sic. Roumania?) but
all its neighbours in Europe except Finland. By the coming into play of this

The reluctance of the Soviet Union's neighbours to enter into closer relations with her of the kind envisaged was, indeed, as clear now as during the earlier negotiations for an Eastern pact.[1] A Warsaw report of 19 April ran:

'Poland has informed Great Britain and Russia that she refuses to participate in any efforts to draw the Soviet Union into the anti-aggression "peace front" being organized by Britain, it was announced officially to-night. Poland has a "negative attitude" towards permitting Soviet troops or planes to march or fly over Polish territory, the announcement said.'[2]

On 18 April the Estonian Foreign Minister told his Parliament that the Estonian and Latvian Governments had exchanged views with the Soviet Government in an atmosphere of mutual confidence on the subject of threats to their independence, the possibility of foreign assistance, and on the maintenance of neutrality in the Baltic Republics in the case of war. Estonian relations with the U.S.S.R. were fixed by the Peace Treaty of 1920 and the Non-Aggression Pact of 1932. Estonia would remain neutral in case of war and fight for her neutrality if it were violated.[3]

---

guarantee, Russia would not engage herself to help these Powers immediately they became the victims of aggression, but only to lend them in time of war, and only when they asked for her assistance, such help, material, financial, military or in the air, as might be asked of her. In brief, the U.S.S.R. would in some sense play the part of a reserve on which one would only call to the extent of one's needs. . . . The British argue that in guaranteeing Poland and Roumania against a German attack, Great Britain gives the U.S.S.R. a shield *ipso facto* and thus justifies the sacrifices which they demand of Moscow. But in addition the British plan does not stop there . . . the London Government seems well-disposed towards concluding a pact of mutual assistance with the Soviet Union.' *L'Europe Nouvelle*, 22 April 1939.

[1] See vol. 1, chap. 12.

[2] The *New York Herald Tribune*, 20 April 1939, quoted by V. A. Yakhontoff, *U.S.S.R. Foreign Policy* (New York, Coward McCann, 1945), p. 201. On 19 April, Moscow radio declared that Great Britain had advised Poland to come to terms with Germany. A Warsaw press statement believed to be 'inspired' stated that Polish-Soviet relations had 'recently been developing quite satisfactorily and it may be said that the Soviet side is showing more and more understanding for the interests of Poland'; *B.I.N.*, XVI, p. 464. According to M. Gafencu, the British Government in a note of 22 April declared itself unable to understand why the Soviet Government affected to believe that H.M. Government was not bound by the declarations which it had made to Poland and Roumania; *Derniers Jours*, p. 166, n.

[3] *B.I.N.*, XVI, p. 448. According to one account Estonia and Latvia sent identical notes to the U.S.S.R. that they were in no danger of attack and had no need of military assistance; Dallin, *Foreign Policy*, p. 23. Estonia was shortly afterwards engaged in talks with Poland, whose policy on the whole she tended to follow. See the articles 'La Douteuse Lettonie', *L'Europe Nouvelle*, 24 June and 29 July 1939.

The position of Roumania was complicated by that country's relationship to her partners of the 'Balkan Entente'; with whom she was endeavouring to strengthen her relations.[1] On 15 April, Fabricius, the German Minister to Bucarest, reported that Roumania had refused to enter into a four-Power pact with Great Britain, Poland, and France, against Germany, and had also refused to extend the scope of the Roumanian-Polish alliance, which was exclusively directed against Russia.[2] On 17 April the Roumanian Government denied a rumour that it had agreed to allow Soviet troops to cross its territory in the event of a conflict.[3]

The Roumanian Foreign Minister, who had visited Turkey earlier in the month, left on 16 April for a visit to Berlin. On his way he stopped at Warsaw, where, according to the 'official' Polish press, he came to an understanding with Beck to take no decisions in the international sphere without prior consultation with Poland.[4]

When he saw Hitler on the 19th, Gafencu 'was warned . . . that Roumania's participation in a scheme of collective security that included the U.S.S.R., and the creation of bonds of mutual assistance between Roumania and Moscow would be regarded in Berlin as an attempt to encircle Germany, against which the Reich was determined to take energetic measures.' Gafencu replied that Roumania 'did not intend to make any particular engagements of assistance' with either Germany or Russia, and he 'maintained the same point of view in London and Paris' to which he went following his visit to Berlin.[5]

The outlook for 'collective security' was thus at its blackest when Litvinov resigned his office as Foreign Commissar on 3 May.[6] He was succeeded by Molotov, and the Moscow radio

[1] Pierre Brossolette, 'Une Histoire Peu Connue: celle de l'Entente Balkanique', L'Europe Nouvelle, 22 April 1939. Gafencu, Prelude, pp. 241–6. In Yugoslavia, the Government of Tsvetkovic which had replaced that of Stoyadinovic on 5 February seemed no more disposed than its predecessor to resist the advance of the Axis. On 21–23 April, its Foreign Minister, Cincar-Markovic, had talks with Ciano at Venice; their results were apparently to the latter's satisfaction.

[2] German White Book, No. 2, p. 291.

[3] L'Europe Nouvelle, 22 April 1939, p. 427.   [4] B.I.N., XVI, p. 463; cf. Gafencu, Derniers Jours, pp. 35–63.   [5] ibid., pp. 64–95.

[6] Questioned in the House of Commons on 2 May as to the negotiations with Russia, the Prime Minister gave guarded indications that the British and Soviet Governments differed as to the form which such an accord should take. The French and British also differed as to how much to concede to the Soviet viewpoint. A French counter-proposal was handed to Suritz on 29 April. Bonnet, op. cit., pp. 182–3.

announced on the following day that the change in personnel did not signify any change in policy. Foreign opinion was nevertheless unanimous in regarding the resignation as a severe blow to the chances of an agreement between the Soviet Union and the Western Powers.[1] Some went so far as to argue that the main reason might be Stalin's desire to remove an obviously unsuitable instrument for a contemplated *rapprochement* with Germany.

The German Chargé d'Affaires, Tippelskirch, wrote from Moscow that Litvinov's departure was believed due to differences of opinion in the Kremlin over the negotiations with the Western Powers, arising presumably from Stalin's distrust of 'the entire surrounding capitalist world'. Astakhov, the Soviet Chargé in Berlin was informed on 5 May that the Skoda contracts would be carried out, and himself commented favourably on the recent moderation of the German press in regard to Russia. He denied that Litvinov's departure could mean a reorientation of Soviet foreign policy since it was a question, not of personal policy but of compliance with general principles.[2]

Litvinov's resignation came at a moment when his principal assistant Potemkin was engaged in what appeared to be an attempt to rally the countries of eastern and south-eastern Europe, in resistance to German aggression.[3] Potemkin reached Ankara on 29 April and left on 5 May.[4] On 7 May he arrived in Sofia for a one-day visit, in the course of which he saw the Prime Minister Kiosseivanov and King Boris. On 8 May he arrived at Bucarest. According to Gafencu's account of the

[1] See e.g. Davies's dispatch from Brussels on 10 May 1939, *Mission to Moscow*, pp. 283–4. According to a German press report Litvinov's resignation came after a quarrel with Voroshilov who had declared that the Red Army would never fight for Poland and that the General Staff were opposed to excessively far-reaching foreign obligations. *Angriff*, quoted *B.I.N.*, XVI, p. 508. Voroshilov, Zhdanov, and Molotov were all rumoured as favouring coming to terms with Hitler if Great Britain would not accept the Soviet terms; Schuman, *Night over Europe*, p. 233.

[2] *Nazi-Soviet Relations*, pp. 2–4.

[3] There is no mention of this tour by Potemkin in either of his works already referred to.

[4] An official communiqué issued in Ankara on 7 May declared that a similarity of views on international questions and on questions of particular interest to Russia and Turkey had once more been established. 'The Soviet and Turkish Governments', it concluded, 'will pursue their respective and parallel efforts for the safeguarding of peace and security and will continue to keep in constant touch with one another in order to exchange all political information bearing upon their common interests, as they have done during M. Potemkin's stay in Ankara.' *B.I.N.*, XVI, p. 530. Turkish circles remained optimistic for some time afterwards as to the prospects of Soviet collaboration; Gafencu, *Derniers Jours*, pp. 207–8.

conversations there, these were very cordial. Potemkin, he writes,

'repeatedly insisted on the necessity of consolidating the Balkan Entente, and expressed his regret that Bulgaria, as he had been forced to observe at Sofia, seemed still less disposed to enter into closer relations with her neighbours.'

Potemkin also tried to reassure his host about the meaning of Litvinov's resignation, declaring that Molotov had shown the continuity of Soviet policy by immediately indicating his approval of the policy of close friendship between the U.S.S.R. and Turkey and of the Anglo-Turkish negotiations which were then in progress. He continued in terms which Gafencu noted as follows:

'The totalitarian Powers are spreading the false rumour that the U.S.S.R. is ready to come to an understanding with Germany and Italy. That is the sort of tactics they use, particularly in Berlin, to prevent an agreement between London, Paris, and Moscow. Hitler himself uses these tactics, and is pleased to insinuate that it will always be possible for him either by means of economic negotiations or by intervention of the German Staff, to tighten relations between the Reich and the U.S.S.R. at the opportune moment. The Italians also are trying to retain non-official links with Moscow in spite of their official pronouncements—so hostile to the Soviet Union. But all that does not change, and will never change, Soviet policy, which does not bend to opportunist exigencies, but follows the end of general peace by pacific measures. . . .'[1]

On 9 and 10 May Potemkin had talks in Warsaw, where Beck had made a firm speech on the 5th, in answer to the German demands about Danzig and the 'Corridor'.[2]

The talks in Warsaw seem to have been regarded by the Poles as highly successful. On 13 May Beck wrote to the Polish Embassy in Paris as follows:

'The conversations with M. Potemkin during his stay in Warsaw on the 10th inst. have made it clear that the Soviet Government takes an understanding attitude to our point of view with regard to Polish-Soviet relations which are now developing quite normally.

'The Soviet realize that the Polish Government is not prepared to enter into any agreement with either one of Poland's great neighbours against the other, and understand the advantages to them of this attitude.

'M. Potemkin also stated that in the event of an armed conflict between Poland and Germany the Soviets will adopt "*une attitude bienveillante*" towards us.

[1] Gafencu, *Prelude*, pp. 239–41; *Derniers Jours*, pp. 199–205.
[2] *Polish White Book*, pp. 84–92.

'As M. Potemkin himself indicated, his statements were made in accordance with special instructions which the Soviet Government sent to Warsaw for him.'[1]

'Recapitulating these conversations' to the Polish Ambassador in Warsaw, Potemkin 'stressed with satisfaction M. Beck's declaration that in the event of such a conflict they (the Poles) would rely inevitably on the Soviets.'

At about the same time Molotov had conversations with the Polish Ambassador in Moscow. The first of these, which has already been referred to, was inconclusive, although Molotov expressed his satisfaction with Beck's speech of 5 May.[2] On the second occasion the Polish Ambassador gave Molotov a résumé of his country's attitude:

'We could not accept a one-sided Soviet guarantee. Nor could we accept a mutual guarantee because in the event of a conflict with Germany our forces would be completely engaged, and so we would not be in any position to give help to the Soviets. Also we could not accept collective negotiations, and make our adoption of a definite attitude conditional on the result of the Anglo-Franco-Soviet negotiations. We rejected all discussions of matters affecting us other than by the bilateral method. Our alliance with Roumania, being purely defensive, could not in any way be regarded as directed against the U.S.S.R.

'In addition, I indicated our favourable attitude to the Anglo-Franco-Soviet negotiations, and once more emphasized our entire loyalty in relation to the Soviets. In the event of conflict we by no means rejected specified forms of Soviet aid, but considered it premature to determine them definitely. We considered it premature to open bilateral negotiations with the Soviets before the Anglo-Franco-Soviet negotiations had achieved a result. Mr. Molotov made no objection whatever.'[3]

Apart from the conversations at Ankara, it was thus hardly possible for the Soviet Government to derive encouragement for a policy of collective security from the results of Potemkin's tour.

On 6 May Ribbentrop saw Ciano in Milan and on the following day it was made known that a military alliance between

---

[1] ibid., p. 183. On 9 May a new Soviet Ambassador to Poland was appointed, N. Sharonov, formerly Minister at Athens. He presented his credentials on 2 June; ibid., p. 184. Since the recall of Sharonov's predecessor Davtian the Soviet Government had had no Ambassador at Warsaw, and not even a Chargé d'Affaires.

[2] Noël, op. cit., p. 376.

[3] *Polish White Book*, p. 208.

Germany and Italy would shortly be signed.[1] On 8 May, the British reply to the Soviet proposals of 17 April was at last delivered to Molotov by Seeds. The contents of the reply were not fully revealed by either side.

A Tass communiqué commented on them as follows:

'In these proposals it is not stated that the Soviet Government must give separate guarantees for the States bordering it.

'The proposals state the Soviet Government must give immediate help to Britain and France in case the latter are involved in military operations in execution of their obligations towards Poland and Roumania.

'However the counter-proposals of the British Government, include no pledge of help to be given by the British and French Governments to the Soviet Union on a reciprocal basis should the Soviet Union become engaged in military operations in execution of the obligations it would undertake concerning any Eastern European State.'[2]

On the other hand, in the course of a long statement made on 10 May, Mr. Chamberlain declared that the modifications in the original British proposals made it

'plain that it is no part of their intention that the Soviet Government should commit themselves to intervene irrespective of whether Britain and France are already intervening in discharge of their own obligations.

'H.M. Government (he went on) added that if the Soviet Government wished to make their own intervention contingent on that of Britain and France, H.M. Government for their part would offer no objection. The Foreign Secretary yesterday saw the Soviet Ambassador, who explained to him that the Soviet Government was still not clear as to whether, under the proposals of H.M. Government, circumstances might not arise wherein the Soviet Government would stand committed to intervention unsupported by H.M. Government and France. . . .'

He had accordingly invited the Soviet Ambassador to inform the British Government of the precise grounds upon which these doubts were based, so that they could be removed.[3]

---

[1] Ciano tried on 8 May to assure the Soviet Chargé d'Affaires, Léon Helfand, that the new pact was not anti-Russian, and attempted to show his goodwill by trying to facilitate the exchange of Russian prisoners held by Franco, *The Ciano Diaries, 1939–1943* (New York, Doubleday, 1946), p. 79. There was at this time a slackening of German press attacks on Poland and rumour attributed it to the moderating influence of Italy. Coulondre to Bonnet, 9 May 1939, *Documents Diplomatiques*, pp. 131–5. The Italo-German treaty was signed in Berlin on 22 May. *B.I.N.*, XVI, pp. 549–60.

[2] It was published in the Soviet press on 10 May. *Istoria Diplomatii*, vol. iii, p. 676.

[3] *House of Commons Debates*, 10 May 1939.

The British Prime Minister's reassurances did not appear to carry conviction and the Soviet attitude was restated with great vehemence in an article in *Izvestia* on 11 May:

'. . . The U.S.S.R. held and continues to hold that if France and Great Britain realy want to create a barrier against aggression in Europe a united front of mutual assistance should be created, primarily of the four principal Powers in Europe—Great Britain, France, the U.S.S.R., and Poland—or, at least of three Powers—Great Britain, France, and the U.S.S.R.—and that these three Powers, bound by a pact of mutual assistance on the principle of reciprocity, should guarantee the other States of Eastern and Central Europe which are threatened by aggression. . . .

'Great Britain's suggestions avoid the subject of a pact of mutual assistance between France, Great Britain, and the U.S.S.R. and consider that the Soviet Government should come to the immediate aid of Great Britain and France should they be involved in hostilities as a result of the obligations they have assumed in guaranteeing Poland and Roumania.

'Great Britain says nothing about the aid which the U.S.S.R. should naturally receive on the principle of reciprocity from France and Great Britain should it be involved in hostilities owing to the fulfilment of the obligations it may assume in guaranteeing any of the States of Eastern Europe.

'It thus follows that under this arrangement, the U.S.S.R. must find itself in a position of inequality, although it would assume exactly the same obligations as France and Great Britain. We say nothing about the highly interesting fact that under this arrangement the actual resistance to aggression and the time of commencement of this resistance are left to be decided only by Great Britain and France, although the brunt of this resistance would fall principally on the U.S.S.R. owing to its geographical situation.

'We are told that by defending Poland and Roumania, Great Britain and France would virtually be defending the western frontier of the U.S.S.R. That is not true.

'Firstly, the western frontier of the U.S.S.R. is not confined to Poland and Roumania. Secondly, and this is the main point, by defending Poland and Roumania, Great Britain and France would be defending themselves and not the western frontier of the U.S.S.R. for they have a pact of mutual assistance with Poland, who in her turn is obliged to defend Great Britain and France from aggression.

'As to Roumania, inasmuch as she has a treaty of alliance with Poland, she will be obliged to follow in Poland's wake—that is Roumania virtually will have to play the part of an indirect ally of Great Britain and France.

'But the situation of the U.S.S.R. is different. Not having a pact of mutual assistance with Great Britain and France, nor with Poland, the U.S.S.R. is to undertake to assist all these states without receiving any assistance from them and moreover, in the event of aggression directly aimed at the U.S.S.R. the latter would have to rely solely upon its own forces. . . .'[1]

On 14 May a Soviet reply, presumably along these lines, was transmitted to London.[2]

Some occasion for optimism was given by the news on 12 May of the successful conclusion of the Anglo-Turkish conversations. London and Ankara issued a joint declaration foreshadowing 'a definite long-term agreement of a reciprocal character in the interest of their national security' and stating that, pending its conclusion, the two Governments would 'in the event of an act of aggression leading to war in the Mediterranean area . . . be prepared to co-operate effectively and to lend each other all the aid and assistance in their power',[3] A similar Franco-Turkish agreement was signed on 23 June after an agreement had been reached concerning the Hatay.[4] The agreement with Britain was welcomed in *Izvestia* on 15 May as 'one of the links in that chain which is the only sure means of preventing the extension of aggression to new parts of Europe', and took the occasion to emphasize the closeness of Russo-Turkish friendship.[5] On the Turkish side also it was made plain that relations with Russia were felt to be as close and cordial as ever.[6]

The hopes placed on the pact in Britain were largely based on the prospect that it would shortly be followed by an agreement between Britain, France, and the U.S.S.R. 'The contact and communication of the Western Allies with Russia through the Dardanelles and the Black Sea', wrote Winston Churchill on the same day upon which the *Izvestia* statement appeared, 'has been proved to be a vital need for the defence of the east of Europe in a war against German invasion. The wheat and trade of southern Russia, as long as British and French sea-power rule in the Mediterranean, can flow freely out to the markets of the world, and whatever is necessary in munitions and the raw materials of war can be brought in return to the Russian Black Sea ports.'[7]

---

[1] Quoted by Schuman, *Night over Europe*, pp. 236–7.
[2] 'The reply stressed that if it were seriously intended to resist aggression then it was absolutely essential to have (a) a three-power pact to resist a direct attack; (b) a military convention side by side with the political agreement; (c) a joint guarantee for all the States bordering on the Soviet Union between the Baltic Sea and the Black Sea.' Coates, op. cit., p. 607.
[3] Chamberlain, *House of Commons Debates*, 12 May 1939.
[4] See 'The Political and Strategic Importance of Turkey', *B.I.N.* 4 November 1939.
[5] Quoted *B.I.N.*, XVI, p. 533.
[6] Turkish official statement of 8 July 1939, ibid., p. 742.
[7] W. S. Churchill, *Step by Step*, p. 335.

But on the main issue of Anglo-Soviet relations, the deadlock appeared to be almost complete, and reports of a Russo-German understanding again multiplied.[1]

It was in fact on 17 May that Astakhov again called on Dr. Schnurre, the economic expert at the German Foreign Office, and 'referred in great detail' to the development of Soviet-German relations. He hoped that the improved tone of the German press would prove a permanent feature. 'Astakhov stated in detail that there were no conflicts in foreign policy between Germany and Soviet Russia, and that therefore there

---

[1] On 17 May 1939 the former notorious German agent, von Rintelen, had an interview with Davies in Brussels. Davies's memorandum of the conversation included the following: 'That Germany is making a desperate effort to succeed in keeping the Soviets neutral and to prevent a new misadventure such as was the case with Turkey. He said that the former Czecho-slovak General Syrovy, who went over to the Nazis after he had succeeded Hodza as Prime Minister, had been sent twice recently to Moscow to contact army officers and friends in Russia as a Hitler emissary.' op. cit., p. 284. In a dispatch on 22 May, Coulondre wrote that Ribbentrop's belief was that the Polish State could have no durable existence and was destined to another partition between Germany and Russia. This partition was intimately linked in Ribbentrop's mind with the idea of a *rapprochement* between Berlin and Moscow, which would give Germany the chance of striking a mortal blow at the British Empire, with the aid of the Soviet Union's material and human resources. This was still opposed by Hitler for ideological reasons, but Ribbentrop had his supporters in the High Command and among the industrialists; *Documents Diplomatiques*, pp. 143–5. An important conference was held in the Reich Chancellery on 23 May 1939. Hitler stressed the importance of extending German *lebensraum* and food supplies in connexion with the Polish question. 'The Polish problem is inseparable from conflict with the West. Poland's internal power of resistance to Bolshevism is doubtful. Thus Poland is of doubtful value as a barrier against Russia. . . . The Polish government will not resist pressure from Russia. Poland sees danger in a German victory in the West, and will attempt to rob us of that victory. There is, therefore, no question of sparing Poland, and we are left with the decision: *to attack Poland at the first suitable opportunity*. . . . Our task is to isolate Poland. . . . The isolation of Poland is a matter of skilful politics. Japan is a weighty problem. Even if at first, for various reasons, her collaboration with us appears to be somewhat cool and restricted, it is nevertheless in Japan's own interest to take the initiative in attacking Russia in good time. Economic relations with Russia are possible only if political relations have improved. A cautious trend is apparent in Press comment. It is not impossible that Russia will show herself to be disinterested in the destruction of Poland. Should Russia take steps to oppose us, our relations with Japan may become closer.' *Nuremberg Trial*, part 1, pp. 166–70. A Berlin message to the French newspaper *L'Ordre*, dated 25 May, declared that Germany had offered Russia as the price of her joining Germany's future activities the eastern half of Poland, Bessarabia, and security against the Ukrainian separatist movement; Bilainkin, *Maisky*, pp. 261–2. On 27 May Goering assured Henderson that Russia would not, out of self-interest, give any assistance to Poland. Henderson to Halifax, 28 May 1939, *British Blue Book*, pp. 18–20.

was no reason for any enmity between the two countries. It was true that in the Soviet Union there was a distinct feeling of being menaced by Germany. It would undoubtedly be possible to eliminate this feeling of being menaced and the distrust in Moscow. During this conversation, he also again mentioned the Treaty of Rapallo. In reply to my incidental question, he commented on the Anglo-Soviet negotiations to the effect that under the present circumstances, the result desired by England would hardly be achieved.'[1]

On 20 May, the German Ambassador, Schulenburg, discussed with Molotov the possibility of sending Schnurre to Moscow to resume the commercial negotiations. Molotov declared that the last attempt at such negotiations had suggested that the Germans were not really in earnest about them, and that 'the Soviet Government could only agree to a resumption of the negotiations if the necessary *political basis* for them had been constructed.' But having dropped this hint, Molotov refused to be drawn into making himself more explicit.[2]

On 15 May a new Russian note was received in London. Unofficial disclosures of its contents in the British press suggested that it marked no advance towards agreement.[3]

Between 15 and 22 May contact between the Soviet Union and the Western Powers was left largely to Maisky, first in London and then in Geneva, where he replaced Potemkin, who was due to be chairman at the meeting of the League Council. Since the Council had been postponed for a week in order to enable Potemkin to report to Moscow after his tour, his absence on 'health grounds' was taken as a further indication of Soviet dissatisfaction with the Western Powers.

From the Soviet viewpoint, the most important matter before the League Council was the Finnish Government's request for permission to fortify the Aaland Islands, at the mouth of the Gulf of Bothnia, which had been demilitarized under a Convention of 1921 to which the Soviet Union was not a party. Soviet opposition prevented the Council from reaching any decision.[4]

[1] Memorandum by Schnurre. *Nazi-Soviet Relations*, pp. 4-5.
[2] ibid, pp. 5-7. Cf. Kordt, op. cit., pp. 156–7.
[3] Namier, op. cit., p. 164.
[4] See Maisky's statement of 27 May 1939, *L.N.O.J.*, 1939, p. 281. Cf. 'Finland and the Aaland Islands', *B.I.N.*, 21 October 1939. Referring to this in his speech of 31 May 1939 Molotov said: 'It is to be expected that the Finnish Government will draw the necessary conclusions from the situation.' Among the subjects dealt with at the meeting was the Italian seizure of Albania. See Maisky's speech of 22 May 1939, *L.N.O.J.*, 1939, p. 246.

The position in the Far East must also have been a factor in
Soviet calculations.[1] During May, trouble broke out on the
borders of Mongolia and Manchuria (in the Nomonhan district
east of Lake Buir). This rapidly developed into fairly large-
scale fighting which continued until after the beginning of the
European War.[2] Soviet relations with China remained satisfactory, and in his speech on 31 May Molotov pointed out that
practical help was being given to China in her struggle for
independence. On 16 June 1939 a Soviet-Chinese trade treaty
was signed in Moscow.[3] But in general, Soviet comment on
the Pacific situation seems to have followed the line indicated
by Stalin's speech of 10 March.[4]

Meanwhile the Germans were weighing up the significance
of the guarded approaches made to them by Molotov and
Astakhov. Reporting his interview of the 20th, Schulenburg
remarked that it was necessary to be cautious until it was
certain that the Russians would not use German proposals
merely as a means of exerting pressure on the Western
Powers. And the German Foreign Office seems to have

[1] The Japanese declared themselves to be worried about the negotiations
between Russia and the Western Powers despite British assurances that only
European matters were involved. J. C. Grew to Secretary of State, 18 May
1939, *Foreign Relations of the United States: Japan 1931–41*, vol. ii, p. 2.

[2] As late as 25 August Soviet naval reinforcements were said to have
reached Vladivostok; L. K. Rosinger, 'The Far East and the New Order in
Europe', *Pacific Affairs*, December 1939. There was also during the summer
a long drawn-out diplomatic duel over the Japanese concessions on Sakhalin; Moore, *Soviet Far Eastern Policy*, pp. 112–14. In February 1946 a
former member of Ataman Semenov's forces was sentenced to twenty-five
years' imprisonment by a Soviet military court for having helped Japan to
provoke the Nomonhan conflict by forging a map of the disputed frontier.
Moscow radio reported by *Soviet Monitor*, 5 February 1946. Early in 1939,
the Japanese Ambassador in Berlin conferred with Himmler on the plans for
the disintegration of Russia by secret German-Japanese activities and the
assasination of Stalin. 'Tokyo War Guilt Trial', *The Times*, 10 March
1947.

[3] It was ratified by the Presidium of the Supreme Soviet on 5 January,
1940 and ratifications were exchanged on 16 March. Text in Moore, op. cit.,
pp. 189–99. On the other hand, May and June saw the renewal of serious
friction between the Kuomintang forces and the Communist 'Eighth
Route' and 'New Fourth' Armies; Wei Meng-pu, 'The Kuomintang in
China: its fabric and future', *Pacific Affairs*, March 1940.

[4] A Soviet work on international relations in the Pacific treated rivalries
in this zone as the affair of four equally 'imperialist' Powers, Great Britain,
the United States, France, and Japan, said nothing about the possibility of
an attack by Japan or Germany on the Soviet Union, but did say that the
Soviet Union might have to intervene to prevent the aggressors becoming
too powerful; V. Motylev, *Zarozhdenie i Razvitie Tikhookeanskovo Uzla
Protivorechii (The Origin and Development of International Rivalries in the Pacific
Zone)* (Moscow, 1939). Reviewed in *Pacific Affairs*, September 1939.

had this much on its mind during the subsequent week or so.[1]

A decision to make a new approach to Moscow was apparently come to at a meeting of the British Cabinet on 24 May 1939.[2] The new Anglo-French proposals were handed to Molotov on 27 May. Once again, their exact contents have not been made public. An informed Soviet account of them rusn as follows:

'In the case of direct aggression against one or other of the negotiating Powers, there was envisaged an obligation of mutual assistance between Great Britain, France, and the U.S.S.R. But these new proposals about mutual assistance were accompanied by such reservations as to make them practically worthless. The new proposals envisaged the assistance of the U.S.S.R. in relation to the five countries to whom Great Britain and France had already given guarantees. But they said nothing of assistance from the side of Great Britain and France to the three Baltic States bordering on the U.S.S.R.—Latvia, Estonia, Finland. It is obvious that there was a danger that the aggressors might, unhindered, make use of one of these small States for an attack on the U.S.S.R.'[3]

Objections on these grounds were amplified in a speech made by Molotov at the conclusion, on 31 May, of the third session of the Supreme Soviet.[4] He then pointed out the likelihood of Germany's using the time-honoured Nazi methods of infiltration and indirect aggression. From the Soviet point of view, he declared, the new proposals showed no advance towards true reciprocity. More ominous still were the doubts which he cast upon the general sincerity of the Western Powers in the current negotiations:

'As yet it cannot even be said whether these countries are seriously desirous of abandoning the policy of non-intervention, the policy of non-resistance to the further development of aggression. May it not turn out that the present endeavour of these countries to resist aggression in some regions will not serve as an obstacle to the unleashing of aggression in other regions? We must therefore be

[1] *Nazi-Soviet Relations*, pp. 8–11.
[2] According to M. Lukasiewicz the terms of the new British proposal had been worked out in accord with the Poles. The Treaty was not to impose any obligations upon third parties—thus the Poles would not be required to admit Soviet troops into their territory. Namier, op. cit., p. 176 *n.*
[3] *Istoria Diplomatii*, vol. iii, p. 681.'
[4] The English text was published (Moscow, 1939) as V. M. Molotov, *The International Situation and Soviet Foreign Policy*. The proceedings were witnessed, it was noticed, by the German and Italian Ambassadors but not by those of Great Britain and France.

vigilant. We stand for peace and for preventing the further development of aggression. But we must remember Comrade Stalin's precept to be cautious and not allow our country to be drawn into conflicts by war-mongers who are accustomed to have others pull the chestnuts out of the fire for them. . . .'[1]

Molotov gave even more point to his remarks when he declared later in his speech that Russia did not intend 'to renounce business relations with countries like Germany and Italy'. A trade treaty with Italy had already been signed.[2] As regards Germany, that country had offered to enter into new trade talks at the beginning of 1938. The Germans had in mind the offer of a new credit of 200,000,000 marks. But the two countries had been unable to come to terms as to the concrete basis for such an agreement and discussions had been broken off. They had been taken up again by Ambassador Schulenburg at the end of 1938, but once more had to be broken off. There were signs now that they might be resumed.

Molotov's statement was followed in June by a new series of reports of moves towards a German-Soviet *rapprochement*.[3]

These rumours were not without foundation. Weizsäcker had a discussion with Astakhov on 30 May and the subject-matter was again switched to political topics, this time on the German's initiative, it seems. Astakhov's principal contribution seems to have been a statement that it was the Germans who

---

[1] On 1 June M. de Monzie, a member of the French cabinet, noted that the negotiations were at a deadlock and that the project of an agreement between the three Powers was dead. According to him the obstacle was the insistence on the part of the Western Powers on submitting everything to the operation of the machinery of the League; *Ci-devant*, p. 121.

[2] The treaty was signed on 7 February 1939.

[3] On 1 June Coulondre reported to Bonnet that the German military leaders were warning Hitler against entering into a war in which Russia was against him and also believed that Turkey would stay out unless Russia came in. On the 13th he wrote that Ribbentrop was still hoping for an agreement between Germany and Russia to partition Poland, and that attacks on Bolshevism had consequently disappeared from the speeches of the German statesmen; *Documents Diplomatiques*, pp. 150–1, 153–4. There was a report of a conversation in Berlin between the Soviet Ambassador Merekalov and the Italian Ambassador Attolico; Blood-Ryan, op. cit., p. 311. On 29 August 1939 the Polish Foreign Under-Secretary wrote to the Polish Ambassador in London as follows: 'On the strength of instructions from Berlin the German representative at Bucarest recently told Roumanian political circles that German-Soviet conversations regarding a non-aggression pact have been in progress for some two and a half months, and that all the details of the Pact have been settled for some time.' *Polish White Book* p. 187.

had erected the ideological barrier between Moscow and Berlin, that they had rejected a Russian offer of an alliance before their treaty with Poland and that until recently, they had shown little understanding of 'the Russian thesis that foreign and domestic policy did not have to interfere with each other'. On the same day, Weizsäcker telegraphed Schulenburg that 'contrary to the policy previously planned' the Germans had now decided to undertake definite negotiations with the Soviet Union.

Writing on 5 June, the Ambassador again commented on his failure to extract any further information as to the nature of the political decisions which Molotov had in mind when he spoke to him and emphasized the need for caution. Commenting on Molotov's speech, he pointed out that it did not exclude a possible demand for support from the Western Powers in the Far East, which Great Britain was believed unwilling to promise, and that Molotov had left unmentioned the British invitations to Mikoyan and Voroshilov. He had received information from a 'generally reliable source' that Potemkin's visit to Ankara had been made in order to block an Anglo-Turkish treaty being concluded before the Soviet Government had acted.[1]

The Soviet reply to the British proposals was transmitted on 2 June.[2] It insisted on the conclusion of an effective pact of mutual assistance between Great Britain, France, and the U.S.S.R.; and upon guarantees against direct and indirect aggression, to be extended to Latvia, Estonia, and Finland, as well as to Poland, Roumania, Turkey, Greece, and Belgium. It was intended that the proposed Pact of Mutual Assistance should come into operation simultaneously with a Military Convention.[3]

The reluctance of the three Baltic States to accept these guarantees was made plain in a series of speeches by their

---

[1] *Nazi-Soviet Relations*, pp. 12-20.

[2] A Tass communiqué on these proposals was published in *Pravda* on 7 June.

[3] *Istoria Diplomatii*, vol. iii, pp. 681-2; Coates, op. cit., p. 609. According to information given by Bonnet to Lukasiewicz the Russian demands also included the deletion of all references to the League Covenant, and of the article precluding the imposition of obligations upon third parties. Mutual help was to be automatic in all cases. In addition to the Powers mentioned help was to be given to neutral powers prepared to defend their neutrality, i.e. Holland and Switzerland. Namier, op. cit., p. 182.

leaders.[1] On 6 June these objections were conveyed to the British Government by the Estonian Minister in London.[2]

According to M. Daladier, the new Soviet demand concerning the Baltic States came at a moment when agreement seemed to have been reached on the essential political issues involved in the three-Power negotiations. The British, he declares, rejected outright the idea of guaranteeing the Baltic States without their consent, but were persuaded to agree, after a few days had elapsed, largely on French insistence.[3] Presumably M. Daladier referred only to British consent to continue the discussions.

On 7 June Mr. Chamberlain informed the House of Commons of the obstacles thus created and of the British Government's intention of sending Mr. William Strang as a 'representative of the Foreign Office to convey full information to H.M. Ambassador' in Moscow to try to overcome the difficulties which had arisen.[4]

The importance of the Baltic issue was underlined by the signature on 7 June of pacts of non-aggression between Germany on the one hand and Estonia and Latvia on the other.[5] Nor was Germany's diplomatic activity confined to this area. At the beginning of June, Prince Paul, the Regent of Yugoslavia

[1] For instance the Finnish Foreign Minister told the Diet on 6 June: 'We realize perfectly well what such an automatic guarantee, if given to Finland, means if offered without her consent and without negotiations. I have every reason to inform you on this occasion that such a guarantee cannot be accepted. It is not compatible with Finland's independance and sovereignty, and Finland is bound to treat as an aggressor every Power that on the strengh of such a self-assumed guarantee intends to extend its socalled assistance when perhaps it considers that tbe guaranteed State needs it.' Quoted by Schuman, *Night over Europe*, p. 248. Finnish suspicions of Russia at this juncture may be the more readily understood if it is correct that at the time of abortive Russo-Finnish trade negotiations in December 1938, Finland was asked for the cession of certain strategic islands near Kronstadt and for a revision of the frontier. The French Communist writer M. Jacques Sadoul has asserted that Germany and Finland had concluded an anti-Soviet offensive alliance in 1935, *Naissance de l'URSS* (Paris, Charlot, 1947).

[2] Cf. 'The Baltic States and the Anglo-Soviet negotiations,' *B.I.N.*, 17 June 1939.

[3] Daladier, speech before French Constituent Assembly, 18 July 1946.

[4] Mr. Strang left for Moscow on 12 June. Much play was made during the summer of 1939 and later with the fact that no leading British political personality was sent to Moscow during the negotiations, and this has even been regarded as one of the contributory causes of their failure. But no high Nazi dignitary visited Moscow before Ribbentrop's arrival for the actual signature of the instrument.

[5] Ratifications of the two pacts were exchanged on 24 July, A similar pact between Germany and Denmark had been signed on 31 May. Finland however declined an offer to conclude one. *B.I.N.*, XVI, p. 595.

made a much-trumpeted visit to Berlin.[1] Later in the
month there were strong press attacks on Turkey and Roumania,
who still appeared to be resisting German blandishments.[2]

As far as Poland was concerned, the Soviet Union still seems
to have been promising support in her continued resistance to
German demands. A conversation on 14 June between the
Polish Under-Secretary for Foreign Affairs and the Soviet
Ambassador seems to have been fairly cordial.[3] But there are
indications that at this stage certain Soviet demands on Poland
were made. A rather obscure passage in the final report of the
Polish Ambassador to Moscow runs as follows:

'In June there was a series of offers on the part of the Soviet to
supply us with armaments materials. It had to be admitted that they
were always accompanied by unacceptable conditions. The Soviet
propaganda never ceased to urge us to resist the German demands.
'It is true that when we raised the question of accelerating the
transit negotiations we met with a refusal, but M. Potemkin assured
me obviously everything would change in the event of a conflict and
in that case we could count on transit.'[4]

It was early made plain that Mr. Strang's mission would find
the Soviet Government in an unyielding mood. An article in
Pravda on 13 June 1939 ridiculed the suggestion that guarantees
would mean a loss of independence for the States concerned.
What about the States already guaranteed by Great Britain
and France? It attributed the reluctance of the Baltic States
to accept the guarantees either to influence from Berlin, or
(more ominously) to influence from 'certain reactionary quarters in the democratic States'.

---

[1] Henderson, *Failure of a Mission*, pp. 232–4. Among the other visitors
to the German capital in the course of the next two months was the Bulgarian Prime Minister, who paid a State visit on 5–7 July.

[2] This did not prevent the former from signing an agreement with France
on 23 June. On 10 June it was reported by the German Minister in Bucarest
that Great Britain and France were still insisting on including Roumania
in their projected arrangements with the Soviet Union; *German White Book*,
No. 2, no. 317.

[3] *Polish White Book*, p. 185.

[4] *Polish White Book*, pp. 208–9. Cf. Noël, op. cit., pp. 377–9. The question
of the transit to Poland of goods through Russia had been left over for future
discussions at the time of the signature of the Soviet-Polish trade treaty on
19 February 1939. Another account based on Polish sources puts it rather
differently. 'In the spring of 1939 the Polish Ambassador in Moscow received
the most formal of assurances that in the case of armed conflict between Poland
and Germany, the question of transit would immediately be favourably
settled and in addition the Soviet Embassy in Warsaw gave promises of war
material. The Russians' first reference to military supplies had already
been made without any question of special terms in December 1938.'
Umiastowski, op. cit., p. 131,

The new talks began on 15 June and on the following day the Soviet press declared that they were not regarded as 'entirely favourable'. On the 16th, the Soviet Government are said to have proposed the conclusion of a triple defensive alliance before tackling the vexed question of the Baltic States.[1] On 20 June Tass denied that Far Eastern questions were holding up the talks. New Anglo-French proposals were presented on the 21st; they were regarded by the Soviet Government as showing no advance on their predecessors.[2] A reply in this sense was apparently delivered on the 22nd.[3]

From a Soviet account of the June-July talks it would appear that the two most serious issues were the question of 'indirect aggression' and the relation between the proposed Mutual Assistance Pact and its accompanying military convention.

'The Anglo-French delegation in Moscow obstinately refused to admit into the text of the agreement with the Soviet Union an undertaking to give assistance in the case of indirect as well as of direct aggression. The British Ambassador Seeds, the French [Ambassador] Naggiar, and the Foreign Office envoy Strang pretended that they did not know in fact what was meant by the expression "indirect aggression". In vain was it explained to them that the abstention of any one of the bordering States from a direct attack on the U.S.S.R. by no means excluded the possibility that an aggressor might use its territory, with or without the consent of its government, for the launching of an attack against the U.S.S.R. . . . The Soviet Government demanded that the political agreement of the three Powers should be concluded simultaneously with a military convention. The latter was to be an inseparable part of the whole political agreement. On the other hand, Anglo-French diplomacy suggested that the two agreements should not be tied up with each other. At most they promised that after the conclusion of a mutual assistance pact they would begin discussions about a military convention. The Soviet Government had every reason not to be satisfied with such a promise. There was sufficient warning in the fate of the Franco-Soviet pact which vanished into thin air for want of support in the form of a military agreement between France and the Soviet Union.'[4]

During the second half of June, Soviet policy seems to have been one of holding out prospects of some agreement with the

---

[1] Coates, op. cit., p. 611.   [2] *Pravda*, 22 June 1939.
[3] Cf. Namier, op. cit., pp. 186–8.
[4] *Istoria Diplomatii*, vol. iii, pp. 682–3. The Anglo-French negotiators took the view that the concept of 'indirect aggression' as the Russians understood it was so wide, that their right to defend themselves against it would amount to a right of unlimited intervention in the political affairs of neighbouring States. Any change of government there could be considered an indirect threat to Soviet security. This only came up on 4 July for the first time.

Germans without committing the Russians any further. On 14 June, Astakhov told the Bulgarian Minister in Berlin that the Soviet Union would be ready to refrain from concluding a treaty with Great Britain, if she could get from Germany a declaration of her readiness to sign a non-aggression pact or other assurances. This hint was duly passed on to the German Foreign Office. But when Hilger, the Counsellor of the German Embassy in Moscow, saw Mikoyan about the proposed resumption of economic talks, he found the Russian anything but forthcoming. On the 29th, Schulenburg made another attempt to find out from Molotov what he had meant by the creation of a new political basis for Soviet-German relations, but received in reply only the assurance that the Soviet Union's policy was one of good relations with all countries, and that this of course applied to Germany, provided there was reciprocity. He seemed to attach importance to receiving an assurance that the Germans still regarded the Soviet-German Treaty of 1926 as being in force.[1] But as late as 12 July, the Germans still appear to have been unwilling to take this matter up any further.[2]

Another public warning was delivered to the Western Powers in the form of an article in *Pravda* on 29 June, by Zhdanov, Chairman of the Foreign Affairs Commission of the Supreme Soviet. In terms so unusual for a member of the *Politbureau* as to give rise to the belief that two alternative lines of policy were causing conflict within that body, Zhdanov declared that for his part, he could not agree with those friends of his who held that the British and French Governments were sincere in their desire for a treaty with the Soviet Union on terms which 'a self-respecting government' could accept:

'. . . I believe, and shall try to prove by facts, that the British and French Governments have no wish for an equal treaty with the U.S.S.R. . . .

'Anglo-Soviet negotiations in the direct sense of this word, that is since we were presented on 15 April with the first British proposals, have been going on for seventy-five days. Of these, the Soviet Government took sixteen days in preparing answers to the various British projects and proposals while the remaining fifty-nine have been consumed by delays and procrastination on the part of the British and French. . . .

'The question of a tripartite guarantee of immediate assistance to Latvia, Estonia, and Finland, in the event of the violation of their

[1] The Soviet-German treaty of friendship of 24 April, 1926 (Treaty of Berlin) had been prolonged in 1931 by a protocol which the German Government had ratified on 5 May, 1933. *Supra*, Vol. I., pp. 63, 68, 97.

[2] *Nazi-Soviet Relations*, pp. 20-32.

neutrality by the aggressors, forms an artificially invented "stumbling-block" to the negotiations. . . .'

He went on to point out that according to the British press the Anglo-Polish agreement included an undertaking to go to war if necessary in case Holland or Lithuania were invaded and that neither of the latter appeared to have been consulted about the 'guarantee'.

The Polish Foreign Minister had also denied in a recent interview that Poland requested a guarantee from the U.S.S.R.

'Wherein then does the position of Poland differ from the position of the ruling circles of the three Baltic States? In nothing whatsoever.

'However, this does not prevent Great Britain and France from demanding from the U.S.S.R. guarantees not only for Poland and for four other States, of whose desire to receive a guarantee from the U.S.S.R. we know nothing, but also Holland and Switzerland, with which the U.S.S.R. does not even maintain ordinary diplomatic relations. . . .

'It seems to me that the British and French desire not a real treaty acceptable to the U.S.S.R. but only talks about a treaty in order to speculate before public opinion in their countries on the imaginary unyielding attitude of the U.S.S.R. and thus make easier for themselves the road to a deal with the aggressors. The next few days must show whether this is so or not.'

The talks in Moscow began again with the presentation of the new Anglo-French proposals on 1 July. These seem to have embodied the suggestion that no names of countries to be guaranteed should appear in the treaty itself but that they should appear instead in a separate annex. On 4 July Molotov seems to have accepted the British formula, but to have objected to the inclusion of Holland and Switzerland among the countries to be guaranteed by the U.S.S.R. He also now suggested that pacts of mutual assistance between the U.S.S.R. on the one hand and Poland and Turkey on the other should be concluded before the Soviet Government guaranteed Holland and Switzerland.[1]

[1] Bonnet, op. cit., p. 193. M. Gafencu gives the text of the first article of Molotovs' proposals, that dealing with indirect aggression: ' Great Britain, France and the U.S.S.R. undertake to lend each other all immediate and effective assistance, if one of the three countries becomes engaged in hostilities with a European State, whether as the result of an act of aggression directed by this Power against one of three countries' or as the result of any act of direct or indirect aggression directed by this Power against any European State. if one the three interested countries considers itself obliged to defend the independence and neutrality of this State.' In an annex it was to be explained that direct aggression would cover the case of an internal *coup d'état* or of a political change favourable to the aggressor; *Derniers Jours*, p. 221,

More important still was the new and far-reaching Soviet demand that the guarantees to be afforded to the Baltic States should cover the eventuality of what the Soviet Government called 'indirect aggression'. Once again, according to M. Daladier, the British demurred, but were eventually persuaded to agree by the French.[1]

The objections of the smaller countries to the proposed arrangements showed no sign of decreasing. The Finnish Prime Minister made a strong protest in a speech on 1 July.[2] On 3 July, the Dutch Government issued a statement objecting to the proposed guarantee, particularly if the guarantors included the Soviet Union, and the Swiss issued an official protest on 7 July.[3]

In the face of these difficulties in the negotiations between the Soviet Union and the Western Powers, the idea that a Soviet-German agreement was on the way continued to gain ground.[4]

On 4 July the French Consul-General reported from Hamburg:

'The German press gives no information on the German-Soviet commercial negotiations now taking place. Economic circles in Hamburg, generally very well informed, believe nevertheless that if an agreement is not speedily reached between London, Paris, and Moscow, the Soviet Government will be ready to sign with the Reich a five-year non-aggression pact.'[5]

On 8 July the Soviet Ambassador in Warsaw denied to the Polish Foreign Under-Secretary that any commercial negotiations between Soviet Russia and Germany were taking place.[6] But the reports continued.

On 8 and 9 July there was a further instalment of the Moscow talks with the British and French representatives.[7] According to one account, Britain and France insisted on the guarantees

---

[1] Daladier, speech of 18 July 1946; Gafencu, *Derniers Jours*, pp. 217–21; Bonnet, *Fin d'une Europe*, pp. 197–8.

[2] On 29 June the Chief of the German General Staff, General Keitel, arrived in Helsinki to return a visit to Berlin of the Finnish Commander-in-Chief.

[3] *B.I.N.*, XVI, pp. 721, 736–7, 741; Schuman, *Europe on the Eve*, p. 254.

[4] Cf. Namier, op. cit., pp. 137–42, 189–90.

[5] *Documents Diplomatiques*, p. 174.   [6] *Polish White Book*, p. 185.

[7] Coates, op. cit., p. 613; According to M. Gafencu both the British and French Governments suggested alternative definitions of indirect aggression designed to allow for the susceptibilities of the Baltic States. M. Bonnet's formula was that an act of indirect aggression was one 'which should have as its effect to bring about an interior *coup d'état* manifestly involving an alienation or alteration of sovereignty for the benefit of the aggressor'.

for Holland and Switzerland, irrespective of the conclusion of
the proposed pacts between the Soviet Union and Poland and
Turkey. There was still no agreement on the definition of
indirect aggression nor on the Soviet demand for a simultaneous
coming into force of the Three-Power Treaty and the Military
Convention.

The possibility of a Soviet-German agreement was by now a
matter of serious concern in the Western capitals. On 15 July
the German Ambassador reported from London:

'According to a report from a very reliable source, the fear of an
arrangement between Germany and Russia, evinced in the leading
political circles here, has lately increased to a considerable degree.
It is feared above all that the logical result of such a compromise
would be an endeavour on the part of Poland to approach Germany
now, since she can no longer reckon on the support of Russia.'[2]

On 18 July President Roosevelt told Davies (who himself said
that Hitler's efforts to alienate Stalin from the Western Powers
were common talk at Brussels, which he had left a week or so
earlier) that he had told Umansky to warn Stalin 'that if his
government joined up with Hitler, it was as certain as the night
followed the day that as soon as Hitler had conquered France,
he would turn on Russia, and it would be the Soviet's turn
next'.[3]

Another meeting took place between the Russians and the
Anglo-French negotiators on 18 July. The latter seem now to
have dropped the question of Holland and Switzerland, leaving
outstanding the two old issues, the definition of indirect aggres-

---

The British formula ran: 'It is agreed that the term aggression shall be
understood as covering also an action accepted by a State, under the threat
of force, and involving the abandonment of its independence or of its
neutrality.' Molotov proposed in reply that indirect aggression should be
defined as acts 'the object of which was to utilize the territory of one of the
States indicated to bring about an act of aggression against that State or
against one of the contracting Powers'. Before the French acceptance of
this could reach M. Molotov he dropped it in favour of a new formula
which combined his own with that of the British. '. . . in the case of indirect
aggression of which the object would be to utilize, under the threat of force,
or without such a threat, the territory of one of the States indicated in order
to carry out an act of aggression against this State or against one of the
contracting Powers'; *Derniers Jours*, pp. 221–3.

[1] Reporting to the Cabinet on 8 July, Bonnet declared that the Russian
demand, at a moment when a political pact was ready, that it should be
subordinated to a military convention, ended all hopes of a useful agreement.
A. de Monzie, op. cit., pp. 126–7.

[2] *German White Book*, No. 2, no. 319.   [3] Davies, op. cit., p. 287.

sion and the relations between the Political Treaty and the Military Convention.[1]

The result of this was several days of agitated negotiations between London and Paris in the course of which the British were persuaded to accept the Soviet definition of 'indirect aggression,' and to agree that the political treaty should enter into effect only when the military convention was concluded.[2]

The Soviet belief that unless they came to terms with Germany, the Western Powers might do so, was no doubt strengthened by the news on 20 July of the presence in London of an economic mission under Dr. Wohltat.[3] The project of a large British loan to Germany was discussed in a statement by Mr. Robert Hudson on 23 July, although the Prime Minister gave it an official disclaimer in the House of Commons on the following day. On 22 July the announcement of a provisional Anglo-Japanese agreement arising out of the difficulties at Tientsin had provided useful ammunition for the critics of British 'appeasement'.[4]

On 22 July the Soviet Commissariat of Foreign Trade announced that negotiations about trade and credits had been renewed at Berlin with the German Government.[5]

On 26 July the Soviet-German talks made a decisive step forward. In the course of an after-dinner discussion with Astakhov and Babarin, the head of the Soviet economic mission, Schnurre sketched the outlines of a scheme for the *rapprochement* by stages of the Soviet Union and Germany, since there were no vital problems to prevent such a relationship in the whole area from the Baltic Sea to the Black Sea or in the Far East. Moreover, Germany, the Soviet Union and Italy had a common ideology in as far as they were all opposed to the capitalist democracies. 'It would appear to us quite paradoxical,' declared Schnurre, 'if the Soviet Union as a Socialist state, were to side with the Western Democracies.'

Astakhov's reply was that such a *rapprochement* would be in the interests of both Germany and the Soviet Union but

---

[1] Coates, op. cit., p. 614. Bonnet had informed Lukasiewicz of this development on 13 July. Namier, op. cit., p. 198 *n*.

[2] Bonnet, op. cit., pp. 198–201.

[3] Schuman, *Soviet Politics*, p. 369; Dallin, *Foreign Policy*, pp. 48–9.

[4] *B.I.N.*, XVI, pp. 779–81. On the other hand the move could be interpreted as due to the British desire to be unhampered in Europe pending the conclusion of the Moscow talks. Dispatch of the German Ambassador in Paris, 28 July 1939; *German White Book*, No. 2, p. 232.

[5] *Nazi-Soviet Relations*, p. 32. There is no indication of the date on which the talks actually began.

that it would have to be a gradual affair. He mentioned as obstacles, the Anti-Comintern Pact, the free hand in Eastern Europe gained as a consequence of Munich, and the German assumption that the Baltic countries, Finland and Roumania lay within the German sphere of interest. Schnurre's attempt to refute the notion that German policy in these areas was a menace to Soviet interests does not appear altogether to have convinced his Russian auditors. But they may have been more impressed with his remark that if an agreement were to be reached the time was now, before the conclusion of a Russian pact with England. 'What could England offer Russia? At best, participation in a European war and the hostility of Germany, but not a single desirable end for Russia. What could we offer on the other hand? Neutrality and staying out of a possible European conflict, and if Moscow wished, a German-Russian understanding on mutual interests which, just as in former times, would work out to the advantage of both countries.' As he pointed out later, Germany's good intentions had been shown in the settlement adopted for the Ukrainian question (i.e. the Hungarian annexation of the Carpatho-Ukraine). The amalgamation of Bolshevism with the national history of Russia had removed the chief obstacle from the German point of view.

This conversation thus laid the real foundations for the agreement signed less than a month later. Its importance was clearly realized by Astakhov, who concluded by asking the Germans whether they 'would maintain similar opinions if a prominent Soviet representative were to discuss these questions with a prominent German representative.' The answer was 'essentially in the affirmative' and on the 29th, Schulenburg was instructed to try once more to sound out Molotov, and if he proved forthcoming to examine with him the method by which Soviet interests might be guaranteed in the event of developments in the Polish question, and ultimately in the Baltic question as well.

On 2 August, Ribbentrop had a conversation with Astakhov. He suggested a remodelling of German-Soviet relations on the basis of abstention from interference in each other's internal affairs and of the abandonment by the Soviet Union of any policies contrary to Germany's vital interests. There was no need for a clash on the Baltic; he hinted at a joint settlement of the fate of Poland, and at the possibility of an ultimate settlement of the differences between Russia and Japan. If the Russians were interested, Molotov could take the matter up with Schulenburg. But on the following day the Germans seem to have become conscious of the need for speed (or possibly some decision had been taken at a higher level), and a telegram was sent to Schulenburg telling him that without prejudice to his conversation with Molotov, Astakhov would be received by Schnurre and told that the Germans were ready for more concrete discussions, if he could get instructions from Moscow enabling him to proceed with them.

In his conversation with Molotov on 4 August, Schulenburg covered again much of the ground traversed by Schnurre and Astakhov on 26 July. On this occasion, Molotov showed himself more interested, although still insisting on the obstacle to an understanding presented by the Anti-Comintern Pact. But he went so far as to seek some clarification of the German proposals and asked, in particular, whether Lithuania was meant to be included in the proposed understanding over the Baltic States. German-Japanese relations also figured prominently.

Reporting this talk to Berlin, Schulenburg said:

'From Molotov's whole attitude it was evident that the Soviet Government was in fact more prepared for improvement in German-Soviet relations but that the old mistrust of Germany persists. My overall impression is that the Soviet Government is at present determined to sign with England and France if they fulfil all Soviet wishes. Negotiations, to be sure, might still last a long time, especially since mistrust of England is also great. I believe that my statements made an impression on Molotov; it will nevertheless take a considerable effort on our part to cause the Soviet Government to swing about.'[1]

And the fact that talks were proceeding between Schulenburg and Molotov was apparently known in London, Paris and Washington by about 4 August.[2]

[1] *Nazi-Soviet Relations*, pp. 32-41, pp. 46-8. A German naval operational order on 4 August dealing with the course to be followed in the event of war with the Western Powers over Poland said: 'Russia's attitude is uncertain, though at first it can be assumed she will remain neutral but with a definite one-sided leaning towards the Western Powers and Poland'; *Fuehrer Conferences on Naval Affairs*, 1939.

[2] Alsop and Kintner, op. cit., p. 71. On 8 August, Bullitt is said to have warned the Chinese Ambassador in Paris of the forthcoming pact and thereby to have prevented the signature of a new Soviet-Chinese treaty; ibid., p. 73. Cf. Bilainkin, op. cit., p. 274. According to Professor Namier two 'reliable sources name the night of August 4th-5th as the date of Hitler's final decision to seek a political understanding with the Soviets— it was immediately communicated over the telephone from Berchtesgaden to Berlin'. Namier, op. cit., p. 284.

The crucial nature of the early days of August was suggested by the renewed acerbity of German-Polish relations after a temporary lull.

Another meeting between the Soviet representatives and the British and French negotiators was held in Moscow on 24 July. On this occasion, there was general agreement on the political side including the naming of the Baltic States in the protocol of the Pact. The only detailed points still to be cleared up were in the definition of 'indirect aggression.' The relationship between the Pact and the proposed Military Convention was established, and Molotov declared himself ready for the military talks to begin in eight or ten days' time. On 25 July the British and French Governments accepted the suggestion that military and naval representatives should be sent to Moscow for discussions.[2] This fact and the names of the members of the missions were announced on 31 July.

The Soviet press at this juncture was still stressing the idea of organizing a genuine Peace Front against the Fascist aggressors. On 1 August Moscow radio broadcast a Tass statement criticizing Mr. R. A. Butler's reported version of the Soviet attitude towards indirect aggression.[3]

'In reality (declared the Soviet statement) the difference is not

---

[1] Cf. Daladier, speech of 18 July 1946; his article, 'Le Procès de Nuremberg et le Pacte Germano-Russe', *Minerve*, 5 April 1946; and his evidence before the Parliamentary Commission of Enquiry into the events of 1939–45 given on 29 May 1947. Bonnet, op. cit., p. 201. The text of the proposed agreement is given. Ibid, pp. 401–3.

[2] *Istoria Diplomatii*, vol. iii, p. 685. According to 'well-informed sources' in Paris, quoted by the German Ambassador there (Welczeck) in his dispatch of 28 July, the Western Powers had accepted the proposal in order to prevent a complete breakdown and in the belief that Germany would not move in the Danzig affair while the Moscow talks were still in progress. It was hoped by the Western Powers that the military missions would improve the atmosphere for a political agreement. 'By means of a possible understanding to be arrived at between the military representatives, the politicians further hope to exert pressure with the object of overcoming the final difficulties, although it is felt that in military discussions, Russia will broach not only the problem of the Border States but also the awkward problem of tolerating military assistance by Poland and Roumania.' *German White Book*, No. 2, no. 323. Once again, it appears that the French had persuaded the British to accept the Soviet demand. *Carnets Secrets de Jean Zay*, p. 60.

[3] *B.I.N.*, XVI, p. 839. Speaking in the House of Commons on 31 July, Mr. Butler said: 'We have proceeded with the utmost vigour to discuss with Russia our outstanding difficulties. The main question has been whether we should encroach on the independence of the Baltic States. We are in agreement that we should not do so, and the difficulty of reaching a formula on this point is one of the main reasons why there has been delay in these negotiations.'

whether to encroach or not to encroach on the independence of the Baltic States, because both sides stand for guaranteeing this independence, but that no loophole should be left in the formula "indirect aggression" for aggressors making an attempt on the independence of the Baltic States.'

As was to prove the fact, this meant that the transfer of the conversations to the military sphere was not going to get over the chief problem of the political negotiators but, instead, to redefine it in a more intractable form, with the Anglo-French rejection probably taken for granted in advance. Further talks between Molotov and the political negotiators were held on 27 July and 2 August, but on 7 August Mr. Strang left Moscow.

In a letter of 7 August, Schulenburg commented on Molotov's reported obduracy in his negotiations with the Western Powers and contrasted it with his amiability towards himself and Hilger. This amiability was not without significance for on 10 August, Astakhov told Schnurre in Berlin 'that he had once again received an express instruction from Moscow to emphasise that the Soviet Government desired an improvement in relations with Germany.' But he had no authority to discuss the concrete question of Poland nor could he say what would be the outcome of the discussions with England. 'The situation had changed since the conversation. But one could not now simply break off something which had been begun after mature consideration. The outcome of the negotiations was uncertain in his opinion, and it was quite possible that his Government likewise considered the question completely open.'[1]

When he visited the German leaders on 11 August, Ciano found the attack upon Poland already firmly decided upon.[2] Ciano's conference with the Germans was interrupted by telegrams from Moscow and Tokyo. 'The Russians agree' run the minutes of the meeting 'to the sending of a German political mediator to Moscow.' The Reich Foreign Minister added that the Russians were completely informed about Germany's intentions against Poland. He himself had informed the Russian Chargé d'Affaires by order of the Fuehrer. The Fuehrer remarked that in his opinion 'Russia would not be willing to pull chestnuts out of the fire for the Western Powers. Stalin's position is endangered as much by a victorious Russian army as by a defeated Russian army. Russia is most interested

---

[1] *Nazi-Soviet Relations*, pp. 48-9. Cf. Kordt, op. cit., pp. 160-1.
[2] *The Ciano Diaries*, p. 119. He was told that the trade negotiations with Russia were going well. Speech of 16 December 1939. *B.I.N.*, XV, p. 1441.

in enlarging her access to the Baltic a little. Germany has no objection to that. Besides Russia would hardly take the part of Poland whom she hated from the bottom of her heart. The sending of the English-French military mission to Moscow had only the purpose of averting the catastrophic state of political negotiations.'[1] The 'telegram' from Moscow clearly refers to the communication made to Schnurre by Astakhov in Berlin on 12 August (the day upon which the military talks with the Western Powers started in Moscow). In this communication Astakhov stated the Soviet readiness to embark on a discussion *by degrees* of the individual questions outstanding between the Soviet Union and Germany, and suggested Moscow as the meeting place, leaving it to the Germans to decide whether to send a special envoy or to rely on their Ambassador.[2] Weizsäcker thus had good reason for telling Henderson on 15 August that he believed that Russian assistance to the Poles would be entirely negligible and that the U.S.S.R. would even, in the end, join in sharing the Polish spoils. The situation, he told the Ambassador, had much deteriorated since 4 August.[3]

The British and French military missions left London on 5 August by sea, arriving in Moscow on 11 August. Discussions began on 12 August.[4] The first awkward point reached concerned the question of the powers granted to the negotiators by their Governments. The Soviet delegation were authorized to sign military agreements for the protection of peace and against the aggressor. Voroshilov found it unsatisfactory that the British delegation had no formal written powers. When it was finally agreed to proceed with the actual discussions, Voroshilov suggested that the missions should give in detail their concrete proposals for action on the two fronts. The representatives of Great Britain and France then gave an account in general terms of their military resources. The Russians (according to M. Reynaud) were struck by the smallness of the British commitment to France where land forces were concerned, and at the small number of divisions which the French expected the Germans to keep in the west in the event of their launching an attack on the eastern front.

---

[1] *Nazi Conspiracy and Aggression*, (Washington, U.S. Government Printing Office, 1946–47), vol. 4, pp. 508–17.

[2] *Nazi-Soviet Relations*, pp. 48–9. Professor Namier, having reached the conclusion that political negotiations did not begin until after this date, dismisses the 'telegram' as a German 'concoction'. op. cit., pp. 267–8, 284.

[3] Henderson to Halifax, 16 August, 1939. Cmd. 6106, pp. 89–91.

[4] See the article by General Doumenc in *Carrefour*, 23 May 1947.

At the end of the session on the 13th, Voroshilov raised the question of what action on the part of the Russians was expected by the Western Powers in the event of an attack by Germany on France, Great Britain, Roumania, Poland, or Turkey. A reply on the following day by General Doumenc was made in very general terms; Voroshilov however insisted on a precise reply to the question whether Poland would allow the passage of Soviet troops through her territory (the 'Vilna corridor' and Galicia) and whether Roumania also would allow it. Voroshilov refused to continue the discussions in any form until this point had been met. Doumenc who knew from Gamelin that the Poles were most unlikely to accept an arrangement of this kind until they were actually attacked could only suggest that the matter be referred back to Paris and London. In view of the possibility that the Germans would launch a sudden attack, the Russians finally agreed to continue discussing a military convention pending the receipt of replies to the inquiries regarding Poland and Roumania. General Doumenc asked permission of Paris to send General Valin direct to Warsaw to treat with the Poles, but he was refused permission to do this on the 16th. On the following day, he telegraphed to Paris again, urging the Government to accept the Soviet position and declaring his confidence in the Soviet intention to conclude a pact of genuine significance.[1]

On 14 August, Ribbentrop took up and developed the suggestion made by Astakhov on the 12th, and instructed Schulenburg to propose to Molotov a short visit by Ribbentrop himself to Moscow, to confer with Molotov *and* Stalin with a view to a comprehensive settlement involving political cooperation between the two countries in the entire area between the Baltic and the Black Sea. Schulenburg saw Molotov on the evening of 15 August and found him appreciative of the importance of the message and ready to report it at once to his Government. For his own part he stressed the importance of adequate preparation for a visit of this kind:

[1] The exchanges between Paris and Warsaw have been further described by M. Lukasiewicz; see Namier, op. cit., pp. 206-8; and by M. Bonnet, *Fin d'une Europe*, pp. 275-94. Cf. *Carnets Secrets de Jean Zay*, pp. 60-1; Noël, op. cit., pp. 420-4. In his speech on 18 July 1946 Daladier stated that he had overborne Lukasiewicz' opposition by declaring to him on the morning of the 21st that if there was any more opposition from the Poles he would suggest to his Cabinet the denunciation of the Franco-Polish alliance. This statement has been categorically denied by the Ambassador himself. Namier, op. cit., pp. 209-10. Umiastowski, op. cit., p. 137. The Roumanians were never asked whether they would permit the passage of Soviet troops. Gafencu, *Derniers Jours*, p. 237.

'In this connection, he was interested in the question of how the German Government was disposed to the idea of concluding a non-aggression pact with the Soviet Union, and further whether the German Government was prepared to influence Japan for the purpose of improvement in Soviet-Japanese relations and settlement of border conflicts and whether a possible joint guarantee of the Baltic States was contemplated by Germany.'

On the afternoon of Wednesday, 16 August, Ribbentrop telegraphed that the Germans were agreeable on all three points but stressed the need for speed, suggesting for Schulenburg's guidance that he come at the end of the week or the beginning of the following one. Clearly, the necessities of the military position in the East were beginning to dictate German policies. But it was not until Friday the 18th, that Molotov gave Schulenburg the Soviet reply to his proposals.

The essential portion of its text ran as follows:

'The Government of the U.S.S.R. is of the opinion that the first step toward such an improvement in relations between the U.S.S.R. and Germany could be the conclusion of a trade and credit agreement . . . The second step to be taken shortly thereafter, could be the conclusion of a non-aggression pact or a reaffirmation of the Neutrality Pact of 1926, with the simultaneous conclusion of a special protocol which would define the interests of the signatory Powers in this or that question of foreign policy, and which would form an integral part of the pact.'

The proposed visit of Ribbentrop, it was again emphasized, would require time to prepare. But at this stage the Germans were in a hurry, and Schulenburg was instructed to try to get agreement to an immediate visit of Ribbentrop before the expected conflict with Poland should break out. He was given a formula for a twenty-five year non-aggression pact, and told that Ribbentrop would be in a position to sign the special protocol settling spheres of interest in the Baltic area, the Baltic States, etc.

On the 19th, Schulenburg had two talks with Molotov. In the first, he found Molotov still holding to his previous position but at the second, he agreed that if the conclusion of an economic agreement were proclaimed on the following day, Ribbentrop might come as early as the 26th or 27th. He also gave Schulenburg a Soviet draft for the proposed non-aggression pact. Schulenburg assumed that an intervention by Stalin was responsible for Molotov's change of mind.

On the evening of the 20th, Hitler himself sent a telegram

for delivery to Stalin and this reached Moscow just after midnight. It accepted the Russian draft but proposed that Ribbentrop should arrive in Moscow on the 22nd or at latest the 23rd. By the late afternoon of 21 August, Schulenburg was able to wire Stalin's message accepting the latter date.[1]

Meanwhile the conversations at Moscow continued. The Russians were prepared to use 70 per cent of their forces in an attack on Germany, should Germany attack the Western Powers. In the event of an attack against Poland or Roumania, the Russian help would be equal to the forces deployed by the Western Powers. Finally if the Russians were attacked through the Baltic States, the Western Powers were to bring to bear on Germany, 70 per cent of the forces used by the Russians. More important however than these numerical calculations, was the Soviet insistence that they should not only have the right to enter Roumanian and Polish territory, but also the right to occupy the principal ports of the Baltic States and the main islands off their coasts in order to forestall aggression from that direction.

The Russians had become increasingly impatient at the lack of a reply about Poland's position and on 17 August, the discussions were adjourned until 21 August. On the 20th Doumenc sent to Warsaw a certain Captain Beauffre to take up the question with the Poles direct. According to M. Reynaud's version Smigly-Rydz replied to him: 'With the Germans we risk losing our liberty; with the Russians, our soul'. On the 21st, when Voroshilov again received the French and British delegations, he suggested an immediate adjournment *sine die* in view of their failure to secure the required assurances. And in spite of the protests of the other delegations, this was done. By now reports of a coming diplomatic sensation were fairly general.

The Soviet-German commercial agreement had been signed on 19 August, in Berlin.[2]

Soviet propaganda was now set to work to justify the

[1] *Nazi-Soviet Relations*, pp. 60-69; cf. Hitler's speech of 22 August 1939 (to his generals), *Nazi Conspiracy and Aggression*, Vol. 3, p. 585; Ribbentrop's account, *Nuremburg Trial*, Part 10, p. 121, and the account by Gustav Hilger summarized in James Byrnes' *Speaking Frankly*, pp. 284-5.

[2] It provided for a German credit to Russia of 200 million marks to run for seven years at 5 per cent. and to be spent on Soviet purchases in Germany. Soviet Russia agreed on its part to export to Germany within two years 180 million marks worth of raw materials. *Nazi-Soviet Relations*, pp. 83-4.

approaching revelation of the Soviet Union's new political alignment. On 19 August Tass issued a denial of a report that difficulties had arisen in the military talks with the Western Powers because of a Soviet demand for assistance in the event of war in the Far East: 'The differences concern an entirely different question and have no relation to the problem of the Far East.' On the same day, *Pravda* reprinted under the headline 'An Attempt at a New Munich' an article which had appeared in the London *Daily Worker* as early as 7 August. This alleged that Lord Kemsley's mission to Germany at the end of July had been part of an attempt by Chamberlain to come to terms with Germany at Poland's expense.[1] On 20 August Tass announced the signature of the Soviet-German trade agreement and the Soviet radio gave prominence to a foreign report of a new British attempt at a 'Munich' through a special economic mission.[2]

On 21 August *Pravda* declared that the commercial agreement might 'turn out to be a significant step towards further improvements not only of economic but also of political relations between the Soviet Union and Germany'. On the night of 21 August it was announced from Berlin that Ribbentrop was flying to Moscow to sign a non-aggression pact. The news was confirmed in Moscow on the 22nd in a Tass communiqué which said that 'after the conclusion of the Soviet-German trade and credit agreement there arose the problem of improving political relations between Germany and the U.S.S.R.' A subsequent exchange of views had established that 'both parties desired to relieve the tension in their political relations, to eliminate the war menace, and to conclude a non-aggression pact'.

Captain Beauffre returned from Warsaw on the 21st, and on that day, General Doumenc received a telegram from Daladier who had been exerting strong pressure on the Polish Ambassador in Paris. Its text, which M. Reynaud

---

[1] Lord Kemsley saw Hitler and other Nazi leaders at Bayreuth on 27 July. For his own account of his mission and its purpose—a press agreement—see *Sunday Times*, 3 March 1940. According to a statement made much later by a French Communist leader, the chief factor influencing the Soviet Union to seek agreement with Germany was the knowledge of the meeting on 7 August between Goering and a group of British industrialists arranged by the Swedish engineer Birger Dahlerus. Florimond Bonté, in French Constituent Assembly, 18 July 1946. On Dahlerus's part in the diplomacy of the weeks preceding the war see the chapter 'An Interloper in Diplomacy', Namier, op. cit., pp. 417-33. Cf. *Nuremberg Trial*, part 9, pp. 210-32, 234, 298

[2] Schuman, *Night over Europe*, p. 258.

describes as somewhat sybilline, ran according to him, as follows:

'Vous êtes autorisé à signer au mieux, dans l'interêt commun, d'accord avec l'ambassadeur, la convention militaire sous réserve de l'approbation du gouvernement francais'.[1]

Although M. Daladier's version is that Poland had given way under the threat of having the Franco-Polish alliance denounced, M. Bonnet writes that Doumenc was simply instructed to go ahead and give the undertaking in Poland's name.[2]

On 21 August (according to M. Bonnet), General Doumenc sent a message to Voroshilov that the desired assurances had arrived and he wished the negotiations to begin again, if possible that day. No reply was received until 6.30 or 7 that evening. Doumenc was then sent for by Voroshilov who told him that he now required a definite reply from the Poles and Roumanians themselves. If the Poles had really been willing to collaborate, they would have insisted on being represented themselves at Moscow. If the political situation did not alter the conclusion of a military pact would not be difficult once the replies were obtained. At all events some days would have to elapse before the negotiations could be resumed.[3]

Ribbentrop arrived in Moscow on the afternoon of 23 August and the pact was signed during that night. What purported to be the full text was published in Moscow on 24 August (and dated the 23rd).

'Guided by the desire to strengthen the cause of peace between Germany and the U.S.S.R., and basing themselves on the fundamental stipulations of the Neutrality Agreement concluded between Germany and the U.S.S.R. in April 1926, the German Government and the Government of the U.S.S.R. have come to the following agreement:

[1] Reynaud, *La France a sauvé l'Europe*, vol. 1, pp. 587–8.
[2] Daladier, speech of 18 July 1946, and article in *Minerve*, loc. cit. In his speech Daladier went on to declare that owing to some unexplained delay, Doumenc only received his telegram at 10 p.m. on the 21st. In his speech on 29 May 1947 Daladier said that the Polish Government 'accepta d'envisager toutes les formes de collaboration militaire' at 6 p.m. on the 23rd. According to General Gamelin, Daladier telegraphed Doumenc first and got Polish consent afterwards; *Servir*, vol. 2, p. 444; cf. Paul-Boncour, *Entre Deux Guerres*, vol. 3, p. 159. This statement is corroborated by Lukasiewicz who adds that Beck informed him that the move was purely a tactical one as no trust could be put in the Soviet Government. Namier, op. cit., pp. 229–3.
[3] M. Reynaud wrongly places this interview on the 22nd.

'1. The two contracting parties undertake to refrain from any act of force, any aggressive act and any attacks against each other undertaken either singly or in conjunction with any other Powers.

'2. If one of the contracting parties should become the object of warlike action on the part of a third Power, the other contracting party will in no way support the third Power.

'3. The Governments of the two contracting parties will in future remain in consultation with one another in order to inform each other about questions which touch their common interests.

'4. Neither of the two contracting parties will join any group of Powers which is directed, mediately or immediately, against the other party.

'5. If disputes or conflicts on questions of any kind should arise between the two contracting parties, the two partners will solve these disputes or conflicts exclusively by the friendly exchange of views or if necessary by arbitration commissions.

'6. The present agreement is concluded for the duration of ten years with the stipulation that unless one of the contracting partners denounces it one year before its expiration, it will automatically be prolonged by five years.

'7. The present agreement shall be ratified in the shortest possible time. The instruments of ratification are to be exchanged in Berlin. The treaty comes into force immediately it has been signed.'[1]

Official Soviet comment came in the form of a leader in *Izvestia* on 24 August, pointing out the great international significance of the commercial and political agreements now concluded:

'It is well understood that the establishment of peaceful and good neighbourly relations, based on broad economic ties between two such powerful States as the Soviet Union and Germany . . . cannot help but aid in the strengthening of peace. . . . [The pact] . . . brings an end to enmity in relations between Germany and the Soviet Union, that enmity which the enemies of both Governments sought to foster and extend. . . . Ideological differences, as well as differences in the political systems of both nations, cannot and must not stand in the way of the establishment and maintenance of good neighbourly relations.'

The full import of the new pact will be discussed later. But it is not surprising that the announcement of its signature, coupled with the knowledge of the far-reaching demands which the Soviet Union had put forward to the Western Powers, led

[1] *Izvestia*, 24 August 1939.

people to believe that the Soviet Union must have received from Hitler more than paper assurances of non-aggression.[1]

For the moment, however, the Soviet Government appears to have thought it wise not to over-emphasize the new departure which the pact involved. At the meeting of the French Cabinet on the afternoon of 22 August, Daladier had not abandoned hope of an agreement with the Russians and suggested a threatening démarche at Warsaw to oblige the Poles to accede to the Soviet demands.[2] The British and French Ambassadors were received by Molotov on 23 August and when they pressed him for a statement as to the effect of this upon the military talks were told to await the outcome of the German negotiations. On the following day, however, there was a semi-official announcement in Berlin that the Franco-Soviet pact was absolutely incompatible with the new German-Soviet pact and was consequently no longer in force. On 24 August Daladier told the Cabinet that the Poles had agreed to the Russians' demands and that everything had been done to let the Russians know this; he was still not without hope of an accord with Moscow. But at the same time there was a telegram from Warsaw saying that the Poles did not agree and never would.[3]

[1] On 24 August, Coulondre wrote to Bonnet as follows: 'I hear that in German official circles, it is believed that by the pact of 23 August, Germany and Russia have agreed to settle among themselves, to the exclusion of every other Power, not only the fate of Poland but also all matters concerning eastern and south-eastern Europe. From the rumours in circulation, it appears that it is believed here that the German-Soviet pact will have as its first consequence the partition of Poland. According to a remark attributed to the Secretary of State, Lammers, Berlin and Moscow have decided to establish their common frontier along the Vistula. Russia would receive a free port at Danzig. According to other rumours Poland would be reduced to the role of a buffer-state; Lithuania would play the same role and would recover Vilna. The provinces of Bohemia and Moravia would obtain a certain independence and would act so to speak as the bridge between Slavism and Germanism. The Reich and Soviet Russia would also revise by mutual agreement the frontiers of the Baltic States and of Roumania.' *Documents Diplomatiques*, pp. 254-5. On 25 August the French Ambassador, M. Naggiar, had an interview with Molotov. 'I thought I ought to ask him', he telegraphed to Paris, 'whether the Soviet Government had not bound itself by secret clauses to give Germany a free hand, excusing him in advance for not answering me, if my question appeared indiscreet. He restricted himself to saying that for his part, he would not ask me if secret clauses existed in treaties signed by France. This rebuff seems definitely to confirm certain indications of mine.' Quoted by Daladier, *Minerve*, 5 May 1946. 'On the 28th Naggiar further asked whether the Soviet-French Pact of Mutual Assistance was still operative, and is reported to have been told that the Soviet Government considered it to have been rendered void by the Franco-German Non-Aggression Pact of December 1938.' Namier, op. cit., p. 289.　　[2] *Carnets Secrets de Jean Zay*, p. 62.

[3] *Carnets Secrets de Jean Zay*, p. 64. Again Noël gives no confirmation of Polish acceptance, nor does Bonnet, and the evidence is decisively against it.

On 25 August Voroshilov told the heads of the military missions that, in view of the Soviet-German agreement, the Soviet Government felt that to continue the conference would be fruitless. The missions left Moscow on the same day.[1]

The failure of the military talks with the Western Powers was discussed by Voroshilov in an interview published in *Izvestia* on 27 August:

'The Soviet military mission took the view that the U.S.S.R. having no common frontier with the aggressor, could only extend aid to France, Great Britain, and Poland through the passage of its troops through Polish territory. The French and British missions did not agree with the position of the Soviet Government and the Polish Government openly announced that they did not require and would not accept the military aid of the U.S.S.R. These circumstances made military collaboration between the U.S.S.R. and these countries impossible.'[2]

On the other hand, regarding the Soviet attitude in the event of war, Voroshilov asserted that help in raw materials and military supplies for Poland was a commercial matter for which no pact of mutual assistance or military convention was necessary.[3]

The German attack on Poland had originally been fixed for the early hours of 26 August.[4] Its postponement was the result, it would appear, of the signature on 25 August of the Anglo-Polish treaty and of subsequent last-moment British efforts to find a peaceful solution.[5] There is in fact good evidence that some at least of Germany's leaders cherished the belief that the Soviet-German pact would result in another 'Munich' and

---

[1] As late as 28 August, some French circles believed in the possibility of an agreement with the Russians, an opinion said to have been shared by Ambassador Naggiar and by General Doumenc. *Carnets Secrets de Jean Zay*, p. 72. Suritz seems to have been encouraging such views as late as the 27th. De Monzie, op. cit., p. 143.

[2] Dallin, *Foreign Policy*, pp. 52–4.

[3] *Polish White Book*, p. 187.

[4] *Nuremberg Trial*, part 2, p. 72.

[5] The final days of peace are dealt with from the 'Coloured Books' and other sources in Namier, *Diplomatic Prelude*, pp. 290–402. A certain amount of new light on this has been thrown by the evidence at the Nuremburg Trial. See also the Introduction in Vol. 1 of *Nazi Conspiracy and Aggression*; *Carnets Secrets de Jean Zay*, pp. 73–87. The Anglo-Polish treaty was printed in Cmd. 6106, pp. 37–9. It has been pointed out that the problem of 'indirect aggression' was faced in the drawing up of this treaty under which the provisions for mutual assistance were to apply (Article 2. (1)), 'in the event of any action by a European Power which clearly threatened directly or indirectly, the independence of one of the Contracting Parties, and was of such nature that the Party in question considered it vital to resist

that they would not have to reckon further with the Western Powers in their dealings with Poland.[1]

The delay in ratification by the Soviet Union has been used to strengthen the argument that the Soviet leaders also thought and indeed hoped that their action would bring about general peace. The latter does not seem very plausible, since there is no evidence that the Soviet Government made any attempt to persuade the Polish Government to come to terms with Germany. On the contrary, Voroshilov's statement on 27 August can only be interpreted as an encouragement to the Poles to resist.[2] On 2 September the Soviet Ambassador in Warsaw asked Beck why the Poles had not taken this hint and opened negotiations for supplies from Russia.[3] Furthermore, the Soviet-German pact went very far in its neutrality provisions towards encouraging Germany to make war, since there was no stipulation that these should only apply in the case of a defensive war.[4]

The importance of this point had been stressed by Litvinov himself in a speech before the Assembly of the League of Nations on 14 September 1935:

'We know of another political conception that is fighting the idea of collective security and advocating bilateral pacts, and this not

---

it with its armed forces.' But, as has been seen, the problem in its Soviet setting was not one which a mere formula could have solved. A secret protocol to this treaty was first published in April 1945 (Cmd. 6616). Article I states that the expression a 'European Power' in the body of the treaty refers specifically to Germany. In the event of aggression by a European Power other than Germany the contracting parties would 'consult together on the measures to be taken in common'.

[1] *Nazi-Soviet Relations*, pp. 79–83. The French Consul-General at Hamburg reported as follows on the afternoon of 22 August: 'I learn from a serious source that the German Government hopes by a lightning aggression to overcome Polish resistance by the end of the month. The Reich is said to be convinced of the non-intervention of Great Britain and France, both disconcerted by the attitude of the U.S.S.R.' Garreau to Bonnet, *Documents Diplomatiques*, pp. 243–4.

[2] Cf. *Polish White Book*, p. 208.

[3] ibid., p. 187.

[4] See Article 2 *supra*. In the Soviet-German treaty of 1926, the corresponding article ran 'Should one of the Contracting Parties, *despite its peaceful attitude*, be attacked by one or more third Powers, the other Contracting Party shall observe neutrality for the whole duration of the conflict'. Article 2 of the Soviet-Polish non-aggression treaty of 1932 released either Party from the obligations of the treaty should the other commit an act of aggression against a third State. (*Polish White Book*, pp. 170–2.) This point was dealt with by Molotov in the speech on 31 August already referred to. 'They go so far as to blame us because the pact, if you please, contains no clause providing for its denunciation in case one of the signatories is drawn into war under conditions which might give someone or other the

even between all states, but only between states arbitrarily chosen for this purpose. This conception can have nothing in common with peaceful intentions. Not every pact of non-aggression is concluded with a view to strengthening general peace. While non-aggression pacts concluded by the Soviet Union include a special clause for suspending the pact in cases of aggression committed by one of the parties against any third state, we know of other pacts of non-aggression which have no such clause. This means that a state which has secured by such a pact of non-aggression its rear or its flank obtains the facility of attacking with impunity, third states.'[1]

On 28 August a special session of the Supreme Soviet opened in Moscow. On the 31st, Voroshilov submitted a new conscription law, lowering the calling-up age and lengthening the period of service. The Soviet Union, he declared 'surrounded by hostile capitalist States', could only rely on its own strength. 'Now that the entire world is preparing for war, we shall not be caught unawares.'

On the same day, Molotov proposed the ratification of the Soviet-German agreement in a lengthy speech.[2]

He began by reviewing the course of the negotiations with the Western Powers. The main obstacle to agreement, according to this version, had been Poland's rejection of military assistance from the Soviet Union. Furthermore, the Anglo-French reservations with regard to indirect aggression were such

'. . . as might convert this assistance into a myth, and provided them with a formal legal excuse for evading assistance and placing the U.S.S.R. in a position of isolation in face of the aggressor.'

After pointing out the delays in the negotiations introduced by the Western Powers, Molotov summed the matter up as follows:

'On the one hand the British and French Governments fear aggression and for that reason would like to have a pact of mutual assistance with the Soviet Union, in so far as it would strengthen them—Great Britain and France. But on the other hand the British and French Governments are afraid that the conclusion of a real pact of mutual assistance with the U.S.S.R. may strengthen our country—the Soviet Union, which it appears does not answer their

---

external pretext to qualify this particular country as an aggressor. But strange to say they forget that such a clause and such a reservation is not to be found either in the Polish-German non-aggression pact signed in 1934, and annulled by Germany in 1939 against the wishes of Poland, or in the Anglo-German declaration on non-aggression signed only a few months ago.' *Soviet Peace Policy*, pp. 20–1. Presumably Molotov had in mind the declaration signed by Hitler and Chamberlain at Munich on 30 September 1938.

[1] *L.N.O.J. Spec. Suppl.*, 138, p. 71.   [2] *Soviet Peace Policy*, pp. 9–23.

purpose. One cannot but see that these fears outweighed other considerations. Only in this way can we understand the position of Poland, which has been acting on the instructions of Great Britain and France.'

On the subject of the Soviet-German pact, Molotov declared that the decision to conclude it had been taken after the military talks had reached an impasse, and after Germany had given evidence of a 'turn towards good neighbourly relations with the Soviet Union'. He referred to Stalin's declaration on 10 March in favour of peace and business relations with all countries, and to his warning against being drawn into conflicts by warmongers, accustomed to having others draw their chestnuts out of the fire for them. 'It must be confessed,' he went on, 'that there were some short-sighted people also in our country, who, carried away by an over-simplified anti-Fascist propaganda, forgot about this provocative work of our enemies'. Later he returned to deal with criticisms of the new pact made from this ideological angle:

'They forget that it is not a question of our attitude towards the internal régime of another country but of foreign relations between two States. They forget that our position is that we do not interfere with the internal affairs of other countries and correspondingly do not tolerate interference in our own internal affairs.'

In spite of the fact that the new pact was only a non-aggression pact and not a mutual-assistance pact such as had been discussed with the Western Powers, it marks 'a turning point in the history of Europe and not of Europe alone. Only yesterday German Fascists were pursuing a foreign policy hostile to us. Yes, only yesterday, we were enemies in the sphere of foreign relations. To-day, however, the situation has changed and we are enemies no longer.' The Russian and German peoples had suffered most in the war of 1914–18; therefore their interests did not lie in mutual enmity.

Molotov did not, it should be noted, claim that general peace had been ensured:

'The chief importance of the Soviet-German non-aggression pact lies in the fact that the two largest States of Europe have agreed to put an end to enmity between them, to eliminate the menace of war and to live at peace one with the other, making narrower thereby the zone of possible military conflicts in Europe.

'Even if military conflicts in Europe should prove unavoidable, the scope of hostilities will now be restricted. Only instigators of a general European war, only those who under the mask of pacifism would like to ignite a general conflagration in Europe, can be dissatisfied at this position of affairs.'

Those people in the Western countries, and particularly Socialist leaders, who demanded that the U.S.S.R. should with- out fail be drawn into war on the side of Great Britain against Germany, were, so Molotov concluded, rabid war-mongers who had taken leave of their senses:

'Is it really difficult for these gentlemen to understand the purpose of the Soviet-German non-aggression pact, on the strength of which the U.S.S.R. is not obliged to involve itself in war either on the side of Great Britain, against Germany, or on the side of Germany against Great Britain?

'Is it really difficult to comprehend that the U.S.S.R. is pursuing and will continue to pursue its own independent policy based on the interests of the peoples of the U.S.S.R. and only these interests?'

Peace, it was clear, was no longer indivisible.

On the day after Molotov's speech, Germany attacked Poland.

On 3 September, Great Britain and France declared war on Germany. These declarations of war were not mentioned in the Soviet press and an official spokesman, questioned on the Soviet attitude towards the war, referred his questioner to Molotov's speech.[1]

---

[1] *B.I.N.*, XVI, p. 960. The question of justifying the Soviet-German pact arose again after the German attack on Russia. The matter was dealt with by Stalin in his radio address on 3 July 1941: 'It may be asked how could the Soviet Government have consented to conclude a non-aggression pact with such a perfidious people, such fiends as Hitler and Ribbentrop? Was this not an error on the part of the Soviet Government? Of course not; non-aggression pacts are pacts between two States. It was such a pact that Germany proposed to us in 1939. Could the Soviet Government have declined such a proposal? I think that not a single peace-loving State could decline a peace treaty with a neighbouring State even though the latter were headed by such monstrous cannibals as Hitler and Ribbentrop. But that, of course, only on one indispensable condition—that this peace treaty did not jeopardize, either directly or indirectly, the territorial in- tegrity, independence, and honour of the peace-loving States. As is well known, the non-aggression pact between Germany and the U.S.S.R. was precisely such a pact.' Stalin, *On the Great Patriotic War of the Soviet Union*, p. 6.

Chapter Twelve

THE SOVIET UNION AND GERMANY: SEPTEMBER 1939 TO MARCH 1940

THE events of the first few months after the signing of the Soviet-German treaty of 23 August 1939 gave ample evidence of the ease with which a State of the Soviet type could carry into effect a new policy, whatever the magnitude of the apparent change involved. The strategic outposts denied by the scruples of Anglo-French diplomacy were rapidly acquired and absorbed. Economic and political co-operation with Germany proceeded according to the letter of the successive treaties and agreements. Relations with the Western Powers became increasingly frigid, quite apart from the inevitable frictions between maritime belligerents and a dubious neutral.[1] Internal propaganda conformed to the new line and all anti-German expressions vanished.[2] But nothing was done to minimize the necesssity for constant preparedness.[3]

As has already been noted, there was a widespread belief that the Soviet-German agreement had gone further than the published text disclosed, and subsequent events as well as German comment upon them bore out this conviction.[4]

Speaking on 17 July 1940, Hitler declared that Germany and Russia had clearly defined, once and for all, their respective spheres of interest and that neither had taken steps to exceed the limits mutually agreed upon. In his proclamation of 22 June 1941, Hitler declared that the sphere assigned to Russia included Estonia, Latvia, Finland, and Bessarabia as well as part of Poland.

Confirmation of this belief had to await the Nuremberg trial.

[1] Anglo-Soviet relations in 1939–40 are described from a pro-Soviet viewpoint in Coates, *A History of Anglo-Soviet Relations*, pp. 619–53.

[2] See Schulenburg's telegram of 6 September, *Nazi-Soviet Relations*, p. 88.

[3] It should perhaps be pointed out that Victor Kravchenko, who occupied important industrial posts during this period, claims that the satisfaction of Germany's economic demands took precedence over the Soviet Union's own armament programme and prevented adequate progress in the latter. He also lays stress on the fact that nothing was done to keep alive the previously inculcated hatred and mistrust of the Nazis. The Soviet propaganda machine took up and maintained the new line without equivocation. V. Kravchenko, *I Chose Freedom* (New York, Scribner, 1946)

[4] The existence of such an agreement was strongly denied at the time by pro-Soviet publicists, particularly as regards Poland. See, e.g. D. N. Pritt, *Light on Moscow* (Penguin Books, 1939), pp. 128–34.

That such a 'secret supplementary protocol' was signed was
confirmed by Ribbentrop in his evidence on 29 March and
1 April 1946.[1] 'Germany hoped to settle matters with Poland
peacefully, but it was possible that an armed conflict might
break out. That was clear any way. For both statesmen, Stalin
as well as Hitler, it was a question of territories which both
countries had lost after an unfortunate war. . . . A line of
demarcation was agreed upon, as is known, in order that in the
event of intolerable Polish provocation, or in the event of war,
there should be a boundary, so that the German and Russian
interests in the Polish theatre could not and would not clash.
The well-known line was agreed upon along the line of the
rivers Vistula, San and Bug in Polish territory, and it was
agreed that in the case of conflict the territories to the west of
these rivers would be the German, and those to the east, would
be the Russian sphere of interest.' Other spheres were defined
involving Finland, the Baltic States and Bessarabia. Both
Hitler and Stalin regarded the absorption of the German
sphere into the Reich as justifiable. 'We were convinced of it
that if, due to the Polish attitude, a war broke out, Russia
would assume a friendly attitude towards us.' Reference to
the contents of the actual document was on several occasions
successfully objected to by the Soviet Prosecutor.[2] But on 21

[1] *Nuremberg Trial*, part 10, pp. 181–2, 210–12. The treaty was also mentioned in the evidence of Ribbentrop's secretary Margarete Blank, on 28
March 1946.
[2] The text of this protocol (Prosecution exhibition GB. 145) was
printed in the *Manchester Guardian* on 30 May 1946; it was signed by Ribbentrop and Molotov and dated 23 August 1939. It ran as follows: 'On the
occasion of the signature of a Pact of Non-Aggression between the German
Reich and the U.S.S.R., the undersigned plenipotentiaries of both parties
raised, in a strictly confidential exchange of views, the question of the
mutual delimitation of the spheres of interest of both parties. This exchange
led to the following results:
    '1. In the event of a territorial and political transformation of the areas
belonging to the Baltic States, Finland, Estonia, Latvia, Lithuania, the
northern frontier of Lithuania automatically constitutes the frontier between the German and Russian spheres of interest, while both parties recognize Lithuania's claim to the territory of Vilna.
    '2. In the event of a territorial and political transformation of the terri-
tories belonging to the Polish State, the spheres of interest of Germany and
the U.S.S.R. will be delimited approximately on the Narev-Vistula-San
line. The question whether in the interests of both parties the maintenance
of an independent Polish State will be considered desirable, will be definitely
decided only in the course of further development of political events. In
any case, both Governments will solve this question in friendly understanding.
    '3. Where South-Eastern Europe is concerned, on the Russian side,
interest in Bessarabia is emphasized. On the German side complete
désintéressement is proclaimed in regard to that territory.

May Weizsäcker, the former German Foreign Under-Secretary, was permitted to describe it from memory.[1]

The agreement drew a line of demarcation between those areas which in given circumstances would be of interest to the Soviet Union and those which would belong to the German sphere. In the Soviet sphere were included Finland, Estonia, Latvia, the eastern part of Poland, and certain areas of Roumania. Everything west of that line went to Germany.[2]

According to a memorandum drawn up by Ribbentrop for Hitler on 24 June, 1940, the formula for Bessarabia was deliberately left vague for fear of indiscretion on the Soviet side. Ribbentrop had been authorized by the Fuehrer 'to declare German disinterestedness in the territories of South-Eastern Europe, even, if necessary, as far as Constantinople and the Straits. However the latter were not discussed.'[3]

The course of the negotiations can be followed in a telegram from Ribbentrop after his first meeting with the Russians on 23 August 1939, and in a German memorandum of the second meeting, as well as in Dr. Gaus's affidavit at Nuremberg.[4] Gaus was present at the second of the two meetings on 23 August 1939. Stalin, who conducted with Molotov the discussions on the Soviet side, objected to a suggested passage in

---

'4. The protocol will be treated by both parties as strictly secret.'
This protocol is said to have been accompanied by more than a dozen maps of Poland and the Baltic countries. Asked in the House of Commons on 23 October 1946 whether he would have the text of the treaty published officially Mr. Bevin replied: 'The text of the secret protocol attached to the non-aggression pact of 23 August 1939, has been published in the British press. No advantage is seen in making any official publication of the text. . . . I think it was published in a reputable newspaper, the *Manchester Guardian* and may be taken as accurate.' A slightly different translation is printed in *Nazi-Soviet Relations*, p. 78.

[1] *Nuremburg Trial*, part 14, pp. 273–5.

[2] As far as Finland is concerned, the former Finnish President Ryti declared at the Finnish War Guilt Trial on 11 December 1945 that Russia had been given a free hand to make frontier adjustments as far as Viipuri (Viborg), but that if Russia went further, Germany was to be permitted to take compensation in western Finland, including the Aaland Islands; *Manchester Guardian*, 12 December 1945.

[3] *Nazi-Soviet Relations*, pp. 157–8. In his letter of 25 August, 1939, to Mussolini explaining his reasons for signing the pact with Russia, Hitler laid much stress on the neutralization of Roumania which was thereby effected. ibid., pp. 80–1.

[4] *Nazi-Soviet Relations*, pp. 71–6; Daladier, 'Le Procès de Nuremberg et le Pacte Germano-Russe', *Minerve*, 5 April 1946. Namier, op. cit., pp. 284–7.

the preamble of the non-aggression pact concerning Russo-German friendship on the ground that the Soviet Government could not make such a declaration in public after the 'buckets of filth' poured over it by the National-Socialist Government for six years. Over the question of the secret protocol, there was a discussion because of the original German wish to include the ice-free ports of Libau and Windau in Latvia as well as the whole of Lithuania in her zone. The Russians would not accept this and the German delegation gave way on receipt of telephonic instructions from Hitler.[1]

This agreement had already been revealed by Stalin during the talks at the Kremlin with the Latvian Foreign Minister, Munters, on 2 and 3 October 1939. Stalin is reported by Munters as saying: 'I tell you frankly a division of spheres of interest has already taken place.' The Germans, he indicated, had originally suggested a line of division in Latvia along the river Dauvaga (Dvina). But the Russians had said that a nation could not be treated in that way and had affirmed their own interest in Liepaja (Libau).[2]

For a few days after the outbreak of war, the precise intention of the Soviet Government remained obscure. On 2 September the Soviet Ambassador in Warsaw asked Beck why the Polish Government had not taken up Voroshilov's hint to ask the Soviet Union for supplies. On 3 September, before the news of the Western Powers' entry into the war, Grzybowski was received by Molotov who asked him whether Poland counted on the intervention of France and Great Britain and at what date. Grzybowski replied that he believed that both Powers would declare war next day. Molotov, he recounted, gave a sceptical smile and said 'We shall see'. On this occasion, Molotov appeared to favour indirect Soviet assistance to Poland in the form of economic aid.[3] Instructions to take the matter up were sent to Grzybowski in Moscow but only reached him on 6 September. By then partial Soviet mobilization seems to have begun, and for two days Grzybowski could not get an interview with Molotov. During the night of 3-4 September, Schulenburg had received from Ribbentrop an urgent message to the effect that the Polish army would be decisively beaten

---

[1] *Nuremberg Trial*, part 10, pp. 210–11.

[2] *Latvia, 1939–1942* (Washington, Latvian Legation, 1942), pp. 95–102. Cf. Byrnes, *Speaking Frankly*, pp. 285–6.

[3] Noël, *L'Agression Allemande contre la Pologne*, pp. 499–500. M. Noël argues that this shows that the Soviet Union based its plans on the likelihood of Great Britain and France failing in their obligations to Poland, which it did not wish to see succumb too rapidly.

in a few weeks, and the Germans would then keep under military occupation the area allotted to them in the Moscow agreement. They would, however, for military reasons have to proceed against Polish forces in the Soviet zone, and the Ambassador was instructed to suggest to Molotov that Soviet forces act against these Polish forces at the proper time and occupy the zone allotted to the Soviet Union. Molotov replied on 5 September, agreeing that concrete action would be necessary at the proper time, but arguing that the moment had not yet come.[1]

On 8 September Molotov informed Grzybowski that the Soviet Union could not help Poland with supplies since the whole situation had been radically altered by the entry of France and Great Britain into the war; nor could the transit of supplies for Poland be considered. On 11 September, the Soviet Ambassador left Poland for 'contact with his Government', after assuring the French Ambassador that France would be able to buy everything it wanted in Russia (presumably for Poland). On the following day the Soviet press launched a strident campaign about the treatment of minorities in Poland.[2]

It was two days earlier, on 9 September, that Molotov had informed Ribbentrop that Soviet intervention could shortly be expected, and that Schulenburg noted external evidence of imminent military activity. But a snag developed on the 10th when Molotov declared that the Russians intended to justify their advance into Poland by declaring that they came to help the White Russians and Ukrainians, threatened by the German advance. This point was not cleared up finally until dealt with by Stalin personally on 16 September.[3]

The Russians also appear to have considered that it would be unwise to commit themselves to a forward policy in Europe until the situation in the Far East was cleared up. The heavy fighting at Nomonhan on the Manchurian-Mongolian frontier was ended by a truce signed on 16 September.[4] On the following day Potemkin communicated to Grzybowski the following note, signed by Molotov:

'The Polish-German war has revealed the internal bankruptcy of the Polish State. During the course of ten days' hostilities Poland

[1] *Nazi-Soviet Relations*, pp. 86–7.
[2] *Polish White Book*, pp. 187–9, 210–11.
[3] *Nazi-Soviet Relations*, pp. 89–96.
[4] Moore, *Soviet Far Eastern Policy*, p. 113.

has lost all her industrial areas and cultural centres. Warsaw no longer exists as the capital of Poland. The Polish Government has disintegrated and no longer shows any signs of life. This means that the Polish State and its Government have, in fact, ceased to exist. Therefore the agreements concluded between the U.S.S.R. and Poland have ceased to operate. Left to her own devices and bereft of leadership, Poland has become a suitable field for all manner of hazards and surprises which may constitute a threat to the U.S.S.R. For these reasons the Soviet Government, which hitherto has preserved neutrality, cannot any longer observe a neutral attitude towards these facts.

'The Soviet Government further cannot view with indifference the fact that the kindred Ukrainian and White Russian people, who live on Polish territory and are at the mercy of fate, are left defenceless.

'In these circumstances, the Soviet Government has directed the High Command of the Red Army to order the troops to cross the frontier and to take under their protection the life and property of the population of Western Ukraine and Western White Russia.

'At the same time the Soviet Government proposes to take all measures to extricate the Polish people from the unfortunate war into which they were dragged by their unwise leaders, and to enable them to live a peaceful life.'[1]

On the same day, 17 September, a note was communicated to all foreign Powers represented in Moscow declaring that the Soviet Union maintained its neutral position with regard to the European war, and Ribbentrop telephoned Ciano that the Russian intervention had taken place according to a pre-arranged plan.[2]

On 18 September the Soviet action was explained in a joint Soviet-German declaration:

'In order to avoid unfounded rumours concerning the aims pursued by Soviet and German forces now in Poland, the Government of the U.S.S.R. and the Government of Germany declare that neither of the troops pursue aims contrary to the interests of Germany or the Soviet Union or contrary to the spirit and letter of the pact of non-aggression signed between Germany and the U.S.S.R. On the contrary, the aim of these troops is to restore order in Poland, disturbed by the disintegration of the Polish State, and to assist the Polish population in the reconstruction of its national existence.'[3]

[1] *Polish White Book*, pp. 189–90.
[2] *New York Times*, 18 September 1939. *Ciano Diaries*, p. 146. On the same day, the U.S.S.R. recognized Slovakia; the Slovak Minister took up his post in Moscow on 12 December 1939.
[3] It was drafted by Stalin himself. *Nazi-Soviet Relations*, pp. 98–100.

The reference to 'the Polish people' in Molotov's note of 17 September, not repeated in subsequent Soviet utterances, has been taken to mean that Soviet troops were prepared to occupy a very considerable portion of ethnic Poland as well as the White Russian and Ukrainian lands.[1] The bombing by the Germans of the Polish town of Zalesczycki near the Roumanian frontier on 15 September has also been taken to mean that a deliberate attempt was made to slow down the Soviet advance.[2]

There was some nervousness on the Soviet side, lest the Germans fail to give up territory in the Soviet zone which they had entered in pursuit of the Poles.[3] The Soviet troops, meeting with little resistance, advanced in fact with considerable speed, and it has been held that the demarcation line fixed on 22 September was to the west of that originally claimed by the Germans and represented on their part a temporary acceptance of the *fait accompli*. According to a joint German-Soviet communiqué issued in Moscow on that date the demarcation line passed along the river Pissa up to its confluence with the Narew, then along the Narew up to its confluence with the Bug, then along the Bug up to its confluence with the Vistula, then along the Vistula up to the mouth of the San, and along the San up to its source. This gave the Russians a long stretch of the Vistula as their frontier and the possession of the Warsaw suburb of Praga on the eastern bank. On the other hand, at least some territories already occupied by the Germans were handed over under this agreement.[4] On 20

---

[1] *Izvestia* published on 18 September a map of Poland showing two-thirds of the country as Soviet. Umiastowski, *Russia and the Polish Republic*, p. 147. 'The German-Soviet Partition of Poland', *B.I.N.*, 7 October 1939; 'The Partitions of Poland', ibid., 21 October 1939; J. Wheeler-Bennett, 'From Brest-Litovsk to Brest-Litovsk', *Foreign Affairs*, January 1940. In a speech at Danzig on 24 October 1939 Ribbentrop declared that Russian troops had occupied Polish territory up to the line agreed on; but this is ambiguous; cf. his statement at Nuremberg quoted *supra*, p. 278.

[2] Maitland, *European Dateline* (Pilot Press, 1946), pp. 71–7. The fact that elements of the Polish administration together with the Corps Diplomatique had taken refuge in this town may have been sufficient reason. On 11 September—that is six days before Soviet troops crossed into Poland—the Soviet Ambassador in Warsaw explained Soviet mobilization measures by declaring that the Germans were apparently 'bombing certain points on the Soviet western frontier'; *Polish White Book*, pp. 188–9.

[3] *Nazi-Soviet Relations*, p. 98

[4] The purpose of Ribbentrop's visit was not revealed to the Italians, to whom his intention of going to Moscow had not been announced. Rosso, the Italian Ambassador, informed Ciano that it appeared that Ribbentrop had gone to Moscow to sign 'a genuine military alliance, to give Bessarabia and Estonia to the Russians and the remaining part of Roumania to the Germans', *Ciano Diaries*, p. 151. For Ribbentrop's account of this visit to Moscow see *Nuremberg Trial*, part 10, p. 195.

September Molotov indicated to Schulenburg that in the Soviet view, the time was now ripe for a definitive settlement of 'the structure of the Polish area'. Stalin's original inclination to leave a residual Polish state had given way to the inclination to partition Poland along the Pissa-Narew-Vistula-San line. On the 23rd, Ribbentrop wired that in view of the inability of the leading Soviet personages to leave Russia, he would come to Moscow himself to negotiate the treaty. Ribbentrop arrived at Moscow on the evening of the 27th and the new treaty with its secret protocols was signed at 5 p.m. on the 28th.[1]

The German treaty included a final demarcation line for the two countries' annexations in Poland. By a secret protocol the greater part of Lithuania was also transferred to the Soviet sphere in return for the emphatic shift eastwards in the Soviet-Polish demarcation line, which now followed the Bug instead of the Vistula for most of its length.[2]

The most notable feature of the fourth partition of Poland was that Russia acquired not only her former provinces as far as the Bug, roughly the line of the third partition of 1795, but

[1] *Nazi-Soviet Relations*, pp. 101–107

[2] Germany allowed the Russians to take over the oil sources of Drohobycz and Boryslav in return for a contract to supply the Germans with 300,000 tons of oil from them and other Soviet sources. It was also agreed that the Soviet Union should facilitate transit traffic between Germany on the one hand and Roumania, Iran, Afghanistan and the Far East on the other. *Nazi-Soviet Relations*, p. 109. Byrnes, op. cit., p. 287. The text of the secret protocol dealing with Lithuania runs (*Manchester Guardian*, 30 May 1946):

'The secret additional protocol signed on 23 August 1939, is changed in its first point in such a way that the area of the Lithuanian State comes into the sphere of influence of the Soviet Union, while, on the other hand, Lublin Province, and part of Warsaw Province come into the sphere of influence of the German Reich. Compare the Map attached to the Frontier and Friendship Agreement signed to-day.'

'From the moment the Soviet Government takes special steps on Lithuanian territory for the purpose of realizing its interests, the present German-Lithuanian frontier will be rectified in such a way that the Lithuanian territory which lies to the south and south-west of the line indicated on the attached map will fall to the Germans.' There is a slightly different translation in *Nazi-Soviet Relations*, p. 107. The Soviet Union occupied the whole of Lithuania in the summer of 1940, including the portion allotted to Germany. On 10 January 1941, an agreement covering this portion of the new Soviet-German frontier was published in Moscow. The Soviet Government had apparently agreed that German protests about overstepping the agreed line in Lithuania were justified but pleaded that the area was hard to separate from the rest of the country. They eventually agreed to pay 31,500,000 reichsmarks for the territory. *Nazi-Soviet Relations*, pp. 113–9, 166, 174, 188, 236–7, 267–8; *infra*, p. 329.

in addition the former Austrian Eastern Galicia.[1] Both in the
north and in the south, the new frontier was considerably more
favourable to the Soviet Union than that of the 'Curzon
line'.[2]

The Soviet annexations in the south had the effect of cutting
the direct line of communication between Roumania and
German-occupied Poland. And it is not surprising that there
were fears that Roumania would be the next sacrifice to Soviet-
German collaboration.[3] In fact, however, it was the Baltic, not
the Danube, towards which Soviet eyes turned first.

The immediate Soviet objectives—mutual assistance pacts
with the three Baltic States and the acquisition of military bases
there—did not take long to achieve. The diplomatic offensive
against the Baltic States began with a Tass communiqué of
18 September accusing Estonia of unneutral conduct. With

[1] For the earlier partitions of Poland, see *Cambridge Modern History Atlas*,
Map 58. The newly incorporated territories with the exception of the Vilna
district, reserved for Lithuania, were annexed to the Ukrainian and White
Russian Republics by resolutions of specially elected assemblies on 26 and
29 October respectively. These territorial changes were duly sanctioned by
the Supreme Soviet on 1 November 1939. *Polish-Soviet Relations, 1918-1943*
(New York, Polish Information Centre, 1943), pp. 102-3. For an account
of the process of Sovietization in the Lvov region, see Z. Sobieski, 'Reminis-
cences from Lwow, 1939-1946', *Journal of Central European Affairs*, January
1947.

[2] See map 2 *infra*. J. T. Shotwell and M. M. Laserson, quote on p. 55 of
their book, *Poland and Russia, 1919-1945* (New York, Carnegie Endowment,
1945) the comment on the new treaty in the article 'Poland' in the
Bolshaya Sovetskaya Entsiklopedia, vol. 46, which was released to the press
on 29 June 1940. 'The treaty of friendship of 28 September 1939, between
the U.S.S.R. and Germany definitely fixed the frontiers of both interested
partners concerning the territory of the former Polish State. Article II
of this treaty states that 'both parties recognize as final the limits set in
Article I to their mutual state interests'. Thus Article II took the ground
from under the feet of those who wanted to have others take their chestnuts
out of the fire. The pharisaical weeping over the 'historical role of Poland'
which we hear from the English and French imperialists and the renegades
of the Second International, are only crocodile tears, for the catastrophic
failure of their hopes.'

[3] The Roumanian Premier Calinescu noted in his papers on 19 September: 'The Russian advance changes the situation. The German danger is
farther off. Now the Russian danger is primary. Inversion of military dis-
positions and concentration of our troops in the valley of the Sereth.' On
the other hand, the collapse of Polish resistance prevented the Polish-
Roumanian alliance being invoked against the Soviet advance and the
Roumanian Government drew up a declaration of neutrality addressed to
Moscow. On 20 September, Calinescu was assassinated. Gafencu, *Prelude
to the Russian Campaign*, pp. 253-5. It has been suggested that the assassination was intended as the signal for a German occupation 'to restore order'
and that this was forestalled by the rapidity of Soviet troop movements in
southern Poland. Maitland, op. cit., p. 78.

clear evidence that no outside help would be forthcoming, the Baltic States could not long hold out and a succession of pilgrimages to Moscow by their representatives resulted in the conclusion of the agreements required of them.[1] The pact with Estonia was signed on 29 September, that with Latvia on 5 October, and that with Lithuania on 10 October.[2] The treaties with Estonia and Latvia involved agreements for mutual assistance against aggression or the menace of aggression, and the leasing to the Soviet Union of naval and air-bases and the right for the Soviet Union to maintain on their territories forces of a strength to be agreed upon. In the case of the Lithuanian treaty the provision for the stationing of troops was included but no exact bases were specified. The treaty also included a provision for the cession to Lithuania of the city and province of Vilna. Vilna was handed over to Lithuania by the Russians on 27 October.[3]

In a speech on 6 October, Hitler admitted in a rather roundabout fashion that Germany had agreed to repatriate all inhabitants of German stock from the Baltic States and from the areas of Poland annexed by Russia. But Moscow denied that this operation had been undertaken as the result of Soviet pressure and the fiction of free negotiations between Germany and the Baltic States was maintained.[4]

[1] The negotiations are summarized in Dallin, *Foreign Policy*, pp. 80–93; Cf. Schuman, *Night over Europe*, pp. 387–9. The Germans were informed by the Estonians of the Soviet demands on 26 September. *Nazi-Soviet Relations*, pp. 103–5.

[2] The treaties with Estonia and Latvia are given in *L.N.T.S.* vol. 198, pp. 223–9, 381–7. Scott gives the Lithuanian treaty as published in *Moscow News*, 16 October 1939; op. cit., Appendix.

[3] The Germans objected to a Soviet suggestion that the Vilna cession should be openly linked to the cession by Lithuania to Germany of the strip of territory allotted to her in the agreement of 28 September, *supra*, p. 284. This would make the Germans appear as 'robbers' of Lithuanian territory while the Russians appeared as 'donors'. They wanted the matter to be left over until Lithuania was actually incorporated in the Soviet Union—a consummation which they appear to have taken as a matter of course. They were also distressed at the fact of the understanding over this piece of territory having been divulged to the Lithuanians by Molotov. But the incident seems to have been passed over. *Nazi-Soviet Relations*, pp. 112–119. For an eye-witness account of events in Lithuania at this time see H. Foster Anderson, *Borderline Russia* (Cresset Press, 1942).

[4] A protocol providing for this movement of populations had been signed by Ribbentrop in Moscow on 28 September. The Germans were to repatriate all persons of Ukrainian and White Russian descent in the territories they occupied. *Nazi-Soviet Relations*, p. 106. Dallin reckons the total of repatriated Germans, including those from the territories later acquired by the Soviet Union from Roumania, at 437,000; *Foreign Policy,*

One of the most significant results of the Soviet invasion of Poland and the second Soviet-German treaty was its effect upon Communist Parties abroad.[1] Hitherto they had maintained their previous support for the policy of resisting Nazi aggression.

On 25 August *L'Humanité* wrote:

'We are in favour of resistance to all acts of aggression and the Communists are ready to fulfil their duties as Frenchmen in the framework of the engagements contracted by their country. They are ready to undertake all their responsibilities. If Poland is attacked the treaty with her must come into play.'

Speaking on the same day Thorez declared:

'If Hitler in spite of everything unleashes war, let him know that he will find before him the united people of France, with the Communists in the front line, to defend the security of the country and the liberty and independence of the nations.'

Similar sentiments were expressed in an open letter from Marcel Cachin to Léon Blum published on 27 August. A formal resolution of the Party on 1 September, while welcoming the Soviet-German pact, advocated aid to Poland. On 6 September Thorez and other Communist deputies of military age joined their regiments with the public approval of their Party. As late as 19 September Cachin wrote to Blum a second open letter in which he said:

'We were the first to proclaim the necessity of making every sacrifice to strike down Hitlerian Nazism. We shall not cease to proclaim it. We receive our *mots d'ordre* only from the French people.'[2]

Now in the course of a few days everything altered. The Comintern swung into line behind the Soviet-German peace

---

pp. 93–101. Cf. 'The Transfer of Populations in North-Eastern Europe', *B.I.N.*, 18 November 1939. On December 5, Keitel complained that the Soviet authorities were trying to force the Germans to take back Jews expelled into Soviet territory from the Polish Government-General. *Nazi-Soviet Relations*, p. 128.

[1] Cf. B. Hopper, 'Narkomindel and Comintern', *Foreign Affairs*, July 1941.

[2] E. Daladier, 'Le Procès de Nuremberg et le Pacte Germano-Russe', *Minerve*, 5 April 1946. See also Daladier's speech to the National Constituent Assembly on 18 July 1946 and the speech on the same occasion by the Communist Florimond Bonté. *L'Humanité* was suppressed on 27 August 1939. Cf. Reynaud, *La France a sauvé l'Europe*, vol. 1, pp. 603–8.

offensive. The Comintern proclamation on 7 November condemned both Germany and the Allies for engaging in a war for world domination, but the emphasis in this period was on Allied responsibility for the war.

Communist Parties which only yesterday had been the most bellicose advocates of collective resistance to an aggressor fell back into the more congenial atmosphere of revolutionary defeatism. In France on 1 October, the 'Workers and Peasants Group' in the Chamber, which had taken this name when the Communist Party was declared illegal on 26 September, addressed a letter to the President of the Chamber, demanding its recall; they protested against the rejection *a priori* of all offers of peace, and declared that Soviet power could help in carrying out a policy of collective security capable of ensuring peace and the independence of France.[1] Propaganda against the 'imperialist war' was carried on in the army; Thorez and other prominent Communists deserted and found asylum in Moscow.[2] General de Gaulle's Free French movement was vilified in the Communist underground press until the time of the German attack on Russia. In England Mr. Harry Pollitt's now inopportune pamphlet *How to Win the War* was withdrawn in mid-September, and Mr. Pollitt himself was forced into temporary obscurity by his failure to comprehend the way the Moscow wind was blowing. The British Communist Party and a large proportion of its fellow-travellers went over to opposition to the war.[3]

In the United States, the Communist Party worked alongside isolationists to prevent help being sent to the Allies, and was still carrying on an anti-war campaign when Germany attacked the Soviet Union in 1941. On the other hand, it has been suggested from certain failures in co-ordination that links between the United States Communist Party and the Comintern were not fully effective after 1939. From the formal point of view, the Party was placed in a dilemma by the 'Voorhis Act' which made illegal all political parties affiliated to non-American bodies. For this reason the American Communist Party announced on 17 November 1940, that it had severed relations

---

[1] Its signatories were arrested. But other members of the group including Thorez were not molested; see Daladier's speech to the Parliamentary Commission of Inquiry, 30 May 1947.

[2] Cf. *Manchester Guardian*, 5 November 1947.

[3] Louis Fischer, *Stalin and Hitler* (Penguin Books, 1940), pp. 54–9; *Men and Politics*, pp. 572–5. Cf. V. Gollancz (ed.), *The Betrayal of the Left* (Gollancz, 1941).

with the Comintern. The *New York Daily Worker* also ceased to be an official Party publication.[1]

More difficult was the problem facing German Communists now that the German Government was in friendly relations with the Soviet Union. In 1939, the anti-war line was strongly played down as far as they were concerned, especially in publications within the Soviet Union, and it has been suggested that an agreement to do so may have formed part of the Soviet-German bargain. Thus an article in the *Communist International* by a German Communist, printed in the English language edition for the United States, did not appear in the Russian edition.[2] In 1940 the German Communist Party, in successive manifestos, published early in June and on 31 July, referred to the imperialist character of the war being waged by the Allies against Germany, thus denying that the German working-class had anything to gain by an Allied victory.[3] The May-Day 1940 proclamation of the Communist International asserted that Germany had invaded Norway as a reply to the Allied Powers' violations of neutrality, while condemning the American bourgeoisie for its attempts to grab Iceland, Greenland, and the British and French possessions in the Caribbean.[4]

[1] Barrington Moore, jun., 'The Communist Party of the U.S.A.', *American Political Science Review*, February 1945. Cf. F. Davis and E. K. Lindley, *How War Came* (New York, Simon and Schuster, 1942), p. 179. The Canadian Communist Party was declared illegal in June 1940. Evidence of its anti-war activities was given in connection with the espionage inquiry in 1946; see the *Report of the Royal Commission*, 27 June 1946 (Ottawa, Edmond Cloutier, 1946).

[2] D. Dallin, 'Komintern v Voine' (The Comintern in the War), *Novy Zhurnal*, January 1942.

[3] *Daily Worker* (London), 9 July 1940; *New York Times*, 31 July 1940. On 23 April 1946 an article in the Berlin newspaper *Der Berliner* alleged that in 1940 Walter Ulbricht, a German Communist leader, published an article urging the German working-class not to fight against Nazism by sabotage and underground activity because the war against Hitler was an imperialist war; *Manchester Guardian*, 24 April 1946.

[4] There is a curious entry in the Ciano diary under the date 20 November 1939 which suggests that in Czechoslovakia the Communists may have taken a rather different line from that elsewhere. 'News from Prague leads us to believe that the situation is more difficult than is admitted in official reports. The Duce is satisfied especially because he thinks that a Bohemian crisis will retard or perhaps torpedo the projected offensive on the western front. For Mussolini, the idea of Hitler's waging war, and worse still winning it, is altogether unbearable. He gives instructions to our consul at Prague to advise the Bohemians to side with the Communists. This will make a German repression harder and will accentuate the causes for disagreement between Moscow and Berlin.' *Ciano Diaries*, p. 170.

It will be seen that the Soviet-German treaty of 28 September 1939 was of more than local significance, and represented indeed the culminating point of Soviet-German co-operation. The first article of the Treaty declared that the 'real interest of all nations' was to end the state of war between the Western Powers and Germany, and that, if the war continued, 'joint consultations' would take place between the German and Soviet Governments on the subject of the 'necessary measures'. Any suggestion that such a 'peace offensive', even if backed by Russia, would stand a chance of success was scotched by the declaration of the British Prime Minister in the House of Commons on 3 October:

'The agreement between Germany and Russia and the subsequent partition of Poland between them has, of course, changed the position in Poland, but it by no means follows that the arrangement will enure to the ultimate advantage of Germany and still less should it affect the aims of His Majesty's Government.'

The peace offensive was duly pursued by Hitler in his speech of 6 October, when he also observed that the pact with the U.S.S.R. was the turning point in German foreign policy and showed the falseness of the idea that Germany cherished aims in the direction of the Urals, the Ukraine, Roumania, and so on.

The Soviet Government seem to have made a tentative effort to bring their endeavours for peace to the favourable notice of the American Government. The European situation was the subject of a discussion between Rubinin, the Soviet Minister to Belgium, and Joseph E. Davies, then American Ambassador at Brussels.[1] Rubinin said:

'that the Soviets would not send their soldiers to the western front; and that it was not to the interest of the Soviets that Britain and France should be destroyed, nor was it to the interest of the Soviets that Germany should be defeated.

'He then made an elaborate argument upon the advisability of accepting the *status quo* and thereby establishing peace in Europe now by a conference of the belligerents . . . in the last analysis the present conflict was simply a conflict between the British Empire which sought to dominate the world and the Germans who demanded the right to develop as equals.'

The suggestion of coming to terms was again rejected by Daladier in a speech on 10 October and by Chamberlain in a speech made two days later. Ribbentrop seems to have intended

---

[1] Davies to Secretary of State, 10 October 1939; *Mission to Moscow,* pp. 294-5.

to include an account of his Moscow negotiations in his speech of 24 October. But Stalin differed from him as to the correct phrasing of Russia's attitude to German policy, and the idea was abandoned.[1] The speech emphasized the absence of subjects of dispute between Germany and Russia, their complementary economies and the likelihood of lasting friendship based on mutual respect for each other's ideologies.[2]

The German 'peace offensive' was, however, supported by Molotov when he addressed the Supreme Soviet on 31 October:[3]

'To-day, as far as the European Great Powers are concerned, Germany is in the position of a State which is striving for the earliest termination of the war and for peace, while Britain and France, which yesterday were declaiming against aggression, are in favour of continuing the war and are opposed to the conclusion of peace.'

Molotov also attacked the recent decision of the American Government to lift the embargo on the export of arms to belligerent countries as likely to intensify, aggravate, and protract the war.[4]

Molotov's speech on the occasion of the anniversary celebrations of the Revolution on 6 November had a decidedly anti-Allied flavour.[5] The 'peace offensive' may be said to have concluded with Hitler's speech at Munich on 8 November. But on 29 November, Stalin himself made a statement in which the Allies were arraigned for their brusque rejection of the Soviet-supported peace proposals.[6]

The Soviet support of the German peace offensive, which was strongly backed by foreign Communist Parties, is not altogether easy to explain. Pro-Soviet commentators at the time had a ready answer:

'It may well be asked why the U.S.S.R. should demand that the Western democracies should bring the war to an end, or assert that the war has no further object. Once one looks at the matter from the Soviet angle, it is easy (without necessarily agreeing with her point of view) to understand why she adopts her attitude. So far as the war aims of the Western democracies have been stated, they are to implement the "guarantee" to Poland by "restoring" her and to put an end to Hitlerism.'

---

[1] *Nazi-Soviet Relations*, pp. 124–7.
[2] *The Times*, 25 October, 1939.
[3] Molotov, *Soviet Peace Policy*, pp. 27–46.
[4] President Roosevelt had repeated his request to Congress to lift the arms embargo imposed by the neutrality act of 1935 in an address on 21 September 1939. The new neutrality act lifting the arms embargo and replacing it by a 'cash and carry' clause became law on 4 November 1939. *Peace and War*, pp. 486–506.
[5] *B.I.N.*, 18 November 1939.　　　　[6] ibid., 16 December 1939.

The writer goes on to argue that the Soviet Government cannot view with favour the restoration of a 'reactionary' Polish State, and cannot trust the Western Democracies to end Hitlerism, or having ended it, not to replace it with another equally capitalist German régime, which could be used by them as the spearhead of an attack against the Soviet Union itself.

'She may rightly or wrongly think that she is better served— and the world too—by bringing such a war to an end, and leaving Hitlerism to be brought to a real end by the establishment of a Socialist Germany which perhaps she believes is not far off.'[1]

Two points arise from this explanation; first: why, if the Western Powers really wished to turn Germany against the Soviet Union, should they assume that any German ruler could be more favourable to the proposal than the author of *Mein Kampf*; second: how was Hitler himself to be restrained from attacking the Soviet Union, once he had made peace in the West?

Alternatively, it has been argued that Stalin, fearing a complete Germany victory, which would obviously imperil the U.S.S.R., preferred the chances of a negotiated settlement which, while leaving Germany with her power greatly increased, would cause internal upheavals in Great Britain and France and 'leave them intact under new leaders who would have no option, if they hoped for national survival, but to seek an entente with Moscow. A new balance of power might thus emerge, with the U.S.S.R. holding the balance.'[2] This, however, assumes that the Russians reckoned with the possibility of a complete German victory in the West as a likely outcome if the war went on, while everything goes to show that the French *débâcle* in May-June 1940 came as a complete surprise to the Kremlin.

While it is possible to assume that the Russians did not take the 'peace offensive' very seriously, and were simply hoping to acquire the prestige of would-be peace-makers, it can be argued that they were convinced that the existence of a state of war involved a danger of its spreading to them, and that even a precarious peace would suit them better. Certainly, the Soviet Government was showing by its home policy and by its actions in Poland and the Baltic States that it put its ultimate trust in its own strength. In his talks with the Latvian Minister at the beginning of October 1939, Stalin claimed that the Soviet demands upon them were based upon the war between

[1] Pritt, op. cit., pp. 153-5.   [2] Schuman, *Night over Europe*, p. 394.

Germany and the Western Powers and that Germany had given Russia a free hand in the matter. As far as Germany was concerned, Russia could occupy Latvia altogether. England had demanded airfields from Sweden and the admission of submarines into Swedish waters; Sweden might be drawn into the war and Russia must be prepared. The English had tried to buy Oesel and Dagoe from Estonia a few years back. Molotov referred to Peter the Great's vision of Russia's need for a western outlet. Finally, Stalin pointed out that Germany's former pretensions could not be forgotten. 'A German attack is also possible. For six years German Fascists and the Communists cursed each other. Now an unexpected turn took place; that happens in the course of history. But one cannot rely upon it. We must be prepared in time. Others who were not ready paid the price.'[1]

The likelihood of Germany committing itself to an all-out struggle with the Western Powers depended to some extent upon how far the Soviet Government was really prepared to give Germany the support indicated by the treaty of 28 September 1939.

An economic mission headed by Dr. Schnurre arrived in Moscow on 8 October, and a new (hitherto unpublished) agreement was concluded on 24 October.[2] Grain, manganese, flax, and other products were to be supplied to Germany and exports actually began in November.[3] In November and December, 1939, the German military authorities complained about the exaggerated and over-meticulous demands of the Russians for war materials.[4] A further agreement was signed on 11 February 1940. A memorandum by Schnurre dated 26 February, gives a full account of its contents. The main feature was that the Soviet deliveries of raw materials over a period of eighteen months were to be met by German deliveries of manufactured goods over twenty-seven months. On the other hand, if German deliveries fell behind their ratio, the Soviet Union would be entitled to suspend its deliveries (and *vice versa*). In the first twelve months, the Soviet deliveries were to be of the value of 650 million reichsmarks as against the 100

[1] *Latvia 1939–42*, pp. 95–102.

[2] Schnurre's instructions are printed in *Nazi-Soviet Relations*, pp. 119–120. The then available evidence on Soviet trade with Germany is summarized in Dallin, *Foreign Policy*, App., together with a note on Soviet trade with other countries after the outbreak of the European war.

[3] A railway agreement was signed on 24 December 1939 and an air transport agreement on 26 December.

[4] *Nazi-Soviet Relations*, pp. 127–9.

million provided for in the August agreement. Grain, mineral oil, cotton, phosphates, and various metals including chrome were among the goods specified. Freight charges on soya beans from Manchukuo were to be reduced, and the Soviet Union was to act as a purchaser on Germany's behalf of metals and other raw materials in third countries to the extent permitted by British counter-measures.

It is not surprising that the negotiations had been lengthy and difficult. The Soviet Government had promised deliveries which would have to be drawn from her own supplies, and where German deliveries of manufactured goods such as machine tools and war material was concerned, German and Soviet bottlenecks often coincided.

'The Agreement', concluded Schnurre, 'means a wide open door to the East for us. The raw material purchases from the Soviet Union and from the countries bordering the Soviet Union can still be considerably increased. But it is essential to meet the German commitments to the extent required. In view of the great volume this will require a special effort. If we succeed in extending and expanding exports to the East in the required volume, the effects of the English blockade will be decisively weakened by the incoming raw materials.'

This secret document confirms the view of one well-informed writer, that 'the economic collaboration between the two empires . . . from the time of the Pact of Moscow, made Russia [Germany's] chief source of supply for cereals, petrol, and raw materials.' He also asserts that the Russian authorities 'made it a point of honour to give delivery with scrupulous punctuality', thus making Soviet collaboration so much the more valuable to German economy.[1]

From his vantage-point as *The Times* correspondent in the Balkans, another observer concluded that Russo-German economic collaboration was fairly extensive and thorough between September 1939 and March 1940. It reached its peak in January–February 1940, when German experts were reported to be working in the Polish oil-producing areas and even

---

[1] Gafencu, *Prelude*, p. 103. According to Karl Ritter, the chief negotiator on the German side in the winter of 1939–40, the goods exported to Russia in the first half of 1940 were so important from the military point of view as to make it very unlikely that Hitler already contemplated attacking her. "New Light on Nazi Foreign Policy," *Foreign Affairs*, October 1946. On 30 March 1940 Hitler commanded that Russian orders for war materials should where necessary have priority over German ones. *Nazi Conspiracy and Aggression*, vol. 4, p. 1082.

in South Russia.[1] At the same time there were reports of a certain amount of sabotage which this observer ascribed to the Soviet desire to keep Germany's strength from growing too fast.[2]

On co-operation involving the armed forces the evidence is naturally even more scanty; there was undoubtedly a measure of co-operation between the Soviet and German naval authorities. The German liner *Bremen* which was on the high seas at the outbreak of war took refuge in a northern Russian port and stayed there until early in December, when it managed to get back to Germany. On 23 October it became known that the *City of Flint*, an American freighter which the Germans had taken as a prize, had put into a Soviet port. The Soviet authorities proved extremely unwilling to furnish the American Ambassador Steinhardt with any information about it, causing considerable feeling in the United States. On 26 October, however, the *City of Flint* was apparently ordered to leave port. It was handed back to its American crew by the Norwegians when it called at a Norwegian port on the way home. The file on Russo-German relations and other documents from the German naval archives submitted as evidence at the Nuremberg Trial provided further proof of naval co-operation.[3]

Raeder, the supreme naval commander, first discussed with Hitler on 23 September 1939 the question of Russia's ceding submarines to Germany, and providing facilities for the fitting out of auxiliary cruisers at Murmansk, and for German ships to call at Russian ports. The German Naval Attaché in Moscow reported on 25 September that the Kremlin was convinced of the necessity for co-operation with Germany.

On 3 October the German Naval Supreme Commander ordered his examination of the possibilities of Russian support for German naval warfare to be forwarded to the Foreign Office. It was considered possible that, with Russian help, bases in

[1] By 11 February 1940 (the date of the Soviet-German trade agreement) 'the existence of a far-reaching German-Soviet agreement for military and economic co-operation in the Ukraine, the Caucasus region, and the Black Sea, had been suggested by circumstantial reports from the Black Sea ports, Istanbul, the Protectorate (?Bohemia-Moravia) and Soviet Poland'; Maitland, op. cit., pp. 114–18. Any talk of co-operation in the Black Sea area was doubtless connected with Soviet fears of an attack from the Allied forces in the Levant at the time of the Finnish War.

[2] The Russians insisted on altering the gauge of the railway linking Roumania with German-occupied Poland where it traversed their territory.

[3] The file on Russo-German relations is printed as Document C.170 in *Nazi Conspiracy and Aggression*, vol. 6, pp. 977–1002. Cf. the British Admiralty publication (mimeographed): *Fuehrer Conferences on Naval Affairs*.

Norway might be secured. On 10 October, on which date one German auxiliary cruiser was at Murmansk for refitting, Raeder recorded that a bay close by had been offered by the Russians as an advanced naval base.

The British-Soviet trade agreement providing for an exchange of lumber for rubber and zinc was well received in Berlin, for it is recorded that rubber and zinc by way of Russia were just as important to Germany as lumber to Britain.[1] Exports of Russian lumber moreover would be made in British or neutral ships from Murmansk 'so that German interference remains possible'. No damage at all, the naval experts believed, was intended by the Russians to German economic warfare. Soviet Russia would fulfil all treaty obligations in full accord with Germany's policy; she would not permit an active hostile position to be taken up by Turkey or permit the passage of British and French warships through the Dardanelles. One entry in the diary referring to the departure of German vessels from Murmansk records that British and other ships were kept back by the Russian authorities until the German craft were safe.[2] On the other hand, in deference to Russian susceptibilities, Germany on 20 October restricted activity in the Baltic to a line W. of 20° East. On its side, Russia was pressing for the delivery of German naval equipment.

Gradually Soviet armament demands were raised. On 4 November they asked for the hulls of the warships *Seidlitz* and *Lutzow*. On 10 October Hitler rejected a proposal for the purchase of Soviet submarines since he was convinced that they were in bad condition and was anxious that the Russians should see no signs of weakness in Germany. He again rejected the idea on 10 November, and also opposed the sale to Russia of the *Prinz Eugen*. Further Russian demands for naval armaments were rejected on 7–8 December.

On 12 and 30 December, negotiations with the Russians for the use of Siberian sea-lanes by German ships were mentioned, and no difficulties were expected.

[1] An Anglo-Soviet agreement for the exchange of rubber and tin against timber was concluded on 11 October 1939. There were no trade talks between the U.S.S.R. and Great Britain during the Finnish War, but on 27 March, Maisky called on Halifax to discuss the detention in the Pacific of two Soviet cargo ships bound for Vladivostok on suspicion that their cargoes of tin, antimony, wolfram, copper, and other metals might be destined for Germany.

[2] In Molotov's speech of 31 October 1939, he dealt with the reply which the Soviet Government had sent on 25 October to the British notes of 6 and 11 September concerning the British blockade. The Soviet reply, published in *Pravda* on 26 October, refused to accept the British definition of contraband.

On 25 November 1939 the Supreme Naval Commander declared himself convinced that this positive attitude on Soviet Russia's part would continue so long as Stalin was in power.[1] Germany supported the expansion of Russia's interests in the direction of the Persian Gulf. Elsewhere their diplomatic collaboration was proving useful: 'For the first time for fifty years a one-front war is possible'. But on 3 December, a declaration by Molotov is reported to the effect that Russia's primary goals lay in south-eastern Europe and that a rapid solution of the Finnish problem was to be attempted in order to free Russian forces for other missions.

The Soviet assurances with regard to Turkey, mentioned in the Turkish documents, related to the renewal of Soviet-Turkish negotiations which had been at a standstill since Potemkin's visit to Ankara in the spring of 1939. Russo-Turkish relations provided, throughout the period with which we are concerned, one of the principal tests of the stability of the new Soviet-German relationship. In the conversation with Davies already quoted from, the Soviet Minister at Brussels had answered Davies's question as to whether Russia would permit Germany to establish herself on the Black Sea 'either at Constanza or at the Dardanelles by stating that in his opinion this was impossible and contrary to the vital interests of Russia'.[2] While the latter remark was no doubt true, the Russians now shared with Germany the immediate objective of excluding all Allied influence from this region. For this reason the Soviet-German pact of 23 August had come as a terrible blow to Turkish hopes.

On 25 August, Hitler had written to Mussolini that the Turks would now be obliged to revise their policy, and in reply, Mussolini pointed out that this would upset the whole

[1] Two days earlier Hitler had addressed a conference of his supreme commanders: 'Russia is at present not dangerous. It is weakened by many incidents to-day. Moreover we have a pact with Russia. Pacts, however, are only held as long as they serve the purpose. Russia will hold herself to it only so long as Russia considers it to be to her benefit. Even Bismarck thought so. Let one think of the pact to assure our back. Now Russia has far reaching goals, above all the strengthening of her position in the Baltic. We can oppose Russia only when we are free in the West. Further Russia is striving to increase her influence in the Balkans and is striking towards the Persian Gulf. That is also the goal of our foreign policy. Russia will do that which she considers to benefit her. At the present moment she has retired from internationalism. In case she renounces this, she will proceed to Pan-Slavism. It is difficult to see into the future. It is a fact that at the present time the Russian army is of little worth. For the next one or two years, the present situation will remain.' *Nazi Conspiracy and Aggression*, vol. 3, pp. 572–80.

[2] Davies, dispatch of 10 October 1939, op. cit., pp. 294–5.

of Anglo-French strategy in the Eastern Mediterranean. On
2 September, Molotov informed Schulenburg that the Soviet
Government was endeavouring to negotiate a non-aggression
pact with Turkey and on 5 September, the Ambassador
impressed upon Molotov the need to secure Turkey's permanent
neutrality and the closure of the Dardanelles in view of the
possibility of Great Britain and France trying to send troops to
the assistance of Roumania. Molotov replied that the Soviet
Government was doing its best to direct Turkey along these
lines, although conversations for a mutual-assistance pact
between the U.S.S.R. and Turkey, which had been carried on
at one time, had been without result.[1]

The definitive pacts with the Western Allies, now on the verge
of signature, had now to be reconsidered by the Turks in the
light of a possible further deterioration in the relationships
between these Powers and the Soviet Union. On 17 September
Stalin told Schulenburg that the Turks had proposed the
conclusion of an assistance pact relating to the Straits and the
Balkans in such a form as not to oblige Turkey to act against
Great Britain and France. The Soviet Government was not
very sympathetic to the proposal in this form.[2] To be pro-
Allied *and* pro-Soviet, as Turkey had wished, was hardly
feasible. A last effort to accomplish this *tour de force* was in fact
made by the Turkish Foreign Minister, M. Sarajoglu, who left
Ankara for Moscow on 22 September.[3] On 12 October, the
Germans learned from the Bulgarian Minister in Berlin that
Bulgaria had recently turned down the offer of a mutual-
assistance pact from the U.S.S.R. The Bulgarians had
proposed a non-aggression pact instead but there had been no
reply from Moscow so far to this suggestion.[4]

Besides continuing the discussions for a Russo-Turkish pact
of mutual assistance, M. Sarajoglu was to explore the Soviet
attitude towards a plan worked out between the members of
the Balkan Entente for settling the Bulgarian question and for
bringing Bulgaria herself into the Entente. The suggestions
were in line with those propounded by Potemkin during his
Balkan tour in the spring. At that time, however, the Soviet
diplomat had warned the statesmen of the Balkan Entente
against a too great readiness to appease Bulgaria. Now Sarajoglu found that the Russians, having adopted a forward policy

[1] *Nazi-Soviet Relations*, pp. 80–2, 85–7.

[2] *Nazi-Soviet Relations*, p. 97

[3] There is an account of M. Sarajoglu's mission in Gafencu, *Prelude*,
pp. 258–64.

[4] *Nazi-Soviet Relations*, p. 124.

of their own, were no longer interested in the prospects of Balkan solidarity.

Sarajoglu's fruitless visit lasted until 17 October. Immediately afterwards, on 19 October, the Turks signed a fifteen-year tripartite treaty of mutual assistance with Great Britain and France.[1] This treaty specifically mentioned Turkish assistance in the fulfilment of the Allied guarantee to Roumania. On the other hand, the Turkish reluctance to be embroiled with Russia led to the addition of the following clause in the protocol of signature: 'the obligations undertaken by Turkey in virtue of the above mentioned Treaty cannot compel that country to take action having as its effect or involving as its consequence armed conflict with the U.S.S.R.'

Speaking on 31 October with reference to Sarajoglu's visit, Molotov denied that the Russian demands in the negotiations with Turkey had included 'the cession of the districts of Ardahan and Kars' or 'changes in the international convention concluded at Montreux and a privileged position as regards the Straits'.

'The question at issue', according to Molotov, 'was the conclusion of a bilateral pact of mutual assistance limited to the regions of the Black Sea and the Straits. The U.S.S.R. considered firstly that the conclusion of such a pact could not induce her to actions which might draw her into armed conflict with Germany; secondly that the U.S.S.R. should have a guarantee that, in view of the war danger, Turkey would not allow warships of non-Black Sea Powers through the Bosphorus to the Black Sea'. Turkey had rejected both these stipulations and having 'definitely discarded a cautious policy of neutrality', had, by tying up its destinies with 'a definite group of European Powers ... entered the orbit of the expanding European war ... whether Turkey will come to regret it', he darkly concluded, 'we shall not try to guess.'[2]

The Turkish reply took the form of a semi-official statement on 3 November that demands made upon her had conflicted with Turkey's international obligations with regard to the Dardanelles under the Montreux Convention.[3]

It would appear that Russia's demands on Turkey had in fact fallen into two categories.[4] In the first place, Russia, with an eye doubtless to her claims on Roumania, and in deference

[1] Text in Shotwell and Déak, *Turkey at the Straits*, App. 4.
[2] Molotov, *Soviet Peace Policy*, pp. 42–3.
[3] *B.I.N.*, XVI, p. 1291.
[4] This account of the negotiations follows that of Dallin, *Foreign Policy*, pp. 105–11; cf. Schuman, *Night over Europe*, pp. 394–6.

to Germany, as has been seen, wanted the Turks to deny to Allied ships the passage of the Straits should they wish to go to Roumania's help.[1] In the second place, the U.S.S.R. wished that any pact with Turkey should fall into place as part of a process of forming the Balkan States into a neutral bloc.[2] According to these sources, the first of these demands was immediately rejected and the Turks prepared to leave Moscow on 1 October as rumours spread that Russia had demanded a base on the Dardanelles. Nevertheless, on the 2nd, the talks were renewed, apparently on Molotov's suggestion. On 2 October, Ribbentrop telegraphed Schulenburg to urge the Russians to try to prevent the Turks from entering into obligations to Great Britain and France. On the following day, Molotov gave assurances that efforts were being made to neutralize Turkey. But on 7 October, the German request was repeated, since there were rumours that a Soviet-Turkish pact was on the way. On the 9th, Molotov indicated that such a pact was unlikely and that Germany's interests were being kept in mind.[3] The Turks insisted on consulting their allies in London and Paris and, having done so, came forward on the 13th with new proposals. They were now willing to sign a mutual assistance pact with Russia and to revise their draft pacts with England and France in order to exclude the possibility of their being called upon to fight Russia. The proposed neutral bloc would also be acceptable to them provided it were negotiated after the signature of their pacts with Britain and France. It would appear that at this point agreement was not impossible, but that the Russians were now induced by the Germans to put forward new demands which proved wholly unacceptable.[4] These demands would seem to have raised the question of the Straits again and also to have included an undertaking that Turkey would not go to war against Germany in association with the Allies.

Russia's annexations, even if justified on security grounds, were regarded by the Turks with apprehension. Whether this new spirit of expansionism was protective or flatly imperialist

[1] Compliance with the Soviet request would have violated the Russians' own cherished Article 19 of the Montreux Convention.

[2] These demands do not appear in a positive form in M. Gafencu's account of the negotiations; but his version contains nothing which contradicts that of Dallin.

[3] *Nazi-Soviet Relations*, pp. 110–111, 113, 117–118, 120.

[4] The German view was probably put forward earlier by Ribbentrop, whose visit to Moscow on 27-28 September coincided with Sarajoglu's stay there. The account in the German Naval War Diary suggests that Germany received assurances from Russia on the points with which it was concerned.

did not concern them. They only saw that the Straits and Constantinople could be seized on grounds of security as well as on any other. The old fear of Russia, bred of two centuries of the 'Eastern Question', reared up in them again. The protocol attached to the Treaty of Ankara was not the outcome of friendship but of fear.[1] At all costs the Turks felt they had to avoid a war on two fronts.[2]

The winter of 1939–40 was marked by steady German and Russian propaganda designed to loosen the alliance with the Western Allies which the Turks regarded as the sheet-anchor of their security.[3] The actual diplomatic moves are obscure. According to the documents which the German Foreign Office published at the beginning of July 1940, with the obvious intention of destroying the perceptible détente in Russo-Turkish relations which had set in since about April, the Allies had definitely been hopeful of obtaining Turkish assistance for their plan of cutting off German oil imports from Russia. According to the dispatch ascribed to M. Massigli under date of 28 March, hopes of a direct Turkish initiative in this respect were not very great. The Turkish attitude was dominated by fear of Russia, and particularly by the fear that the Allies might come to terms with Germany, thus leaving the Turks unsupported to face the Russian might.[4] The ill-success of Russian arms in the Finnish war was only partially consoling. M. Massigli pointed out that France and Britain could not extend their blockading operations into the Black Sea without infringing the terms of the Montreux Convention and that Turkey, if she permitted them to do so, could for conniving at its infringement be held liable by any of its signatories (e.g. Russia or Italy). Nor could a blockade be effective with no examining port. A direct attack upon the Caucasian oilfields would be better; but here again Turkish co-operation would be needed. M. Massigli's dispatches of 1 April and 25 April and General Weygand's dispatch of 17 April hardly lend themselves to the interpretation that the Turks were willing listeners to these overtures, which

---

[1] It has been stated that Daladier prevented the British from acceding to a Soviet-inspired demand by the Turks that their pact with the Allies should only cover aggression by Italy; 'Pertinax', *Les Fossoyeurs*, vol. 1, p. 130.

[2] Ward, *Turkey*, pp. 105–6.

[3] P. P. Graves, *Briton and Turk* (Hutchinson, 1941), pp. 246–7.

[4] On the other hand an informed Turkish commentator pointed out that Germany, which then encouraged Russia to turn on Turkey, would only await the time to turn on Russia. Halidé Edib, 'Turkey and her Allies', *Foreign Affairs*, April 1940.

they were in no position to rebuff altogether in as far as they concerned questions of Turkey's own defence, for which Allied supplies were and remained, throughout the period in question, indispensable.[1]

The new Balkan policy of the Soviet Union, revealed at the time of the Sarajoglu mission, became more clearly defined in the succeeding months.

'This policy in the first place threatened Roumania. The Turkish Minister for Foreign Affairs expressed himself in . . . definite terms to the Soviet Ambassador, M. Terentiev, when, in December 1939, he asked what Turkey would do in the event of the U.S.S.R. being called upon to take "certain military measures" with regard to Roumania. M. Sarajoglu replied . . . that Turkey was interested in the peace of Roumania, and that she intended to respect the engagements in relation to the Franco-British guarantee given to that country.'[2]

Soviet patronage was transferred from the 'status quo' countries of the Balkan Entente to revisionist Bulgaria. On 6 November 1939, Lavrentiev, the new Soviet Minister to Bulgaria, presented his credentials and referred in his speech to the 'historic affinities' between Russia and Bulgaria.[3] The Soviet press had begun to give increasing attention to the Bessarabian question. An issue of the *Communist International*, published at the beginning of December, included an article by a Bulgarian Communist, Boris Stefanov, formerly resident in Roumania but now in Moscow, demanding the immediate conclusion of a Soviet-Roumanian mutual assistance pact on the model of the pacts with the Baltic States.[4] Although a Tass statement on 8 December denied that the article represented the views of the Soviet Government, and in spite of assurances given on the same day by Paul Kukoliev, the Soviet Chargé d'Affaires at Bucarest, to the effect that the Russians did not intend to occupy Bessarabia, circumstantial rumours of Soviet designs continued to circulate.[5]

---

[1] In his speech on 29 March 1940, Molotov coupled Turkey with Iran as countries with whom relations were determined by the Soviet Union's 'existing pacts of non-aggression and by an unswerving desire of the Soviet Union for the observance of mutual obligation arising out of them'.

[2] Gafencu, *Prelude*, pp. 276–7.

[3] A. Mousset, *Le Monde Slave* (Paris, Société d'Editions Françaises et Internationales, 1946), p. 143. Bulgaria had recognized the U.S.S.R. on 23 July 1934.

[4] Dallin, *Foreign Policy*, pp. 173–4.

[5] The newspaper *Stampa* of Milan declared in an article on 3 December that Hitler and Stalin had reached an agreement on Roumania by which Soviet Russia was to acquire Bessarabia, and Hungary, Transylvania, while

The fact that Soviet plans envisaged more than the recovery of Bessarabia seems to have been known in Bucarest before the end of the year. For on 1 January the Roumanian Prime

---

the rest of Roumania was to fall within the German sphere of influence. Dallin, loc. cit. This would appear to be part of an effort by Italy to carve out for herself a sphere of influence in south-eastern Europe, from which the Soviet-German agreement appeared to have excluded her. Italy had not followed Germany in the latter's *rapprochement* with Soviet Russia and Soviet-Italian relations had deteriorated sharply after the outbreak of the Finnish War. On 8 December, the Fascist Grand Council reaffirmed Italy's continued interest in all matters affecting the Danube basin. The newly appointed Soviet Ambassador Gorelkin informed the Italian Government on 9 December that he had been recalled to Moscow and would not be able to present his credentials. *Ciano Diaries*, p. 177. On 16 December, Ciano made a speech in which he violently attacked Bolshevism (although in his diary he described it as in substance anti-German), ibid., p. 179. In discussions with Carol's special envoy Antonescu on 23–26 December, Ciano declared that Italy was anti-Bolshevik but would avoid commitments; ibid., pp. 182–4. The Roumanian envoy seems nevertheless to have reported a promise of concrete assistance in the event of a Soviet attack. 'Italy', repeated Ciano to the Roumanian Minister N. Bossi on 10 January 1940, 'has supported the armed resistance of Spain and Finland against Bolshevism. She will do the same for Roumania; the more so since Italy had only indirect interests in Finland and in Spain, while she has a direct interest in maintaining Roumania, the first barrier in the way of the U.S.S.R., whose menace extends over the whole of the Balkans, where Italy has taken and intends to retain the position of a Great Power.' Gafencu, *Prelude*, p. 277. On the previous day, the Italian Ambassador in Moscow for the past two years, Augusto Rosso, who had been recalled on 28 December, had arrived back in Rome for what proved to be a long stay. Italy's attempt to re-enter the Balkan scene as an anti-Soviet bulwark was facilitated by the fact that Great Britain had been forced to inform the Roumanian Government that they could fulfil their guarantee to Roumania in the case of *Soviet* aggression, only in the event of Italy remaining neutral and of Turkey giving immediate assistance. Communication from Sir Reginald Hoare to M. Gafencu, 14 December 1939, ibid., p. 274. In these circumstances, Soviet-Italian hostility became increasingly marked. The press and radio of the two countries vied with one another in mutual vilification and the commercial agreement which lapsed on 31 December was not renewed. Dallin, *Foreign Policy*, pp. 175–6. See also the letter from Mussolini to Hitler dated 4 January 1940 in *Les Lettres secrètes échangées par Hitler et Mussolini* (Paris, Éditions du Pavois, 1946), pp. 50–1. German propaganda was more circumspect but also did not cease attempting to combat Soviet influence in the Balkans even during the period of closest diplomatic co-operation. It was directed in particular towards arousing fears of Russian designs in Roumania. If there were a threat to Sub-Carpathian Russia from the Soviet Ukraine, the Roumanians were told, the Hungarians would be forced to take Transylvania in self-defence; Maitland, op. cit. p. 79. Strong Roumanian forces were henceforward concentrated on the Russian (as well as the Hungarian) frontier, and the consequent burden on the population made for unrest from which both native political extremists and their foreign backers might hope to profit. Cf. H. Seton-Watson, *Eastern Europe between the Wars*, pp. 397–400.

Minister, Tatarescu, declared that Roumania was 'prepared to fight to defend Bessarabia and Bukovina which joined the Roumanian State of their own volition after the World War'.[1]

A last attempt to consolidate the Balkan Entente and make it effective against aggression from outside the area was made at a conference of the Entente which met at Belgrade on 2 February 1940.[2] The Council decided that the General Staffs of the four States should draw up a common plan of defence to meet all contingencies. This involved coming to terms with Hungary and Bulgaria. The former was unapproachable but there were signs that Bulgaria would be willing to consider some arrangement, and it has been said that an assurance had in fact been received that Bulgaria's territorial claims would not be pressed during the war.[3] On 15 February, however, the Bulgarian Prime Minister, Kiosseivanov, resigned. This event was hailed in Moscow as a victory for Germany and Russia and as an Allied defeat. Although the new Prime Minister, Filov, declared his intention of following the foreign policy of his predecessor, it soon became clear that Bulgarian revisionism, encouraged by both Germany and the Soviet Union, would henceforward be increasingly active, although it was not clear whether this would redound to Russia's or Germany's advantage.[4]

The Finnish War was perhaps the most significant and paradoxical event in the winter of 1939–40 from the point of view of Soviet-German relations.[5] Russia's demands on Finland, if taken together with those on the Baltic States, were clearly strategic in their immediate intention. The fact that on this

---

[1] Bukovina, formerly part of Moldavia, was ceded to Austria by the Turks in 1777. Part of it was included in the 'independent' Ukrainian state recognized under the Treaty of Brest-Litovsk. In November 1918 political leaders in Bukovina had proclaimed its reunion with Roumania, which had been promised a part of the province by the Allies in August 1916, to the dissatisfaction of the Ukrainian (or Ruthenian) element in the population—about 40 per cent of the whole according to the Austrian statistics.

[2] Communiqué of 5 February 1940 in *B.I.N.*, 10 February 1940. Cf. Gafencu, *Prelude*, p. 277.

[3] Cf. 'The Bulgarian Claim to Southern Dobrudja', *B.I.N.*, 24 February 1940.

[4] Cf. Maitland, op. cit., pp. 107–8.

[5] See *The Development of Finnish-Soviet Relations during the Autumn of 1939, including the Official Documents* (*Finnish Blue Book*) (Finnish Ministry of Foreign Affairs: Harrap, 1940). Cf. Dallin, *Foreign Policy*, pp. 112–98, Schuman, *Night over Europe*, pp. 397–427; H. B. Elliston, *Finland Fights* (Harrap, 1940). For further sources, see P. Grierson, *Books on Soviet Russia* (Methuen, 1943), pp. 171–3.

occasion they involved actual territorial cessions as well as the lease of bases was incidental, except to the Finns. Once more, the only aggressor which could seriously be envisaged was Germany. In the case of Finland, suspicions might well be strengthened by recent evidence that Finnish sympathies with Germany, dating back to the latter's help in crushing the Communist revolution in Finland in 1918, had not ceased to operate. Nevertheless, in spite of the frequent occasions of friction in the past few years, Finland, if resolutely opposed to the idea of a Soviet guarantee during the negotiations of the summer of 1939, had also refused in May to be a party to a bilateral non-aggression pact with Germany.

Negotiations with Finland began with the summoning of a Finnish representative to Moscow on 5 October. From the beginning it was evident that progress was not going to be as rapid as in the case of the talks with the Baltic States.[1]

Molotov gave a detailed account of them in his speech of 31 October:

'We began negotiations with the Finnish representatives MM. Paasikivi and Tanner, sent for this purpose by the Finnish Government to Moscow, by proposing the conclusion of a Soviet-Finnish pact of Mutual Assistance approximately on the lines of our Pacts of Mutual Assistance with the other Baltic States, but inasmuch as the Finnish Government declared that the conclusion of such a Pact would contradict its position of absolute neutrality, we did not insist on our proposal. We then proposed that we proceed to discuss concrete questions in which we are interested from the standpoint of safeguarding the security of the U.S.S.R. and especially of Leningrad, both from the sea—on the Gulf of Finland—and from land, in view of the extreme proximity of the border to Leningrad.

'We further proposed that an agreement be reached to shift the Soviet-Finnish frontier in the Isthmus of Karelia a few dozen kilometres further to the north of Leningrad. In exchange for this we proposed to transfer to Finland a part of Soviet Karelia, double the size of the territory which Finland would transfer to the Soviet Union.

'We further proposed that an agreement be reached for Finland to lease to us for a definite term a small section of her territory near the entrance to the Gulf of Finland where we might establish a naval base. With a Soviet naval base at the southern entrance to the Gulf of Finland, namely at Baltiski port, as provided for by the Soviet-Estonian Pact of Mutual Assistance, the establishment of a naval base at the northern entrance to the Gulf of Finland would fully safeguard the Gulf of Finland against hostile attempts on the

[1] The Germans indicated to the Finns that they would not intervene on their behalf. *Nazi-Soviet Relations*, pp. 111, 121–3.

part of other States. We have no doubt that the establishment of such a base would not only be in the interests of the Soviet Union but also of the security of Finland herself.

'Our other proposals, in particular our proposal as regards the exchange of certain islands in the Gulf of Finland, as well as parts of the Rybachi and Sredni Peninsulas, for territory twice as large in Soviet Karelia, evidently do not meet with any objections on the part of the Finnish Government. Differences with regard to certain of our proposals have not yet been overcome, and concessions made by Finland in this respect, as, for instance, the cession of part of the territory of the Isthmus of Karelia, obviously do not meet the purpose.

'We have further taken a number of new steps to meet Finland half-way. We declared that if our main proposals were accepted we should be prepared to drop our objections to the fortification of the Aaland Islands on which the Finnish Government has been insisting for a long time. We only made one stipulation: we said that we would drop our objection to the fortification of the Aaland Islands on condition that the fortification is done by Finland's own national forces without the participation of any third country, inasmuch as the U.S.S.R. will take no part in it.

'We also proposed to Finland the disarming of the fortified zones along the entire Soviet-Finnish border on the Isthmus of Karelia, which should fully accord with the interests of Finland. We further expressed our desire to reinforce the Soviet-Finnish Pact of Non-Aggression with additional mutual guarantees. Lastly, the consolidation of Soviet-Finnish political relations would undoubtedly form a splendid basis for the rapid development of economic relations between the two countries. Thus we are ready to meet Finland in matters in which she is particularly interested.

'In view of all this we do not think that Finland will seek a pretext to frustrate the proposed agreement. . . .'[1]

The negotiations did not, however, solve the deadlock on the most vital issues involved, and it is clear that the Soviet Government was determined to have its way. On 26 November a 'frontier incident' occurred; on 28 November the U.S.S.R. denounced its non-aggression pact with Finland; and on 29 November, the Soviet assault began.[2]

The Soviet Government did not, however, see fit to proceed by a declaration of war. On 1 December, it announced that it had recognized a new Finnish Government set up in the border town of Terijoki under Otto Kuusinen, a Finnish Communist, resident in the Soviet Union ever since the failure of the Communists in Finland in 1918, and formerly secretary of the Com-

[1] Molotov, *Soviet Peace Policy*, pp. 39–41.
[2] Soviet note to Finland of 28 November in Scott, op. cit., App. 12.

munist International.[1] On 2 December the U.S.S.R. signed a treaty with the new Government, in which the latter conceded the Soviet claims.[2]

Although the move against Finland might be considered a move against Germany, it was clear that the situation would not allow this to be hinted. It was therefore necessary for the Russians to make out that Finland was likely to become the spearhead of an attack against the Soviet Union on the part of the Allies.[3] The effect of this propaganda, of the attack itself, of the setting up of the Kuusinen puppet government, and of the determined and well-publicized resistance of the Finns, was to provoke widespread sympathy for the Finns in the Western democracies and particularly in the United States.[4]

The long-cherished distrust of the Soviet Union on the part of some political circles in the West, genuine indignation at the recent treachery of the local Communist Parties, particularly in France, the violent reaction against the Soviet Union after the pact with Germany on the part of some of her erstwhile admirers—all these combined, with a general underestimation of both Soviet and German strength, to suggest the idea that the two enemies of Western civilization might be dealt a blow simultaneously, first by aid to Finland, and secondly by a direct attack on the Caucasian oil-fields on the part of the Allied armies under General Weygand's command in the Middle East.[5] The idea that the Soviet Union itself contemplated any Middle Eastern adventures at this juncture can probably be dismissed. But Molotov failed to point out, when denouncing those who spread this idea, that its source was clearly German rather than Allied.[6]

For Germany, to remain neutral without letting the situation

[1] Tass communiqué, 1 December 1939, quoted by Dallin, *Foreign Policy*, p. 134.   [2] Text of treaty in Scott, op. cit., App. 13.
[3] German missions abroad were instructed to support the Soviet thesis. *Nazi-Soviet Relations*, pp. 127–130.
[4] D. Smith, *America and the Axis War* (Cape, 1942), pp. 211–12, 298. Molotov had commented acidly in his speech on 31 October on a note sent to Kalinin by Roosevelt on 12 October, in which the American President had expressed his country's interest in a peaceful outcome of the negotiations. The most important result of American disapproval of Russia's actions was a 'moral embargo' on the export of certain goods to Russia proclaimed on 2 December 1939 and extended to further items on 15 and 20 December. It was only lifted on 21 January 1941; Dallin, *Foreign Policy*, p. 177; *Documents on Foreign Relations*, 1939–40, vol. 2, pp. 382–98, 725–8. See also the speech by Roosevelt on 10 February 1940, *B.I.N.*, XVII, p. 255. The Finnish War is not dealt with in the State Department compilation, *Peace and War*.
[5] For the feeling in France see E. J. Bois, *Truth on the Tragedy of France* (Hodder and Stoughton, 1941), pp. 175–7.
[6] Speech of 29 March 1940, *Soviet Peace Policy*, p. 52.

get out of hand was to enjoy the advantage of the widening breach between the U.S.S.R. and the Western Powers.[1] This was taken a stage further by the Finnish appeal to the League of Nations on 3 December, under Articles 11 and 15 of the League Covenant.[2] In response to a communication from the League Secretary-General M. Avenol, Molotov replied on 4 December refusing to participate in the proposed special session.

'The Soviet Union is not at war with Finland and does not threaten the Finnish people. The Soviet Union maintains peaceful relations with the Democratic Republic of Finland. The People in whose name Holsti (the Finnish representative at Geneva) appeals to the League are not the real representatives of the people of Finland.'

The League Assembly opened on 11 December and a Committee of Thirteen, appointed to study the situation, again communicated with Moscow, inviting the Soviet Government to suspend hostilities and to send a representative to Geneva.[3] The Soviet reply refused on the grounds already stated by Molotov. On 13 December the League Assembly passed a resolution to the effect that the U.S.S.R. had violated its agreements with Finland, Article 12 of the League Covenant, and the Kellogg-Briand Pact, condemned the Soviet Government's action, and appealed to League members to give Finland what aid they could. It also passed over to the Council the question of applying Article XVI of the Covenant, in view of the U.S.S.R.'s neglect of the provisions of Article XV. On 14 December the League Council considered the matter and unanimously adopted the following resolution:

'The Council having taken cognizance of the resolution adopted by the Assembly on 14 December 1939, regarding the appeal of the Finnish Government, (1) associates itself with the condemnation of the Assembly of the action of the U.S.S.R. against the Finnish state, and (2) for the reasons set forth in the resolution of the Assembly, in virtue of Article 16 para. 4 of the Covenant finds that, by its act, the U.S.S.R. has placed itself outside the League of Nations. It follows that the U.S.S.R. is no longer a member of the League.'[4]

---

[1] There was a current belief, which may have had its adherents in Moscow, that Finnish obstinacy during the negotiations was due to secret German encouragement. Elliston, op. cit., pp. 114–15, 176.

[2] *L.N.O.J.*, 1939, pp. 505–42.

[3] As *Pravda* later pointed out, nine of the thirteen Powers represented on it had no diplomatic relations with the Soviet Union; later Poland was added to the Committee.

[4] China, Finland, Greece, and Poland abstained from voting. Affirmative votes came from Great Britain, France, Belgium, South Africa, Egypt, Bolivia, and the Dominican Republic. Eleven members of the League had also made reservations about the Assembly resolution. They were Estonia, Latvia, Lithuania, Bulgaria, China, Sweden, Norway, Denmark, Switzerland and the Netherlands.

Germany therefore made it clear from the first that she would do nothing in connexion with the Finnish affair which might harm her relations with the Soviet Union. On 8 December the Finnish Minister in Rome told Ciano that Germany had supplied arms to Finland, particularly from captured Polish stocks.[1] Berlin reacted strongly to a Tass report on 10 December, which quoted neutral sources for the information that Germany had sold arms to Finland and that Great Britain had not.[2] It was also denied, apparently with truth, that Germany was giving facilities for the flying of Italian aircraft to Finland. German pressure also forced Hungary to deny that she had any hostile intentions towards the U.S.S.R.

The German naval archives show that on 12 December the Supreme Naval Commander was opposed to Germany favouring Finland. But on 17 December it was noted that the war had shown up Russia's weakness. On 31 December the German General Staff circulated a survey of the campaign which rated very low the fighting qualities of the Red Army.[3]

By January 1940 it began to seem possible that the rising indignation at Russia's action might lead to Great Britain and France taking more active steps than hitherto in support of Finland.[4] The ultimate object would have been to proceed beyond actual assistance to Finland, to attack the Russian sources of German supplies, and to open up a new front in the Balkans or Scandinavia. Plans of this kind appear to have been the subject of serious discussion in the first weeks of the new year.[5]

[1] *Ciano Diaries*, p. 177.
[2] See the note on the conversation, on 11 December, between Ribbentrop and the Soviet Ambassador Shkvartsev. *Nazi-Soviet Relations*, pp. 130-1.
[3] *Nazi Conspiracy and Aggression*, vol. 6, pp. 981-2.
[4] Daladier is said to have cherished the idea that French national unity (and his Government) would have been strengthened by a decision to support Finland. 'Pertinax', op. cit., vol. i, pp. 174-7.
[5] The most important evidence so far available is that contained in the *German White Books*, Nos. 4 and 6. These contain documents said to have been discovered by the Germans during the French retreat in the summer of 1940. A narrative based on these documents will be found in Schuman, *Night over Europe*, pp. 415-24. The author does not doubt their authenticity, although he does not commit himself on the question of how they were obtained; cf. Dallin, *Foreign Policy*, pp. 166-72. The latter accepts as an admission that the documents were in principle correct, a statement made in the House of Commons by Mr. R. A. Butler on 11 July 1940. 'Pertinax' writes as follows: 'In March-April the British and even the Turks began to incline towards the French project which included not only air raids on the Caucasian oil-wells but also naval action in the Black Sea. M. Massigli, French Ambassador at Ankara, was at the centre of the negotiations'; op. cit., vol. 1, p. 61.

Such plans were forestalled by the conclusion on 12 March, as a result of the Soviet breach of the Finnish defences on the Karelian Isthmus, of a Treaty of Peace, whose terms were substantially those offered by the Soviet Union during the negotiations of October-November 1939.[1] On the same day, Daladier had declared that on 5 March, the Allied Supreme War Council had taken the decision to help Finland with troops as well as with supplies. On 7 March, he stated, Finland had been informed that troops would be sent in the event of a direct appeal from the Finnish Government, as nothing short of this would justify the necessary pressure on Norway and Sweden to permit their passage. This account was confirmed by Chamberlain in the House of Commons on 19 March 1940.[2]

The Russians' readiness to throw over Kuusinen and sign a treaty with the Finnish Government was not caused by any doubt of the Red Army's ability to crush the Finns in the spring. Indeed, the Army's achievements in the last weeks of the war were very considerable.[3] It was rather that the administrative and economic strain had been heavier than justified by the military effort required, and with so much uncertainty on all sides, the Soviet Union clearly required a breathing space to put its house in order.[4] In addition it is possible that Stalin believed that the Allies genuinely intended to help Finland and that the Soviet Union might find itself engaged in a major war.

[1] Text in *Documents on American Foreign Relations*, vol. 2, 1939–40, pp. 392–6

[2] The Swedish Foreign Minister Gunther stated in a speech on 16 March 1940 that the Russians had announced in a note on 29 January that they were not in principle opposed to a settlement; *B.I.N.*, 23 March 1940.

[3] If Mr. Churchill really believed that the Finns had 'exposed for all the world to see the military incapacity of the Red Army and the Red Air Force', he was for once the sharer in a common illusion. Broadcast address, 20 January 1940, in W. S. Churchill, *Into Battle* (Cassell, 1941), p. 160.

[4] For the internal effects of the Finnish War on the Soviet Union and for the measures taken to cope with the weaknesses which it revealed, see J. Scott, op. cit. There were important changes in the Army after Timoshenko replaced Voroshilov as Defence Commissar on 8 March 1940. On 12 August the 'Political Commissars' were again abolished and unity of command reintroduced. On 12 October a new and severer disciplinary code was promulgated. Growing attention was given in army training to the record of Russia's past military prowess; Fedotoff White, *The Growth of the Red Army*, pp. 384 ff. It has been estimated that the Red Army increased in size from roughly two million men in 1938 to six or seven million men in the spring of 1941; Scott, *Behind the Urals*, pp. 200–1. On the industrial side a considerable advance seems to have been made in building up industries away from the western frontier and particularly in the Urals, but the dependence on the older industrial areas was still very great in 1941; M. L. Harvey and M. J. Ruggles, 'Eastward Course of Soviet Industry and the War', *Russian Review*, April 1942.

The treaty included the cession to the Soviet Union of the entire Karelian isthmus with the town of Viborg (Viipuri), Viborg Bay with its islands, the western and northern shores of Lake Ladoga with the towns of Keksholm (Kakisalmi), Sortavala and Suojärvi, and a number of islands in the Gulf of Finland, the territory east of Merkjärvi with the town of Kuoljärvi, and part of the Rybachi and Sredni peninsulas. It also included a thirty years' lease to the Soviet Union of the peninsula of Hangoe, the grant of transit rights across the Petsamo region to Norway, the right of transit to Sweden and the construction, in order to facilitate this, of a railway between Kandalaksha and Kemijärvi. Finland also agreed to demilitarize her Arctic coastline and waters and the two countries entered into mutual obligations of non-aggression and abstention from hostile alliances or coalitions.[1]

Reviewing these events in his speech of 29 March Molotov said: 'We were obliged to put the question of the security of Leningrad on a more reliable basis; in addition we could not but raise the question of the security of the Murmansk railway and Murmansk, which is our only ice-free port in the west and is therefore of extreme importance for our foreign trade and for communication between the Soviet Union and other countries generally.'[2]

The Soviet attitude to Finland after the treaty was that no outside nation should be allowed to show any interest in Finland's fate and when, on 14 March, Norway and Sweden indicated their readiness to consider some form of defensive alliance with Finland, the Soviet reaction was strong enough to make them abandon the idea. There is, however, a certain amount of evidence for the belief that the Germans had led the Finns to believe that their sacrifices would only be temporary and that Germany was prepared at some more favourable date to assume again her old role of protector of Finland against Bolshevism.[3]

If the Finnish question might in the long run complicate

---

[1] See Map 3 *infra*.

[2] *Soviet Peace Policy*, p. 62. For a Finnish view of the peace terms see *Finland reveals her Secret Documents on Soviet Policy, March 1940—June 1941 (Finnish Blue and White Book)*, (New York, Funk, 1941), p. 1. On 31 March the Karelian isthmus was incorporated in the Karelian Autonomous Republic, which became the Karelian–Finnish Union Republic.

[3] Dallin, *Foreign Policy*, pp. 194–8. The Finnish delegate Paasikivi said in a conversation with Molotov on 21 March 1940, 'We are not at all thinking of revenge. Sweden and Norway would not be the right allies if we were to seek revenge. We should strive for an alliance with quite different states, if we really wanted revenge. Sweden and Norway are politically wholly defensive.' *Finnish Blue and White Book*, p. 43.

relations with Germany, the more immediate result of the war was, as already indicated, a further exacerbation of Soviet relations with the Western Powers. This was particularly the case with regard to France, where pressure on the Government to intervene had been stronger than in Great Britain.[1] The drive against Communism in France led on 5 February to a search by the police of the premises of the Soviet Trade Delegation and Soviet travel agency in Paris. This produced a sharp protest from the Soviet Ambassador, Suritz, who immediately afterwards returned to Moscow for a short time. Some time after his return to France, the Soviet Government was informed (on 19 March) that Suritz had become *persona non grata*, as the result of a congratulatory telegram he had sent to Moscow on the conclusion of the Finnish Peace, in which he had talked of the collapse of the plans of the 'Anglo-French' warmongers. In its reply on 26 March, the Soviet Government declared that it saw no justification for the French complaint but agreed to withdraw the Ambassador, who left on 1 April and was not replaced.[2]

This deterioration in relations with the Western Powers was a principal theme of the speech made by Molotov at a session of the Supreme Soviet on 29 March 1940—a speech which may be taken as marking the end of the first phase in the wartime foreign policy of the Soviet Union.

The hostility which Great Britain and France had shown towards the Soviet Union was attributed by Molotov to the Soviet Union's refusal to become an abettor of France and Great Britain in their 'imperialist policy towards Germany'. They had thus demonstrated how profound were 'the class roots of the hostile policy of the imperialists towards the Socialist State'. The only comfort to be drawn by the Allies was Molotov's assertion that the basis of the peace with Finland was that it properly ensured 'the safety of Leningrad and of Murmansk and the Murmansk railway'. For it could hardly be overlooked that the Murmansk railway had originally been built to link Russia with the Western Powers in an earlier war and that, whatever use the Germans might be making of it at the time, Murmansk was a port for communication with the West and not with Central Europe.

[1] The Soviet-Finnish Treaty was the proximate cause of the fall of the Daladier Government, and the assumption of the premiership by Reynaud on 21 March.

[2] Dallin, *Foreign Policy*, pp. 171–2. In his speech on 29 March Molotov declared that this had been done in order to show that the Soviet Union was 'no more interested in relations between the two countries' than was France.

In defining the general policy of the Soviet Union with regard to the war, Molotov was content to reiterate its unswerving adherence to the policy of neutrality proclaimed at the outset. Relations with Germany itself were treated rather laconically:

'A radical change for the better in the relations between the Soviet Union and Germany found its expression in the Non-Aggression Pact signed last August. These new, good relations between the U.S.S.R. and Germany have been tested in practice in connexion with events in former Poland and their strength has been sufficiently proved. The development of economic relations which was envisaged even then, last autumn, found concrete expression already in the August 1939 Trade Agreement, and subsequently in the February 1940 Trade Agreement. Trade between Germany and the U.S.S.R. began to increase on the basis of mutual economic advantage and there is ground for its further development.'[1]

The remainder of the speech was largely devoted to presenting the Soviet view of the Finnish War and of its international repercussions:

'What was going on in Finland was not merely our collision with Finnish troops. It was a collision with the combined forces of a number of imperialist States most hostile towards the Soviet Union. By smashing these combined forces of our enemies the Red Army and the Red Fleet have added another glorious page to their history, and have shown that the springs of valour, self-sacrifice, and heroism among our people are inexhaustible.'

For the future, the most significant passage was that in which Molotov dealt with Roumania:

'Of the southern neighbouring States . . . Roumania is one with whom we have no Pact of Non-aggression. This is due to the existence of an unsettled dispute, the question of Bessarabia, whose seizure by Roumania the Soviet Union has never recognized although we have never raised the question of recovering Bessarabia by military means. Hence there are no grounds for deterioration in Soviet-Roumanian relations.'

[1] The Germans seem to have thought the moment perhaps propitious for a further attempt at a general clarification of German-Soviet relations. Ribbentrop had during his own visit to Moscow issued an invitation to Molotov and Stalin to visit Berlin, and Schulenburg had obtained from Molotov on 17 October, 1939 an acceptance in principle. Ribbentrop discussed the project during his visit to Rome on 10–11 March and on 28 March telegraphed to Schulenburg for his opinion. Replying on the 30th, Schulenburg pointed to the accent on neutrality in Molotov's speech as evidence for his view that the Russians would be unlikely now to take so meaningful a step. The matter was dropped for the time being. *Nazi-Soviet Relations*, pp. 134–7.

The fact that the Soviet Government was still only represented at Bucarest by a Chargé d'Affaires was explained by the Butenko affair. But the verbal reassurances which were thus conveyed did not counterbalance the fact that the Bessarabian issue had now been raised officially, and confirms that the Soviet Union was definitely preparing to secure a remodelling in its favour of existing arrangements in the Balkans.

Towards the end of his speech, Molotov touched briefly on relations with Japan. These had on the whole shown some improvement since the Nomonhan truce. On 6 November a new Soviet Ambassador, Smetanin, had arrived in Tokyo, where the Soviet Embassy had been in charge of a mere Secretary since Slavutsky's departure in June 1938.[1]

'In our relations with Japan,' declared Molotov, 'we have, not without some difficulty, settled several questions. This is evidenced by the conclusion on 31 December last (1939) of the Soviet-Japanese Fisheries Convention for the current year, and also by Japan's consent to pay the last instalment for the Chinese Eastern Railway which had long been overdue.[2] Nevertheless we cannot express great satisfaction in regard to our relations with Japan. To this day, for example, notwithstanding the prolonged negotiations between the Soviet-Mongolian and Japan-Manchurian delegates, the important question of determining the frontier line on the territory in the area of the military conflict of last year has remained unsettled.'[3]

After referring to other outstanding elements of friction, Molotov ended this part of his speech by mentioning a proposal made in the Japanese Diet that conflicts between Japan and the U.S.S.R. might be ended once and for all by Japan's purchasing the Maritime Province and other eastern territories. 'If, however,' declared Molotov, 'the Japanese Parliament is so keen on trading, why should not its members raise the question of selling South Sakhalin? I have no doubt that purchasers would be found in the U.S.S.R.'

It may be assumed that this remark was not uncalculated. Japan, with its maturing plans for an attack on the Western

---

[1] The Japanese Government had been trying to use the idea of a *rapprochement* with the U.S.S.R. as a diplomatic weapon to secure concessions from the U.S.A. Memorandum by Sumner Welles, 24 November 1939. *Foreign Relations of the United States: Japan, 1931–41*, vol. 2, pp. 36–9; cf. ibid., p. 44.

[2] Cf. Moore, op. cit., pp. 115–16, 119, 140.

[3] The discussions of the border commission set up after the Nomonhan fighting broke down on 31 January 1940. They were subsequently resumed and an agreement was reached on 9 June 1940. *Problems of the Pacific, 1939*, ed. W. L. Holland and K. Mitchell (New York, I.P.R., 1940), p. 91. Cf. Buss, *War and Diplomacy in Eastern Asia*, pp. 248–52.

Powers' Pacific domains, required assurances from the Soviet Union as to its neutrality in that event, no less than the Soviet Union required assurances from Japan that its Far Eastern territories would be secure while the European emergency lasted. There was clearly to be some hard bargaining before the terms of such an understanding were arrived at.[1]

Soviet relations with China did not form part of Molotov's theme. Soviet assistance to China continued even after the outbreak of the European War.[2] From 1940, the pressure on Soviet resources exerted by the new home defence programme seems to have been felt in China. One result was the withdrawal of Russian technical personnel from the Chinese North-West.[3] In Sinkiang, on the other hand, Soviet influence continued to predominate, although the extent of this was difficult to determine in view of the Soviet control of all the facilities for entering the country, of air and road transport, and the denial of passage to almost all non-Russian foreigners. There was certainly considerable Soviet participation in the economic development of the country and as late as 1941, the Soviet Government advanced the Sinkiang administration a loan of 15 million roubles for developing industry and transport and for stabilizing the currency.[4]

In so far as Soviet influence in China proper was connected with the national status of the Chinese Communist Party, it suffered a series of setbacks from the autumn of 1939 onwards.

The Soviet-German pact provided for the Chinese Communists, as for Communists elsewhere, a test of morale from which they emerged triumphant. Their leader Mao Tse-tung declared in an interview that outside the borders of the capitalist world there existed another, a bright world—the Soviet Union. The Soviet-German pact had raised the international significance of the U.S.S.R.[5]

Kuomintang spokesmen, however, sharply criticized the arguments now put forward and the conclusions as to future

[1] In March 1940, the Emperor approved a plan of campaign against Russia drawn up by the Japanese General Staff; 'Tokyo War Guilt Trial', *The Times*, 10 March 1947.

[2] Moore, op. cit., p. 118.

[3] Hogg, *I see a New China*, pp. 146-9. Soviet influence in this area was still very marked at the end of 1939 when the Russians were stationed all along the North-west Highway and had an air-base at Lanchow. See F. T. Durdin's dispatch from Chungking, dated 30 November 1939, in *New York Times*, 2 January 1940.

[4] See the articles 'Chinese Routes of Supply from Abroad', and 'China and Soviet Russia in Sinkiang', *B.I.N.*, 19 October, 16 November 1940. Cf. M. R. Norins, *Gateway to Asia: Sinkiang* (New York, John Day, 1944).

[5] Dallin, *The Big Three*, pp. 173-4.

action drawn at this juncture by Mao Tse-tung and his associates, namely that China's foreign policy should be orientated towards the U.S.S.R., and even 'approach Germany'. While they expressed incredulity as to the possibility of a serious *rapprochement* between the Russians and the Japanese, they knew that such was indeed Germany's plan and stressed the need for caution. If this did come off, where would the Communists stand? Would they stick to the 'Communist' in their party's title and join Wang Ching-wei or 'stick to the word "Chinese" and cancel the word "Communism"?'[1] Some justification for this sharp comment was to be found in Mao's interview with Edgar Snow, published in the *China Weekly Review* in January 1940. He then, it would seem, 'asserted that the Chinese Communist Party was not reformist but revolutionary', and that the continuance of Russian aid to China would depend on whether China 'co-operated closely with the Soviet Union'.[2] When questioned as to whether Soviet aid to China might take the form of the aid given to the subjects of the Polish State, Mao replied that such a possibility existed.[3]

The political differences between the Kuomintang and the Chinese Communist Party had already led to armed clashes in the summer of 1939 and these became more frequent from about October 1939. National troops would seem to have begun what amounted to a real armed blockade of the Special Area. In November 1939 fairly severe clashes occurred between the Kuomintang and the Communist forces; these continued into the following year, when clashes also took place on the Shensi-Kansu border, in Hunan and with the Border Government's force.[4] At this time the Communist Party was believed to control North Shensi and an area between the Yellow River and Inner Mongolia, including part of Shantung (The latter, the area under the Border Government, with its three Communist members, was said to have twelve million inhabitants.) At this time the Eighth Route Army itself consisted of only three

---

[1] Chen Kuo-hsiu, 'A Discussion of Mao Tse-tung's Comments on the Present State of International Relations', translated in Linebarger, *The China of Chiang Kai-shek*, pp. 403–17. For contemporary discussion from differing points of view of the new situation, see the articles under the general title 'The Asiatic Aspects of the War in Europe', *Asia*, March 1940.

[2] Cf. the analysis of Mao Tse-tung, *The New Democracy* (Yenan, 1940) in White and Jacoby, *Thunder Out of China*, pp. 220 ff.

[3] Quoted by F. Utley, 'Will Russia betray China?' *Asia*, April 1941.

[4] *China and Japan* (R.I.I.A. 3rd ed.), pp. 14–15; H. S. Quigley, *The Far Eastern War, 1937–41* (Boston, World Peace Foundation, 1942), pp. 110–12. G. E. Taylor, *The Struggle for North China* (New York, I.P.R., 1940), p. 163; Carlson, *The Chinese Army*, p. 82.

divisions, and the bulk of these men were new recruits from all over China; but the partisan groups which it had trained were reckoned as being ten times as numerous. In addition their prospects in the event of a real trial of strength were affected by the possibility that some Kuomintang troops would prove unreliable against them.[1]

There does not seem to have been any leftward swing in the internal policy of the Special or Border Areas to account for the worsening of relationships between these and the central authority. The priority of peasant rights was recognized and no measures of socialization seem to have been undertaken.

At a slightly later date the Communists were reported as upholding internal free trade against government control and the monopoly of the co-operatives.[2] Nevertheless the future of the United Front was, by the spring of 1940, not held to be over-bright. It was still true that 'its first condition was the post-ponement of all major changes in the social structure', but in view of China's continued dependence on Russia for supplies, much seemed to depend on whether Russia would continue loyally to accept the principle of non-intervention in China's internal affairs, or rather continue to interpret this as demand-ing that the Comintern discourage the Chinese Communists from pursuing their social aims. On 10 June a further step in the Russo-Japanese *rapprochement* seemed to have been reached in the Mongolian-Manchukuoan frontier agreement, but on the 16th of the same month the Soviet Union extended to China a credit for the purchase of supplies. Russian supplies for Chung-king were given new importance by the French closure of the Yunnan route in June, the closing of the Burma Road from July to October, and the tripartite Axis pact in September. It is possible too that Chiang feared 'Anglo-American "appease-ment" efforts . . . to lure Japan from the Axis at the expense of China.'[3] One result may have been the new agreement arrived at in July between Chiang and the Communists.[4]

The newly restored harmony was not, however, of long duration. In October the New Fourth Army was ordered to

[1] Carlson, op. cit., pp. 22–3; Taylor, op. cit., pp. 100–1.

[2] Hsu Tung-ying, 'Critics of Economic Control in China', *Pacific Affairs*, June 1942.

[3] E. Snow, 'Is it Civil War in China?', *Asia*, April 1941. Cf. his article in *Pacific Affairs*, June 1941.

[4] *China and Japan*, p. 15. A Japanese interpretation of the situation was that Russia had two policies, both of them anti-Japanese. One was to supply Chungking. The other was to use the North-West as a base for the Sovietization of China. Saburo Okazaki, 'Moscow, Yenan, Chungking', *Kaizo* (Tokyo), 2 November 1940; translated in *Pacific Affairs*, March 1941.

leave its position south of the Yangtse and to retire northwards. In spite of the fact that the move had apparently begun by December, the Army was declared to have defied the order and in January 1941 its rear column was attacked in southern Anwhei.[1] The Army was thereupon officially declared to have been disbanded; this order was certainly ineffective and not long afterwards the Army's new northern Kiangsu head-quarters claimed to have 150,000 men at its orders.[2]

From the point of view of the Communists things were not going well. Chou En-lai in an interview in February 1941 declared that the position was unsatisfactory, that fighting was going on in several ways, and that there existed the possibility of a general civil war.[3] At the capital, the Communist daily paper was being subjected to serious interference, and in the circumstances the Communists would not attend the next session of the People's Political Council.[4] On the other hand, Chou gave no countenance to Mao's hint of the previous year that a Soviet China might break away from China and join the U.S.S.R. 'I asked Chou how it was possible to answer those who claimed that in the Far East the Soviet Union had certain territorial objectives. Chou said that as far as the Chinese Communists were concerned the Border Regions in the North West had no contact with Mongolia and Sinkiang, and that the direction towards which the Communist forces moved was eastward and southward into Japanese-occupied areas—not further west. Communists, moreover, were primarily concerned with being constantly on the move against Japan rather than in setting up a permanent base.' They had received no aid from the Soviet Government.

The Communists submitted a series of demands to the People's Political Council for its March session. The demands included the reconstruction of the New Fourth Army and the release of its commander General Yeh Ting, who had been wounded and imprisoned, the punishment of the generals who

---

[1] A Communist Party declaration of 26 February 1941 gave its version of these events and put forward the Party's political demands. Quoted by Rosinger, *China's Wartime Politics*, pp. 111–14. Cf. *Strany Tikhovo Okeana* (Countries of the Pacific) (Moscow 1942). For a description of the Communist-controlled areas of China at this time see *Oriental Affairs*, January 1941.

[2] E. Snow, *Asia*, April 1941, pp. 168–9. 'Asiaticus', 'The New Fourth Army Area Revisited', *Amerasia*, September 1941.

[3] The interview was described in a dispatch by R. W. Barnett, printed in *Amerasia*, May 1941.

[4] For the constitution and role of this body, see Linebarger, op. cit., pp. 69–70.

had attacked it, and the abolition of the Kuomintang 'one party dictatorship'. The seven Communist members of the Council refused to attend unless these demands were granted.[1] They were actually rejected, and with some violence of expression, in a speech by Chiang Kai-shek on 6 March 1941. He compared the demands of the Communists to those of the Japanese militarists before July 1937, and likened the Border Governments to the Nanking and Manchukuoan puppet régimes.[2] After these sallies, reports of further friction were not surprising, but some observers believed that the leaders on both sides were still anxious to avoid a real civil war. And it was also clear that the Communist position was still a formidable one.[3] There is, however, no evidence that the Chinese Communists were in receipt of any material aid from the Soviet Union.

[1] *China and Japan*, p. 15.
[2] Text in Rosinger, op. cit., pp. 115–21. Cf. 'Asiaticus', 'China's Internal Friction aids Japan', *Amerasia*, May 1941.
[3] H. Deane, 'Political Reaction in Kuomintang China', *Amerasia*, 8 July 1941. Cf. White and Jacoby, op. cit., pp. 77–9 and *passim*.

Chapter Thirteen

THE SOVIET UNION AND THE WAR IN THE WEST:
APRIL TO NOVEMBER 1940

THE months of April, May, and June 1940 which saw the German conquest of most of Western Europe, put a new complexion upon Soviet-German relations. Instead of a divided 'capitalist' Europe weakening itself by internecine strife, the Soviet Union now saw before it a single Great Power controlling the larger part of Europe's resources and with the prospect, if Britain too should fall, of being able to throw all those resources into a campaign for *lebensraum* in the East. The speed with which the Soviet Union gathered in the remaining fruits of the partition agreements of August-September 1939, and the rigorous measures for increasing industrial productivity, were suggestive of Moscow's alarm at the new turn of events, and of a far from passive reaction to them.

Once the territorial gains had been consolidated, the policy of the Soviet Government again appeared to be wholly defensive, but the internal tension was not relaxed. Although Soviet economic aid for Germany was still forthcoming, the acute hostility earlier shown towards Great Britain was slightly moderated in favour of a more genuine neutrality. Soviet encouragement to Britain to continue resistance was given, although with caution.[1] Germany tried to secure a free hand in the Danube basin and the Balkans by offering the Soviet Union support for any plans of expansion in the Middle East.[2] The Soviet Government, however, did its best to insist on participation in all matters concerning eastern Europe, and, where this failed, to preserve for the time being at least the impression that it was being consulted by Germany before decisions were taken. Meanwhile it gave more or less veiled encouragement to such forces in the Balkans as might seem likely to oppose the establishment of complete German domination in that area. On the other hand, just as Germany tried to

[1] M. Maisky's expressions of confidence in Great Britain's ability to stand alone after the fall of France are undoubtedly to be interpreted in this light. See, e.g., the account of his attitude in Bilainkin, *Maisky*, pp. 311 ff.
[2] See German naval file on Russo-German relations, under the date 26 September, where it is stated that Germany's campaign in the Near East is to bring Turkey into her power while Russia is to be directed towards Persia and India; *Nazi Conspiracy and Aggression*, vol. 6, p. 988.

divert Soviet attention towards areas in which its own interests were secondary, so the Soviet Government in its turn tried to divert Japanese aggression from its own frontiers towards the gleaming prizes of the South Seas. Finally, the accent on Soviet preparedness was still further marked by a variety of measures in the military, economic, and social fields.

These developments, whose full significance only became apparent in the period between the French armistice on 22 June 1940 and Molotov's visit to Berlin on 12–14 November 1940, had to some extent been foreshadowed by scarcely concealed Soviet-German friction as early as March 1940.[1] Molotov's speech of 29 March 1940, coming together with other indications of the Soviet Union's increasing interest in the Balkans, was not very cordially received in Berlin. There was also some anxiety at the renewal of contacts between Maisky and the British Foreign Office after the interlude of the Finnish War.[2] The Soviet Government was clearly averse to being drawn into open conflict with the Western Powers.[3] But with France as yet unconquered, the basis for general co-operation with Germany still existed. It was the specific question of the Balkans which was the more serious, particularly in view of the approaching full belligerency of Germany's Italian ally, which had a Balkan policy of its own.

In a dispatch from Moscow on 4 June, Schulenburg made known that Molotov had indicated that he hoped that Balkan problems would be solved peacefully by collaboration between the U.S.S.R., Germany and Italy.[4]

In the period before the fall of France there were two episodes of some importance from this point of view—the beginning of

[1] When Ciano saw Sumner Welles on 19 March, the day after Mussolini's meeting with Hitler on the Brenner pass, he said that he had gained the impression that Hitler expected to use the agreement with Russia for his own purposes and then to turn against her and recover German positions in Finland and the Baltic States. Sumner Welles, *A Time for Decision*, p. 115.

[2] Maisky called on Halifax on 27 March, the main subject of discussion being the detention in the Pacific of two Soviet ships on the suspicion that they might ultimately be destined for Germany. The Soviet view, which the British Government refused to accept, was that Soviet merchant shipping being state-owned was not subject to contraband control.

[3] The following note appears in the German naval file under the date 5 April 1940: 'Temporary limitations in the use of "Base North" and Molotov's attitude of refusal in the question of the use of a Far Eastern base are to be traced to present Russian nervousness because of the future position of England and France towards Russia.' *Nazi Conspiracy and Aggression*, vol. 6, p. 983.

[4] *Nazi-Soviet Relations*, p. 144, 148

contacts between the Soviet Union and Yugoslavia, and the demonstration of the Soviet Union's interest in the future of the Danube and its delta.

As has been seen, Yugoslavia alone of the Slav countries had hitherto abstained from entering into relations with the Soviet Union. Nevertheless, sympathies for Russia remained strong in the people, and it has been suggested that at Belgrade (as at Sofia) the Government feared that the establishment of a Russian mission would create a focus for these feelings and so endanger the prestige of the régime.[1]

In the spring of 1940, Axis pressure on Yugoslavia brought about a change.[2] Negotiations apparently began in Ankara at the end of March. On 20 April *Izvestia* reported that it was the Yugoslav Government which had taken the initiative and that the matter was one for the Commissar for Foreign Trade. On the following day, the Yugoslav Minister of Finance, Grigorevic, left Belgrade for Moscow. The Soviet Government continued to stress the purely economic nature of the talks and on 10 May issued a denial that Soviet aid had been promised in the event of Yugoslavia being attacked. On 11 May a series of economic agreements was signed. The text of the trade treaty, which was published on 26 May, showed that the trade delegations were to have diplomatic immunity, and their premises extra-territorial status. Meanwhile, Lavrentiev, the Soviet Minister to Bulgaria, had visited Belgrade, and there were hints from Moscow that the Soviet Union would look favourably on attempts by Turkey, Bulgaria, and Yugoslavia to resist Italian penetration of the Balkans.[3] On 6 June, four days before Italy's entry into the war, Moscow radio made the following announcement:

'The Soviet Government has made it unequivocally clear to Italy that it will not remain passive in the face of a threat to the Balkans. The foreign policy of Soviet Russia is based upon a sincere desire to maintain peace, and also upon the fact that the independence of certain states is a vital condition for Soviet security. The Italian Government would do well to take this warning into account.'[4]

---

[1] A. Mousset, *Le Monde Slave*, pp. 92–8.

[2] Dallin, *Foreign Policy*, pp. 202–6.

[3] On 18 May the German Foreign Office opposed a plan for the use of German auxiliary cruisers in the Black Sea in deference to the susceptibilities of Russia and other Black Sea Powers. *Nazi Conspiracy and Aggression*, vol. 6, p. 983.

[4] Dallin, *Foreign Policy*, pp. 209–11. Germany seems to have been trying at this juncture to bring about better relations between the U.S.S.R. and Italy and on 20 May suggested that she should mediate between them. On 8 June an agreement was concluded for the return of the Italian Ambassador Rosso to Moscow. *Ciano Diaries*, pp. 230, 242, 253, 262.

On 25 June, Molotov discussed with the Italian Ambassador, Rosso, the Soviet desire to have relations with Italy placed on the same basis as those with Germany. After discussing the Bessarabian question and the claims of Hungary and Bulgaria on Roumania which the Russians considered largely justified, and also the menacing attitude (in the Russian view) of Turkey, Molotov suggested as a basis for such an agreement that Italy should recognize Soviet hegemony in the Black Sea, and the U.S.S.R. Italian hegemony in the Mediterranean.[1]

The events of June hastened on *rapprochement* with Yugoslavia and on the 24th the resumption of diplomatic relations was announced. Milan Gavrilovic, leader of the Serb Agrarian Party, was sent to Moscow as Minister. Dr. Gavrilovic arrived in Moscow early in July 1940. After a short talk with Kalinin and a long conversation with Molotov and a general survey of the position he wrote to his government that there must have been a written agreement between the U.S.S.R. and Germany covering spheres of influence in the whole area from the Baltic to the Straits. In Dr. Gavrilovic's view, the Russians wanted the Yugoslavs to resist the Germans and would help them with war material and underground propaganda. But the U.S.S.R. would not at any price declare war on Germany. The agreement of 1939 might have appeared to Hitler as a renunciation of the Balkans on Russia's part; by encouraging the Balkan States to resist German pressure in 1940, she tried to give these States the impression that such was not the case. The impression formed by members of the Yugoslav Foreign Office as a result of their conversations with V. Plotnikov, the new Soviet Minister, who had formerly been posted at Oslo, was that the Soviet Government had not abandoned the Balkans to Germany.[2]

At the outbreak of war in September 1939, formal authority on the Danube was still divided between two international bodies.[3] Control of traffic on the 'maritime Danube', between Braila and the sea, was in the hands of the European Danube Commission set up in 1856 by the Treaty of Paris. Since the

---

[1] *Nazi-Soviet Relations*, pp. 160–1.

[2] See the two anonymous articles 'Le Coup d'Etat de Simovich' in *La France Intérieure*, September–October 1945. On the other hand it has been stated that the (underground) Yugoslav Communist Party continued to propagate the orthodox Communist doctrine of indifference towards the outcome of the war in the West. 'The Yugoslav Political Situation', *The World To-day*, January 1946. In the middle of July 1940, German official quarters were commenting on the increase of Soviet influence in Yugoslavia and on the evident Soviet desire for closer relations with Bulgaria; *Nazi Conspiracy and Aggression*, vol. 6, p. 985.

[3] 'The Germans on the Lower Danube', *B.I.N.*, 19 October 1940. Cf. 'Control of the Danube', *The Times*, 5 July 1946; Gafencu, *Prelude*, pp. 66–8.

Russian Revolution, the Commission, which sat at Galatz, had been composed of representatives of Great Britain, France, Italy, and Roumania; Germany had been added in May 1939. The Commission's rights had been limited in favour of Roumania at the Sinaia Conference in September 1938. The 'fluvial Danube', from Braila upstream to Ulm, had been subject to the technical regulation of the International Danube Commission set up in 1920, and composed of the riparian States, together with Great Britain, France, and Italy.

On 16 February, with the Danube playing an increasingly important role in Germany's supply system, the European Commission met at Galatz. It then became known that the Soviet Government was demanding representation on the Commission, as it had done as early as 1925. On 19 May *Izvestia* announced that Molotov had raised the question officially. On this occasion there was no evidence of German support for the idea. A month earlier, on 17 April, the executive committee of the International Commission, meeting at Belgrade, announced restrictions on the use of the river for the transport of warlike materials and a scheme of policing by the only four riparian States now represented on the Commission: Hungary, Yugoslavia, Roumania, and Bulgaria. On 23 May this scheme was extended to the maritime Danube. From the point of view of the Danube route, as well as because of the claims raised by the Soviet Union to Bessarabia, and by Bulgaria to the Dobrudja, Roumania continued to be subjected to considerable pressure.[1] As late as 19 April the Roumanian Government still envisaged resistance in case of German or Soviet aggression, direct or indirect. The military disasters of the Western Powers in May removed the basis for a policy of this kind, and on 29 May a Crown Council decided to abandon neutrality and to accept German protection against the threat from Soviet Russia.[2]

Events in northern Europe seemed for the time being of less interest to the Soviet Government.[3] When Germany invaded Denmark and Norway on 9 April, Soviet press comment suggested that British and French violations of Norway's neutrality

---

[1] 'Special Problems of Roumania', *B.I.N.*, 1 June 1940.

[2] Gafencu, *Prelude*, pp. 279–87. Gafencu resigned as Foreign Minister on 1 June.

[3] After the signing of the new German-Soviet trade agreement on 11 February 1940, it was suggested in German naval quarters that the demarcation line laid down for German naval operations in the Baltic might be shifted, but Hitler would not allow the Russians to be pressed on this point. *Nazi Conspiracy and Aggression*, vol. 6, pp. 982–3.

were responsible for spreading the area of the conflict.[1] The
Soviet Government had only been informed by the Germans of
this action and their reasons for it on the day it began. According to Schulenburg, the result of the German move was a
very happy one for Soviet-German relations which had recently
shown signs of strain. Schulenburg attributed this to the relief
of the U.S.S.R. at the thought that there was now no chance
of the Western Powers intervening in the Baltic, with the
possible result of bringing the U.S.S.R. into the war through
a re-opening of the Finnish question.[2] There is no known
evidence to support Schulenburg's view that the Russians
genuinely expected an Anglo-French invasion of Norway and
Sweden. The position of Sweden was however, an obvious
matter of concern and the Soviet desire to see its neutrality
preserved was made clear to Schulenburg by Molotov on 13
April. German assurances on this point, already given on
9 April, were repeated almost at once.[3] On 3 May a Tass
communiqué announced that it was the view of both Germany
and the Soviet Union that their mutual interests required the
neutrality of Sweden. On 11 May Moscow radio stated:
'Soviet Russia has saved Sweden from war. The Soviets have
erected a barrier against the spread of the war to the east of
Europe.'[4]

On 21 May the German Ambassador in Moscow could find
no sign of uneasiness over the German victory.[5]

On the other hand, the moment seemed opportune to the
British Government for another attempt to end the existing
tension in Anglo-Soviet relations. On 19 April 1940 Halifax
informed Maisky that the British Government was prepared to

[1] This accusation was repeated in the Comintern May-Day proclamation. In the Western world the Communist Parties maintained this line to
the end. In Denmark, for instance, the Communist Party did not join the
resistance movement until after Russia had been attacked. H. H. Fisher,
America and Russia in the World Community (Claremont College, California,
1946), p. 83. M. Daladier showed in a speech before the French Constituent Assembly on 18 July 1946, that the same was true of the French Communist Party. Cf. Reynaud, *La France a sauvé l'Europe*, vol. 2, pp. 407 ff.
In Washington, a Communist-sponsored demonstration against American
aid to Britain took place a few hours before the German attack on Russia.
Smith, *America and the Axis War*, p. 297.

[2] *Nazi-Soviet Relations*, pp. 137–140.

[3] *Nazi-Soviet Relations*, pp. 140–1. It had been suggested in some German
quarters that the Russians be allowed to occupy Tromsoe, but this was
vetoed by Hitler. *Nazi Conspiracy and Aggression*, vol. 6, p. 283.

[4] Dallin, *Foreign Policy*, p. 209. On 14 May a Swedish trade delegation
arrived in Moscow and a new agreement was signed on 7 September.

[5] *Nazi Conspiracy and Aggression*, vol. 6, p. 983.

explore the possible basis of a new trade agreement which should take into account the exigencies of the war. A Soviet note in reply was sent on 29 April. According to a presumably well-informed source, its contents amounted to the following:

'. . . (1) A denial that the U.S.S.R. was supplying Germany with foreign goods imported by the former; Soviet imports were exclusively for her own use. The increased importation of metals from the United States and other countries via Vladivostok was due to the fact that before the war these were purchased on the British market and imported via European ports, which had now, of course, become impossible, and to the increased Soviet need for these metals. (2) The Soviet Government was prepared to discuss guarantees that British products imported into the U.S.S.R. would not go to Germany. (3) They were also prepared to discuss Soviet trade with neutrals. (4) They absolutely refused any discussion as to what they would or would not do with their own products.'[1]

This reply was regarded as unsatisfactory in London, and a new British memorandum was sent on 8 May, two days before the new British Government under Winston Churchill assumed office. As the situation of the Western Powers grew more critical, there was increasing pressure on the British Government from many sides to take more active steps towards a *rapprochement* with the Soviet Union. The latter's reply to the British memorandum sent on 20 May was not encouraging. The Soviet Government did not, it was stated, consider it possible to subordinate questions of trade to the military requirements of other countries. The Soviet Union would continue to trade with belligerents and neutrals on the principle of equality and would not discuss with Great Britain questions of Soviet-German trade.[2]

The effort to renew contact was not abandoned on the British side. On 23 May the British Government informed the Soviet Government that Sir William Seeds, who had left Moscow after the outbreak of the Finnish War, would not be returning to his post, and inquired whether the U.S.S.R. would be prepared to receive Sir Stafford Cripps as special envoy. On 27 May Sir Stafford Cripps set out for Moscow. On 29 May, however, it was made known that his proposed status as special trade delegate was unacceptable to the Russians. On 5 June, therefore, he was formally nominated as Ambassador and in this capacity he arrived in Moscow on 12 June.[3] Owing to further

[1] Coates, *A History of Anglo-Soviet Relations*, p. 638.

[2] Cf. Schulenburg's dispatch of 29 May, *Nazi-Soviet Relations*, pp. 142–3.

[3] On 5 June 1940 the Soviet Government accepted the nomination of M. Erik Labonne as French Ambassador. He arrived on the same plane as Sir Stafford Cripps, and had an interview with Molotov on 16 June. M. Labonne presented his credentials to Stalin on 22 June, the day of the Franco-German armistice. Reynaud, op. cit., vol. 2, pp. 333–4.

difficulties, his credentials did not reach him until 21 June, and not until 28 June did he finally present them to Kalinin. On 1 July Sir Stafford Cripps was received by Stalin, although news of this was not released until the 17th of that month.[1]

The re-establishment of Anglo-Soviet contacts coincided with the crisis in Great Britain's fortunes following the French armistice. The German intentions were not communicated in advance to the Russians.[2] The Soviet Government, to judge by Russian press and radio comment, had followed the course of the campaign in the West with surprise and consternation.[3] For a short while, according to some foreign observers, it was apparently thought possible in Moscow that the German victory might be followed by an immediate attack upon Russia. As shown by the German naval archives, these anxieties were evident to the Germans as well. In June 1940 neither *Izvestia* nor *Pravda* published a single leading article on the war; and through the subsequent months press comment upon the general situation was very scanty.[4]

In so far as a general line could be deduced from the Soviet press, it would seem to have been a dual one. On the one hand the hopes placed on Great Britain's survival were shown by the increasingly appreciative comment on the achievements of the R.A.F. On the other hand there was obviously a strong desire to propitiate Germany. This was manifest, first, in direct assurances that Soviet action in eastern Europe was not to be

[1] The Germans were given an account of the talk on the 13th. Stalin had declared that he saw no danger of a German hegemony in Europe. He was prepared to trade with Great Britain, but not to allow Great Britain to interfere with the Soviet Union's right to trade with others. The Soviet Union was opposed to a single Power controlling the Balkans, to the exclusive domination of the Straits by Turkey, and to that Power's dictation of terms in the Black Sea. *Nazi-Soviet Relations*, pp. 167–8.

[2] *Nazi-Soviet Relations*, pp. 141–2.

[3] By 5 June the Germans were noticing Russian fears of an immediate German attack. *Nazi Conspiracy and Aggression*, vol. 6, p. 984. On 14 June, the Germans noted a report from Stockholm that the Soviet Minister there, Alexandra Kollontai, had told the Belgian Minister there recently that it was in the common interest of European powers to place themselves in opposition to German imperialism. Schulenburg was instructed to raise the matter tactfully with Molotov. *Nazi-Soviet Relations*, p. 147. On their side, the Germans took care to avoid Soviet distrust by forbidding Ukrainian organisations such as that of Skoropadsky to carry on political activity in Germany or German-occupied territories. ibid., p. 145.

[4] The previously publicized plans for cultural exchanges with Germany were dropped in June. It is said that work was stopped on waterways between German Poland and the Bug and Dnieper, and that contacts with German missions in Russia were cut down. Davis and Lindley, *How War Came*, p. 164.

interpreted by the Germans or anyone else as due to Soviet suspicions of Germany, and second, by the direct attacks upon the Western Powers for which the Soviet press still occasionally found room. The most conspicuous of these was the wide publicity given in the Soviet press on 5 July, to the Fifth and Sixth German White Books, and the evidence therein contained of British and French hostility towards the Soviet Union at the time of the Finnish War.[1] Great Britain and France were still reproached for having rejected Hitler's 'peace offer' in October 1939. On the other hand, Hitler's new 'peace offer' in his speech of 19 July 1940 received little comment, since the consequences for the Soviet Union of a peace in the West on Germany's terms were obvious.

The Soviet press continued to stress the permanent importance of the Soviet-German pact and its value to Germany, supporting this with quotations from the German press. In the *Izvestia* leader on the first anniversary of the pact of 23 August, it was emphasized that the pact helped to neutralize the effects of the British blockade. But nothing was said about the new Soviet-German trade negotiations which began on 28 August and there was generally no sign of any attempt to popularize Soviet-German friendship with the Russian people at large.

It was deeds rather than words, perhaps, which spoke in Europe in the summer of 1940. From Soviet action in the Baltic and in south-eastern Europe it may be hazarded that the Soviet Union would have liked to go beyond the partition line laid down in the secret agreement of August 1939, but with limited exceptions forbore from doing so in order not to provoke Germany.

Until after the Finnish War, the situation in the Baltic States had remained stable in spite of the presence of a considerable number of Soviet troops—about 90,000 according to one estimate.[2] On 15 April the Soviet newspaper *Trud* stated that the Soviet Union would aid the Baltic countries in the event of an attack. Unlike the neutrality of the Scandinavians, which had leaned towards the Allies, the neutrality of the Baltic States was real, because their pacts with the Soviet Union guaranteed it.[3]

---

[1] See C. Prince, 'Legal and Economic Factors affecting Russian Foreign Policy', *American Political Science Review*, August–October, 1944.

[2] The events leading up to the annexation of the Baltic States are recounted in detail in Dallin, *Foreign Policy*, pp. 241–59. Cf. *Latvia, 1939–42*.

[3] *B.I.N.*, XVII, p. 518. On the other hand, German official quarters were noting as early as 22 April that Russia's intention to incorporate the border States had become recognizable. *Nazi Conspiracy and Aggression*, vol. 6, p. 983.

The Soviet attitude towards the Baltic States altered with the triumphant progress of Germany's western campaign.

Further Soviet action in this area began on 28 May, when a Soviet note was sent to Lithuania complaining about the alleged kidnapping of Red Army men in Lithuania. A visit of the Lithuanian Prime Minister to Moscow was followed on 15 June by a Soviet ultimatum. This accused the Lithuanian Government of fostering hostility to the Soviet garrisons with a view to attacking them later, and of entering into a military alliance with Latvia and Estonia obviously directed against the Soviet Union. It demanded the arrest and trial of the Lithuanian Minister of the Interior and of the head of the political police, the stationing of Soviet troops in all the major centres of the country and the formation of a new government prepared to work loyally under the provisions of the Soviet-Lithuanian pact of mutual assistance. The occupation was carried out on the same day and a new government was formed on 17 June with the assistance of Dekanozov, the Soviet Assistant Commissar for Foreign Affairs.

The occupation of Lithuania by Soviet troops extended to the area assigned to Germany under the secret agreement of 28 September 1939. Subsequent negotiations with Germany led (as has been seen) to a new frontier agreement (on 10 January 1941) together with an agreement for the exchange of population, presumably covering the repatriation of the 35,000 Germans still said to be in Lithuania at the time of the Soviet occupation.[1]

Similar proceedings with regard to Latvia and Estonia culminated in ultimatums on 16 June 1940. As in the case of Lithuania, both countries immediately complied with the Soviet ultimatum. A new Latvian Government was formed on 20 June and a new Estonian Government on 22 June. The part played in Lithuania by Dekanozov was taken in the other two countries by Vyshinsky and Zhdanov respectively. A memorandum by Schnurre dated 17 June, 1940 pointed out that as a result of secret agreements during the past six months, the Germans were receiving about 70 per cent. of their total exports. These goods—foodstuffs, timber, flax and Estonian shale-oil—were of considerable importance to the German war effort and he feared that the Soviet occupation would endanger their supply. In spite of this however, the Germans

---

[1] On 30 August, the U.S.S.R. vainly protested to Germany about the denial of rights to the Lithuanian Soviet Republic (as it had become) in the Memel Free Port zone. *Nazi-Soviet Relations*, pp. 175–178, 187.

refused to give any encouragement to the idea that they were interesting themselves in the fate of any of those countries.[1]

Conditions in all three Baltic States now resembled each other closely. The establishment of new Governments, democratic and left-wing although non-Communist, the promulgation of radical legislative programmes, the arrest of prominent personalities of the former régimes—those who fled to Germany were interned there—the release of political prisoners, the presence of large contingents of the Red Army—all these helped to create a quasi-revolutionary atmosphere. But the Soviet authorities soon showed that they had no intention of being hustled out of their carefully conceived programme by the enthusiasm of local revolutionary elements.

Within ten days the obnoxious alliances had been annulled and the existing Parliaments dissolved. New elections were held on 14 July. These were on the Soviet model. No party other than the Communist Party was permitted to function, and a single list made up of Communist candidates and of non-Communist sympathizers was put forward under the title of 'The Union of the Toiling People'. The vote recorded for these lists was over 90 per cent in each of the three countries, the number of abstentions and negative votes being lowest in Lithuania and highest in Estonia. On 21 July the newly elected Parliaments petitioned for the incorporation of the Baltic States into the Soviet Union. On 1 August a special session of the Supreme Soviet admitted Lithuania as a Soviet Socialist Republic, adding to it certain territories previously belonging to the White Russian Republic; Latvia was admitted on 5 August and Estonia on 8 August.[2]

At the end of May 1940, the Soviet press had also begun to attack Finland. This was the prelude to Soviet attempts to secure a new agreement which would have replaced British by Soviet interests in the Petsamo nickel mines and divided their output between the Soviet Union and Germany. The Soviet Government also began to show increasing interest in

---

[1] *Nazi-Soviet Relations*, pp. 146–154, 168–173.

[2] Between August 1940 and June 1941 the relations between the Soviet Union and the Baltic States were part of the internal history of the Soviet Union and fall outside the scope of this narrative. It is worth noting that the progress towards the identification of their economies with that of the remainder of the U.S.S.R. was gradual and not complete at the time of the German attack. The agrarian policy involved primarily not collectivization, but the redistribution of the land into small farms. The economic system in the Baltic Republics corresponded roughly to that of Soviet Russia under the N.E.P. R. Schlesinger, *Federalism in Central and Eastern Europe* (Kegan Paul, 1945), pp. 389–90.

the fortunes of pro-Soviet forces in Finland—an interest which developed later in the year to a powerful patronage of the 'Society for Peace and Friendship between Finland and the U.S.S.R.'[1]

Germany seems to have been officially informed of the new moves only at the meeting between Molotov and Schulenburg on 15 June. Care was taken, however, on both sides, to preserve the outward appearance of agreement.[2] Denials were put forth that an excessive number of Soviet troops was concentrated upon the Lithuanian-German border. On 22 June Tass stated that not more than eighteen or twenty Soviet divisions were stationed in the whole Baltic area and that rumours and propaganda would be unable to undermine the good neighbourly relations between Russia and Germany.[3] The efforts of British diplomacy to exploit Russian fears of the possible consequences of the German victories were not assisted by the hostile British attitude to Soviet actions in the Baltic States, and by the British refusal on 13 July to hand over to Soviet banks the gold assets of the Baltic States in London and the impounding of their ships in British ports.[4] On 23 July the Germans were noting Sir Stafford Cripps's failure to split Russia from Germany.[5]

Friction between the Soviet Union and Germany seemed more likely as a result of Balkan developments. The occupation of the Baltic States was rapidly followed by an increase in Soviet pressure on Roumania.[6] Evidence of Soviet preparations to solve the Bessarabian question had been noted by the Germans as early as 24 May, and by 20 June it was reckoned that the Russian entry into Bessarabia was imminent.[7] Meanwhile the German domination of Roumania had become still

---

[1] *Finnish Blue and White Book*, pp. 15–17, 22–8. At the end of July, the Germans were noting Russian pressure on Finland with the object of eventually including it in the Soviet zone; *Nazi Conspiracy and Aggression*, vol. 6, p. 986.

[2] Cf. Hitler's speech before the Reichstag on 17 July 1940 where he indicated that Soviet expansion had not gone beyond its allotted sphere.

[3] *Nazi-Soviet Relations*, pp. 156–7. Schulenburg inferred that Stalin himself was the author of the communiqué. In his proclamation of 22 June 1941 Hitler referred to Molotov's admission that there were 22 divisions in the Baltic States 'in the spring of 1941'. Giving evidence at the Nuremberg trial on 30 March 1946, Ribbentrop said that Hitler was very disturbed after the fall of France by Russian troop concentrations near the East Prussian border, and by a report that the Russian trade delegation was a centre for Communist propaganda in German factories; *Nuremberg Trial*, part 10, p. 196.   [4] Coates, op. cit., p. 644.

[5] *Nazi Conspiracy and Aggression*, vol. 6, pp. 985–6.

[6] For events in Roumania in June-July 1940, see Dallin, *Foreign Policy*, pp. 234–41 and Gafencu, *Prelude*, pp. 288–97.

[7] *Nazi Conspiracy and Aggression*, vol. 6, pp. 983–4.

more marked.[1] On 20 June, Lavrentiev, now appointed to the long vacant post of Soviet Minister, arrived in Bucarest where he made two fruitless efforts to have an audience with the King. The fear that Germany might soon be in a position to frustrate any action may have decided the Soviet Government upon immediate action.

The Soviet intention to annex at once not only Bessarabia but also Bukovina, which had not been included in the secret agreement of 23 August 1939, was first conveyed by Molotov to Schulenburg on 13 June.[2] Instructions to the latter to call attention to this as inimical to German economic interests in Roumania and to the position of the German minorities in the two provinces, were sent on 25 June. Schulenburg also pointed out to Molotov that a renunciation of Bukovina which had never belonged to Russia would substantially facilitate a peaceful solution. Molotov declared that the province was the last missing part of the Ukraine. But on the following day, he told Schulenburg that the Soviet Union had decided to limit its demands to Czernowitz and Northern Bukovina.[3] The Soviet Union proceeded with the knowledge that no German assistance for Roumania would be available.[4] Nor was Italy in a position to make good her claims to be the protector of the Balkans against Bolshevism.[5] By this time Italy had clearly abandoned any hopes of stabilizing the Balkan situation and was contemplating an attack on Yugoslavia as well as on Greece.

On 26 June 1940 at 11 p.m. the Roumanian Minister in Moscow was summoned to the Kremlin and handed a note by

[1] For a first-hand account of German penetration in Roumania and of the reaction there to the Soviet advance see R. G. Waldeck, *Athene Palace: Bucharest* (Faber, 1943).

[2] By the treaty of 17 August 1916 between Roumania and the Entente Powers, the former had been promised the Bukovina as far as the Pruth, with the remainder presumably going to Russia. The Russian Revolution enabled Roumania to upset this arrangement and acquire almost the whole province.

[3] *Nazi-Soviet Relations*, pp. 155–162.

[4] In a despatch on 11 July, Schulenburg gave it as his opinion that the demand for Northern Bukovina had been prompted by Ukrainian circles in the Kremlin whose influence had also been felt during the negotiations on the Polish frontier. *Nazi-Soviet Relations*, pp. 164–5.

[5] Ciano entered the following in his diary under the date 24 June 1940: 'Russia is preparing to attack Roumania. That is what Molotov has told Schulenburg. Germany can do no more than acquiesce, but it is clear that Russian policy is increasingly anti-German. The capital in which there is the greatest amount of conspiracy against German victory is Moscow. The situation appeared quite otherwise when in August and September the

Molotov which took the form of a twenty-four-hours ultimatum for the cession of Bessarabia and Northern Bukovina.[1] The text reminds the Roumanian Government that the U.S.S.R. had

'never acquiesced in the separation of Bessarabian territory—a territory populated mostly by Ukrainians—from the U.S.S.R. Therefore the Government of the U.S.S.R. regards it as necessary and timely and in the interest of justice to begin with Roumania immediate negotiations regarding the return of Bessarabia to the Soviet Union. This question is organically linked with the question of transferring to the Soviet Union the part of Bukovina which, in the composition of the population, is historically and linguistically bound up with the Soviet Ukraine. Such an act would compensate—only to a small degree of course—for the great wrong done to the Soviet Union and to the population of Bessarabia by the twenty-two years of Roumanian domination of Bessarabia. The transfer of these territories to the Soviet Union would thus be an act of justice.'[2]

Upon the ultimatum being transmitted to the Roumanian Government, it appealed to Germany and Italy, both of which strongly urged acceptance. Efforts to give the reply a temporizing character were brushed aside by the Russians on receipt of German assurances that the Roumanian acceptance was unconditional, and a term of three days was fixed for Roumanian evacuation of the disputed provinces.

On 2 August the Moldavian Autonomous Republic, enlarged by the addition of the predominantly Roumanian-speaking districts of Bessarabia, was detached from the Ukraine and formed into the Moldavian S.S.R. Bukovina and the predominantly Ukrainian-speaking districts of Bessarabia were incorporated in the Soviet Ukraine.

In Roumania itself the annexations were a prelude to a further strengthening of the German hold.[3] In the middle of July 1940, a German mission arrived in Galatz to assist in the repatriation of the Germans of the ceded provinces and this

---

Bolsheviks signed pacts with the Nazis. At that time they did not believe in a German triumph. They wanted to push Germany into a conflict and Europe into a crisis because they were thinking of a long and exhausting struggle between the democracies and Hitler. Things have moved fast, and now Moscow is trying to trouble the waters.' *Ciano Diaries*, p. 269.

[1] The line drawn by Molotov included in the territory claimed the district of Hertza in northern Moldavia. The Russians insisted on retaining this additional piece of territory, which gave them direct railway communication from Lvov into Bessarabia via Czernowitz.

[2] The Soviet note was published in Moscow on 28 June 1940. See Map No. 4, *infra*.

[3] Cf. Maitland, *European Dateline*, pp. 120–7.

proved to be the real beginning of the German military occupation of the country.[1]

The session of the Supreme Soviet called to deal with the territorial acquisitions of the summer of 1940 provided Molotov on 1 August with an opportunity to give another survey of the international position.

After pointing out that Great Britain had rejected the proposal to come to terms with Germany contained in Hitler's speech of 19 July, he forecast an intensification of the war between Germany and Italy on the one side and Great Britain assisted by the United States on the other. True to her policy of peace and neutrality, the Soviet Union was not taking part in the war. But the Soviet-German non-aggression pact which had prevented Soviet-German friction during the recent measures on the Soviet western frontiers, had acquired new significance. He repudiated the suggestions abroad that disagreements might arise owing to Soviet fears of the growing German might and noted the recent improvement in relations with Italy.[2]

As a result of the gains of territory from Roumania, 'the frontiers of the Soviet Union', he said, 'have shifted to the west and reached the Danube which, next to the Volga, is the biggest river in Europe and one of the most important commercial routes for a number of European countries'.

In the Baltic, the mutual assistance pacts with Lithuania, Latvia, and Estonia had not led to the hoped for *rapprochement* with these countries because this was 'opposed by the ruling groups of the Baltic countries'. This had made the recent measures necessary. As the result of the affiliation to the Soviet Union of the Baltic countries and of Bessarabia and Northern Bukovina the population of the Soviet Union would be increased by about ten millions, in addition to the thirteen millions in the territories acquired from Poland.

'It should be noted that nineteen-twentieths of this population previously formed part of the population of Soviet Russia, but had been forcibly torn from her by the Western imperialist Powers at a time when Soviet Russia was militarily weak. Now this population has been re-united with the Soviet Union . . . the U.S.S.R. will now be able to speak in the powerful voice in the name of a population of 193,000,000 not counting the natural increase in the population in 1939 and 1940. The fact that the frontier of the Soviet Union will

---

[1] Leigh White, *The Long Balkan Night* (New York, Scribner's, 1940), p. 110.
[2] Molotov, *Soviet Peace Policy*, pp. 71–82.

now be shifted to the Baltic coast is of first-rate importance for our country. At the same time we shall now have ice-free ports in the Baltic of which we stand so much in need.'

A rapid survey of relations with other countries included a warning to Finland that the expected improvement in Soviet-Finnish relations might not materialize if 'certain elements in the Finnish ruling circles' did not cease their 'persecution of elements in Finland' which were 'striving to strengthen the good neighbourly relations with the U.S.S.R.' Satisfaction was expressed with the state of Soviet relations with Yugoslavia and Bulgaria, but both Turkey and Iran came in for some criticism. Relations with Japan had begun to assume a more normal character and relations with China remained friendly.

After criticizing Great Britain and, more forcibly, the United States for their attitude to events in the Baltic, Molotov concluded by another general survey of the world scene and the dangers which it presented of 'a further extension and fanning of the war and of its transformation into a world imperialist war.

'Under these conditions the Soviet Union must enhance her vigilance in regard to external security as well as in regard to strengthening all her positions both at home and abroad. We have introduced an eight-hour working day instead of a seven-hour day and have carried out other measures.' The enhancement of discipline among all the working-people and the raising of the productivity of labour were essential. Finally, quoting Stalin, he repeated: 'We must keep our entire people in a state of mobilization, preparedness in the face of the danger of military attack so that no "accident" and no tricks of our foreign enemies could catch us unawares.'[1]

The emphasis upon preparedness in Molotov's speech more than balanced the complacent enumeration of his country's recent successes, and events in the Balkans in the following

[1] Texts of the following important decrees are given in the Appendix to John Scott, *Duel for Europe*; Decree for the Obligatory Transfer of Workers, 19 October 1940; Decree on the Reintroduction of Tuition Fees in Secondary and Higher Education, 3 October 1940; Decree on the Establishment of State Labour Reserves, 2 October 1940. In addition to the significance of these measures for industrial preparedness, the educational system itself was given a new 'general line' in the shape of emphasis on discipline, production and patriotism. The keynote was struck in a much publicized speech by Kalinin delivered on 2 October and printed in *Pravda* on 30 October. The increase in the hours of labour referred to by Molotov was decided upon by the trade unions and sanctioned by the Praesidium of the Supreme Soviet on 26 June 1940. In the same month the seven-day week replaced the six-day week in all branches of Soviet economy.

weeks were not such as to increase Soviet confidence. Mussolini's wish for a spectacular agreement with Russia as a preparation for an Italian attack on Yugoslavia was frustrated by German opposition.[1] Germany now considered that to her alone, with Italy as a junior partner or satellite, belonged the decision on the future of the Balkans, and Soviet Russia was left to make what little use she could of underground sympathies felt for her on ideological and racial grounds.[2]

The immediate issue was that provided by the claims of Bulgaria and Hungary against Roumania.[3] Roumanian-Bulgarian negotiations for the cession to the latter of the southern Dobrudja began in July; early in August it was openly admitted in Bucarest that some territory would have to be ceded to Hungary and on 16 August negotiations to that end were begun.[4]

Soviet policy showed some hesitancy.[5] At first it appeared as though Russia would favour the cession to Bulgaria of the entire Dobrudja, which would in effect have provided a possible barrier against the German advance to the Black Sea.[6] In mid-August, however, this policy was seemingly reversed in favour of a suggestion that Russia would prefer a friendly and undiminished Roumania, and Balkan Communists began to advocate a new bloc between Yugoslavia, Bulgaria, and Roumania.[7]

Gafencu, who had taken up his new post as Roumanian Minister in Moscow on 10 August, was received by Molotov on 15 August and 'given categorical assurances that the Soviet

[1] *Ciano Diaries*, entries of 6 and 17 August 1940, pp. 281 and 285.

[2] According to some accounts Communist propaganda in the Balkans, especially in Yugoslavia, Greece, and Bulgaria now became anti-German, in spite of the fact that the former line continued to be followed elsewhere. Scott, op. cit., p. 136. On 20 August the German Chief of Naval Operations noted that 'Panslavic Communist Propaganda' was having some success in Yugoslavia and Bulgaria; *Nazi Conspiracy and Aggrssion*, vol. 6, p. 986. On 14 August the Soviet Government informed the Germans that an article in a Latvian Communist paper declaring that German Communists were opposed to the 'Compiégne Dictate' (the armistice with France) had appeared as the result of a misunderstanding. *Nazi-Soviet Relations*, pp. 175–177.

[3] For the following paragraphs, see Dallin, *Foreign Policy*, pp. 260–7; Gafencu, *Prelude*, pp. 51–64.

[4] P. E. Mosely, 'Transylvania Partitioned', *Foreign Affairs*, October 1940.

[5] On 29 July, before making his speech on foreign policy, Molotov asked Schulenburg for information about recent German and Italian talks with Balkan statesmen. Schulenburg was instructed to tell him that they arose from German advice to Roumania to negotiate directly with Hungary and Bulgaria for a settlement of their claims. *Nazi-Soviet Relations*, pp. 173–4.

[6] Maitland, op. cit., p. 114.   [7] Leigh White, op. cit., p. 74.

Union had no further claims on Roumania and that she wished to develop peaceful relations and good neighbourliness with Roumania'.[1] Nevertheless on 19 August a strong note was sent to Roumania protesting against recent frontier incidents and threatening that if these were to continue, events might take a serious turn. On 22 August Roumania and Bulgaria reached an agreement for the cession to the latter of the southern Dobrudja but on 24 August negotiations with the Hungarians were broken off. The events of the next few days were so involved and 'the political interplay between Germany and the Soviet . . . was so close that even those witnesses best placed to judge had the greatest difficulty in discovering whether they were watching a carefully disguised complicity or the beginnings of an hostility which would have great consequences.'[2]

On 24 August the Roumanian Government, acting on information supplied by the German General Staff, instructed Gafencu to seek an explanation of suspicious concentrations of Russian troops on the Roumanian frontier. The existence of such concentrations was categorically denied by Dekanozov. On 29 August the Roumanian Foreign Minister Manoilescu arrived in Vienna on the summons of the German and Italian Foreign Ministers, who had come to a decision to settle the Transylvanian dispute. There can be little doubt that the prospect of a Soviet invasion of Roumania was held out as the major argument for the acceptance by Roumania of the Axis award. This was made the more plausible by a note presented to Gafencu by Dekanozov on the night of 29 August, containing another serious warning as to the possible consequences of the alleged frontier incidents. This note was made public by Tass on the following morning, 30 August. On the same day the partition of Transylvania was announced from Vienna, together with Roumania's acceptance of a German-Italian guarantee of her new frontiers. While it could be argued from the facts as then known that the Soviet Union and Germany were acting in collusion, it is now clear that the Soviet note of 29 August was a last-minute effort to give the world the impression that it was actually being excluded. It was only on 31 August that Schulenburg was instructed to inform Molotov officially of the Vienna award and of the German guarantee to Roumania. Molotov was distinctly reserved and pointed out that Germany's failure to consult the Soviet Union was a breach of Article 3 of the Soviet-German pact. On 3 August Ribbentrop instructed Schulenburg to reject this interpretation of the clause on the

[1] Gafencu, *Prelude*, p. 51.   [2] ibid., p. 56.

ground that the territories involved were not of direct interest to the Soviet Union. He was also to point out that the Soviet Union had not given notice in regard to Lithuania, where territory promised to Germany had been occupied, and had given only short notice of the move into Bessarabia and Northern Bukovina. After correspondence between Schulenburg and Ribbentrop on the form which the memorandum should take, it was handed to Molotov on 10 September. On the 21st, Molotov as promised, gave Schulenburg (who was about to leave for Berlin) a written reply. This repeated the Soviet point of view, and made the assertion (to which Schulenburg only partially assented) that Molotov had made it clear on 24 June that the Soviet Union would eventually expect German support for its claim on Southern Bukovina. If the Germans were no longer satisfied with Article 3 of the Pact, the Soviet Government was prepared to negotiate on its amendment or deletion.[1]

A further exchange of notes between the U.S.S.R. and Roumania on 'frontier incidents' took place on 12-13 September, but thereafter Soviet pressure upon Roumania ceased, and Roumania fell into complete bondage to Germany.

The economic relations of Russia and Germany began now to be a source of worry. On 14 August it was made known to the German officials concerned that Hitler wished for punctual deliveries to Russia only till the spring of 1941.[2] There were inconclusive negotiations in Moscow from 24 August to 12 September on Russia's initiative, in order to examine the state of deliveries under the agreement of 11 February. It appears that the German deliveries had fallen short and the Russians announced that their own deliveries would be discontinued unless Germany made arrangements to remedy the deficit. They were also re-arranging their demands and cancelling all long-range agreements. 'That means', wrote Dr. Schnurre in the secret memorandum of 28 September 1940, from which this information is derived, 'that they do not want any processes, installations and equipment to be delivered over a long period, but that they want to restrict themselves to goods which will benefit their economy, especially their armament within the next 8–10 months. Therefore the conflict with our own military demands in the remaining small sector of deliveries of machinery and rolling mill products is still very much stronger

[1] *Nazi-Soviet Relations*, pp. 178–194.
[2] *Nazi Conspiracy and Aggression*, vol. 4, p. 1082.

than it used to be'. Since Russian deliveries to date had been 'a very substantial support of the German war economy' it is not surprising that the German ministers involved and the Army, had asked the Fuehrer for a decision regarding a continuance of these economic relations with the U.S.S.R.[1]

As shown in the evidence of Goering, von Paulus, and others at the Nuremberg Trial, Hitler was by the beginning of September 1940 firmly resolved to attack Russia and directions were given for a regrouping of German forces in the east. The elaboration of the plan for the attack—the Barbarossa plan—henceforth went steadily forward.[2]

On the Soviet side, the principal result of the Vienna award was the abandonment of attempts to give an impression of continued close Soviet-German collaboration in favour of reiterated manifestations of Soviet determination to pursue an independent policy. On 9 October, the Russians were given by the Germans an explanation of their reasons for sending German army elements into Roumania, a country which they declared to be menaced by British plans.[3] But on 15 October, the Narkomindel denied a Danish report to the effect that the Soviet Government had been informed in advance of Germany's intentions and of the objects and numbers of the troops sent.

Since the end of August the Soviet press had more than once stressed that from the Soviet point of view there were still open questions in the Balkans from whose solution Russia could not be excluded; on the other hand it was still made clear that the Soviet Government was neutral in as far as the Anglo-German

[1] *Nazi-Soviet Relations*, pp. 199–201; cf. his memorandum of 26 September, ibid, pp. 196–7.

[2] On 6 September a directive was sent from the Fuehrer's headquarters to the German counter-intelligence service abroad: 'The Eastern Territory will be manned stronger in the weeks to come. By the end of October the status shown on the enclosed map is supposed to be reached. These regroupings must not create the impression in Russia that we are preparing an offensive in the East. On the other hand Russia will realize that strong and highly trained German troops are stationed in the Gouvernement, in the Eastern provinces, and in the Protektorat; she should draw the conclusion that we can at any time protect our interests—especially the Balkans—with strong forces against Russian seizure.' *Nazi Conspiracy and Aggression*, vol. 3, pp. 849–50. According to a lecture delivered by Jodl on 7 November 1943, Hitler had told him during the Western campaign of his fundamental decision to turn against the Soviet Union, ibid., vol. 7, p. 920. Hitler is said in some German accounts to have announced this intention at a meeting on 29 July 1940; 'New Light on Nazi Foreign Policy', *Foreign Affairs*, October 1946.

[3] *Nazi-Soviet Relations*, pp. 206–7.

struggle in this area was concerned.[1] The first such question to be raised was that of the Danube.[2]

As has already been seen, Germany wished for a change in the existing régime for the Danube and the elimination of the representation given to British and French interests. At the beginning of September 1940, it became known that Germany was convening a conference at Vienna with the object of substituting a new organization for the International Commission controlling the upper reaches of the Danube. To this conference were invited all the riparian States together with Italy. On 11 September Vyshinsky, recently appointed Assistant Commissar for Foreign Affairs, informed Schulenburg that the Soviet Union was surprised to have received no invitation to the conference. All Danubian problems were of interest to the Soviet Union and he refused to accept the suggestion that Soviet interests were confined to the lower reaches of the river. This Soviet protest was made public on the following day.

On 14 September Molotov received from Shkvartsev, the Soviet Ambassador in Berlin, Ribbentrop's reply to this protest. The Vienna conference, it stated, had as its object the liquidation of the International Commission at Belgrade; Germany was, however, prepared to recognize the Soviet right to a seat on the European Commission at Galatz. Molotov in turn handed Schulenburg a note in which the Soviet proposals for the future of the Danube were set out in full. This suggested the dissolution of both existing bodies and the substitution for them of a single Danubian Commission for the whole length of the river from Bratislava to the sea. The Commission was to be confined to the riparian States—Germany, Slovakia, Hungary, Yugoslavia, Bulgaria, Roumania, and the U.S.S.R. France, Great Britain, and Italy were thus excluded. According to Gafencu, Schulenburg told him that Molotov, in giving the history of the Russian claim, declared that he was concerned to get rid of the inferior status imposed upon Russia by 'the unhappy Crimean War'.

The Soviet proposal, more far-reaching than the German, and suggestive of Russian plans for pushing on once more towards the control of the Black Sea and the Straits, would have the effect of bringing Russia for the first time into the affairs

[1] The strength of Soviet interest in Balkan questions was affirmed by Schulenburg when he returned to Berlin for consultations on 23 September; Gafencu, *Prelude*, pp. 64–5. Cf. *Nazi Conspiracy and Aggression*, vol. 6, pp. 987–8.

[2] Dallin, *Foreign Policy*, pp. 267–9; Gafencu, *Prelude*, pp. 65–84; 'Control of the Danube', *The Times*, 5 July 1946.

of the upper reaches of the Danube, and give her a new position from which to influence the policies of the lesser Slav States. The German reply was delayed until after Schulenburg's return to Moscow on 15 October. In the meantime the seriousness of Soviet intentions had been shown by the action of its representatives on the joint commission set up to demarcate the new Soviet-Roumanian frontier. They demanded a line in the delta itself which would give the Russians control of the principal channels. Germany refused to give Roumania any support in the matter and the disputed zone was occupied by the Russians later in the year.[1] The German reply to Molotov's proposals went very far towards meeting the Soviet demands, although the Germans insisted that Italy be brought into the new scheme and that 'provisionally' there should remain in being a special régime for the lower reaches of the river.

On 25 October a Tass communiqué announced that an agreement had been reached as follows:

'It is stated by the U.S.S.R. and Germany with the assent of Italy that it is necessary to liquidate the two existing Danubian Commissions and to replace them by a single Commission composed of the States bordering the river and of Italy, whose powers will extend from Bratislava to the sea. The purpose of the conference which will meet at Bucarest will be to establish the provisional international administration of the maritime Danube from Braila to the sea.'

On 28 October the delegates from Germany, Italy, Roumania, and Soviet Russia met at Bucarest and were at once confronted with a Soviet scheme for handing over the administration of the lower reaches of the river to a Russo-Roumanian commission which, under its proposed powers, would effectively assure to the Russians command of the whole maritime Danube. These Soviet proposals ran completely contrary to Germany s desire for the unhampered and unobserved movement of military and civilian shipping along the entire river, and the counter-proposals of the Axis Powers were equally unacceptable to the Russians. The Bucarest conference lingered on until 21 December, adjourning on that date, not to be recalled.

Another possible cause of Soviet-German friction was Finland. On 27 September a rumour spread in diplomatic circles in Moscow that Germany and Finland had concluded a military

---

[1] Soviet infiltration into the Danube delta, which was accompanied by some fighting, is described by C. Hollingworth, *There's a German Close Behind Me* (Secker and Warburg, 1942), pp. 208-12.

alliance. In response to their enquiries, the Russians were assured that all that was involved was the right of transit on Finnish railways for German soldiers joining their units in northern Norway.[1] On 28 September the Soviet Union raised with Finland the question of the latter's alleged negotiations for a Swedish alliance—a charge returned to on 7 December. The Russians also strongly pressed for the demilitarization of the Aaland Islands, a demand to which Finland acceded on 11 October. Negotiations concerning the control of the Petsamo nickel mines went on throughout the winter and were still unresolved in March. Finally, the Soviet Government brought pressure to bear on the Finns to exclude certain personalities from the Government.[2]

More important than the local clashes between Soviet and German interests, was the importance for the Soviet Union of the redefinition of the relations between the Axis Powers and Japan.[3] Japan, previously averse to military commitments, was now preparing for an assault upon the British Empire and anxious to secure German assistance in the event of America being involved. For Germany, while Japanese pressure was looked upon as a means for keeping America out of the European war, the motive may have been more complicated.[4] Knowledge of closer ties between Germany and Japan might prevent Russia giving too much attention to developments in the Balkans. If Soviet-Japanese relations could be themselves improved, Japan would be freed from anxieties on the score of Russia and would be able to go ahead with her Pacific plans.[5]

---

[1] Gafencu, *Prelude*, p. 85; *Nazi-Soviet Relations*, pp. 197–9, 203–5. As early as October the Germans, whose own interests were involved, were encouraging the Finns to resist the Soviet demands. ibid., p. 205.

[2] *Finnish Blue and White Book*, pp. 6–17; Dallin, *Foreign Policy*, pp. 293–6.

[3] A. W. Griswold, 'European Factors in Far Eastern Diplomacy', *Foreign Affairs*, January 1941.

[4] Mussolini urged on Hitler in a letter on 27 August the desirability of trying to diminish Soviet-Japanese tension and to increase friction between the United States and the Soviet Union; *Lettres secrètes échangées par Hitler et Mussolini*, p. 79.

[5] According to Dallin, the German envoy to Tokyo, Stahmer, through whom the Pact was negotiated, stopped in Moscow on his way to Japan in August 1940, to give the Soviet Government the necessary assurances, and to inquire as to the terms upon which the Soviet Union would enter into friendly relations with Japan. The conditions, said to have been advanced by the Soviet Union, included a far-reaching revision of the terms of the Treaty of Portsmouth; but the mere fact of the Soviet Union being willing to negotiate is said to have been taken by the Japanese as a reassuring sign. The Soviet Government is also said to have informed Germany that the Soviet Union would remain neutral in the Far East, even in the event of Japan refusing the proposed terms; *Foreign Policy*, pp. 337–8.

Agreement between Germany and Japan was reached during September, and Ribbentrop arrived in Rome on the 19th to enlist the Italian Government in the scheme. Ciano's diary is interesting on the point:

'In the car Ribbentrop speaks at once of the surprise in his bag: a military alliance with Japan to be signed within the next few days at Berlin. The Russian dream vanished forever in the rooms of the Belvedere at Vienna after the guarantee to Roumania. He thinks such a move will have a double advantage: against Russia and against America.'[1]

The signing of the Tripartite Pact took place in Berlin on 27 September. By Article 3, the three Powers, Germany, Italy, and Japan, undertook to 'assist one another with all political, economic, and military means, if one of the high contracting parties should be attacked by a power not at present involved in the European conflict or the Sino-Japanese war'. By Article 5, the three Powers affirmed that the terms of the Pact did not in any way affect the existing political status as between each of the three contracting parties and Soviet Russia.[2]

On 29 September the German radio followed this up with further assurances. 'Political circles in the Soviet Union who, of course, were informed of the signing of the Pact, note with particular attention the fact that it will in no way change the relations between the three Powers and the Soviet Union. On the contrary the Pact provides for a further development of these relations.'[3]

On 30 September *Pravda* confirmed the Soviet Union's fore-knowledge of the Pact and declared that the reservation with regard to the Soviet Union showed respect for the Soviet policy of neutrality and proved the value of the Soviet-German and Soviet-Italian pacts of non-aggression. On the other hand, while cautious as to the future of the spheres of influence marked out for themselves by the signatories of the agreement, the writer forecast that the upshot of the pact would be to spread the area of the conflict.[4]

Since the imminent conclusion of the Pact was apparently only communicated to Molotov by the German Chargé d'Affaires, von Tippelskirch, some twenty-four hours in advance

---

[1] *Ciano Diaries*, p. 293.
[2] This was repeated by Matsuoka in his radio address of 27 September 1940. *Foreign Relations of the United States: Japan, 1931–41*, vol. 2, pp. 166–8. Cf. 'Tokyo War Guilt Trial', *The Times*, 10 March 1947.
[3] *B.I.N.*, XVII, pp. 1313–19.
[4] The article is printed in translation in Moore, *Soviet Far Eastern Policy*, pp. 249–50.

of its signature, the object of Soviet comment seems to have
been to signalize the fact that no important diplomatic event
could take place without it, while emphasizing the continued
independence of Soviet policy itself. In his interview with
Molotov (on 26 September), von Tippelskirch had indicated
that the Tripartite Pact did not affect the relations between
any of the signatories and the Soviet Union. He also told
Molotov that the Russians could soon expect an answer from
Ribbentrop to the Soviet memorandum of 21 September, and
that this would contain an invitation to Molotov to visit Berlin.
Molotov showed himself particularly concerned with the
Japanese aspect of the pact and declared that by the Soviet
interpretation of the Soviet-German Pact, (Articles 3 and 4),
the Soviet Government was entitled to receive the full text of
the pact, including any secret protocols. Finnish questions
also came up for discussion, as has already been seen. On
4 October, von Tippelskirch communicated Ribbentrop's
reply to the effect that no questions arose under the terms of
the Soviet-German pact, since the new treaty, which had no
secret protocols, showed by its published text that Soviet-
German relations were not involved. Molotov reserved his
Government's reply.[1] German efforts to bring about a Russo-
Japanese understanding seem to have continued. But the
Japanese reactions were more favourable than were those of
the Russians. Soviet reluctance to fall in completely with
German plans may have helped to increase Hilter's determination to attack the Soviet Union with the least possible
delay.[2] When he met Mussolini on the Brenner Pass on 4
October, the latter found him 'energetic and again extremely
anti-Bolshevist. "Bolshevism," he said, "is the doctrine of
people who are lowest in the scale of civilization."'[3]

It rapidly became clear that Germany intended to use the
Tripartite Pact as a basis for the further consolidation of her
position in Europe. The Soviet reaction to the first step in this
process—the German occupation of Roumania in the first half
of October—has already been noted.

In Bulgaria, opinion showed itself divided as to the respective
shares of Germany and Russia in securing the return of the
southern Dobrudja. On 10 September the Bulgarian envoy

[1] *Nazi-Soviet Relations*, pp. 195–9, 201–4. Cf. Grew to Secretary of
State, 29 September 1940; *Foreign Relations of the United States: Japan
1931–41*, vol. 2, pp. 169–71.
[2] There is reason to believe that on 10 October 1940 the Soviet Government approached the Polish General Berling with a view to forming a
fighting force out of the Polish prisoners in Russia in the event of a German
attack on the Soviet Union.   [3] *Ciano Diaries*, pp. 298–9.

Stamenev had called on Molotov to express his country's gratitude for the Soviet Union's moral support. According to a Tass statement on the following day, Molotov expressed satisfaction with the Bulgarian declaration. Subsequently, the Soviet Union seems to have encouraged Bulgaria to maintain a policy independent of that of the Axis Powers, while Bulgarian Communists denounced Germany's alleged intention of occupying the country and called for a mutual-assistance pact with the Soviet Union.[1] But such activities in no way committed the Soviet Union to active intervention, and the Yugoslav minister Gavrilovic is said to have tried in vain to elicit from Molotov a statement as to what the Soviet attitude would be should German troops enter Bulgaria.[2]

Most important of all was the question of Turkey.[3] The revelations in the German Sixth White Book about the Allies' Black Sea plans, had marked the culminating point of Soviet-Turkish friction. The Soviet Ambassador Terentiev left Ankara and for a time there was virtually no contact between the two Governments. Italy's decision to attack Greece, which was carried into effect on 28 October, was said to have been influenced by the belief that fear of the Soviet Union would prevent Turkey coming to Greece's assistance.[4]

By this time, however, an effort at a *rapprochement* in face of the German advance appears to have been initiated by the departure for Moscow on 8 October of the Turkish Ambassador Haydar Aktay after two months' leave, and by the arrival in Ankara of a new Soviet Ambassador, Vinogradov, who was received by the Turkish President on 12 October. While the Turks do not seem to have received any assurances of Soviet opposition to further German advances in the Balkans, the Russians apparently indicated that Turkey had nothing to fear from their side should she become involved in the war. The fact that no specific Soviet demands were put forward seems to have led to the belief that there was a genuine détente in Soviet-Turkish relations. Indeed, after a long talk between Molotov and the Turkish Ambassador on 15 October, it was reported

[1] Dallin, *Foreign Policy*, pp. 279–81; Maitland, op. cit., p. 141; Scott, op. cit., p. 136. It has been stated that in October Bulgaria was offered and refused a mutual assistance pact with the U.S.S.R.; J. T. Murphy, *Russia on the March* (Lane, 1941), pp. 97–8.

[2] 'Le Coup d'Etat de Simovich', *France Intérieure*, 15 September 1945.

[3] See the article 'Turkey since 1940', *B.I.N.*, 5 September 1942.

[4] Graves, *Briton and Turk*, pp. 249–50; C. Mackenzie, *Wind of Freedom* (Chatto and Windus, 1943), p. 53. The same author, however, attributes to Soviet pressure Bulgaria's failure to enter the war against Greece in November; ibid., p. 78.

that the Foreign Commissar considered Russo-Turkish relations much improved.[1]

According to a document in the German archives Schulenburg reported on 19 October that the slight deterioration in Soviet-German relations due to the transit of German troops through Finland had apparently been alleviated. On 2 November, the Soviet Commissar for Foreign Trade, Mikoyan, who was conducting trade negotiations with a German delegation under Schnurre which had arrived in Moscow in mid-October, pointed out that the Germans were refusing to deliver war material to Russia while they were delivering it to Finland and other countries. This was the first time the subject of deliveries to Finland had been raised.[2] A note appended to this points out that 'Renunciation by Moscow of interference in Balkan interests permits very well the possibilities of compensation in other areas'. On 30 October the same German document recorded that there was no anxiety about Russia's attitude to the Italo-Greek conflict, that economic deliveries were proceeding according to plan, and that Russo-Japanese tension was relaxed.[3]

Schulenburg arrived back at his post in Moscow on 15 October. On 17 October, he handed to Molotov the letter from Ribbentrop to Stalin, having decided that it would be inopportune to try to deliver it to Stalin direct since Stalin had recently shown strong reserve in public and might refuse to see the Ambassador, especially in view of a statement in the Soviet press early in September that he had not seen him for more than six months. The letter, which was dated 13 September, contained a review of events since the signing of the Soviet-German pact. He again produced the possibility of action by Great Britain as an explanation for action in Finland and the Balkans. The Tripartite Pact was directed against British attempts to bring the United States into the war. Germany was working to bring about Soviet-Japanese friendship as a logical corollary to Soviet-German friendship.

'In summing up,' he went on, 'I should like to state that in the opinion of the Fuehrer also, it appears to be the historical mission of the Four Powers—the Soviet Union, Italy, Japan and Germany—to adopt a long-range policy and to direct the future development

---

[1] Dallin, *Foreign Policy*, pp. 305–7; Gafencu, *Prelude*, p. 62.

[2] *Nazi-Soviet Relations*, p. 217.

[3] *Nazi Conspiracy and Aggression*, vol. 6, pp. 988–9. On 20 November a trade delegation from the German vassal-state of Slovakia arrived in Moscow. In October Goering again pressed for deliveries to Russia to be accelerated; ibid., vol. 4, p. 1082.

of their peoples into the right channels by delimitation of their interests on a world-wide scale.'

He therefore suggested a visit by Molotov to Berlin, to be followed by one by himself to Moscow for the discussion, possibly with Japanese and Italian representatives as well, of a policy of practical advantage to all concerned.[1]

Thus by the end of October 1940, the Soviet Government had at least given some indication that it did not intend to have the future of south-eastern Europe decided without its participation. From the German point of view, this manifestation of independence could only evoke anxiety.

In addition, Schulenburg had no doubt had the task of making Germany's own actions seem as acceptable as possible to the Russians:

'The heads of foreign missions most closely informed as to the affairs of the German Embassy thought it certain that the Ambassador had received precise instructions bearing on four points: he was to justify the dispatch of German troops to Roumania, to be accommodating regarding Danubian affairs, to expedite the conclusion of a Russo-Japanese understanding and to reconcile Moscow to the Tripartite Pact by pressing her on the road to Iran and the Persian gulf.

'Even if the instructions were not so precise as they were said to be, it was in this direction that the activities of the German Embassy turned.'[2]

Stalin's reply to Ribbentrop, which Schulenburg had no doubt was composed by him personally, was handed to him on 21 October. It ran as follows:

My Dear Herr Von Ribbentrop,

I have received your letter. I thank you sincerely for your confidence, as well as for the instructive analysis of recent events which is contained in your letter.

I agree with you that a further improvement in the relations between our countries is entirely possible on the permanent basis of a long-range delimitation of mutual interests.

Herr Molotov admits that he is under obligation to pay you a return visit in Berlin. He hereby accepts your invitation.

It remains for us to agree on the date of arrival in Berlin. The time from the 10th to the 12th of November is most convenient for Herr Molotov. If it is also agreeable to the German Government, the question may be considered as settled.

[1] *Nazi-Soviet Relations*, pp. 207–215.
[2] Gafencu, *Prelude*, p. 99.

I welcome the desire expressed by you to come to Moscow again in order to resume the exchange of ideas begun last year on questions of interest to both our countries, and I hope that this wish will be realized after Herr Molotov's trip to Berlin.

As to joint deliberation on some issues with Japanese and Italian participation, I am of the opinion (without being opposed to this idea in principle) that this question would have to be submitted to a previous examination.

Most respectfully yours,

Marshal Timoshenko's speech on 7 November, with its emphasis on the Red Army as the sole guarantee of Soviet security, was not reassuring. But on 9 November it was duly announced that Molotov had accepted an invitation to Berlin. The Soviet Foreign Minister left Moscow on the following day and returned on the 15th. The obvious importance of the Berlin conversations was only matched by the lack of precise information as to their contents. An official German statement on the 12th—the day of Molotov's arrival and of his first conversation with Hitler—described the visit as

'the logical outcome of the evolution of the European situation and the signing by Germany, Italy, and Japan of the Tripartite Pact. In view of the new situation created by the developments of the war and the triple alliance it has become necessary to define positively and clearly the position of the Soviet Union.

'M. Molotov's visit has the following aims: first, to fix the basis for the political and economic collaboration of the Soviet Union with the Axis Powers and eventually with Japan; secondly, to reconsider from the point of view of a more extensive collaboration the bases of the German-Soviet agreement.'

Two days later, on the conclusion of the talks, an official German communiqué declared that the exchange of views had taken place in 'an atmosphere of mutual confidence' and that it had led to agreement 'on all important questions of interest to Germany and the Soviet Union'.[1] On 14 November the Red Army paper *Krasnaya Zvezda* (*Red Star*) included a note on the Molotov visit to Berlin in its regular weekly survey of foreign affairs. It pointed out that the Berlin talks were the centre of attention for the entire world and that the German

---

[1] *B.I.N.*, XVII, pp. 1584–5. Cf. *Nazi-Soviet Relations*, p. 255. Molotov's visit was followed by a change in Soviet representation in the German capital. On 23 November the Ambassador Shkvartsev, who had taken up his post on 2 September 1939, was replaced by Dekanozov, the Foreign Assistant Commissar who had been one of Molotov's party of sixty-five accompanying officials.

and Italian press were emphasizing their outstanding importance. 'There is no doubt that the renewal of personal contacts
and friendly exchanges of views with the leaders of the German
Government serves the interests of both countries by strengthening and developing Soviet-German relations.'

On the other hand, the statement on the opening day of the
conference in Ribbentrop's organ, the *Diplomatisch-politische
Korrespondenz*, that Russia would be invited to join in building
the new world order in harmony with Germany, Italy, and
Japan, gave significance to a Tass statement on 15 November
—after the conference—that a report of a Russo-Japanese
agreement involving a division of spheres of influence in the Far
East and of a Soviet undertaking to stop helping China was
'devoid of reality'.[1] The Soviet press published no editorials
on Molotov's journey, although Hitler's portrait appeared in
Soviet newspapers for the first time.

Indeed, after the publication of the official communiqués
on Molotov's visit 'both countries refrained scrupulously from
any reference to it. On the surface it had been neither significant nor fruitful'.[2]

It was only on 22 June 1941, when justifying the German
decision to attack Russia, that Hitler and Ribbentrop gave
their versions of what had taken place—versions coloured, of
course, by the desire to blacken the Soviet Union in the eyes
of the other countries concerned. From the German side there
are now contemporary documents.[3] There is also the evidence
given at the Nuremberg Trial by Ribbentrop and Goering.[4]
There is no Soviet account.[5]

The first of the Berlin conversations was that between Molotov
and Ribbentrop on 12 November. After a general survey of the
world situation, Ribbentrop declared that the Fuehrer now

---

[1] *B.I.N.*, XVII, p. 1604. On 19 April 1941 *Pravda* wrote: 'In November
1940, a proposal was made to the Soviet Government to join the Tripartite
Pact and to convert it into a four-Power Pact. The Soviet Government did
not deem it possible to accept the offer.' Dallin, *Foreign Policy*, p. 273 *n*.

[2] ibid., p. 272. Berlin circles are said to have shown little optimism as to
the outcome of the visit; H. W. Flannery, *Assignment to Berlin* (Michael
Joseph, 1942), p. 36.

[3] Memoranda by the interpreter, Dr. Paul Schmidt, *Nazi-Soviet Relations*,
pp. 217–254.

[4] *Nuremberg Trial*, part 9, pp. 134–5; part 10, pp. 196–8, 249–51.

[5] Dallin makes use of some remarks by Lozovsky made at a press conference on 7 October 1941 and quoted in *Pravda* on the following day. He
also makes use of reports from the Ankara correspondent of the *Neue
Züricher Zeitung* which gave the impression that his information 'emanated
from Soviet circles'. Dallin. *Foreign Policy*, pp. 272–5.

held that it would be advantageous if the attempt were made 'to establish the spheres of influence between Russia, Germany, Italy and Japan along very broad lines'—Japan in the South, Germany, after the establishment of the New Order in Europe, in Central Africa, Italy in North and East Africa. He, the Foreign Minister, wondered whether Russia in the long run would not also turn to the South for the natural outlet to the open sea that was so important for Russia'.

Pressed by Molotov to define his ideas more exactly, Ribbentrop commented on the successful results so far achieved by German-Soviet collaboration. The question was whether in the future, Russia could not profit from 'the new order of things in the British Empire', i.e., 'whether in the long run the most advantageous access to the sea for Russia could not be found in the direction of the Persian Gulf and the Arabian Sea, and whether at the same time, certain aspirations of Russia in this part of Asia—in which Germany was completely disinterested—could not also be realized'.

The second sphere in which joint action by the Four Powers was envisaged was that of Turkey and the Straits, where the Montreux Convention should be replaced by an agreement more beneficial to Russia, particularly with regard to her access to the Mediterranean.

Finally, there was the question of the possibility of finding a basis for mediation between Japan and China.

On his side Molotov, while agreeing with Ribbentrop's remark about the advantages of a Sino-Japanese accord, contented himself for the most part by asserting the need for greater definition of the plans put forward. There was a hint of trouble to come in his remark that the existing delimitation of spheres of influence in Europe between the Soviet Union and Germany, had been rendered 'obsolete and meaningless' by recent events (except for unsettled issues in Finland), and that a new understanding with Germany must precede any wider settlement.

The attitudes taken up at the beginning were maintained throughout the conversations. On the German side, the emphasis was on a wide four-power agreement for the future domination of the world; on the Soviet side, there was a series of definable issues relating to Europe upon which preliminary satisfaction was demanded.

When Molotov saw Hitler later in the day, the latter again ranged widely over the whole political field, and renewed assurances as to the German desire to avoid interfering with Russia's vital interests. The German occupation of Roumania was a temporary measure which would end with the coming of peace.

On his side, Molotov put a series of questions to Hitler: was the Russo-German agreement still in force where Finland was concerned? what was the meaning of the New Order in Europe and Asia and what was to be the Soviet Union's role in it? But Russia was prepared to participate in the Tripartite Pact provided it 'was to co-operate as a partner and not be merely an object'.

In another meeting on the following day, Hitler tried to satisfy Molotov on the Finnish question. Germany had shown consideration for Soviet claims with regard to Lithuania and the Bukovina which were not within the original Soviet sphere. On her side she could claim consideration for her military and economic interests in Finland, which were considerable while the war lasted. In reply, Molotov raised, among other matters, the question of Southern Bukovina following the German guarantee to Roumania. But there was more significance in the statement that Russia's revisions were much less than Germany had undertaken elsewhere by force of arms.

The idea that the Soviet Union was entitled to new accretions of power to make up for those which Germany had gained as a result of the war, was hardly likely to commend itself to Hitler. The important thing was that Germany should have the prerequisites for a successful conclusion of the war. Then there would exist the basis for a far wider collaboration.

But Molotov was not to be moved from his point that minor issues must be settled first. And some argument followed his blunt demand that there must be no German troops in Finland and no demonstrations there of anti-Soviet feeling. After an inconclusive argument, the conversation was again turned by Hitler towards the problems of a new world alignment of powers.

Molotov once again insisted on Europe first, and after mentioning the German guarantee to Roumania and the Danube Commission's deliberations, passed on to the question of Turkey, the Straits and the proposed Soviet guarantee to Bulgaria. Hitler again pointed out Germany's readiness to accept a revision of the Straits Convention but demanded to be assured that Bulgaria itself had asked for a guarantee, and pointed out that in this matter, Italy, too, would have to be consulted. Molotov, on the other hand, pointed out that in the Straits, the Soviet Union would require more than a paper guarantee.

In the final conversation on the 13th, only Ribbentrop again took part on the German side. It was now that Ribbentrop produced the German formula. This took the form of a ten-year agreement between the Soviet Union and the Powers of the Tripartite Pact, to co-operate politically, to respect 'each other's natural spheres of influence' and to consult on problems arising from their contact, to join no hostile combinations directed against any one of them, and finally to co-operate economically.

Besides this pact, which should be public and include the customary phrases about the desire to restore world peace, there should be a secret protocol, 'establishing the focal points in the territorial aspirations of the Four Countries.' . . . 'The focal points in the territorial aspirations of the Soviet Union would presumably be centred south of the territory of the Soviet Union in the direction of the Indian Ocean'.

There would also be an agreement between the Soviet Union, Germany and Italy over the question of Turkey and the Straits, and finally, the Germans would like to see the conclusion of a non-aggression pact between the Soviet Union and Japan, and were prepared to mediate if necessary. If such a pact were concluded, the Japanese would be prepared to meet the Russians half-way over the coal and oil concessions on Sakhalin.

Molotov informed Ribbentrop that exchanges over the question of a non-aggression pact were proceeding with the Japanese. On the Straits, he again stressed the question of real guarantees of Russian security. There was also the question of the pact with Bulgaria, and the Soviet Government did not disinterest itself from the fate of Hungary, Roumania and Yugoslavia. Did the Germans regard as still in force the protocol providing for German-Soviet consultations over the future form of Poland? What about Swedish neutrality? And the passages out of the Baltic Sea—the Soviet Government believed this a suitable subject for discussions like those being held on the Danube question. On Finland, the Soviet Government had made its position clear.

Ribbentrop's reply took the line that Molotov had questioned him too closely; but he was at pains to be reassuring, and to indicate that military necessity could explain those actions and omissions by Germany of which the Russians had complained.

On the question of spheres of influence and the outlet to the Indian Ocean, Molotov refused to commit the Soviet Government; the Germans were assuming the war against

England had already been won. First the immediate issues must be settled and the task was one for the ordinary diplomatic channels.

On 25 November, Molotov gave Schulenburg the Soviet answer.[1]

The Soviet Government were prepared to accept the German proposals subject to conditions. These run as follows (in Schulenburg's dispatch):

'1. Provided that the German troops are immediately withdrawn from Finland which under the compact of 1939, belongs to the Soviet sphere of influence. At the same time the Soviet Union undertakes to ensure peaceful relations with Finland and to protect German economic interests in Finland (export of lumber and nickel).

'2. Provided that within the next few months the security of the Soviet Union in the Straits is assured by the conclusion of a mutual assistance pact between the Soviet Union and Bulgaria, which geographically is situated inside the security zone of the Black Sea boundaries of the Soviet Union, and by the establishment of a base for land and naval forces of the U.S.S.R. within range of the Bosphorus and the Dardanelles by means of a long-term lease.

'3. Provided that the area south of Batum and Baku in the general direction of the Persian Gulf is recognized as the centre of the aspirations of the Soviet Union.

'4. Provided that Japan (renounces) her rights to concessions for coal and oil in Northern Sakhalin.'

This would involve amending the two proposed protocols, and three further ones would be required to cover the points about Finland, Sakhalin and Bulgaria.

The statement of the German view on these proposals which Molotov requested was never given.[2] The Russians had asked for too much. These exchanges marked the end of any prospect of a further development of German-Soviet collaboration.[3] On the other hand, the two Governments seem to have agreed to press on with the negotiations for a new economic agreement

---

[1] What was presumably intended as a draft of the proposed agreements was found in Germany among what had been the files of the German Embassy in Moscow, and is printed in *Nazi-Soviet Relations*, pp. 255–8.
[2] ibid., pp. 258–9.
[3] Hitler wrote to Mussolini on 20 November of his difficulties in trying to get the Russians to turn their attention from the Balkans to the East; *Lettres Secretes*, pp. 83–9.

which had been going on in Moscow for some time. The German delegates under Schnurre continued their task throughout December and a new agreement was signed on 10 January 1941.[4]

[4] Gafencu, *Prelude*, pp. 118–19. 'The Soviet negotiators insisted upon a provision that the exports and imports of the two countries be balanced every quarter, a stipulation which was finally inserted in the treaty. The official communiqués issued upon the conclusion of this agreement spoke of its broad scope, of wheat transactions of a volume never known before and so forth. What they failed to mention was that the provision for equalizing their trade every quarter actually greatly decreased the turnover between the two countries, and that the entire treaty, which had been heralded with much fanfare by both countries, was merely "the frame of a trade agreement" the real significance of which could only be determined in actual day-by-day practice.' Dallin, *Foreign Policy*, p. 424.

Chapter Fourteen

SOVIET POLICY ON THE EVE OF WAR: NOVEMBER 1940 TO JUNE 1941

IT is clear in retrospect that the dominant factor in the international situation after Molotov's visit to Berlin was Hitler's determination to attack the Soviet Union at the earliest possible moment, and his military and diplomatic preparations to that end.[1] The master-plan for the attack on the Soviet Union—'Case Barbarossa'—was issued from Hitler's headquarters on 18 December 1940, and the date for the completion of the necessary preparations was fixed at 15 May 1941.[2] But it is by no means certain to what extent the Soviet

[1] For a summary of the development of Hitler's plans to attack the U.S.S.R., see *Nazi Conspiracy and Aggression*, vol. 1, pp. 794 ff. On 12 November a directive of the Fuehrer's informed his senior commanders that discussions with the Soviet Union had been entered into with the aim of clarifying the Soviet Union's intentions for the time being. Irrespective of the results of these discussions, all the preparations for a campaign in the cast, already verbally ordered, would be continued; ibid., vol. 3, pp. 403–7. German naval circles noted that the Fuehrer was still inclined to instigate a conflict with Russia, although it was not believed that the Russians would initiate a conflict during the ensuing year in view of the importance of German assistance in building up Russia's naval strength; ibid., vol. 6, pp. 989–91. On 5 December 1940, the German Chief of Staff presented a report to Hitler on the proposed operations in the east; ibid., vol. 4, pp. 374–5.

[2] ibid., vol. 3, pp. 407–9. Cf. *Nuremberg Trial*, part I, p. 176. On the other hand, it should be noted that Hitler was still outwardly cautious. Writing to Mussolini on 31 December 1940, he declared that he did not foresee any likely Russian initiative against Germany as long as Stalin was alive, and provided Germany was not itself the victim of a major crisis. The Germany army must nevertheless be prepared for all eventualities in the east. A satisfactory commercial treaty was about to be signed. The only things at present dividing Germany and Russia were the questions of Finland and Constantinople. The major German interest where Finland was concerned was to avoid a second war there. It was not to Germany's interest to abandon Constantinople and Bulgaria to Bolshevism; but even here a solution was not impossible; *Lettres Secrètes*, p. 109. On 8 January 1941 Hitler was reported as perturbed by evidence of British diplomatic activity in Russia and as declaring that the Russian threat would have to be removed for the sake of the war against England. On 17 January the Germans rejected a Russian request to allow Russian naval officers to sail on a German heavy cruiser for training purposes, on the ground that the voyage would be an operational one. It was agreed that the Russians might participate in the shipyard test voyages. Soviet pressure on Finland was again causing concern and relations with Russia were discussed at the meeting between Hitler and Mussolini at Salzburg on 20 January. Finland, declared Hitler, was of great

Union realized the imminence of the danger confronting it, in spite of the various military and industrial measures undertaken during the period.[1] As has already been pointed out, there are differences of opinion as to the extent to which psychological preparation for a war with Germany were carried out. They seem to have been almost entirely confined to military circles.[2]

On the diplomatic side, Soviet activity seems to have passed through two fairly distinct phases. Between October 1940 and the time of the German campaign in the Balkans in April 1941, the Soviet Union seems to have attempted, although with great caution, to use its influence in the Balkans to counter the spread of German domination. After the German victories, the Soviet Government seems to have decided upon a final desperate effort to avert the blow and a new period of total appeasement followed. Throughout the Soviet Union honoured its economic agreements with Germany.[3] The only tangible diplomatic achievement was the non-aggression pact with Japan.

A more positive Soviet policy was indeed precluded throughout by the obvious Soviet determination to give no grounds for belief that it was acting in concert with Great Britain or the

---

importance because of its nickel resources and should not be touched any more. Germany had rejected Russian complaints about the concentration of German troops in Roumania. The purposes of the German concentrations were (1) operations against Greece; (2) the protection of Bulgaria against Russia and Turkey; (3) as a security measure and for the guarantee of Roumania. The United States, he said, should not be regarded as a serious danger even if it were to enter the war. A greater danger, despite the favourable political and economic treaties, was Russia, and this led to the tying down of considerable German forces on the Russo-Roumanian frontier. But there was no danger so long as Stalin was alive. *Ciano Diaries*, p. 338. Cf. *Nazi Conspiracy and Aggression*, vol. 6, p. 993. An important conference on the Barbarossa plan was held on 3 February 1941. ibid., vol. 3, pp. 623–6. A document dated 5 February 1941 ordered that mobilization against Russia should be camouflaged as long as possible. When this was no longer possible it should be explained as a deceptive diversion from the invasion of England. On 13 March, a supplementary directive was issued giving the plans for the occupation and administration of the Russian territories to be conquered. ibid., vol. 3, pp. 409–13.

[1] On these, see John Scott, *Duel for Europe*. The Eighteenth Conference of the All-Union Communist Party, which met in February 1941, was mainly devoted to problems of production.

[2] On 20 January 1941, it was reported in German naval circles that Stalin had made a speech in which he had declared that he was working tirelessly for the strengthening of the Russian State and army: 'the international situation is complicated and confused and even Russia is threatened by the danger of war'; *Nazi Conspiracy and Aggression*, vol. 6, p. 993.

[3] M. T. Florinsky, 'The Soviet Union and International Agreements,' *Political Science Quarterly*, March 1946.

United States. Relations between the Soviet Union and Great Britain since the summer of 1940 had continued to be far from cordial.[1] The main outstanding issue was the failure to solve the various financial and other claims arising from the Soviet Union's annexation of the Baltic States. A British proposal for settling these, made on 13 September, was rejected, and on 17 October the Soviet Ambassador again protested against the detention of the Baltic States' ships and the freezing of their funds.[2] On 22 October Sir Stafford Cripps is understood to have submitted to the Soviet Vice-Commissar, Vyshinsky, new proposals for a settlement of existing disputes. This seems to have suggested, on the British side, a *de facto* recognition of the incorporation of the Baltic States—the formal question of their status to be left over for the Peace Conference; a guarantee of Soviet participation in any post-war peace settlement; and finally, an assurance that Great Britain would not participate in any attack on the Soviet Union. In return, the Soviet Government was to pledge its neutrality and give an undertaking not to conduct any anti-British propaganda on British territory.[3] These proposals were regarded by the Russians as conceding nothing. No formal reply to them was ever given.[4]

Soviet relations with Great Britain deteriorated still further when, on 29 October, the British Government formally protested against the Soviet attitude on the question of the Danubian Commissions. The Soviet reply, sent on 2 November, denied that the Soviet participation in the Bucarest negotiations was a departure from neutrality and explained the Soviet viewpoint as follows:

'The Danube Commission must naturally be composed of representatives of the States situated on the Danube or closely connected with the Danube and using the Danube as a trade channel—for instance Italy.

'It is clear that Great Britain, being removed thousands of kilometres from the Danube, cannot be classed as such a State.'[5]

But it was the general world situation, not specific disagreements, that governed Soviet relations with Great Britain. These continued substantially unchanged even after Anthony Eden—a reputed supporter of closer relations with the Soviet Union—replaced Lord Halifax at the Foreign Office on 22 December

[1] Dallin, *Soviet Russia's Foreign Policy*, pp. 321 ff.
[2] As a reprisal the Soviet Government refused to pay further instalments due under the settlement of the Lena Goldfields case. See vol. i, p. 111 *n.* 2.
[3] Coates, *A History of Anglo-Soviet Relations*, p. 651.
[4] F. Davis and E. K. Lindley, *How War Came*, p. 167.
[5] Coates, op. cit., pp. 649–50.

1940. Indeed, in the new year, and particularly after the signature on 11 January of a new Soviet-German trade treaty, yet another major cause of Anglo-Soviet friction came into prominence. This took the form of British charges that United States goods were reaching Germany by way of the Trans-Siberian railway, and that excess purchases by the Soviet Union of goods from America were enabling it to increase its exports to Germany.[1]

Relations with the United States had been far from good after the placing by the Americans of restrictions upon Soviet trade at the time of the Finnish War.[2] 'By the spring of 1940,' writes the then Under-Secretary of State, Mr. Sumner Welles, 'official relations between the two countries were only nominal.' In the summer of 1940, however, the United States Government decided to attempt to improve matters, and on 27 July, Sumner Welles had the first of what was to be a series of twenty-seven conferences with the Soviet Ambassador Umansky, between that date and the German attack on Russia. After this renewal of contacts, Soviet orders were to some extent facilitated. On 21 January 1941 the 'moral embargo' on exports to the Soviet Union was formally lifted, but supplies were curtailed by the needs of America's own defence programme and from March by lend-lease. During the last months of 1940, information about Hitler's projected assault on Russia reached the State Department, and early in January 1941 it became known that this had been fixed for the spring of that year. Some time in February, Welles conveyed this information to Umansky and at the Soviet Government's request this was repeated in a conversation between them on 20 March.[3]

Negotiations for an improvement in relations with Italy had begun late in 1940. Ciano's diary contains the following entry under the date 1 January 1941.

'I write to Alfieri to acquaint him with our negotiations with Russia and to inform Ribbentrop also. These are no longer in the

---

[1] Mr. Dalton, Minister for Economic Warfare, *House of Commons Debates*, 28 January, 25 March 1941.

[2] See letter of Cordell Hull to Senator Key Pittman on 30 January 1940 on the Soviet failure to live up to the obligations of the 1933 agreement, and exchange of letters 10–19 February with Representative F. C. Hook on the proposed embargo on oil exports to the U.S.S.R. *Documents on American Foreign Relations, 1939–1940*, vol. ii, pp. 495–500.

[3] When an account of this interview was first given out unofficially in 1942, it was alleged that Umansky had informed the German Chargé d'Affaires of the warning. Umansky, then in Moscow, denied the allegation. *Peace and War*, p. 638; Sumner Welles, *A Time for Decision*, pp. 168–71; Davis and Lindley, op. cit., pp. 162–78; Dallin, *Foreign Policy*, pp. 332–3.

stage of broad and superficial conversations; the Russians wish to go to the bottom of many fundamental and important questions on which I would consider it imprudent to commit ourselves without first having agreed with the Germans.'[1]

For the Italians, continued access to Russian oil would seem to have been the most important consideration. On 27 May Ciano noted:

'In the afternoon the Duce telephoned me asking me to speed up the negotiations with Russia, so that we can get a little bit of fuel oil. "Otherwise," said the Duce, "a little while longer and we will be compelled to sit with folded hands."'[2]

The first additional signatory to the Tripartite Pact was Hungary, which adhered on 20 November 1940. In spite of a specific reference to Article 5, which excluded relations with Russia from the scope of the Pact, made by the Hungarian Premier Teleki in his speech on the occasion, the Soviet Government signified its displeasure in the normal roundabout fashion. A Tass communiqué on 23 November denied a German press report that Hungary's action had received prior Soviet approval. On 23 November it was Roumania's turn to sign.[3] On 24 November Slovakia gave its adhesion.[4]

It was thus Bulgaria which became the focal point of Soviet-German rivalry. King Boris arrived in Berlin two days after Molotov's departure, but was apparently able to provide adequate reasons, based no doubt on the pro-Russian sympathies of the Bulgars, for refusing to adhere to the Pact or to admit German troops into his country. Soviet diplomacy continued its attempts to fortify Bulgaria's resolution, and on 25 November Boris was visited by Sobelev, Secretary-General of the Narkomindel.[5] But the knowledge of the increasing German concentrations in Roumania and pressure from pro-German elements within Bulgaria itself made the Bulgarian

[1] *Ciano Diaries*, p. 331.   [2] ibid., p. 358.

[3] When the Iron Guard broke out in revolt on 19 January 1941, the Communists were accused by the Roumanian Government of being implicated in the affair and Russo-Roumanian relations became still **more tense**. In spite of this, however, a new trade agreement with Roumania was signed on 26 February. Dallin, *Foreign Policy*, pp. 266–7, 428.

[4] The Soviet Government had recognized the German Protectorate over Slovakia on 6 November and had signed a trade agreement with the Slovak Government on the same day.

[5] Sobelev was believed to have proposed a guarantee of Bulgaria's frontiers which Boris rejected. Dallin, *Foreign Policy*, p. 282. According to other versions, the Soviet proposal was for a pact of mutual assistance. See the pamphlet, *Resistance Movements in Occupied and Satellite Europe*, No. 4, **Bulgaria** (Union of Democratic Control, 1944).

standpoint increasingly difficult to maintain.[1] There were reports of a secret meeting on 6 January between the Bulgarian Premier, Filov, and Ribbentrop.[2] German quarters noted on the same day that Soviet pressure was being exerted on Bulgaria not to join the Tripartite Pact. On 8 January, Schulenburg reported that the Russians were likely to be alarmed by the reports of large-scale German troops movements into Roumania, but was instructed not to broach the subject himself, and if approached to justify the move by British moves in Greece.[3] On 8 January Hitler was reported as saying that the Soviet attitude concerning the imminent German action in Bulgaria was not yet clear, and that the Soviet Union required Bulgaria itself for the assembly of troops for an advance on the Bosphorus.[4] At about this time a conference was apparently held in Moscow, attended by the Soviet envoys to Bulgaria, Yugoslavia, Roumania, and Hungary. It was followed on 12 January by a public warning to Bulgaria which involved an oblique reproach to Germany as well. A Tass communiqué on 12 January ran as follows:

'Recently stories have appeared in the foreign press, said to emanate from informed Bulgarian circles, to the effect that a number of German troops had entered Bulgaria, and that this was done with the knowledge and consent of the U.S.S.R.; that the U.S.S.R. responded favourably to Bulgaria's inquiry on the passage of German troops. Tass is authorized to state:

'1. If German troops are actually in Bulgaria and if they are continuing to enter the country, this has taken place without the prior knowledge or consent of the U.S.S.R., in as much as Germany has never broached to the U.S.S.R. the question of either garrisoning such troops in Bulgaria or of their passage through the country.

'2. The Bulgarian Government has never discussed with the U.S.S.R. the question of allowing German troops to pass through Bulgaria and hence could not have received any kind of reply from the U.S.S.R.'

On 17 January, Dekanozov called upon Weizsäcker to inform him that there were reports that the German troops in Roumania were intending to march into Bulgaria and to occupy that country, Greece and the Straits. This would lead Great Britain, in alliance with Turkey, to try to forestall the German moves, and Bulgaria would become a theatre of operations:

[1] Hitler wrote to Mussolini about Soviet pressure on Bulgaria and his hope that the obstacle to Bulgarian adhesion could be overcome, on 5 December 1940 and again in his letter of 31 December; *Lettres secrètes*, pp. 96 and 107.

[2] Dallin, loc. cit.   [3] *Nazi-Soviet Relations*, pp. 264-7.

[4] *Nazi Conspiracy and Aggression*, vol. 6, p. 992.

'The Soviet Government has stated repeatedly to the German Government that it considers the territory of Bulgaria and of the Straits as the security zone of the U.S.S.R. and that it cannot be indifferent to events which threaten the security interests of the U.S.S.R. In view of all this the Soviet Government regards it as its duty to give warning that it will consider the appearance of any foreign armed forces on the territory of Bulgaria and of the Straits as a violation of the security interests of the U.S.S.R.'

Weizsäcker's reply was distinctly non-committal.

Molotov made the same statement to Schulenburg on the same day, but preceded it with the remark that the Soviet Government was surprised to have received no reply to its communication of 25 November (regarding the proposed new treaty with the Powers of the Tripartite Pact). Schulenburg gave as the reason for this, the necessity for Germany of consulting Italy and Japan.

On the 22nd and 23rd replies to the Russian communications were made in Berlin and Moscow. These were to the effect that there was no reason to believe that Great Britain contemplated occupying the Straits, and Germany would respect Turkish territory unless Turkey committed a hostile act against her armies. But Great Britain was about to attempt to gain a foothold on Greek territory which Germany could not allow. A movement through Bulgaria would be necessary in the event of operations in Greece. There was no intention of violating the interests of Soviet security:

'The Reich Government—as it indicated on the occasion of the Berlin visit of Chairman (i.e. Premier) Molotov—has an understanding of the Soviet interest in the Straits question and is prepared to endorse a revision of the Montreux Convention at the proper time. Germany on her part is politically not interested in the Straits question and will withdraw her troops from there (*sic*) after having carried out her operations in the Balkans.'

With regard to the wider question raised by Molotov, it was repeated that consultations were proceeding with Italy and Japan. The German Government hoped to be able 'to resume the political discussion with the Soviet Government in the near future'.

In Berlin, Dekanozov repeated that the presence of any foreign troops on Bulgarian territory would be a violation of Soviet security, but Molotov's comment to Schulenburg seems to have been more guarded.[1]

[1] *Nazi-Soviet Relations*, pp. 264–74.

Towards the end of the month, the Bulgarian Communist Party again demanded a mutual-assistance pact with the U.S.S.R.[1] Early in February, Sobelev visited Sofia and there were once more reports that he had proposed such an agreement.[2]

The problem of Bulgaria was now a part of the wider efforts of Anglo-American diplomacy to build up resistance to Germany in the Balkans. These efforts hinged upon the attitude of Turkey, which was not receiving any overt support from Russia.[1] On 17 February the signature of a non-aggression pact between Turkey and Bulgaria was announced and this could only be interpreted as an indication of Turkey's unwillingness to risk intervention. Soviet disapproval of the Turkish step was made clear in a Tass communiqué on 22 February:

'The Swiss newspaper *Baseler Nachrichten*, recently published a story to the effect that the latest agreement between Bulgaria and Turkey had been concluded with the active participation of the Soviet Union. Tass is authorized to state that this report does not correspond to fact.'

On 22 February, Schulenburg was instructed to let it be known abroad that the number of German troops in Roumania was now very large—the actual figure was 680,000. On 27 February he was instructed to see Molotov on the 28th and inform him that on 1 March, Bulgaria would sign the Tripartite Pact. On 1 March, he was to inform Molotov that German troops were entering Bulgaria forthwith, and to renew assurances that only Greece was envisaged. Molotov received the second communication with great gravity and immediately drafted a note which ran:

'1. It is to be regretted that despite the caution contained in the *démarche* of November 25, 1940, on the part of the Soviet Government the German Reich Government has deemed it possible to take a course that involves injury to the security interests of the U.S.S.R. and has decided to effect the military occupation of Bulgaria.

---

[1] Dallin, *Foreign Policy*, pp. 282–4. On 20 January, Hitler told Mussolini he had rejected a Soviet protest about the concentration of German troops in Roumania, *Fuehrer Conferences on Naval Affairs*, 1941, p. 15.

[2] Mackenzie, *Wind of Freedom*, p. 138. On 11 February the Bulgarian Government took steps against certain Soviet agencies without provoking any reaction from the Russians. Leigh White, *The Long Balkan Night*, pp. 105–6.

[3] On 4 February, Tass issued a formal denial of a report that a secret agreement had been concluded with Turkey, under which the Soviet Union undertook to supply her with armaments to counteract possible German activity in the Balkans.

'2. In view of the fact that the Soviet Government maintains the same basic position as in its *démarche* of November 25, the German Government must understand that it cannot count on support from the U.S.S.R. for its acts in Bulgaria.'[1]

On the same day Bulgaria duly signed the Tripartite Pact, and German troops crossed the Danube and entered the country. A statement broadcast by the Soviet radio on 3 March ran as follows:

'On 1 March a representative of the Bulgarian Minister for Foreign Affairs, M. Altinov, stated to the Minister of the U.S.S.R. at Sofia that the Bulgarian Government had given its consent to the entry of German troops into Bulgaria, in order to ensure peace in the Balkans. On 3 March, the Deputy Foreign Commissar Vyshin-sky replied as follows to the Bulgarian Minister in Moscow:

'In reply to the communication of 1 March . . . the Soviet Government deems it necessary to say: (1) The Soviet Government cannot share the view of the Bulgarian Government as to the correctness of its attitude in this question: as this attitude, independently of whether the Bulgarian Government wishes it, leads not to the consolidation of peace, but to an extension of the sphere of war and the involving of Bulgaria in war; (2) The Soviet Government, true to its peace policy, is not in a position to render any support whatever to the Bulgarian Government in the execution of its present policy. It finds it necessary to make this statement, particularly in view of unhindered rumours spread in the Bulgarian press which fundamentally misrepresent the real attitude of the Soviet Government.'[2]

This statement was noted in German quarters as symptomatic of a general stiffening of the Soviet attitude over the Balkans.[3]

With Bulgaria in Germany's grasp, the position of Yugoslavia became critical. The visit to Ankara at the end of February of Mr. Eden and Sir John Dill failed to secure any

---

[1] *Nazi-Soviet Relations,* pp. 274–9.

[2] The direct protest to Germany was not made public.

[3] *Nazi Conspiracy and Aggression,* vol. 6, pp. 994–5. Cf. Ribbentrop's account in his statement of 22 June 1941. There seems to have been a certain amount of contact at this time between the Russians and the British mission in Moscow. Sir Stafford Cripps returned there after his meeting with Mr. Eden at Ankara on 28 February convinced of the imminence of a German attack on Russia. Similar sentiments were now heard in Soviet military circles. Gafencu, *Prelude,* pp. 133–9. The Soviet press also took up a fairly favourable attitude towards Allied prospects in the Eastern Mediterranean. On 1 March 1941, John Scott sailed from Odessa in a ship carrying 200 Czech airmen, interned after serving with the Polish forces and now released to join the R.A.F. in the Middle East; *Duel for Europe,* p. 191.

definite promise of Turkish support for Greece or Yugoslavia;
on the other hand Turkey still seemed prepared to resist any
German demands on herself.

Gavrilovic's efforts to secure Soviet undertakings on Yugoslavia's behalf came up against the Soviet Government's habi-
tual reserve. On 28 November he had felt able to telegraph
that the Soviet Union was prepared to help Yugoslavia in the
matter of armaments, but there does not seem to have been any
practical sequel. On 28 November the Yugoslav Foreign
Minister Cincar-Markovic left Belgrade for talks with Hitler
and Ribbentrop. At this juncture, no definite demands on
Yugoslavia seem to have been made. Hitler and Ribbentrop
underlined the complete agreement existing between Berlin
and Moscow.[1] Pressure increased, however, with the approach
of the spring campaigning season. On 14 February the Yugoslav Foreign Minister, this time accompanied by the Prime
Minister Tsvetkovic, again saw the Fuehrer. They were now
confronted with a definite demand for Yugoslavia's adherence
to the Tripartite Pact. This demand was confirmed and probably agreed to when the Regent, Prince Paul, saw Hitler at
Berchtesgaden on 5 March.[2]

The reason for the ensuing delay is not quite clear; it may
have been largely due to internal political considerations.[3]

On 23 March the text of the German demands became known
in Belgrade.[4] At a Cabinet meeting on the same day, three
Serbian Ministers voted against accepting the pact; the Prime
Minister and Minister of War abstained; the other Serbian and
all the Croat and Slovene Ministers voted for acceptance. The
three opponents of the pact thereupon resigned. The Foreign
Minister telegraphed to Gavrilovic on the 24th that the Prime

[1] 'Le Coup d'Etat de Simovitch', *France Intérieure*, September 1945.

[2] On 27 February, Yugoslavia had signed a pact of friendship with
Hungary, itself a signatory of the Tripartite Pact.

[3] On 15 March it was understood in Belgrade that Yugoslavia had in
fact rejected the German proposals and had suggested a non-aggression
pact with an undertaking to resist by force any violation of her neutrality.
The Germans were believed to have replied that this was insufficient and to
have given till 19 March for the acceptance of their original demands;
B.I.N., XVIII, p. 383. According to Compton Mackenzie, the departure
of the Yugoslav Ministers to sign the pact was actually announced for the
13 March but was postponed because of pressure from the U.S.S.R. which
on 16 March definitely advised Yugoslavia not to sign; op. cit., pp. 158–9.

[4] *B.I.N.*, XVIII, pp. 458–9. *Nazi Conspiracy and Aggression*, vol. 6, p. 995.
As compared with previous signatories Yugoslavia secured important
concessions. She was not required to participate in military action arising
from the provisions of the Pact and she was promised eventual German
support for her demands for an outlet on the Aegean (i.e. Salonika).

Minister and himself were about to leave for Vienna to sign the pact and Gavrilovic telegraphed his resignation on the same day. On 25 March, the Yugoslav Ministers signed the Tripartite Pact at Vienna.

The Soviet Government's own attitude towards developments in the Balkans had been made still clearer on 22 March, when it was stated in Ankara that Turkey had been assured that the Soviet Union would do nothing to embarrass Turkey should that country's relations with a third Power (i.e. Germany) deteriorate. This was followed up on 25 March by a Narkomindel communiqué:

'Since certain rumours are being circulated in the foreign press, according to which, if Turkey were obliged to go to war, the U.S.S.R. would take advantage of her difficulties in order to attack her, the Soviet Government, having in mind the questions put to it on this subject, has made known to the Turkish Government that:

'1. These rumours do not correspond in the least with the position taken by the U.S.S.R.

'2. Should Turkey in fact be exposed to aggression, and if she were compelled in defence of her territory to go to war, she would be able by virtue of the Russo-Turkish Pact of Non-Aggression (of 17 December 1925) to rely on the complete understanding and neutrality of the U.S.S.R.

'3. In taking cognisance of this declaration, the Turkish Government has expressed to the Soviet Government its sincerest thanks and has declared in its turn, that in the event of the U.S.S.R. finding itself in a similar situation it can rely upon the complete understanding and neutrality of Turkey.[1]

This was naturally considered by the Germans to be a hostile step; but the terms of the declaration seem to have been so narrowly drawn as to suggest that Turkey would take care not to go to war in defence of Greece and were thus of no assistance in the building up of a common front among the still independent nations of south-eastern Europe.[2]

---

[1] *B.I.N.*, XVIII, pp. 451–2.

[2] In an article by Kalinin published during the Soviet-German war, the chairman of the Presidium of the Supreme Soviet claimed that Soviet action had helped to save Britain's position in the Middle East, since after the occupation of the Balkan Peninsula 'a move against Egypt through Turkey was well within the power of the German army. . . .' Apparently the fact that the Soviet Union took a definite stand on the Yugoslav question and then warned the Germans, in a statement to the Turkish Government in March 1941, that it could count on the complete understanding and neutrality of the U.S.S.R. 'played quite an important part in causing the Germans to reject this path'; M. Kalinin, 'Slavs and the War', *Soviet War News*, 11 April 1944. There seems to be no confirmation of a story put out on the basis of documents allegedly discovered in Germany to the effect that Molotov visited Berlin in March 1941 and offered the Germans a

This cautious demonstration of Soviet hostility to the expansion of German rule in the Balkans may have encouraged the revolt which overthrew the Yugoslav Regency and Government on the night of 26–27 March. But there is no evidence of Soviet participation.[1] The Germans themselves blamed American intrigues.[2] Belgrade Communists signalized the event by demonstrating impartially against 'imperialist England' and against Germany, and demanded a mutual-assistance pact with the U.S.S.R.[3]

Although the new Foreign Minister Nincic announced Yugoslavia's neutrality and said that the revolt was of purely internal significance, the Germans demanded, on 30 March, the fulfilment of his predecessor's pledges and Yugoslav demobilization.   Gavrilovic again tried to secure active assistance from the Soviet Union to parry the inevitable attack. The new Yugoslav Government informed Gavrilovic that Molotov acting through the Soviet Chargé d'Affaires in Belgrade had offered Yugoslavia a military convention and that they were sending to Moscow two officers to act as delegates along with Gavrilovic for the negotiation and signature of the convention.

---

military alliance in return for complete control of the Dardanelles, a free hand in Iraq and Iran and a position in Saudi Arabia to secure Soviet domination of the Persian Gulf and the Gulf of Aden; R. Lacoste, *La Russie Soviétique et la Question d'Orient* (Paris, Editions Internationales, 1946), p. 37, quoting *New York Times*, 19 March 1946 and *New York Post*, 26 March 1946.

[1] 'The Yugoslav revolt was inspired by hopes pinned on Moscow not on London, and ... at a long view it was a demonstration of pro-Russian sentiment.' Mackenzie, op. cit., p. 162. Cf. the account in 'Le Coup d'Etat de Simovitch', *France Intérieure*, September-October 1945. Cf. R. West, *Black Lamb and Grey Falcon* (Macmillan, 1941), vol. 2, pp. 530–46. The *coup* postponed the movement of German troops into Yugoslavia which had been ordered for the 27th; *Fuehrer Conferences on Naval Affairs*, 1941, p. 41. It is difficult in view of the evidence now available to accept the claim put forward by Goering that the German attack on Russia might not have taken place but for the alleged complicity of the Russians in the Belgrade *coup*; *Nuremberg Trial*, part 9, pp. 128–9.

[2] *Nazi Conspiracy and Aggression*, vol. 6, pp. 895–6. The same document mentions a report from Roumania that it was believed there that events were influenced by the prospect of an agreement with the U.S.S.R. and of obtaining arms from Russia.

[3] Dallin, *Foreign Policy*, p. 303. The statement that 'The Communist and Fascist groups alone refused their support and continued their Quisling role' (*The World To-day*, January 1946, p. 18), is thus rather misleading. What is clear, is that Communist opposition to the Germans was organized independently. Once Russia had been attacked this emerged as the 'Partisan' movement which could otherwise hardly have got going as early as the summer of 1941, as it did according to Brigadier F. H. R. Maclean, 'Tito and Mikhailovitc', *The Times*, 11 June 1946.

On the evening of 4 April, Molotov summoned Schulenburg to the Kremlin to inform him that the Soviet Government had accepted the Yugoslav offer of a non-aggression pact and that this would be signed that night or on the following day. Schulenburg pointed out that the moment was unfortunate as Yugoslavia's attitude towards Germany was an ambiguous one. But Molotov refused to accept this view, and declared himself convinced of the Yugoslav Government's peaceful intentions. The Soviet Government would stand by its decision and urgently hoped that Germany too would do everything possible to preserve peace in the Balkans.[1]

At the first meeting with the Yugoslavs on 5 April, Vyshinsky declared that there must have been a misunderstanding; no military convention was ever intended. He offered them an ordinary treaty of friendship with the usual clause providing for neutrality in case of war. The Yugoslavs argued all day to try to get at least this clause replaced by one providing that in case of war friendly relations would continue. Finally the Russians agreed and it was in consequence of the delay while the change was made that the pact was signed after midnight on the night of 5–6 April although dated 5 April.[2] A few hours later at 5.15 a.m. on 6 April, the Germans invaded Yugoslavia and Greece. The Yugoslav treaty was given unusual publicity in the Soviet press. But the Russians, as Gavrilovic telephoned to Simovic during the night, would go no further.[3] When Schulenburg, as instructed, called on Molotov on 6 April to inform him that Germany had been compelled to attack Greece and Yugoslavia because of their plans for co-operating with Great Britain against her, neither the Ambassador nor Molotov mentioned the Soviet-Yugoslav Pact.[4] The treaty was never published in the Yugoslav press and had no effect on the course of the Balkan campaign which ended with the capitulation of the Yugoslav Army on 17 April, the German conquest of Greece, and the evacuation by British forces of the Greek mainland, which was completed after heavy losses by the end of the month.[5] The Turkish decision not to intervene was made known on 9 April.

[1] *Nazi-Soviet Relations*, pp. 316–18.
[2] Text in Scott, op. cit., App.
[3] Evidence of Simovic during the trial of Mihailovic, *Manchester Guardian*, 29 June 1946.
[4] *Nazi-Soviet Relations*, pp. 319–20.
[5] According to German reports, the Russians hesitated between 6 and 8 April as to what attitude to adopt to the conflict. *Nazi Conspiracy and Aggression*, vol. 6, pp. 996–7. After the first two days, the overwhelming superiority of the enemy's forces had already made the outcome obvious.

On 12 April the Hungarian Minister in Moscow informed
Vyshinsky of his country's occupation of portions of Yugoslav
territory.   In his reply, Vyshinsky declared that a particularly
bad impression had been created by Hungary's acting so soon
after her Pact of Friendship with Yugoslavia. 'It could easily
be understood,' he added, 'in what a position Hungary might
find herself if she, while in misfortune, should be subjected in
her turn to an attack of this kind'—since in Hungary there
were also 'substantial national minorities'.[1]

The conduct of the U.S.S.R. towards Yugoslavia at this juncture was significant of the change in relations with Germany.[2]
Co-operation, particularly on the economic side, had not yet
come to an end.   But it was clear that such co-operation would
continue to be limited by the Soviet Union's regards for its own
vital interests.[3] A memorandum by Schnurre on 5 April
pointed out that whereas political tension had caused considerable restraint on the Soviet side in the carrying out of
deliveries after the Agreement of 10 January, 1941, 'deliveries
in March rose by leaps and bounds' and a new very favourable
grain contract was secured. Transit traffic through Siberia
was also proceeding favourably. Hitherto German deliveries
had been kept to schedule but this would not be possible later
because of labour shortage and the priority of the military
programme.[4] Some German circles remained convinced that
the policy of friendship with the Soviet Union should be
continued. Such was the view of Schulenburg, who left
Moscow for Berlin on 13 April and did not return to his post
until 30 April.[5] But according to Ribbentrop, Hitler forbade

---

On 10 April, *Red Star* declared that the Soviet-Yugoslav treaty was 'all the
more valuable under the new conditions because the Soviet Union always
fulfils its international pledges'; quoted by Schuman, *Soviet Politics at
Home and Abroad*, p. 405.

[1] Text in Scott, op. cit., App. On 9 April, Vyshinsky had made a friendly
suggestion to the Roumanian Ambassador that Soviet-Roumanian relations
should be put on a better footing, but later refused to consider any territorial concession. Gafencu, *Prelude*, p. 196.

[2] Instructions were given in Berlin on 13 March that no Russian
boundary or repatriation commissions should be allowed to remain on the
German side of the Lithuanian frontier after 25 March. The massing of
German troops in the North-East had begun. *Nazi-Soviet Relations*, p. 279.

[3] Further German assistance for training personnel for the rapidly growing Soviet fleet was asked for as late as 28 March. *Nazi Conspiracy and
Aggression*, vol. 6, p. 996.

[4] *Nazi-Soviet Relations*, pp. 318–9.

[5] Ribbentrop's secretary asserted at the Nuremberg Trial that Schulenburg and Hilger, the economic adviser to the Moscow Embassy, were recalled
by Ribbentrop in order to reinforce Ribbentrop's warning to Hitler against

any further negotiations with the Soviet Union after the conclusion of the Soviet-Yugoslav pact.[1]

The Balkan campaign following upon the *coup d'état* in Yugoslavia did in fact have the effect of postponing the date of the attack on Russia, originally intended for 15 May. At a conference on 30 April, the date was fixed for 22 June.[2] But the Soviet Union's actions had hardened Hitler's determination that the attack should be made. Giving evidence at the Nuremberg Trial on 15 March 1941, Goering said:

'The affair of the Simovich undertaking was a very late and decisive reason to remove the very last hopes of the Fuehrer in regard to Russia, and to convince them that he had to take the first steps in that direction. Before the Simovich incident it is probable that although preparations had been undertaken, they would have doubted the necessity of an attack against the Soviet Union.'

In addition the general course of the war indicated reasons for Germany turning its attention to the east. *Red Star* said on 9 April that there could be no question of an invasion of Britain. The central burden of the war had been shifted from west to east.[3] The Germans also appear to have believed that the war could only be continued if all their armed forces were 'fed by Russia' in the third year of the fighting.[4]

Germany's intentions were certainly not altogether unsuspected in some Moscow circles. Soviet anxieties were manifest

---

going to war with Russia. *Nuremberg Trial*, Part 10, p. 83. Ribbentrop himself declared that the Moscow Embassy reported favourably on Russia's intentions in the spring of 1941; ibid., pp. 249–51. Cf. Byrnes, op. cit., p. 291.

[1] *Nuremberg Trial*, part 10, p. 192.

[2] *Nazi Conspiracy and Aggression*, vol. 3, pp. 633–4. Cf. 'New Light on Nazi Foreign Policy', *Foreign Affairs*, October 1946, pp. 50–1. It is not clear whether the campaign in Crete (20 May–2 June) affected the planning of the German attack on Russia; it was of considerable importance for the situation in Iraq.

[3] Louis Fischer, *Dawn of Victory* (New York, Duell, Sloan and Pearce, 1942), p. 148. According to Kalinin, in the article already quoted, 'the Germans by attacking the Soviet Union hoped that victory would cover their flanks for a further advance eastwards to India'; *Soviet War News*, 11 April 1944.

[4] Memorandum of a conference on 'Plan Barbarossa', 2 May 1941; *Nuremberg Trial*, part 1, p. 177. 'Moscow knew that only too well. An article in *Red Star*, commenting on the downfall of Belgrade, in more than usually reserved terms, observed not without malice that the destruction of Yugloslavia deprived Germany of an important source of food supply, and consequently increased the value of the economic relations between Germany and the U.S.S.R.' Gafencu, *Prelude*, pp. 171–2.

in further military precautions.[1] But the most spectacular result was in the field of Far Eastern diplomacy.

As has already been noted, only slow progress had been made in the negotiations with Japan begun after the conclusion of the Tripartite Pact. On 15 November Tass denied a foreign press report that the Soviet Union and Japan had reached an agreement for the division of their respective spheres of influence in Asia, and that this had involved a Soviet undertaking to give no further help to China.[2] On 5 December a more authoritative statement was published in connexion with the Japanese treaty with the Nanking 'puppet' Government of Wang Ching-wei. The Japanese Government, it was made known, had given the Soviet Government assurances that the anti-Communist clauses of this treaty were not directed against the U.S.S.R. and that the treaty was no impediment to the Japanese desire for better relations with the U.S.S.R. The Soviet Ambassador, Smetanin, had found it necessary to state that the 'policy of the U.S.S.R. had not changed in the least with regard to its relations with China'. New trade agreements with China were in fact concluded on 11 December 1940 and on 3 and 12 January 1941.[3] In January, it appears that Soviet supplies for China were increased.[4]

From the Japanese point of view the only hopeful features were the renewal of the fisheries agreement for one more year on 20 January, the settlement at the same time of an outstanding financial dispute, and the establishment on 12 March of diplomatic relations between the U.S.S.R. and Thailand, now in fact a Japanese vassal state.[5] It was generally believed, however, that Japan was doing its best to secure an agreement.[6] The state of Japanese-Soviet relations was thought to be a

[1] German reconnaissance flights over Soviet territory became more numerous. *Pravda*, 29 June 1941. On 24 April, the German Naval Attaché in Moscow reported that many rumours of a Russo-German war were in circulation and that Sir Stafford Cripps had forecast 22 June as the date. *Nazi Conspiracy and Aggression*, vol. 6, p. 997. On 30 April, *Pravda* for the first time reported the presence of German troops in Finland. On 17 April a twenty-day ban was enforced on the entry of foreigners into the Soviet Union via Manchouli. This was believed to be due to exceptionally heavy troop movements to the west. O. D. Tolischus, *Tokyo Record* (New York, Reynal and Hitchcock, 1943), p. 103.

[2] On the following day, Tass denied a report that Japan had offered British India to Russia in return for Eastern Siberia.

[3] Dallin, *Foreign Policy*, p. 429.

[4] Davis and Lindley, op. cit., p. 177.

[5] Moore, *Soviet Far Eastern Policy*, p. 121.

[6] In January, there were reports that Japan had offered to cede southern Sakhalin in return for a political agreement. Scott, op. cit., p. 189.

primary reason for the journey to Europe in March 1941 of the Japanese Foreign Minister, Matsuoka.

Travelling via Moscow, Matsuoka had a discussion with Stalin and Molotov on 24 March. Although there was no positive outcome, Japanese press comment suggested that the atmosphere had not been unfavourable.[1] According to the account given by Matsuoka to Hitler three days later, the talk was on the initiative of the Russians. It seems to have begun on a high ideological level with Matsuoka explaining how the traditional Japanese 'moral communism' had been overthrown by Western liberalism, individualism and egoism. Hence the ideological bitterness of the struggle against the Anglo-Saxons. He had represented to Stalin that the latter were the common foe of Japan, Germany and Russia and that after the elimination of the British Empire, the difficulties between Japan and Russia could be eliminated. 'Stalin had arranged to give him an answer when he passed through Moscow again on his return journey to Japan; he had, however, after some reflection stated that Soviet Russia had never gotten along well with Great Britain and never would'.

In a subsequent talk with Ribbentrop, Matsuoka stated that he had proposed a non-aggression pact to Molotov to which the latter had replied with the proposal of a neutrality agreement. On his return to Moscow he would be forced to take a positive stand on these matters. He also intended to try to get the Russians to give up Northern Sakhalin, where the Russians were putting obstacles in the way of the Japanese working their important oil concessions.[2]

From Moscow, Matsuoka proceeded to Berlin which he reached on 26 March. On 27 March, he had a lengthy talk with Ribbentrop, followed by another with Ribbentrop and Hitler. On the 28th and 29th, he again saw Ribbentrop. The question of Russia joining the Tripartite Pact, he was informed, no longer arose. The Soviet demands, which he expounded, could not be met. Besides, Russia was still internationally-minded. Stalin had hoped for a long war which would render the peoples ripe for revolution. The fall of France had not been to his liking. Now Russia was trying to push forward in the Balkans; 'in connection with recent happenings in Yugoslavia, activity was now increasing, partly with the aid of the

---

[1] There is reason to believe that American diplomacy was trying to prevent the Soviet Union from acceding to the Japanese request for an agreement. Dallin, *Foreign Policy*, pp. 333–4.

[2] *Nazi-Soviet Relations*, pp. 280–1, 296–7, 308–9.

Sokol organisation, or through direct Communist influence'. Matsuoka thereupon stated that Chiang Kai-shek 'with whom he was in personal touch, who knew him and trusted him, was greatly alarmed as to the further increase of the influence of the Red Army in China'. Ribbentrop declared that the conditions described might lead to a Soviet-German conflict. 'If Germany should feel herself endangered she would immediately attack and put an end to Bolshevism'.[1] Ribbentrop advised Matsuoka not to carry the discussions with the Russians too far as he did not know how the situation would develop. But Germany would strike at Russia at once if Russia attacked Japan and the largest part of the German army was now on the eastern frontier ready to attack if necessary. Japan could therefore strike south at Singapore without fear of complications with Russia. Ribbentrop did not himself believe Russia would fight; if she did, she would be finished off in a few months. 'He could not know of course, just how things with Russia would develop. It was uncertain whether or not Stalin would intensify his present unfriendly policy against Germany . . . a conflict with Russia was anyhow within the realm of possibility.' After visiting Rome, Matsuoka returned to Berlin. He saw Hitler on 4 April and discussed with him the possibility of keeping the United States out of the war after the Japanese attack on Great Britain. Hitler declared that for his part he would not hesitate a moment to reply instantly to any extension of the war, whether by Russia, or by America.[2] In his proclamation of 22 June Hitler declared that he had advised Matsuoka, 'to ease the tension with Russia hoping . . . to serve the cause of peace'. This is confirmed in a note of a conversation between Hitler and the German Supreme Naval Commander.[3] Hitler also told the latter that he had said to Matsuoka that Russia would not be attacked it she behaved in a friendly fashion and observed the Soviet-German treaty. Germany acquiesced in the idea of a Soviet-Japanese pact. At the moment, Russia was acting favourably and was not expecting an attack.[4] For his part, Ribbentrop again appears to have told Matsuoka on 5 April not to go too far in his negotiations with the Russians. Germany might fight Russia anyhow, if Stalin's attitude continued hostile, and would guarantee to do so, if Russia attacked Japan. The largest part

[1] *Nazi-Soviet Relations*, pp. 281–311.
[2] *Nazi-Soviet Relations*, pp. 311–6.
[3] *Nazi Conspiracy and Aggression*, vol. 6, p. 997.
[4] Hitler's object was to persuade Japan into an immediate declaration of war on Great Britain. *Fuehrer Conferences on Naval Affairs*, 1941, pp. 47–8.

of Germany's army was on the eastern frontiers and ready to launch an attack at any moment.[1]

By the time that Matsuoka returned to Moscow on 7 April, events in Yugoslavia had given a new twist to Soviet-German relations, and his statement to the press that he did not believe this to be the case can hardly be taken at its face value. There was considerable nervousness in Japan at the thought that (whatever might have passed in Berlin), Japan was bound under the Tripartite Pact to come to Germany's aid, but that Germany was not reciprocally bound where Russia was concerned. Matsuoka's resignation after the German attack on Russia, suggests that he had decided that such an event was unlikely, possibly because he believed that the Soviet Union could still satisfy Germany by further peaceful collaboration. The course of Matsuoka's negotiations in Moscow can be followed to some extent from Schulenburg's dispatches, although he noted Matsuoka's reticence in their early stages. By the evening of 10 April, Matsuoka had waived the original Japanese demand for a non-aggression pact coupled with the purchase by Japan of North Sakhalin. The proposal was now for a neutrality pact, but the Soviet Government was insisting on the abandonment of the Japanese concessions in Northern Sakhalin. But in a final interview on the 12th, the Russians gave up the latter as an immediate demand, and the pact was agreed upon.[2]

By the treaty, which was signed and published on the 13th, each party pledged itself to neutrality should the other 'become the object of hostilities on the part of one or several third powers'. In an appended declaration, the U.S.S.R. and Japan respectively bound themselves to observe the territorial integrity and inviolability of Manchukuo, and of the Mongol Peoples' Republic.[3] Only on 31 March 1944 was it revealed that the Soviet negotiators had secured an important concession as the price of the pact:

'In the spring of 1941, during negotiations for the conclusion of the Soviet-Japanese neutrality pact, the Soviet Government raised before the Japanese Government the question of the liquidation of [the Japanese oil and coal concessions on Northern Sakhalin]. On 13 April 1941, simultaneously with the signing of the neutrality pact, M. Matsuoka . . . gave to the Soviet Government a pledge in writing to settle the matter of the liquidation of the concessions in Northern

[1] Nuremberg Trial, United States Document C. 33. (Not printed.) Cf. *Nazi Conspiracy and Aggression*, vol. 4, pp. 526–8.

[2] *Nazi-Soviet Relations*, pp. 321–4; Cf. Gafencu, *Prelude*, pp. 154–61.

[3] The text is in Moore, op. cit., pp. 200–1. Scott suggests that the change was in the Soviet attitude and was due to the Yugoslav collapse and to increasing doubts about German intentions, op. cit., pp. 224–8.

Sakhalin within several months. On 31 May 1941 M. Matsuoka confirmed this pledge by a new statement conveyed to the Soviet Government through M. Tatekawa, the Japanese Ambassador in Moscow. At that time the Japanese party undertook to settle this matter not later than six months [after] the date of the signing of the neutrality pact. This undertaking of the Japanese party was not fulfilled...'[1]

In spite of the fact that the new treaty was simply one of neutrality and made no mention of mutual consultation, the circumstances of its signature and the fact that Stalin made a demonstrative appearance at the station to bid Matsuoka the fondest of farewells on his departure from Moscow, suggested that the Russians attached great importance to the pact.[2] An article in *Izvestia* on 15 April was entitled 'The Historic Reversal in the Relations between Russia and Japan'.[3]

'The documents signed on 13 April in Moscow', it said, 'not only assist in strengthening peace, but also open the way to real good neighbour friendly relations between the two great peoples of both countries. The historic paths of development of both the Soviet Union and Japan demand such relations. Enmity between these two Powers can only serve as an obstacle to the realization of the tasks each one has set for itself. It is not by chance that at various historical stages various third countries have tried to support and stir up this enmity. Having passed through a multitude of difficult experiences, Soviet-Japanese relations are now passing through a new phase which promises to bear good fruit.'

On 16 April, Molotov asked the Japanese Ambassador to call on him to continue negotiations regarding a trade pact.[4]

Alleged attempts in the British and American press to belittle the significance of the pact were answered in an article in *Pravda* on 19 April. This also denied that German mediation had been responsible for the conclusion of the pact, and pointed out that it was time it was realized that the U.S.S.R. followed its own policy, independent, and free of all external influences. This article traced back the idea of such a pact for a whole decade and revealed for the first time the Soviet rejection, in October 1940, of a pact with Japan similar to the Soviet-German pact, and the Soviet refusal in November to adhere to the Tripartite Pact.

[1] *Moscow News*, 1 April 1944, quoted in Moore, op. cit., pp. 257–9. The agreement was only concluded on 30 March 1944.

[2] Cf. 'Asiaticus', 'Soviet Relations with Japan', *Pacific Affairs*, September 1941.   Schulenburg and the German military attaché also came in for a share of Stalin's cordiality.   *Nazi-Soviet Relations*, p. 324.

[3] Moore, op. cit., pp. 251–3.

[4] *Nazi-Soviet Relations*, pp. 326–7.

The Japanese press, in welcoming the treaty, forecast that the Soviet Union would compensate itself in central Asia and particularly in Iran for its concessions elsewhere.[1]

Of more immediate interest was the effect which the treaty would have upon the Soviet position in China. The Chinese Communists proved fully capable of justifying the new turn in Soviet policy. A pamphlet published by them in Yenan declared that the new treaty was a victory for the Soviet peace policy, consolidating the Far Eastern front. It would have the effect of raising the international status of the Soviet Union, making her voice as audible in the east as in the west. It did not restrict aid for China, and as for the assurances about Manchukuo, Soviet Russia had never intended to invade it. The reconquest of the Four North-Eastern Provinces (Manchukuo), which, like Outer Mongolia, formed an integral part of the Republic of China, was a matter for the Chinese themselves to undertake. Collaboration between the Kuomintang and the Communists continued to be indispensable.[2] This statement was in accordance with the current Comintern 'line' which was

[1] Soviet relations with Iran had been rather strained for some time. The trade treaty of 25 March 1940 had indeed embodied substantial concessions to Iran, including transit facilities for her trade with Germany. Further commercial and technical discussions had continued throughout the year. Meanwhile, broadcasting in Persian and the export of Soviet films were added to the Soviet propaganda armoury. On the other hand, Russian troop concentrations on the frontier were reported and there were rumours of requests for air bases and railway concessions in northern Iran. Molotov, in his speech on 1 August 1940, had connected Iran as well as Turkey with the recent revelations about Allied designs on the Baku oilfields and had drawn the conclusion that it was necessary to intensify vigilance on Russia's southern borders; Elwell-Sutton, *Modern Iran*, pp. 184–5; 'Iran, Its Position To-day', *B.I.N.*, 14 June 1941; 'The Land of Iran', ibid., 6 September 1941. From the autumn of 1940, Germany replaced the Allies as the main source of Soviet anxieties in the Middle East. German trade with Iran continued to flourish and in the year ending March 1941 its value was more than four times that of Soviet trade with the country in the same period; Haas, *Iran*, p. 222. Teheran, an important centre of Axis propaganda, became fuller than ever of German and Italian nationals; Sir Percy Sykes, 'The Role of the Middle East', *J.R.C.A.S.*, January 1941. In April there were reports of the arrival of German instructors and of stocks of war material, in May of 6,000 German 'tourists'. On 8 May, Tass denied that the Soviet Union had dispatched light naval units to the Caspian and that a military mission had left for Teheran to arrange for the use of air bases in Iran in the event of Turkey becoming involved in war. Rumours of a Soviet-German deal for the partition of central and southern Asia continued to spread. Dallin, *The Big Three*, p. 140 n.

[2] *Oriental Affairs*, May 1941; cf. P. J. Jaffe, 'The Soviet-Japanese Neutrality Pact', *Amerasia*, May 1941. On the other hand, there were unconfirmed reports that after the announcement of the treaty, the Chinese Communists had taken up a neutral attitude towards Japan.

that the lesser States, Yugoslavia, Greece, Norway, and China, were right to continue their struggle for independence but should do so without alliances with Great Britain or the United States.[1]

On 16 April Molotov had given assurances to the Chinese Ambassador that nothing would be altered in Soviet relations with China.[2] And the subsequent course of trade relations tended to bear out this assurance. Once this aspect of the question became apparent to the Japanese, there were demands that the agreement should be extended. Further Soviet-Japanese talks were held in the next two months. A number of frontier questions were settled. When a German trade delegation arrived in Tokyo at the end of May, the Japanese press announced that the treaty with Russia had opened up the trans-Siberian route to Germany. On 11 June a new trade agreement for five years was initialled, and on 17 June an agreement was reached for the demarcation of the Mongolian-Manchurian frontier.[3]

By the end of April signs of Soviet awareness of the danger from Germany and of preparations, material and psychological, to meet it, were multiplying.[4] On 22 April, the Russians made a verbal protest to the German Chargé in Moscow about violations of the Soviet frontier by German aircraft. On the

---

[1] *World News and Views*, 3 May 1941.

[2] He also explained that the word Manchukuo had been used for want of a satisfactory substitute. *Oriental Affairs*, loc. cit.

[3] Moore, op. cit., p. 124; Dallin, *Foreign Policy*, pp. 348-9.

[4] On 29 April, the transit of all war materials through Soviet territory was forbidden. Evidence on the Soviet Government's own military preparations is not easy to come by. On 24 June 1941, the German newspaper *Angriff* published what purported to be reports on this subject made by German military commanders during the previous months. General Jodl had reported violations of the frontier by aircraft and reconnaissance parties ever since January and particularly since the beginning of April. Keitel in a report to Ribbentrop on 11 May had referred to Soviet concentrations, including facilities for bombers, on the frontier since January and particularly since the signing of the Soviet-Japanese pact. On 11 June another report by Keitel made an interesting admission: 'If the Soviet Union has shown a variable mien in its political attitude, and *if the fulfilling of the Treaty in the economic field has in essentials given no occasions for objection* . . . the military measures of the Soviet Union have been unequivocally directed towards the preparation of an attack on the German Reich.' The number of troops in the Baltic States, which had stood at 57,000 in February 1940 and 250,000 in the early summer of that year, now stood at 650,000. In addition there had been concentrations in Bessarabia and northern Bukovina since the dispatch of the German military mission to Roumania in October 1940. A report of Jodl's dated 20 June and released in the *Voelkischer Beobachter* on 25 June, gave details of Soviet concentrations on the borders of East Prussia.

following day the German High Command reported an increasing number of Soviet flights over German territory.[1] It was apparently being made plain that the limit of Soviet concessions had been reached.[2] At the First of May parade, Timoshenko, the Commissar for Defence, declared that although the Soviet Union stood for peace and for good relations with all its neighbours, the Party, the Government, and the whole people realized that the country lay in 'a capitalist encirclement' and must be ready for all eventualities.[3]

Hitler's speech on 4 May, with its ominous lack of any reference to Russia, was not commented upon. But on 5 May, Stalin, speaking to officer-graduates in Moscow, was reported to have told them that the Red Army had been re-equipped and reorganized in the light of the lessons of the war.[4]

Economic factors still continued to exercise a favourable influence on Soviet-German relations. In April, there was a conference in Berlin between Schnurre and Krutikov, the Deputy-Commissar for foreign trade, to examine the state of deliveries under the trade agreements. It was calculated that Soviet deliveries up to 11 February 1941 amounted to 310.3 million reichsmarks and that Germany was obliged to deliver at least up to this sum by 11 May. A generally favourable picture from the German point of view was again drawn by Schnurre in a memorandum of 15 May giving details of Soviet deliveries. There were difficulties on the German side because of the refusal of the Reich Ministry for Air to release aircraft already

---

[1] *Nazi-Soviet Relations*, pp. 328-9. On 17 May, the Narkomindel was informed that these were being investigated, but its Secretary-General pointed out that the violations were continuing. ibid., pp. 341-3.

[2] When Gaston Bergery, the new French Ambassador, presented his credentials to Kalinin in the presence of Molotov on 6 May, he is reported to have referred to the fact that France proposed to become part of a new pacific order in Europe and his hope that the U.S.S.R. would do likewise. On the following day he is said to have received an answer in the shape of a remark by Bogomolov, the Soviet Ambassador in Vichy, at this time in Moscow, to the effect that the U.S.S.R. did not see how it could become part of a Europe at the orders of a nation whose workers and peasants did not enjoy the same rights as in the U.S.S.R. Gafencu, *Prelude*, pp. 194-5.

[3] It was noted that Litvinov, who had as recently as 20 February been dropped from the Central Committee of the Party, was placed next to Stalin on the tribune. But Dekanozov, the Ambassador to Germany, was equally prominent. Another sign of the times was the ostentatious revival of the film 'Alexander Nevsky', which had been withdrawn at the time of the Soviet-German pact. A. U. Pope, *Maxim Litvinoff* (Secker and Warburg, 1945), p. 460.

[4] It was rumoured that in private Stalin had told the officers that they should be ready if necessary to take the offensive against the Powers claiming world domination; Gafencu, loc. cit.

sold to the Russians, but at that date there were still about seventy German technicians working under the direction of a German Admiral on the construction of a cruiser in Leningrad.

'I am under the impression,' wrote Schnurre on 15 May 1941, 'that we could make economic demands on Moscow which would even go beyond the scope of the treaty of January 10, 1941, demands designed to secure German food and raw-material requirements beyond the extent now contracted for. The quantities of raw materials now being contracted for are being delivered punctually by the Russians, despite the heavy burden this imposes on them, which, especially with regard to grain, is a notable performance'.[1]

Schulenburg left Moscow for Berlin on 13 April. On 28 April, before returning to his post he had an interview with Hitler in which he endeavoured to explain all Russia's recent actions as dictated entirely by apprehensions for her own security, and declared that in his view Stalin had no intention of going over from the side of the Axis powers to that of Great Britain. On the contrary, he was convinced that Stalin was prepared to make even further concessions. It had been intimated that if the Germans applied in due time, the Russians could supply up to five million tons of grain in the following year.[2]

On 6 May the gravity of the situation was emphasized by the news that Stalin had succeeded Molotov as Chairman of the Council of People's Commissars, leaving the latter as Foreign Commissar and Vice-Chairman. Soviet actions during the next few days suggested that this move marked the beginning of one more effort to come to terms with Germany. On 8 May Tass denied reports of troop concentrations in the West.[3] On 9 May the Soviet Government withdrew its recognition from the legations of the Governments-in-exile of Belgium, Norway, and Yugoslavia.[4] On 12 May the Soviet Government established relations with the Iraq Government of Rashid Ali

---

[1] *Nazi-Soviet Relations*, pp. 327, 339-41.

[2] ibid., p. 331-2. Weizsäcker's comment on Schulenburg's view was that while Germany would certainly defeat Russia, she might well be unable to exploit her victory from the economic point of view. A German attack on Russia might therefore postpone rather than bring nearer the victory over Great Britain which was the thing which really mattered. ibid., pp. 333-4.

[3] On 17 May, however, foreign diplomats were barred from all frontier zones.

[4] Recognition of the Greek Government-in-exile was withdrawn on 3 June.

who had brought off an anti-British *coup d'état* five weeks earlier.[1]

These moves were regarded by the Germans as denoting the 'return of Russia to her previously correct attitude' in consequence of Germany's Balkan victories.[2] Nevertheless German preparations for an attack continued unabated.[3] Rumours of the coming attack continued to circulate despite German attempts to stifle them.[4] Germany's failure to react to British moves in Iraq and Syria also suggested that the next blow would fall elsewhere and must have increased Soviet anxieties.

At the same time there were various reports that the Germans were seeking a preliminary understanding which would neutralize Great Britain during the attack on Russia, on the old plea of an anti-Communist crusade.[5] These reports were brought to a head by the flight to England on 10 May of Rudolf Hess.[6] The Soviet press, however, gave no prominence

[1] An account of previous negotiations with Iraq was given at the same time. This said that the Iraq Government had suggested entering into diplomatic relations with the U.S.S.R. at the end of 1940, but had then suggested that the U.S.S.R. should publish a declaration recognizing the independence of the Arab countries as a whole. The U.S.S.R. did not consider that it could make the establishment of relations dependent upon a condition of this kind. On 3 May, however, the Iraq Government had proposed the unconditional establishment of relations and this had been accepted. Notes to this effect were exchanged at Ankara on 16 May. British counter-measures resulted in the overthrow of Rashid Ali shortly afterwards and by 2 June he was a fugitive at Teheran. The Soviet haste to recognize his régime can only be taken as a friendly gesture to Germany, although a long-term desire to curry favour with Arab nationalism may have played some part.

[2] *Nazi Conspiracy and Aggression*, vol. 6, p. 998. Cf. *Nazi-Soviet Relations*, pp. 335–9, 344–5. When Ribbentrop saw Mussolini on 13 May, he told him that Russia would not act. If she did, she would be destroyed in three months. ibid., vol. 4, pp. 499–508.

[3] An order signed by Keitel and received by 6 June gave a complete timetable for the attack, setting zero hour as 3.30 a.m. on 22 June; ibid., pp. 857–67. On 15 April, the Russians had suddenly accepted the German proposals for settling the Soviet-German boundary questions arising from the agreement over Lithuania on 10 January. But the Germans clearly did not wish a mixed boundary commission to operate now. *Nazi-Soviet Relations*, pp. 325–6, 343–4.

[4] *Nazi-Soviet Relations*, pp. 330, 334–5; Dallin, *Foreign Policy*, p. 368; Schuman, *Soviet Politics*, pp. 414–15.

[5] Dallin, *Foreign Policy*, pp. 369–71.

[6] Evidence of Hess's statements after his landing was given at the Nuremberg Trial on 7 February 1946. He gave various conditions upon which Hitler would be prepared to negotiate peace, including a free hand for Germany in Europe and the return of German colonies. To Mr. Kirkpatrick of the Foreign Office he said that Russia was to be 'included in Asia' but that Germany had certain demands to make on Russia which would have to be satisfied either by negotiation or as a result of war. Hess claimed that there was no truth in the rumours that Hitler contemplated an early attack on the Soviet Union; *Nuremberg Trial*, part 6, pp. 159–62.

to this sensational event, which it reported with great caution.

Indeed, from the Soviet press, it would have been impossible to gather that there was any serious tension at all between the Soviet Union and Germany.[1] The tone of its reporting of foreign news remained unchanged. As before, communiqués and other military news were given from both sides, with the German communiqués put first. There was complete silence about Hitler's 'New Order' and about Soviet economic relations with Germany, and very little on internal conditions there.

The first intimation which the Soviet public received of the general speculation abroad as to a possible new accord between the Soviet Union and Germany came on 25 May with an article in *Pravda* by Zaslavsky, which branded as 'nonsense or a simple lie' the report by the Berlin correspondent of a Finnish newspaper that large concessions would be made to Germany including a 'lease' of the Ukraine.

The Germans admitted privately that there was no outward change in Soviet-German relations.[2] On 6 June Schulenburg reported that Russia would only fight if attacked and that all military preparations were purely defensive and being made as quietly as possible. On the following day, he reported that Stalin and Molotov were solely responsible for the conduct of Soviet foreign policy and that they were doing everything possible to avoid a conflict.[3]

Even at this late stage nothing was done to improve Soviet relations with the Anglo-Saxon Powers. Relations with the United States had actually deteriorated after the Soviet-Japanese pact and American supplies had been further curtailed.[4] London had reacted favourably to the Soviet-Turkish declaration of 22 March. In April, Maisky had further conversations with Eden, but once again a solution of the Baltic States' dispute was made by the Soviet Government a precondition of any general agreement.[5] In Moscow, Sir Stafford Cripps was completely ignored, and there was hardly any

---

[1] The German consul at Harbin secured an intercepted Soviet dispatch of 9 May telling Soviet representatives abroad to report on likely reactions if a conflict with Germany should be forced on the Soviet Union by Germany's dictatorial attitude. *Nazi-Soviet Relations*, p. 339. There was talk in both Soviet and German circles of Russian troop concentrations in the West. ibid., p. 342.

[2] On 24 May, Schulenburg was instructed to tell the Russians that Hitler had signed the ratification of the treaty of 10 January. *Nazi-Soviet Relations*, pp. 341–2.

[3] *Nazi Conspiracy and Aggression*, vol. 6, pp. 999–1000.

[4] Dallin, *Foreign Policy*, p. 334.

[5] Bilainkin, *Maisky*, pp. 330–1.

contact between the Embassy and the Narkomindel.[1] On 6 June the Ambassador was recalled to London for consultation. Sir Stafford Cripps arrived in London on 11 June, and there were reports that the results of his mission were so discouraging that he would not be returning.

On 13 June Sir Stafford Cripps's journey was made the excuse for a Tass statement, designed apparently both to reassure the Germans and to sound out their intentions.[2] The text ran as follows:

'Even before the arrival in London of the British Ambassador to the U.S.S.R. Cripps, and particularly after his arrival, the British and, in general, the foreign press began to disseminate rumours about the "proximity of war between the U.S.S.R. and Germany". According to these rumours:

'First, Germany allegedly presented to the U.S.S.R. claims of a territorial and economic nature, and negotiations are now under way between Germany and the U.S.S.R. concerning the conclusion of a new·closer agreement between them.

'Second, the U.S.S.R. allegedly rejected these claims in consequence of which Germany began concentrating her troops on the borders of the U.S.S.R. for the purpose of attacking the U.S.S.R.

'Third, the Soviet Union on its part, has allegedly begun intensive preparations for war with Germany and is concentrating troops at the latter's borders.

'Despite the obviously nonsensical character of these rumours, responsible Moscow quarters still found it necessary, in view of the rumours, to authorize Tass to state that these rumours constitute clumsily concocted propaganda of forces hostile to the U.S.S.R. and to Germany and interested in the further extension and unleashing of war.

'Tass declares that:

'First, Germany did not present any claims to the U.S.S.R. and does not propose any new, close agreement, in view of which no negotiations on this subject could have taken place.

'Second, according to information at the disposal of the U.S.S.R., Germany is abiding by the provisions of the Soviet-German pact of non-aggression as steadfastly as is the Soviet Union, in view of which,

[1] Schulenburg had been able to point out to Hitler that Cripps had not succeeded in even speaking to Molotov's deputy Vyshinsky until six days after the Soviet-Yugoslav pact. *Nazi-Soviet Relations*, p. 332.

[2] It was handed to Schulenburg by Molotov that evening. *Nazi-Soviet Relations*, pp. 345–6. On 28 June Lozovsky told the press that the statement had been made 'in order to elicit from Germany her precise attitude. Since the Nazi press and that of the satellite countries did not publish the Tass statement, it was a clear indication that Hitler did not mean and did not want to observe the pact. That cleared the air and showed Germany's innovation in international law—namely that the object of a non-aggression pact is the careful preparation of aggression.' Schuman, *Soviet Politics*, p. 417.

in the opinion of Soviet quarters, rumours about Germany's intentions to disrupt the pact and to undertake an attack upon the
U.S.S.R. are devoid of any foundation, whereas the dispatching of
German troops relieved from operations in the Balkans to the eastern
and north-eastern districts of Germany, which is now taking place,
is connected, it should be assumed, with other motives having no
bearing on Soviet-German relations.

'Third, the U.S.S.R., as follows from its peace policy, has abided
and intends to abide by the provisions of the Soviet-German non-
aggression pact, in view of which rumours to the effect that the
U.S.S.R. is preparing for war with Germany are false and
provocative.

'Fourth, the summer camp drill of Red Army reservists now being
held, and forthcoming manœuvres, have no purpose other than the
training of reservists and the checking of the work of railroad
organizations, which is carried out every year as is well known, in
view of which to present these measures of the Red Army as inimical
to Germany is, to say the least, absurd.'

During this time, Soviet and German diplomacy had been
active at either end of the prospective front. Soviet-Finnish
relations had continued tense. At the beginning of January,
the Soviet Union had stopped exports to Finland on the alleged
grounds that Finland had not fulfilled its quota.[1] On 21 April,
however, there were reports of Soviet concessions leading to
improved relations.[2] On 5 May the question of the Petsamo
nickel mines was again discussed in Helsinki, and on 10 May,
for the last time, in Moscow. On 12 May a protocol finally
regulating the Soviet-Finnish frontier was published. Trade
talks were resumed, and Soviet radio propaganda against the
Finnish Government came to an end. On 1 June the retiring
Finnish Ambassador, Paasikivi, was received by Stalin, who
agreed to send 20,000 tons of wheat to Finland, in spite of the
arrears in Finland's own deliveries.[3] It is clear, however, that
there were no serious hopes of detaching Finland from the
Germans. Talks between the German and Finnish General
Staffs, to regulate Finnish participation in the assault on Russia,
began on 25 May.[4]

German pressure on Turkey had also been growing, and
although the desired military alliance was not forthcoming, a

[1] *Finnish Blue and White Book*, p. 29.

[2] *Nazi Conspiracy and Aggression*, vol. 6, p. 997. Nevertheless, as already
noted, *Pravda* released on 29 April the news that there were as many as
10,000 German troops in Finland.

[3] Dallin, *Foreign Policy*, pp. 294-7.

[4] According to evidence submitted at the Finnish War Guilt Trial on
11 January 1946, Finnish-German negotiations for a military alliance had
begun in December 1940.

Treaty of Friendship signed at Ankara on 18 June ensured to
the Germans the benevolent neutrality of Turkey during the
forthcoming conflict.[1] On 15 June, the German Minister in
Budapest was instructed to inform the Hungarian Premier
that the Germans would be compelled to clarify the situation
with Russia by the beginning of July at the latest, and that
Hungary should take steps at once to secure her frontiers.[2]

The Soviet Government appears still to have refused to
credit the worst. The British intelligence service had shown
that Germany would probably attack Russia, but warnings to
this effect were discounted as the product of wishful thinking.
On 20 June, the American Ambassador was able to tell Mr.
Churchill that should Germany attack Russia, the Americans
would support any statement made by Mr. Churchill in favour
of regarding Russia as an ally in the war against Nazi aggression.[3] It may have been believed in Moscow that the Germans
would put forward some proposals before actually attacking.[4]
On 21 June, German reconnaissance flights over the Baltic
found signs of Russian preparedness such as mine-barriers,
but no evidence that an attack was thought to be imminent.[5]
Orlov, the Soviet Minister to Helsinki, assured Witting, the
Finnish Foreign Minister, that there was not even a likelihood
that war would break out.[6] In Berlin, Dekanozov handed
Weizsäcker a memorandum complaining of German aircraft violating the Soviet frontier. Weizsäcker remarked that the reverse
was true.[7] In Moscow, in the evening, Molotov summoned
Schulenburg to his office and after mentioning the question of
border violations, pointed out the existence of indications that
Germany was dissatisfied with the Soviet Union, and that
there were even rumours of imminent war. The Soviet
Government could not understand why this should be.

[1] *B.I.N.*, XVIII, pp. 864–5. For the Turkish attitude and the role of the
Pan-Turanians, see A. C. Edwards, 'The Impact of the War on Turkey',
International Affairs, July 1946.
[2] *Nazi-Soviet Relations*, p. 346.
[3] J. G. Winant, *A Letter from Grosvenor Square* (Hodder and Stoughton,
1947), pp. 145–6.
[4] This would explain Molotov's twice repeated statement in his broadcast
on 22 June 1941 that Germany had attacked without 'presenting any complaints' to the Soviet Union; *Soviet Foreign Policy during the Patriotic War*
(Hutchinson, 1946), vol. I, p. 75. There is good reason to believe that at
about the end of the first week in June, Soviet anxieties quickened and that
Dekanozov was sent back to Berlin to make a last effort to seek agreement.
[5] *Nazi Conspiracy and Aggression*, vol. 6, p. 1002.
[6] *Finnish Blue and White Book*, Document 73.
[7] For Hitler's explanation of his decision to attack, see his letter to
Mussolini of 21 June, *Nazi-Soviet Relations*, pp. 349–53.

Molotov believed his earlier communications had cleared up the question of Yugoslavia. He would appreciate it if Schulenburg could tell him what had brought about the present state of affairs. Schulenburg professed himself unable to answer the question. On the same night he received the note to hand to Molotov, announcing the beginning of the German attack and the German reasons for it. Ribbentrop in Berlin made a similar communication to Dekanozov.[1]

It was left to Hitler, on 22 June, to speak the epilogue to this chapter of Soviet diplomacy.

'United with their Finnish comrades, the warriors who won the victory at Narvik are manning the shores of the Arctic Ocean. German divisions commanded by the conqueror of Norway, together with the champions of Finnish liberty commanded by their Marshal, are protecting Finnish territory. From East Prussia to the Carpathians fresh formations mass along the German eastern front. Along the lower regions of the Danube down to the shores of the Black Sea, German and Roumanian soldiers are united under the Roumanian premier, General Antonescu.'

While, on the night of 22 June, the Kremlin was silent, Russia and the world waited on the voice of the British arch-'imperialist', Winston Churchill.

[1] *Nazi-Soviet Relations*, pp. 347–57.

VI. THE PRINCIPLES OF SOVIET FOREIGN POLICY

Chapter Fifteen

THE PRINCIPLES OF SOVIET FOREIGN POLICY

IT must be clear that a narrative such as that which has just been brought to an end can furnish only an introduction to the problems with which the student of Soviet foreign policy finds himself faced. The formative years, for reasons already indicated, have not been treated in more than the barest outline; and during the years which have elapsed since the date chosen for bringing the story to an end, the actions of the Soviet Government on the international scene have provided a great deal of new evidence which it would be the sheerest pedantry to ignore. On the other hand, this is not the place to attempt a current evaluation of Soviet policies, still less a prognostication of their future course.

The most that one can hope for by way of a conclusion is some indication of the general way in which these problems of interpretation may most profitably be tackled, and some warning of the major pitfalls that beset the path of the would-be interpreter.

The first point which must be made, and made as forcibly as possible, is that for very much of the history of Soviet foreign policy we still lack the factual information necessary before one can proceed to an analysis of motives.[1] Neglect of this elementary fact, and a willingness to accept instead, at their face value, the contemporary speculations of foreign journalists, diminishes the value of some otherwise important works on the subject.[2] Nor is this problem adequately faced by those who go to the other extreme and attempt to write the history of Soviet foreign policy solely from the pronouncements of Soviet leaders, and statements in the Soviet press.[3] In the case of the Soviet Union, as in the case of other countries, there may be reasons, and good reasons, why some agreement or other diplo-

---

[1] For some of the questions of method involved in such studies, see the present writer's article: 'The Study of Contemporary History: Some Further Reflections', *History*, March 1945.

[2] This applies even to so useful a work as Dallin's *Soviet Russia's Foreign Policy, 1939–42*.

[3] This point has been elaborated in the present writer's review of Miss Harriet L. Moore's study *Soviet Far Eastern Policy, 1931–45* (*International Affairs*, July 1946).

matic event should not be made public.[1] One has only to consider the extent to which the production of portions of the German archives at the Nuremberg Trial, and the evidence there given, have thrown light upon the diplomatic history of the last few years to appreciate how much of its inner development remains concealed. The continued publication of materials from the German archives and of the American documents, the beginning of the publication of British diplomatic documents of the inter-war period, and the possible emergence of material from the French archives—all these will probably involve a continued re-writing of the international history of recent times.[2] Personal testimony from diplomats and others is also likely, to judge by precedent, to be forthcoming in considerable volume.

Such problems, which are general to the study of recent international relations, are particularly marked when one comes to deal with the U.S.S.R. In the democratic countries of the West, the necessity imposed upon ministers to defend their policies in person or by deputy, before a parliament which includes their political adversaries, and before the electorate, together with the existence of a free press, enables the observer and student to define and assess the various alternative policies and trends. In the case of the Soviet Union and of other totalitarian régimes, the evidence of public debate is not available.

By the opening of the period dealt with in the preceding pages not only had the Communist Party long established complete control over the machinery of the Soviet State and over the media for the expression of opinion, but intra-party democracy itself had also disappeared as far as major issues of policy were concerned, in favour of a centralization of decisions in the Party's Political Bureau. Thus neither the Party Congresses nor the rare sessions of the Supreme Soviet have debated foreign policy. If the conduct of the Foreign Commissariat was criticized, as in January 1938, there could be little doubt but that the initiative came from above as in the case of other outbursts of criticism. Normally the procedure has been for the Commissar for Foreign Affairs to make a declaration to the Supreme Soviet and for the latter to resolve unanimously to refrain from debate. On the occasion of the ratification of the Soviet-

[1] As has been noted, the Soviet-Japanese agreement on the Sakhalin concessions of 13 April 1941 was not published until 30 March 1944.

[2] Over most of continental Europe the possibility of archival material becoming available will depend upon the political future of the countries concerned, as well as upon the extent to which such material has survived the chances of war.

German pact on 31 August 1939, discussion was formally renounced because of the 'clarity and consistence of the Soviet Government'.[1]

It is true that once a decision has been taken it is likely to be expounded, together with the reasons for it, through all the available media of propaganda. At one time it was apparently considered that some preparation of this kind was desirable before the announcement of an important new move.[2] But recent experience suggests that the Soviet Government is more confident than formerly of its ability to command consent for any policy which it chooses to adopt. To some extent therefore the Soviet press provides evidence on the Government's views which is not paralleled in the press of countries where the Government possesses no recognized mouthpiece. But interpretation along these lines must not be pushed too far. What appears in the press is the 'line' which the Soviet Government wants the ordinary citizen to follow at the moment or one which it wishes brought to the notice of foreign governments. At the same time of course the inner hierarchy of the Party may be working along quite a different 'line' towards a goal of which no intimation is allowed to appear. Thus for instance the negotiations with Germany in the summer of 1939 had reached the stage at which Ribbentrop's flight to Moscow could be announced without the Soviet press giving any inkling of the fact that they were in progress. Nevertheless, those who go to the other extreme, and dismiss the evidence to be got from studying the Soviet press as 'mere propaganda', are missing an all-essential source of enlightenment. For if the Soviet press fails to reveal the internal play of forces which result in the adoption by the Soviet Union of particular policies, it does reveal the basic approach to problems of international affairs, the temper in which they are discussed, and the basic assumptions upon which the Soviet leaders conduct their affairs. A work like the *History of Diplomacy* published in three volumes between 1941 and 1946, and frequently referred to in the preceding pages, is of interest not because of any revelations of Soviet policy—for there are none—but because of the categories in which international relations generally are discussed.

From what has been said, it will be seen that it has not been

[1] *Izvestia*, 1 September 1939.

[2] Thus when discussions on the proposed Franco-Soviet pact were carried on in Paris at the end of 1933 between Paul-Boncour and the Soviet Ambassador, Dovgalevsky, the French Foreign Minister reports the latter as insisting that the talks be kept secret. 'You understand . . . after all our previous attitudes, this could disconcert our public opinion and we must prepare it for this.' J. Paul-Boncour, *Entre Deux Guerres*, vol. 2, pp. 361 ff.

found possible to subscribe to the notion that the totalitarian façade which such a régime imposes necessarily involves complete agreement at every stage on matters of external (or internal) policy. Nor is it possible to assume that disagreement with what has proved to be the policy of the ruling group has been synonymous with treason. But it is clear that we have not at our disposal the means to see even in outline the nature of the conflicting interests and objectives whose tensions have to be resolved. Once again, there are obvious and easy over-simplifications.[1] But the bare fact remains, that we know so little about the foreign policy of the Soviet Union because we are so far as yet from understanding to the full the working of its institutions.

It is obvious that in saying this, one is assuming that foreign policy is itself a matter of reasoned choice, and that its determinants are objectives set by the conscious or unconscious political philosophy of those responsible. One must admit, in dealing with Soviet foreign policy, the weight of a body of opinion of a contrary tendency.

Such contrary interpretations stress the physical, automatic, and compulsive elements in foreign policy. Once the Bolsheviks had got control of the territories making up the nucleus of the former Russian Empire, they were bound, we are told, to follow in foreign policy essentially the lines along which Tsarist policy had developed. While they were weak, the Bolsheviks sought, by exploiting the divergencies between their enemies, to frustrate any hostile designs against them. Once they were strong, they were bound to seek to recover lost ground and to press on with the tasks dictated by their need for warm water ports, for securer frontiers, for additional natural resources, and for other material advantages.[2] For the proponents of this way of thought, the outstanding problems of interpretation have

[1] A favourite method of interpretation at various junctures has been to analyse alternative policies in terms of a clash between the military and civilian elements in the régime. Thus one writer in dealing with the mid-nineteen-thirties describes the army leaders as demanding an 'activization' of Soviet foreign policy, as objecting to the toleration of the depredations of Japanese imperialism and as forcing Stalin after three months of neutrality to intervene in Spain. E. Wollenberg, *The Red Army*, pp. 247–8. All this may be true, but there is nothing that could be called historical evidence to justify one in accepting any of these statements.

[2] 'It may be concluded that the urge to the sea is one of the most fundamental of all basic trends in Russian development and that it will be continued regardless of the doctrines or methods used.' R. J. Kerner, 'The Foreign Policies of Russia' in *Foreign Policies of the Great Powers* (California University Press, 1939). Cf. the same author's *The Urge to the Sea* (California University Press, 1942).

been those of priority. Would the Russians concentrate their
efforts towards the Straits, towards the Persian Gulf or towards
the Yellow Sea—and what would be the corollaries of such
concentration? Such experts pay great attention to the gradual
and long-term eastwards shift in the Russian economic and
demographic axis. They rightly stress the importance of internal
colonization in Russian history. And sometimes they go on to
suggest that the acceleration of these movements under the
Soviet régime, together with the greater symbiosis between the
Slav and Asiatic peoples of the Soviet Union, has meant an
even greater accent upon the eastern motif in its policy.[1]

Other writers attach the greatest significance to the evolution
of the Soviet régime itself. They point out that by the middle
1930's the revolutionary process had passed its culminating
point. After the great upheaval, the structure of the State and
of the economy received a new stabilization. Still more important, new class stratifications arose and were consolidated; a
new ruling class with the characteristics of its kind occupied
the seat of power.[2] Foreign policy, it was argued, was bound
in these circumstances to become once more a matter of *raison
d'état*. Furthermore, the new ruling-class appeared at one time
at least eager to salvage what it could of the elements of
authority and prestige which clung to the memories of its predecessor. There was a rewriting of Russian history on patriotic
lines, the re-establishment of the Great Russians as the dominant nationality within the Union,[3] the rehabilitation of military ranks and dignities and—after the period covered by our
narrative—a *modus vivendi* with the Orthodox Church and a
guarded appeal to Pan-Slav sentiment. The Napoleonic
analogy—the Légion d'Honneur, the Concordat, the Habsburg marriage! To some historians it was irresistible! If the
Soviet régime was a new Tsardom then the new priorities would
be the same as the old ones. Russia as before would sacrifice
her chances in the east to her European ambitions. 'Russia has
gazed much more intently through Peter the Great's window on

[1] See for instance the writings of the 'Eurasian' school of émigré historio-
graphy of which the leader is G. Vernadsky. These are briefly discussed in
A. G. Mazour, *An Outline of Modern Russian Historiography* (University of
California, 1939). There is a very persuasive article along these lines by
G. Fedotov, 'Zagadki Rossii' (The Riddles of Russia), in *Novy Zhurnal*
(*New Review*), No. 5, 1943.

[2] The best such exposition of Soviet history is N. S. Timasheff, *The Great
Retreat* (New York, Dutton, 1946).

[3] The early and not unnatural prominence of Jews in the official hierarchy of the Soviet Union has been succeeded by their virtual elimination
from the posts of command in favour of Great Russians; this is particularly
striking in the Foreign Ministry and the diplomatic service.

the west, eyed the Bosphorus more hungrily than Tsushima, and dreamed the Pan-Slav dream, not the Pan-Asiatic.'[1]

For the partisans of both schools of thought, one thing was clear: the prime objective of the Soviet Government after the expulsion of Trotsky from its councils was not a revolutionary one. The fact that according to the Trotskyist interpretation also, Stalin's régime was a Thermidorean one, gave them additional self-confidence.[2] The adoption by the U.S.S.R. in 1936 of a simulacrum of Western constitutionalism, and on the other hand, the adoption by the West of 'planning', all combined to make such views at least temporarily plausible.

During the period when the Soviet Union was a member of the League of Nations and the advocate of 'collective security' under the slogan 'peace is indivisible', it could be held that Soviet policy as thus defined held out the promise of a long period of stability in the relations between the Soviet Union and the Western democracies. And both then, and after 1941, there were those who proceeded further, and assumed that the difference in ideologies merely cloaked alternative methods of attaining basically identical objectives, the amelioration of the human lot through the control of economic life. In so far as the ideologies were different, the principle adopted in order to prevent trouble would be that of *cujus regio, ejus religio*.

The comparative eclipse of the Comintern during the 'collective security' period and the dissolution of that institution on 22 May 1943, gave further support to those who argued that the Soviet Union was a State among other States, pursuing clearly defined ends by the conventional methods of *realpolitik*. It was not until after 1945 that the re-emergence of men like Togliatti, Dimitrov, and Thorez on the world-scene, together with many less prominent but equally thoroughly trained technicians of Socialist transformation, suggested that the residence in Moscow of foreign Communists might have any other object than the occasional signature of a manifesto. Similarly, the weight of historical evidence is now overwhelmingly against those who asserted that Communist Parties in other countries—in France or in China—could be anything but obedient executants of a policy settled in Moscow. No nation-State could acquire similar loyalty from non-nationals. An explanation of Soviet policy which dismisses the Revolution would seem to be an explanation which neither the facts nor Soviet writings warrant.

[1] A. W. Griswold, 'European Factors in Far Eastern Diplomacy' *Foreign Affairs*, January 1941.
[2] See, e.g. L. Trotsky, *The Revolution Betrayed* (Faber, 1937).

There would seem to be a legitimate field here for the use of historical analogy. For the basic problem involved is not a new one. The marriage between a territorial or ethnic power-complex and an ideology (divine or secular) is no new thing. If the expansion of Islam and of Arab rule offers the most striking parallel, there is perhaps a closer one in the inter-relations of the Counter-Reformation and the Habsburg dynasty. For a crucial century of the development of modern Europe, it is indeed impossible to say where religious zeal and dynastic aggrandizement respectively begin and end; and in a figure like that of Philip II of Spain, the enigma is reduced to an insoluble personal equation.

It is clear that such alliances when once formed have normally proved extremely durable, and it would have been surprising if anything less than a successful counter-revolution had sufficed to put an end to the Russo-Marxist alliance of 1917. The bearers of an ideology of this kind, once they are in power, are bound to put the preservation of their régime above all other considerations. It was the dominant consideration in the Bolsheviks' first great decision in foreign policy—the acceptance of the peace of Brest-Litovsk. Then and since they have been dominated by 'the idea that, whatever may happen, it is vital even at the cost of great territorial sacrifices and loss of face to maintain control of the government of a limited territory in the hands of the Bolsheviks as a symbol and as a hope of a better future.'[1]

It is further necessary to keep clearly in mind, that by virtue of the Marxist-Leninist ideology itself, the régime is bound to be continually threatened so long as non-Communist States exist. For between a society like that of Soviet Russia, where the proletarian revolution is in the past, and the 'capitalist' world, where this revolution is in the future, there is an unbridgeable gulf. Even bourgeois democracy, the most highly developed social form known to the capitalist world, is incapable of autonomous development into Socialism. The soi-disant Democratic Socialism of the West—all those Socialist Parties which do not accept the leadership of the Russian Communist Party—is simply an element of confusion designed to prevent the working-class seeing clearly the historical issues involved. The effectiveness of such a highly simplified distinction between what are in effect the elect and the reprobate, is a commonplace of group psychology, and the world has recently seen a terrifying example of its power when it takes a racial rather than a class line of division. It is worth remembering,

[1] Kerner, *The Foreign Policies of the Great Powers*, loc. cit.

too, that the methods of physical and moral coercion possessed by a modern government of the single-party pattern are of incomparable power and that the three decades which have elapsed since the Russian Revolution have permitted the emergence of a generation all of whose upbringing has been governed by this ideology.

What it means in the international field, can be deduced without difficulty from actual practice, and finds adequate expression in Soviet writings. The introduction to the third volume of the *History of Diplomacy*—the volume dealing with the years 1919–39—gives an authoritative summary of the Soviet viewpoint:

'The end of the world war and the victory in Russia of the October Socialist Revolution meant the beginning of a new period in the history of diplomacy. The essential contents of this period are characterized by two factors: in the first place, the co-existence, the inter-relationship and the conflict of two opposed systems—capitalism and socialism; in the second place the extreme exacerbation of all the capitalist contradictions which led humanity into the second world war.'[1]

This means in effect that since class-conflicts are beyond all doubt the most important political phenomena in the non-Soviet world, all political action by other governments is determined first of all by such conflicts. Such governments are fundamentally and permanently anti-Soviet, whatever apparently friendly attitudes necessity may drive them to adopt, because the existence of the Soviet State is in itself a source of strength to their oppressed classes (or to the oppressed nations of colonial and 'semi-colonial' areas which they exploit). The basic and inescapable relation of the Soviet State to other States, is one of conflict. And for a full understanding of the Soviet attitude, it is necessary to realize that the conflict is one in which the outcome is a foreordained victory for the Soviet State and, with it, the international proletariat. To try to comprehend the Soviet outlook and to dismiss the inevitability of the world proletarian revolution is as idle as to try to comprehend the outlook of medieval man and to dismiss the reality of the Last Judgment.

It is correct of course—and the events which have been chronicled go to prove it—that the eschatological aspects of the new secular religion exercised a rather less immediate effect upon the imagination of believers once the psychological effect of the first dramatic victory had worn off. What must be realized is the continued psychological advantage which the

[1] P. 1.

belief in inevitable victory—in working with the inexorable laws of history and not against them—has conferred upon the Communist faithful, and above all the extreme flexibility in daily action which they have derived from the conviction of their own absolute righteousness. It is essential if one is to understand the technique and the language of Soviet diplomacy to realize that one is at grips with a dual system of morality— that what is permitted to the faithful in the service of the faith is morally reprehensible among the infidels. Morality is meaningless apart from its context in the class struggle. This explains the curious paradox that whereas according to the Communists' own theory, the behaviour of the bourgeois States is conditioned by objective material conditions, it is nevertheless correct to condemn this behaviour in the conventional terms of bourgeois morality. The phenomenon as it appears in the pronouncements of Soviet leaders, will be sufficiently familiar to the reader of the foregoing pages, but it is worth calling attention to the curious section in the concluding chapter of the *History of Diplomacy* in which the well-known historian of the Napoleonic era, E. V. Tarlé, discusses 'The Methods of Bourgeois Diplomacy'.

The history of European and world diplomacy since the eighteenth century is discussed by Tarlé under a series of headings intended as categories of diplomatic activity. Thus we have a paragraph on 'aggression concealed under the motive of self-defence' with appropriate historical examples, another on 'the use of pacifist propaganda for the purpose of misleading an enemy', and others on the use of pacts of friendship in order to disarm suspicion and the use of phrases like the 'localization of conflict' and 'the protection of small nations' in order to further the plans of an aggressor.

Bourgeois diplomacy is thus pictured as the servitor of forces whose sole motivation is aggression, a blind desire for conquest. Among the excuses for aggression which Tarlé chronicles are 'disinterested ideological motives' and 'the combatting of Bolshevism and the U.S.S.R.' Tarlé indicates the way in which aggressors have made use of intervention in the internal affairs of other countries as a cloak for their own designs and adds the following curious comment:

'It is interesting to note that in the seventeenth and eighteenth centuries, diplomacy did not think it necessary to envelop intervention in the internal affairs of other countries in any lofty rules of conduct and principles. Only beginning with the period of the French Revolution did such intervention begin zealously to mask itself behind every kind of high principle.'[1]

[1] *Istoria Diplomatii*, vol. iii, p. 730.

Thus bourgeois diplomacy and its objectives are branded according to its own moral terminology, and in non-Marxist language. And this in turn leads to the analysis of the fundamental characteristics of the alternative system, Soviet diplomacy:

'Lenin and Stalin', writes Professor Tarlé, 'have created a new Soviet diplomacy. By laying down its conditions, defining its objectives and methods in the conditions of capitalist encirclement, and pointing out the paths which lead to the attainment of its peaceful, liberating, and progressive aims, Lenin and Stalin have opened a new era in international relations.

'. . . Soviet diplomacy is built on conditions which are in principle entirely new. That is—it is the diplomacy of the only Socialist State in the world. . . . The high vocation of Soviet diplomacy is made easier by the fact that it wields a weapon possessed by none of its rivals or opponents. Soviet diplomacy is fortified with the scientific theory of Marxism-Leninism. This doctrine lays down the unshakable laws of social development. By revealing these norms, it gives the possibility not only of understanding the current tendencies of international life, but also of permitting the desirable collaboration with the march of events. Such are the great advantages held by Soviet diplomacy. They give it a special position in international life and explain its outstanding successes.'[1]

If one assumes that such utterances are a sincere reflection of the Soviet mind, the picture of Soviet foreign policy which emerges, is at least a credible and a coherent one. The Soviet Government is then like other governments necessarily and at all times faced with a possible divergence between its short term objectives—security and consequent progress within its own frontiers—and long term objectives—the extension of the area of Sovietization. Which alternative will hold the field at any particular time will on this analysis, depend on the external situation as viewed through Marxist-Leninist spectacles. Where a single powerful enemy has emerged in the capitalist environment, Soviet diplomacy has sought to isolate it, as during the 'collective security' period from 1934–38. Where the outside world is in turmoil, and the capitalist powers indulging in internecine strife, the opportunity for expansion recurs, as in 1939–41.

If one accepts this, one is faced with the difficult problem of how far, in the former circumstances, Soviet diplomacy can be regarded as 'sincere'; how far, in other words, its inherent dualism is still conscious. But without embarking on so perilous a discussion, one can at least suggest that the Soviet leaders have consistently adhered to one precept. Never have they

[1] ibid., pp. 763–4.

acted during such periods of collaboration with non-Soviet Powers in such a way as to sacrifice important long-term advantages. The ideological slate has been kept clean, and the building up of the cadres of international action has not been abandoned.

The same dualism has, of course, been marked in the Soviet attitude to international law, whose norms have been accepted as those for the conduct of Soviet relations with non-Soviet States, but on the understanding, on the Soviet side, that this is a limited concession to the necessities of a situation which cannot of its very nature be durable.[1] Even if the original formulation of the Soviet theorists—the 'international law of the transition period'—is no longer fashionable, it is difficult to see that later attempts to clarify the situation have done more than embroider the same theme.[2]

If this approach to the study of Soviet foreign policy is adopted certain lines of inquiry suggest themselves while others are automatically ruled out. It is obvious that a policy so conceived does not permit an inquiry directed towards ascertaining what deficiencies in international machinery have been responsible for the catastrophes of the past three decades. The gulf between the Soviet world and the non-Soviet world has never on the Soviet side been regarded as bridgeable by machinery—for such machinery must logically involve the sacrifice of sovereignty to a partially non-Socialist organ which could not but be biased against the U.S.S.R. On the other hand, such an approach permits a valid appreciation of each concrete situation and the assessment both of how the Soviet Government envisaged that situation and how it sought to deal with it. For the Marxist, of course, the problem is hardly one at all. The Soviet appreciation was correct and the action taken, necessary. But for the non-Marxist Soviet policy is as imperfect and arbitrary and non-scientific as that of any other State. The history of the revolution in China, of Hitler's rise to power in Germany, and of the course of events in Europe in 1940 and 1941, are none of them testimonies to the infallibility of the Marxist prognosis. The student of Soviet foreign policy is likely to arise from his task with a strengthened conviction that history above all is the study of the imperfect, the contingent, and the unique.

[1] Cf. Taracouzio, *The Soviet Union and International Law* (New York, Macmillan, 1935); cf. 'Laws among Nations: The Impact of Soviet Principles', *The Times*, 11 December 1947.
[2] See R. Schlesinger, *Soviet Legal Theory* (Kegan Paul, 1945), chap. X.

Appendix A

THE CONDUCT OF FOREIGN AFFAIRS UNDER THE CONSTITUTION OF THE U.S.S.R.

WHATEVER one's view may be on the inner meaning and purpose of the Soviet Union's activity in the international field, its formal relations with other States have had perforce to be conducted along lines for the most part already laid down, before its own arrival on the international scene.[1] In spite of the fact that no Commissariat inherited so little of the Tsarist bureaucracy as the People's Commissariat for Foreign Affairs, the Narkomindel, it did not long retain many outward peculiarities, and has tended to approximate together with the diplomatic and consular services it controls to the foreign offices of non-Soviet Powers.[2] Its particular formal features arise partly from the Socialist nature of the Soviet economy and partly from the federal nature of the Soviet State.[3]

The Narkomindel was originally headed by a 'collegium' consisting of the Commissar and three or four other members. This system was abolished in favour of a single Commissar in 1934. In recent years, an important role has been played by a number of deputy-commissars. The Narkomindel itself is divided 'according to the main geographical divisions of the world and to the main functions of the department'.[4]

[1] This appendix is based on two Soviet accounts: 'The Formulation and Administration of Soviet Foreign Policy' by A. F. Neymann, First Secretary of the Soviet Embassy in Washington, printed as an appendix to S. N. Harper (ed.), *The Soviet Union and World Problems* (Chicago, 1935); and I. P. Kolchanovsky, 'Organizatsionie formy, mezhdunarodnopravovie osnovy i tekhnika sovremennoy diplomatii' (The Organizational Forms, International-Legal Bases and Technique of Contemporary Diplomacy), in *Istoria Diplomatii*, vol. 3. Cf. T. A. Taracouzio, *The Soviet Union and International Law*; M. T. Florinsky, 'The Soviet Union and International Agreements', *Political Science Quarterly*, March 1946.

[2] At its Session in March 1946, the Supreme Soviet abolished the name Commissariat in favour of that of Ministry for all departments.

[3] It is not possible for want of evidence to go into the extent to which the hierarchy of the Soviet foreign service is interpenetrated by the organization and hierarchy of the Communist Party, nor can anything useful be said about the frequent charges that Soviet diplomatic representation abroad is used for purposes of organizing Communist propaganda. Kolchanovsky points out that such activity is forbidden to Soviet diplomats by the decree of 1924 governing their conduct abroad. *Istoria Diplomatii*, vol. 3, pp. 791–2. See on this point, *The Report of the Royal Commission* (Canada) (27 June 1946) on 'The circumstances surrounding the communication . . . of secret and confidential information to a foreign power'.

[4] Neymann. loc. cit.

By a decree of 4 June 1918, the new régime signalized its breach with the past by abolishing the traditional diplomatic ranks of ambassador and minister in favour of representation abroad by heads of missions with the uniform title of *Polpred* (plenipotentiary representative).[1] The necessities of the situation brought about the practice of referring to them in their letters of credence according to the traditional ranks. By a decree of the Presidium of the Supreme Soviet of 9 May 1941, the Soviet Government introduced three official ranks among its diplomatic representatives: ambassador, minister, and chargé d'affaires. By a further decree of 14 June 1943, the Soviet diplomatic service as a whole was divided into eleven classes.[2]

The main difference between the representation abroad of the Soviet Union and that of other countries is the special status which the Soviet trade monopoly is held to confer upon the Soviet trade representative (*Torgpred*) for whom it is customary to claim diplomatic immunity when the appropriate treaties or agreements are concluded.[3]

The status of foreign diplomatic representatives in the U.S.S.R. is governed by international law and by a decree of 14 January 1927.[4] This decree also governs the activity of foreign consulates. Since the U.S.S.R. has no private interests of its citizens to guard abroad and few of its own nationals to protect, consular activities are rather circumscribed and the U.S.S.R. has tended to diminish as far as possible the consular representation of foreign countries within its own territories. It does not recognize the institution of 'honorary' consuls.[5]

The Narkomindel works directly under what is now the Council of Ministers which is generally responsible for the conduct of the Union's foreign relations (Constitution of 1936, Article 68).[6] The ratification of treaties requiring it (those involving changes of territory and the making of peace or containing a provision for ratification in their text) was under the Constitution of 1923 executed by

[1] The basic decree governing the Soviet diplomatic and consular service which is a single unit, is that of 27 August 1927 printed in the appendix to Taracouzio, op. cit.

[2] The professionalization of the foreign service through specialized training began in the early nineteen-thirties. An institute for the purpose was set up and attached to the Narkomindel in 1934. By a decree of 28 May 1943, the foreign service acquired an official uniform for full-dress occasions.

[3] Cf. I. V. Boyeff, 'The Soviet State Monopoly of Foreign Trade' in Harper, op. cit.

[4] The text of this is given in the appendix to Taracouzio, op. cit. One point is perhaps worth noting here. Foreign diplomats present their credentials to the Chairman of the Presidium of the Supreme Soviet and this has led superficial observers of the Soviet system to regard his office as on a par with that of President under such constitutions as that of the Third French Republic.

[5] Cf. *Istoria Diplomatii*, vol. 3, pp. 797–803.

[6] Prior to 16 March 1946 the Council of Ministers was known as the Sovnarkom (Council of People's Commissars).

either by the Central Executive Committee of the Supreme Soviet or by the Presidium. With the abolition under the new Constitution, of the Central Executive Committee, ratification has become a function of the Presidium. The Presidium also has the power in between Sessions of the Supreme Soviet to proclaim a state of war 'in the event of armed attack on the U.S.S.R., or whenever necessary to fulfil international treaty obligations concerning mutual defence against aggression' (Article 49).

As already remarked, the federal nature of the Soviet Union has involved certain complications from the point of view of foreign relations. Prior to the coming into force of the Union Constitution of 1923, the separate Soviet republics had their own diplomatic representation in some countries, and were represented on delegations to international conferences. Thus both the Ukraine and Georgia were represented at the Lausanne Conference in 1923.

Under the Constitution the function of representing the entire Soviet Union was entrusted to the Narkomindel and the same was true under the Constitution of 1936. The decree of 12 November 1923 governing the functioning of the Narkomindel described its duties as follows:

'(a) the protection of the foreign political and economic interests of the U.S.S.R. and of its citizens abroad;

(b) the carrying out of decisions concerning the conclusion of treaties and agreements with foreign governments;

(c) the carrying into effect of treaties and agreements concluded with foreign governments and co-operation with the relevant organs of the U.S.S.R. and the Union-Republics in making effective the rights based upon such treaties;

(d) the control of the execution, by the relevant organs of the State, of the agreements and conventions, agreed upon with foreign governments.'

For these purposes it was the practice to attach to the Sovnarkoms of the Union Republics representatives of the Narkomindel. The Sovnarkoms of the Union Republics were also consulted about appointments to diplomatic posts in the capitals of countries in which they had special interests.

Much speculation was caused abroad by a constitutional amendment passed by the Supreme Soviet on 1 February 1944. By the Constitution as then amended, each Union Republic was given the right 'to enter into direct relations with foreign States, to conclude agreements with them and exchange diplomatic and consular representatives with them'. This involved changing the status of the Narkomindel to that of a Union-Republican instead of an All-Union Commissariat.

The admission of the Ukraine and White Russia (Belorussia) to the United Nations involved the acceptance of the new arrangement in international law. The reasons for the change are obviously bound up with policy and fall outside the scope of the present appendix. It should, however, be pointed out that the independence of the

Union-Republics in the conduct of their foreign relations is governed
by the same principle of 'dual subordination' as governs the Soviet
federal system in general. That is to say that the Union-Republican
Ministers for Foreign Affairs are not only responsible to their
respective Supreme Soviets but also to the relevant Minister of
the Federal Government, and to the Federal Council of Ministers
(Constitution, Articles 69 and 76). And it appears that any treaties
concluded by the Union-Republics which required ratification
would have to be ratified centrally. Finally of course the general
control of the U.S.S.R. by the single All-Union Communist Party
assures complete identity of policy at every level.

Appendix B

THE FRANCO-SOVIET PACT

According to M. Paul-Boncour, the subject of a Franco-Soviet pact of mutual assistance was first broached by him to Litvinov in their talk on 31 October 1933. The negotiations were continued with Dovgalevsky, the Soviet Ambassador, and were complete when Barthou became foreign minister in February 1934. It was thought best to leave the credit for negotiating the pact to Barthou, since M. Paul-Boncour as a man of the Left would be more suspect in circles from which opposition might be expected. M. Paul-Boncour confirms that the idea of the pact was supported by General Weygand and other military leaders. (J. Paul-Boncour, *Entre Deux Guerres*, vol. 2, pp. 361 ff.)

M. Reynaud deals at some length with France's failure to conclude a military convention as a sequel to the Franco-Soviet pact (*La France a Sauvé l'Europe*, vol. I, pp. 115 ff.). He quotes from a book by Colonel Jean Fabry, published under the German occupation, with the title *De la place de la Concorde au cours de l'Intendance*. Fabry was Laval's Minister for War from June 1935 to January 1936. In his book he recounts a conversation with Potemkin, then Soviet Ambassador to France, which took place in July 1935. Potemkin, suggested a military convention analogous to that of 17 August 1892 which specified the forces to be engaged under the terms of the Franco-Russian alliance. M. Reynaud quotes Fabry's text as follows:

'I received from M. Potemkin the renewed assurance that Moscow wished the Franco-Soviet Pact to be accompanied by a "military convention." Having avoided, in the articles of the pact, binding France by a too rigid text, the Prime Minister (Laval) had no taste for the brutal automatism of a military convention. I was personally resolved not to enter upon this path which left too many opportunities open for war. As M. Potemkin soon perceived this attitude, he ended the second interview by putting directly the question: "Why don't you want a precise military agreement with us? You certainly have such agreements with others, with the Rumanians for instance."

'I replied that one reason made it unnecessary to give any others. The Government of France was sincerely attached to peace; any risk of war made it attentive and suspicious. The Soviet Government for its part seemed to accept without fear the hypothesis of a European conflict, and to consider it if not as desirable, at least as inevitable.

'Potemkin then said unambiguously: "Why should war frighten us? Soviet Russia emerged from the last war. Soviet Europe will emerge from the next".'

The account by A. M. Pankratova in the *Istoria Diplomatii* (vol. iii, pp. 497–8), attaches importance in respect of the Franco-Soviet *rapprochement* to the commercial treaty of 11 January 1934, signed by Paul-Boncour, but emphasizes the role of Barthou.

THE bibliography of books and pamphlets in English relating to the U.S.S.R. is amply covered in P. Grierson, *Books on Soviet Russia, 1917–1942* (Methuen, 1943). It is planned to keep this bibliography up to date by articles in the *Slavonic Review*, of which the first appeared in the issue for January 1946. There are lists of sources in Russian and chronologies of treaties in T. A. Taracouzio, *The Soviet Union and International Law*, and *War and Peace in Soviet Diplomacy*. Reference may also be made to *Foreign Affairs Bibliography, 1919–1932* edited by W. L. Langer and H. F. Armstrong (New York, Harper, for Council on Foreign Relations, 1933) and to its continuation, *Foreign Affairs Bibliography, 1932-42*, edited by R. G. Woolbert (New York, Harper, 1945).

The following is therefore intended to be only a list of the principal works used in the writing of the present work and does not include all the books and pamphlets mentioned in the footnotes. Unless otherwise stated, the place of publication of all works in Russian is Moscow, and of all works in English, London. Where there has been more than one edition of a particular book, reference is normally made only to the one actually used.

Books marked with an asterisk have useful bibliographies.

I. Soviet Sources.

1. *Documents dealing with foreign relations*

Conférence de Moscou pour la limitation des armements (Moscow, 1923).

The Soviet Union and Peace (Martin Lawrence, 1929).

L'URSS à la Conférence du Désarmement (Moscow, 1932).

Documents relating to the Foreign Economic Relations of the U.S.S.R. (Moscow, 1933).

Sbornik Konsulskikh Dokladov: Severnaya Persia, 1933 (Collection of Consular Reports on Northern Persia).

Sovetsko-Amerikanskie Otnoshenia, 1919–33 (Soviet-American Relations 1919–33), 1936.

2. *Miscellaneous Documents*

Vsesoyuznaya Kommunisticheskaya Partia (B) v rezolutsiakh i resheniakh s'ezdov, konferentsii i plenumov ts. k., 1898–1935 (The All-Union Communist Party [of Bolsheviks] in the resolutions and decisions of its congresses, conferences, and of the plenums of the Executive Committee 1898–1935). (Fifth Edition, 2 vols., 1936).

Shestnadtsaty S'ezd Vsesoyuznoy Kommunisticheskoy Partii (The Sixteenth Congress of the All-Union Communist Party, 1936).

Semnadtsaty S'ezd Vsesoyuznoy Kommunisticheskoy Partii (The Seventeenth Congress of the All-Union Communist Party, 1934); cf. *Socialism Victorious* (Martin Lawrence, 1934).

Vosemnadtsaty S'ezd Vsesoyuznoy Kommunisticheskoy Partii (The Eighteenth Congress of the All-Union Communist Party, 1939); cf. *The Land of Socialism To-day and To-morrow* (Moscow 1939).

Court Proceedings in the Case of the Anti-Soviet Trotskyite Centre (Moscow, 1937).

Report of Court Proceedings in the Case of the Anti-Soviet Bloc of Rights and Trotskyites (Moscow, 1938).

3. *Speeches and Articles by Soviet Leaders*

LITVINOV, M. M.   Vneshnaya Politika S.S.S.R. (The Foreign Policy of the U.S.S.R., 1937).

Against Aggression (Lawrence and Wishart, 1939).

MOLOTOV, V.   The New Phase in the Soviet Union (Modern Books, 1930).

MOLOTOV, V.   Soviet Peace Policy (Lawrence and Wishart, 1941).

RADEK, K.   Podgotovka Borby za Novy Peredel Mira (The Preparation of the Struggle for a New Partition of the World, 1934).

STALIN, J. V.   Political Report to the Sixteenth Party Congress (Martin Lawrence, 1930).

Marxism and the National and Colonial Questions (Martin Lawrence, 1936).

Leninism (Allen and Unwin, 1940).

On the Great Patriotic War of the Soviet Union (Hutchinson, 1943).

4. *Other Works*

Summary of the Fulfilment of the First Five Year Plan (Gosplan, 1933).

O Mezhdunarodnom Polozhenii: sbornik (On the International Situation: a collection) (1937).

Istoria Vsesoyuznoy Kommunisticheskoy Partii (B): kratki kurs (History of the All-Union Communist Party [of Bolsheviks]: short course) (1938).

(English edition: Short History of the All-Union Communist Party, Moscow, 1939).

Strany Tikhovo Okeana (Countries of the Pacific Ocean) (1942).

BARANSKY, I. I.   Ekonomicheskaya Geografia S.S.S.R. (Economic Geography of the U.S.S.R.) (1939).

KOROWIN, E. A.   Das Völkerrecht der Ubergangszeit (translated from the Russian, Berlin, Rothschild, 1929).

POTEMKIN, V. P.   Politika Umirotvorenia Agressorov i Borba Sovetskovo Soyuza za Mir (The Policy of Appeasement and the Struggle of the Soviet Union for Peace) (Moscow, 1943).

POTEMKIN, V. P. (ed.) *Istoria Diplomatii (History of Diplomacy), 3 vols. (Moscow, 1941–5).

5. *Works of Reference*

Bolshaya Sovetskaya Entsiklopedia (in progress).
Sibirskaya Sovetskaya Entsiklopedia (1932).

II. Works on Soviet Russia.

1. *Works dealing generally with Soviet Foreign Policy*

COATES, W. P. & Z. World Affairs and the U.S.S.R. (Lawrence and Wishart, 1939).

DALLIN, D. J.   Soviet Russia's Foreign Policy 1939–42 (New Haven, Yale University Press, 1942).
Russia and Post-War Europe (New Haven, Yale University Press, 1943).

DAVIS, K. W.   The Soviets at Geneva (Geneva, Kundig, 1934).

FISCHER, L.   The Soviets in World Affairs, 2 vols. (Cape, 1930).

FLORINSKY, M. T.   World Revolution and the U.S.S.R. (Macmillan, 1933).

GAFENCU, G.   Prelude to the Russian Campaign (Muller, 1945).
Derniers Jours de l'Europe (Paris, Egloff, 1946).

HARPER, S. (ed.)   The Soviet Union and World Problems (Chicago University Press, 1935).

HARTLIEB, W. W.   Das Politische Vertragssystem der Sowjetunion, 1920–35 (Leipzig, 1936).

HOETZSCH, O.   Le Caractère et la Situation Internationale de l'Union des Soviets (Geneva, Kundig, 1932).

LASERSON, M. M.   Russia and the Western World (New York, Macmillan, 1945).

MAHANEY, W. L. jun.   The Soviet Union, the League of Nations and Disarmament (University of Pennsylvania, 1940).

MARQUÈS-RIVIÈRE, J. L'U.R.S.S. dans le Monde (Paris, Payot, 1935).

MILIOUKOV, P.   La Politique Extérieure des Soviets. 2nd Edition (Paris, Librairie Générale de Droit et de Jurisprudence, 1936).

SCOTT, J.   Duel for Europe (Boston, Houghton Mifflin, 1942).

STEWART, G. R.   The White Armies of Russia (Macmillan, 1933).

LORENZ, H.   Handbuch des Aussenhandels und des Verkehrs
                     mit der U.d.S.S.R.
TARACOUZIO, T. A.   *The Soviet Union and International Law (New
                     York, Macmillan, 1935).
                     *War and Peace in Soviet Diplomacy (New
                     York, Macmillan, 1940).
WHEELER-   *Brest Litovsk: The Forgotten Peace (Macmil-
BENNETT, J. W.   lan, 1938).

2. *Works dealing with specific aspects of Soviet Foreign Policy.*

COATES, W. P. & Z.   A History of Anglo-Soviet Relations (Lawrence
                     and Wishart and Pilot Press, 1943).
DULLES, F. R.   The Road to Teheran (Relations with the
                     U.S.A.) (Princeton University Press, 1944).
FISHER, H. H.   America and Russia in the World Community
                     (California, Claremont College, 1946).
KONOVALOV, S. (ed.) Russo-Polish Relations (Cresset Press, 1945).
MOORE, H.   Soviet Far Eastern Policy, 1931–1945 (Princeton
                     University Press, I.P.R., 1945).
SCHUMAN, F. L.   American Policy towards Russia since 1917
                     (New York, International Publishers, 1928).
SHOTWELL, J. T. &   Russia and Poland, 1919–1945 (New York,
LASERSON, M. M.   Carnegie, 1945).
SLOVÈS, H.   La France et l'Union Soviétique (Paris, Rieder,
                     1935).
TARACOUZIO T. A.   *The Soviets in the Arctic (New York, Mac-
                     millan, 1938).
UMIASTOWSKI, R.   Russia and the Polish Republic, 1918–1941
                     (Aquafondata, 1945).
YAKHONTOFF, V. A.   Russia and the Soviet Union in the Far East
                     (Allen and Unwin, 1932).

3. *Collective works containing articles on Soviet Foreign Policy*

The Foreign Policies of the Powers (New York, Harpers, 1935;
   ed. Armstrong, H. F.).
The Foreign Policies of the Great Powers (University of California,
   1939).
The Renaissance of Asia (University of California, 1944).

4. *Works on Soviet foreign economic relations*

The Prospects of British and American Trade with the Soviet Union
   (School of Slavonic Studies, 1935).
CONOLLY, V.   *Soviet Economic Policy in the East (Oxford
                     University Press, 1933).
                     *Soviet Trade from the Pacific to the Levant
                     (Oxford University Press, 1935).

KNICKERBOCKER, H. R.   Soviet Trade and World Depression (Lane, 1931).
The Soviet Five Year Plan and its Effect on World Trade (Lane, 1931).

5. *General Works on Soviet Russia*

BASILY, N. DE   Russia under Soviet Rule (Allen and Unwin, 1938).

BASSECHES, N.   The Unknown Army. The Nature and History of the Russian Military Forces (Heinemann, 1943).

BATSELL, W. R.   *Soviet Rule in Russia (New York, Macmillan, 1929).

CHAMBERLIN, W. H.   *The Russian Revolution. 2 vols. (Macmillan, 1935).

HARPER, S. N.   The Government of the Soviet Union (New York, Van Nostrand, 1937).

HOOVER, C. B.   The Economic Life of Soviet Russia (Macmillan, 1931).

MALEVSKY-MALE-VITCH, P. (ed.)   Russia: U.S.S.R. A Complete Handbook (New York, Farquhar Payson, 1933).

MANDEL, W.   The Soviet Far East and Central Asia (New York, Institute of Pacific Relations, 1944).

MAYNARD, SIR JOHN   The Russian Peasant and Other Studies (Gollancz, 1942).

ROSENBERG, A.   History of Bolshevism (Oxford University Press, 1939).

SCHUMAN, F. L.   Soviet Politics at Home and Abroad (New York, Knopf, 1946).

TIMASHEFF, N. S.   The Great Retreat (New York, Dutton, 1946).

TROTSKY, L.   The Revolution Betrayed (Faber, 1937).

TURIN, S. P.   The U.S.S.R.: An Economic and Social Survey (Methuen, 1944).

WEBB, S. & B.   Soviet Communism, A New Civilization? (Longmans, 1935).

WHITE, D. FEDO-TOFF   The Growth of the Red Army (Princeton University Press, 1944).

WOLLENBERG, E.   The Red Army, (2nd edition : Secker and Warburg, 1940).

YUGOW, A.   Russia's Economic Front for War and Peace (Watts, 1943).

6. *Biographies and Personal Narratives*

BARMINE, A.   Memoirs of a Soviet Diplomat (Lovat Dickson, 1938).

BILAINKIN, G.   Maisky: Ten Years Ambassador (Allen and Unwin, 1944).

DAVIES, J. E.   Mission to Moscow (Gollancz, 1942).

FISCHER, L.   Men and Politics (Cape, 1941).

KRAVCHENKO, V.   I Chose Freedom (New York, Scribner's, 1946).

KRIVITSKY, W. G.   I was Stalin's Agent (Hamilton, 1939).

LITTLEPAGE, J. D. & BESS, D. In Search of Soviet Gold (Harrap, 1939).

MONKHOUSE, A. Moscow 1911–33 (Gollancz, 1933).
POPE, A. U. Maxim Litvinoff (Secker and Warburg, 1945).
SCOTT, J. Behind the Urals (Secker and Warburg, 1943).
SOUVARINE, B. Stalin (Secker and Warburg, 1939).
TROTSKY, L. Stalin (New York, Harper, 1946).

III. Works dealing wholly or mainly with Pre-Revolutionary Russia.

1. *Works dealing mainly with Foreign Policy*

GORIAINOV, S. Le Bosphore et les Dardanelles (Paris, Plon, 1910).

LOBANOV-ROSTOV-SKY, A. Russia and Asia (New York, Macmillan, 1933).

MOSELY, P. E. Russian Diplomacy and the Opening of the Eastern Question in 1838–9 (Harvard University Press, 1934).

NOLDE, B. E. Russia in the Economic War (New Haven, Carnegie, Endowment series, Yale University Press, 1928).

PRICE, E. B. The Russo-Japanese Treaties of 1907–16 concerning Manchuria and Mongolia (Baltimore, John Hopkins University Press, 1933).

ROSEN, R. R. Forty Years of Diplomacy. 2 vols. (Allen and Unwin, 1932).

SUMNER, B. H. Tsardom and Imperialism in the Far East and the Middle East, 1880–1914 (Oxford University Press and British Academy, 1942).

TAUBE, M. M. La Politique Russe d'Avant Guerre et la Fin de l'Empire des Tsars (Paris, Leroux, 1928).

2. *Miscellaneous*

ALLEN, W. E. D. The Ukraine (Cambridge University Press, 1940).

BOLSHAKOFF, S. The Foreign Missions of the Russian Orthodox Church (S.P.C.K., 1943).

JOCHELSON, W. Peoples of Asiatic Russia (American Museum of Natural History, 1928).

SUMNER, B. H. *Survey of Russian History (Duckworth, 1944).

IV. The Third International: Comintern.

BORKENAU, F. The Communist International (Faber, 1938).
DIMITROV, G. The United Front (Lawrence and Wishart, 1938).

Kommunisticheski Internatsional v Dokumentakh: ed. Bela Kun (The Communist International in Documents, 1932).

Twelfth Plenum of the Executive Committee of the Communist International: Theses and Resolutions (Modern Books, 1932).

Kommunisticheski Internatsional Pered VII Vsemirnym Kongressom (The Communist International before the 7th World Congress, 1935).

Report of the 7th World Congress of the Communist International (Modern Books, 1936).

Seventh Congress of the Communist International: abridged report (Moscow, 1939).

V. The International Labour Movement.

DOLLÉANS, E.   Histoire du Mouvement Ouvrier. 2 vols. (Paris, Colin, 1936–9).

PRICE, J.   The International Labour Movement (Oxford University Press, R.I.I.A., 1945).

STURMTHAL, A.   The Tragedy of European Labour (Gollancz, 1944).

VI. General International Relations.

1. *Documents*

FELLER, A. H. &   Diplomatic and Consular Laws and Regulations.
HUDSON, M. O. (ed.)   2 vols. (Washington, Carnegie, 1933).

KEITH, A. B. (ed.)   Speeches and Documents on International Affairs. 2 vols. (Oxford University Press, 1938).

Publications of the League of Nations

Official Journal (Records of the Council).

Official Journal. Special Supplements (Records of the Assembly).

Reports and Proceedings of the International Economic Conference (Geneva, 1927).

Minutes of the Preparatory Commission for the Disarmament Conference.

Records, Minutes and Documents of the Conference for the Reduction and Limitation of Armaments.

International Trade Statistics (Annual).

Armaments Year Book.

World Economic Survey.

The International Labour Organization (I.L.O.) Year Book.

The Lausanne Conference on Near Eastern Affairs, 1922–3 (Cmd. 1814).

Documents diplomatiques de la Conferénce de Lausanne. 2 vols. (Paris, Ministère des Affaires Etrangères, 1923).

Actes de la Conférence de Montreux (Paris, Pedone, 1936).

The Trial of German Major War Criminals:
Proceedings of the International Military Tribunal sitting at
Nuremberg, Germany. Taken from the Official Transcript
(London, H.M. Stationery Office, 1946–8).
Documents on International Affairs (Royal Institute of International
Affairs, 1928 . . . in progress).

2. *Secondary Works*

ARMSTRONG, H. F. Where there is no Peace (Macmillan, 1939).
CARR, E. H. International Relations since the Peace Treaties
(Macmillan, 1937).
The Twenty Years' Crisis (Macmillan, 1939).
ENGEL, S. League Reform, 1936–9 (Geneva Research
Centre, 1940).
GATHORNE- A Short History of International Affairs, 1920–
HARDY, G. M. 39. 3rd edition (Oxford University Press,
R.I.I.A., 1942).
JORDAN, W. M. Great Britain, France, and the German Problem
(Oxford University Press, R.I.I.A., 1943).
MARSHALL-CORN- Geographic Disarmament (Oxford University
WALL, J. H. Press, R.I.I.A., 1935).
MAUGHAM, VIS- The Truth about the Munich Crisis (Heine-
COUNT mann, 1944).
SCHUMAN, F. L. Europe on the Eve (Hale, 1939).
Night over Europe (Hale, 1941).
SETON-WATSON, Munich and the Dictators (Methuen, 1939).
R. W. From Munich to Danzig (3rd edition of the
above, Methuen, 1939).
SPENDER, J. A. Between two Wars (Cassell, 1943).
TEMPERLEY, A History of the Peace Conference of Paris.
H. W. V. (ed.) 6 vols. (British Institute of International
Affairs, H. Frowde, Hodder and Stoughton,
1924).
TOYNBEE, A. J. Survey of International Affairs (Oxford Univer-
sity Press, R.I.I.A., 1924 . . . in progress).
WISKEMANN, E. Undeclared War (Constable, 1939).
WOLFERS, A. *Britain and France between two Wars (New
York, Harcourt Brace, 1940).
Problems of Peace, 11th Series (Allen and Unwin, 1937).
Problems of Peace, 12th Series (Allen and Unwin, 1938).
Royal Institute of International Affairs, The Future of the League
of Nations (R.I.I.A., 1936).

VII. Works dealing with other Countries and throwing Light on their Relations with Soviet Russia.

1. *Great Britain and the British Commonwealth*

CHURCHILL, W. S. Step by Step (Cassell, 1939).
Into Battle (Cassell, 1941).

FRIEDMANN, I. S.   British Relations with China, 1931–9 (New York, I.P.R., 1940).

HALIFAX, VISCOUNT Speeches on Foreign Policy (Oxford University Press, 1940).

HENDERSON, SIR N. Failure of a Mission (Hodder and Stoughton, 1940).

LONDONDERRY,   Ourselves and Germany (Hale, 1938).
MARQUESS OF   Wings of Destiny (Macmillan, 1943).
SETON-WATSON, Britain and the Dictators (Cambridge, 1933).
R. W.   Britain in Europe (Cambridge, 1937).

Correspondence showing the course of certain discussions directed towards securing a European Settlement (Cmd. 5143, 1936).

Documents concerning German-Polish relations and the outbreak of hostilities between Great Britain and Germany (British Blue Book) (Cmd. 6106, 1939).

2. *United States*

ALSOP, J. &   American White Paper (Michael Joseph, 1940).
KINTNER, R.

ALSTYNE,   American Diplomacy in Action (Stanford Uni-
R. W. van   versity Press, 1944).

BEMIS, S. F.   A Diplomatic History of the United States (Cape, 1937).

BISSON, T. A. American Policy in the Far East, 1931–40 (New York, I.P.R., 1940).

DAVIS, FORREST How War Came (New York, Simon and Schus-
& LINDLEY, E. K. ter, 1942) (Published in England by Allen and Unwin under the title: How War Came to America).

DODD, W. E.   Ambassador Dodd's Diary (Gollancz, 1941).

HICKS, G.   John Reed (Macmillan, 1937).

ROOSEVELT, F. D. Addresses and Messages (Washington and His Majesty's Stationery Office, 1943).
               Public Papers and Addresses (ed. S. Rosen-man...in progress).

SMITH, D.   America and the Axis War (Cape, 1942).

WELLES, SUMNER A Time for Decision (New York, Harper, 1944).

WILSON, H.   A Diplomat between Wars (New York, Long-mans, 1941).

United States Department of State. Papers relating to the Foreign Relations of the United States (in progress).

Peace and War. United States Foreign Policy 1931–1941 (1943).

World Peace Foundation. Documents on American Foreign Relations (in progress).

Council on Foreign Relations. The United States in World Affairs (Annual 1931 onwards).

3. *France*

BLUM, L.   Léon Blum before his Judges (Routledge, 1943).

BOIS, E. J.   Truth on the Tragedy of France (Hodder and Stoughton, 1941).

BONNETT, G.   Défense de la Paix: De Washington au Quai d'Orsay (Geneva, Bourquin, 1946).

BROGAN, D. W.   The Development of Modern France (Hamilton, 1940).

CAMERON, E. R.   Prologue to Appeasement, 1933–6 (Philadelphia, University of Pennsylvania, 1942).

COT, PIERRE   Triumph of Treason (Chicago, Ziff Davies, 1944).

MICAUD, C. A.   The French Right Wing and Nazi Germany, 1933–39 (Durham, N.C., Duke University Press, 1944).

MONZIE, ANATOLE DE   Ci-devant (Paris, Flammarion, 1942).

PAUL-BONCOUR, J.   Entre deux Guerres. 3 vols. (Paris Plon, 1945; New York, Bretanos, 1946).

'PERTINAX' (GERAUD, A.)   Les Fossoyeurs. 2 vols. (New York, Maison Française, 1943).

THOREZ, M.   France today and the People's Front (Gollancz, 1941).

WERTH, A.   France and Munich (Hamilton, 1939).

ZAY, J.   Carnets Secrets de Jean Zay. Ed. P. Henriot. (Paris, Editions de France, 1942).

Documents Diplomatiques, 1938–9 (Ministère des Affaires Etrangères, 1939) (French Yellow Book).

4. *Germany*

BAYNES, N. H. (ed.)   *Hitler's Speeches, 1922–39. 2 vols. (Oxford University Press, R.I.I.A., 1942).

BLOCH, K.   Germany's Interests and Policies in the Far East (New York, I.P.R., 1940).

CLARK, R. T.   The Fall of the German Republic (Allen and Unwin, 1935).

HEIDEN, K.   Der Fuehrer (Gollancz, 1944).

KLOTZ, H. (ed.)   The Berlin Diaries (New York, Morrow and Co., 1934).

KNIGHT-PATTERSON, W. M.   Germany from Defeat to Conquest (Allen and Unwin, 1945).

MELVILLE, C. F.   The Russian Face of Germany (Wishart, 1932).

MORGAN, J. H.   Assize of Arms, vol. 1 (Methuen, 1945).

REIMANN, G.   Germany: World Empire or World Revolution (Secker and Warburg, 1938).

ROSENBERG, A.   History of the German Republic (Methuen, 1936).

ROSINSKI, H.   The German Army (Hogarth Press, 1939).

TAYLOR, A. J. P.   The Course of German History (Hamilton, 1945).

VALTIN, J.   Out of the Night (Heinemann, 1941).
WEIGERT, H.   Generals and Geographers (New York, Oxford
                      University Press, 1942).
WHEELER-   Hindenburg: The Wooden Titan (Macmillan,
BENNETT, J. W.   1936).
Documents on the Events preceding the Outbreak of the War (New
   York, German Library of Information, 1940) (German White
   Book, No. 2).
The German White Paper. Polish Documents issued by the German
   Foreign Office (New York, Howell Soskin, 1940) (German White
   Book, No. 3).
Die Geheimakten des Französischen Generalstabes (Berlin, 1940)
   (German White Book, No. 6).

5. *Italy*

CIANO, GALEAZZO   The Ciano Diaries, 1939–43, ed. Hugh Gibson
                   (New York, Doubleday, 1946).
MACARTNEY,M.H.H. Italy's Foreign and Colonial Policy, 1914–37
& CREMONA, P.   (Oxford University Press, 1938).
MASSOCK, R. G.   Italy from Within (Macmillan, 1943).

6. *Spain*

BAREA, A.   The Clash (Faber, 1946).
BORKENAU, F.   The Spanish Cockpit (Faber, 1937).
BRENAN, G.   The Spanish Labyrinth (Cambridge University
                   Press, 1943).
BUCKLEY, H.   Life and Death of the Spanish Republic (Hamil-
                   ton, 1940).
'HISPANICUS' (ed.) Foreign Intervention in Spain. Vol. I (United
                   Editorial, 1938).
PADELFORD, N. J.   International Law and Diplomacy in the Spanish
                   Civil Strife (New York, Macmillan, 1939).
VAYO, JULIUS   Freedom's Battle (Heinemann, 1940).
ALVAREZ DEL

7. *Poland*

BUELL, R.   Poland, Key to Europe. 3rd Edition (New York,
                   Knopf, 1939).
DONNADIEU, J.   La Lutte des Aigles aux Marches Orientales
                   (Paris, Alcan, 1939).
HARLEY, J. H.   The Authentic Biography of Colonel Beck
                   (Hutchinson, 1939).
MACKIEWICZ, S.   Colonel Beck and his Policy (Eyre and Spottis-
                   woode, 1944).
NOËL, LÉON   L'Agression Allemande contre la Pologne (Paris,
                   Flammarion, 1946).
SCHMITT, B. (ed.) Poland (Berkeley, California University Press,
                   1945).

Official Documents concerning Polish-German and Polish-Soviet Relations (Polish Ministry for Foreign Affairs, 1939) (Polish White Book).

Polish-Soviet Relations, 1918–1943, Documents. (New York, Polish Information Centre, 1943).

Cambridge History of Poland (Cambridge University Press, 1941).

8. *Finland and the Baltic States*

ANDERSON, H. FOSTER	Borderline Russia (Cresset Press, 1942).
HAMPDEN JACK-SON, J.	Finland (Allen and Unwin, 1938).

The Development of Finnish-Soviet Relations in the Autumn of 1939 (Finnish Ministry of Foreign Affairs, Harrap, 1940) (Finnish Blue Book).

Finland Reveals her Secret Documents on Soviet Policy (New York, Funk, 1940) (Finnish Blue and White Book).

Latvia in 1939–42 (Washington, D.C., Latvian Legation, 1942).

9. *Czechoslovakia*

BILEK, B.	Fifth Column at Work (Trinity Press, Lindsay Drummond, 1946).
GEDYE, G. E. R.	Fallen Bastions (Gollancz, 1939).
HENDERSON, A.	Eyewitness in Czechoslovakia (Harrap, 1939).
KERNER, R. J. (ed.)	Czechoslovakia, Twenty Years of Independence (Berkeley, California University Press, 1940).
RIPKA, H.	Munich, Before and After (Gollancz, 1939).
SETON-WATSON, R. W.	A History of the Czechs and Slovaks (Hutchinson, 1943).
THOMSON, S. HARRISON	Czechoslovakia in European History (Princeton University Press, 1943).
VONDRACEK, F. J.	The Foreign Policy of Czechoslovakia, 1918–1936 (New York, Columbia University Press, 1937).
WINCH, M.	Republic for a Day (Hale, 1939).

10. *The Danube and the Balkans*

GESHKOFF, T. I.	Balkan Union (New York, Columbia University Press, 1940).
GOMME, A. W.	Greece (Oxford University Press, 1945).
KERNER, R. J. and HOWARD, H. N.	The Balkan Conferences and the Balkan Entente (Berkeley, University of California Press, 1936).
MACARTNEY, C. A.	Hungary and her Successors (Oxford University Press, 1937).
	Problems of the Danube Basin (Cambridge University Press, 1942).
MOUSSET, A.	Le Monde Slave (Paris, S.E.F.I., 1946).

POPOVICI, A.   The Political Status of Bessarabia (Washington,
                      D.C., Georgetown University, 1931).
ROUCEK, J. S.   Contemporary Roumania (Stanford University
                      Press, 1932).
SETON-WATSON,   Eastern Europe between the Wars (Cambridge
HUGH   University Press, 1945).

11. *Turkey and the Straits*

ADAMOV, E. A.   Konstantinopol i Prolivy, 2 vols. (1925–6)
                      (Translated as E. A. Adamow, Konstantinopel
                      und die Meerengen. Dresden, 1932).
GRAVES, P. P.   The Question of the Straits (Benn, 1931).
                      Briton and Turk (Hutchinson, 1941).
HOWARD, H. N.   The Partition of Turkey (Norman, University
                      of Oklahoma Press, 1931).
MANDELSTAM, A.   Le Sort de l'Empire Ottoman (Paris, Payot,
                      1917).
SHOTWELL, J. T.   Turkey at the Straits (New York, Macmillan,
and DÉAK, F.   1940).

12. *The Middle East*

ARBERY, A. J. and Islam To-day (Faber, 1943).
LANDAU, R. (ed.)
ELWELL-SUTTON,   Modern Iran (Routledge, 1941).
L. P.
MESBAH ZADEH, M.   La Politique d'Iran dans la Société des Nations
                   (Paris, Pedone, 1936).
HAAS, W. S.   Iran (New York, Columbia University Press,
                   1946).
MONROE, E.   The Mediterranean in Politics (Oxford Univer-
                   sity Press, 1938).
SYKES, SIR PERCY   A History of Persia. 2nd Edition. 2 vols. (Mac-
                   millan, 1931).
                   A History of Afghanistan. 2 vols. (Macmillan,
                   1940).
Department of Overseas Trade, Economic Conditions in Iran (1937)

13. *The Far East*
(a) *General*

BIENSTOCK, G.   The Struggle for the Pacific (Allen and Unwin,
                   1937).
BUSS, C. A.   War and Diplomacy in Eastern Asia (New York,
                   Macmillan, 1941).
GAYN, M. J.   The Fight for the Pacific (Lane, 1941).
HOLLAND, W. L.   Problems of the Pacific, 1936. (Sixth I.P.R.
& MITCHELL, K.   Conference) (Oxford University Press, 1936).
                   Problems of the Pacific, 1939 (Seventh I.P.R.
                   Conference) (New York, Institute of Pacific
                   Relations, 1940).

HUDSON, G. F.　　　The Far East in World Politics (Oxford, Claren-
don Press, 1937).

HUDSON, G. F. &　　An Explanatory Atlas of the Far East (Faber,
RAJCHMAN, M.　　1942).

LATTIMORE, OWEN　Solution in Asia (Cresset Press, 1945).

MORSE, H. B. &　　Far Eastern International Relations. 2nd
MACNAIR, H. F.　　Edition (Boston, Houghton Mifflin, 1931).

QUIGLEY, H. S.　　The Far Eastern War (Boston, World Peace
Foundation, 1942).

QUIGLEY, H. S. &　The Far East (Boston, World Peace Foundation,
BLAKESLEE, G. H.　1938).

Royal Institute of International Affairs, China and Japan (3rd
edition, 1941).

War and Peace in the Pacific (1942 I.P.R. Conference) (R.I.I.A.,
1943).

(b) China

BERTRAM, J. M.　　Crisis in China (Macmillan, 1939).

CARLSON, E. F.　　The Chinese Army (New York, I.P.R., 1940).

CRESSY-MARCKS, V. Journey into China (Hodder and Stoughton,
1940).

HOLCOMBE, A. N.　The Chinese Revolution. 2nd Edition. (Harvard University Press, 1931).

ISAACS, H. R.　　The Tragedy of the Chinese Revolution (Secker
and Warburg, 1938).

JOHANSON, E. &　Soviety v Kitae, 1927–1932 (The Soviets in
TAUBE, E.　　　China) (Moscow, 1933).

KUN, BELA (ed.)　The Fundamental Laws of the Chinese Soviet
Republic (Martin Lawrence, 1934).

LINEBARGER,　　The China of Chiang Kai-shek (Boston, World
P. M. A.　　　　Peace Foundation, 1941).

PRATT, SIR J.　　War and Politics in China (Cape, 1943).

ROSINGER, L. K.　China's Wartime Politics (Princeton University
Press, I.P.R., 1944).

SNOW, E.　　　Red Star over China (Gollancz, 1937).

TAWNEY, R. H.　Land and Labour in China (Allen and Unwin,
(ed.)　　　　　1932).

TAYLOR, G. F.　　The Struggle for North China (New York,
I.P.R., 1940).

TONG, H. K.　　Chiang Kai-shek. 2 vols. (Hurst and Blackett,
1938).

YAKHONTOFF, V.　The Chinese Soviets (New York, Coward
McCann, 1934).

Treaties and Agreements with and concerning China, 1894–1919.
ed. J. V. A. Macmurray. 2 vols. (New York, Carnegie, 1921).

Treaties and Agreements with and concerning China, 1919–1929
(New York, Carnegie, 1929).

China Year Book (Annual. Shanghai, North China Daily News).

Wellington Koo, V. K. Memoranda presented to the Lytton Commission (New York, 1932).

Agrarian China. Selected source material from Chinese authors. Introduction by R. H. Tawney (Allen and Unwin, I.P.R., 1939)

(c) *Sinkiang and Mongolia*

CABLE, M. &   The Challenge of Central Asia (World Dominion
OTHERS   Press, 1929).
CABLE, M. &   The Gobi Desert (Hodder and Stoughton, 1942).
FRENCH, F.
FILCHNER, W.   A Scientist in Tartary (Faber, 1939).
FLEMING, P.   News from Tartary (Cape, 1936).
FRITERS, G. M.   The International Position of Outer Mongolia
                   (Dijon, 1939).
HASLUND, H.   Men and Gods in Mongolia (Kegan, Paul, 1933).
                   Tents in Mongolia (Kegan Paul, 1934).
HEDIN, S.   Big Horse's Flight (Macmillan, 1936).
                   The Silk Road (Routledge, 1938).
KAZAK, F.   Ostturkistan zwischen den Grossmächten
                   (Königsberg, Osteuropa, 1937).
LARSON, F. A.   Larson, Duke of Mongolia (Boston, Little,
                   Brown, 1930).
LATTIMORE, O.   Inner Asian Frontiers of China (New York,
                   American Geographical Society, 1940).
NORINS, M. R.   Gateway to Asia: Sinkiang (New York, John
                   Day, 1944).
TEICHMAN, SIR ERIC Journey to Turkistan (Hodder and Stoughton,
                   1937).
VERBRUGGE, R.   La Mongolie, un instant autonome (Antwerp,
                   1926).
WU, A. K.   Turkistan Tumult (Methuen, 1940).
Treaties and Agreements concerning Outer Mongolia, 1881–1916
    (Washington, Carnegie, 1921).
Mongolia, Yesterday and To-day (Tientsin, c. 1924–5).
(*Note:* The bibliography by P. Grierson already referred to has
    sections on Sinkiang (Chinese Turkestan), Mongolia, and the
    Chinese Communists.)

(d) *Japan and Manchuria*

AKAGI, R.   Japan's Foreign Relations (Tokyo, 1936).
HIDEMICHI
GREW, J. C.   Ten Years in Japan (New York, Simon and
                   Schuster, 1944).
LATTIMORE, O.   Manchuria, Cradle of Conflict, 2nd edition (New
                   York, Macmillan, 1935).
LYTTON REPORT: Appeal of the Chinese Government, Report of the
                   Commission of Inquiry (League of Nations,
                   Document C. 663 M. 320, 1932, VII, 12).
SCHUMPETER, E. B. The Industrialization of Japan and Manchukuo
(ed.)   (New York, Macmillan, 1940).
TOLISCHUS, O. D.   Tokyo Record (New York, Reynal and Hitch-
                   cock, 1943).

WILLOUGHBY, W. W.   Japan's Case Examined (Baltimore, Johns Hopkins University Press, 1940).

VIII. Miscellaneous.

BROGAN, D. W.   Is Innocence enough? (Hamilton, 1941).

COBBAN, A.   National Self-Determination (Oxford University Press, R.I.I.A., 1945).

EARLE, E. (ed.)   Makers of Modern Strategy (Princeton University Press, 1943).

SCHLESINGER, R.   Federalism in Central and Eastern Europe (Kegan Paul, 1945).

SCHUMPETER, J. A.   Capitalism, Socialism, and Democracy (Allen and Unwin, 1943).

American Geographical Society.   Pioneer Settlement (New York, 1932).

Royal Institute of International Affairs.   Nationalism (Oxford University Press, 1939).

ADDENDA

BAYKOV, A.   Soviet Foreign Trade (Princeton University Press, 1946).

BYRNES, J. F.   Speaking Frankly (Heinemann, 1947).

CONDOIDE, M. V.   Russian-American Trade: a study of the Soviet Foreign Trade Monopoly (Ohio State University, 1946).

GAMELIN, MAURICE   Servir, vol. II: Le Prologue du Drame (Paris, Plon, 1946).

NAMIER, L. B.   Diplomatic Prelude, 1938–9 (Macmillan, 1948).

REYNAUD, P.   La France a Sauvé l'Europe. 2 vols. (Paris, Flammarion, 1947).

WHEELER-BENNETT, J. W.   Munich : Prologue to Tragedy, (Macmillan, 1948)

Foreign Relations of the United States: Japan, 1931–41. 2 vols. (Washington, Government Printing Office, 1943).

Fuehrer Conferences on Naval Affairs (London, Admiralty, mimeographed, 1947).

League of Nations. Report of the High Commissioner for Danzig. C.42.M.38. 1940. VII.

Les Lettres secrètes échangées par Hitler et Mussolini. Introduction de André François-Poncet. (Paris, Editions du Pavois, 1946).

Nazi Conspiracy and Aggression. Office of the U.S. Chief of Counsel for the prosecution of Axis Criminality. 8 vols. (Washington, U.S. Government Printing Office, 1946).

Report of the Royal Commission appointed under Order in Council. P.C. 411 of 5 February 1946 (Ottawa, 27 June 1946).

Nazi-Soviet Relations, 1939-1941 (Documents from the Archives of the German Foreign Office) ed. by R. J. Sontag and J. S. Beddie (Washington, U.S. Department of State, 1948).

LIST OF ABBREVIATIONS

I.P.R. Institute of Pacific Relations.

L.N.T.S. League of Nations Publications: *Treaty Series.*

L.N.O.J. *League of Nations: Official Journal.*

L.N.O.J. Spec. Suppl. League of Nations: Official Journal: Special Supplement.

C.P.S.U. Communist Party of the Soviet Union.

R.I.I.A. Royal Institute of International Affairs.

Survey for . . . A. J. Toynbee: *Survey of International Affairs.* (R.I.I.A., O.U.P., 1920–1938.)

Documents for . . . *Documents on International Affairs* (ed. J. Wheeler-Bennett, and others. R.I.I.A., O.U.P., 1928—in progress).

J.R.C.A.S. Journal of the Royal Central Asian Society.

Int. Conc. International Conciliation. (Documents: Carnegie Endowment for International Peace.)

B.I.N. Bulletin of International News. (R.I.I.A.)

1. EASTERN EUROPE 1938—1941

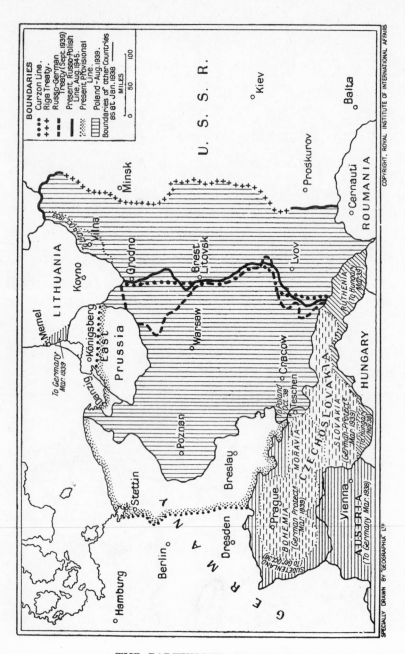

2. THE PARTITIONS OF POLAND

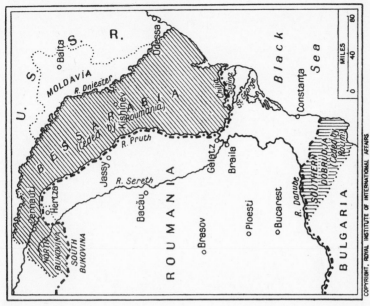

COPYRIGHT, ROYAL INSTITUTE OF INTERNATIONAL AFFAIRS

4. THE U.S.S.R. AND ROUMANIA

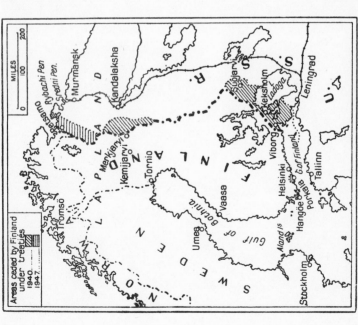

SPECIALLY DRAWN BY 'GEOGRAPHIA' LTD

3. THE U.S.S.R. AND FINLAND

INDEX